IMAGES
of America

MONMOUTH

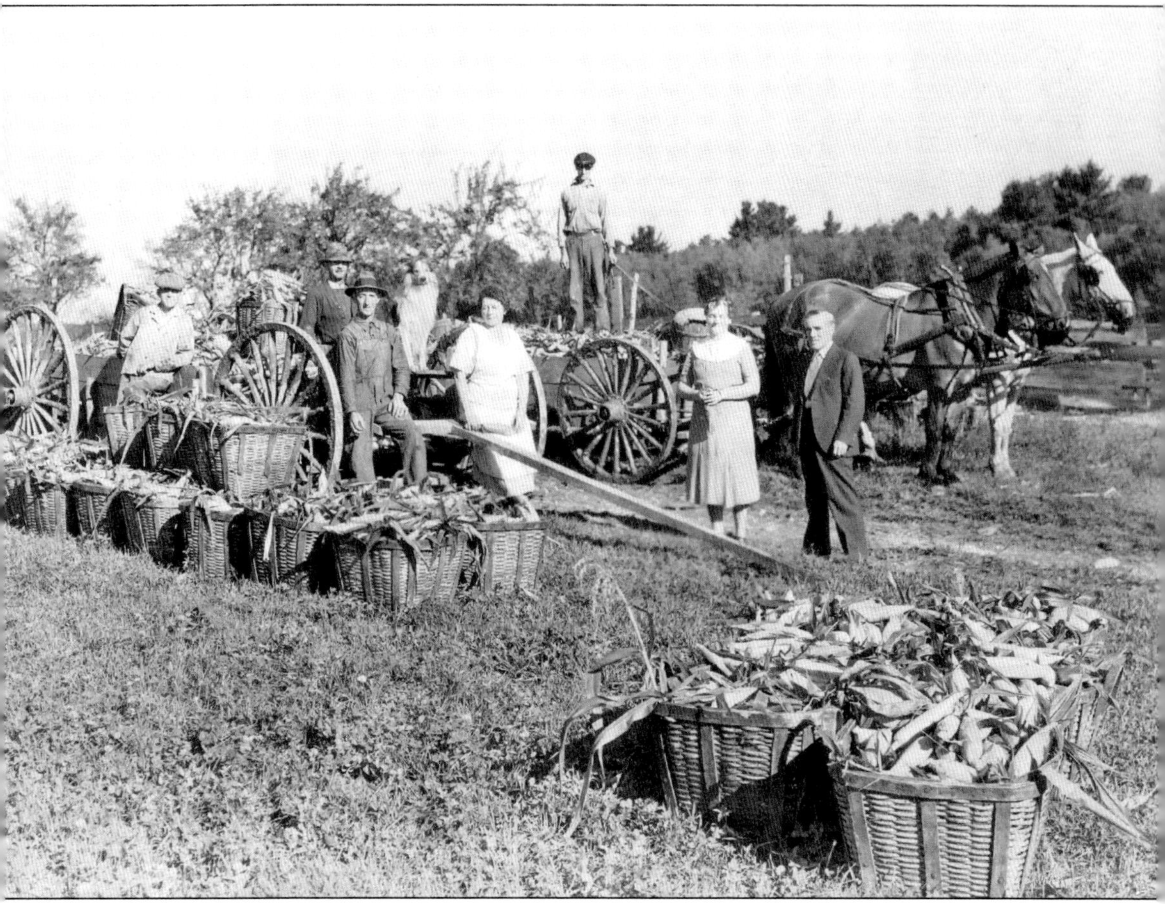

On the Cover: The photograph shown on the cover and above depicts Emil and Hulda Peterson standing by the tongue (pole) of their wagon, George and Madeline Peterson in front of the horses, several baskets full of ears of corn, and three unidentified men on the Petersons' farm in South Monmouth. (Courtesy of the Monmouth Museum.)

IMAGES
of America

MONMOUTH

Bobbie M. Bowler

ARCADIA
PUBLISHING

ISBN 978-0-7385-7345-8

Published by Arcadia Publishing
Charleston SC, Chicago IL, Portsmouth NH, San Francisco CA

Printed in the United States of America

Library of Congress Control Number: 2010921767

For all general information contact Arcadia Publishing at:
Telephone 843-853-2070
Fax 843-853-0044
E-mail sales@arcadiapublishing.com
For customer service and orders:
Toll-Free 1-888-313-2665

Visit us on the Internet at www.arcadiapublishing.com

This book is dedicated to the late Earle and late Mildred Flanders, the founders of the Monmouth Museum. This book was made possible thanks to their dedication and hard work for the preservation of the history of Monmouth and its surrounding towns. I would also like to dedicate this book to the late Roland LaVallee of Winthrop, who photographed Monmouth people and events for over 40 years. He was kind enough to donate his collection of some 1,500 negatives to the Monmouth Museum before he passed away.

Contents

ACKNOWLEDGMENTS

I would like to thank all of those people who have volunteered their energy and time in the preservation of Monmouth's history. Many of those who were so important to these efforts have passed on before they could be properly acknowledged. I would also like to thank the following for the use of their photographs in the making of this book: the Monmouth Museum, the late Lewis Horzempa, the late Wilfred Frost, the late Doris Andrews Johnson, the late Alberta Keene, the late Clason Dixon, Natalie Hall Jones, Audrey and David Walker, Stan DeOrsey, Dr. Stanley Painter, Frederick Chenery III, Thomas McDonald, Shelia Sanford, Dora King, Alberta Burnham, Marcia Brophy, Marge Maxim, Carol and Ted Johnson, Bertha Johnson, Harland Kennison, Jayne Robinson, Edson Donnell, Marion Donnell, Roscoe Scott, and Mildred Robinson. A special thank you goes to Dr. Larry Buggia, who brought me so many wonderful old photographs from the farmers he visited on his veterinary calls over the years. His insight into protecting the legacy of these images, before they were lost to time, was crucial to the preservation of Monmouth's photographic history. Finally, I would like to thank my mother Bessie Bowler and my father the late Everett Bowler, who passed their love for history and storytelling on to me.

Introduction

From the age of 15, I have wanted to do a photographic history of Monmouth, Maine. I became interested in Monmouth history after Earle Flanders came to give a presentation on Monmouth history to my eighth-grade class. I began working for Earle in the summer of 1974 as a guide for the Monmouth Museum, where I learned to appreciate the importance of preserving Monmouth history. It began as a small collection of 100 Monmouth photographs, and between the Monmouth Museum and myself, it has grown to a collection of over 2,400 photographs. Most of the photographs document life in Monmouth during early 1900s; however, 1,500 negatives document Monmouth life from the late 1940s until the early 1980s.

The center of Monmouth is the heart of the community. Throughout the history of the town, the villages at the center, north, east and south have been hubs of activity. The Monmouth area is famous for its apples and agriculture. The town was named in honor of Gen. Henry Dearborn for his participation at the Battle of Monmouth during the Revolutionary War.

The business of making moccasins in Monmouth has a long history covering nearly 100 years. Charles P. Blake, the grand nephew of Gen. Henry Dearborn, began what would become a very important part of Monmouth's economy. In 1880, there were two moccasin factories in Monmouth Center; by 1900, this was reduced to one; and by the 1970s, Monmouth saw the last moccasins made by the late Alden Grant.

In 1885, Monmouth Center experienced the first in a number of devastating fires, with the "Great Fire" of 1888 being the most destructive. There were also significant fires in 1903, 1907, and 1913. In 1963, the Clough Block, the former Grand Army of the Republic Hall, was lost to fire, to be followed a few years later with the loss to fire of the old Day and Richardson Hardware and Crockery building in the late 1960s. With each fire, another piece of Monmouth history vanished from the center landscape. The old Corn Shop near the Monmouth beach was destroyed by fire in the early 1970s, and in 2008 came the great loss of Leone's restaurant, the former Bungalow, home to Ally and Martha Kemp Jotham during the 1930s.

For over 100 years, Monmouth has been a popular area for summer people, who have camps and cottages on the local lakes. The first cottages were built along the east shore, and by 1909, there were 15 stretching the length of the east side of Lake Cochnewagan. The town of Monmouth is also the home of the Theater at Monmouth; it is a theater company that performs plays during the summer months at the prestigious Cumston Hall. The Theater at Monmouth celebrated its 40th season in 2009.

Monmouth's famous son Harry Cochrane was the architect of Cumston Hall, which was the first building in town to have electricity when it opened in 1900. Harry Cochrane was a man of many talents, including his authorship of the two-volume *History of Monmouth and Wales*. He was also an artist, fresco painter, musician, photographer, and poet.

To the north of the town center is the little village of North Monmouth. Early efforts to construct four dams and mill ponds helped to harness the local water power and promoted several successful factories. In the early 1900s, the construction of a new woolen mill at North Monmouth brought emigrants from Poland and so grew a small Polish community, which was unique to this area.

In the early to mid-1900s, Monmouth, like so many other towns in Maine, had a tradition of celebrating the Fourth of July with a grand parade, baseball games, and other festive activities. The "night before the Fourth" also used to hold a tradition of pranks and practical jokes. For a number of years throughout the first part of the 20th century, many of the young people in Monmouth would take great pains to collect everything that was not nailed down and carry it to the center of town. The next morning, most people could be found collecting their bicycles, front steps, hitching posts, and even their outhouses and returning them to their rightful places. There was one such occasion when a town farmer had to collect his hay-raking machine from the roof of the Monmouth Center railroad station. The items were never destroyed, just relocated for a brief period of time.

The railroad was the main link to the outside world for the town of Monmouth. The building of the railroad in 1849 boosted economic development and built work opportunities for the townspeople. Will Lord was a well-known section man for the Maine Central Railroad who spent over 29 years working on the Monmouth section. Work could be hazardous on section 36, and Will Lord had several close calls during his railroad service. He was caught up in the snow plow of an engine clearing the tracks, when the engineer mistakenly thought he was a dead tramp. It was not until the flailing arms, legs, and finally Will's head popped out of the snow that the engineer realized he had nearly killed the section man. This story and other "thrilling stories" of Will Lord were run in the July 31, 1922, issue of the *Lewiston Evening Journal.*

During World War II, Monmouth lost 10 of its young men in the service of their country. They were Allen Dunn, Roy H. Rolfe, Wendell Hanson, Matthew Klopot, F. Raynald Bonin, Delmont Johnston, Glendon E. Harris, Merton E. Willard, E. Franklin Bryant, and Clayton W. Leavitt.

Monmouth has seen the rise and fall of the industry and agriculture over the last 100 years. The once plentiful and beautiful apple orchards are disappearing. No longer are blankets of apple blossoms spread over the landscape. The sound of the apple sprayers in the spring no longer fills the air, and the sound of the old yellow airplane swooping down over the apple trees can no longer be heard. There are no more canning of vegetables, no more making of moccasins, no more weaving of woolen blankets, and no more doctors making house calls. The beauty of simplicity seems lost to technology and progress.

I have many fond memories of time spent interviewing the people who lived their lives in Monmouth during the early to mid-20th century. Many of them have passed and are missed as dear friends. It is my hope with this book to provide a way of preserving their memories for others to appreciate the contributions these people made to their community.

One

Monmouth Center

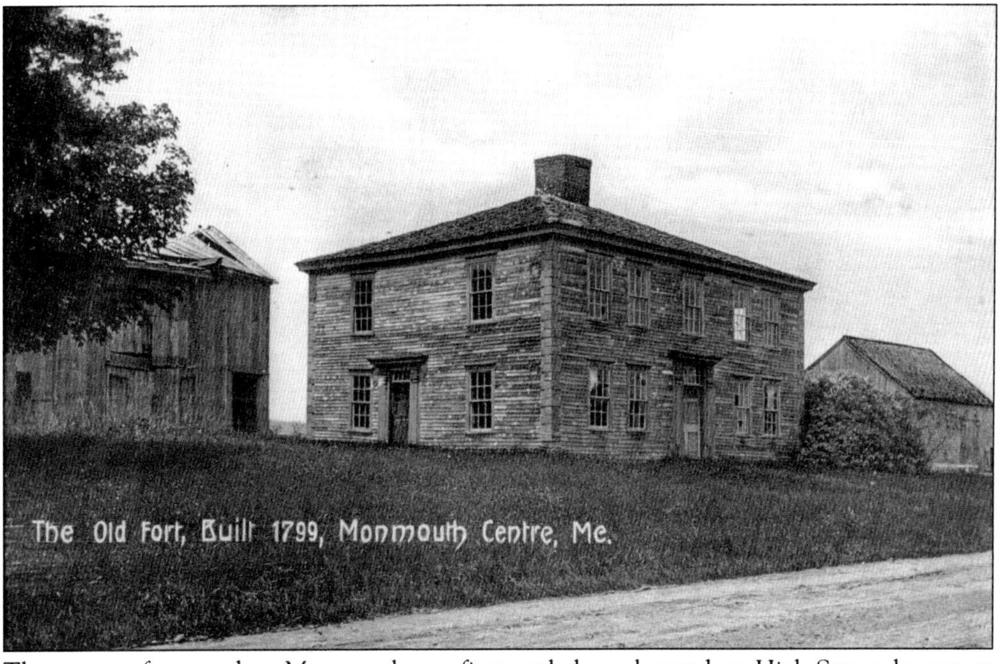

The center of town when Monmouth was first settled was located on High Street, known as Academy Street today, near what is now the Henry L. Cottrell School. A little to the north of the school, the Old Fort was built by Sewall Prescott around 1798. In 1802, Bishop Francis Asbury preached here at the New England Methodist Conference with nearly 2,000 people in attendance. The Old Fort, also known as Prescott's Tavern, was so named because the local militia mustered in the field across the street from it and would come to the tavern for liquid refreshment following their muster. (Courtesy of the author.)

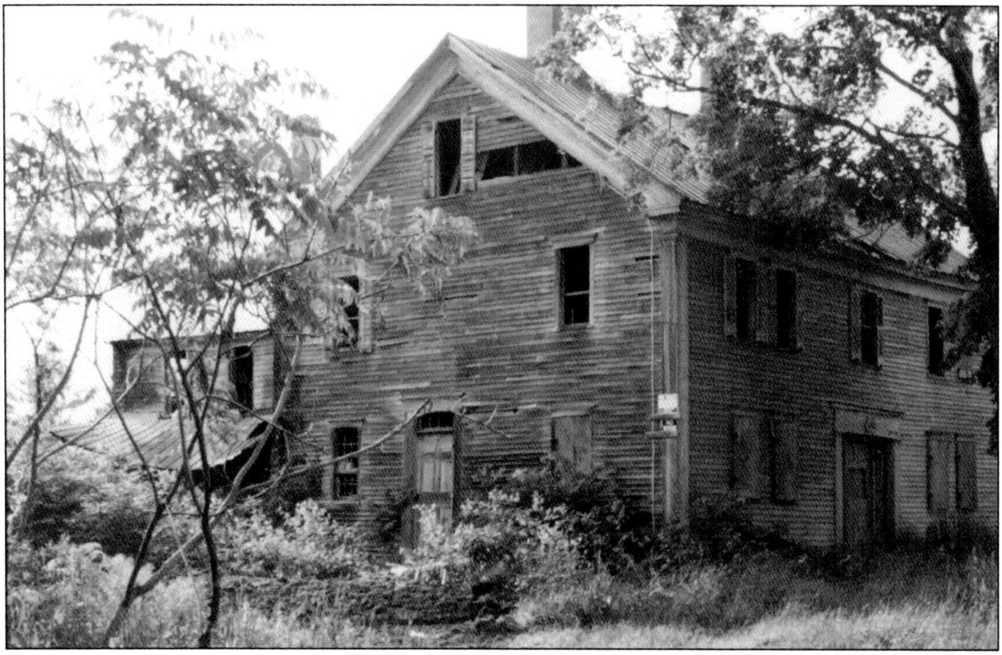

The next residence to the northeast of the Old Fort was the home of the noted Rev. Caleb Fogg. Reverend Fogg, a Revolutionary soldier from Epping, New Hampshire, was well known for his practical jokes. The photograph here shows his old home in a sad state of decay just prior to its destruction by fire in 1973. (Photograph by the author.)

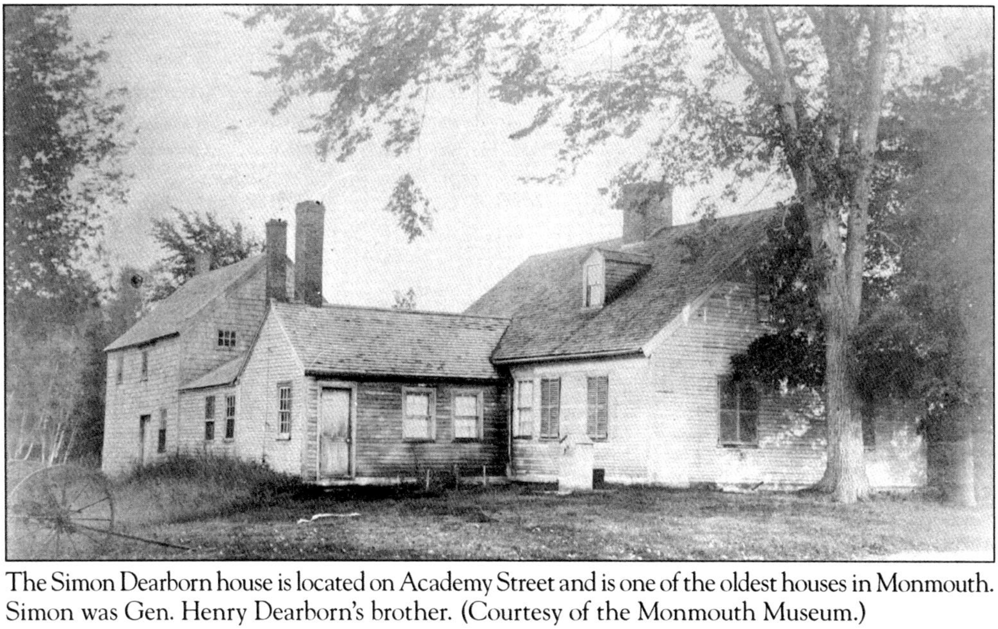

The Simon Dearborn house is located on Academy Street and is one of the oldest houses in Monmouth. Simon was Gen. Henry Dearborn's brother. (Courtesy of the Monmouth Museum.)

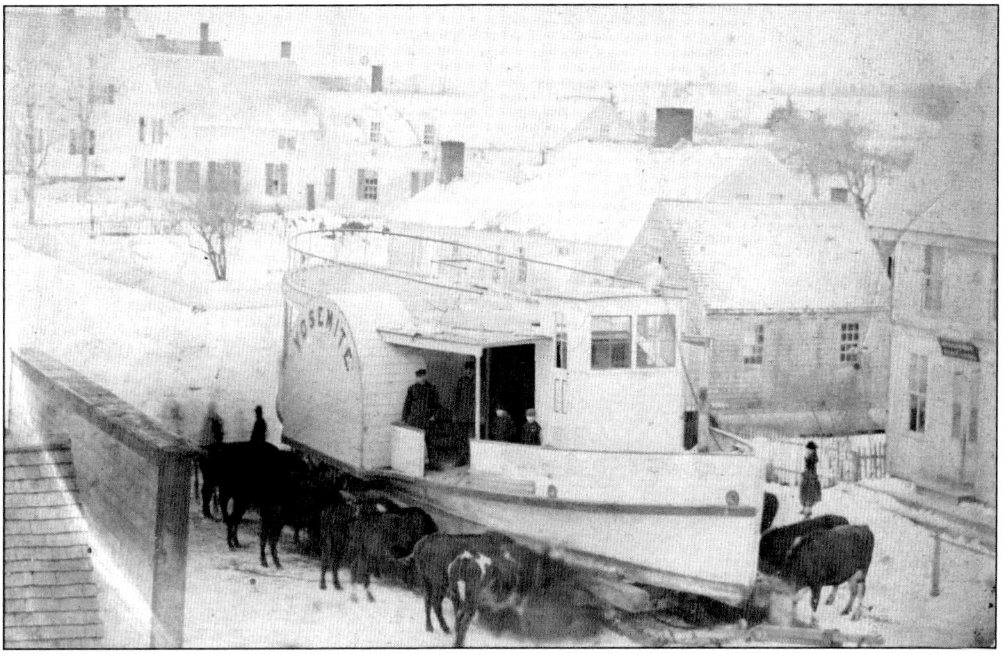

The *Daily Kennebec Journal* reported on December 11, 1880, that the *Yosemite Steamer* was being relocated from Lake Auburn to Lake Maranacook in Winthrop. The photograph here shows the oxen being fed alongside the steamer on Main Street. In the background, the present-day Blossom House of the Monmouth Museum can be seen. (Harry Cochrane photograph, courtesy of the Monmouth Museum.)

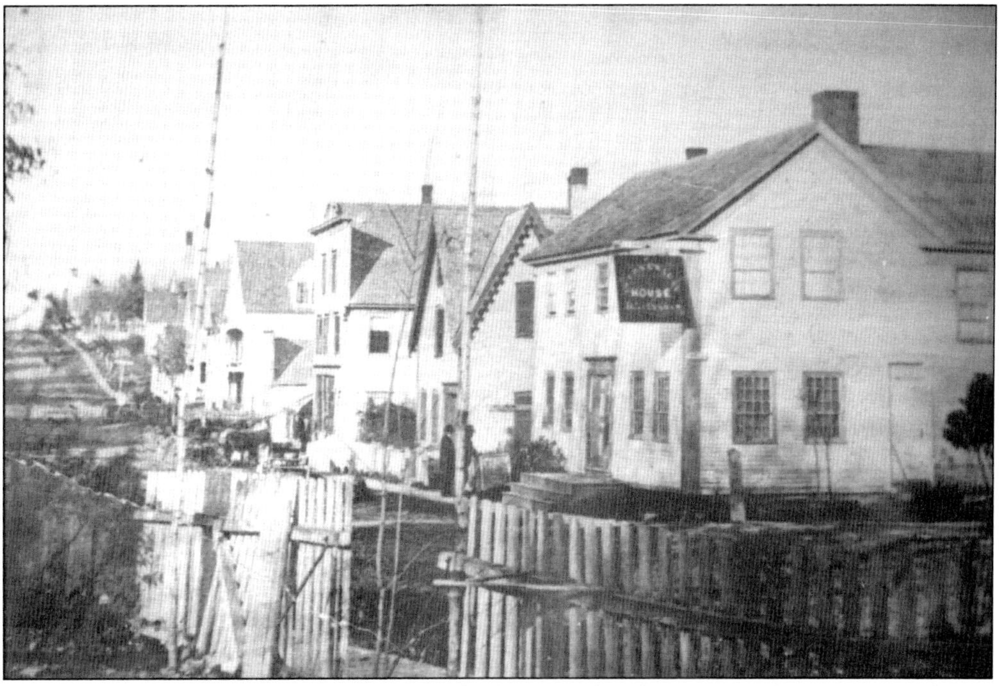

This is a view of the east side of Main Street looking north, taken prior to the Great Fire of 1888. (Courtesy of the Monmouth Museum.)

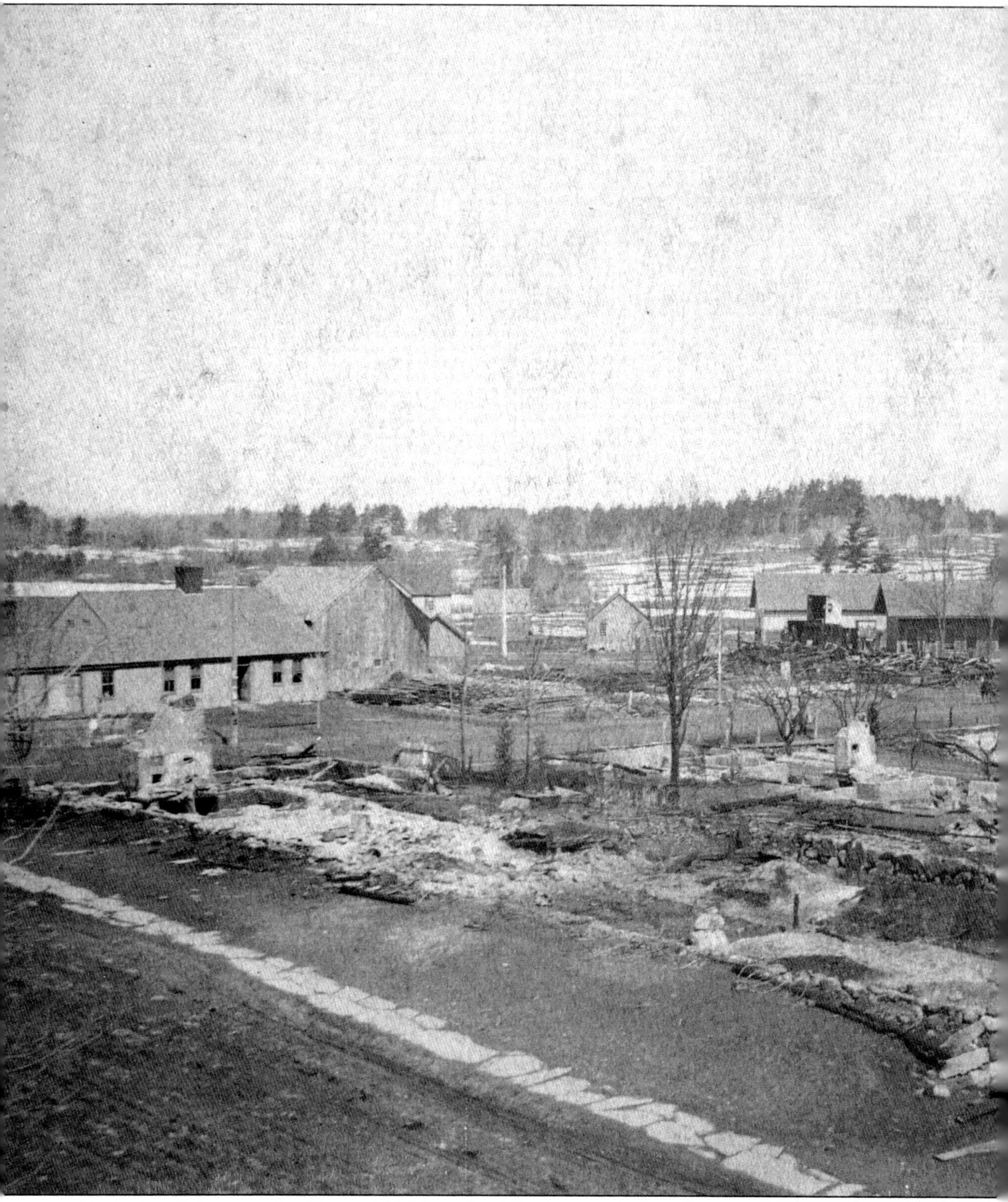

Professional photographer George F. McIntosh of Gardiner took this photograph the morning after the fire of April 19, 1888, which devastated the entire downtown section of Monmouth, known as Monmouth Center. No lives were lost. The photograph was taken from Maple Street facing

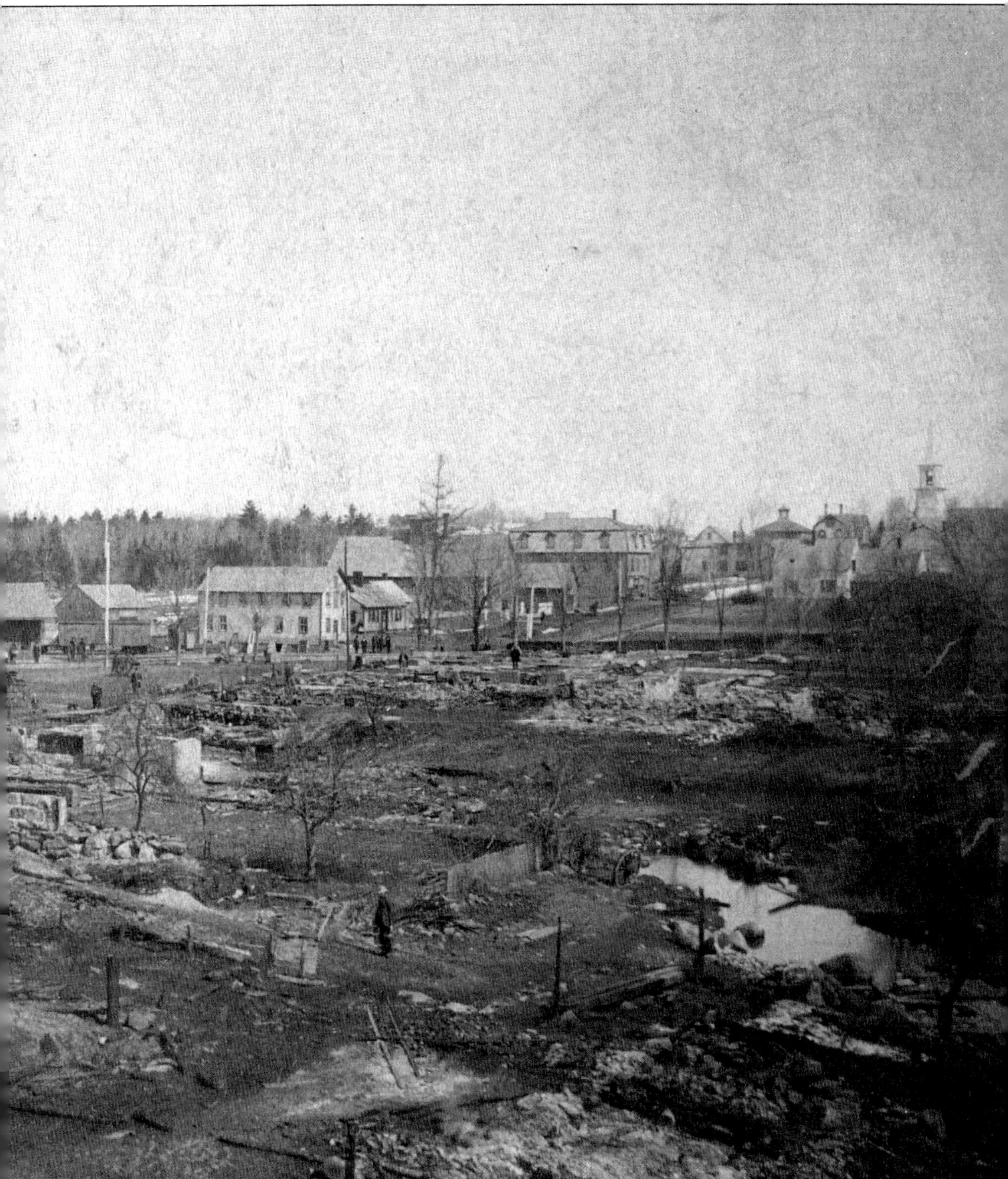

northwest toward Main Street and was perhaps taken out of the upstairs window of the blacksmith shop. On the far left is the Blossom House. The long building in the middle was the train depot, which missed the fire by only 10 feet and 5 minutes. (Courtesy of the Monmouth Museum.)

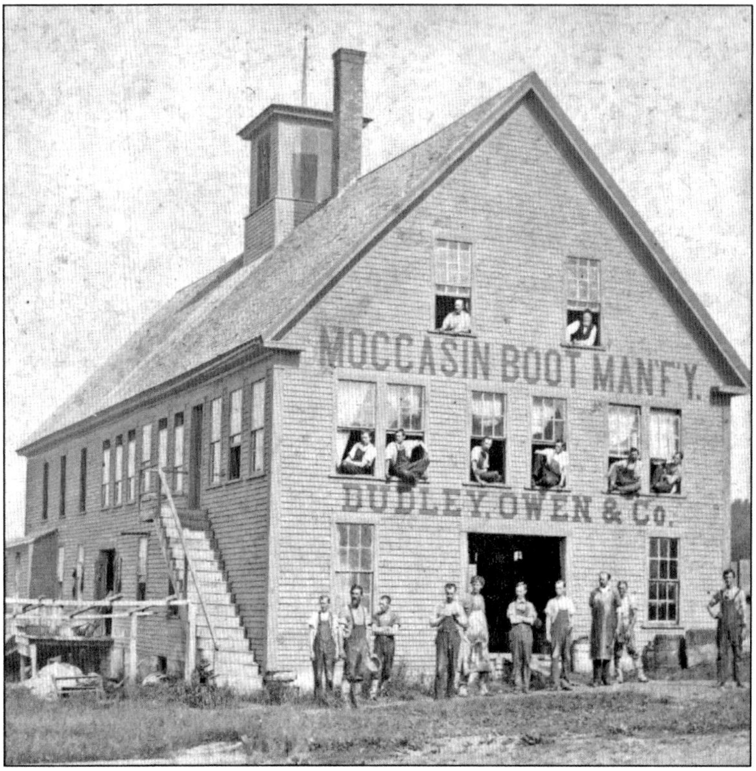

The Dudley Owen Moccasin Factory, later known as the M. L. Getchell Company, was located at the present-day site of Don's Electric on Main Street at Monmouth Center. Note Cyrus Owen, left, and William Dudley, right, are in the top two windows of the building. (Courtesy of Audrey and David Walker.)

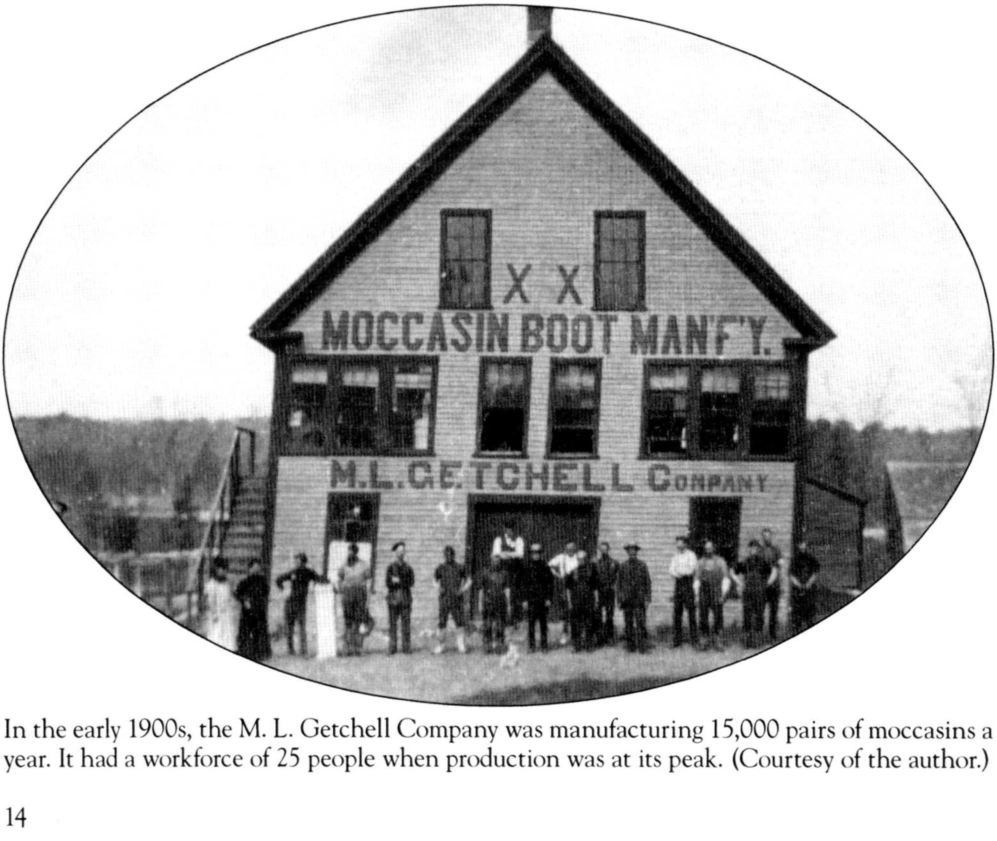

In the early 1900s, the M. L. Getchell Company was manufacturing 15,000 pairs of moccasins a year. It had a workforce of 25 people when production was at its peak. (Courtesy of the author.)

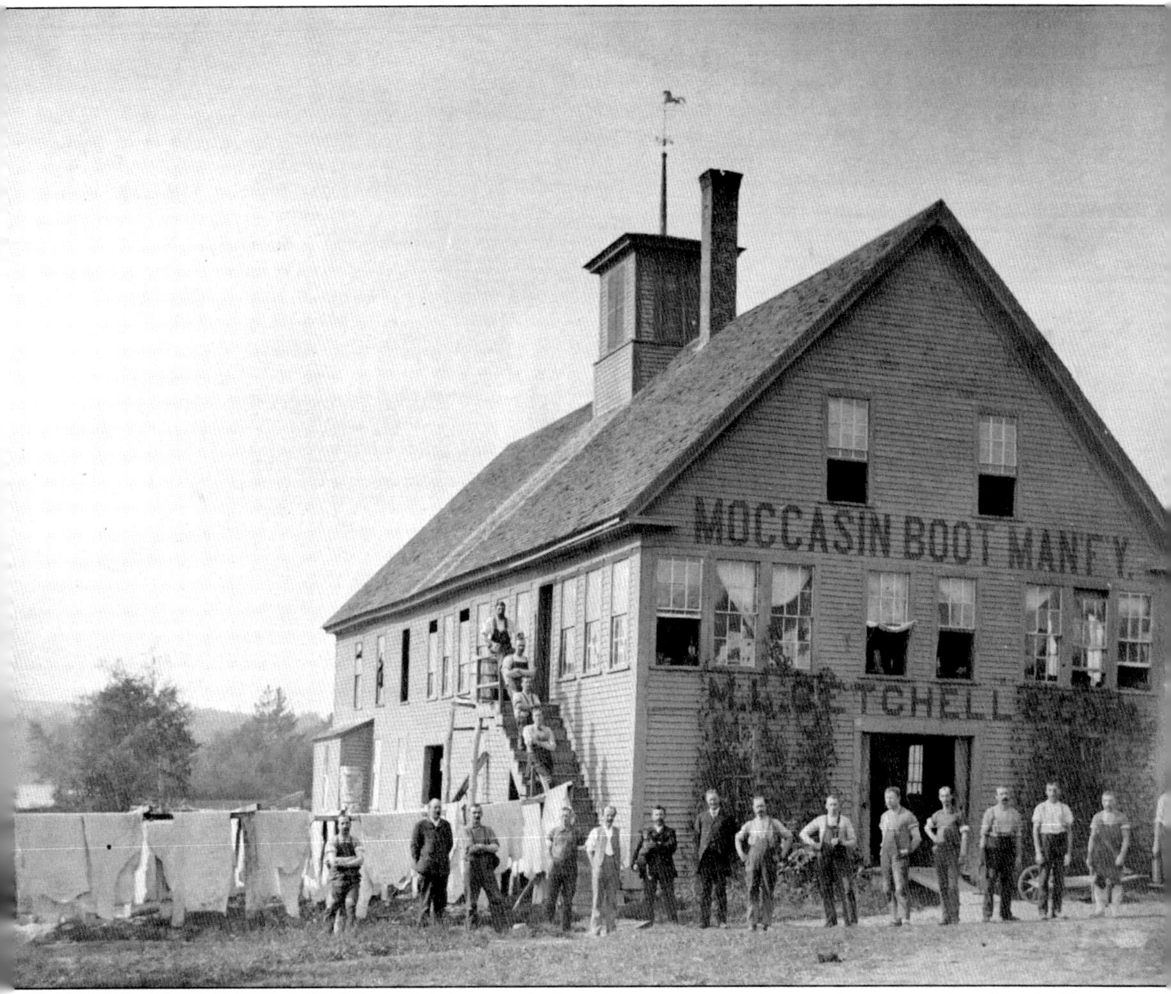

This instantaneous view of the M. L. Getchell and Company and its workers was taken by H. W. Blaisdell of Greene. He specialized in landscape and general view photography. The workers in the photograph are identified as follows, starting at the top of the stairs going down and then from left to right: John McCulla, Charles Towle, Frank Greenlief, Ed Prescott, Pete Frost, Horace Frost, Millard Richardson, Frank Wadsworth, Cyrus Richmond, Warren Plummer, Amasiah Getchell, Will Norris, Frank Rowell, Jack Cowan, John Frost, Fred Flanders, Charles Curtis, Will (Bill) Curtis, and Henry Jacobs. (Courtesy of the Monmouth Museum.)

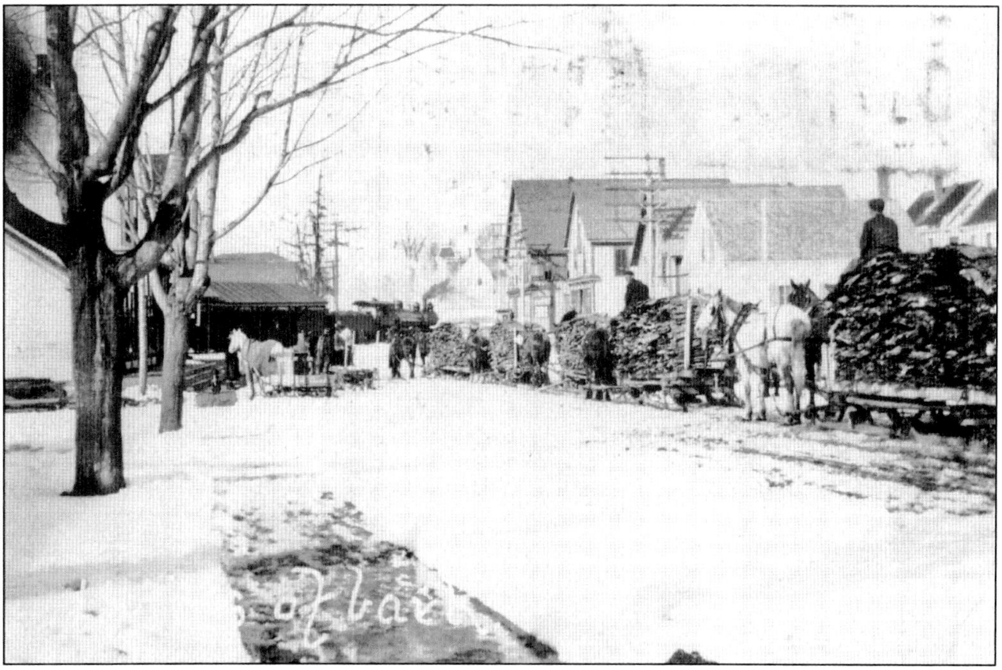

Main Street in Monmouth Center was a flourish of activity during the early 1900s. Here sleds of bark are waiting for the train, which is headed for Winthrop. They were on their way to the tannery for the M. L. Getchell Moccasin Factory, which was just beyond the tracks. Trees were cut in the early spring, when the sap was beginning to run, and the bark was removed in large strips to take to the tannery. Hemlock bark was used for producing a dark-colored leather, while oak bark was used to produce a lighter-colored leather. (Courtesy of Harland Kennison.)

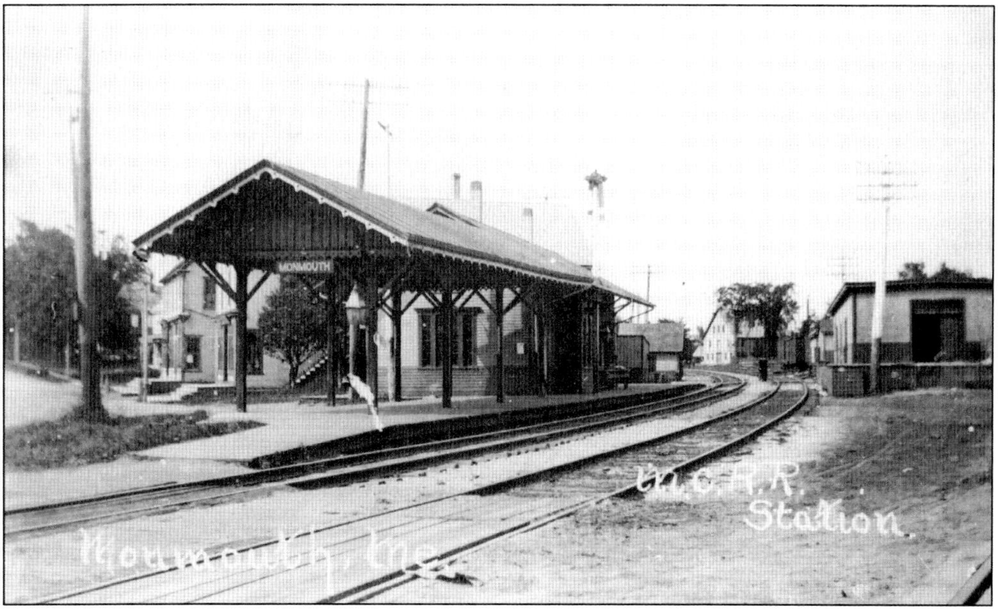

The railroad line through Monmouth was completed in late June 1849, and the first passenger train passed over the rails on July 4, 1849. This is the second Monmouth station, built in 1894, which replaced the smaller original station. It was dismantled in 1953. (Courtesy of the author.)

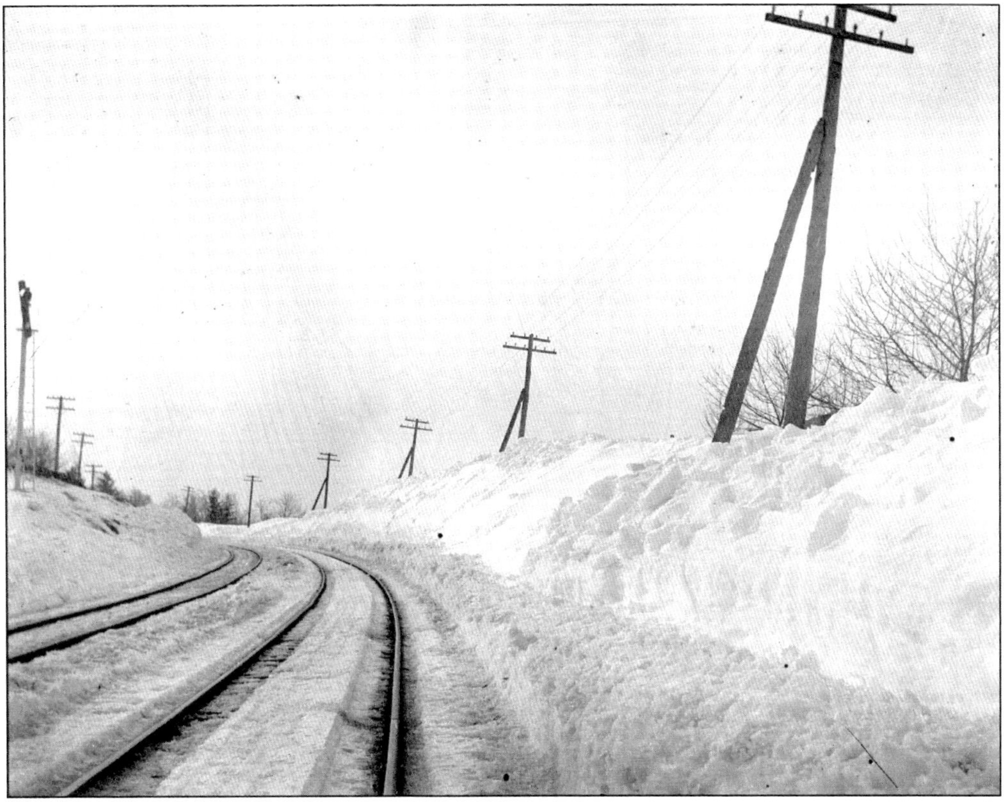

This photograph from the early 1900s shows the high snow banks heading out of Monmouth towards Portland along the railroad. (Courtesy of the Monmouth Museum.)

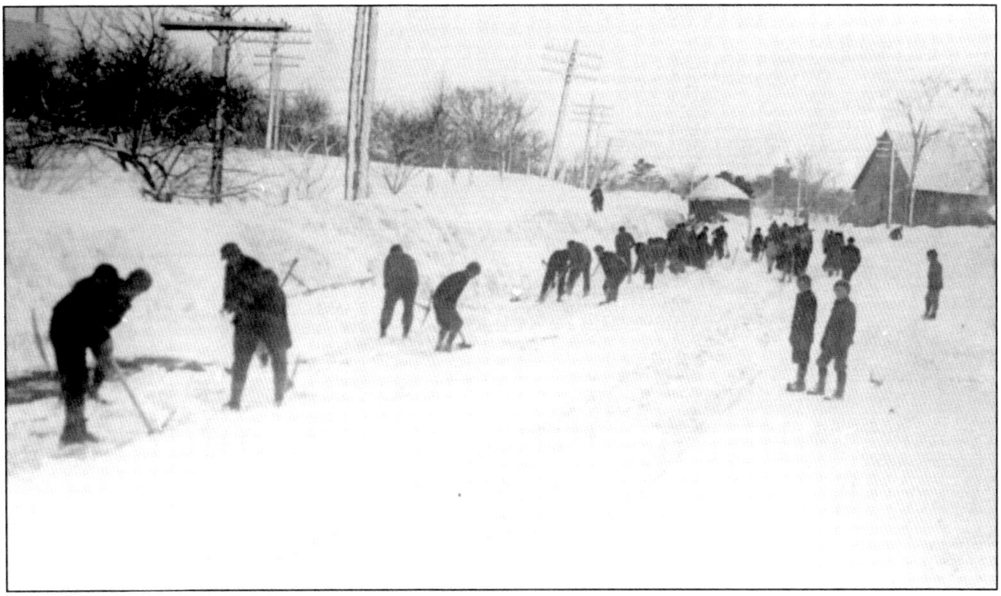

Men are clearing the tracks of snow just south of the center station. On the right side of the photograph is the Corn Shop, which was located near the present-day beach. (Courtesy of the Monmouth Museum.)

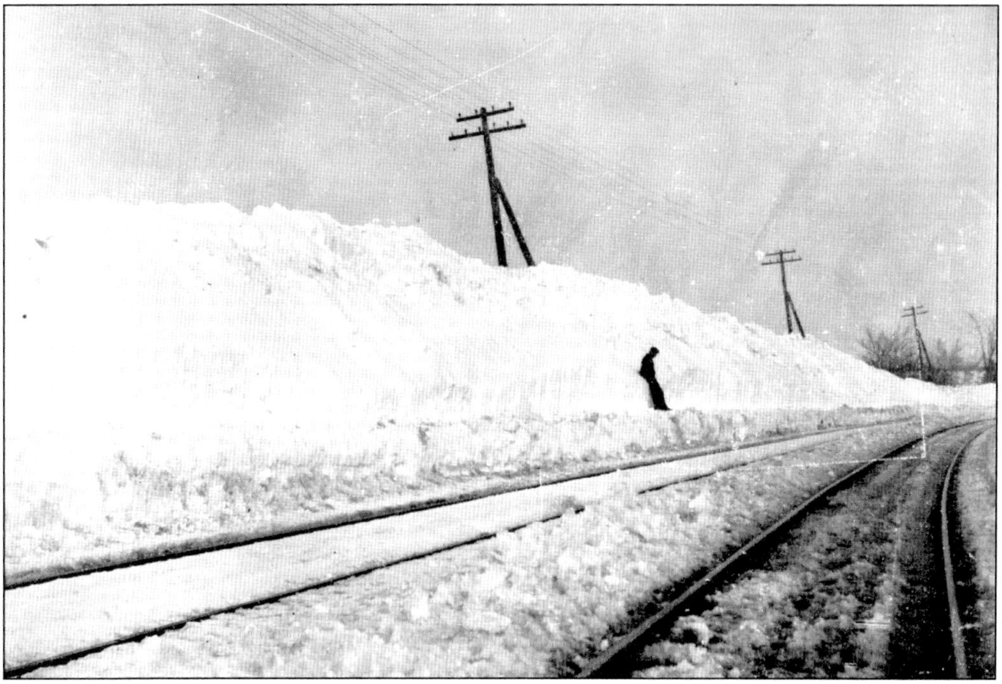

Leading away from the center of town along the shores of Cochnewagan, this photograph from a glass negative was taken in the early 1900s. Note the man standing at the bottom of the bank on the left side of the tracks. (Courtesy of the Monmouth Museum.)

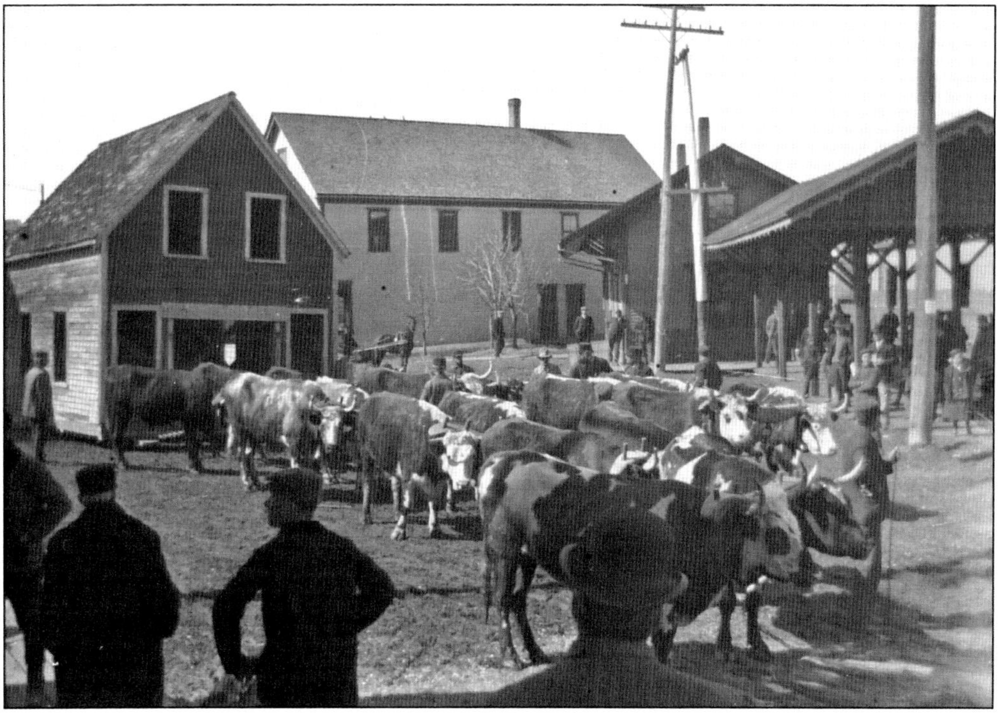

Oxen are moving a building on Main Street. Nearby is the train station and Woodbury's clothing store. (Courtesy of the Monmouth Museum.)

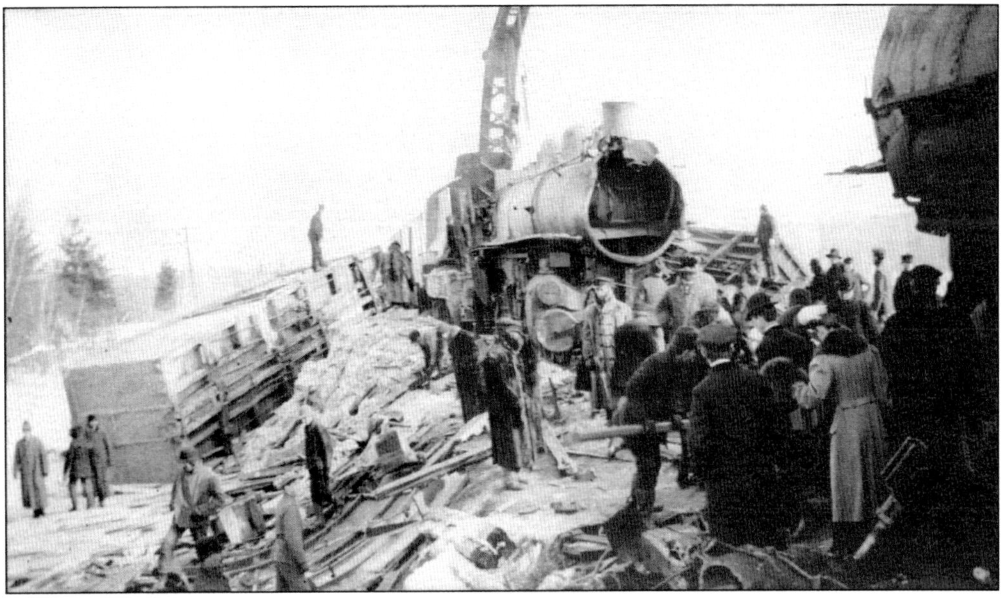

December 7, 1906, marked one of the worst train wrecks in Maine's railroad history. The wreck took place in Monmouth on a curve of track between the Annabessacook station and the Monmouth Center station. According to an article that ran in the *Daily Kennebec Journal* on December 8, the collision of freight train No. 22 from Waterville to Portland and an extra train from Portland to Waterville took place just before midnight on the 7th. Of the 12 trainmen, 4 were killed, and 3 were seriously injured. (Courtesy of the Monmouth Museum.)

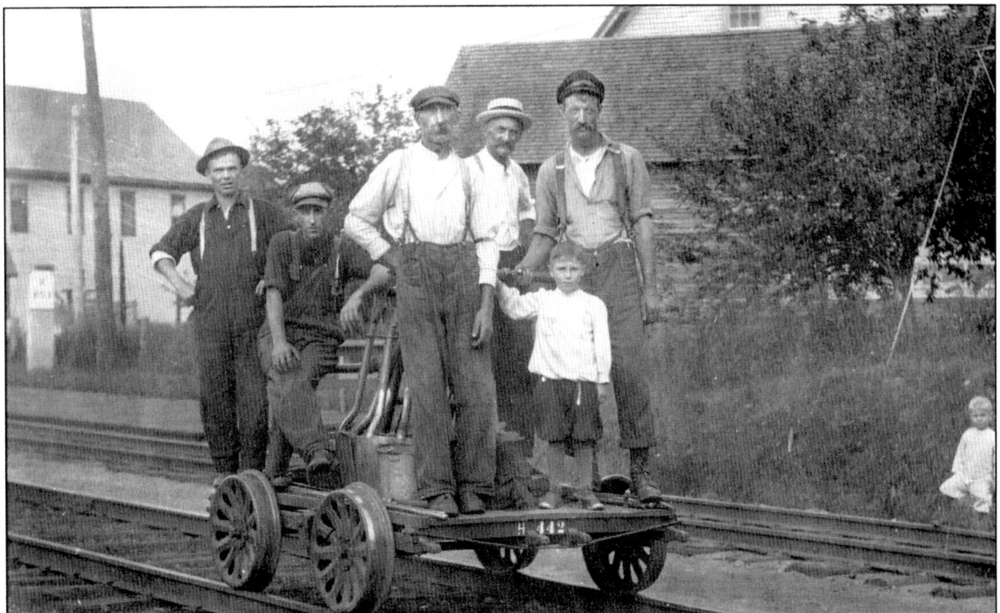

From left to right are Henry Dube, Willie Chandler, Charles Curtis, Will Lord, and Ed Burnham. The children are Raymond Stetson on the handcar and Merle Gordon on the side of the track. (Courtesy of Audrey and David Walker.)

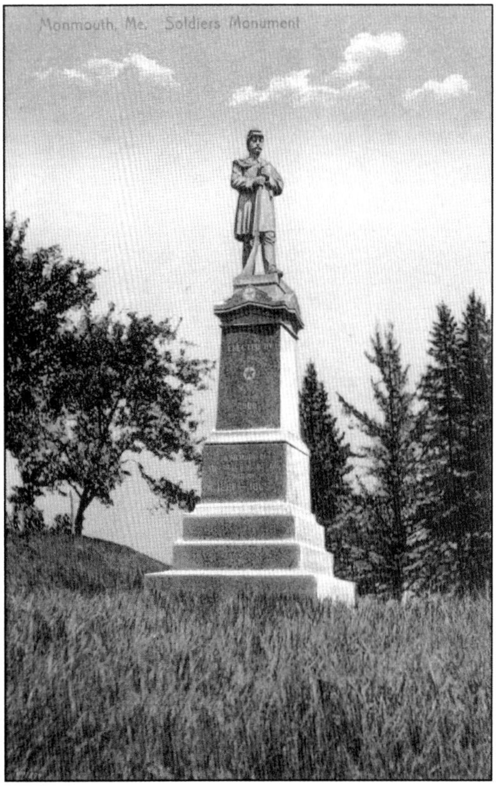

The ceremony for the dedication of the town's Civil War monument took place on Tuesday, May 29, 1900, under the auspices of the Monmouth Chapter of the G. K. Norris Woman's Relief Corps. The Woman's Soldiers Monument Association purchased the land that the monument stands on for $50 on May 22, 1900. (Courtesy of the Monmouth Museum.)

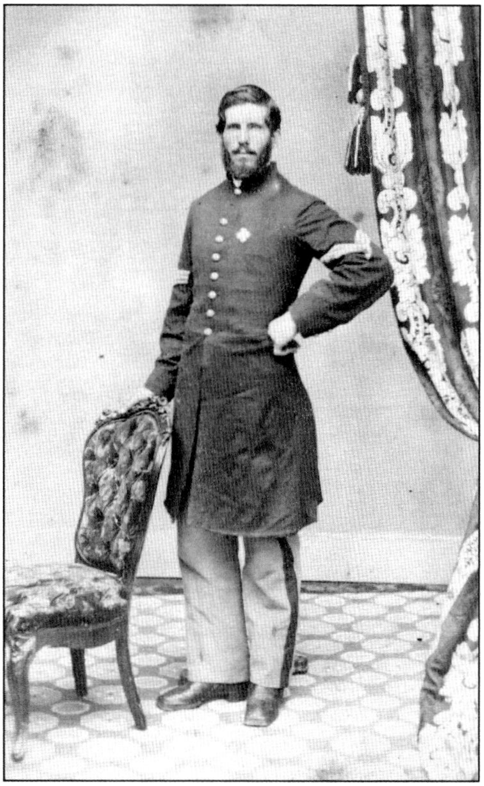

Sgt. Charles Hinkley paid the ultimate price by giving his life for his country during the Civil War. He enlisted in Company K of the 7th Maine Regiment on August 21, 1861, at the age of 21. He was killed in action on May 12, 1864, at the battle of Spotsylvania Court House and was buried on the battlefield. (Courtesy of the author.)

William H. Briggs of Monmouth enlisted in Company B of the 3rd Maine Regiment on June 4, 1861, at the age of 24. He was wounded in five places at the battle of Fair Oaks in 1862. He survived his wounds and returned to service. He rose from the rank of sergeant to first lieutenant during his three years of service. He was killed at Bethesda Church on May 30, 1864, at the age of 27. He is buried at Yorktown National Cemetery in Yorktown, Virginia, grave No. 258. (Courtesy of Tom McDonald.)

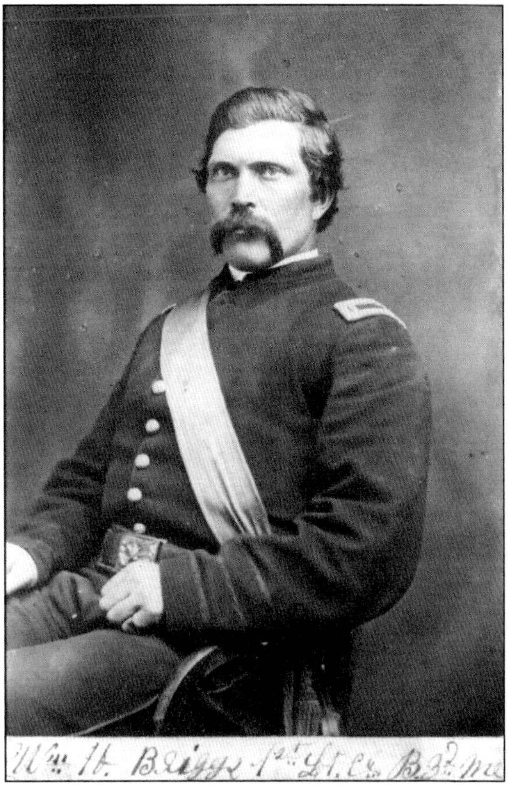

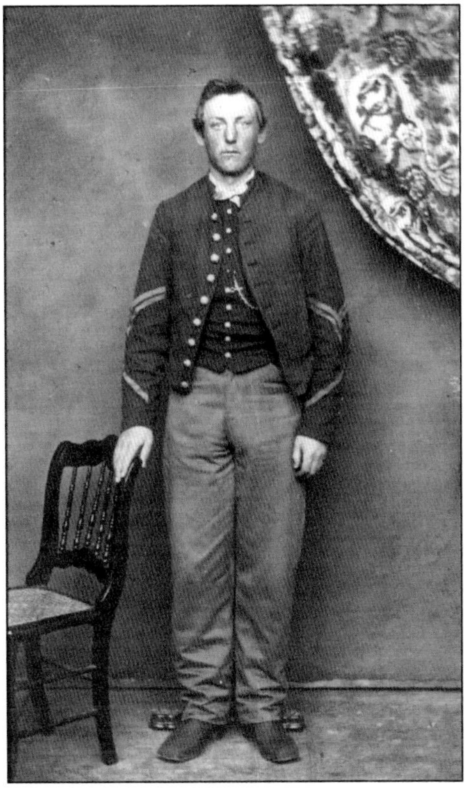

Sgt. Charles Plummer of Company K, 1st Maine Veteran Infantry lost his life fighting for his country during the Civil War. He enlisted in Company K of the 7th Maine Regiment on September 7, 1861, at the age of 18. In 1863, he became a corporal. He was killed on May 23, 1865, before Petersburg. He was originally buried at Flower's Farm. His final resting place is now in Poplar Grove Cemetery in Petersburg, Virginia, grave No. 1595. (Courtesy of the author.)

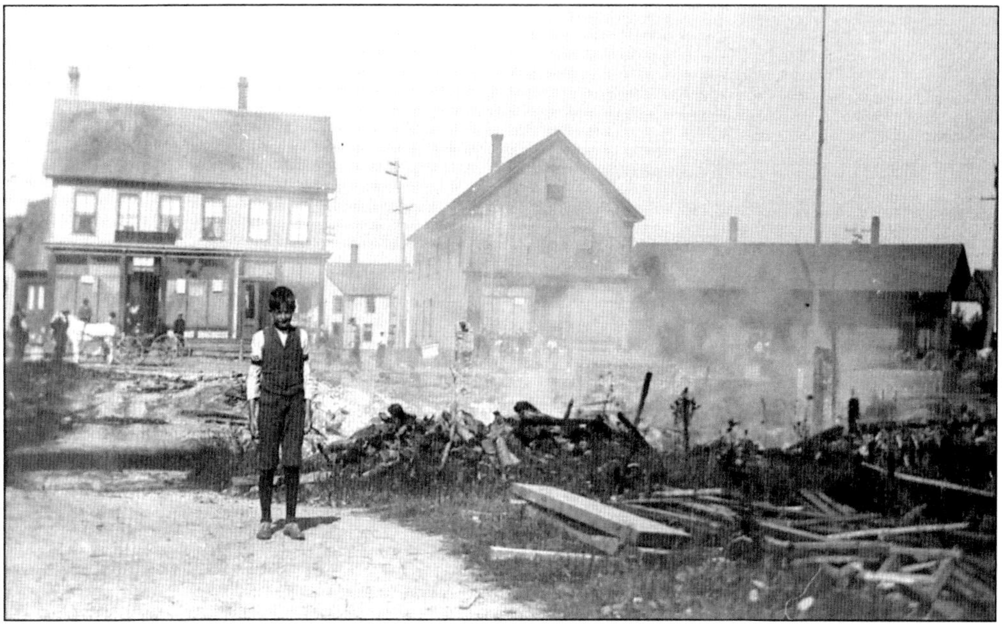

On August 28, 1903, Monmouth Center, once again came close to total destruction. The hard-working townspeople were able to save 7 of the 10 buildings that caught fire that morning. This is a view of the east side of Main Street looking west after the fire had run its course. (Courtesy of Natalie Hall Jones.)

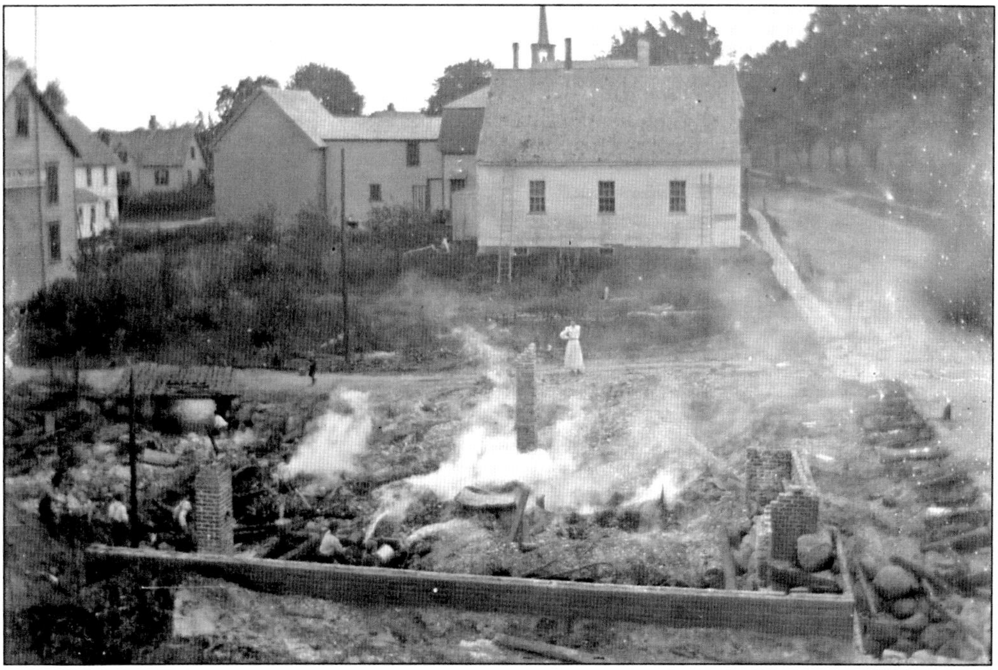

A woman in the center of the photograph is looking at the destruction on the east side of Main Street from the fire of 1903. In the background, one can see what is now the Monmouth Museum Town Hall building, the Whitehouse Block, and the steeple of the Congregational church, now the Masonic hall. (Courtesy of the Monmouth Museum.)

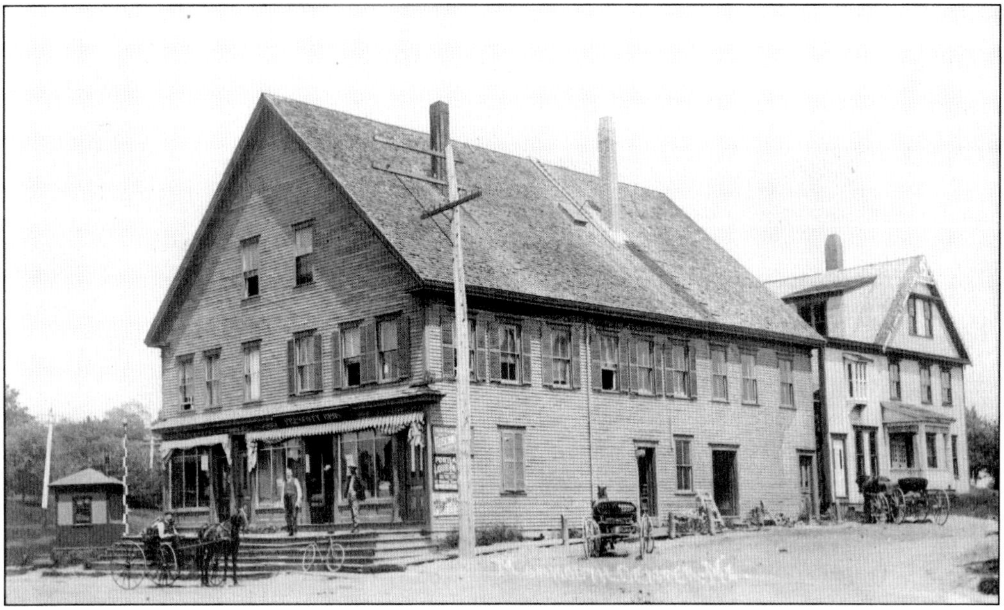

C. W. Prescott once occupied what is presently called the Monmouth General Store. (Courtesy of the author.)

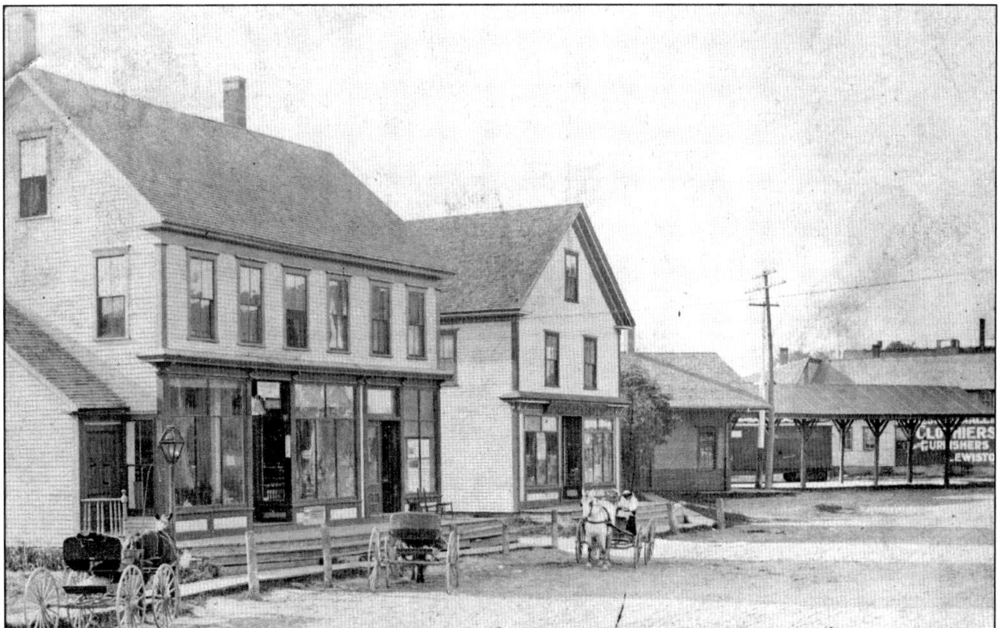

This is a Main Street view looking at the Prescott brothers' store and the Woodbury's clothing store with the train station in the background. (Courtesy of the Monmouth Museum.)

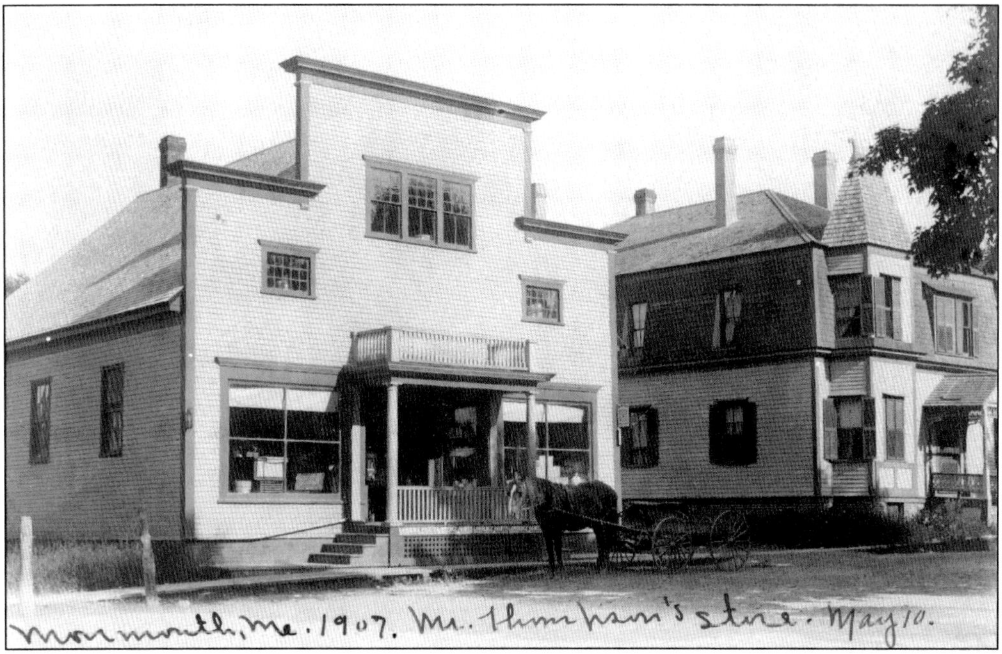

In 1907, this building, currently part of the Monmouth Museum, was known as the C. L. Thompson Store. Originally, the building was located where Cumston Hall now stands. When the building was moved, it was put in backwards, so that the front of the building actually faces the back. (Courtesy of the author.)

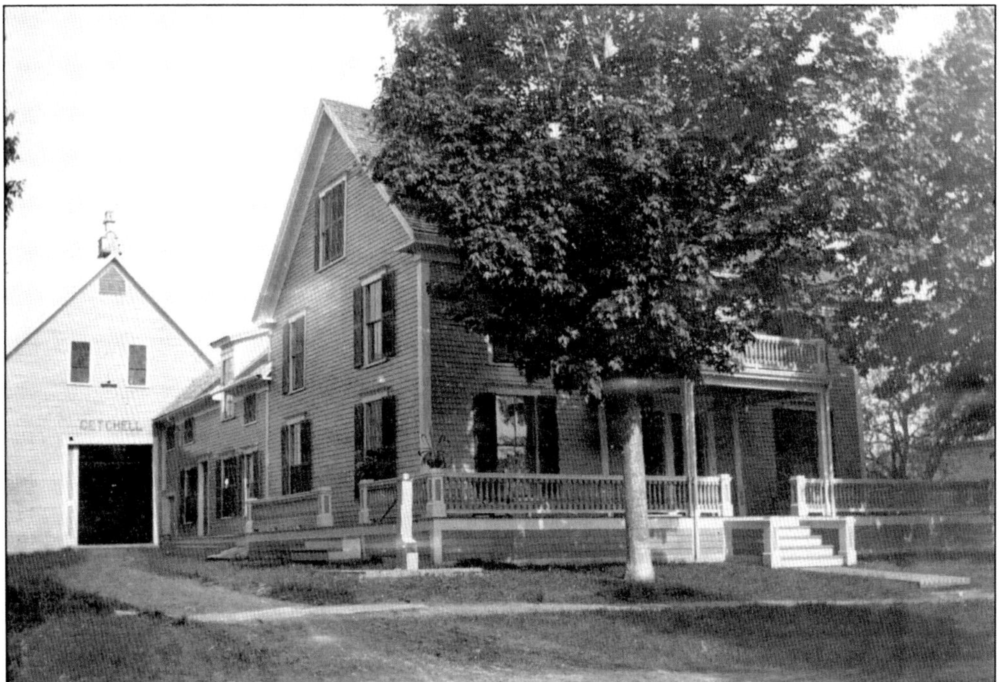

This is the Getchell Homestead on Main Street, next to the current Bragdon-Finley Funeral Home, as it appeared in the early 1900s. (Courtesy of Stan DeOrsey.)

The Day family lived on Maple Street during the early 1900s. From left to right are (seated) Ross Day, Myra Day, and Ruby Day; (standing) unidentified, Millard Day, and Willard Day. (Courtesy of the Monmouth Museum.)

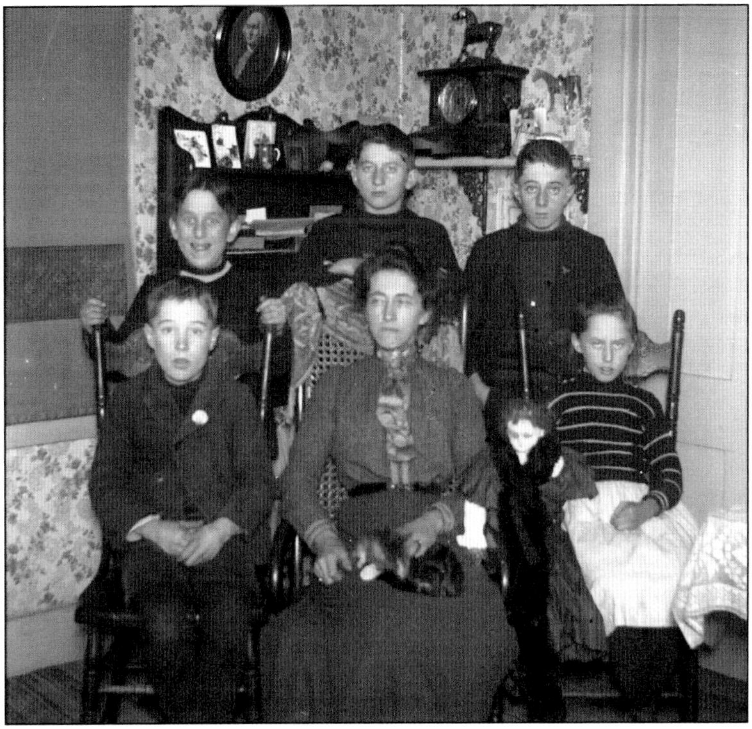

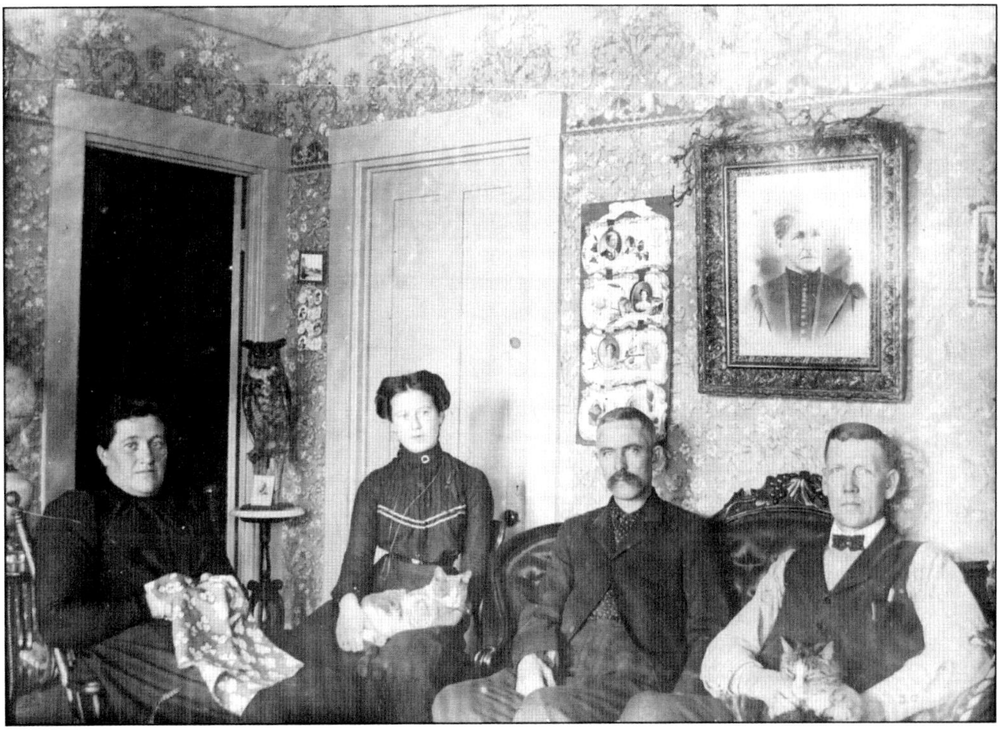

From left to right, Mary Dudley Blake, Anna Blake, Herbert Blake, and John Prescott, one of the heros of the Great Fire of 1888, are pictured at the Blakes' home on Maple Street. (Courtesy of the Monmouth Museum.)

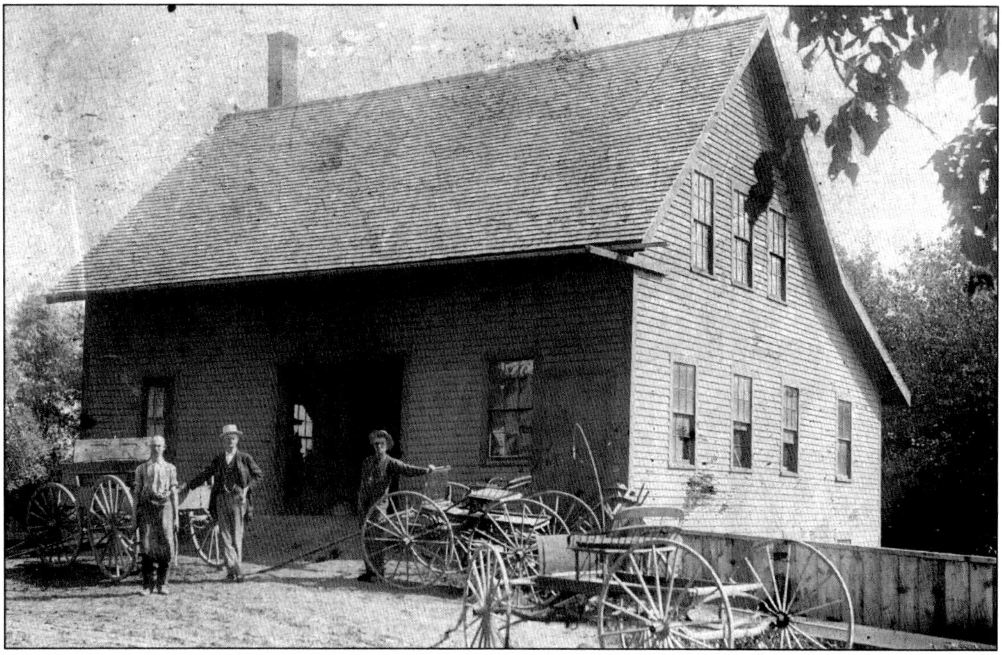

The blacksmith shop located on Maple Street at Monmouth Center was built by Wilbur Maxwell around the time of the Civil War and operated as a working blacksmith shop into the 20th century. It later was home to Rollins Feed Store in the 1960s. Now restored, the blacksmith shop is one of the buildings belonging to the Monmouth Museum complex. The blacksmith shop was the first building opened at the museum in 1970 by the founder, H. Earle Flanders. (Courtesy of the Monmouth Museum.)

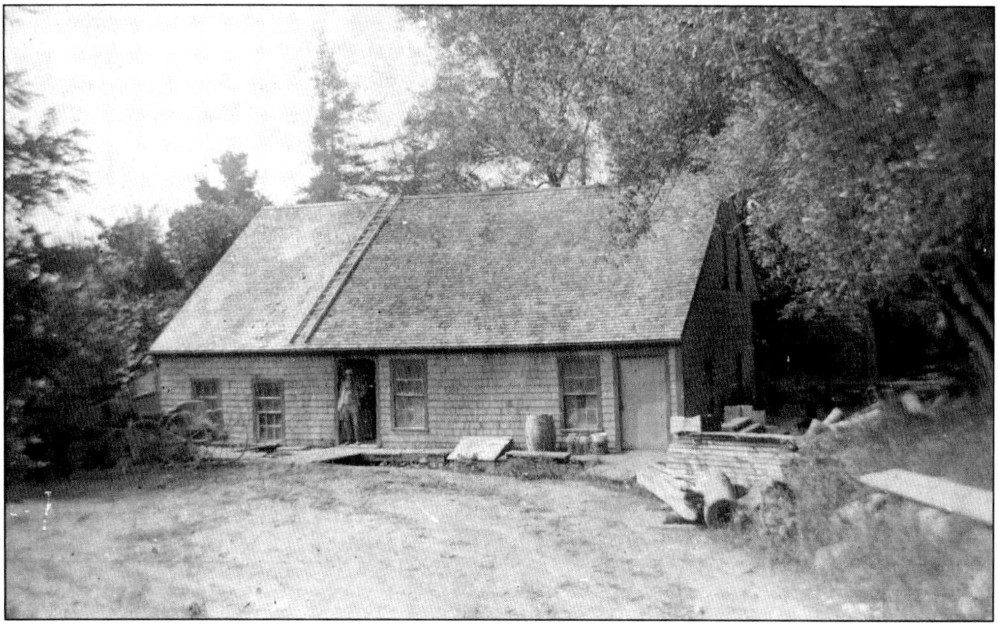

The gristmill on Maple Street was operated by Oscar Frost, Monmouth's poet and hen fancier. He is noted for developing the White Plymouth Rock variety of poultry. (Courtesy of the Monmouth Museum.)

George Pottle (left) and Eugene Day are pictured at Day's store. (Courtesy of Audrey and David Walker.)

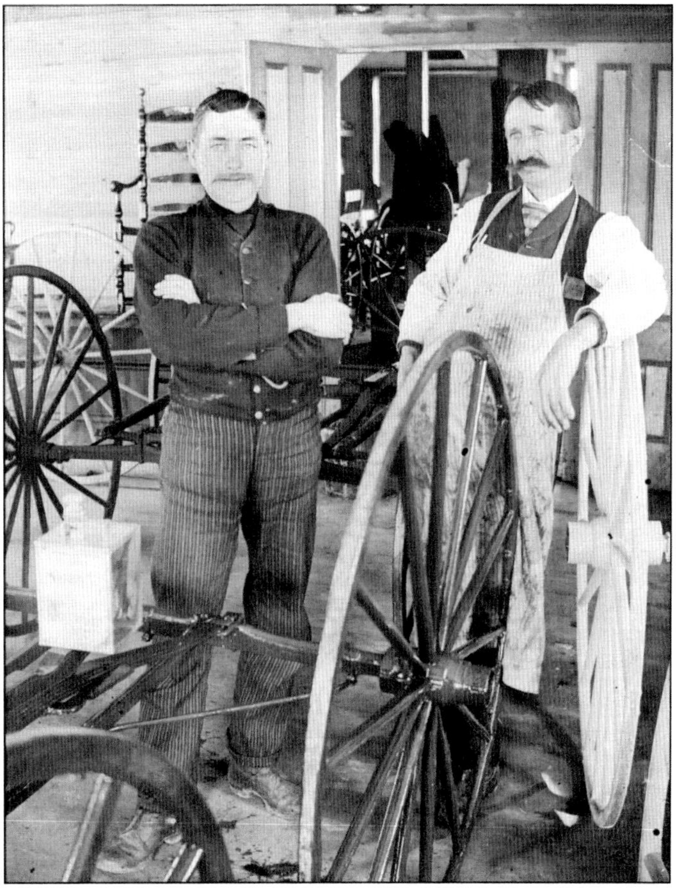

The present-day home of Ruth and Phil Prescott was moved from the Donnell opening to sit on Blue Road in 1908. It was moved with the help of 19 pairs of oxen, 20 pairs of horses, and old-fashioned community hauling led by G. O. Bishop Leeds. (Courtesy of Louise Smith.)

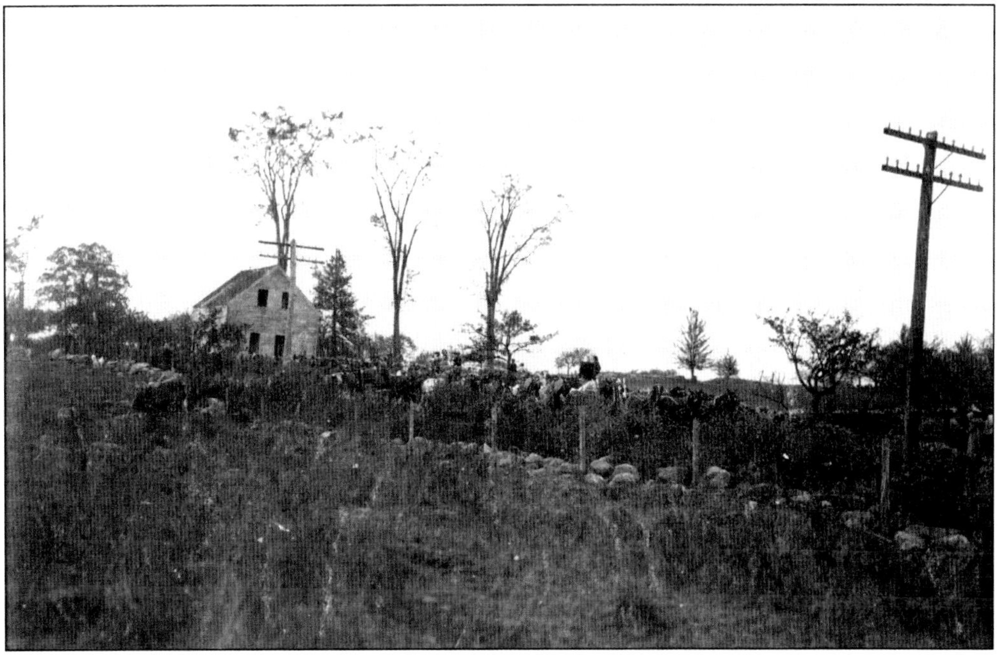

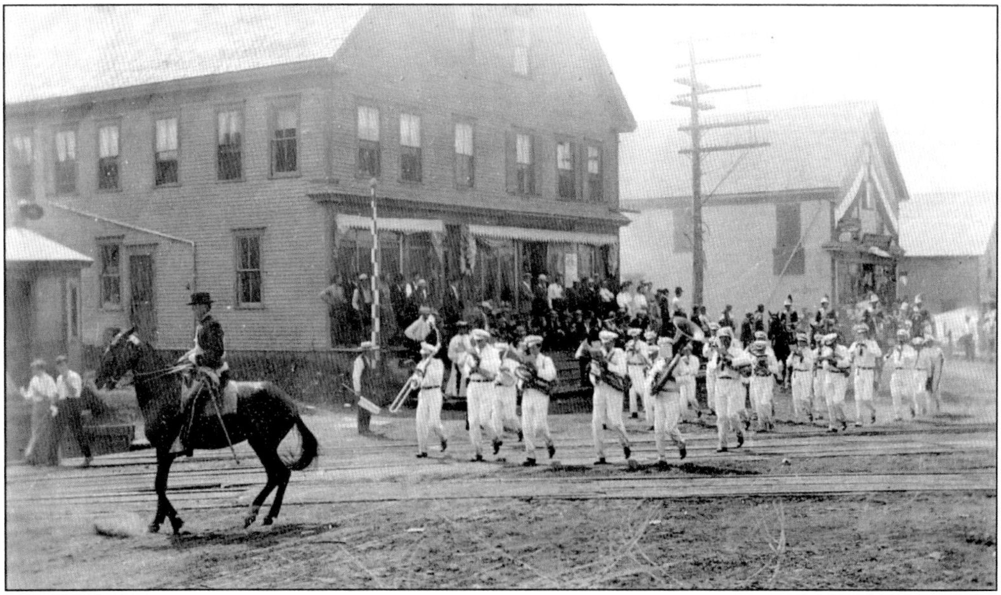

The parade of July 4, 1908, is passing over the railroad tracks led by Civil War veteran A. C. Sherman. Note the bicycle hanging from the telephone pole next to the first building on the left side of the photograph. (Courtesy of the Monmouth Museum.)

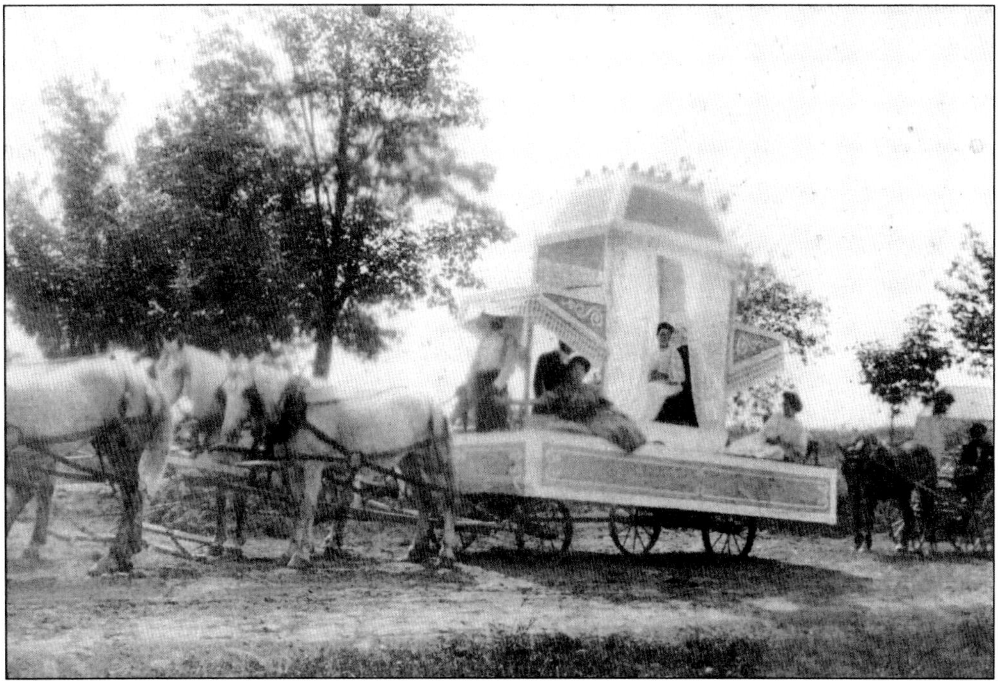

This float was one of several designed by Harry Cochrane for the Fourth of July parade that Monmouth held in 1908. The local newspapers wrote that Independence Day in Monmouth was celebrated on a scale seldom known in the town's history. The parade was headed by the marshal of the day, A. J. Chick. The line of the parade was unbroken from South Main Street to North Monmouth. Arthur J. Chick was a longtime principal of Monmouth Academy during the first half of the 20th century. (Courtesy of the Monmouth Museum.)

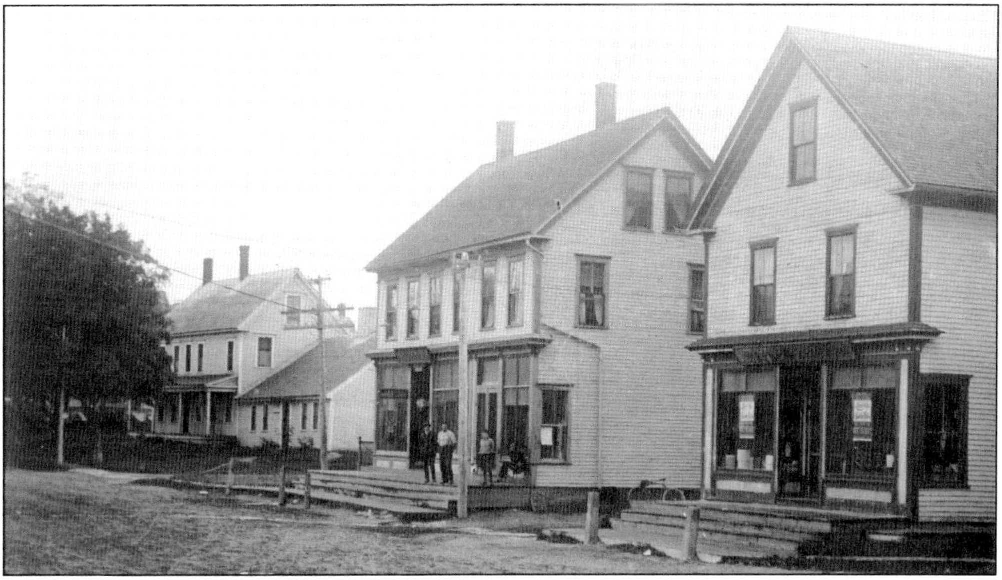

This is a view of the west side of Main Street facing south. In the background, the residence of Terry King and the Monmouth Museum's Blossom house can be seen. (Courtesy of the Monmouth Museum.)

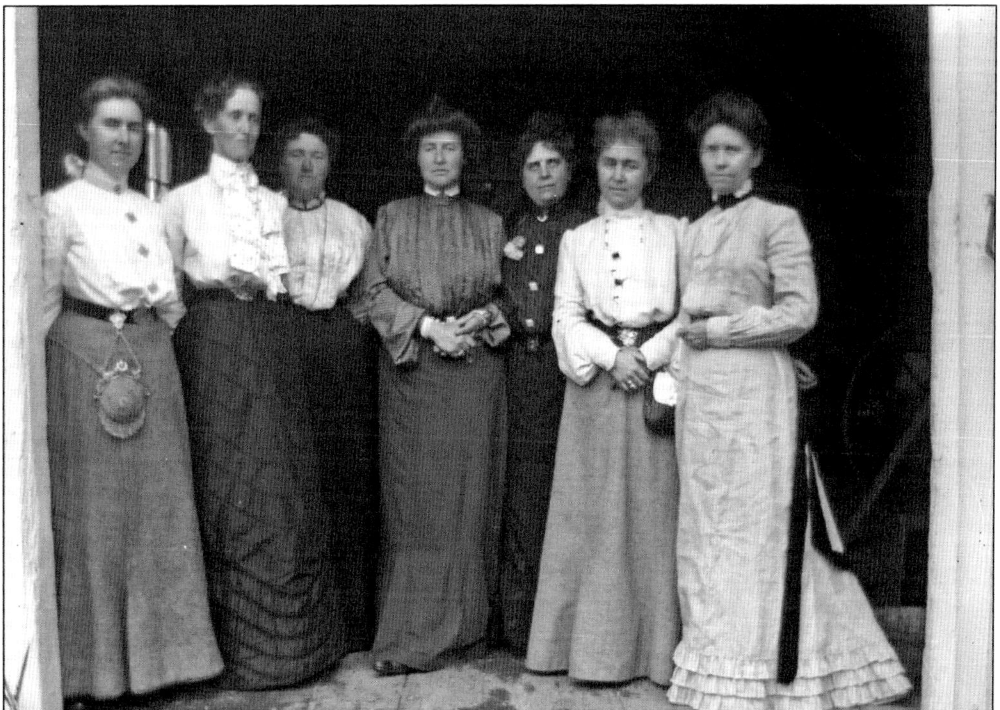

Earl Flander's grandmother Mary D. Blake is the third from left in this group of seven ladies. Rose Wellman, Mary Greenlief, and Augusta (Smith) Owen, as well as three other unidentified women, are also in this group. They appear to be standing in the doorway of someone's barn. (Courtesy of the Monmouth Museum.)

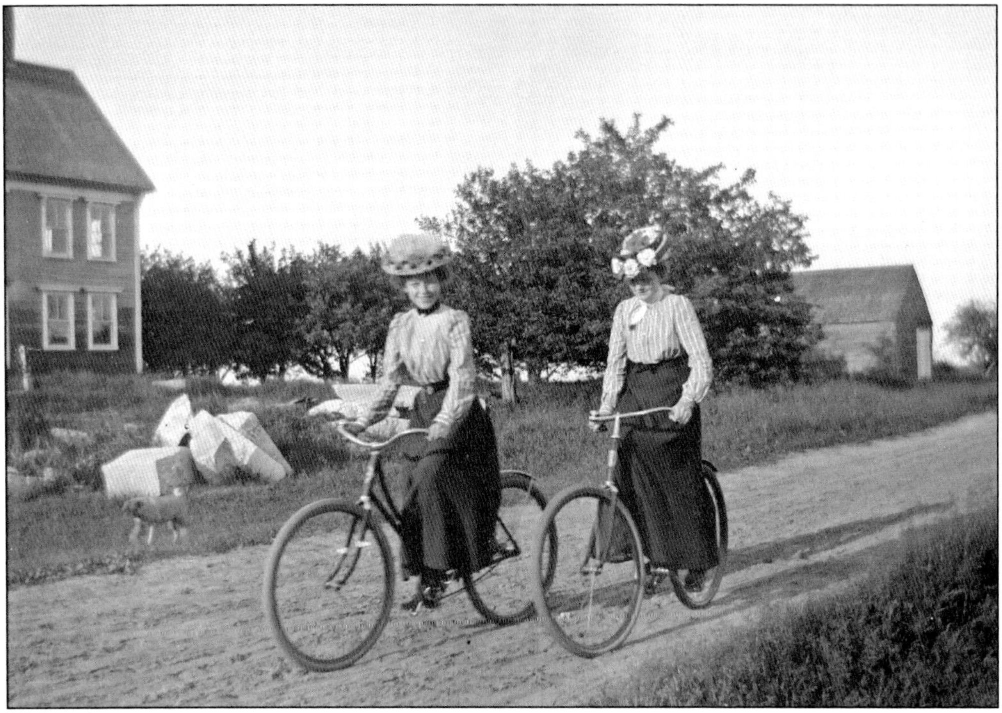

Two lovely young ladies are out for a ride on the outskirts of town. A little dog keeps them company to the left. (Courtesy of the Monmouth Museum.)

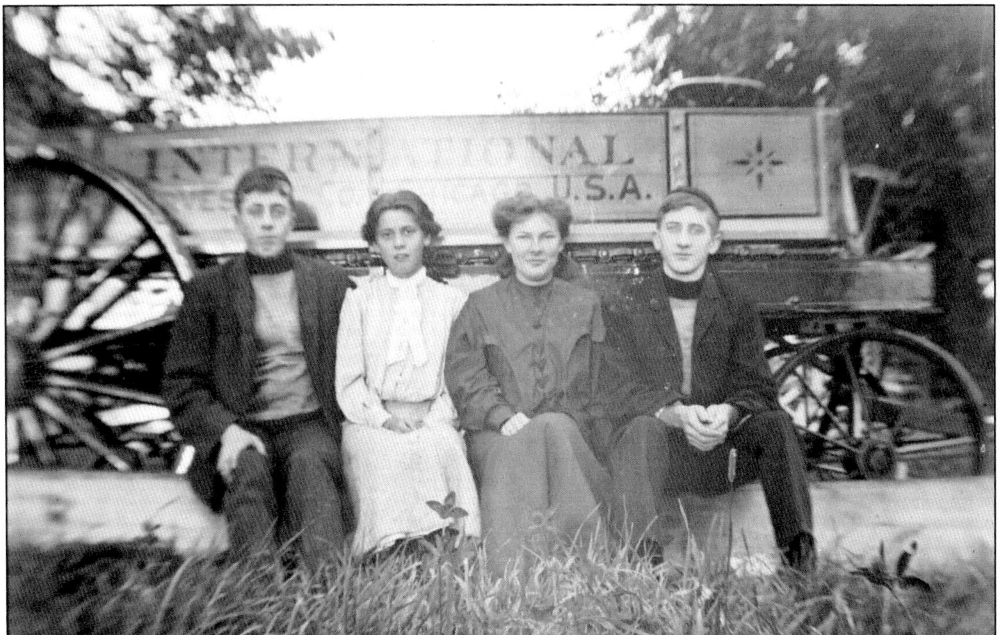

From left to right, Willard Day, Ruby Day, an unidentified friend, and Millard Day pose beside a International Harvester wagon. The Days lived on and grew up on Maple Street. Ruby would later marry Elmer Haskell. (Courtesy of the Monmouth Museum.)

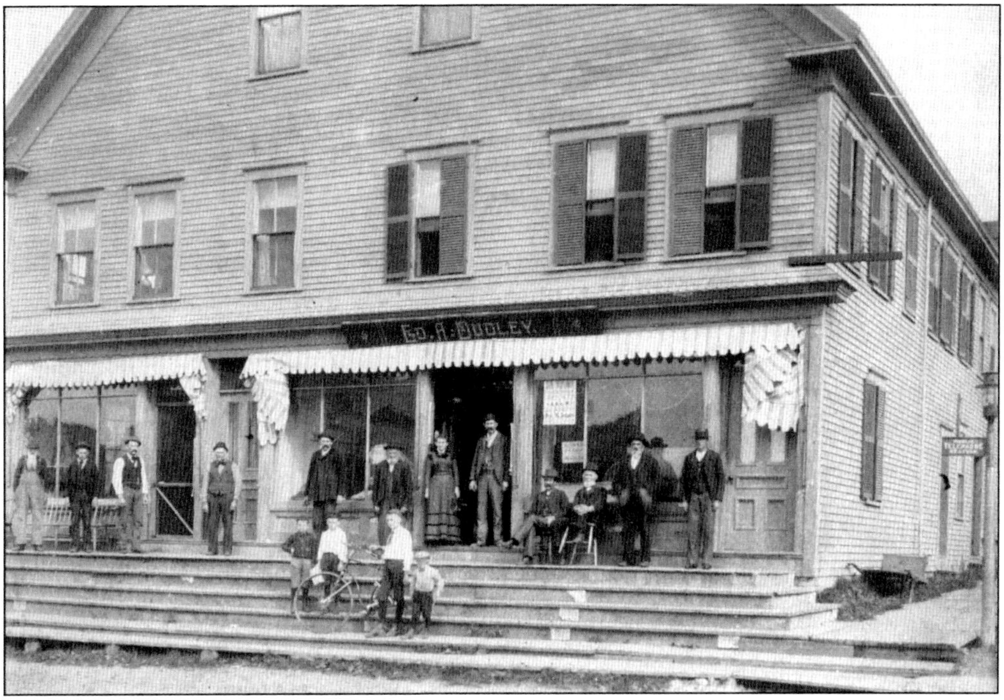

At the beginning of the 20th century, the building that now is home to the Monmouth General Store was the Ed A. Dudley Store. Ed and Mary Dudley can be seen here standing in the doorway to their store. (Courtesy of the Monmouth Museum.)

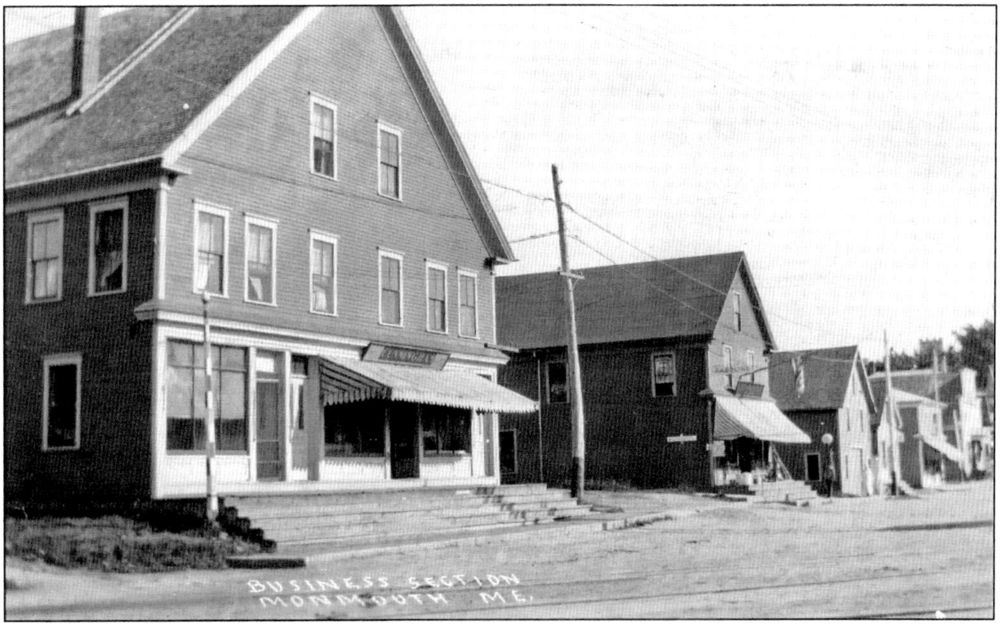

This view of the current Monmouth General Store shows it when it was run by the Cunningham family. (Courtesy of the Monmouth Museum.)

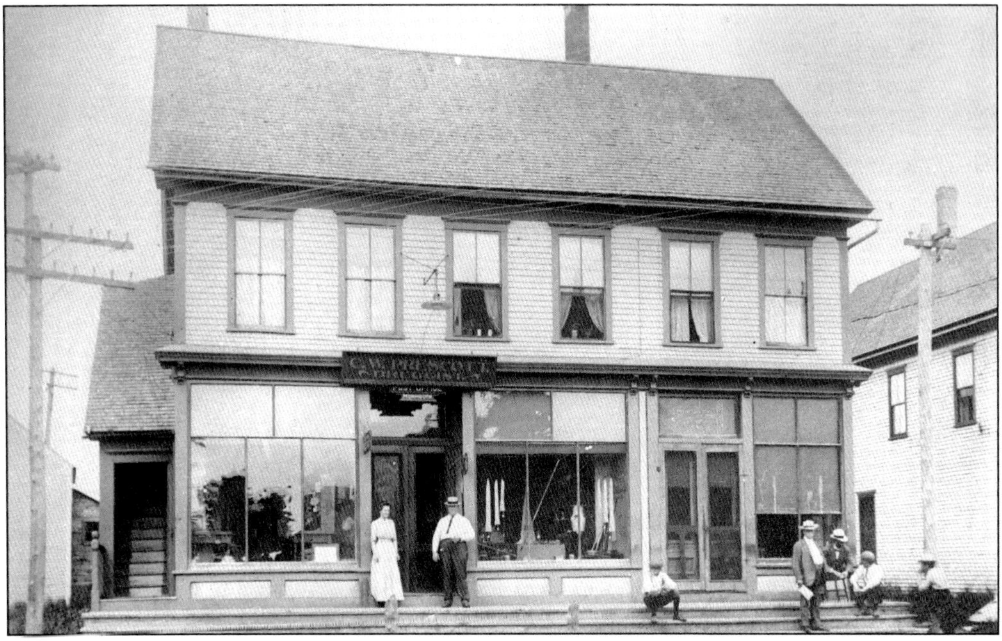

The town post office, the C. W. Prescott drugstore, and the C. O. Flanders Meat Market were housed in this building, which was owned by T. E. Frost. It was one of two buildings destroyed on October 20, 1913. The building stood on the lot that now is home to the Monmouth Museum's Stencil Shop. (Courtesy of the Monmouth Museum.)

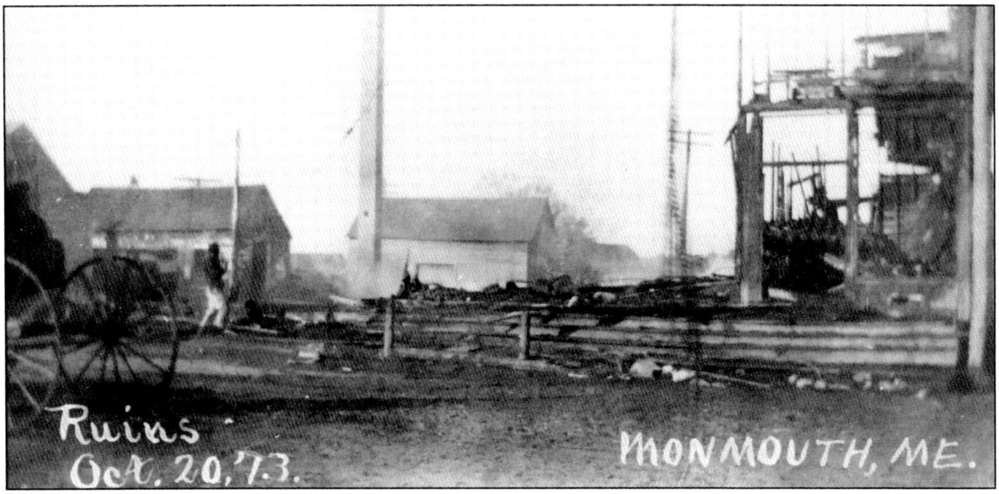

The 1913 fire destroyed the two-story, 30-by-60-foot building of the R. E. Woodbury Company, Inc., with all of its stock and fixtures. The valuation placed upon the building and Woodbury's losses was estimated around $10,000. He had only partial insurance at the time of the fire. Pictured here is the building adjacent, containing the post office of Postmaster Edward A. Prescott, the C. W. Prescott drugstore, and the C. O. Flanders Meat Market, which all totaled losses of $3,000. The mail was saved by heroic efforts. Willard Day and his family lived in the Woodbury structure and completely lost their household furniture, for he had no insurance. C. Wesley Prescott was away on a hunting trip. It is believed that cinders from the previous evening at the Cochnewagan stables had drifted into the Woodbury building through a broken windowpane and were responsible for the devastation. (Courtesy of the author.)

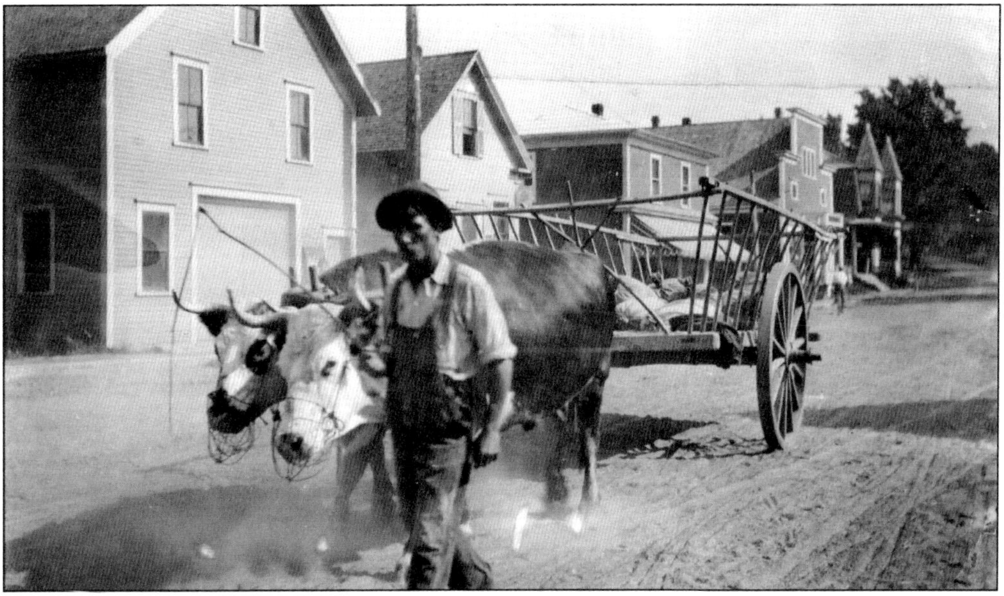

A young man with his muzzled oxen and their wooden hay cart is heading north on Main Street. The wire muzzle prevented the oxen from eating grass. (Courtesy of the Monmouth Museum.)

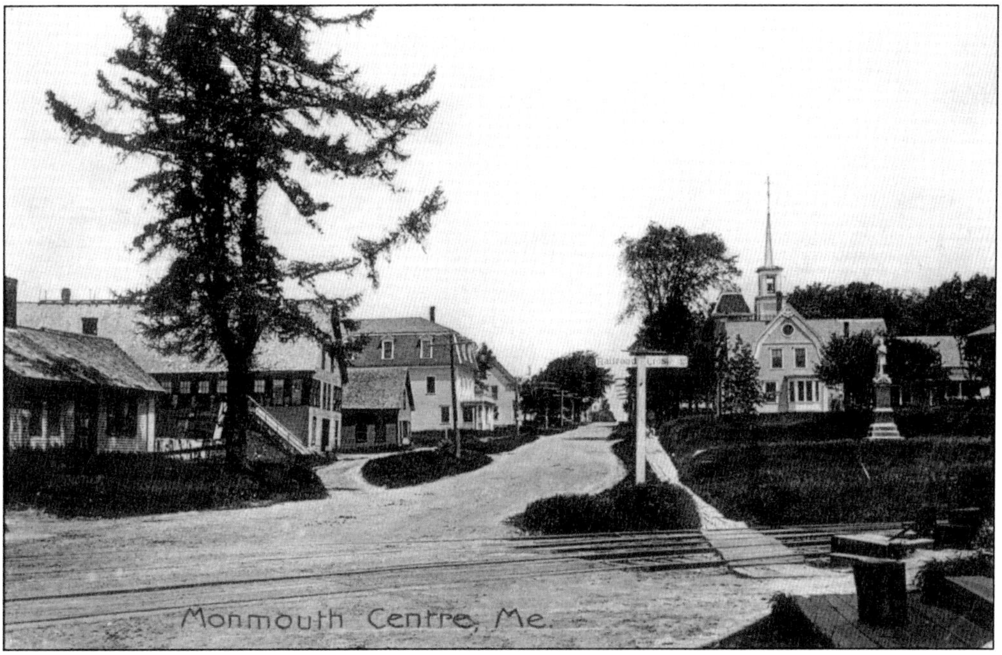

In the early 1900s, this view north of the railroad tracks shows the Civil War Monument, the Methodist church parsonage, and the Methodist church. The small Cape Cod to the left was the former home of Leone's Sandwich and Pizza Place, which was destroyed by fire in 2007. The Getchell and Company Moccasin and Boot Factory is the second building on the left heading north. The Monmouth Garage and the Monmouth Grange are the third and fourth buildings on the left. (Courtesy of the author.)

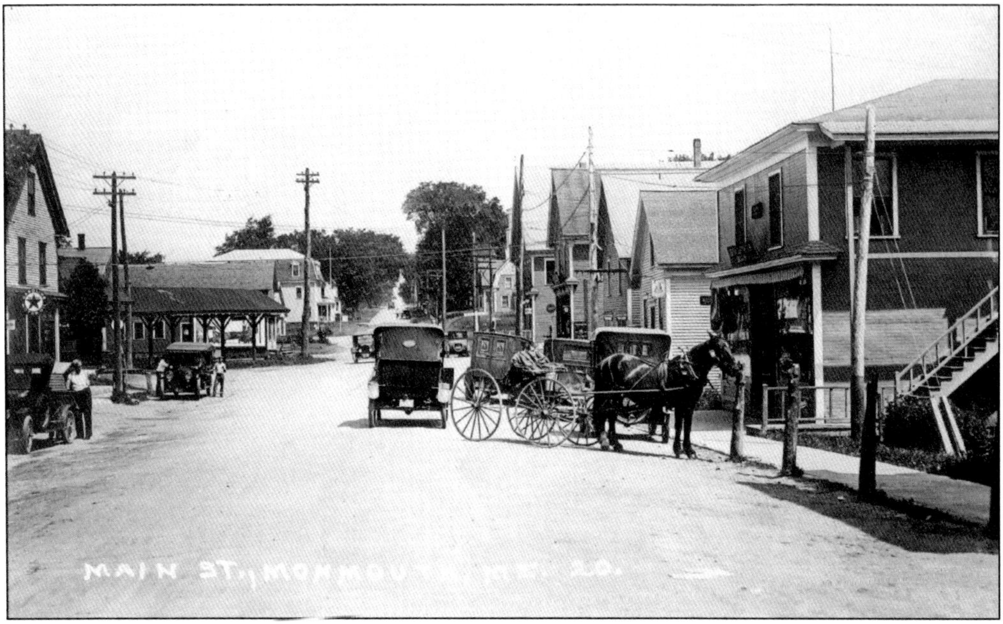

In 1928, the center of town was a busy place. The first store on the right belonged to Roy A. DeFratus, druggist. The next building heading north on Main Street was the Lewiston, Greene, and Monmouth Telephone Company, which was followed by the Monmouth Fire Department, Richardson's Hardware, and finally George Dudley's Store. On the west side of the street was Day's Hardware and the train station. (Courtesy of the Monmouth Museum.)

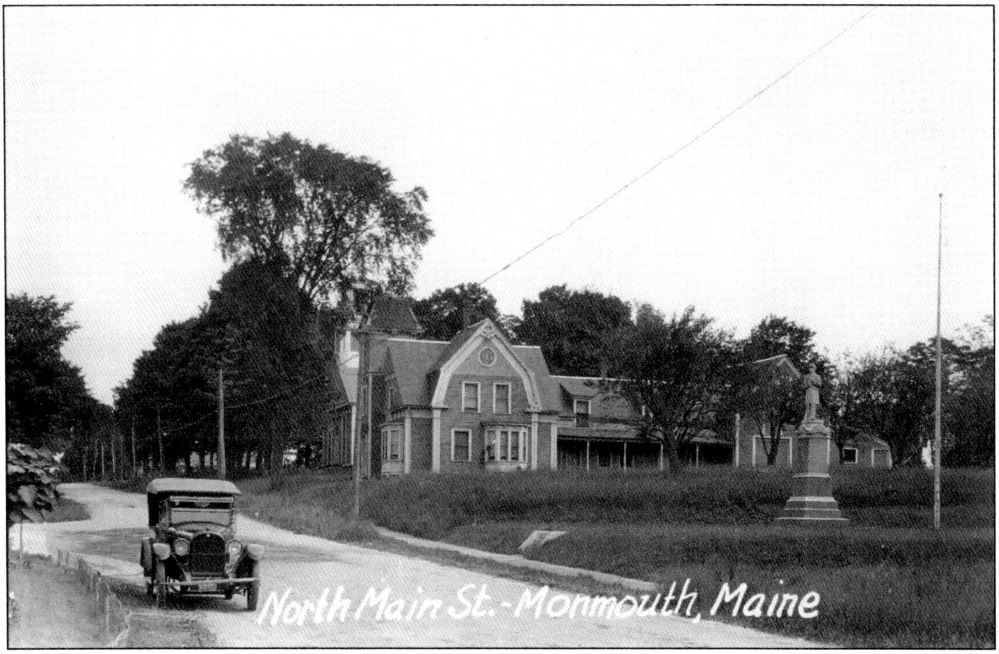

In 1920, the view of the east side Main Street looking north had not changed a great deal from the earlier photographs. (Courtesy of the author.)

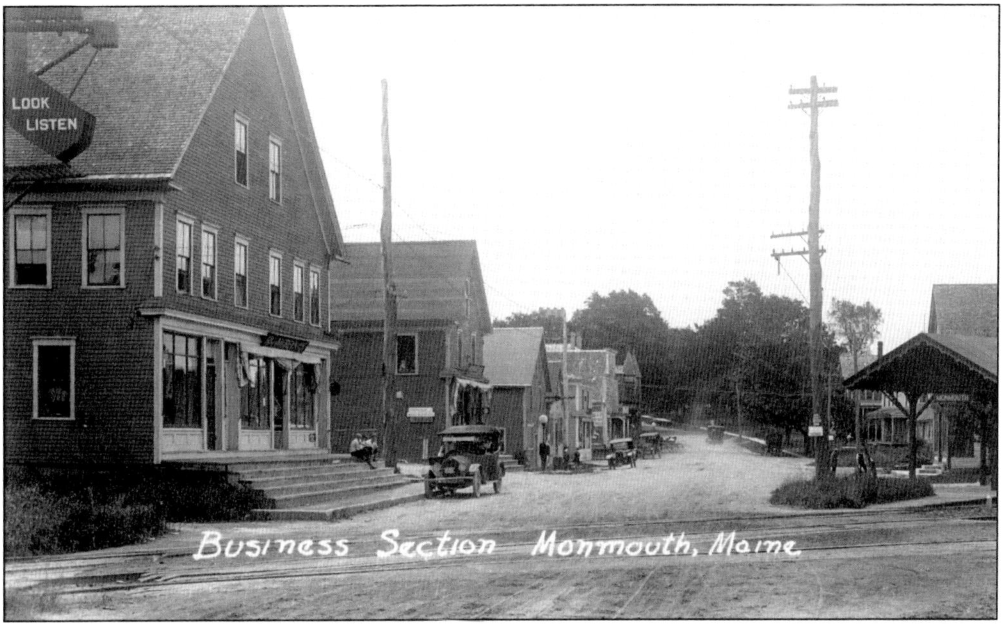

The first building on the left was a market run by Eugene Andrews in 1920. He later became the superintendent of the Monmouth Canning Company, which is also known as the Corn Shop. (Courtesy of the author.)

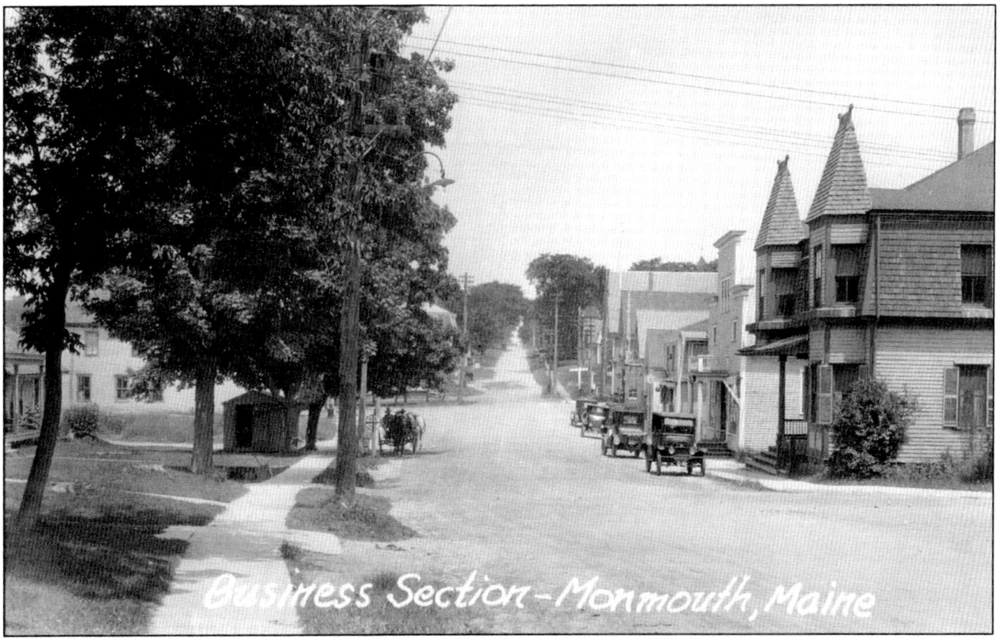

Taken just south of the Whitehouse Block on Main Street, this real photograph postcard was the third in a series of Monmouth's business section around 1920. (Courtesy of the author.)

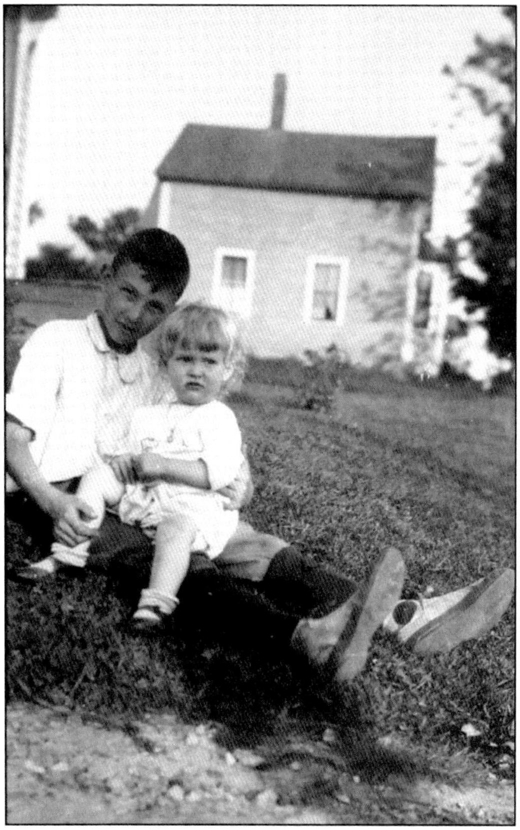

Chester Rolfe and Natalie Hall Jones are sitting beside Blue Road. (Courtesy Natalie Hall Jones.)

The old Shorey Homestead at the corner of Blue Road and Main Street is pictured around 1900. This large house is now residence for the Theater at Monmouth's summer performers and is fondly named Toad Hall. (Courtesy of the Monmouth Museum.)

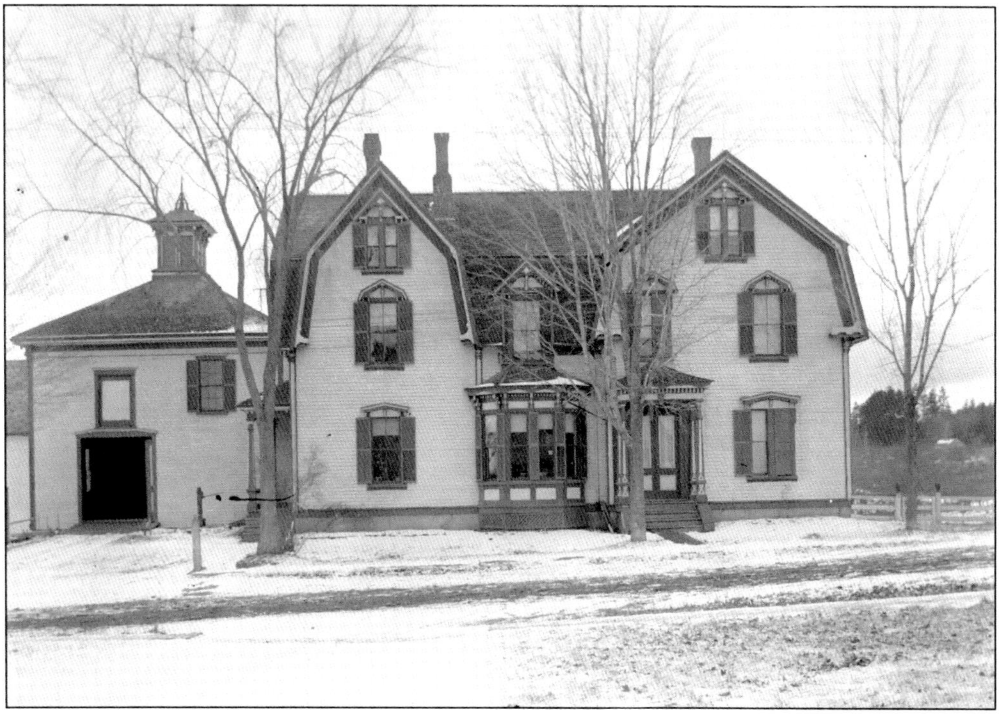

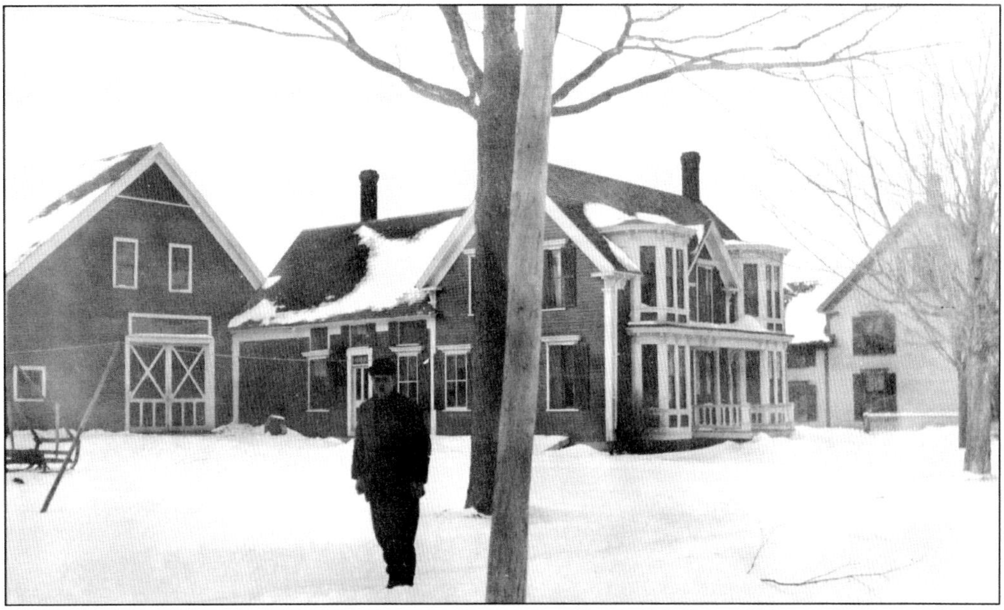

Prior to becoming the Bragdon-Flanders Funeral Home, this stately house on Main Street belonged to the Gilman family. (Courtesy of the Monmouth Museum.)

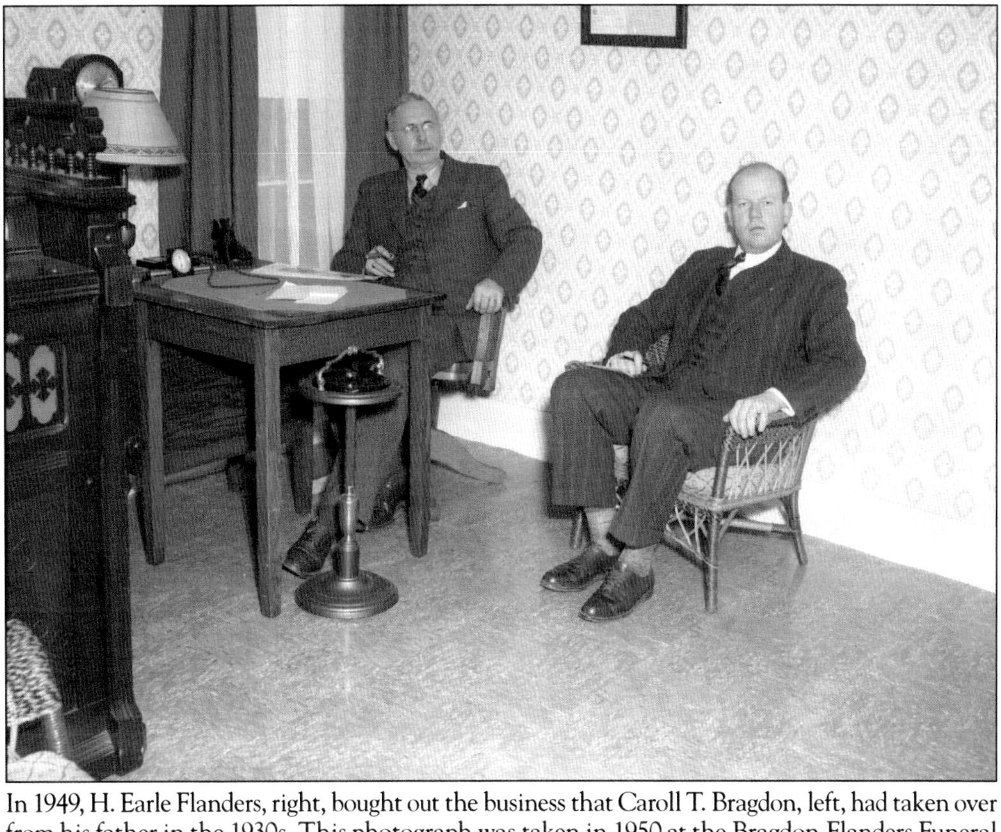

In 1949, H. Earle Flanders, right, bought out the business that Caroll T. Bragdon, left, had taken over from his father in the 1930s. This photograph was taken in 1950 at the Bragdon-Flanders Funeral Home on Main Street. (Photograph by Roland LaVallee, courtesy of the Monmouth Museum.)

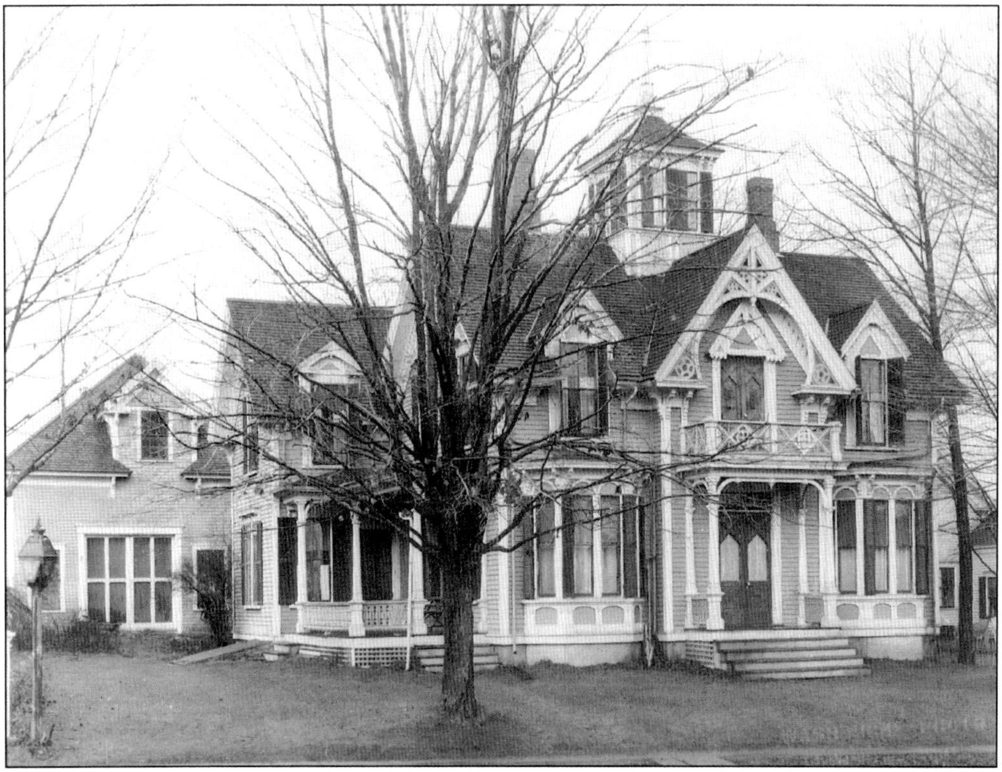

The Oscar Frost house was located on the west side of Main Street. It was later home to C. O. Flanders and Dr. Frederick Chenery Jr. (Washburn photograph, courtesy of Frederick Chenery III.)

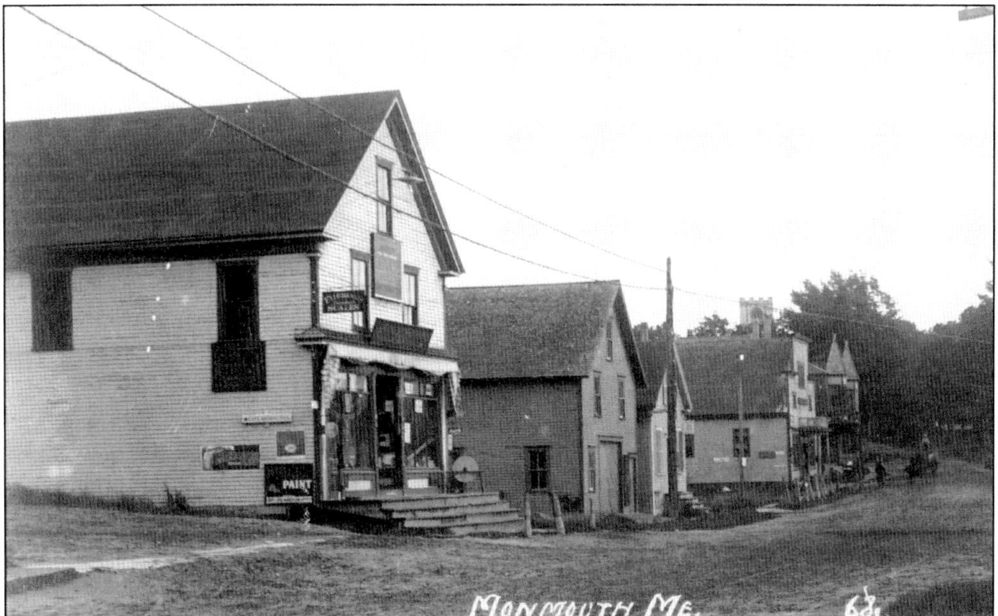

This view of Main Street shows the businesses on the west side of the street looking south from the corner of Pleasant Street. (Courtesy of Stan DeOrsey.)

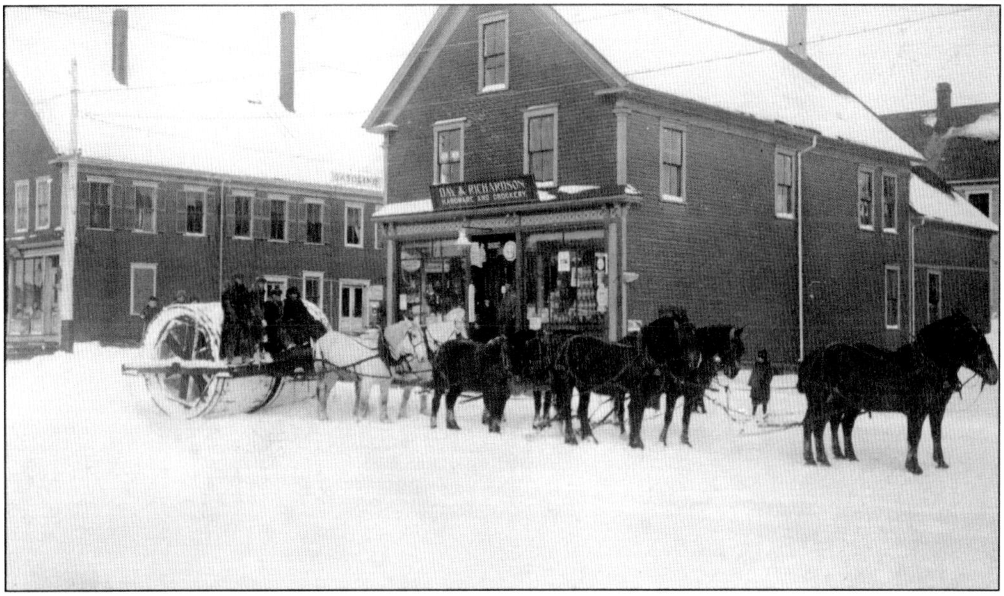

This large snow roller required four teams of horses to pull it along Main Street. The present-day Richardson Hardware and Crockery is in the background. (Courtesy of the author.)

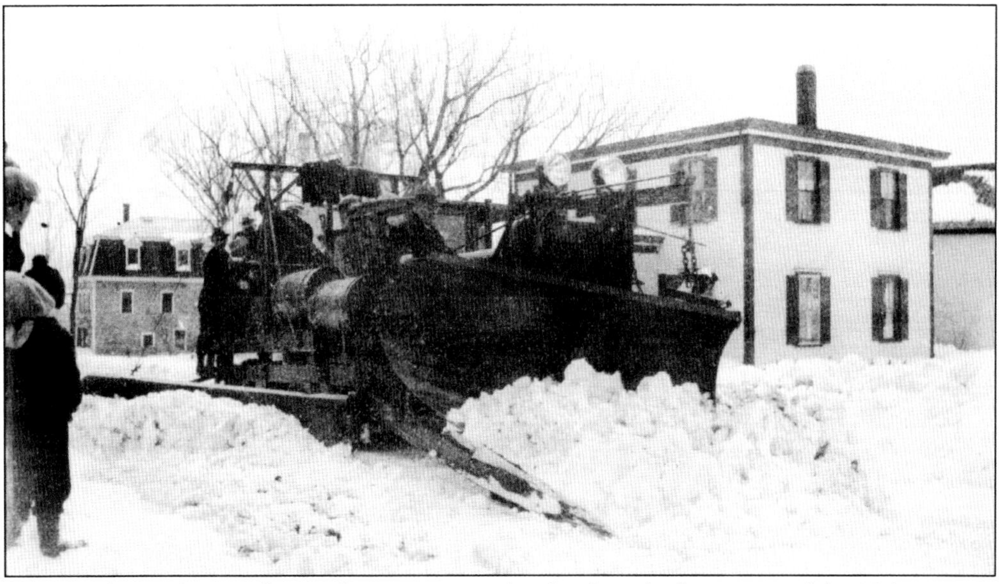

Keeping the roads open during the winter was a hard task at the beginning of the 20th century. This Lombard tractor with plow is shown going north on Main Street. The house in the background was moved in 2001 onto the Blue Road to make way for the Monmouth branch of the Bangor Savings Bank. The late Joe Bergeron and his family had lived in the house for a number of years when it was located on Main Street. (Courtesy of Audrey and David Walker.)

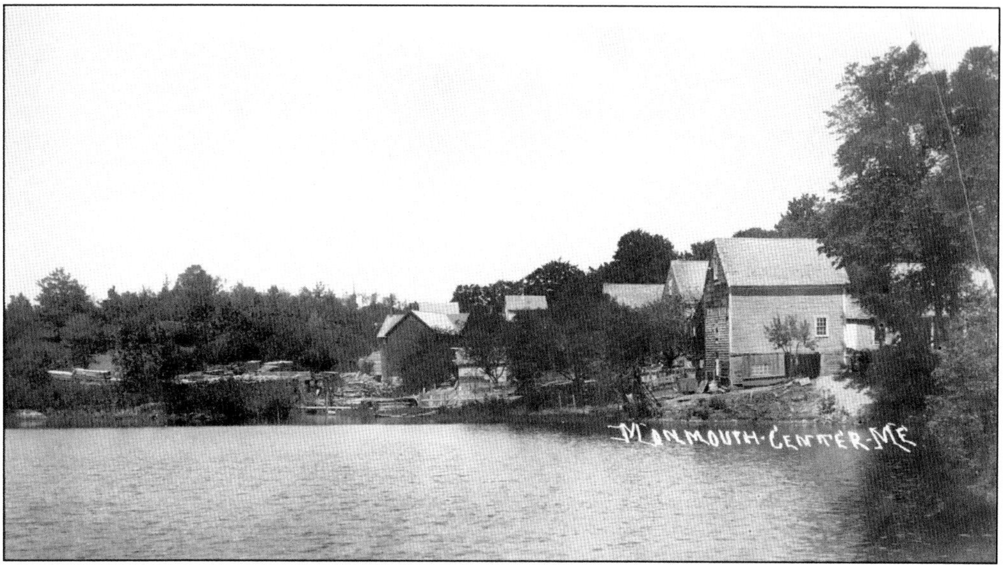

This view looking west along the stream on the south side of Maple Street shows the second of four millponds that once existed. The back side of the Merrill and Witherell Shingle and Planing Mill can be seen in the upper right. (Courtesy of Stan DeOrsey.)

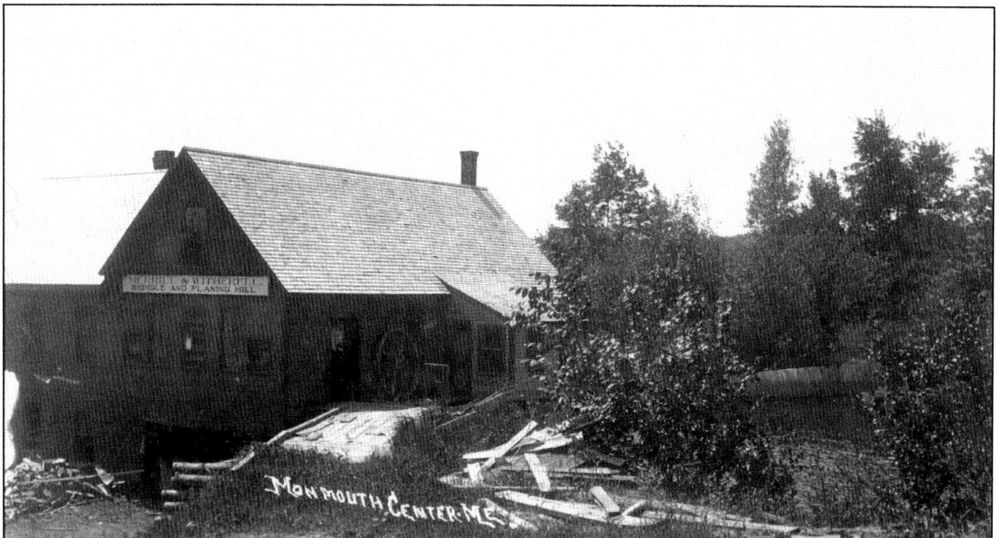

The Merrill and Witherell Shingle and Planing Mill operated on the stream that ran behind the blacksmith shop on Maple Street. Note the lathe wheel leaning against the side of the building. (Courtesy of the author.)

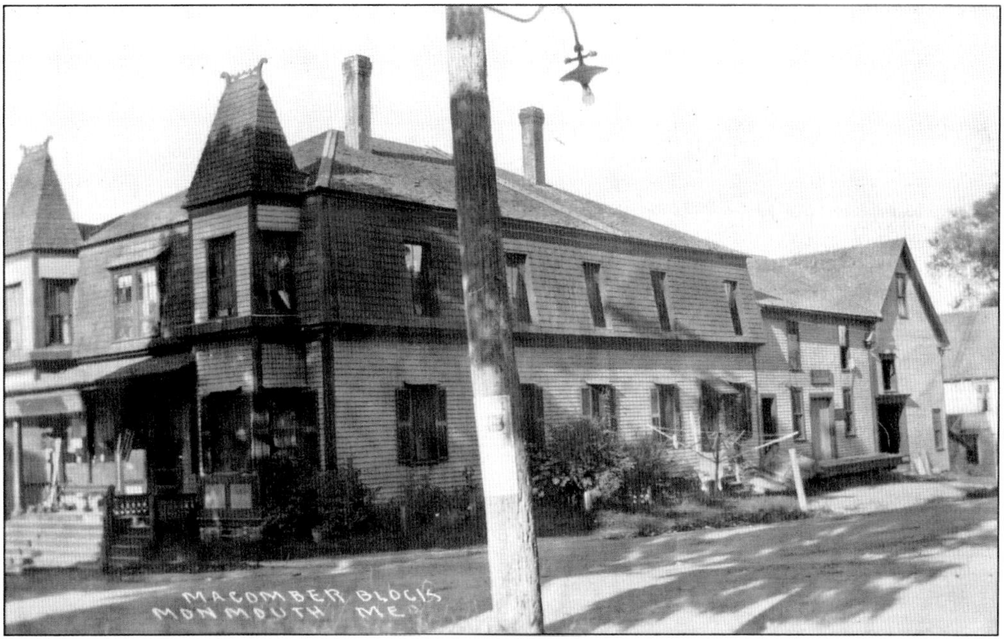

The Whitehouse Block sat on the corner of Maple and Main Streets on the old site of the Cochnewagan House, which was destroyed by the fire of 1888. On the first floor of the block, William C. Carr, Doris Poole's father, ran a meat market during the early 1900s; it closed in 1931. There were two rents upstairs in the block. (Courtesy of the author.)

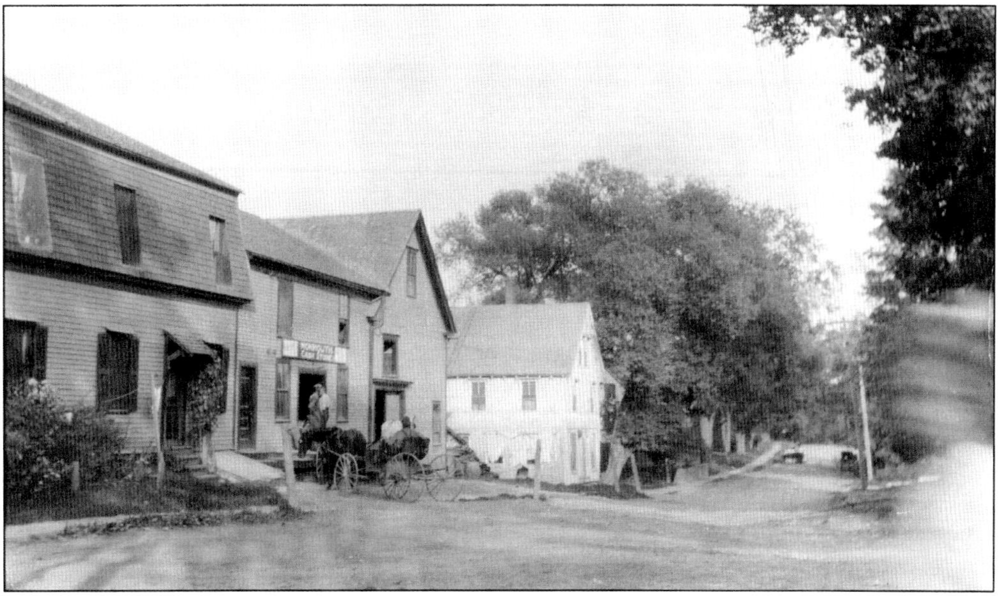

The indication of how large a structure it was is shown in this extended view of the Whitehouse Block going down Maple Street. The middle section of the block is where George Albert Randlette, son of Dr. C. M. Randlette, ran a gaming room and beer parlor. This was the first place in town to serve liquor following Prohibition. (Courtesy of the Monmouth Museum.)

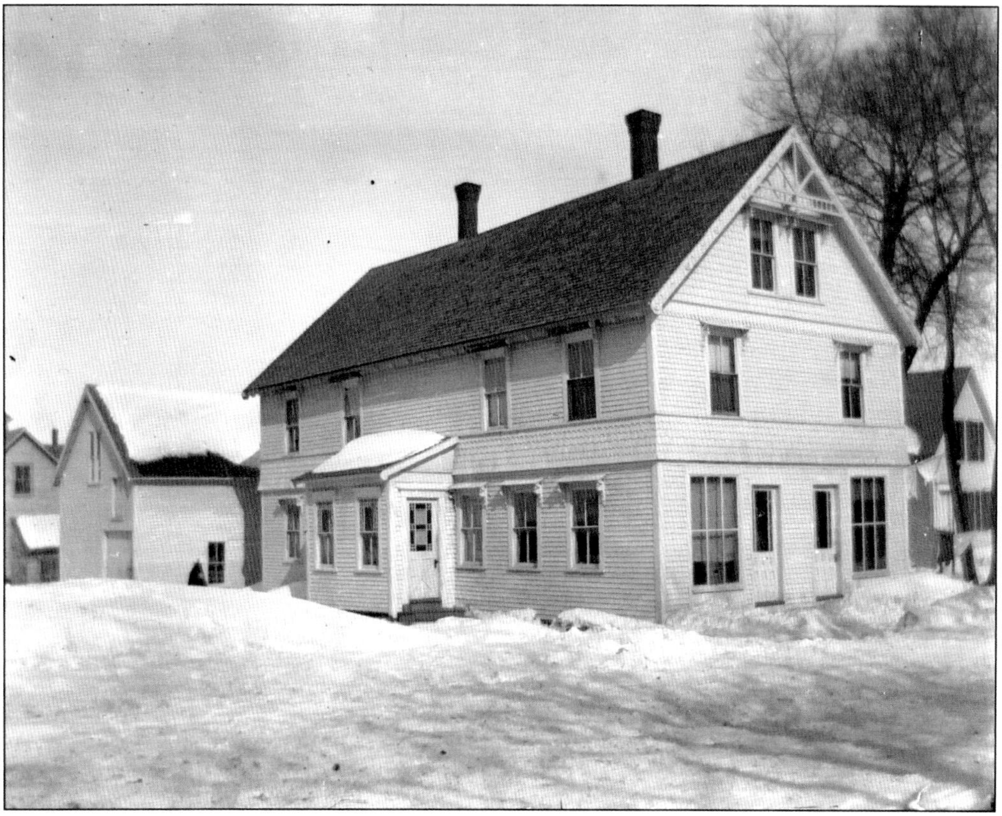

This store sat behind the Whitehouse Block going east on Maple Street. Elmer Haskell was one of several people to have a business here. (Courtesy of the Monmouth Museum.)

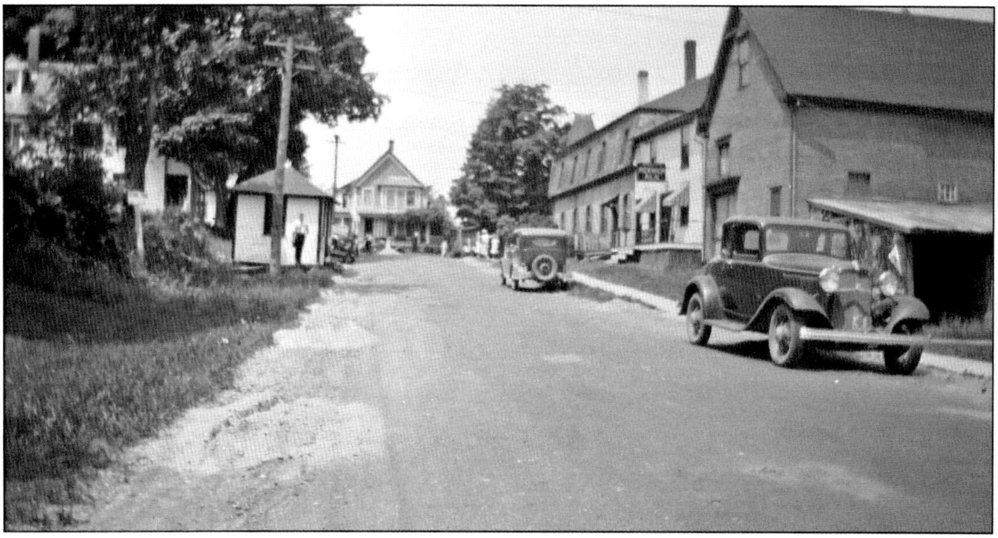

This view looking west on Maple Street shows the Whitehouse Block to the right and the home of the late Virginia Richardson on Main Street. The sign on the side of the Whitehouse Block says "Pickwick Ale." This was the first place in Monmouth that liquor was served following Prohibition. (Courtesy of Audrey and David Walker.)

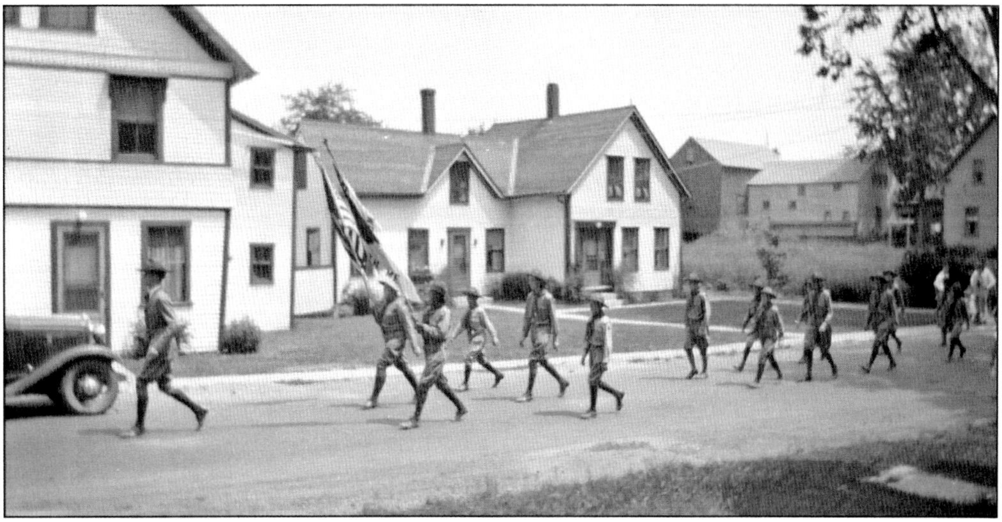

The Monmouth Boy Scouts are marching west on Maple Street during a Fourth of July parade around 1930. (Courtesy of Audrey and David Walker.)

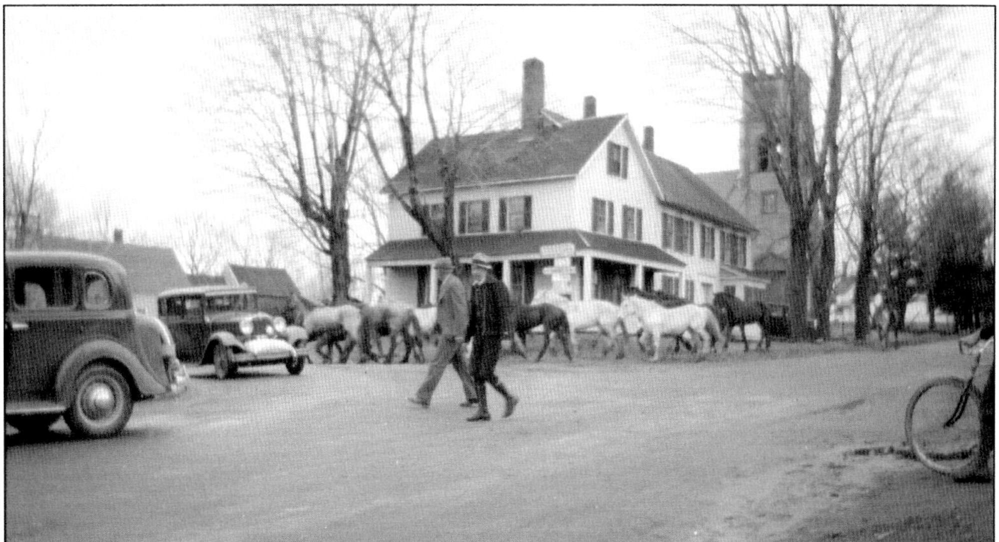

A large group of horses turns right onto Maple Street from Main Street. The house in the background is where Frank Greenlief grew up, and in 1909, a Mrs. King owned it. The Congregational church can be seen behind the large house. (Courtesy of Audrey and David Walker.)

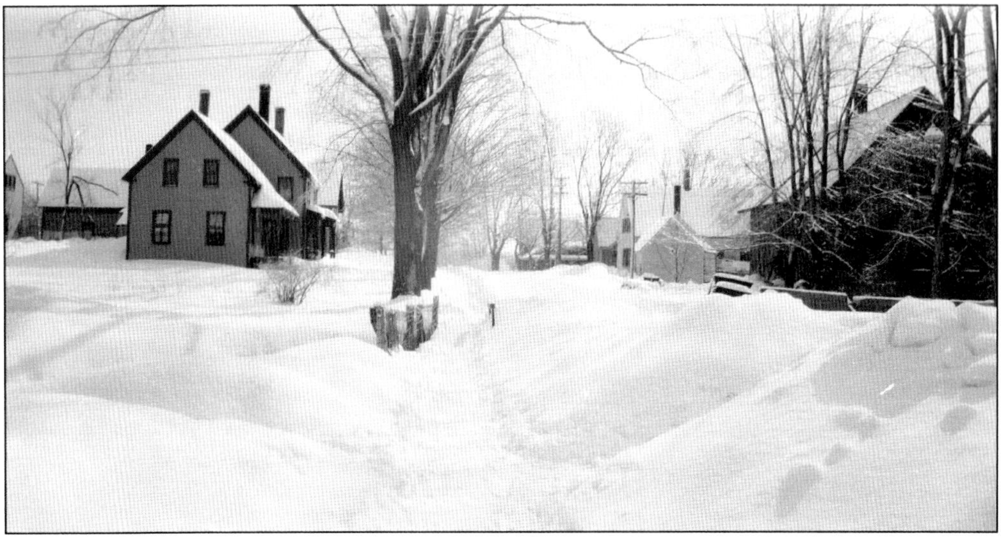

Elmer Haskell took this photograph on Maple Street looking east toward the blacksmith shop. Note the small path heading east along the snow-laden street. (Courtesy of Audrey and David Walker.)

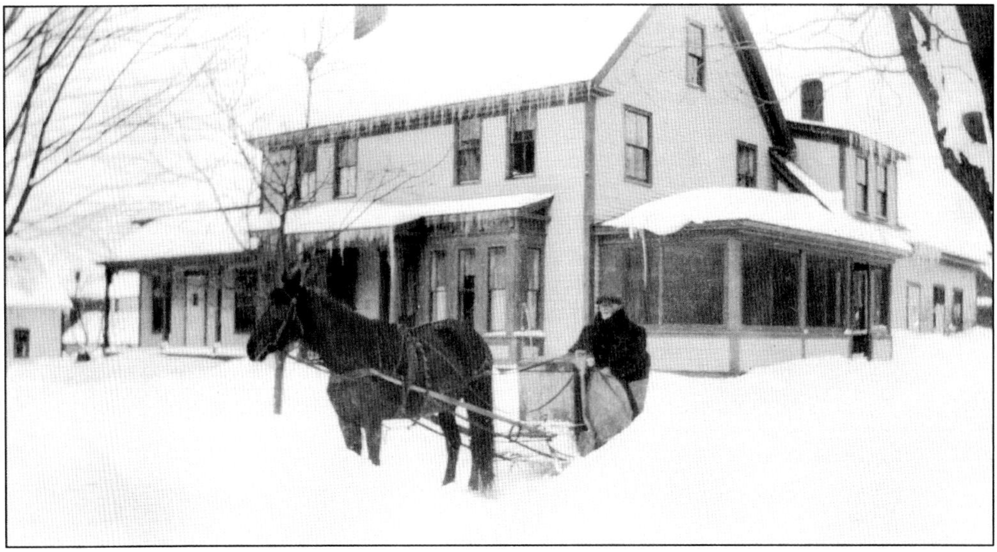

This wintery scene shows John Pinkham in his sleigh at his house on Maple Street. The current owners of this house are Dick and Caroline Allen. (Courtesy of the Monmouth Museum.)

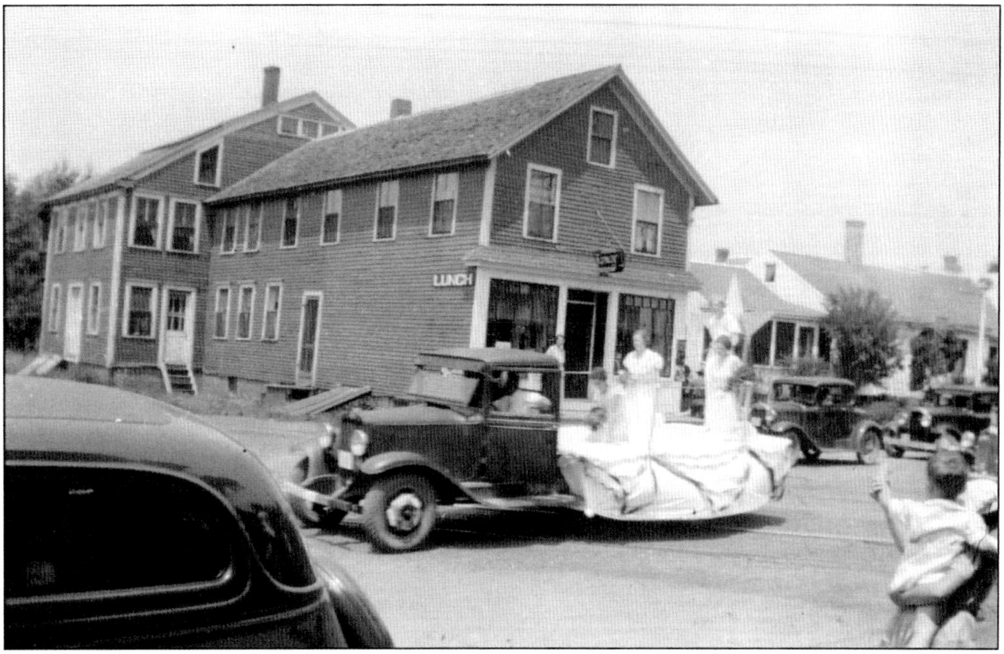

This July 4, 1934, parade shows the Eastern Star float. In the background is the old Clough Block building, which once served as the GAR hall, built by Simon Clough. The little Cape Cod to the right of the Clough Block was known as the Bungalow; it was the home of Ally and Martha Kemp Jotham. (Courtesy of Edson Donnell.)

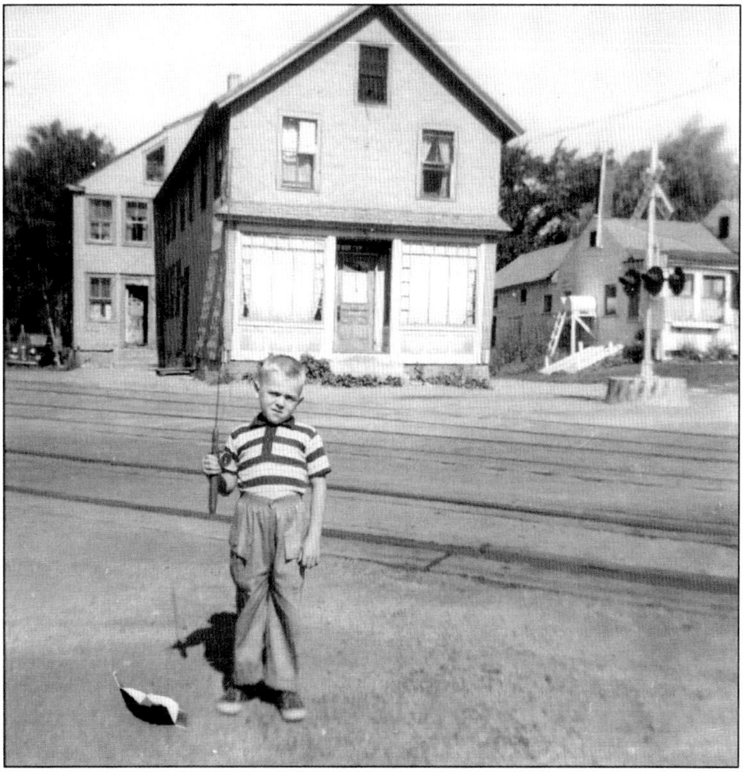

The son of the late Lawrence and Ruth Bragg, Jim is all set to go fishing at the lake. The building in the background was home to the old tearoom, a lunchroom that was run by Clara DeRoche and her daughter Maggie. The DeRoche family lived upstairs over the lunchroom. (Courtesy of Ruth Bragg.)

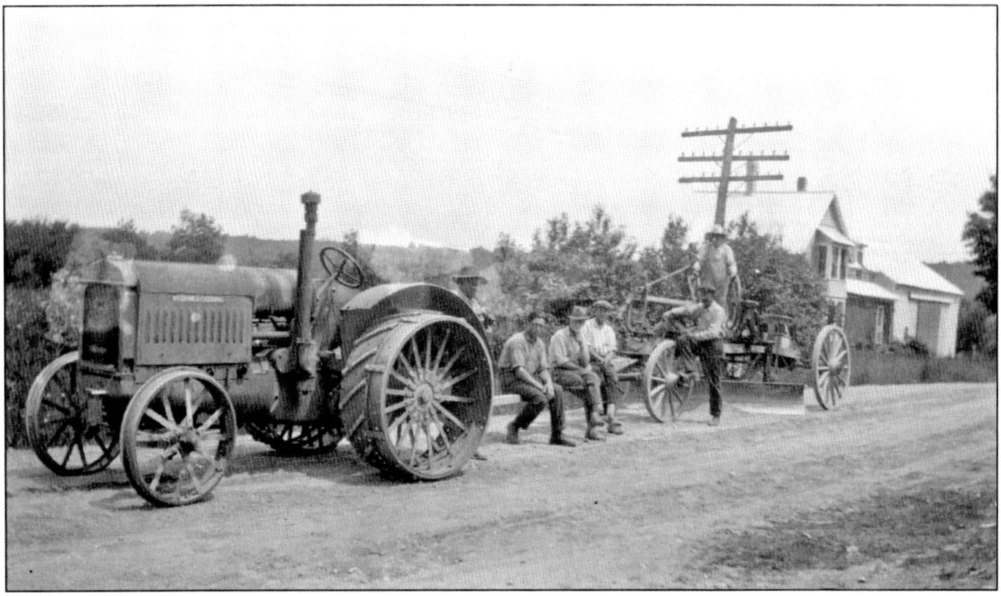

The town road crew is taking a break from grading on the outer edge of Maple Street, which is just west of where Laura Gilman Sanborn grew up and later raised her family. (Courtesy of the Monmouth Museum.)

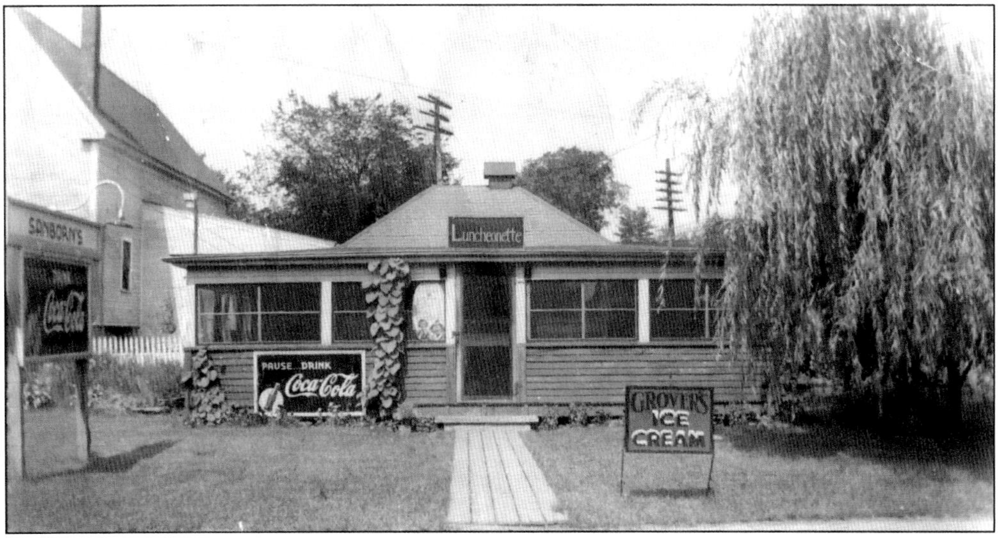

Nellie Sanborn's Tea Room stood on the lot where the current Monmouth Museum Stencil Shop stands. She was in business during the late 1930s and early 1940s. After World War II, Bertha Johnson and Eleanor Ramsdell operated a lunchroom there for one year. (Courtesy of Jessie Sanborn.)

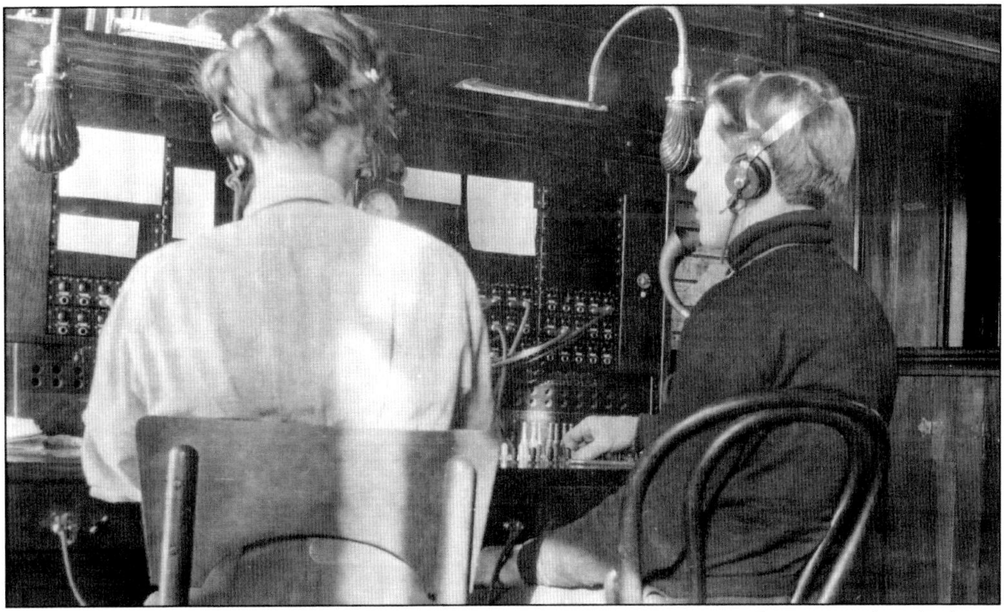

Ruby Day Haskell and Ross Day are at work in the Lewiston, Greene, and Monmouth Telephone Company at the corner of Main Street and what is now known as Grover Road. (Courtesy of Audrey and David Walker.)

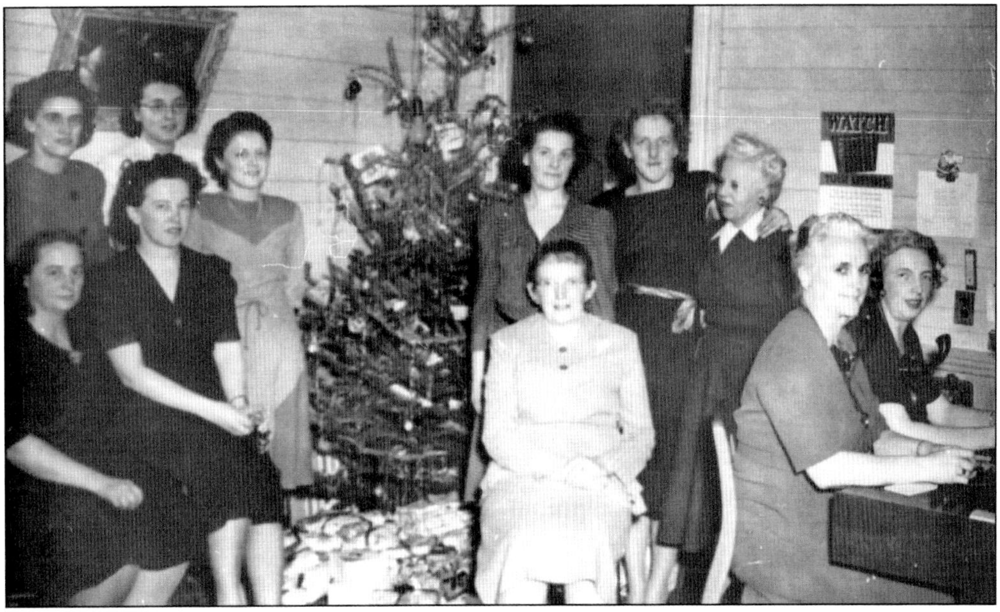

Shown here is the 1955 or 1956 Christmas party at the Monmouth central office of the Lewiston, Greene, and Monmouth Telephone Company. Normally, two ladies worked the magneto switchboards by day and one at night. From left to right are (standing) Margory Ham (substitute/weekends), Esther Prince (substitute/weekends), Nora Holloway (day), Katherine Flynn (night), Ellie Hill (substitute /weekends), and Virginia Richardson (retired operator); (seated) Marcia Johnson (night), Eleanor Flanders (day), Margaret Smith (retired operator), Susie McKenney (day/chief operator), and Phyllis Witherell (day). (Photograph by Roland LaVallee, courtesy of the Monmouth Museum.)

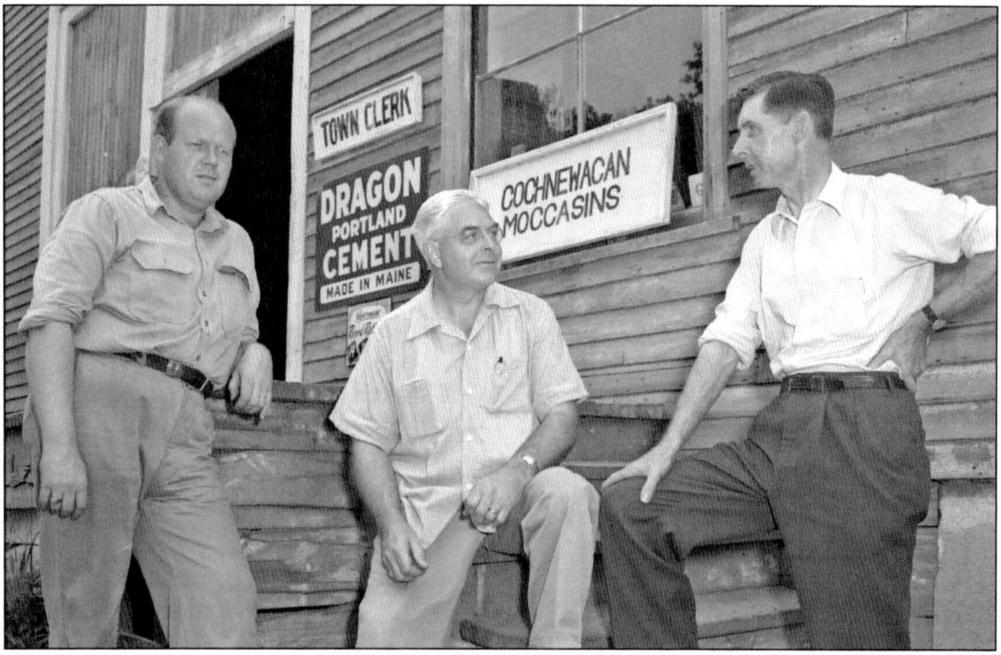

The Monmouth Improvement and Beach Association is, from left to right, Earle Flanders, Robert Hanson, and Elmer Haskell. Elmer Haskell managed the grain store that was a branch of a business in Greene. Earle Flanders made moccasins upstairs over the town clerk's office. (Photograph by Roland LaVallee, courtesy of the Monmouth Museum.)

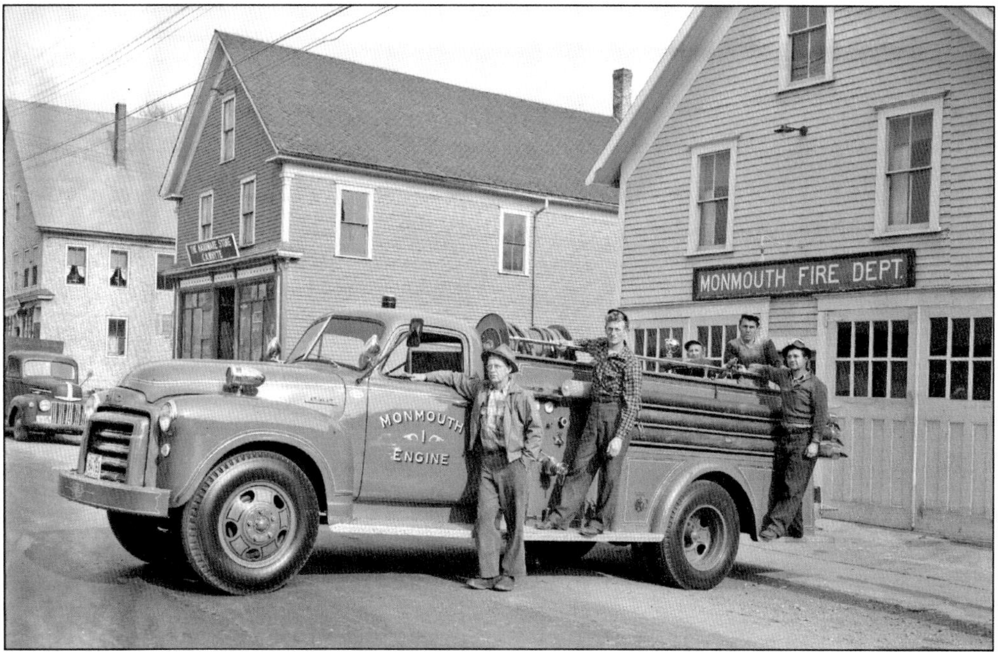

Monmouth's new pumper was purchased in 1953. Pictured are, from left to right, Chief Engineer Cyrille Chretien, Robert Mains, Alton Berry, Dick Kenney, and Frank Gray. In the background is the old Monmouth Fire Department building. (Photograph by Roland LaVallee, courtesy of the Monmouth Museum.)

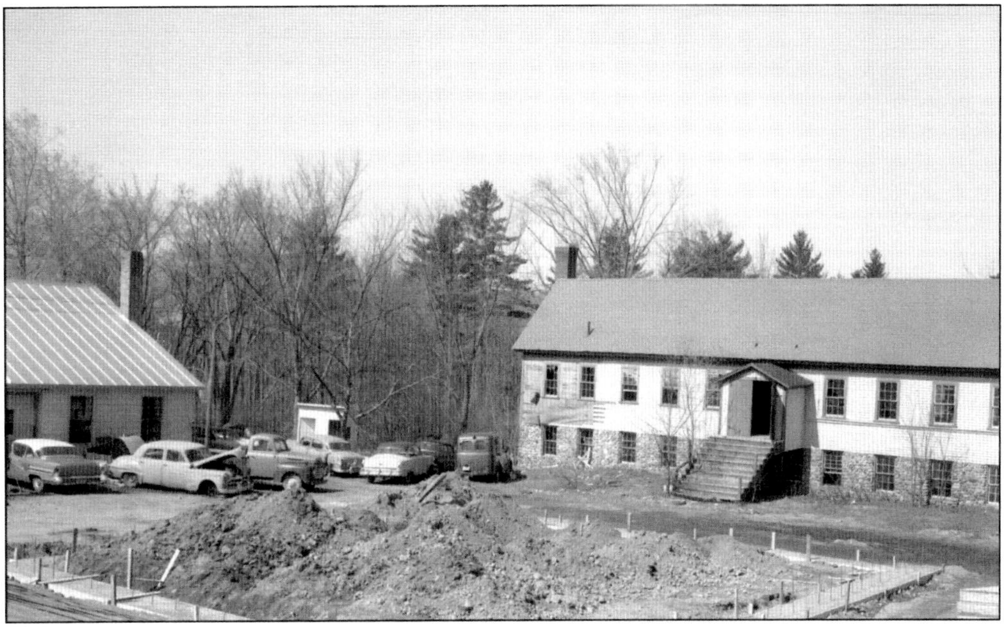

Shown here are preparations for the construction of the Carol T. Bragdon Fire Station on Main Street. The old Lunn Moccasin Factory can be seen in the background. The moccasin shop that was built and run by John D. Lunn in the 1920s sat behind the present-day fire station on Main Street. The Lunn Company was well known for the Monmouth moccasins. (Photograph by Roland LaVallee, courtesy of the Monmouth Museum.)

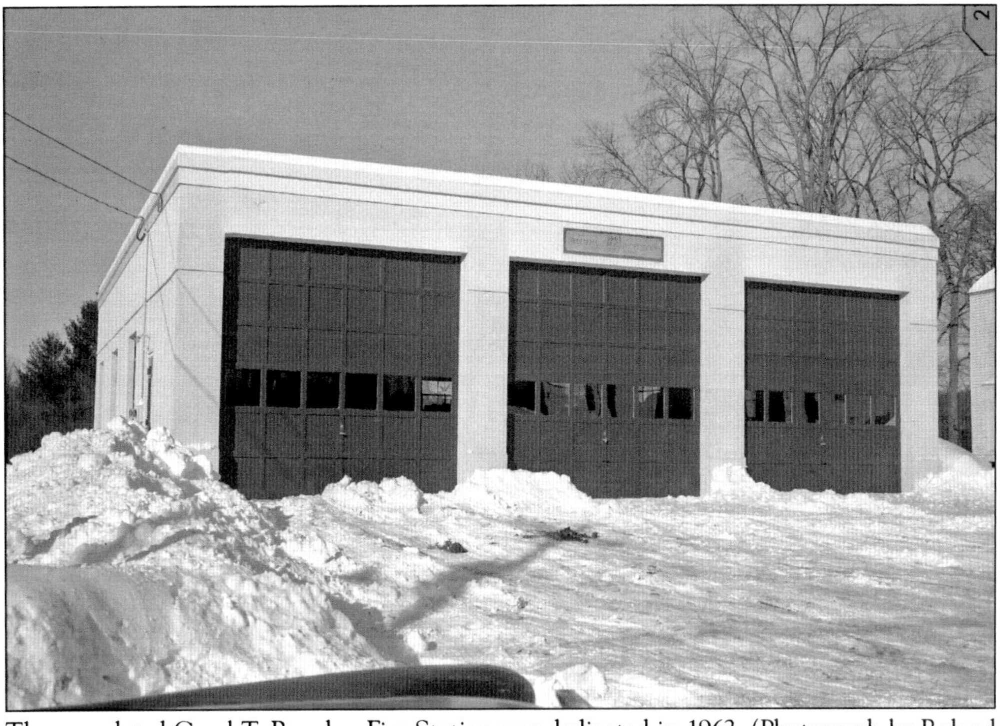

The completed Carol T. Bragdon Fire Station was dedicated in 1962. (Photograph by Roland LaVallee, courtesy of the Monmouth Museum.)

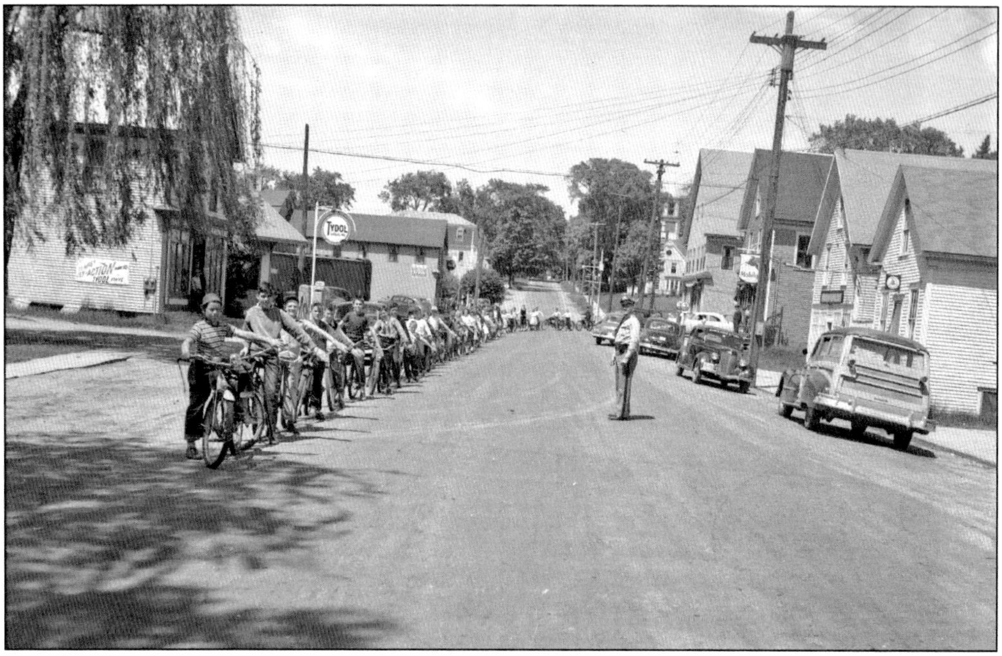

Bicycle safety became important as the automobile became more abundant. This bicycle parade on Main Street shows a policeman supervising the use of hand signals. With hands demonstrating the stop signal, Monmouth boys and girls line up for this parade in the early 1950s. (Photograph by Roland LaVallee, courtesy of the Monmouth Museum.)

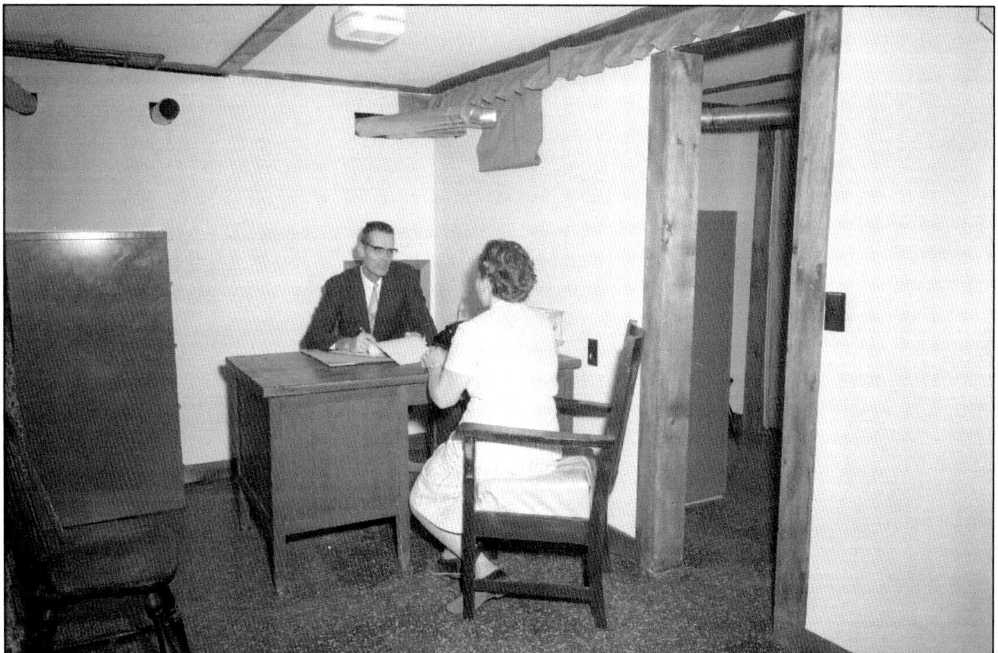

Robert Walker opened the Monmouth Federal Credit Union at Monmouth Center in 1953. He still serves on the board of directors at the credit union's new location on north Main Street near Route 202. (Photograph by Roland LaVallee, courtesy of the Monmouth Museum.)

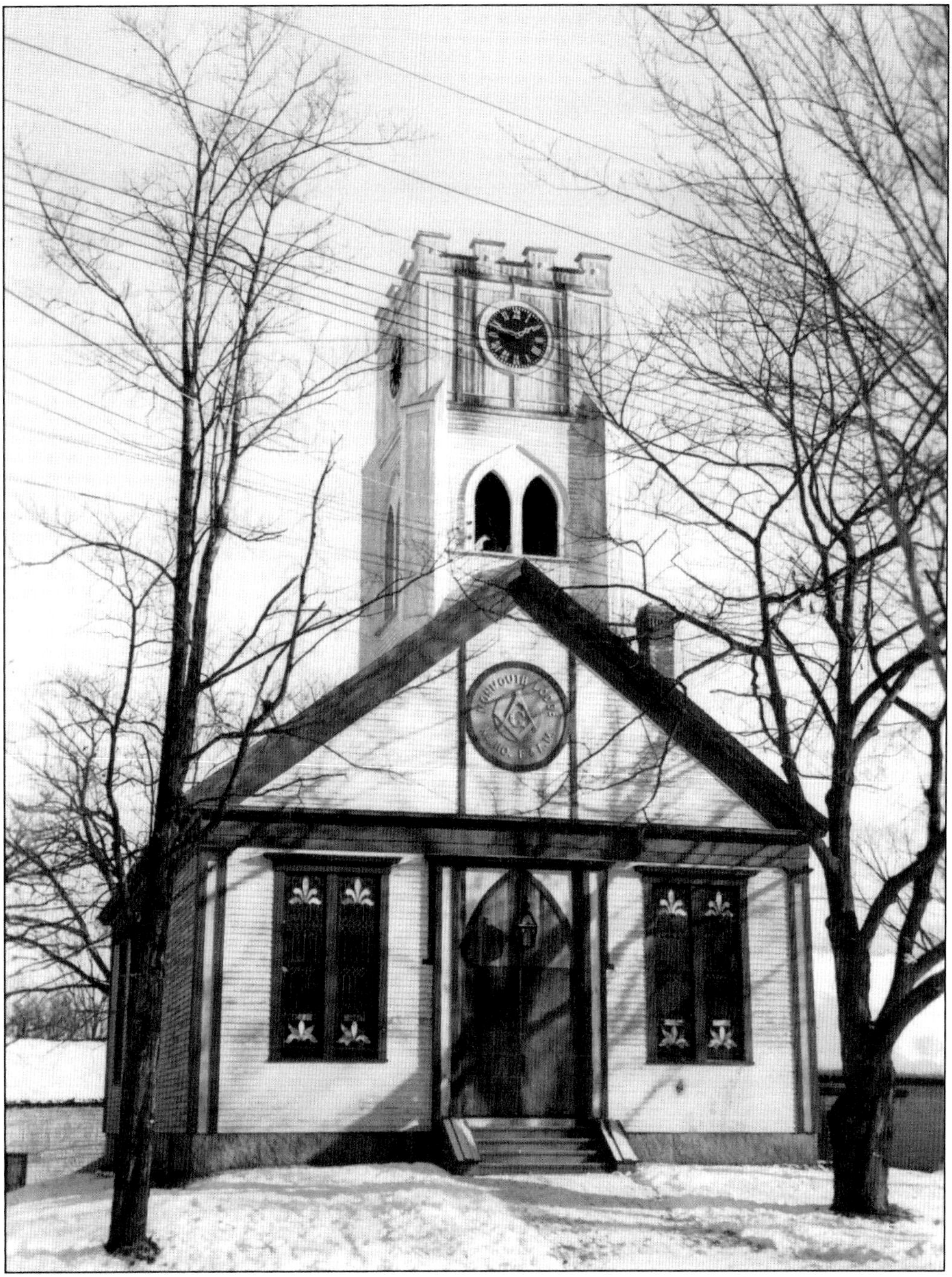

The Masons purchased their hall from the Congregational church and had their first functions there in 1939. The Congregational church merged with the Center Methodist Church to become the United Church of Monmouth. The tower's clock, which was donated to the church by the children of George H. and Sarah Safford Andrews in their memory, was maintained by the Congregational society. The tower is known as the Leander Macomber Tower and was a gift from former church member Mrs. A. W. Strauss of Cambridge, Massachusetts. She was Wealthy Macomber prior to her marriage. (Courtesy of the author.)

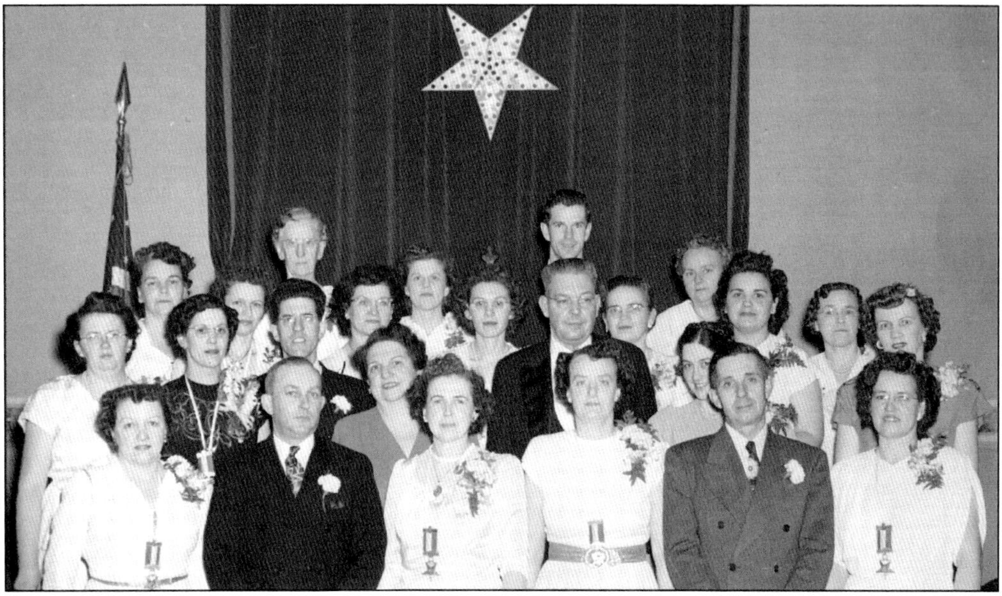

This photograph shows the installation of the 1949 Order of the Eastern Star in Monmouth. From left to right, those in the photograph are as follows: (first row) Jane Plummer, Eugene Donnelly, Ruby Pettingill, Evelyn Rolfe, Clarence Maxim, and Ella Robinson; (second row) Dorothy Peasley, Laura Sanborn, Thomas Peasley, three unidentified officers from the Grand Chapter of Maine, and Madeline Riggs; (third row) Eleanor Ramsdell, Evelyn Chick, Bernice Hathaway, Marion Donnell, Lyle Withers, Louise Otis, and Bernice Day; (fourth row) Stella Peasley, Mildred Covell, Robert Covell, and Thelma Maxim. (Courtesy of the Monmouth Museum).

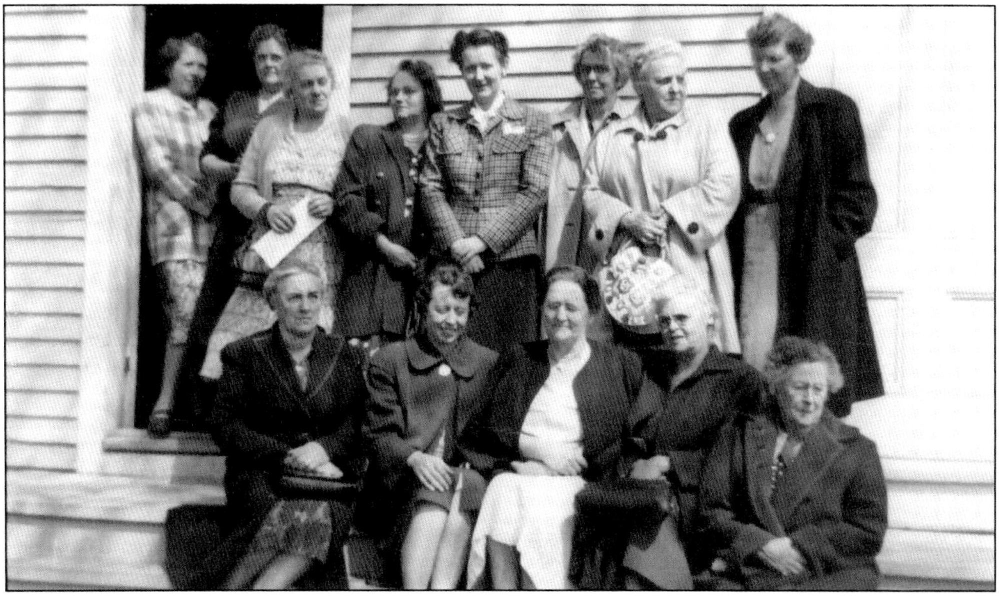

Members of the Monmouth Extension Group are, from left to right, (standing) Leana Hight, Millie Emmerson, Madelyn Foster, Annie Hill, an unidentified home demonstration agent, Pauline Chretien, Ada Painter, and Dorcas Knowlton; (sitting) Elizabeth Hutchinson, an unidentified home demonstration agent, Daisy Berry, Edna Woodbury, and Grace Dudley. (Courtesy of Dr. Stanley Painter.)

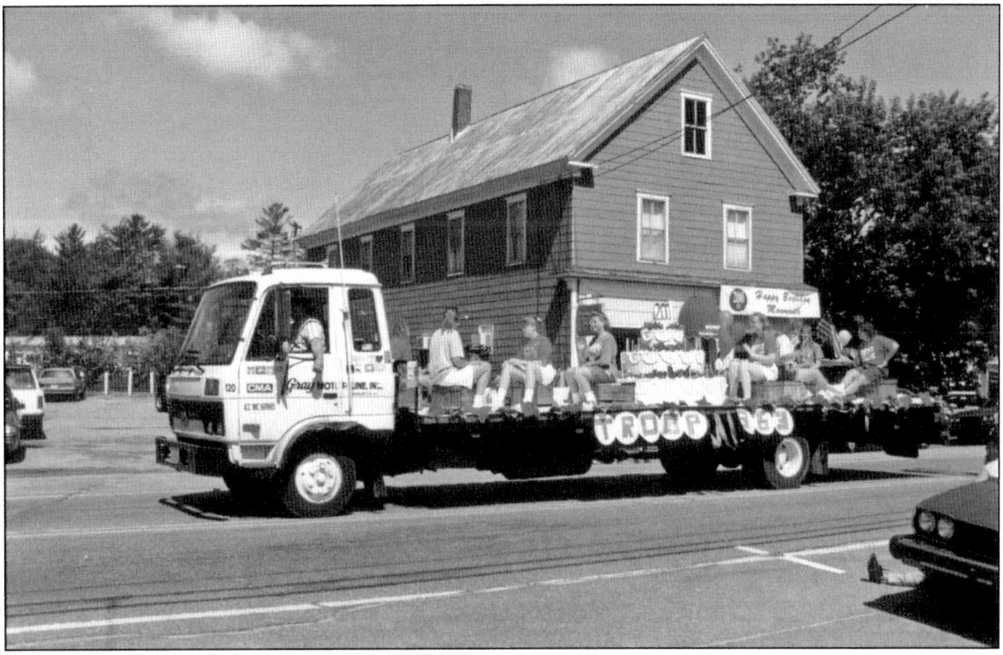

The Monmouth bicentennial was celebrated on July 18, 1992, with a large parade down Main Street. Girl Scout Troop 863 supplied the Monmouth bicentennial cake, which they recycled from the town of Greene's 1988 bicentennial celebration. (Photograph by the author.)

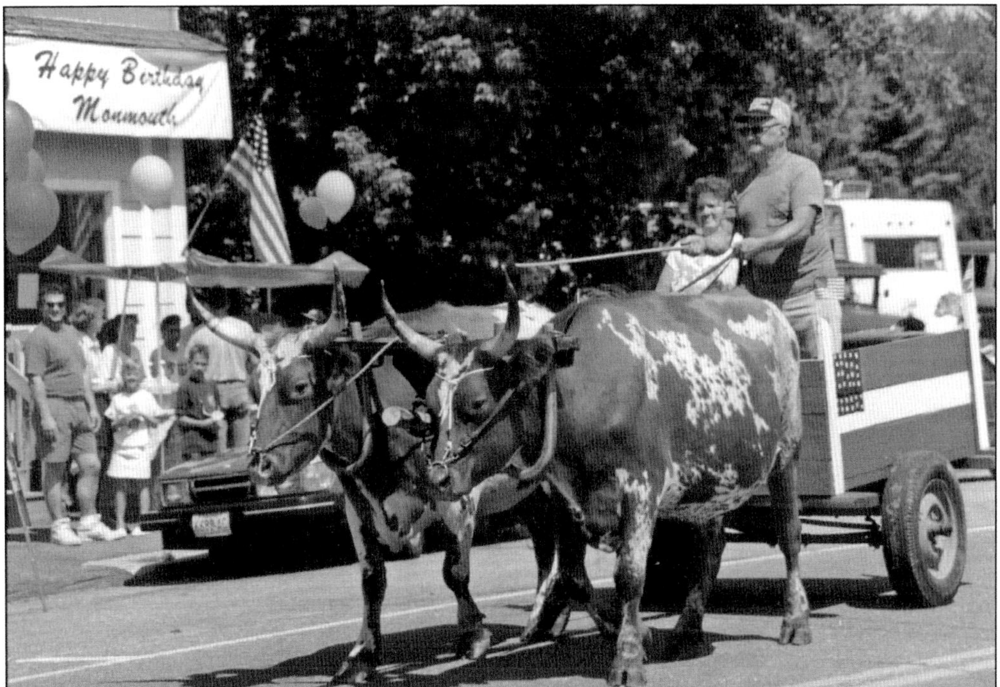

Jim and Carol Mosher of Monmouth are pictured with their oxen, Tim and Tom, at the Monmouth Bicentennial Parade. (Photograph by the author.)

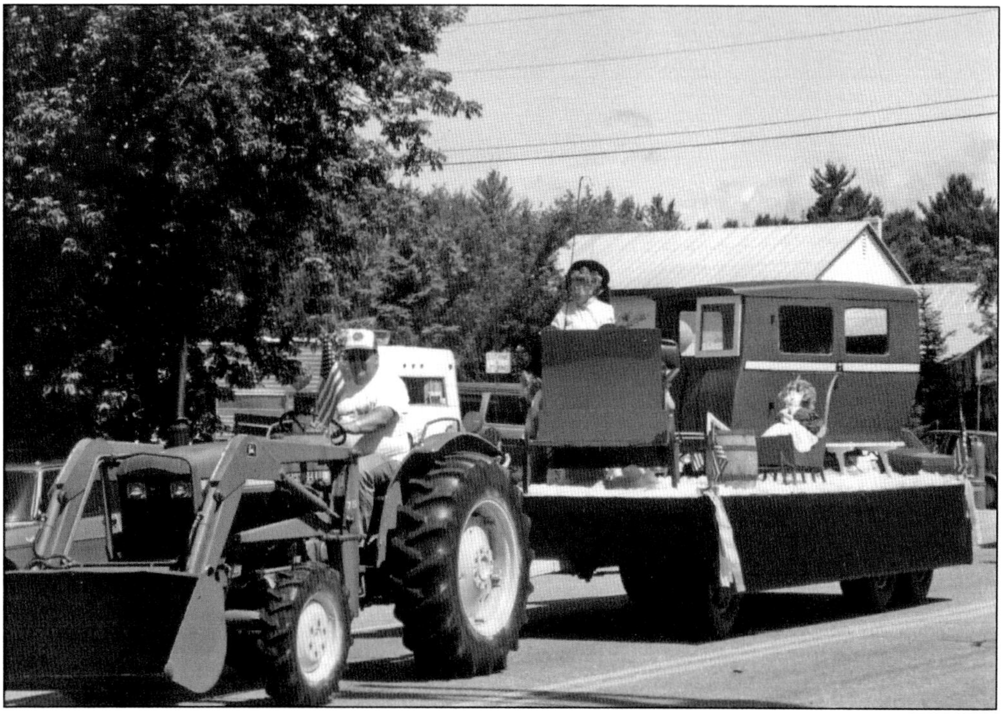

Ted Johnson of Monmouth is pulling his float with two pungs (sleighs) he restored. Bessie Bowler went for a wintry ride in July. (Photograph by the author.)

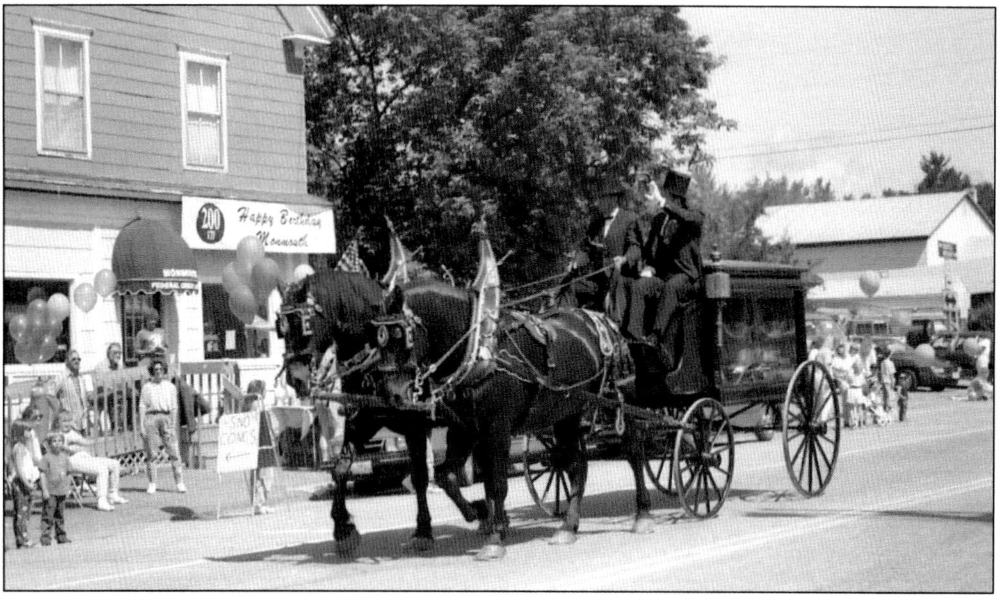

The Monmouth hearse even made an appearance for the bicentennial parade. Funeral director Hugh LeMaster of Bragdon-Finley Funeral Home waves to the crowd as Dwight (Pete) Tripp drives his team of black Percherons, Doc and Captain. Doc (left) is now 26 years old and living out his retirement at Trippcrest Farm in Harrison, Maine. The hearse was the last one purchased by the town in 1911 and is part of the Monmouth Museum collection. It even had sleigh runners for winter usage. (Photograph by the author.)

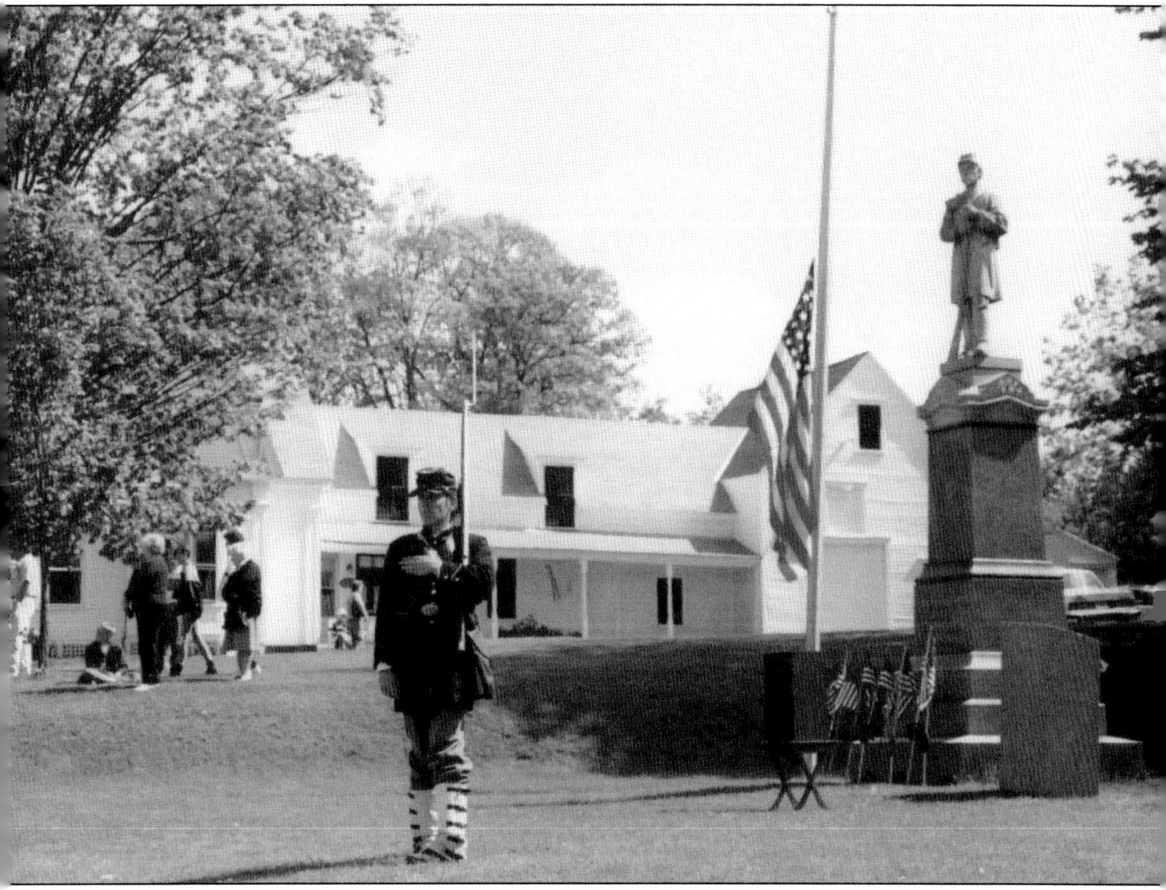

In 1860, a year before the American Civil War began, the population of Monmouth was documented at 1,854. During the four years that the war was fought, 154 men who listed Monmouth as their residence enlisted to serve their country. A total of 28 men would give their lives to preserve this great nation. Three of those men were killed in action, four died of wounds received in battle, and 21 died from disease. Pictured here, the late Mark Quinlivan serves as sentinel at Monmouth's Civil War monument on Memorial Day, 1992, Monmouth's bicentennial year. (Photograph by the author.)

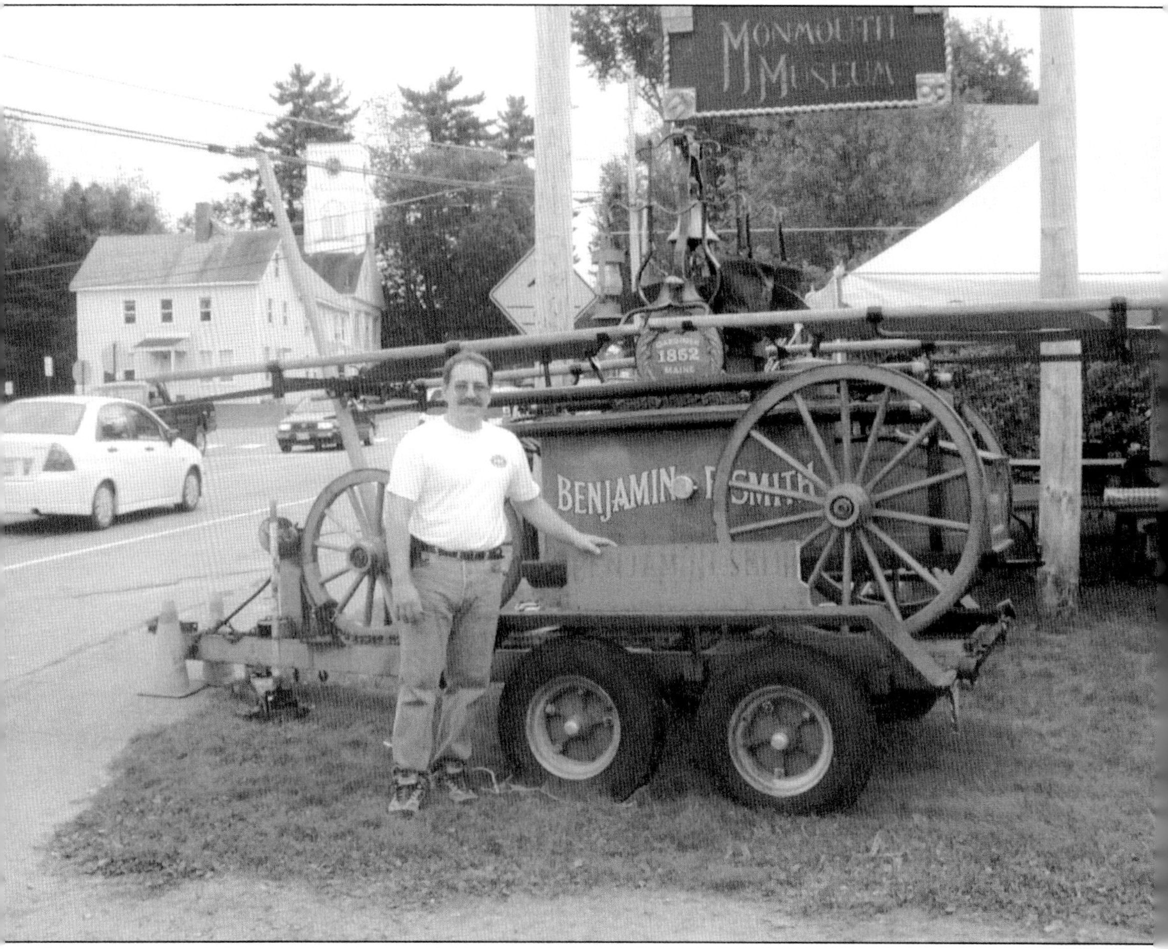

Fire chief Andre Poulin stands with the original hand tub that Monmouth purchased in 1904. The hand tub was on loan from the Gardiner Fire Department, the current owners. Monmouth Fire Department celebrated 100 years of service in 2004; it participated in the Monmouth Museum Apple Fest and brought the old hand tub back for a reunion. (Photograph by the author.)

Two

North Monmouth

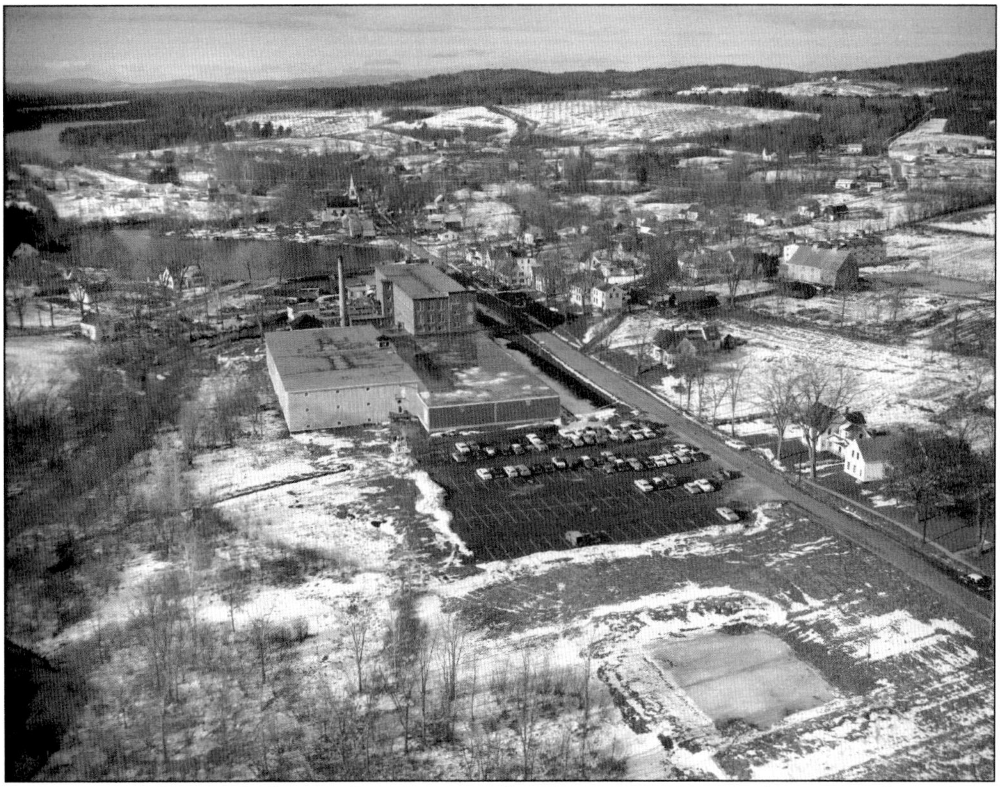

This is an aerial view of Albany Felt, now Tex-Tech Industries, Inc., in North Monmouth. Looking to the upper left corner, one can see the millpond that is fed by a stream from Wilson Pond at the very top. A large portion of the North Monmouth Village is also visible. (Photograph by Roland LaVallee, courtesy of the Monmouth Museum.)

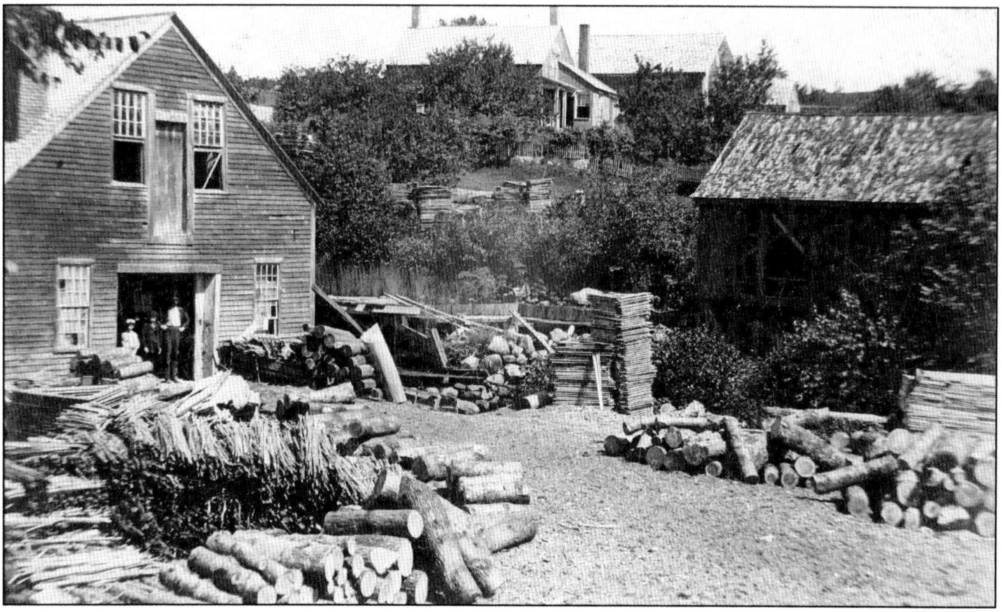

Depicted in this photograph is the box factory that was situated near the intersection of Wilson Pond Road and North Main Street in North Monmouth, across the road from present-day home of Grace Burnham. The box factory, owned by Rufus Moody, was in operation during the late 1800s. (Courtesy of the author.)

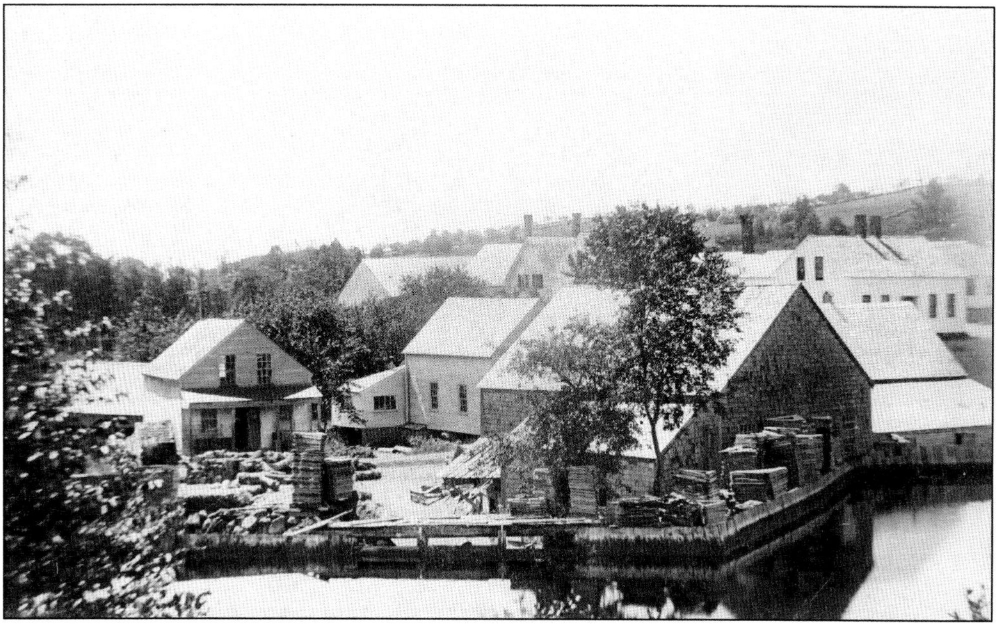

This view is from behind the box factory and was taken by an unknown photographer. Barrels for shipping apples were also manufactured at the box factory. (Courtesy of the author.)

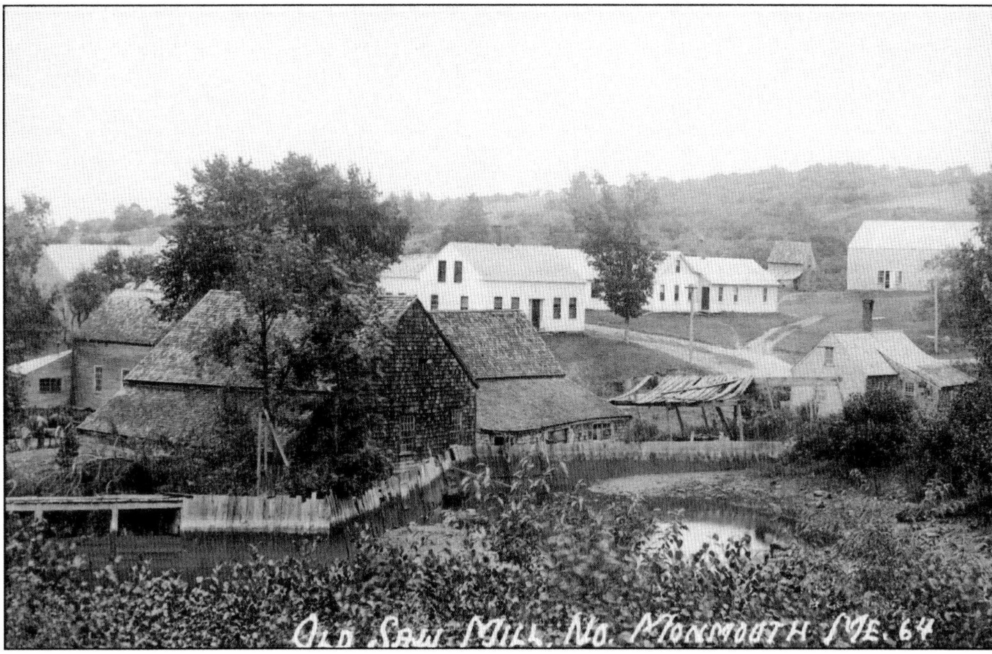

Leonidas Pettingill also owned and operated the box factory at one time. He made dowels, apple barrels, and packing cases. The old sawmill was located right next to the box factory on Wilson Pond Road. (Courtesy of the author.)

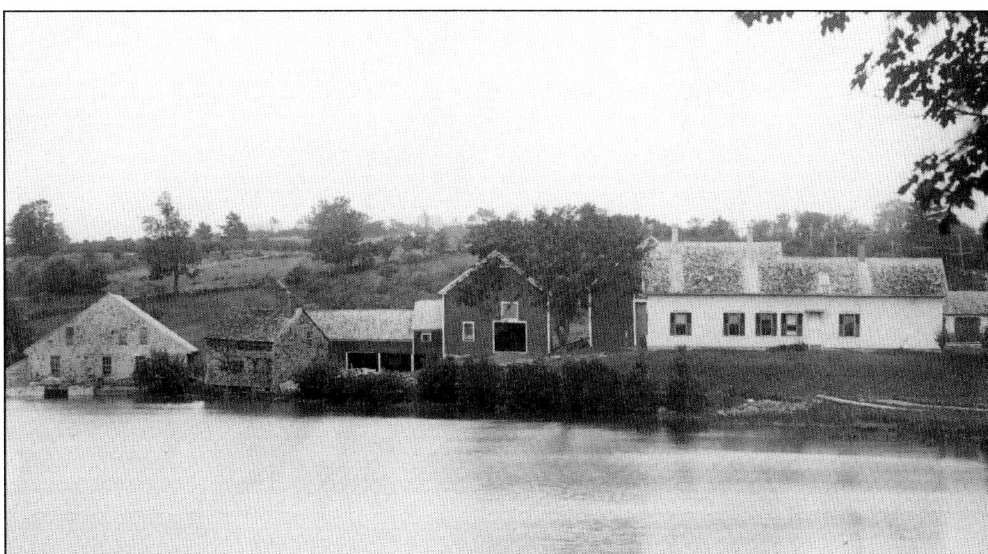

Here is the old gristmill and the third millpond along Wilson Stream. It was run by Jeremiah Gordon during the early 1900s and later by George "Walter" Whiting. (Courtesy of the author.)

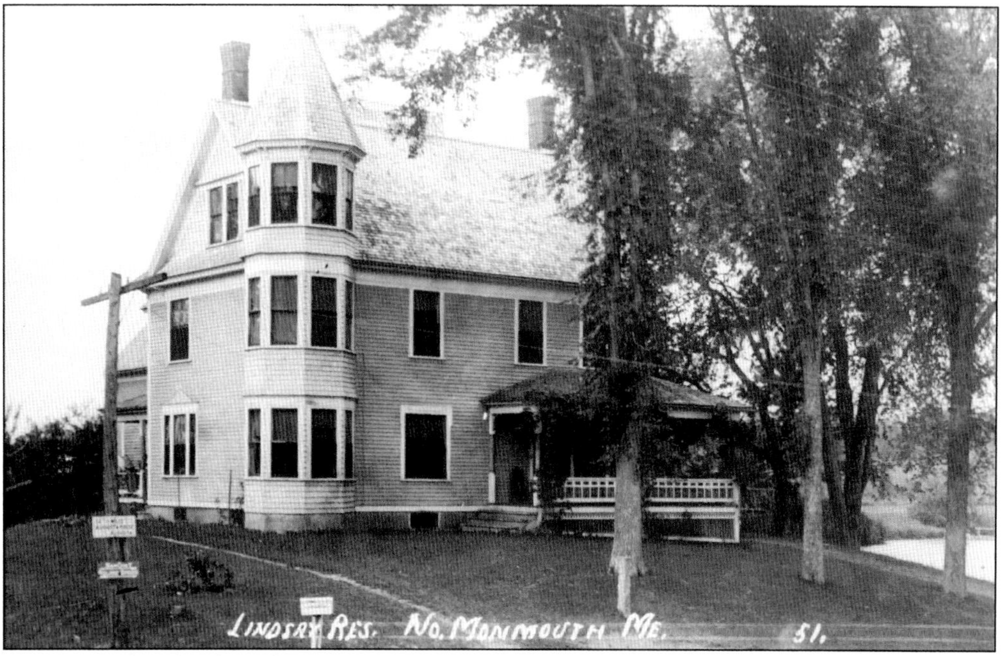

Everett Lindsay lived on the corner of Old Lewiston Road and what is currently called North Main Street. He was in charge of the axe and hoe factory, which was located on Wilson Stream until it was destroyed by fire. The Lindsay House was destroyed by fire in the late 1960s. (Courtesy of the author.)

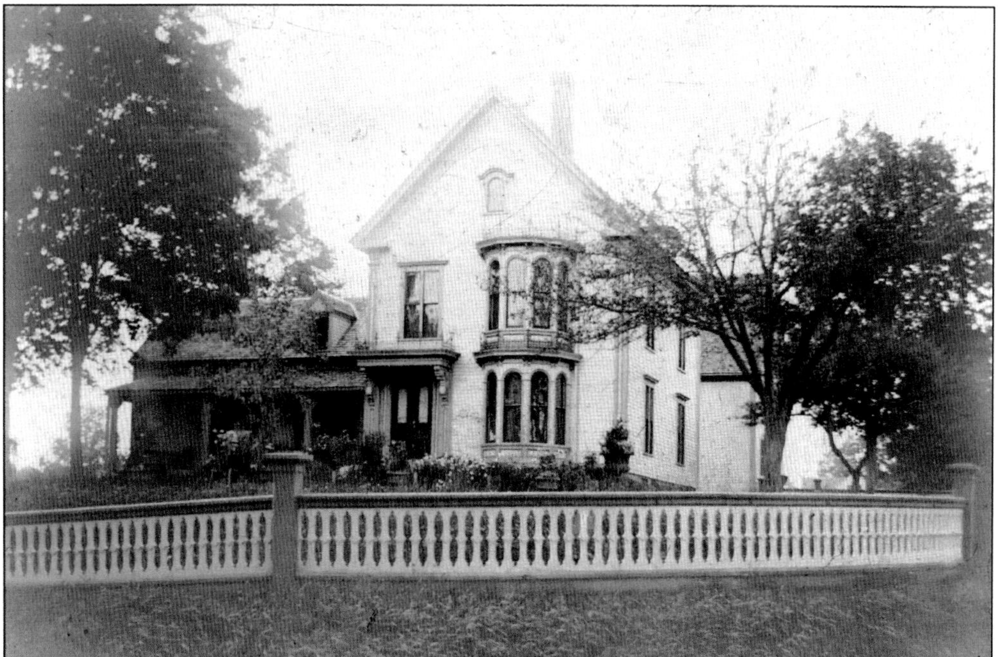

The Ambrose House is located on the corner of Old Lewiston Road and what is currently called North Main Street. It is directly across from where the Lindsay House once stood. Today it is the residence of Dennis Cripps. (Courtesy of the Monmouth Museum.)

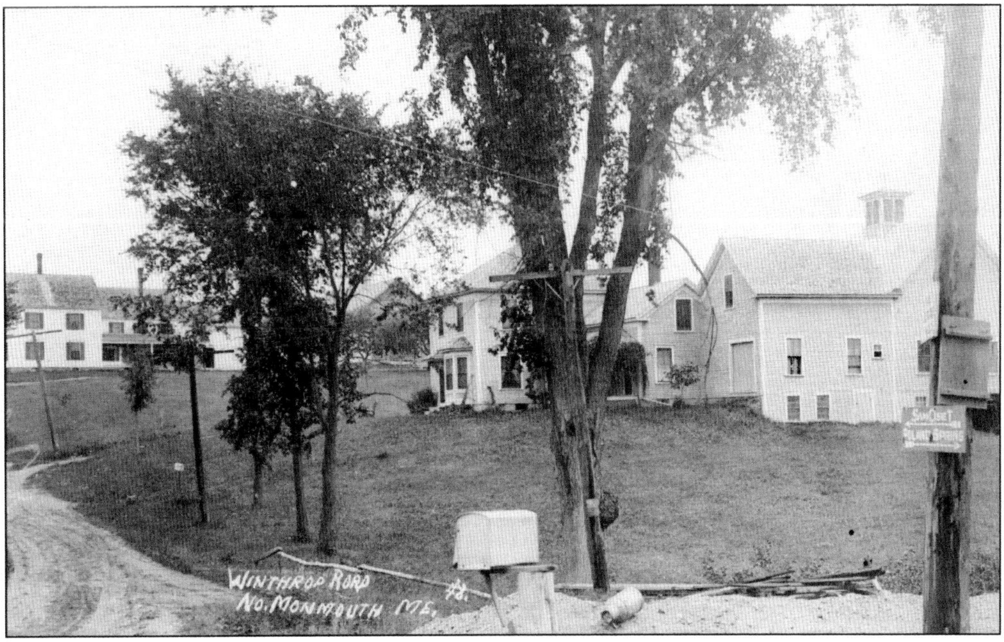

The residence of E. E. Walker was on Old Lewiston Road just past the four-way intersection of North Main Street. (Courtesy of the author.)

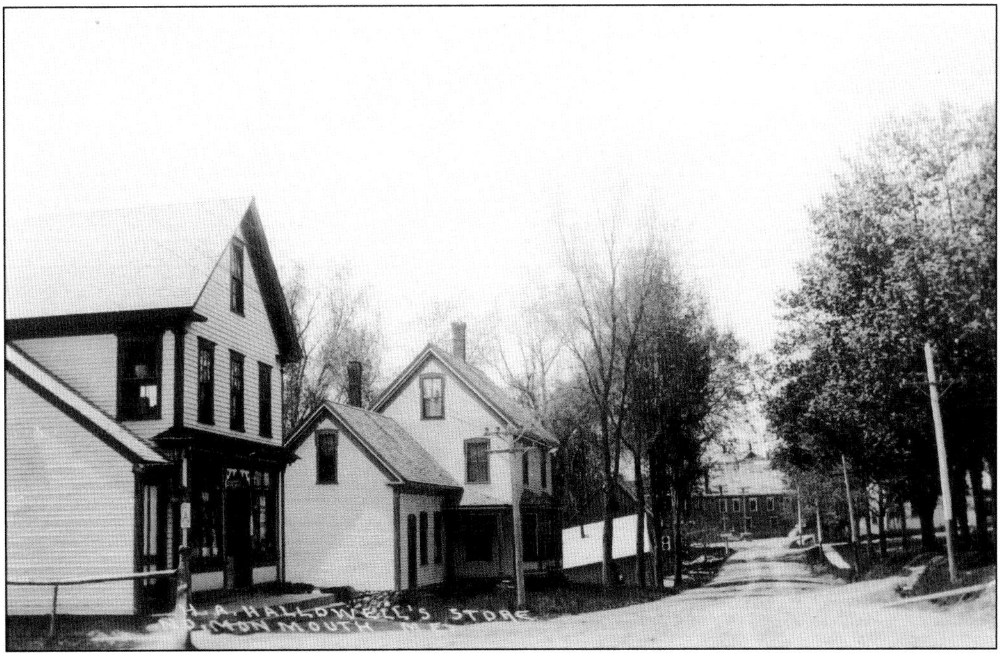

This view is looking down North Main Street past Harry Hallowell's store on the left. At the end of the street stands the old brick mill, which was built by Samuel King as a starch factory. According to Harry Cochrane's *History of Monmouth and Wales*, Joseph King bought the business from his father in 1850 and remodeled the mill to put in new machinery for the manufacture of webbing. (Courtesy of the author.)

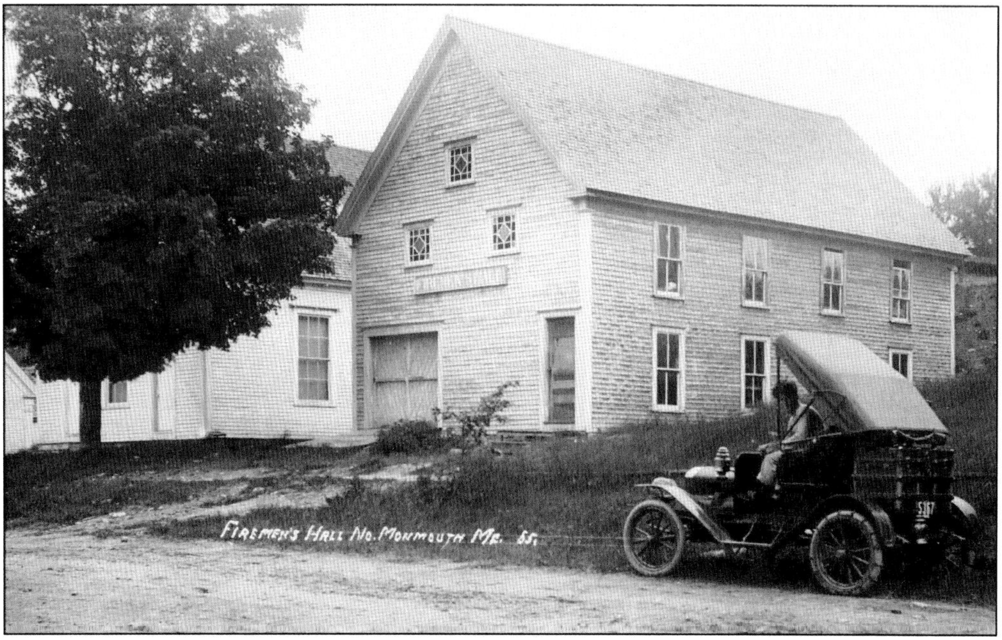

Fireman's Hall was built in 1909 and is located on North Main Street. It hosted a wide variety of social activities over the ages. It now is a private residence. (Courtesy of the author.)

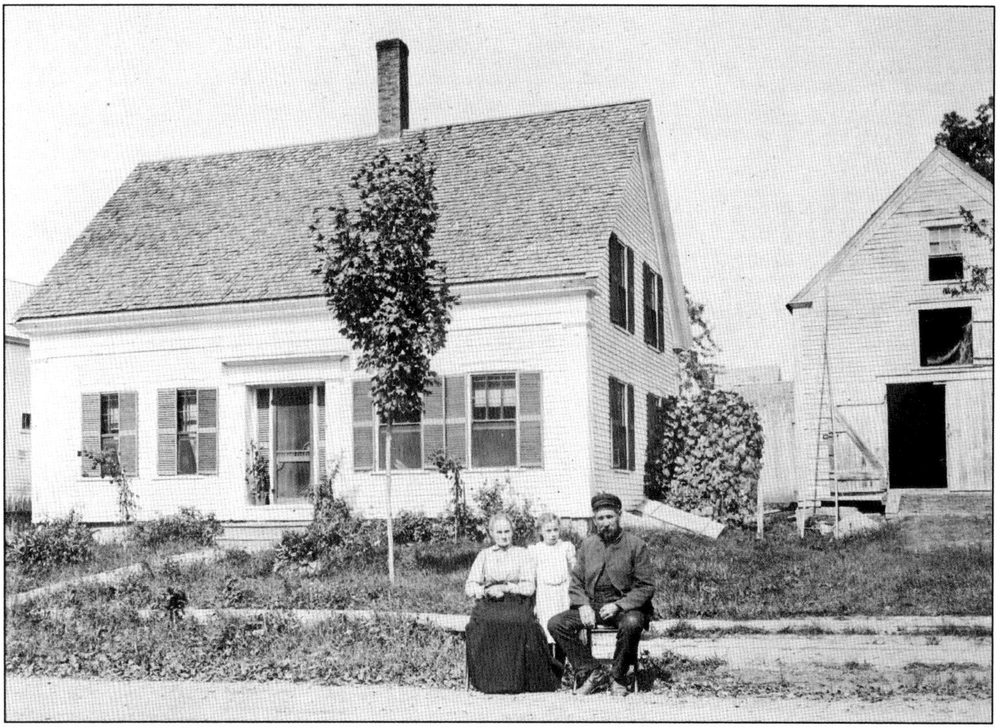

Pictured in North Monmouth is a homestead on North Main Street that sat across from the mill that belonged to the late Alice and Irving House. Louis Robinson, who lived behind this beautiful Cape Cod, is shown sitting with his daughter Gertrude and perhaps his mother-in-law Mary Withers. (Courtesy of Roscoe Scott.)

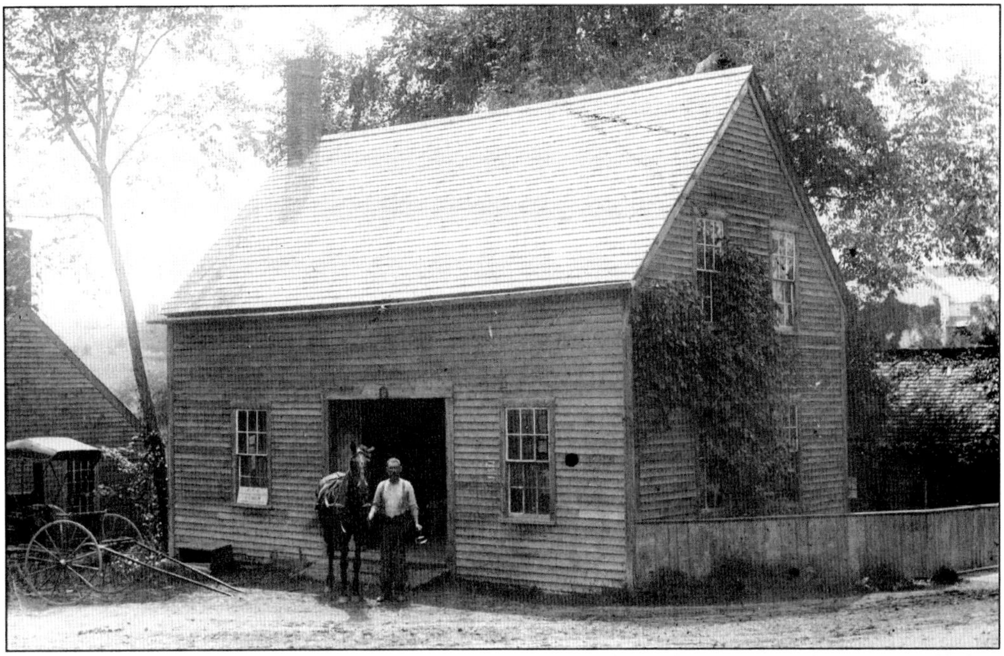

The blacksmith shop at the north end of North Main Street is shown here. Louis Robinson, grandfather of the late Ruby Pettingill, is the man in the photograph. (Courtesy of Roscoe Scott.)

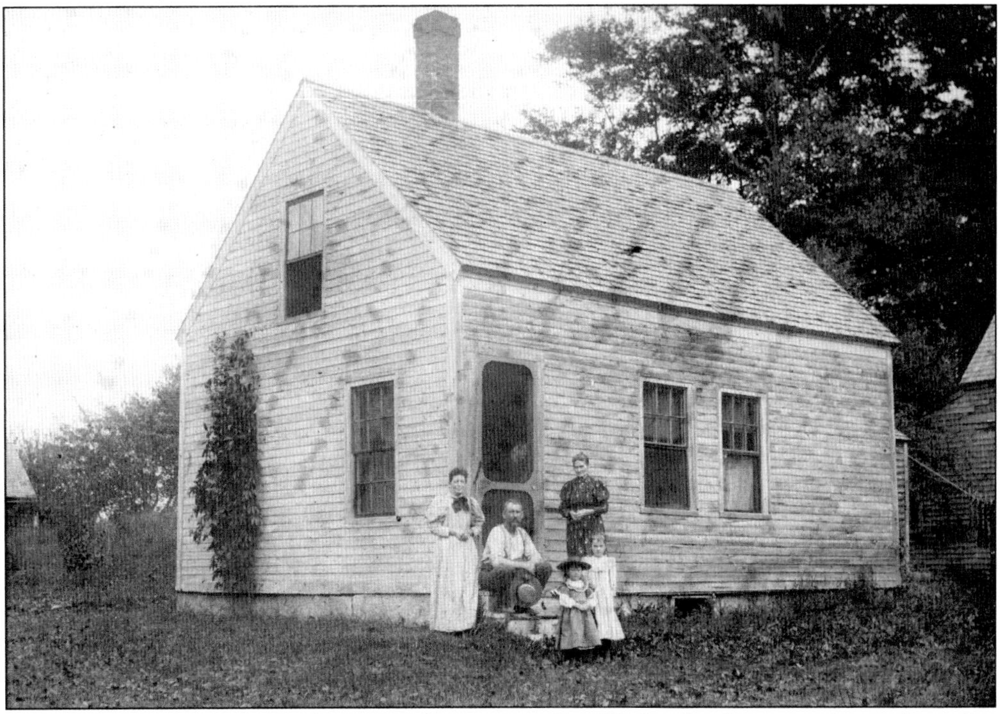

This is the home of Louis Robinson and his wife Nellie (Withers), who is standing to his right. Nellie's twin sister, Rosetta (Nettie Withers) stands to Louis's left. The smaller child is unidentified. The young girl is Louis and Nellie's daughter Gertrude. The Robinsons lived directly behind the home of the late Alice and Irving House on North Main Street. (Courtesy of Roscoe Scott.)

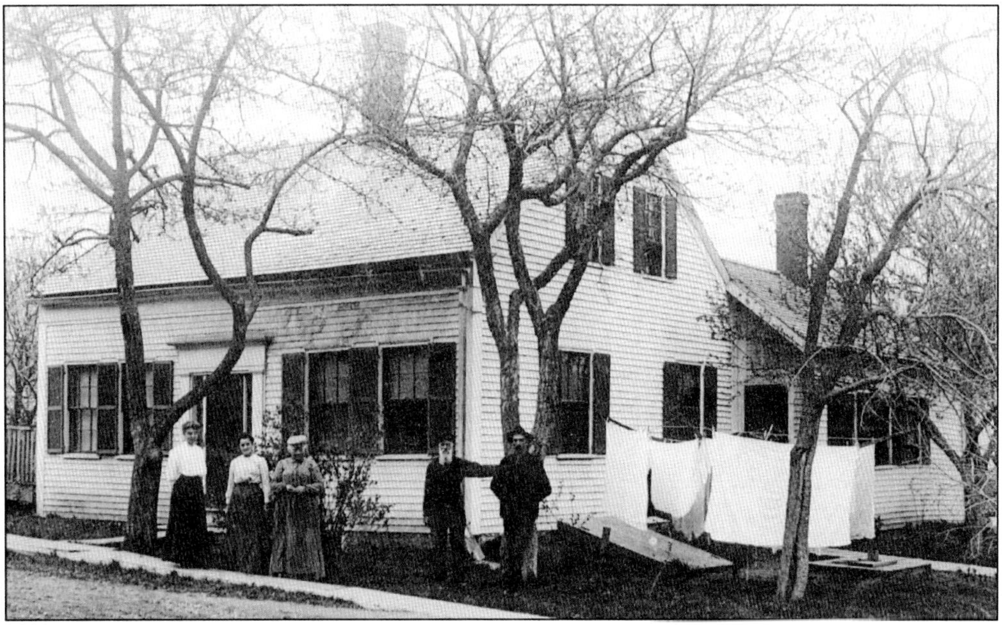

James Withers's house was located at the corner of what is now North Main Street and Wilson Pond Road. The older couple in the photograph is James and his wife, Mary E. Whipple Withers. The two young ladies are their twin daughters Nettie (left) and Nellie. The young man standing next to James Withers is perhaps one of his sons or Nellie's husband. James Withers was a Civil War veteran and served with Company C of the 30th Maine. (Courtesy of Shelia Sanford.)

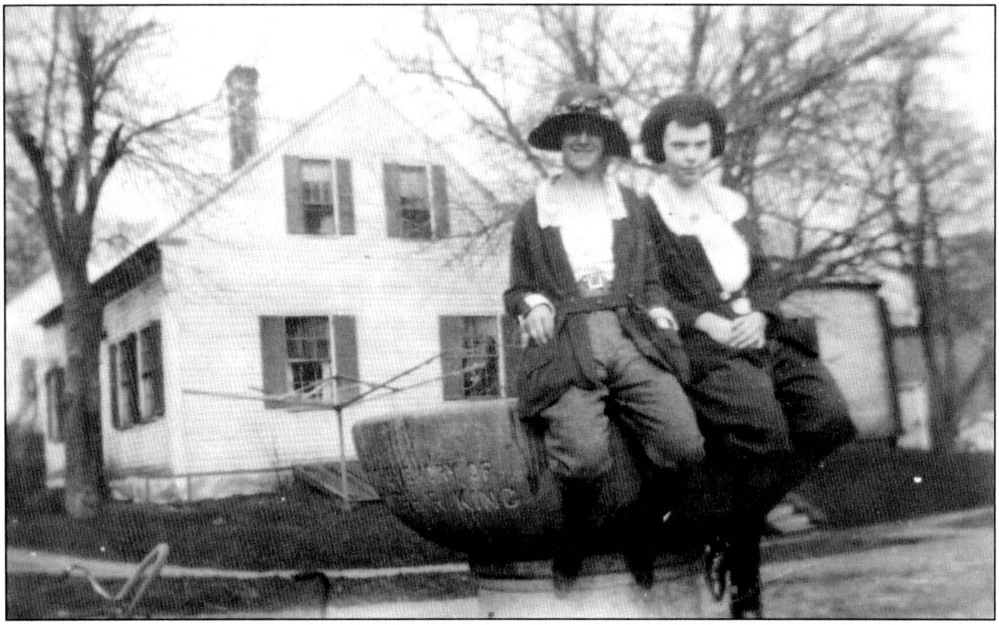

Verna Whittier (right) and a friend are relaxing on the old watering tub that sat at the intersection of what is now Wilson Pond Road and North Main Street. The water tub was given to the village in honor of Joseph R. King by his family. Around 1980, the tub was taken down for a number of years, but it has since been reinstalled a short distance from where it stood. (Courtesy of Shelia Sanford.)

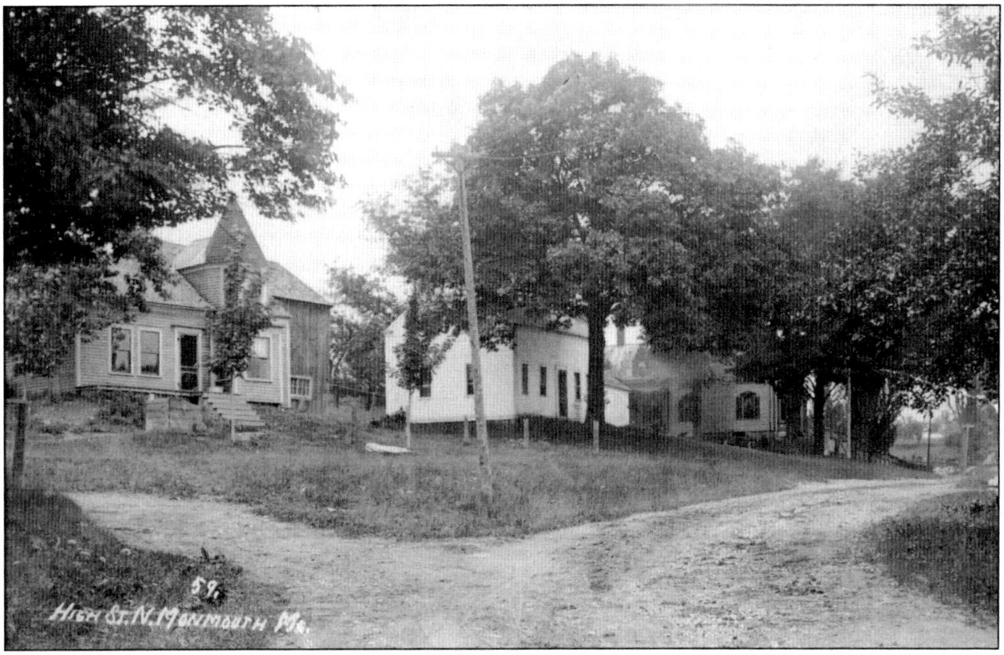

The High Street section of North Monmouth is shown here. Two of the houses pictured here are no longer standing. (Courtesy of Shelia Sanford.)

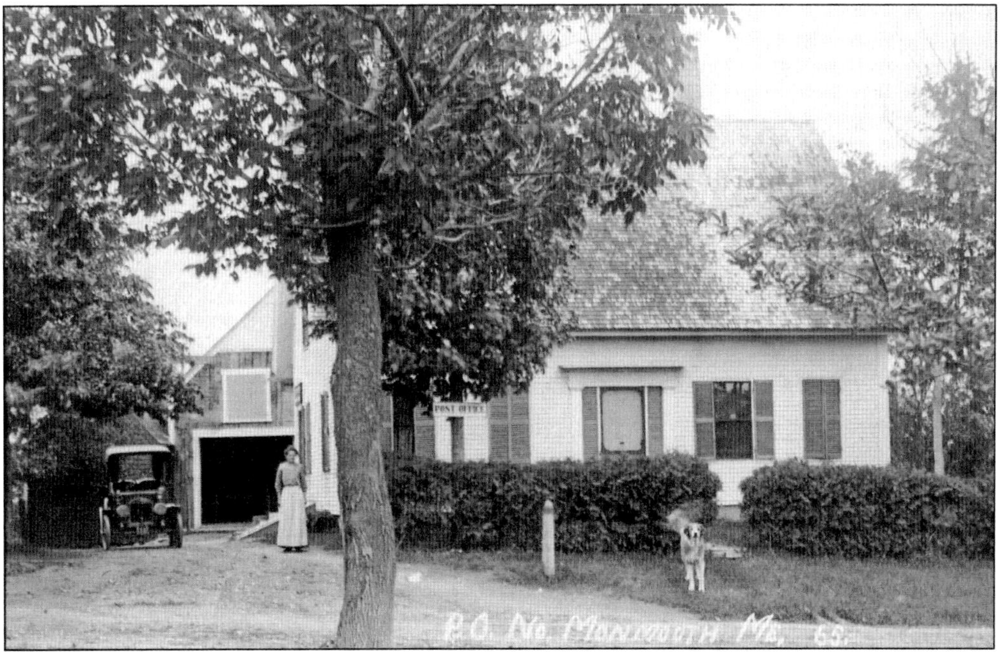

Picture is the North Monmouth Post Office on the corner of Wilson Pond Road and New Street. Melzer and Arobina Cunningham Peaslee also ran a meat market here. (Courtesy of Shelia Sanford.)

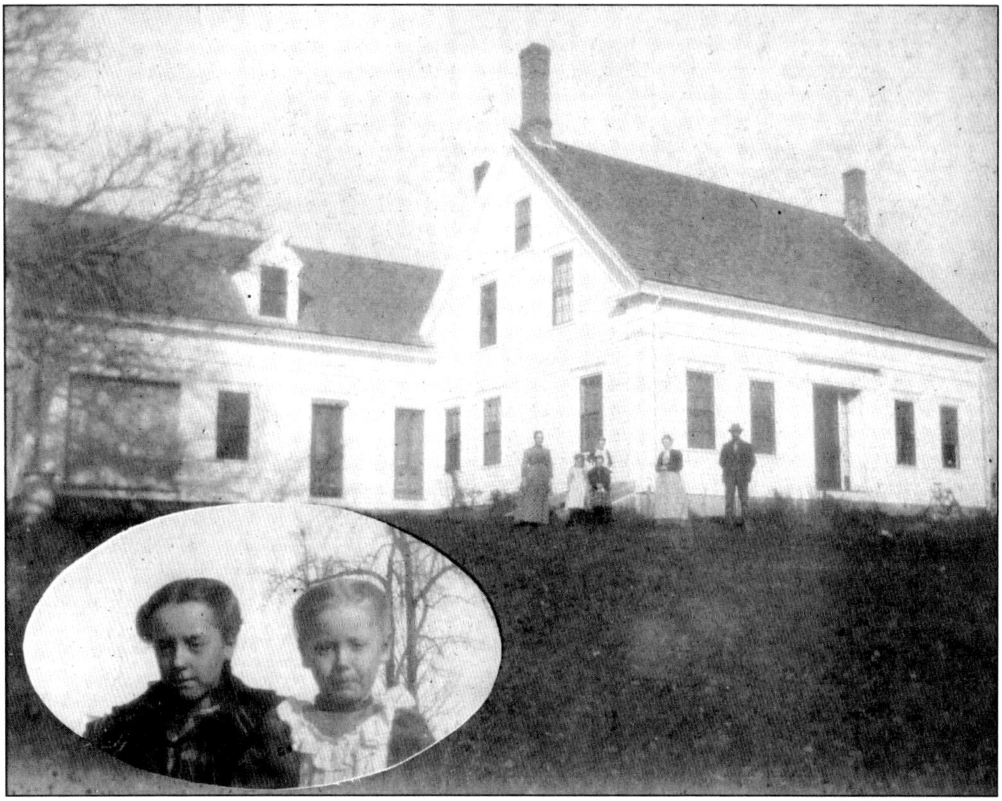

Just past the four-way stop at the intersection of Wilson Pond Road is a home that once belonged to the Manwell family. The two little girls in the lower left corner are believed to be Myrtle Fairbanks (left) and Ethel Chandler (right). (Courtesy of Valerie House Coffin.)

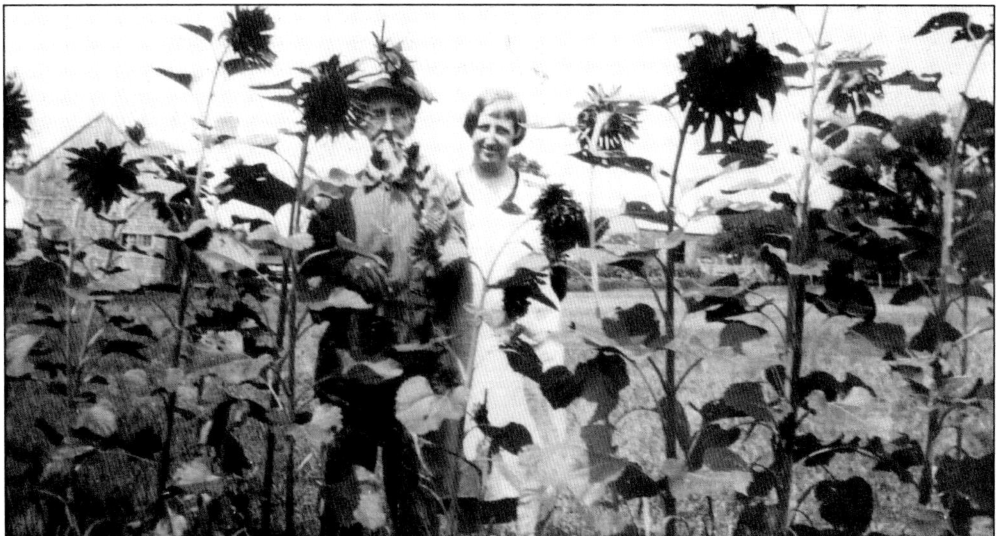

Charles R. Chandler and his daughter, Ethel Chandler Brown, are seen peeking through the sunflowers in the backyard of the late Jack and Libby Williams, which was on Wilson Pond Road. (Courtesy of Valerie House Coffin.)

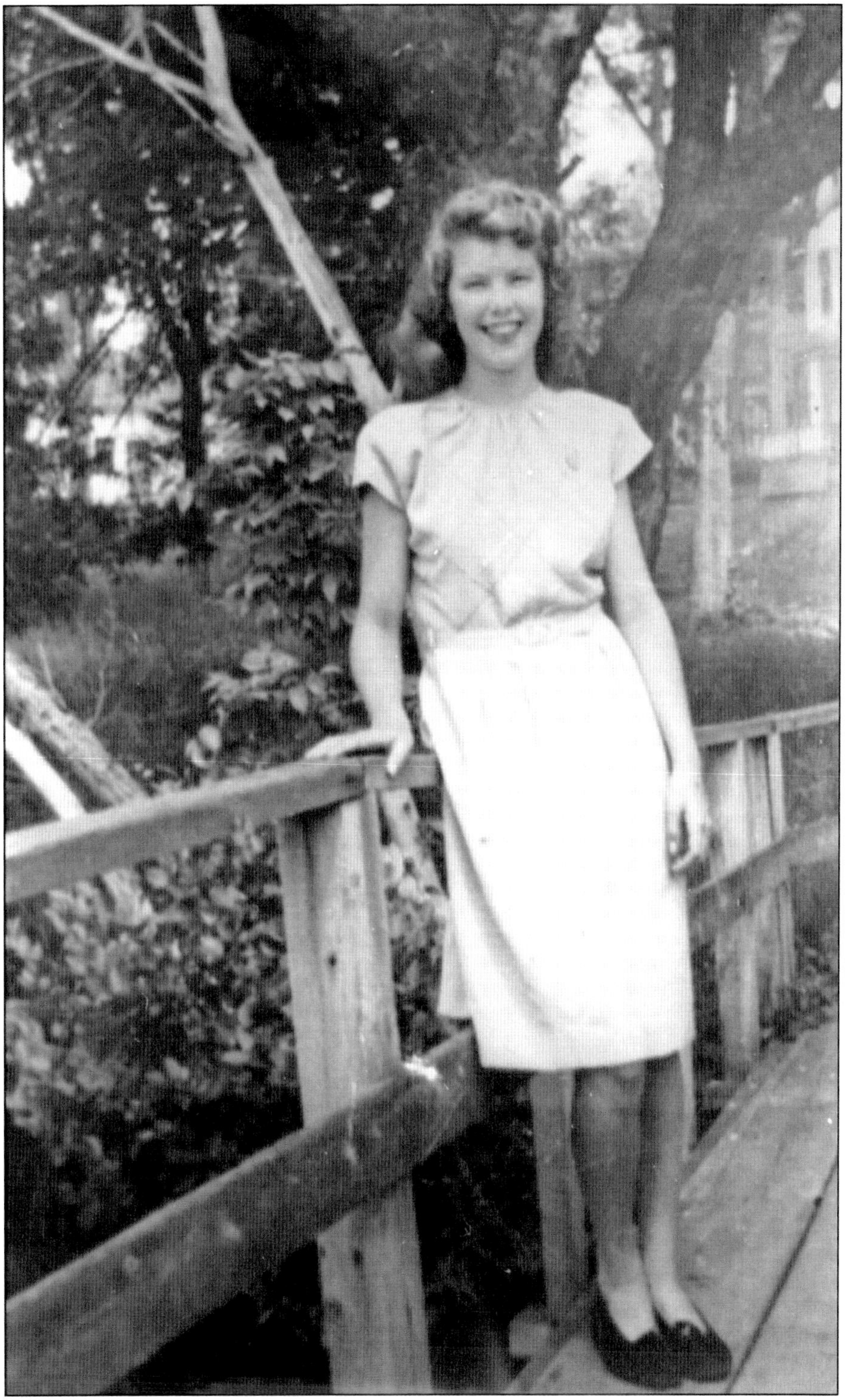

The late Alberta Dunn Keane is standing on Harry Hallowell's wooden bridge that crossed over Wilson Stream. (Courtesy of the late Alberta Dunn Keane.)

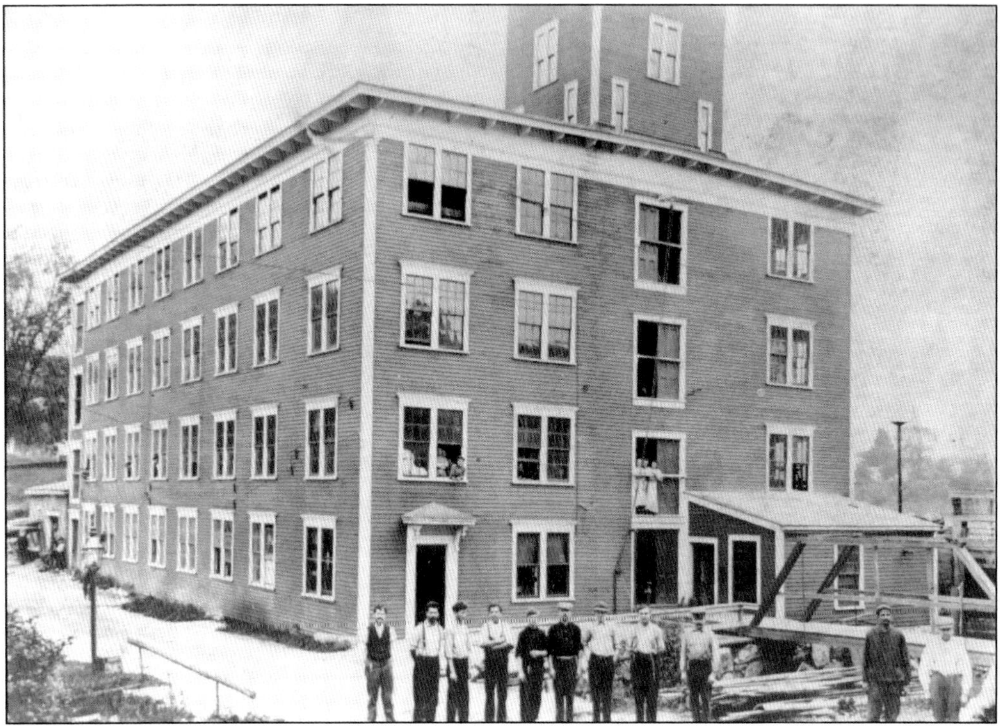

The wooden woolen mill at North Monmouth was built in 1896 and was used with the brick mill, which was built in 1914 by the Winthrop Mill Company. The wooden mill was dismantled in 1949. (Courtesy of the late Lewis Horzempa.)

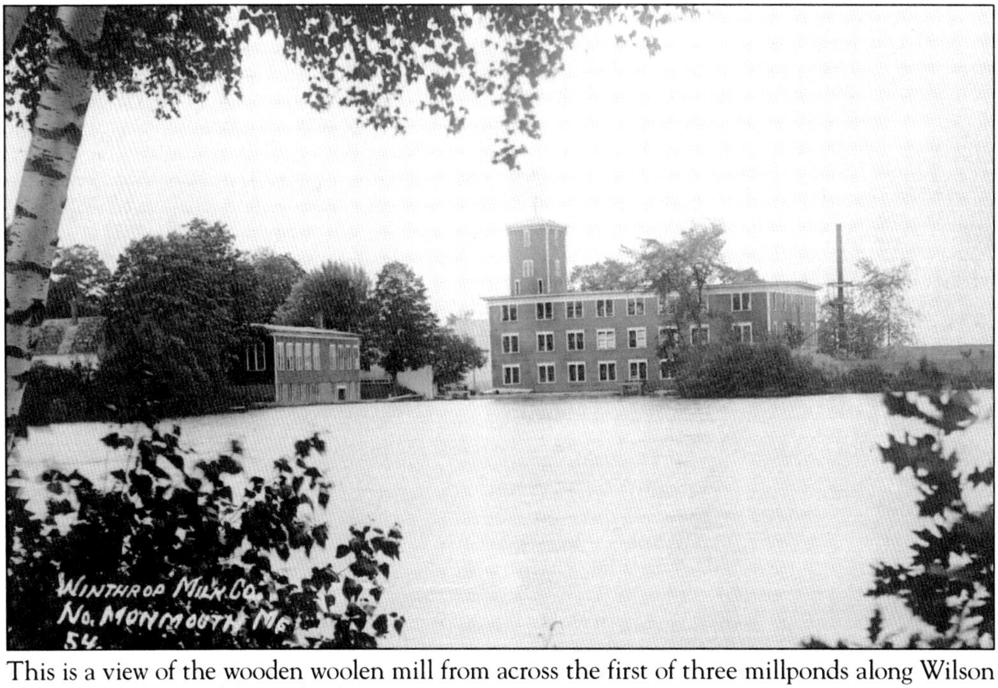

This is a view of the wooden woolen mill from across the first of three millponds along Wilson Stream. (Courtesy of the author.)

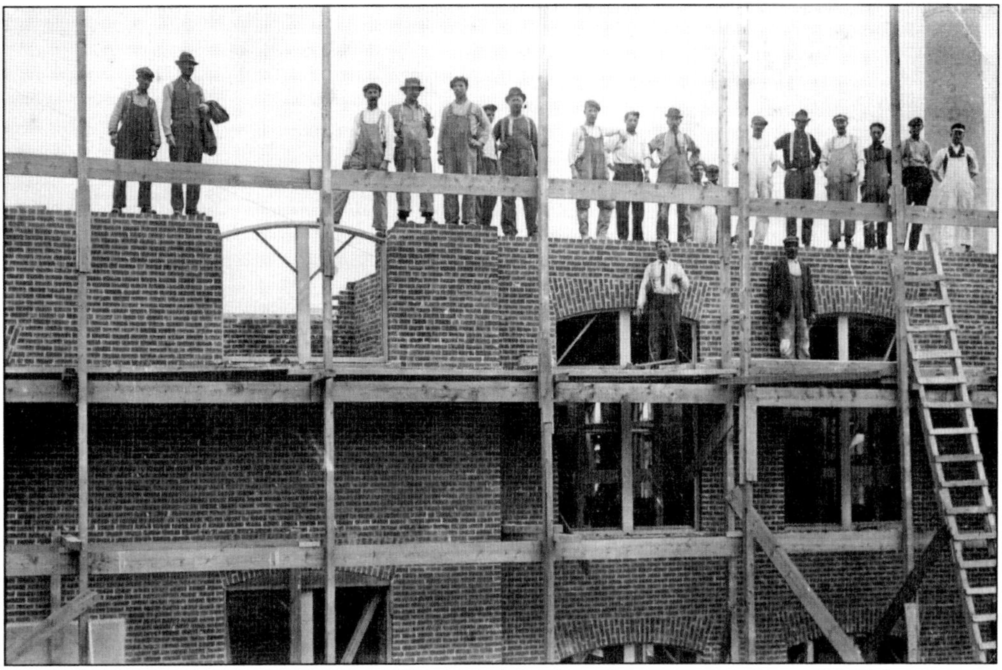

This photograph shows the new Annabessacook Mill under construction in 1914. The original wooden structure, know as the Fairbanks Mill and later the Annabessacook Mill, was built in 1829 by Joseph Fairbanks. The construction of this new mill would attract a small group of emigrants from Poland who settled in North Monmouth and added a special uniqueness to the town. (Courtesy of the author.)

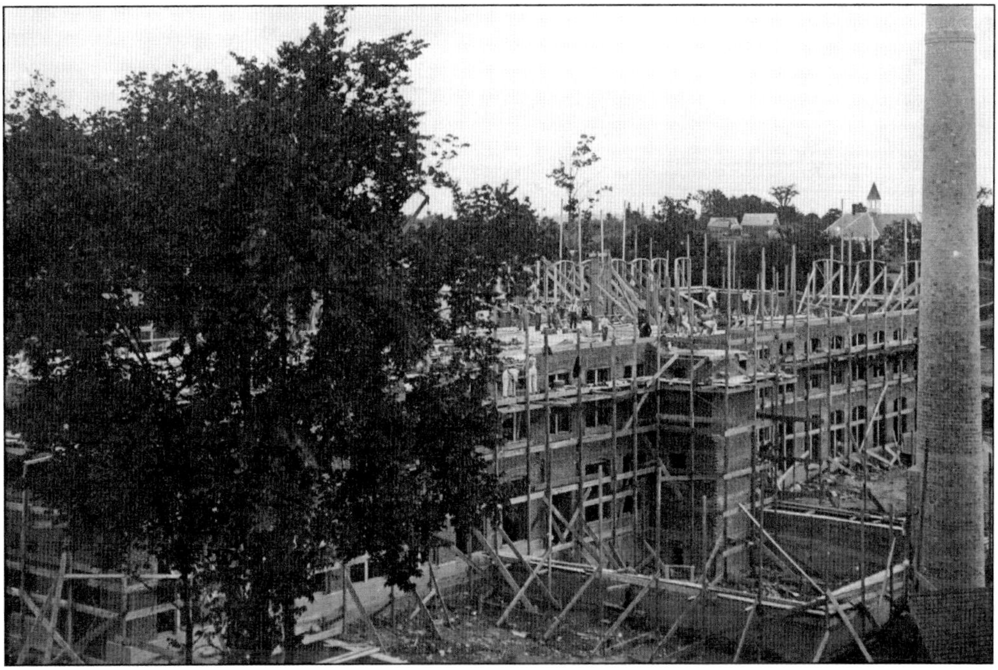

This is another perspective of the mill under construction in 1914. In the distant background is the belfry of the North Monmouth School. (Courtesy of the Monmouth Museum.)

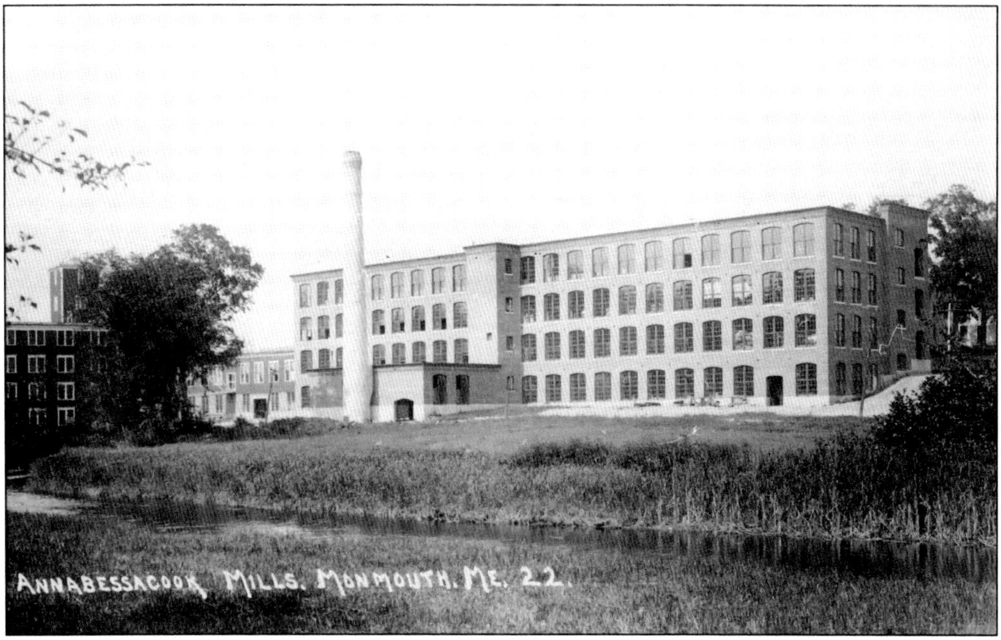

Annabessacook Mills are shown here with the recently completed new mill on what is known today as North Main Street. (Courtesy of Stan DeOrsey.)

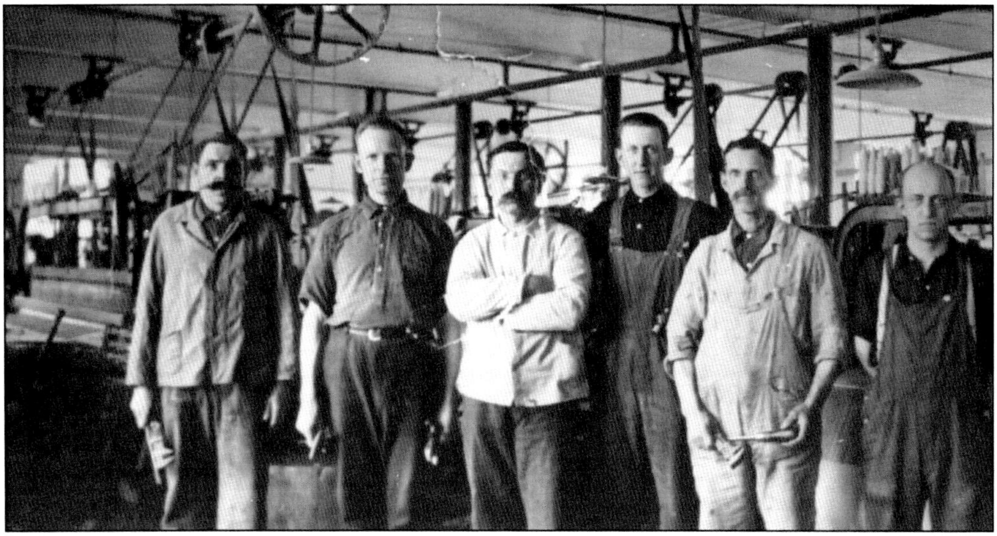

Pictured around 1919 are, from left to right, William Horzempa, Martin Slez, William Piela, Ozro Cram, Leo Dow, and Henry Hodgdon at the North Monmouth Mill (Annabessacook Mill). (Courtesy of Lewis Horzempa.)

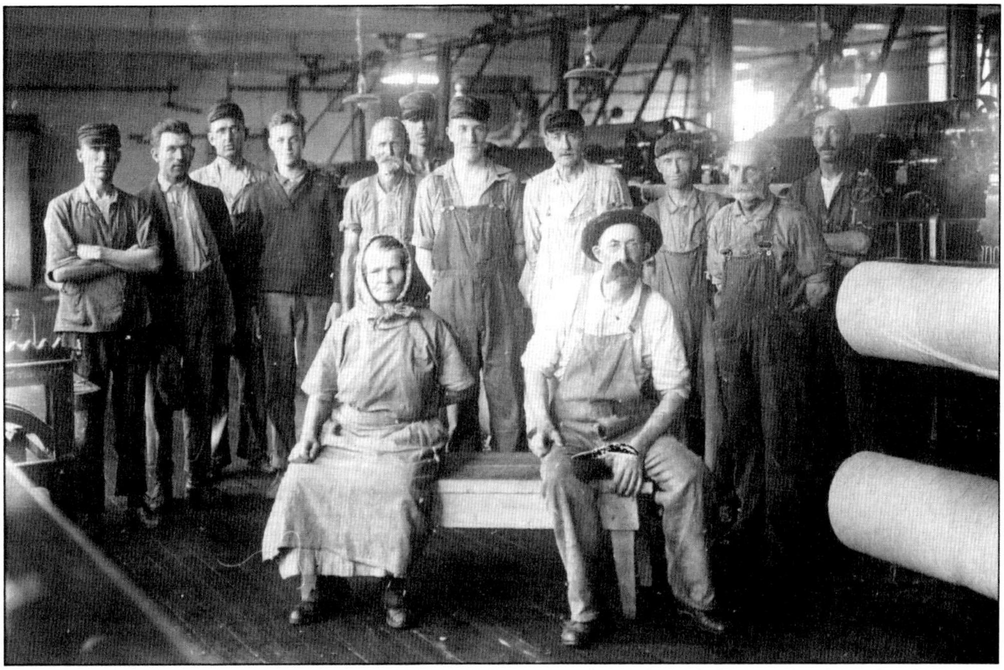

At the North Monmouth Mill around 1920, those pictured are, from left to right, (standing) Austin Carter, Fred Hooker, Carl Richardson, Alton Espionghnette, Allie Warren, Roy Morse, James Ridlon, Herbert Arris, Edward Souviney, Willie Higgins, and Arthur Payne; (seated) Victoria Pickor and Harry Prescott. (Courtesy of the Monmouth Museum.)

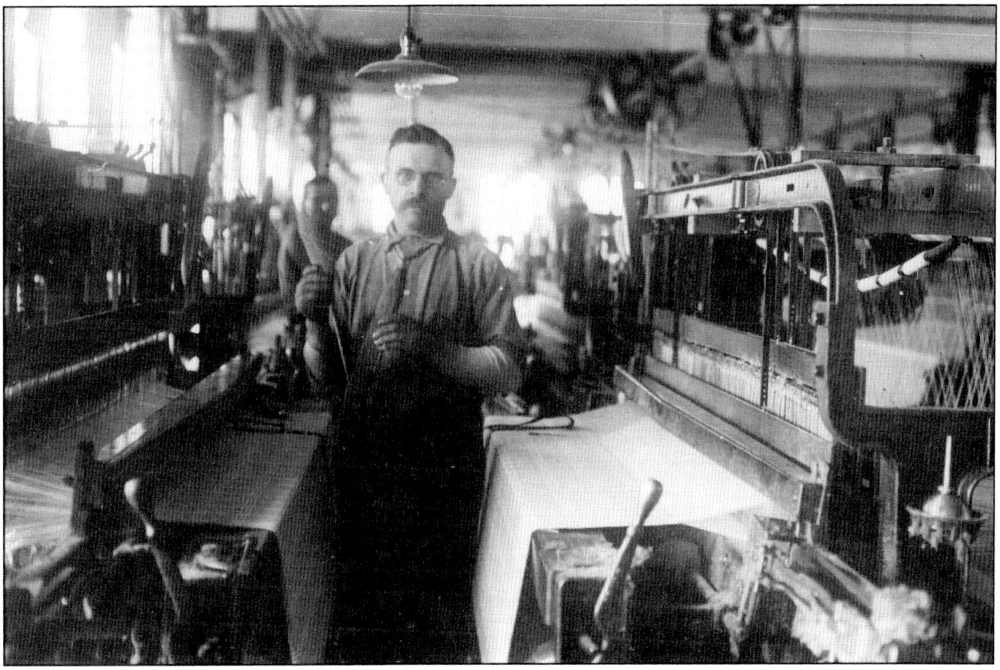

William Horzempa is pictured at the North Monmouth Mill around 1920. He served in the Polish Austrian army before he immigrated to the United States in 1909. (Courtesy the Monmouth Museum.)

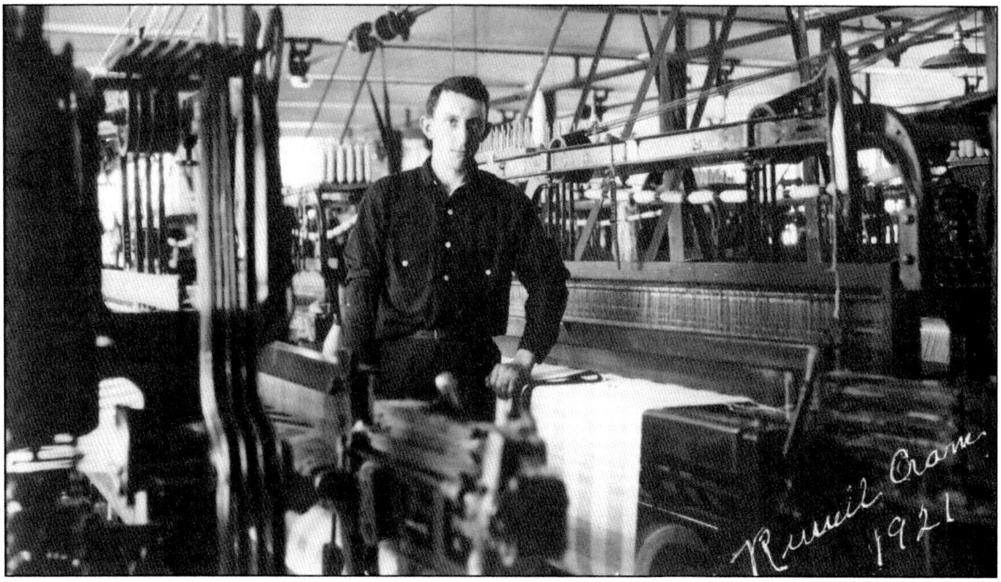

Russell Cram is shown here at the North Monmouth Mill in 1921. (Courtesy of the author.)

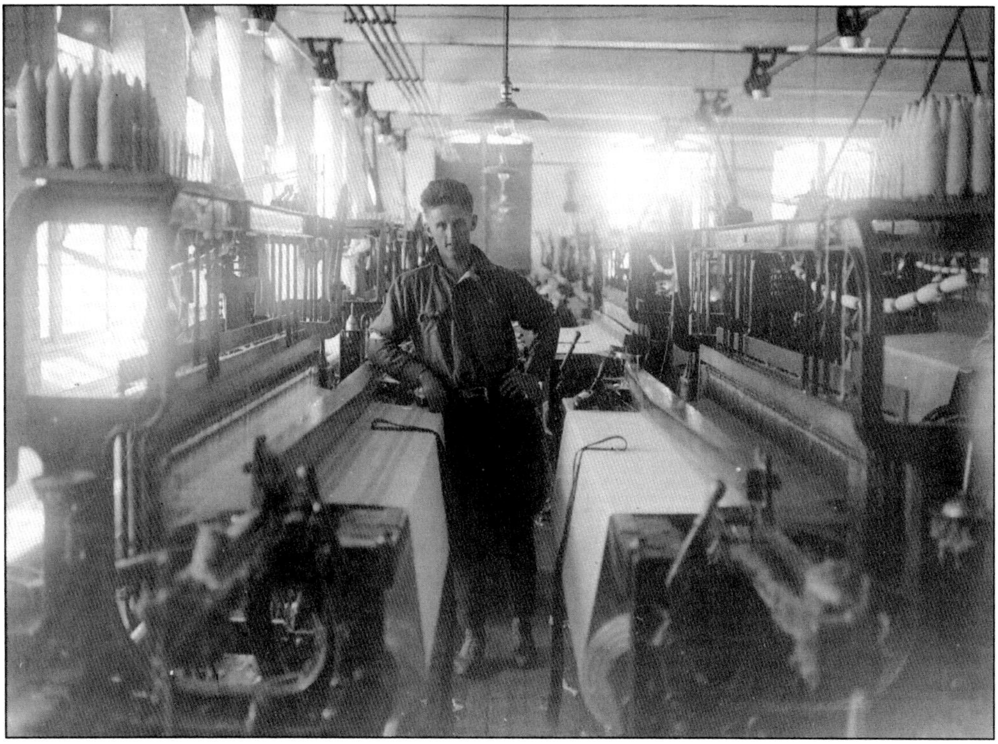

This photograph shows Sam Berry at the North Monmouth Mill around 1920. (Courtesy of the Monmouth Museum.)

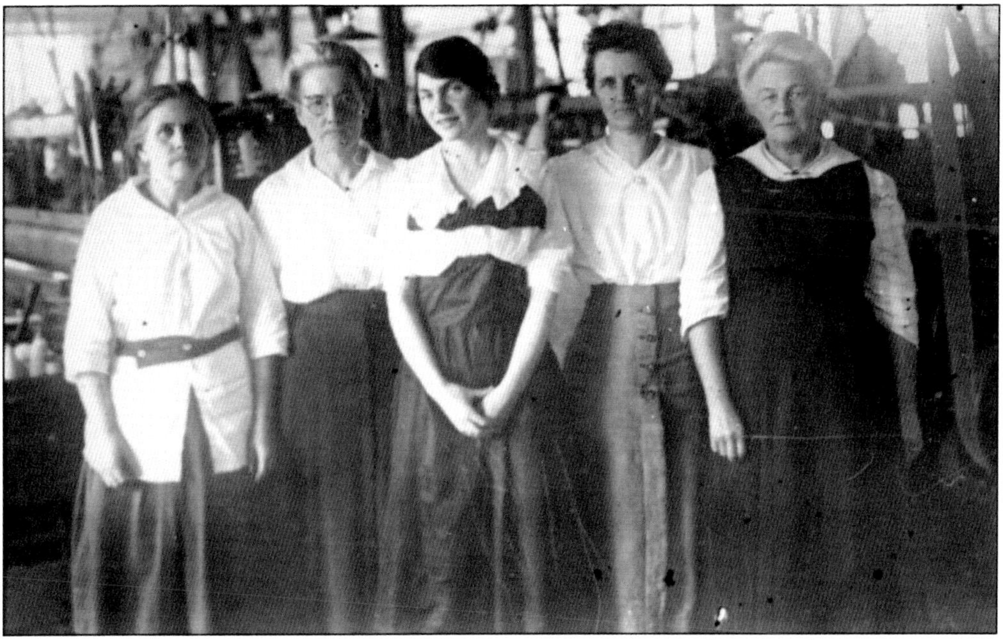

From left to right are Mary Canwell, Ella Thurston, Geneva Canwell, Gertrude Berry, and Dora Hanson at the North Monmouth Mill around 1919. (Courtesy of the Monmouth Museum.)

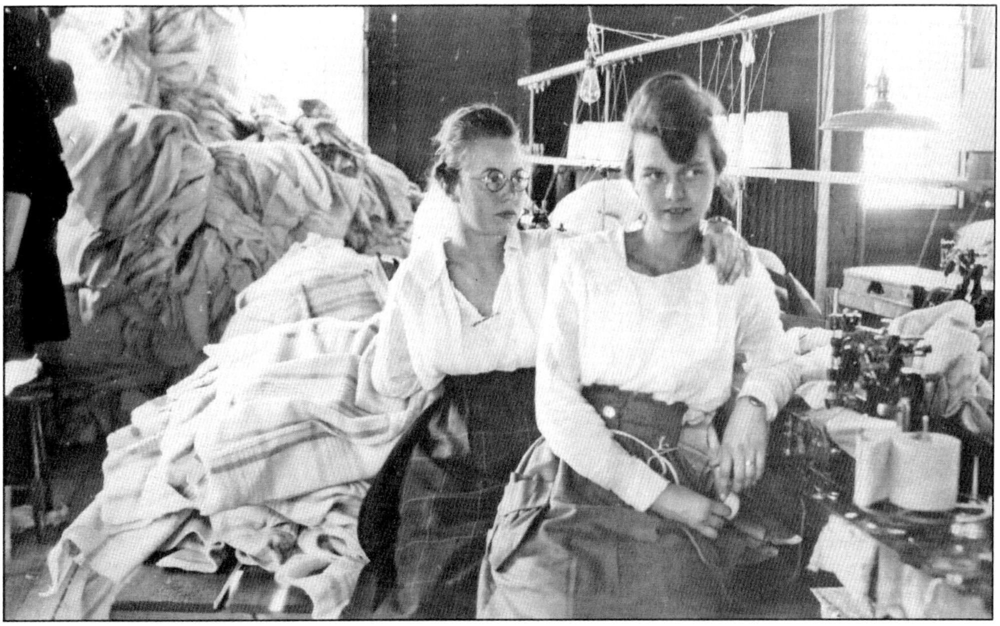

Marion Prescott Dunn (left) and Lida Whittier Prout (right) are pictured in the North Monmouth Mill around 1920. (Courtesy of the Monmouth Museum.)

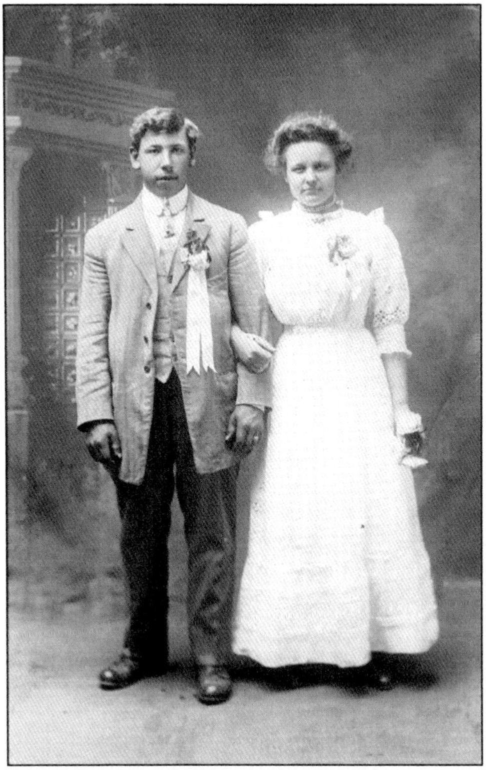

Members of the Polish community in North Monmouth, Albert Horzempa and Katie Sciuk are at a wedding. (Courtesy of the Monmouth Museum.)

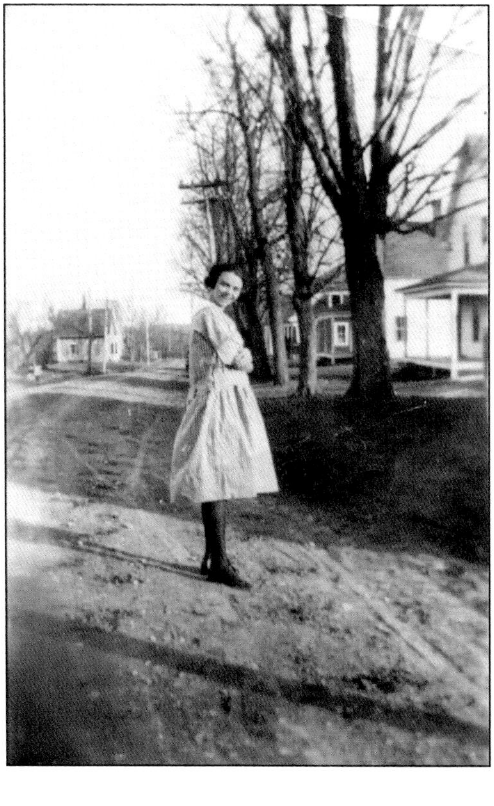

Valeria Piela Plossay is on the lower end of North Main Street, where she lived with her husband, Frank, and their children. (Courtesy of Shelia Sanford.)

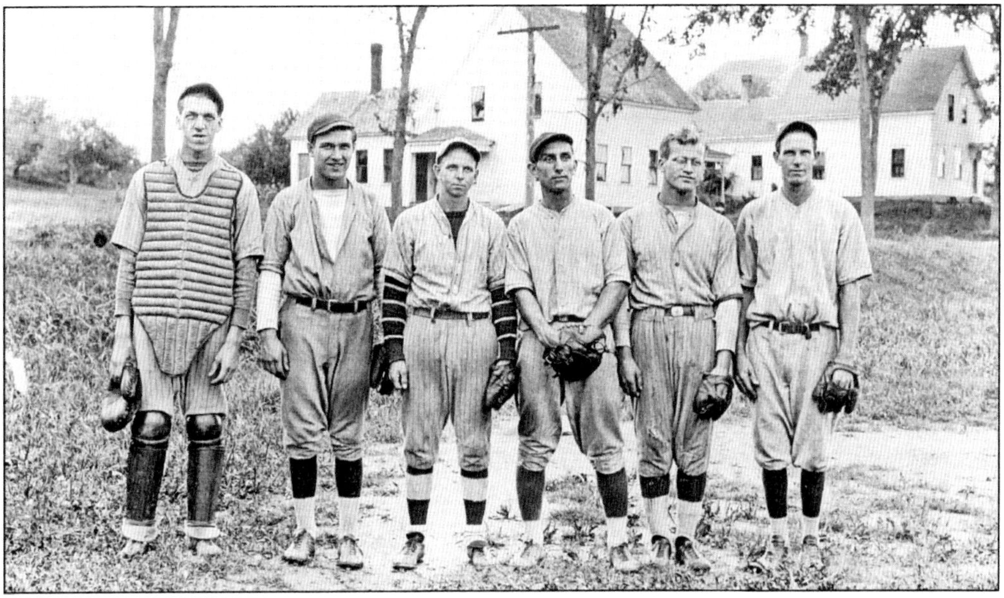

Members of the North Monmouth ball team are, from left to right, Alden Hutchinson, Frank Rodzen, "Smelt" Frost, "Eddie" Piela, "Lou" Sulya, and "Buster" Whittier. (Courtesy of Shelia Sanford).

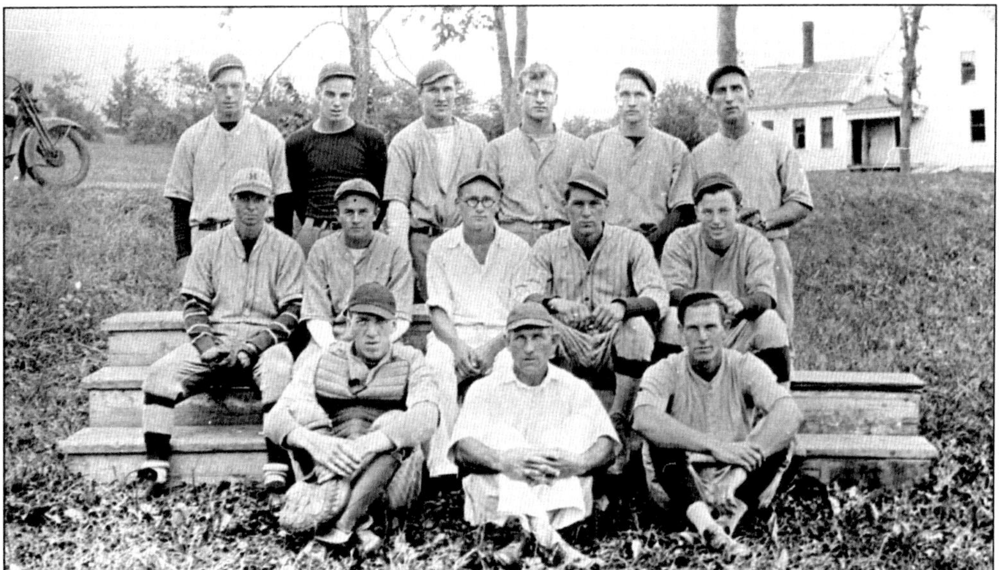

A North Monmouth ball team from the late 1930s is shown here. Those pictured are, from left to right, (first row) Alden Hutchinson, manager Fred Hooker, and Everett Whittier; (second row) "Smelt" Frost, "Shookie" William Pyska, Carl Sulya, Martin Sulya, and "Mont" La Mont Grant; (third row) Phil Riggs, "Wally" Littlefield, Frank Rodzen, "Lou" Sulya, Everett Day, and Ed Piela. The house to the right in the background is where La Mont Grant lived on North Main Street. The ball field was across the road from La Mont's house, where the mill parking lot is today. (Courtesy of Shelia Sanford.)

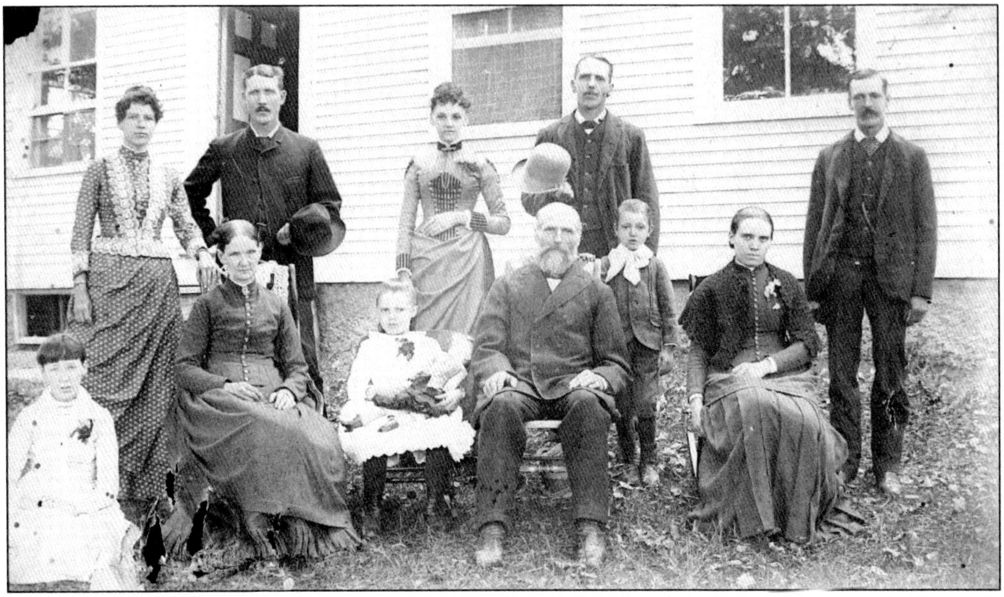

Jacob and Elizabeth Stanton Robinson are pictured with their family in North Monmouth. Elizabeth attended Monmouth Academy, which is where she learned to paint. One of her paintings of the North Monmouth Village during the 1860s is at the Bowdoin College Museum of Art. (Courtesy of the Monmouth Museum.)

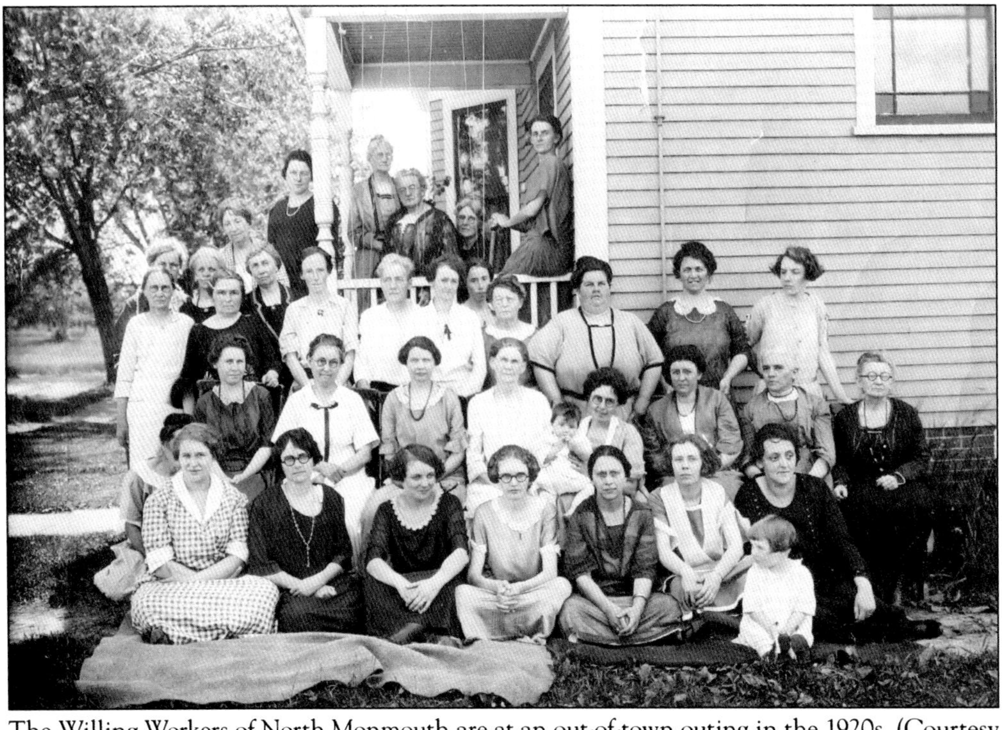

The Willing Workers of North Monmouth are at an out-of-town outing in the 1920s. (Courtesy of Shelia Sanford.)

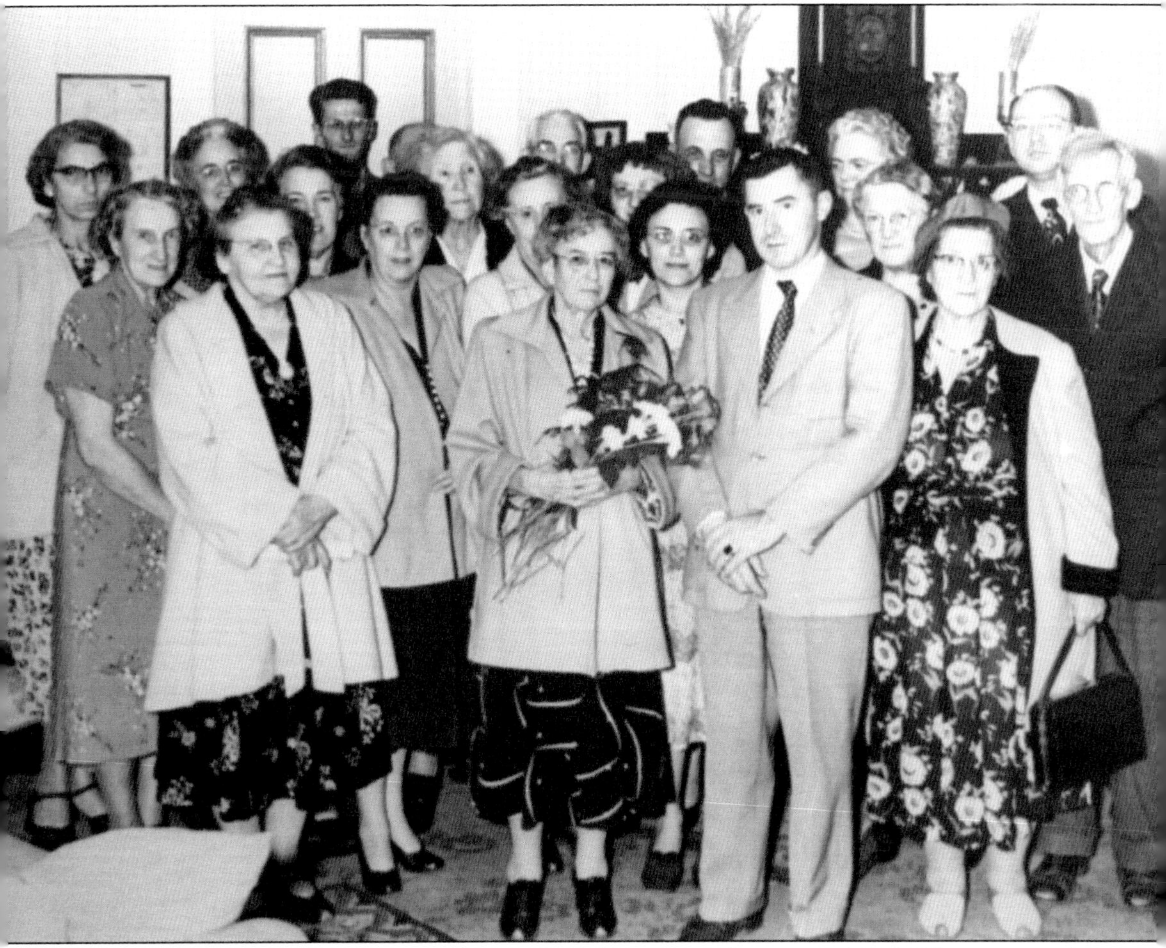

This group photograph at Rev. Joseph LeMaster's house was taken around 1950. Those pictured are, from left to right, (first row) Anna Leighton, Mildred Lindsey (with flowers), Sheldon Clark, and Clara Frost; (second row) Catherine Crafts, Mattie Hooker, Marion Dunn, Hazel Clark, Dot Gile, Nellie Daggett, and Percy Jefferies; (third row) Ethel Pelky, Bertha Morse, Jud Gile, Fred Hooker (hidden), Emma Garrett Hallowell, George Dunn, Bertha Wright, Millet Howard, Gertrude Howard, and Rev. Joseph E. LeMaster. (Courtesy of the late Alberta Keene.)

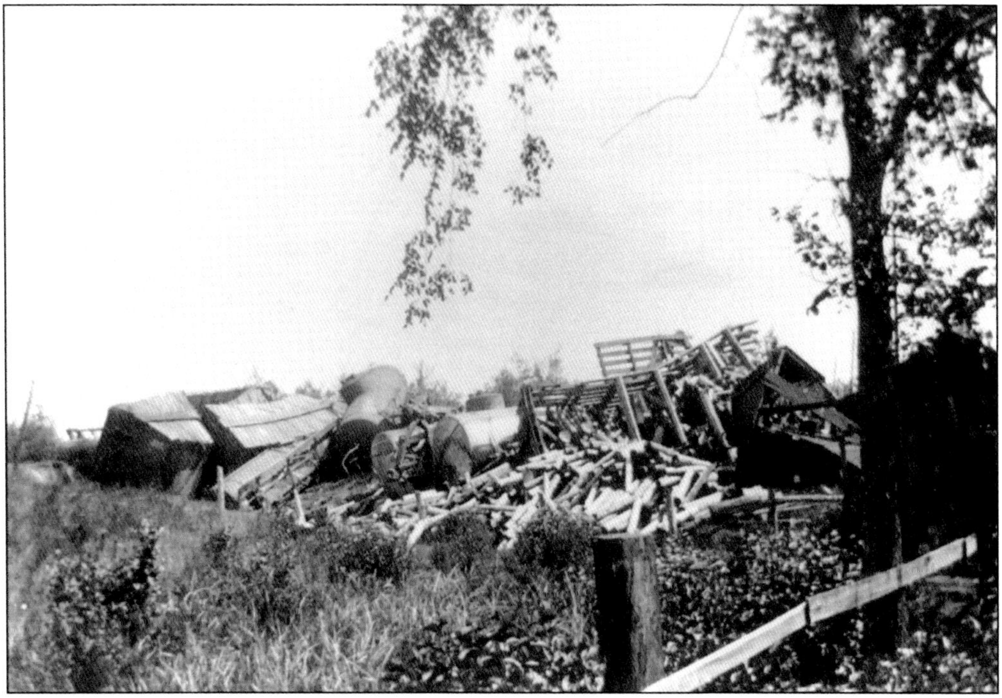
Pictured is a train derailed at the Annabessacook crossing in North Monmouth in 1930. (Courtesy of the late Forrest Ridlon.)

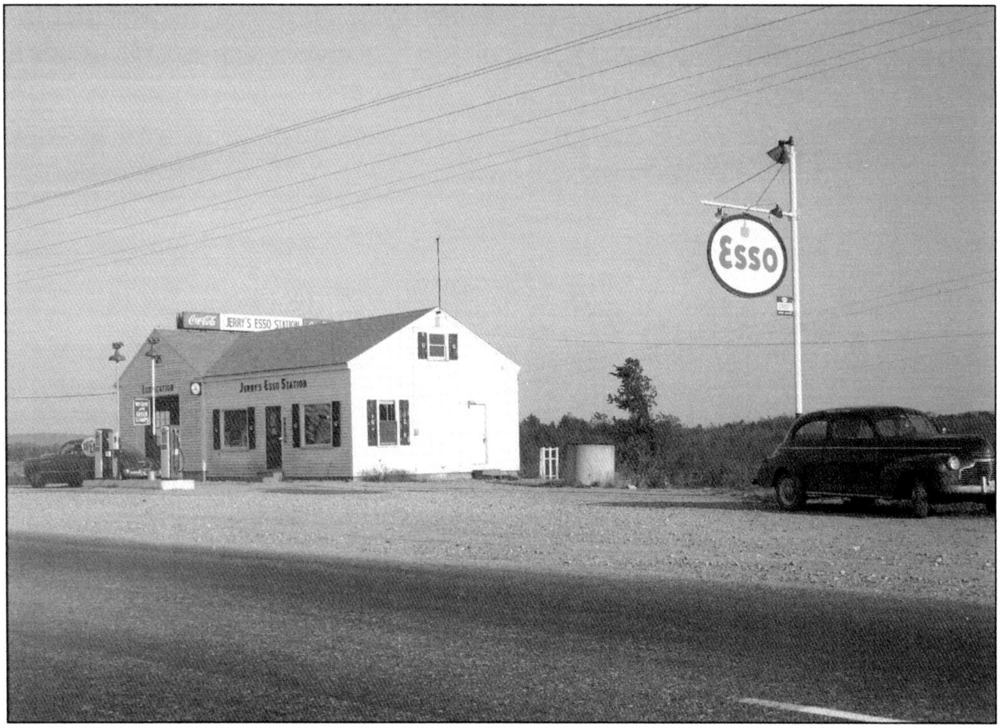

Jerry's Esso station on the new Route 202 in North Monmouth is pictured here. (Photograph by Roland LaVallee, courtesy of the Monmouth Museum.)

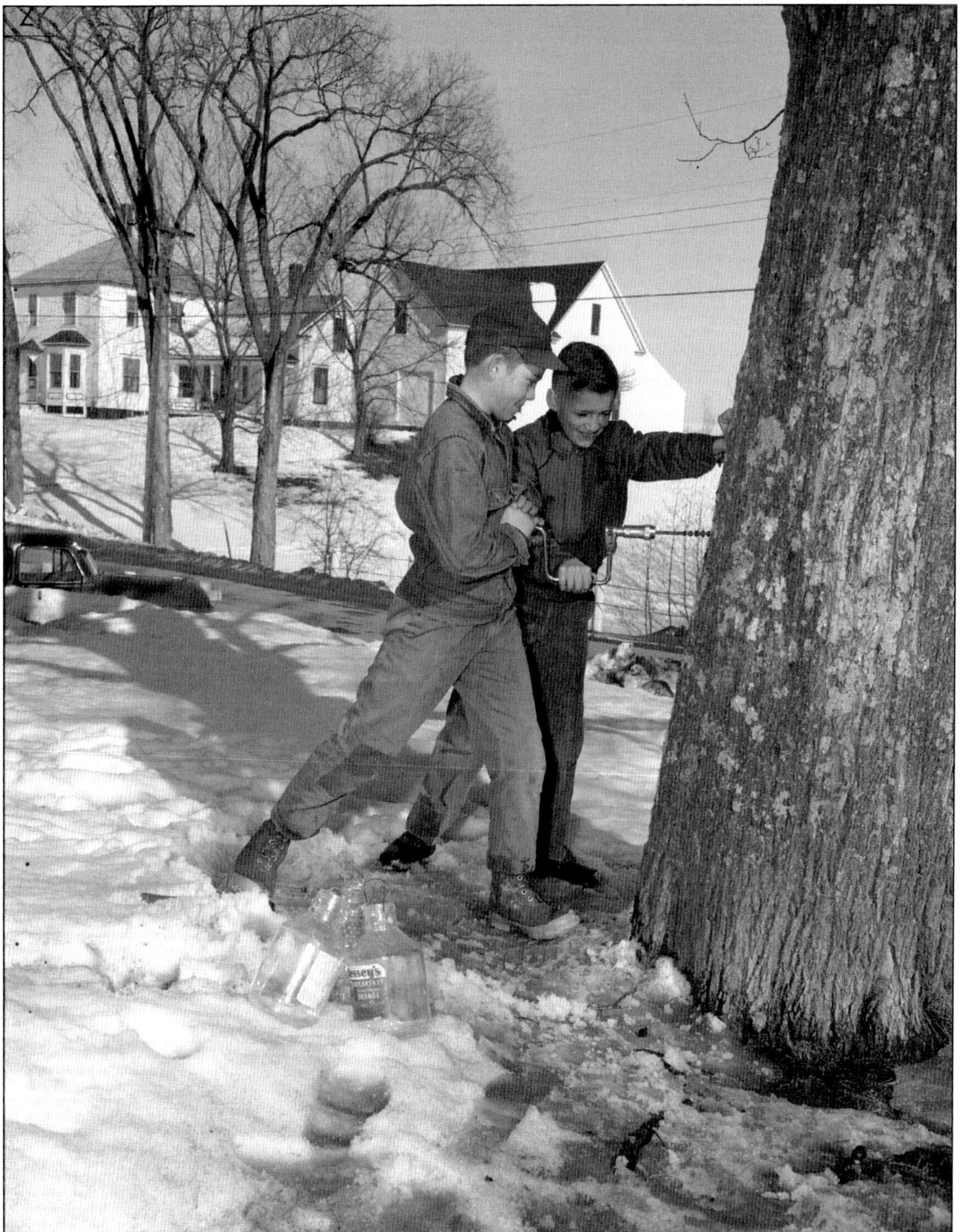

Dan Niles (right) and a friend try tapping a tree in the spring of 1960. (Photograph by Roland LaVallee, courtesy of the Monmouth Museum.)

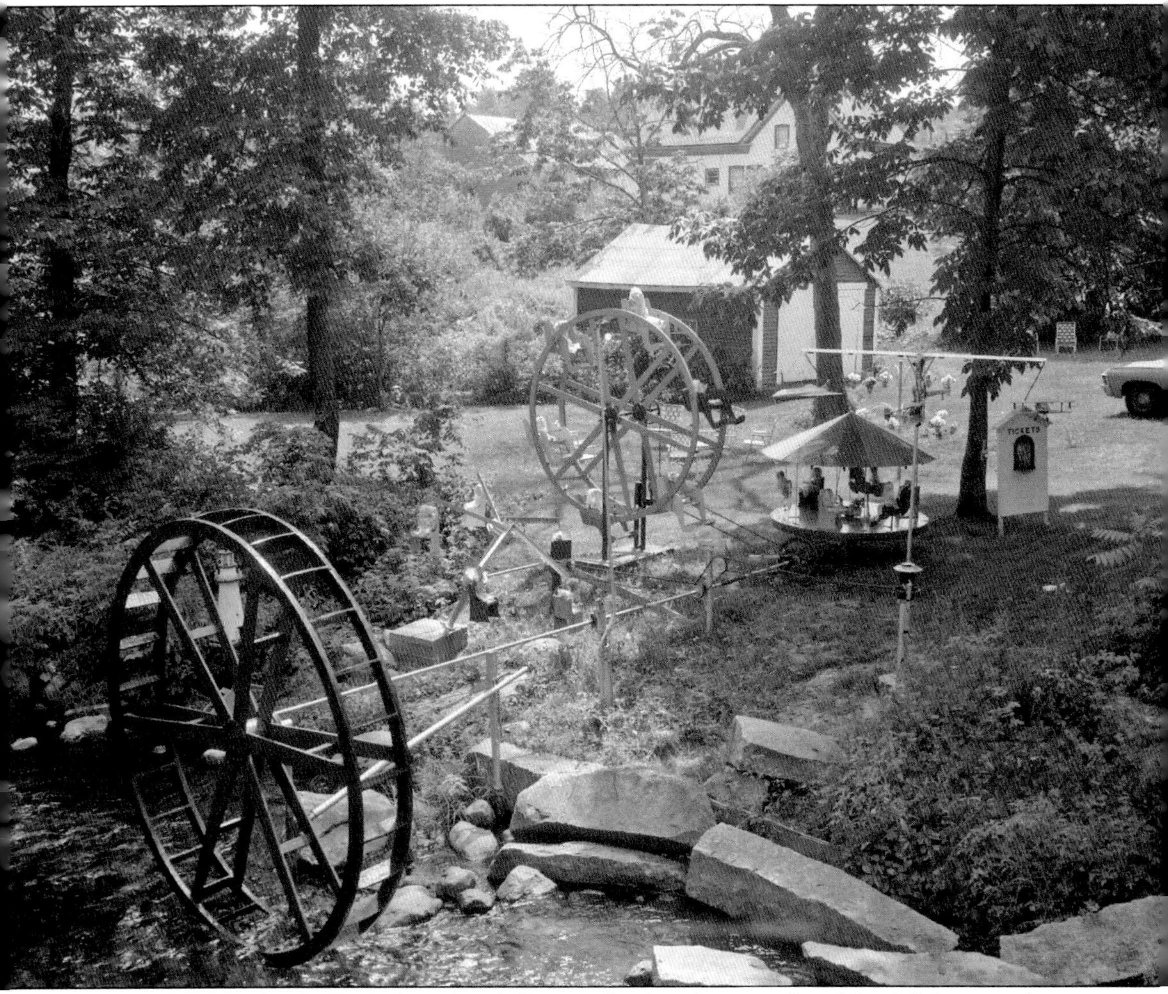

This photograph of Myrtle Burnham's Ferris wheel and carousel in North Monmouth was taken in August 1970. Herbie Frost of Winthrop did the construction of Myrtle's little fun town. (Photograph by Roland LaVallee, courtesy of the Monmouth Museum.)

Three

East and South Monmouth

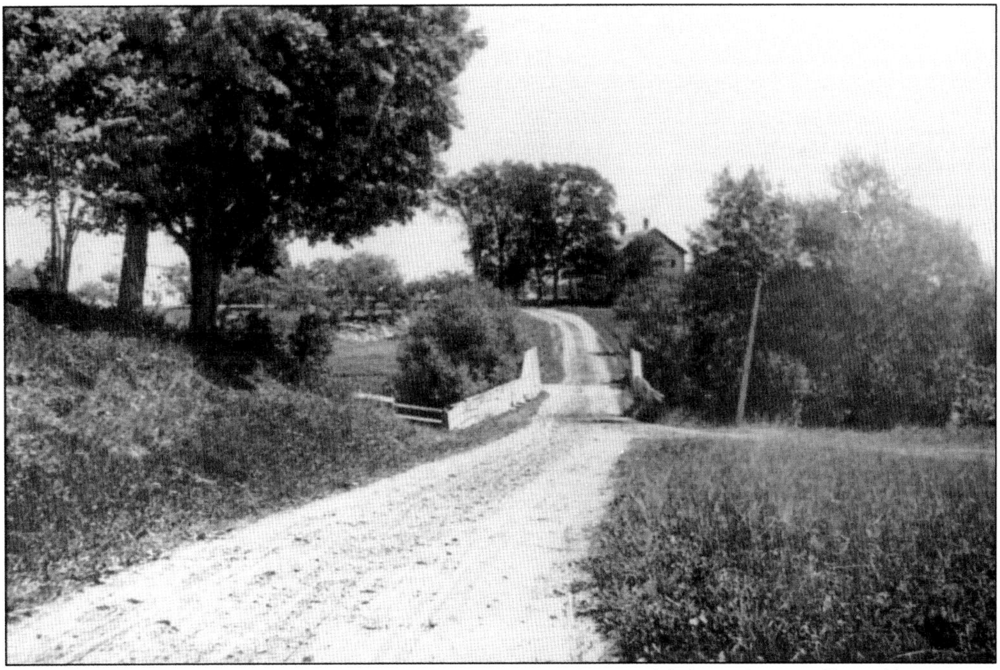

In East Monmouth, like the Center and North villages, the availability of water allowed businesses to develop and flourish. Taken in the early 1900s, this view of the bridge over Jocmunyaw Stream shows the Norris family homestead in the background. (Courtesy of Natalie Hall Jones.)

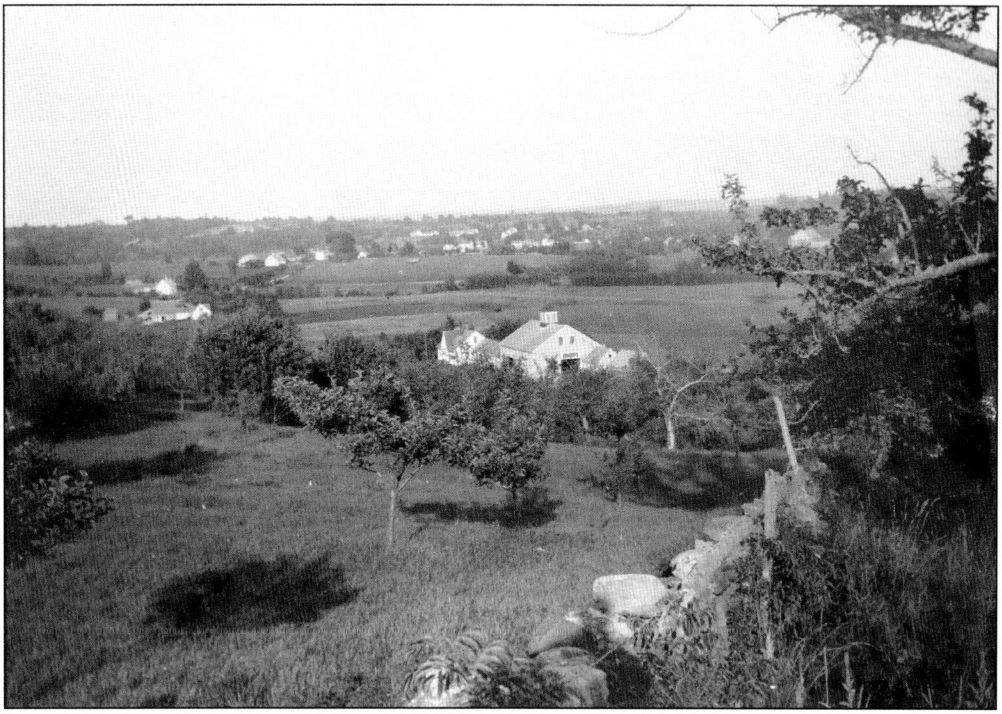

Gerald Hall took the view from Prescott Hill Road in Monmouth looking northeast in the early 1900s. (Courtesy of Natalie Hall Jones.)

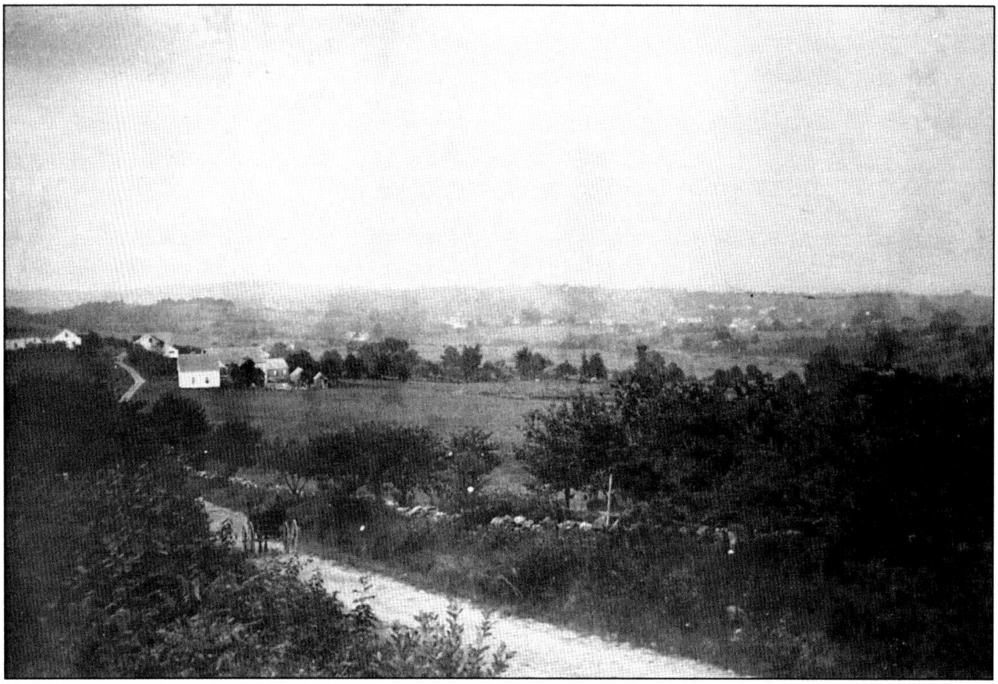

Taken by Gerald Hall, this photograph shows a horse and carriage heading down Prescott Hill towards East View Farm, which is where he lived with his parents. (Courtesy of Natalie Hall Jones.)

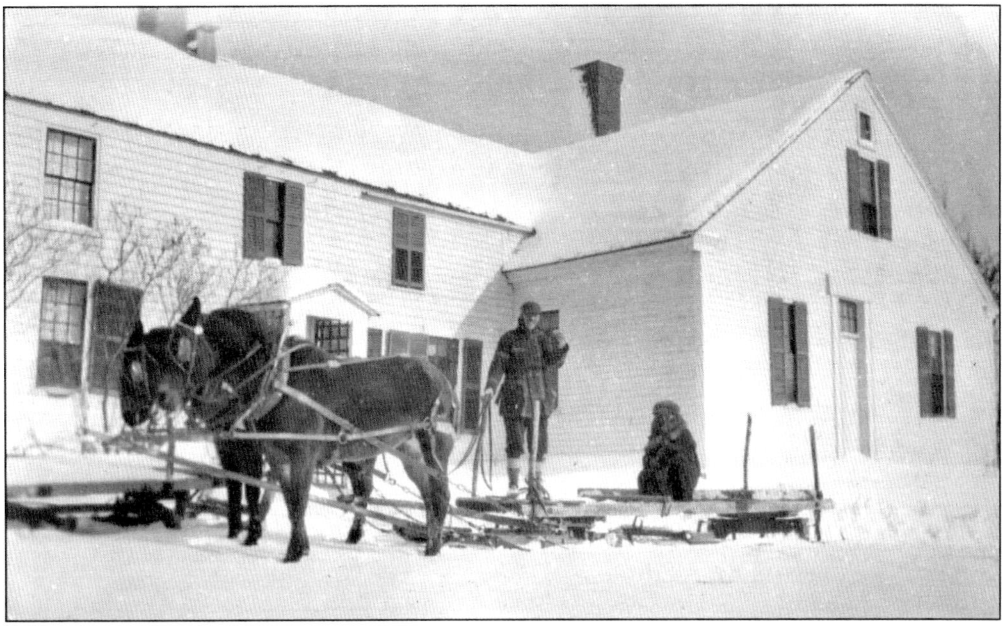

Gerald Hall is with his team of horses at East View Farm. His mother is sitting on the logging sled. (Courtesy of Natalie Hall Jones.)

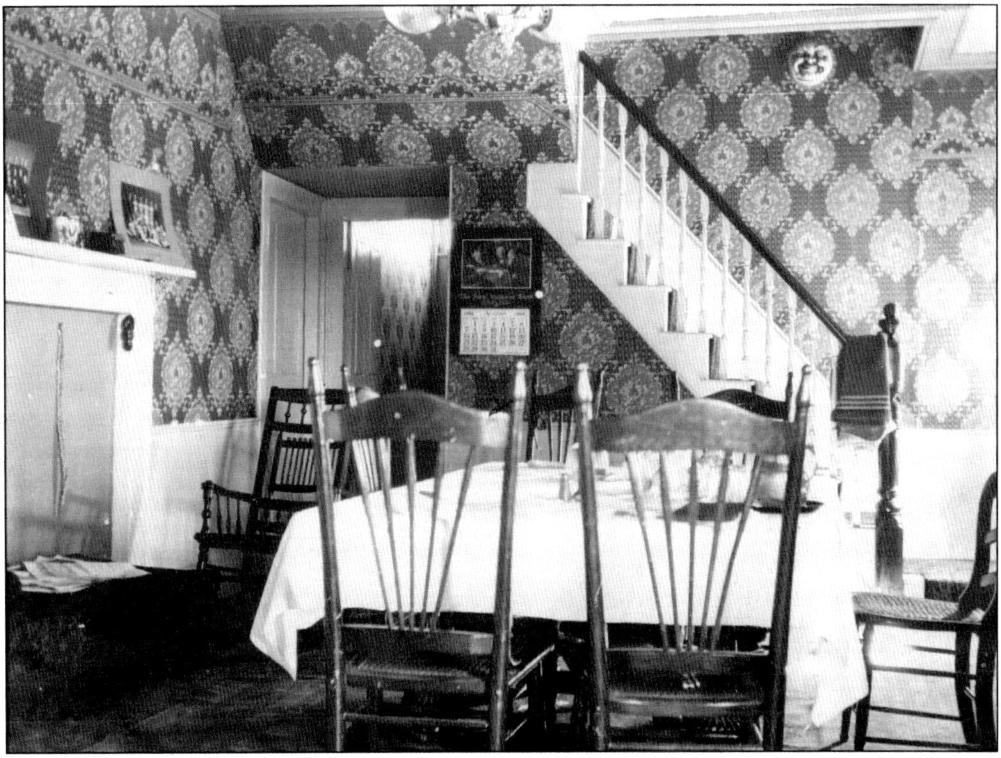

This is an interior view of East View Farm. The calendar on the back wall is dated August 1904. (Courtesy of Natalie Hall Jones.)

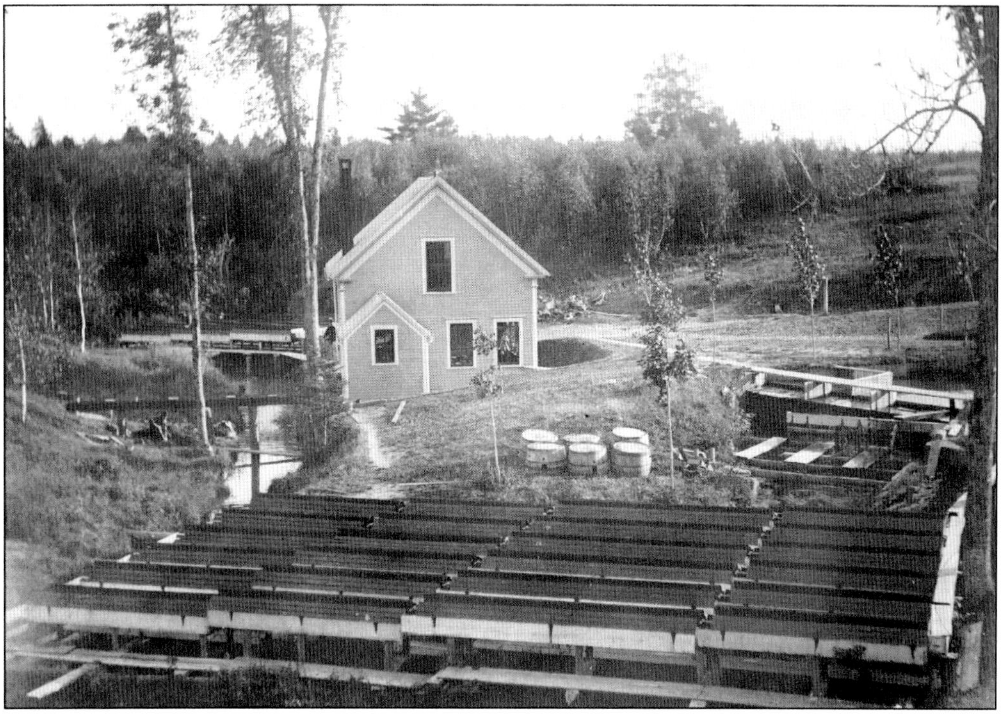

The Monmouth Fish Hatchery was located on what is now called Fish Hatchery Road, which is on the way to South Monmouth. The hatchery was one of eight such facilities in the early 1900s. Built around 1900, the capacity of the plant was about 500,000 young fish per season in 1907. The superintendent at that time was W. A. Whiting of Winthrop. (Photograph by H. A. Morton Portland, courtesy of Marge Maxim.)

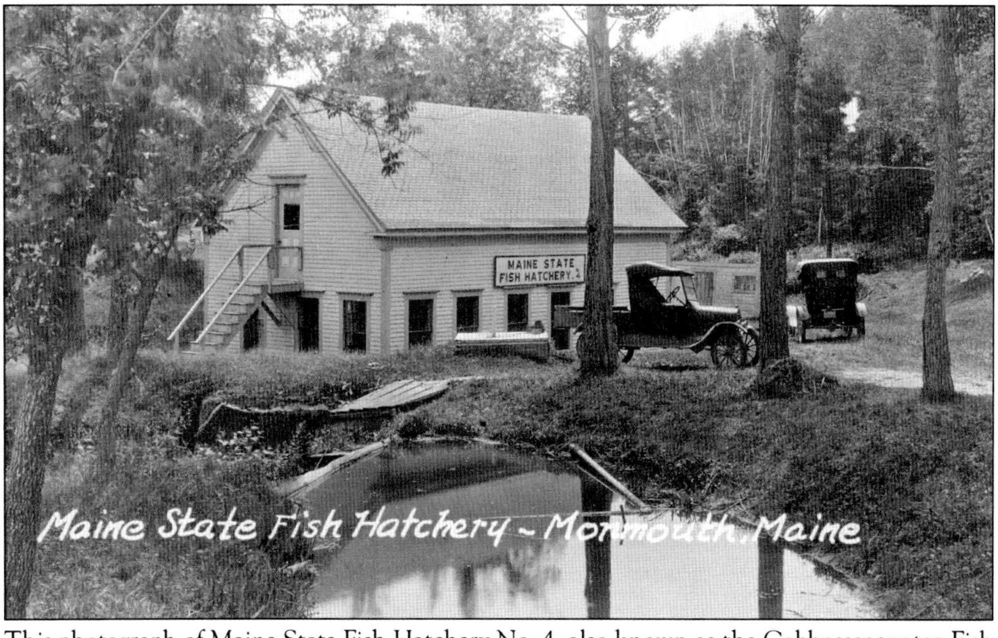

This photograph of Maine State Fish Hatchery No. 4, also known as the Cobbosseecontee Fish Hatchery, was taken in the 1920s. (Courtesy of the author.)

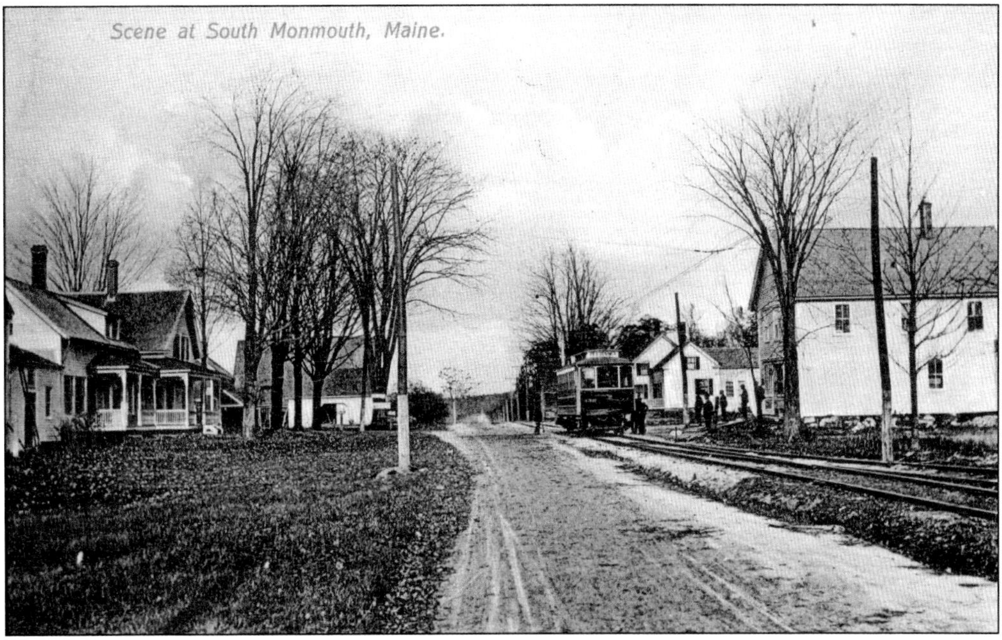

The construction of the Sabattus-Gardiner line, which ran through Days Corner in South Monmouth, began in 1907. The car in this photograph, No. 332, was 28 feet, 10 inches long. This Brill Semi-Convertible was manufactured in 1908 with a seating capacity of 42 passengers. According to O. R. Cummings's 1963 book, *Lewiston, Augusta, and Waterville Street Railway*, car No. 332 was scrapped between 1920 and 1932. (Courtesy of the author.)

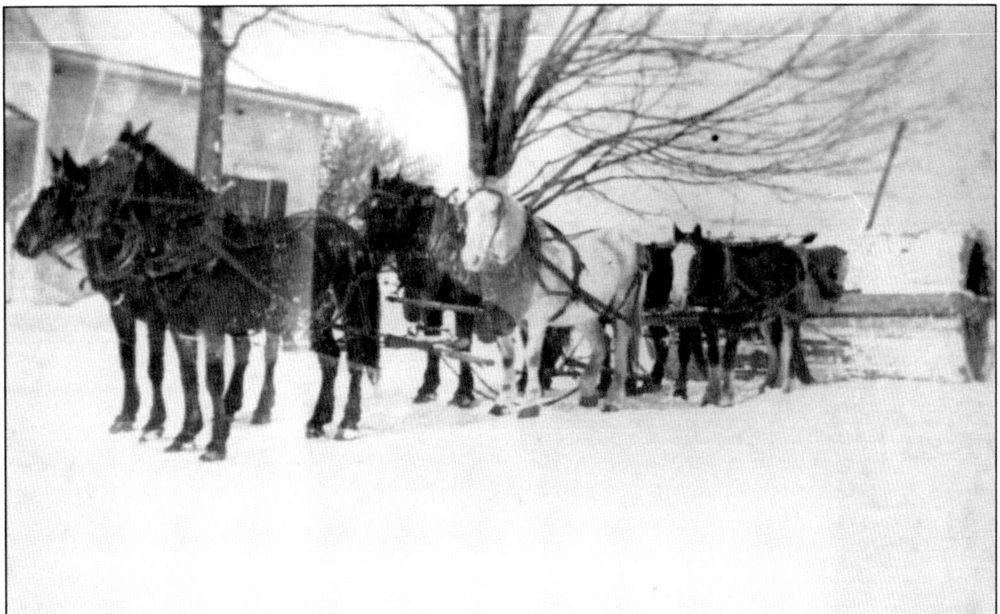

At the turn of the century, it was a common sight to see a snow roller packing down the snow on local roads. This picture was taken at Days Corner in South Monmouth at the beginning of the 1900s. Lester Young owned the first team of horses, Emil Peterson owned the second team, and Clifton Newcity owned the third team. (Courtesy of the late Clason Dixon.)

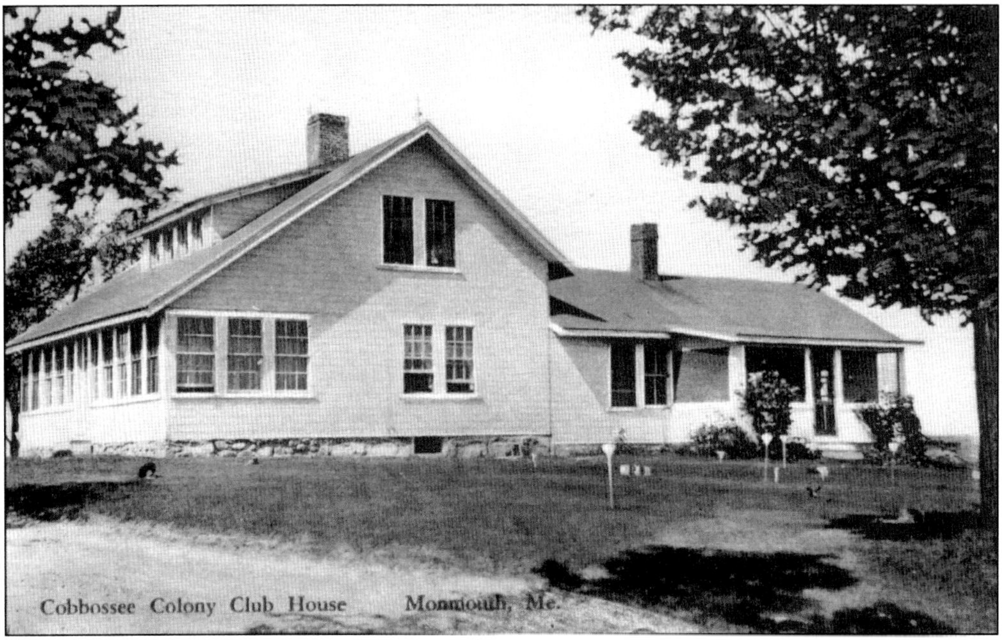

Cobbossee Colony opened in 1913 under the direction of Harry Rich Mooney. It boasted many wonderful features, including its own Cobbossee spring water. The clubhouse pictured here is for the golf course. The colony was also later owned and operated by the Cottrell brothers. (Courtesy of the author.)

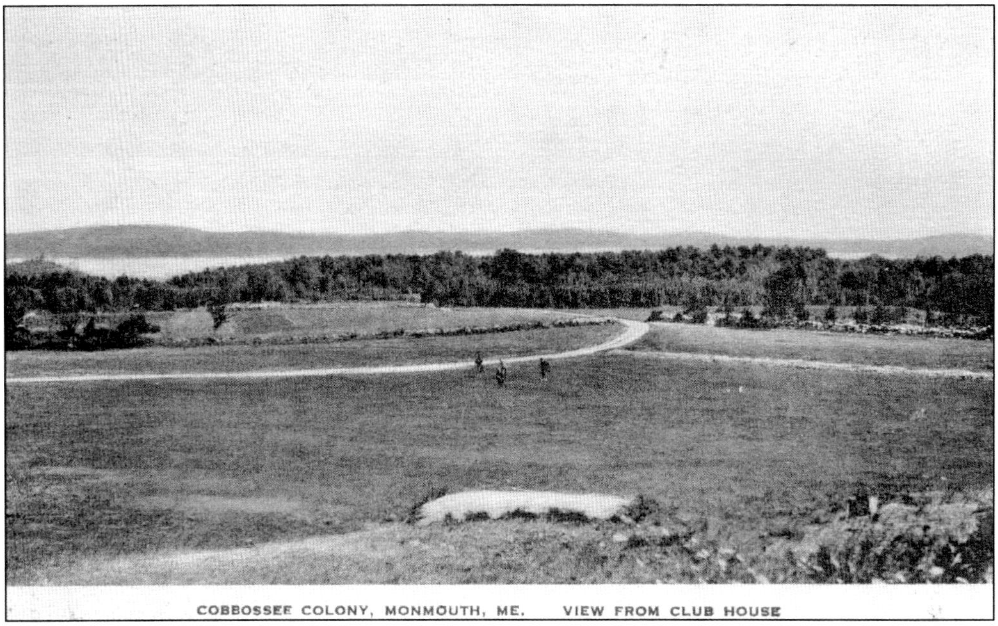

This is the view from the clubhouse looking toward Lake Cobbosseecontee. (Courtesy of the author.)

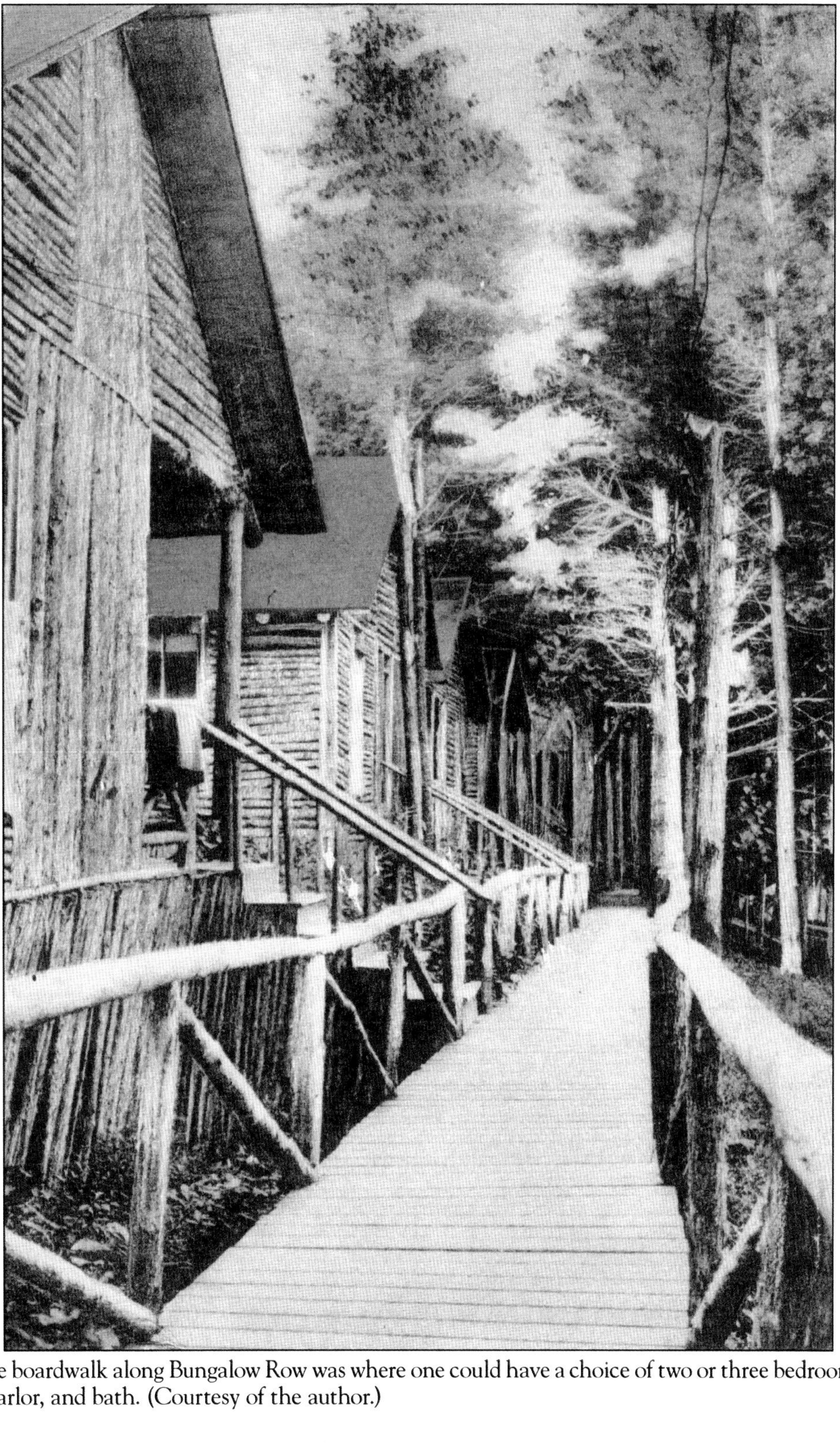

The boardwalk along Bungalow Row was where one could have a choice of two or three bedrooms, a parlor, and bath. (Courtesy of the author.)

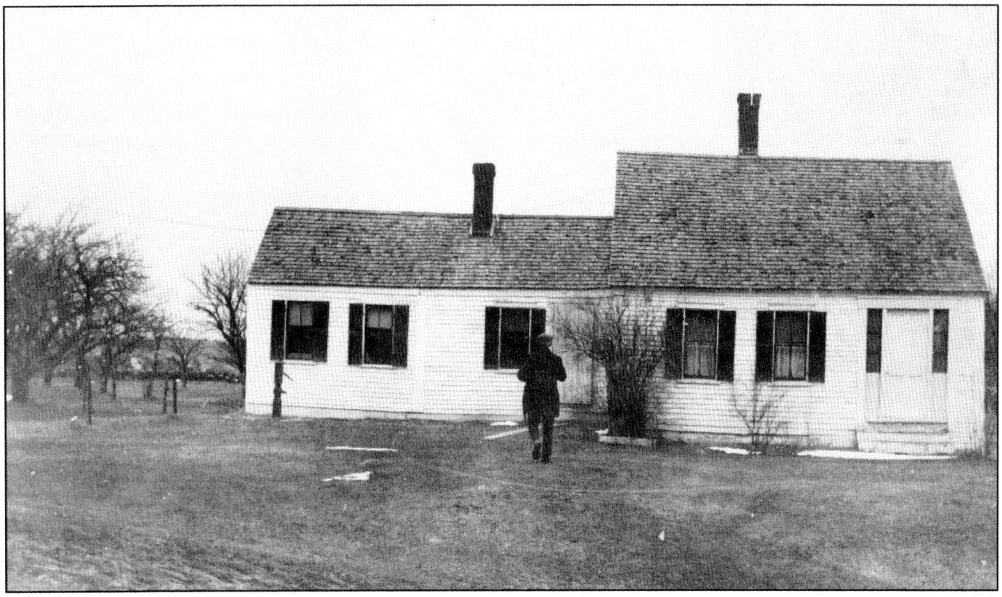

Located on Ridge Road, this house is the birthplace of Lulu Safford. Her father was the third in a line of noted redware potters. Their pottery shop was across the road from Lulu's homestead. (Courtesy of the Monmouth Museum.)

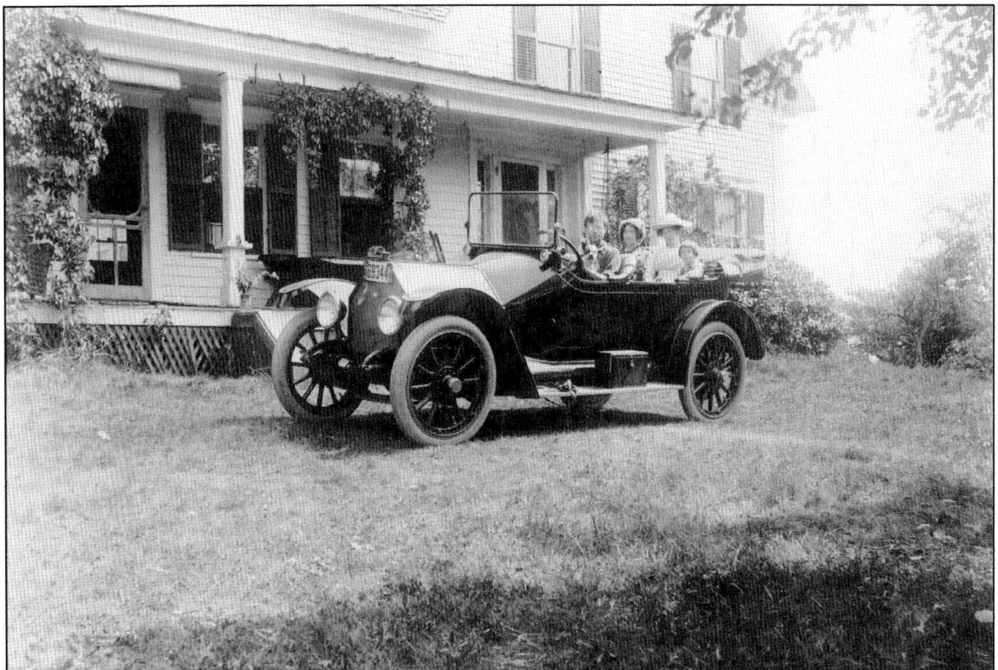

This photograph was taken of H. O. Pierce's homestead on Ridge Road. Pierce's daughter Carrie was a longtime librarian for the Cumston Public Library, located in Cumston Hall. (Courtesy of the author.)

Four

Summers in Monmouth

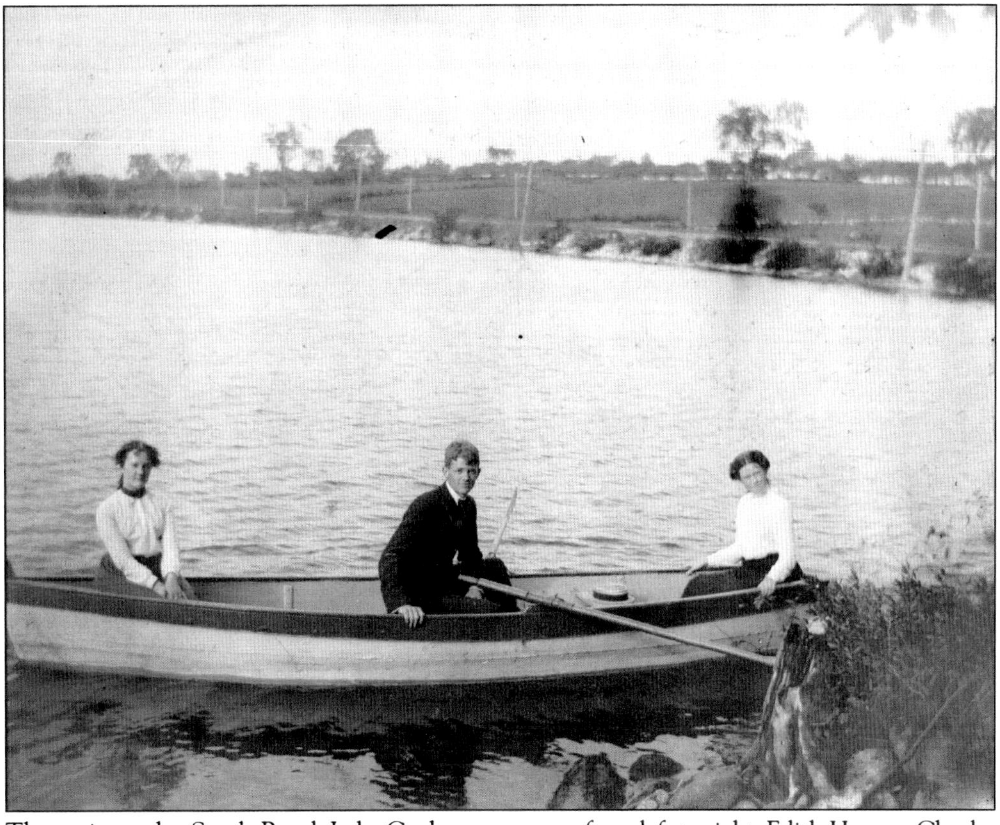

Those pictured at Sandy Beach Lake Cochnewagan are, from left to right, Edith Haynes, Charles Dinsmore, and Anna Blake. (Courtesy of Audrey and David Walker.)

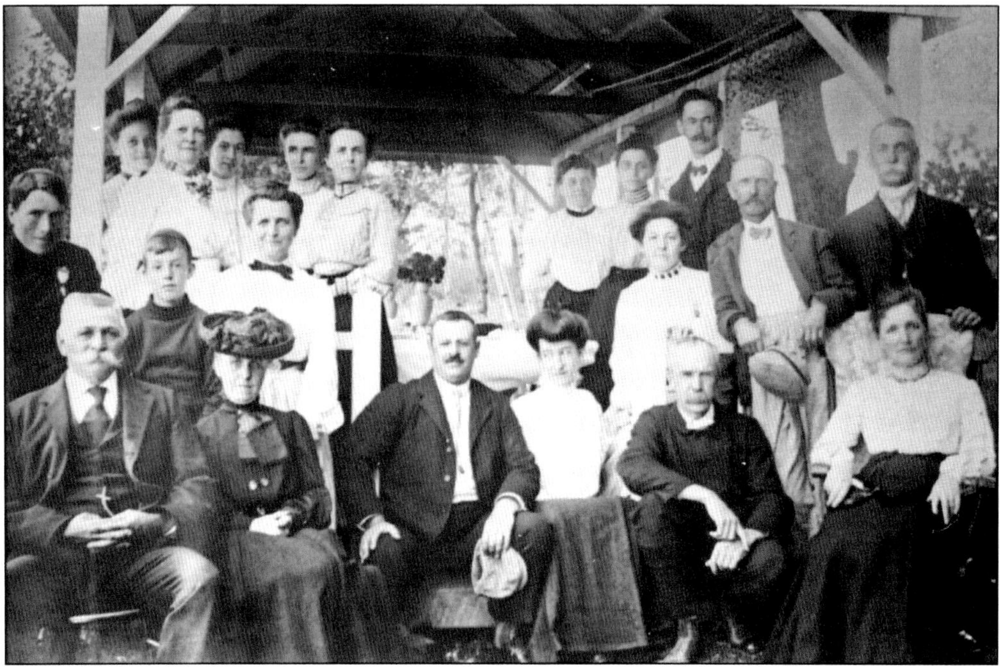

In this group photograph of vacationers at Lake Cochnewagan are Harry and Ida Cochrane. They are the first two on the right in the back row of the photograph. (Courtesy of Natalie Hall Jones.)

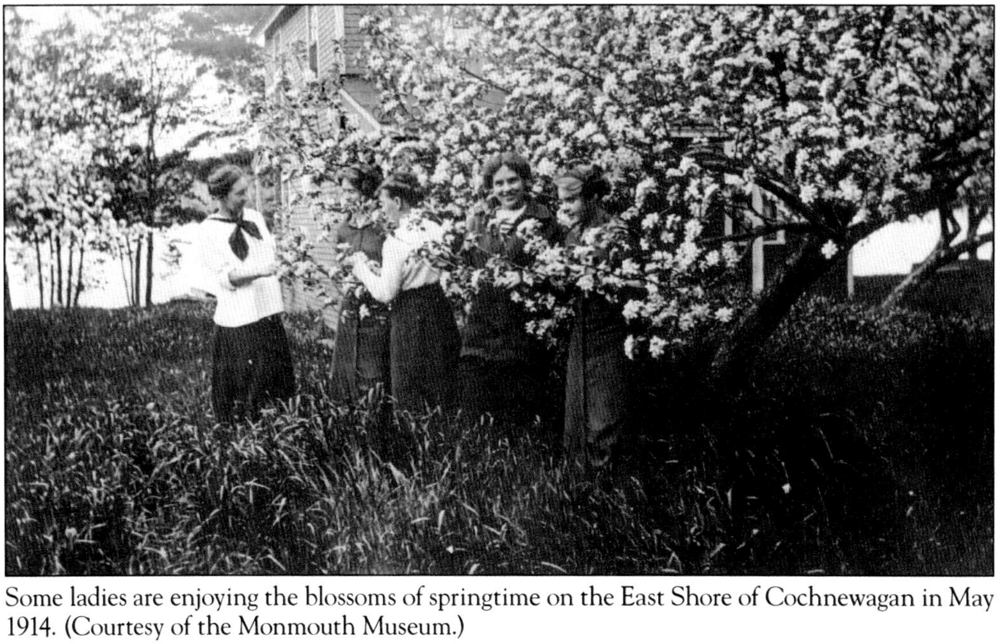

Some ladies are enjoying the blossoms of springtime on the East Shore of Cochnewagan in May 1914. (Courtesy of the Monmouth Museum.)

Pictured are vacationers enjoying the springtime on the East Shore of Cochnewagan Lake, known today as Beach Road, in May 1914. (Courtesy of the Monmouth Museum.)

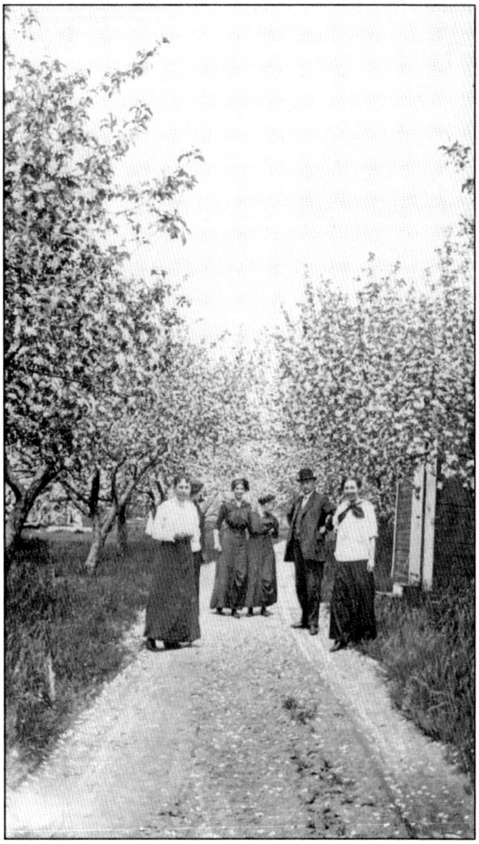

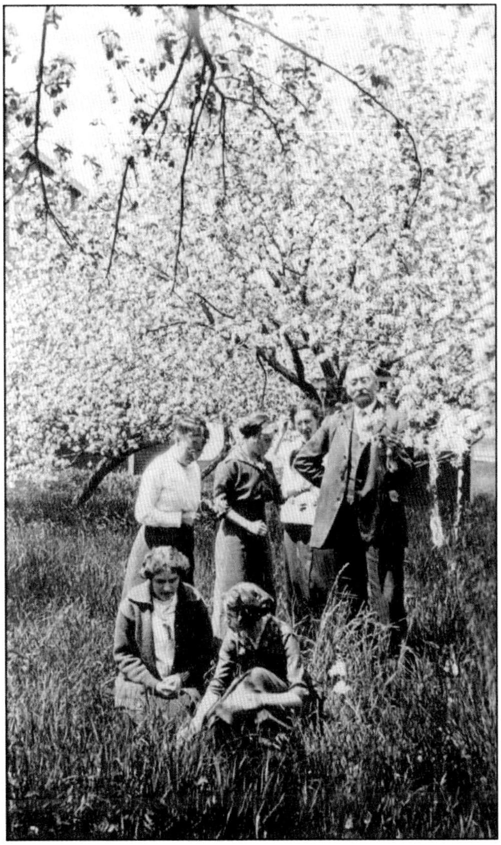

A gentleman is enjoying some fun among the blossoms in May 1914 on the East Shore of Cochnewagan. (Courtesy of the Monmouth Museum.)

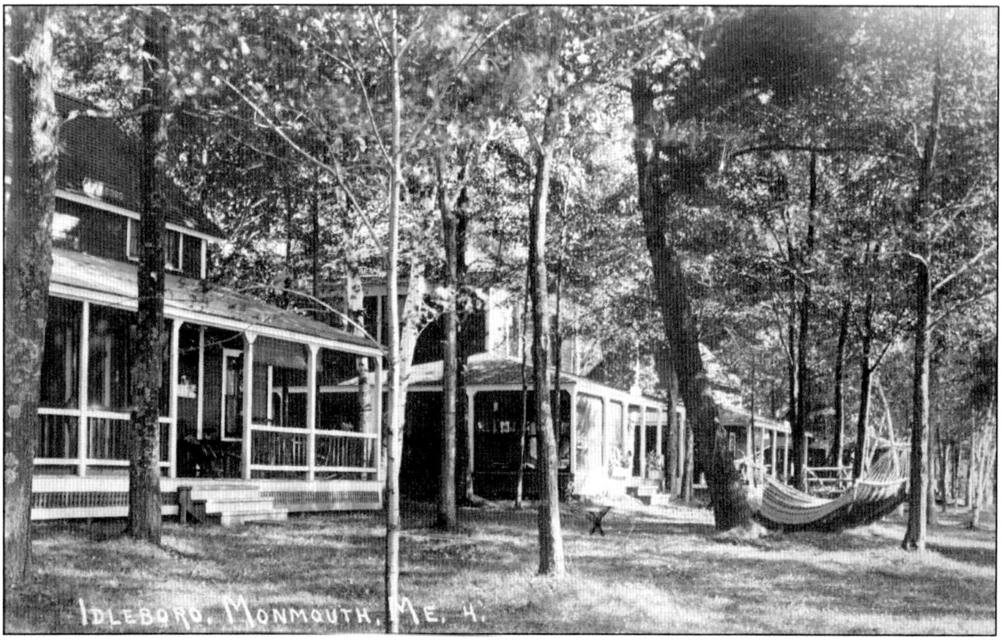

The first two cottages in this photograph of the East Shore of Cochnewagan are Idleboro and Rest-a-while. (Courtesy of the author.)

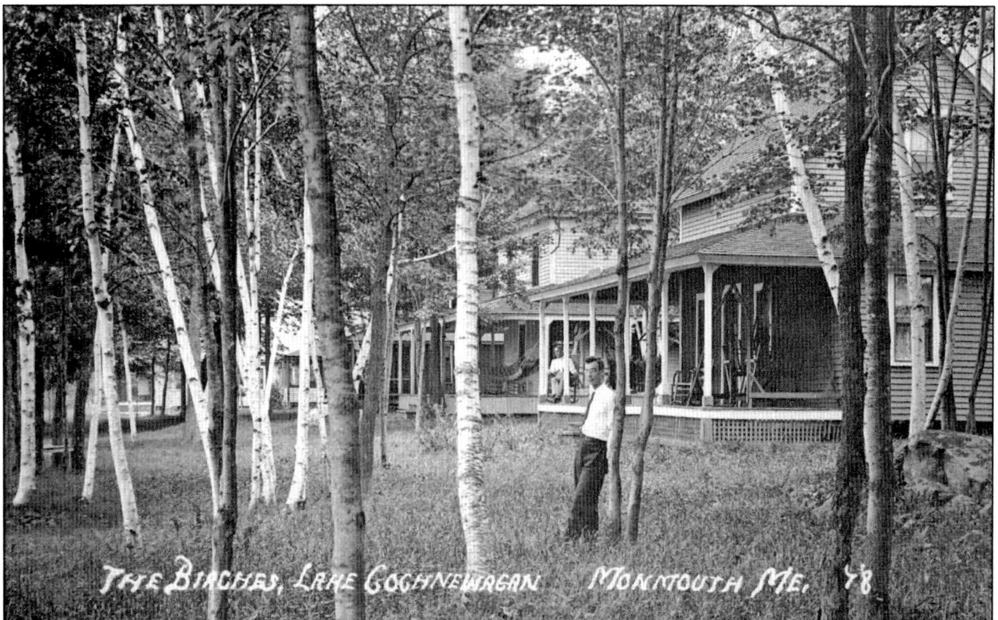

This image looking north on the East Shore of Cochnewagan shows the birches. (Courtesy of the author.)

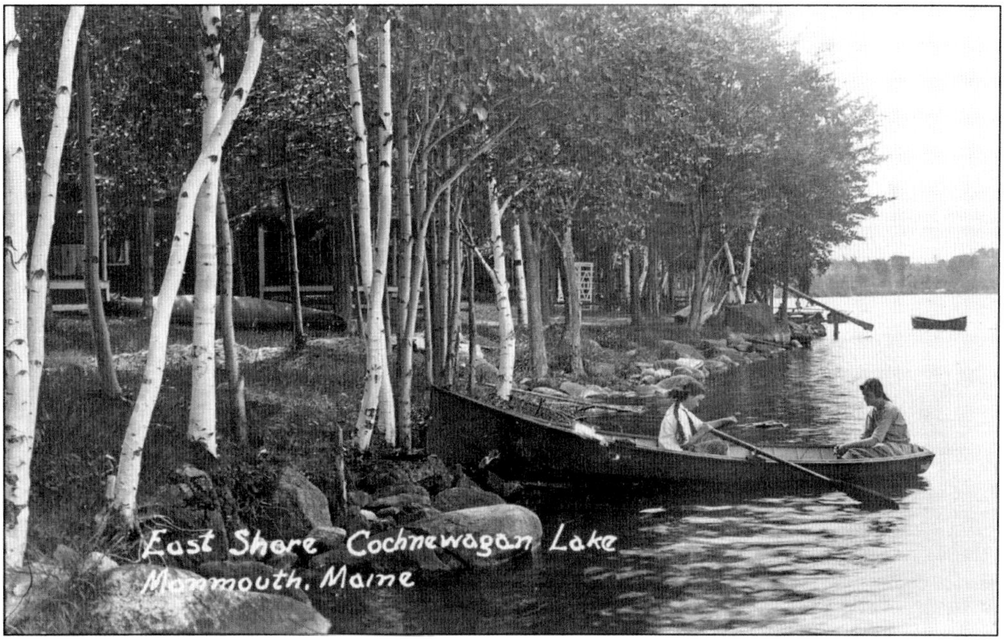

Two young ladies are enjoying some boating on Lake Cochnewagan. (Courtesy of the author.)

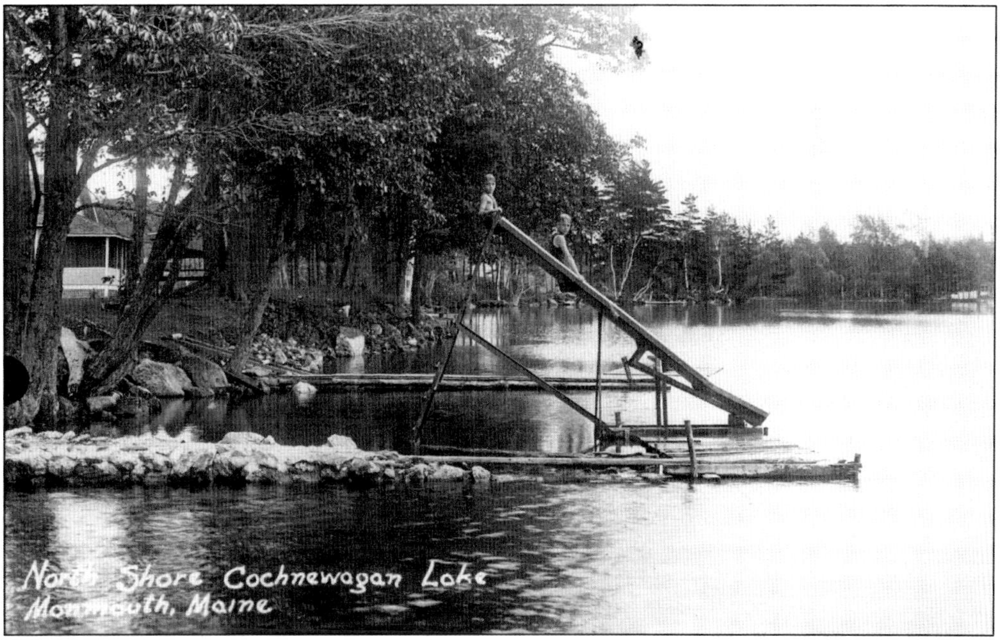

The people in this photograph are enjoying the Fourth of July in the 1920s on the North Shore of Cochnewagan. (Courtesy of the author.)

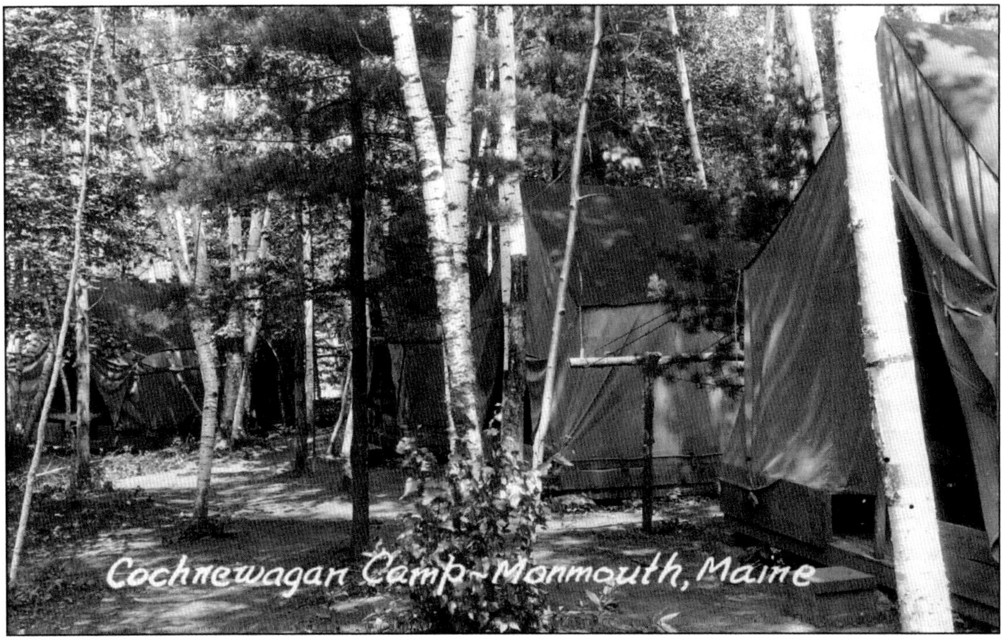

Edith Haynes ran the Cochnewagan Camp for Girls in the 1920s and 1930s. (Courtesy of the author.)

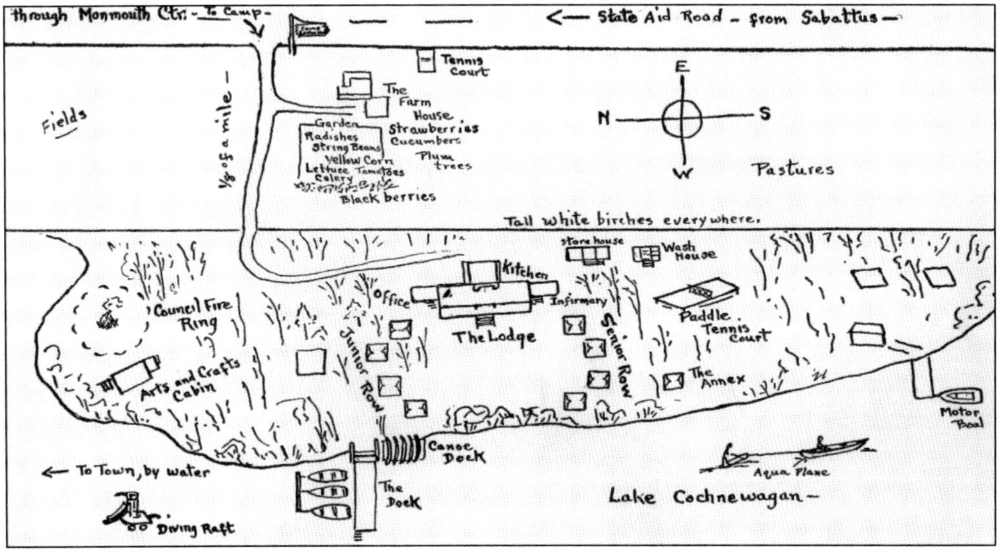

This is a map of the Cochnewagan Camp for Girls, which was on the east shore of the lake. (Courtesy of the Monmouth Museum.)

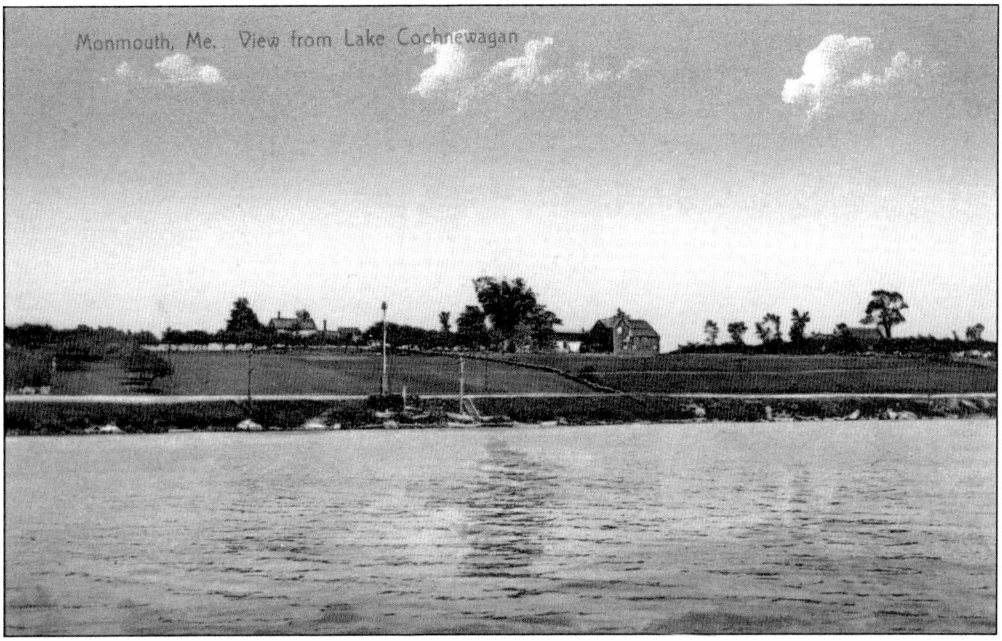

This is a view looking at the East Shore and the southern part of Main Street. (Courtesy of the author.)

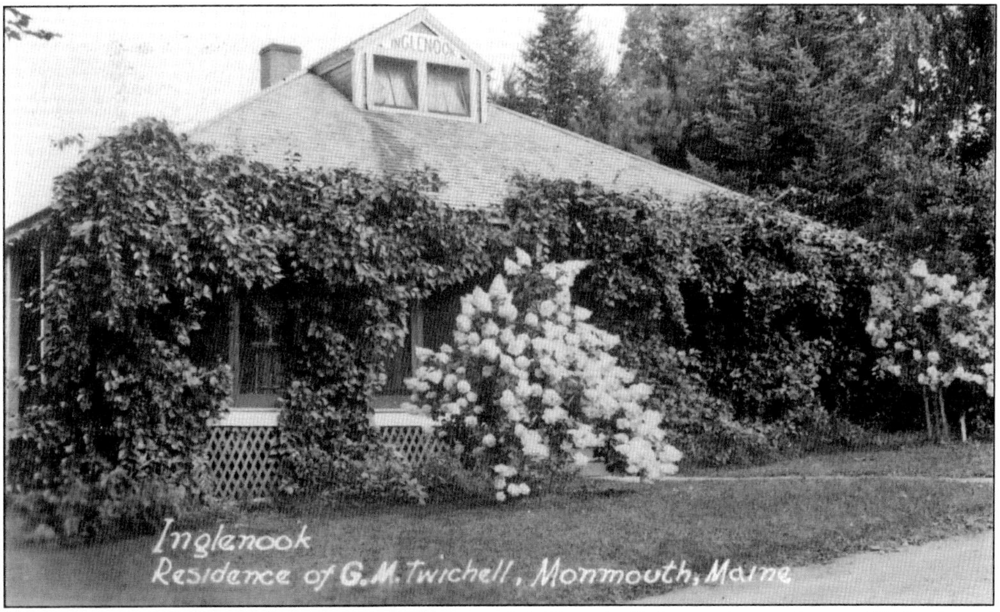

Inglenook was the summer residence of George M. Twitchell. It was located just off Blue Road on what is currently called Robertson Drive. Twitchell had wonderful gardens along his side of Blue Road. (Courtesy of the author.)

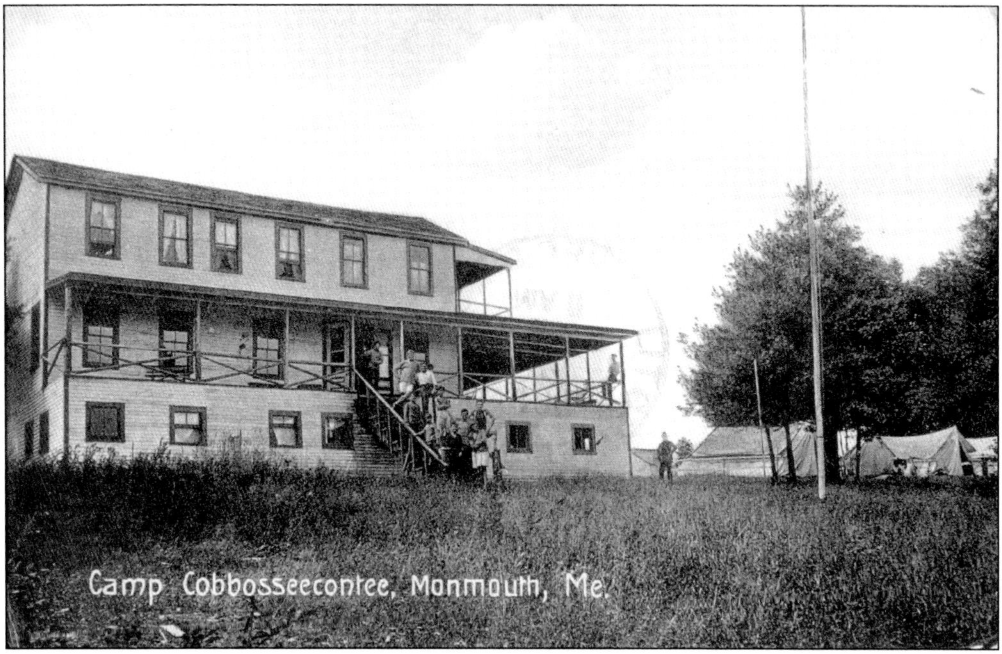

The main building at Camp Cobbossee for Boys in East Monmouth is pictured here. (Courtesy of the author.)

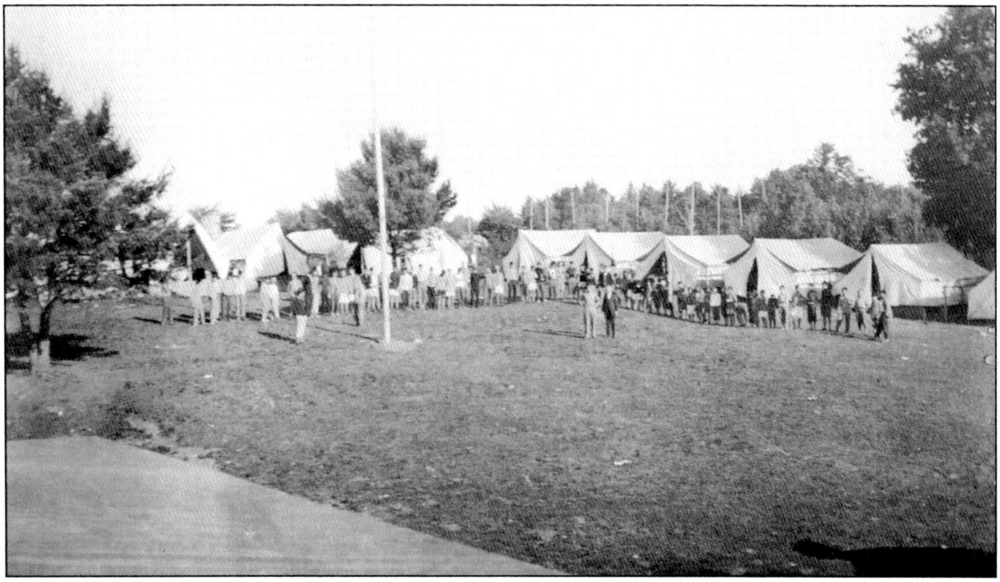

This is the tent grounds at the Camp Cobbossee for Boys. The camp was run by Harry Rich Mooney. (Courtesy of the author.)

Five

EDUCATION AND RELIGION

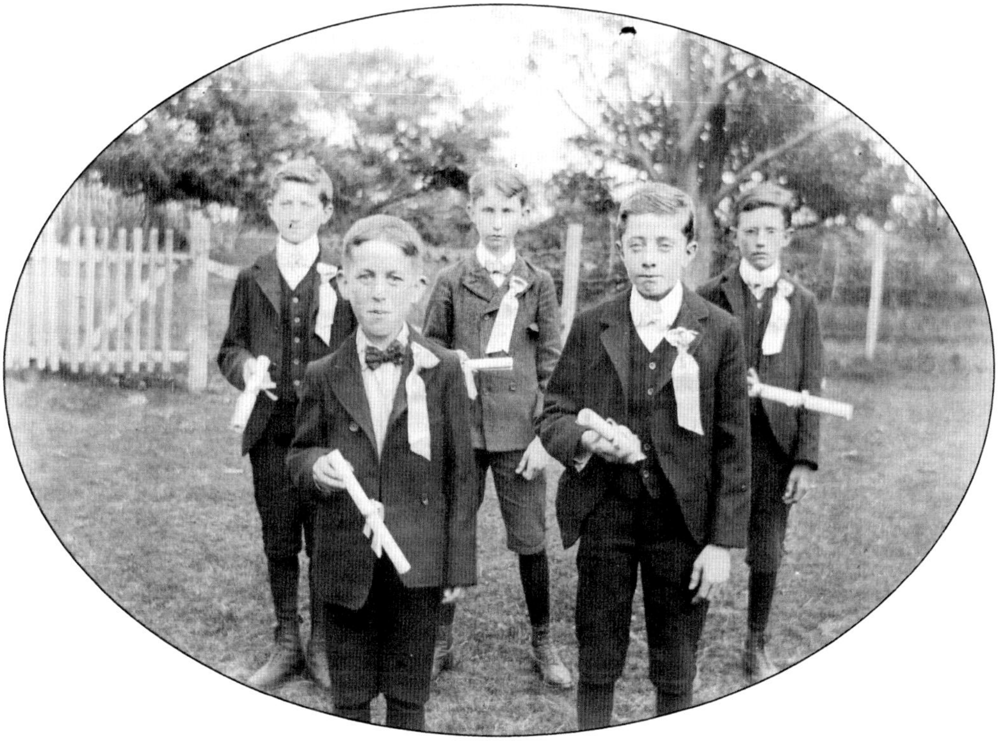

This Monmouth Center Grammar School graduation shows five boys with grade school diplomas. Those pictured are, from left to right, (first row) Walter Sanderson and Willard Day; (second row) Millard Day, Walter Drake, and Frank Richardson. (Courtesy of Audrey and David Walker.)

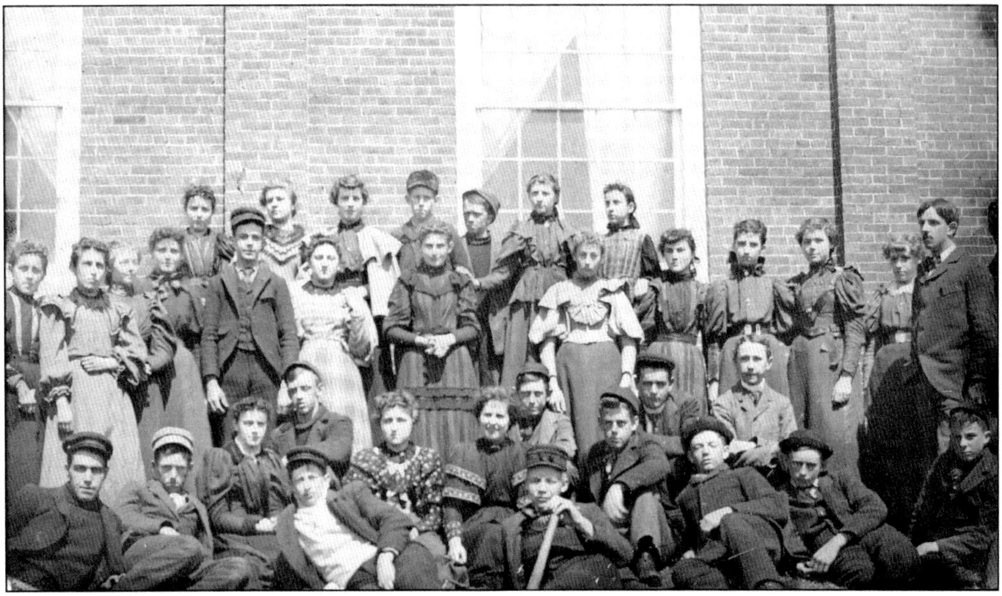

Monmouth Academy student Ralph E. Woodbury is located in the front row. He is wearing a cap with the letters "R. W." and holding baseball bat. This photograph was taken around 1895. (Courtesy of the Monmouth Museum.)

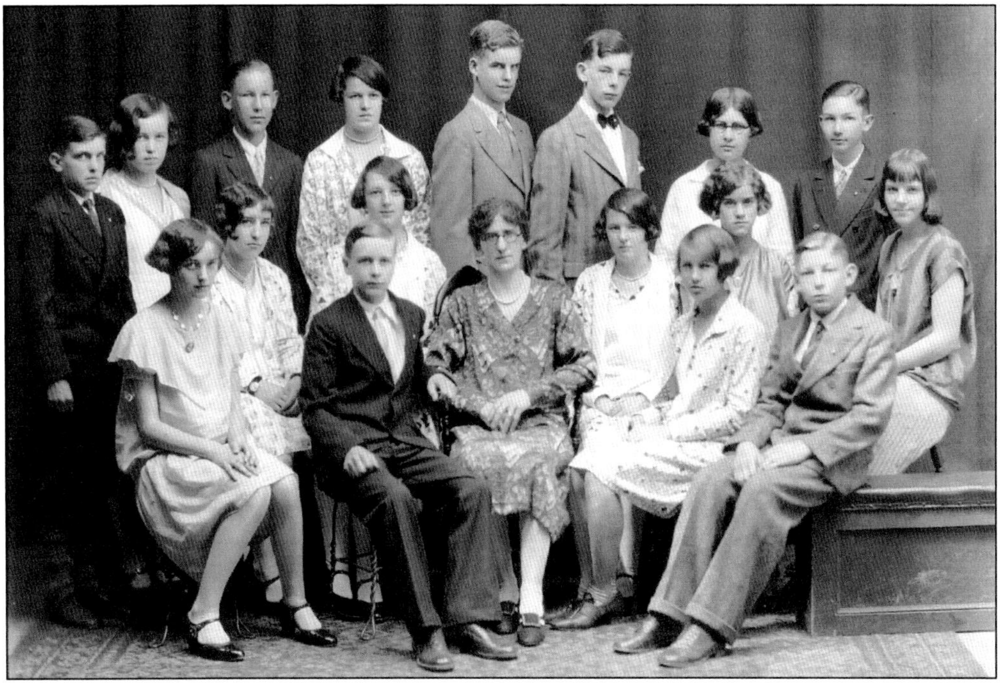

This eighth-grade graduation class photograph was taken in 1929. From left to right are (first row) Helen Donnell (Niles), Mildred Carr (Clark/Cooper), Malcom Day, Marjorie Parsons (Merrill), teacher Stella Peasley, Dorothy Parsons (Peasley), Isabelle Berry (Maguire), Marjorie Anderson (Ham), Arthur Chick Jr., and Beulah Slaunwhite (Prout); (second row) Carroll Hines, Eleanor Flanders, Carl Huntington, Amy Pettingill (Cooper), Walter Bragdon, Richard Kennedy, Jennie (Jewell), and Chester Rolfe. (Hammond Brothers photography, courtesy of Stan DeOrsey.)

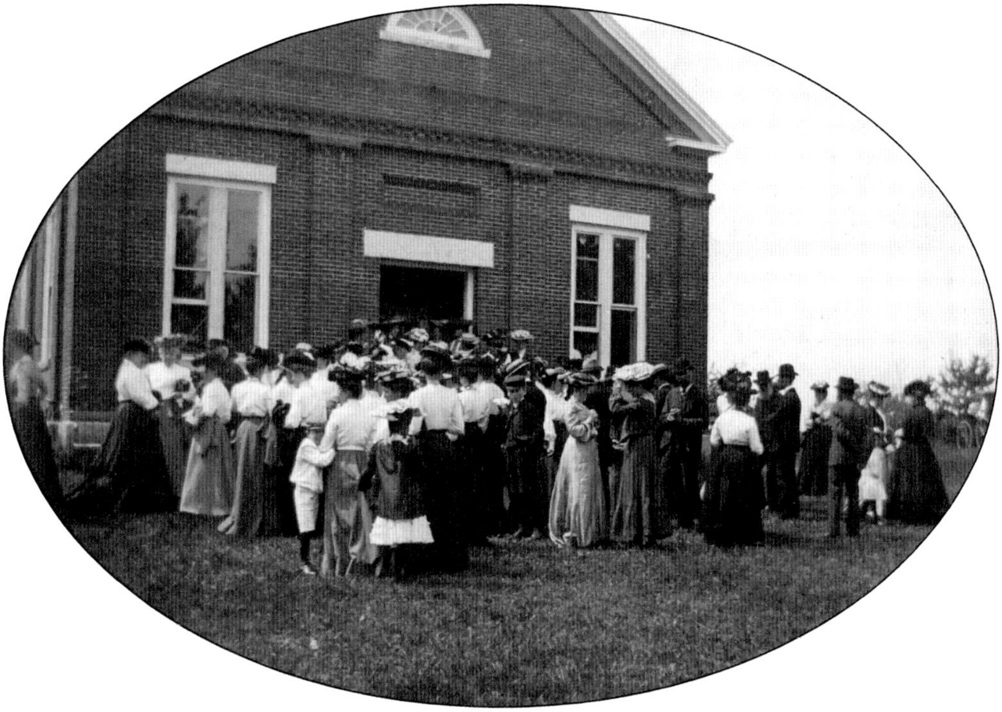

A Monmouth Academy reunion during early 1900s is pictured here. (Courtesy of Audrey and David Walker.)

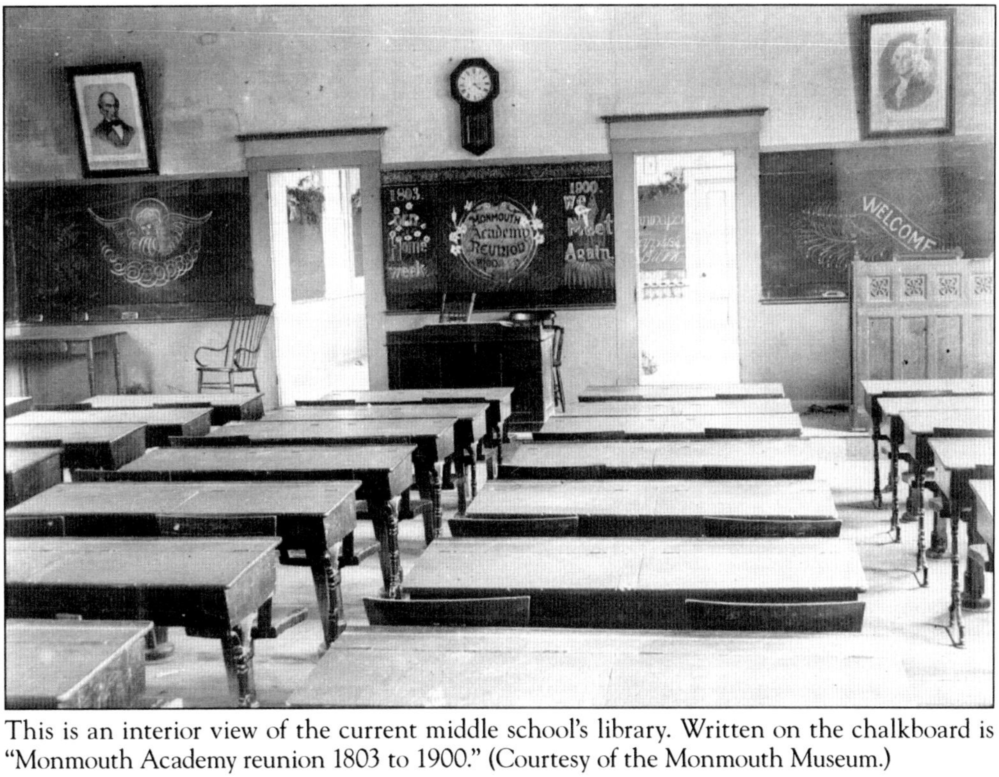

This is an interior view of the current middle school's library. Written on the chalkboard is "Monmouth Academy reunion 1803 to 1900." (Courtesy of the Monmouth Museum.)

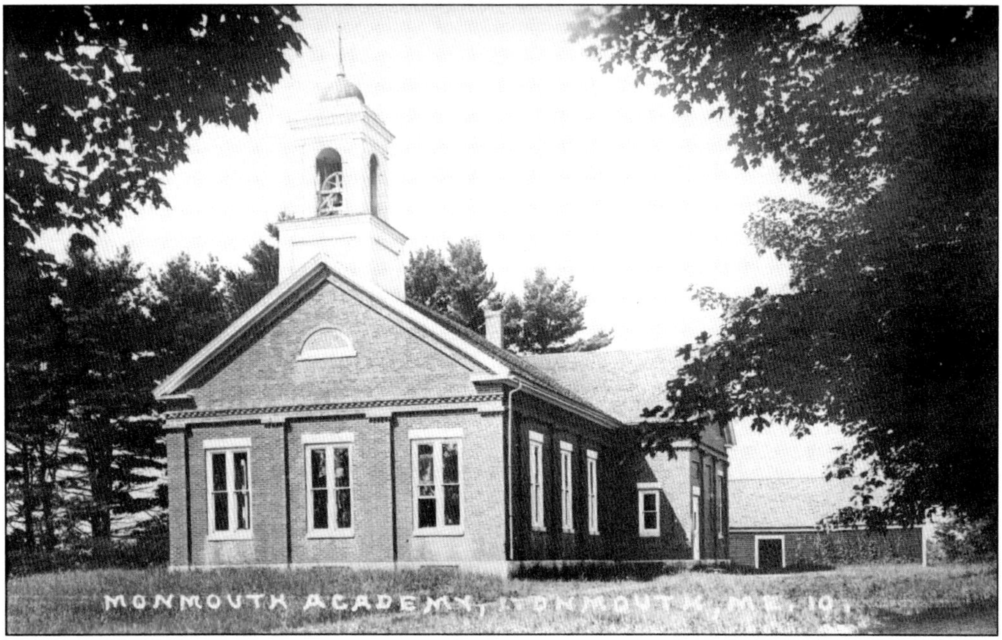

Monmouth Academy is shown here as it appeared in the early 1900s. (Courtesy of the author.)

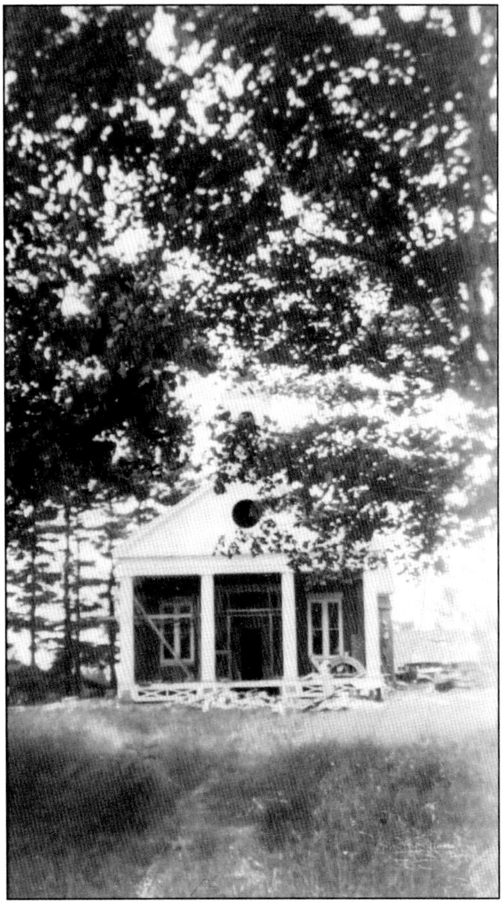

One of the last projects that Harry Cochrane worked on before he died in 1946 was the design of the porch and column area of the front of the old Monmouth Academy. (Courtesy of Natalie Hall Jones).

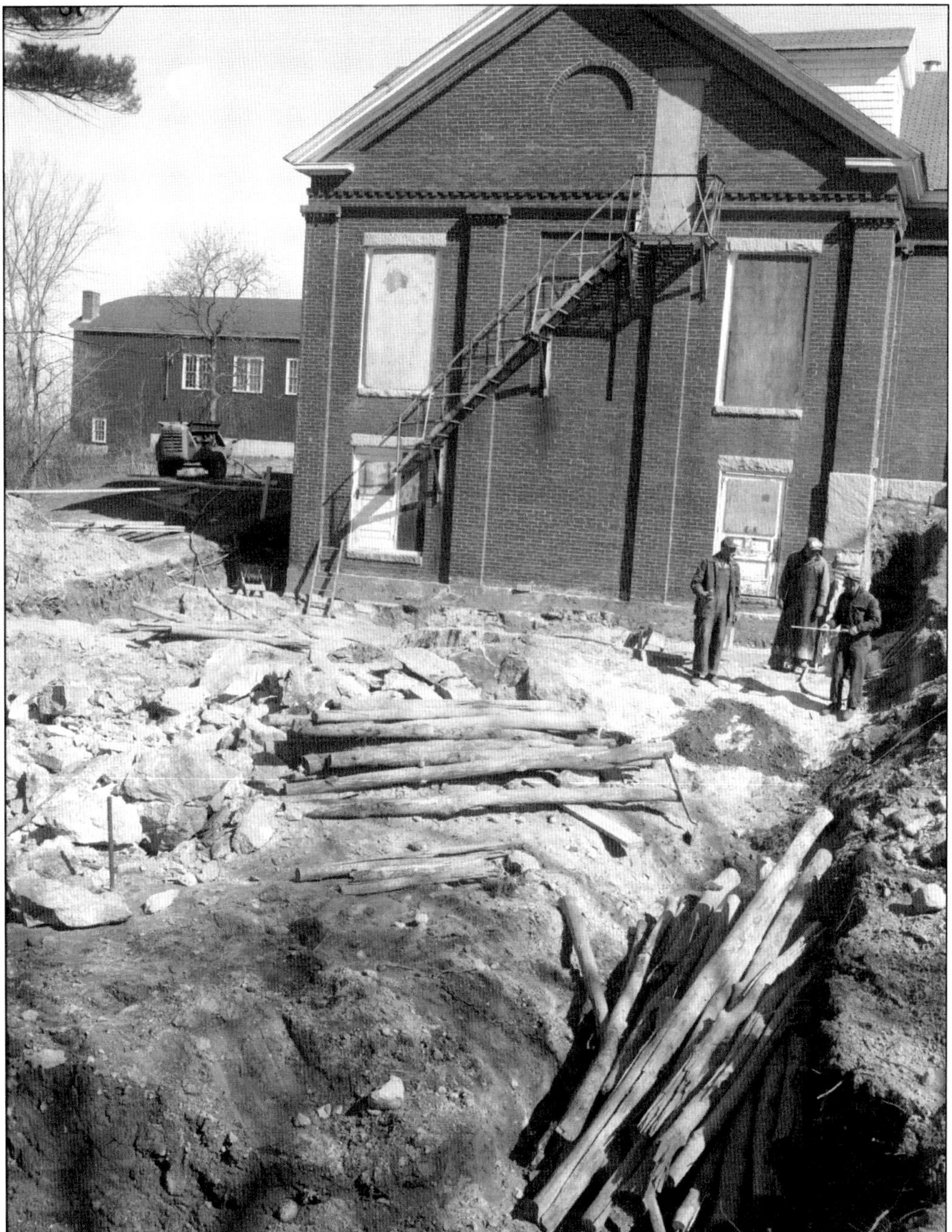

Construction of the Monmouth Academy wings occurred in 1952. (Photograph by Roland LaVallee, courtesy of the Monmouth Museum.)

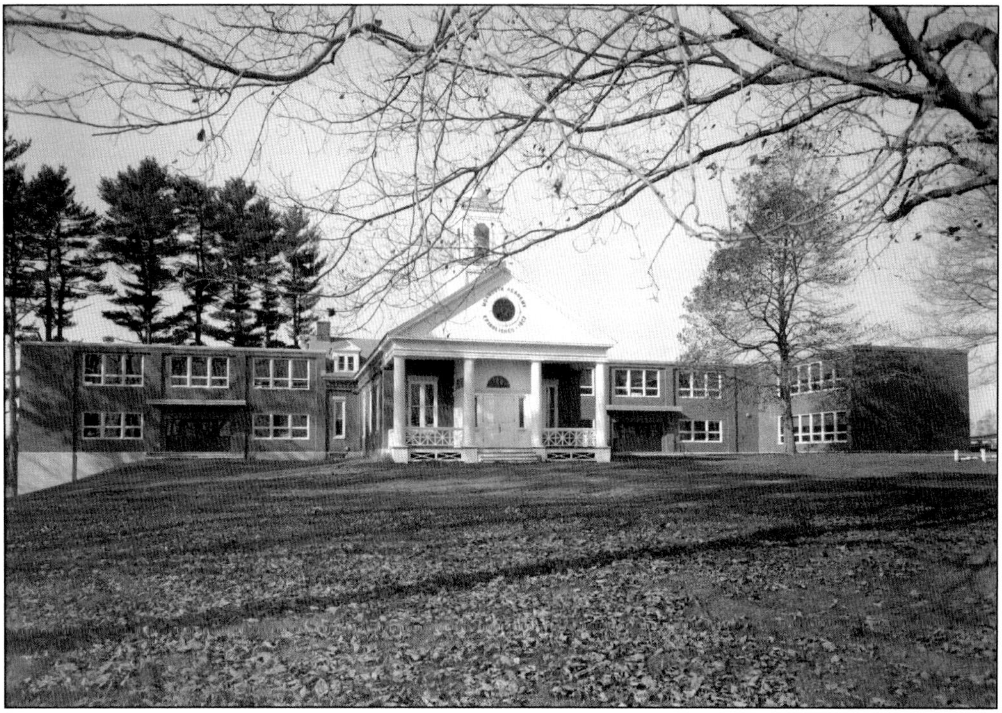

Monmouth Academy is shown here with more revisions completed in 1964. (Photograph by Roland LaVallee, courtesy of the Monmouth Museum.)

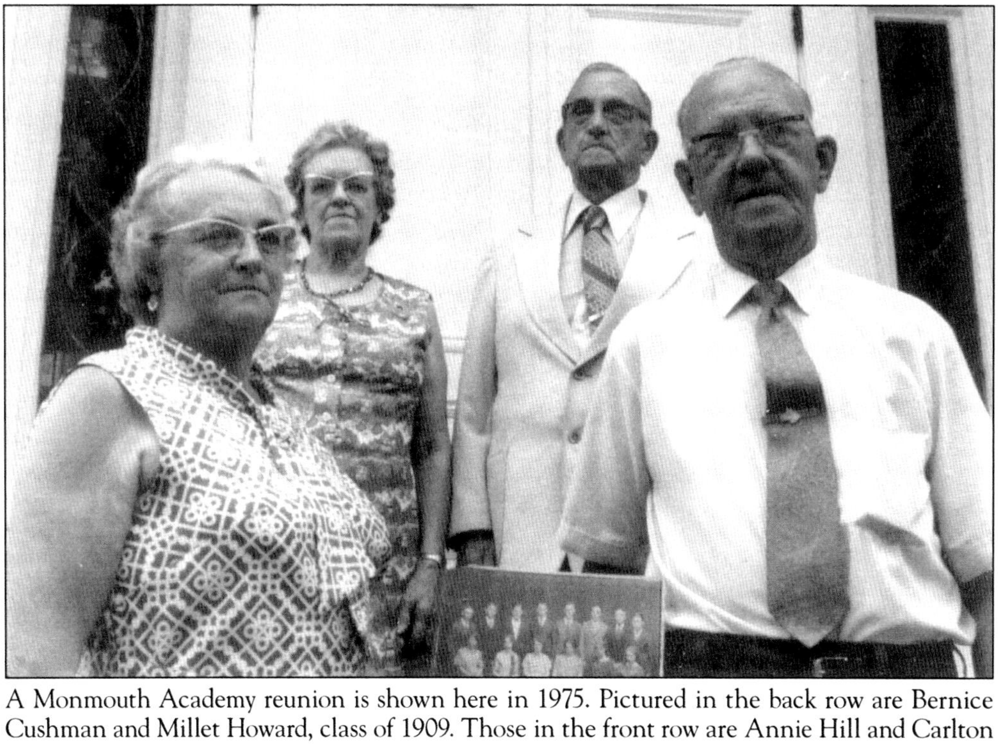

A Monmouth Academy reunion is shown here in 1975. Pictured in the back row are Bernice Cushman and Millet Howard, class of 1909. Those in the front row are Annie Hill and Carlton Turner, class of 1925. (Courtesy of Dr. Stanley Painter.)

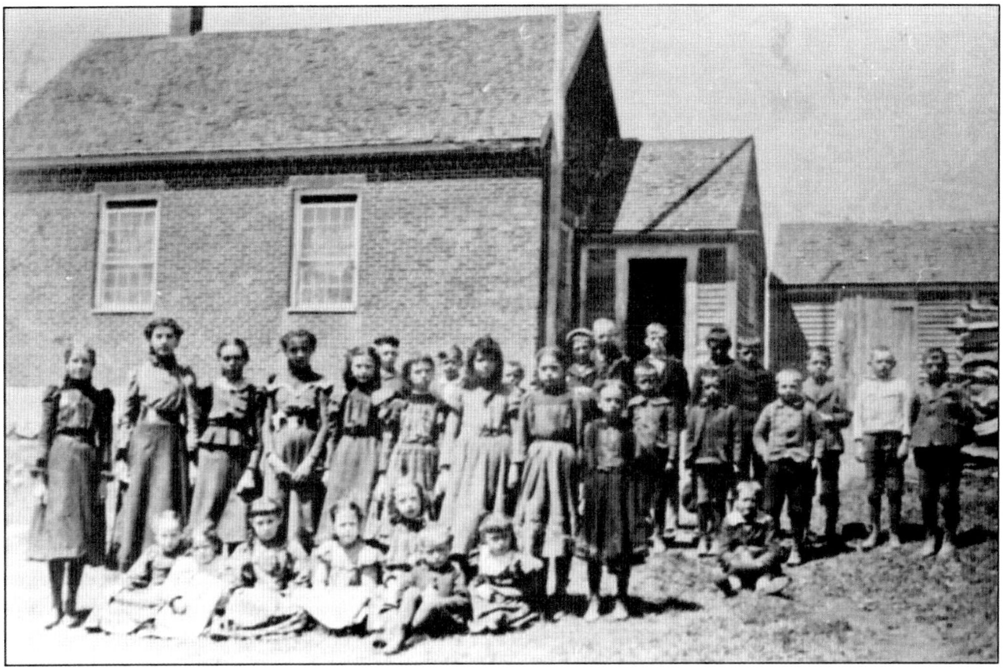

North Monmouth's brick schoolhouse on Wilson Pond Road is shown here with students from the late 1800s. Later members of the Polish community purchased it for use as a Catholic church. Today it is a private residence. (Courtesy of the Monmouth Museum.)

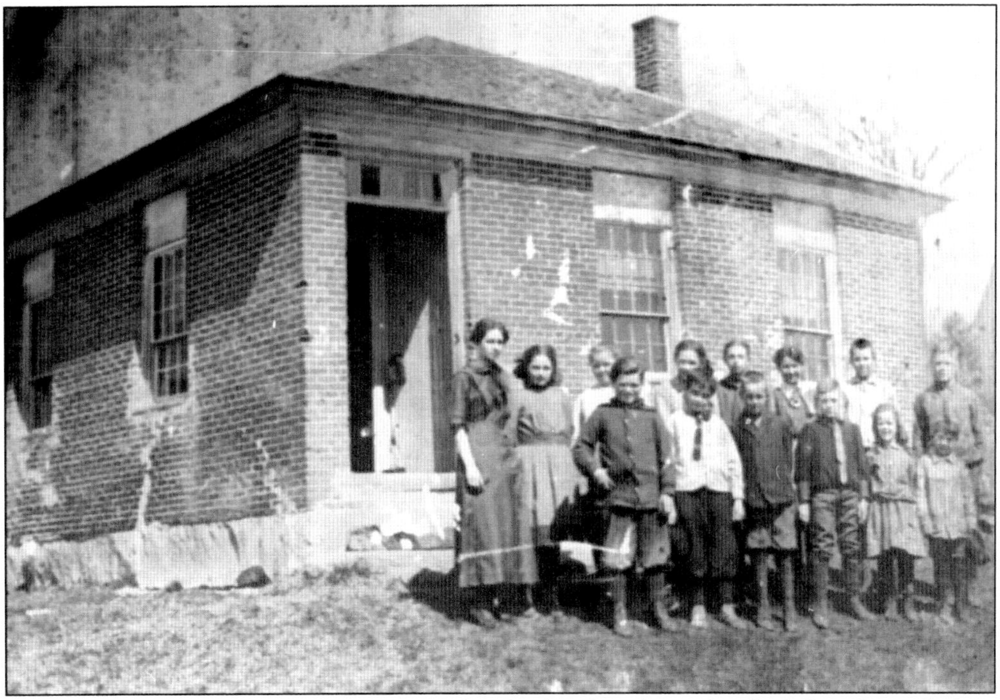

This brick schoolhouse was known as the Neck School and was located at the fork in the road where East Monmouth Road meets Route 135. At one time, Monmouth had 12 one-room schoolhouses and 16 school districts. (Courtesy of the Monmouth Museum.)

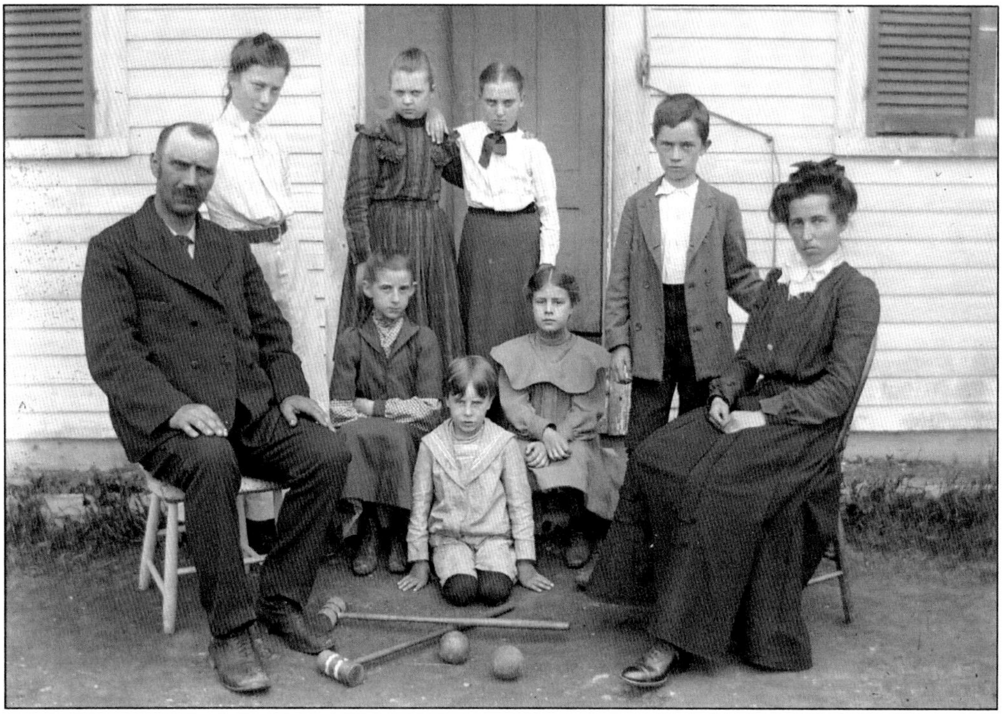

Superintendent James Packard and schoolteacher Inez Marston are pictured at the Norris Hill School in the early 1900s. (Courtesy of the Monmouth Museum.)

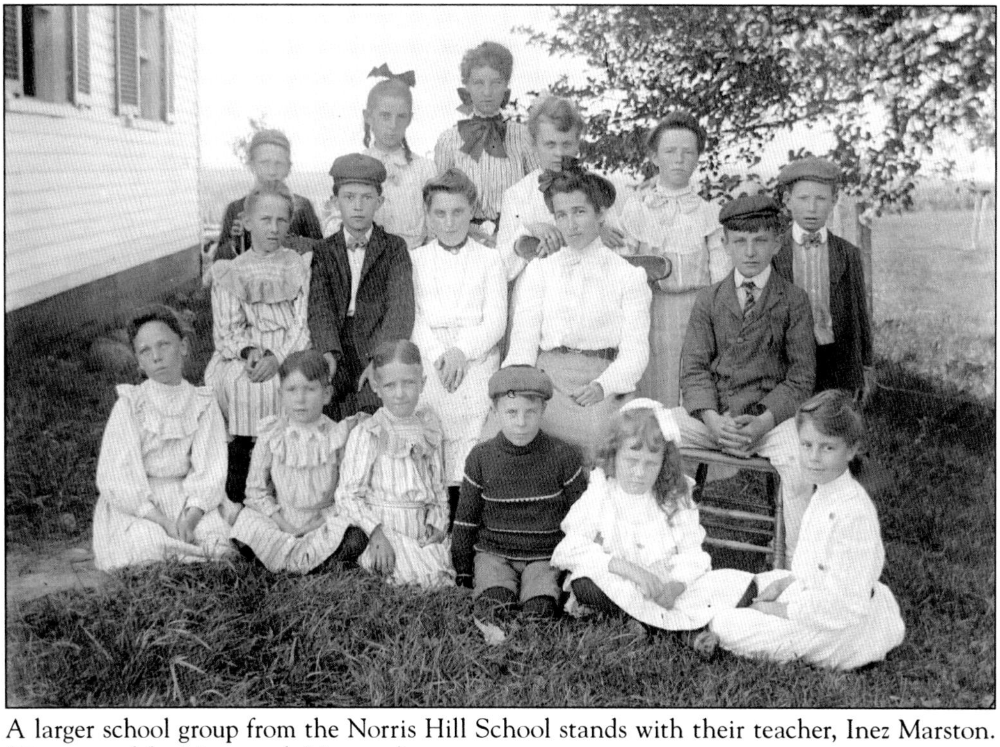

A larger school group from the Norris Hill School stands with their teacher, Inez Marston. (Courtesy of the Monmouth Museum.)

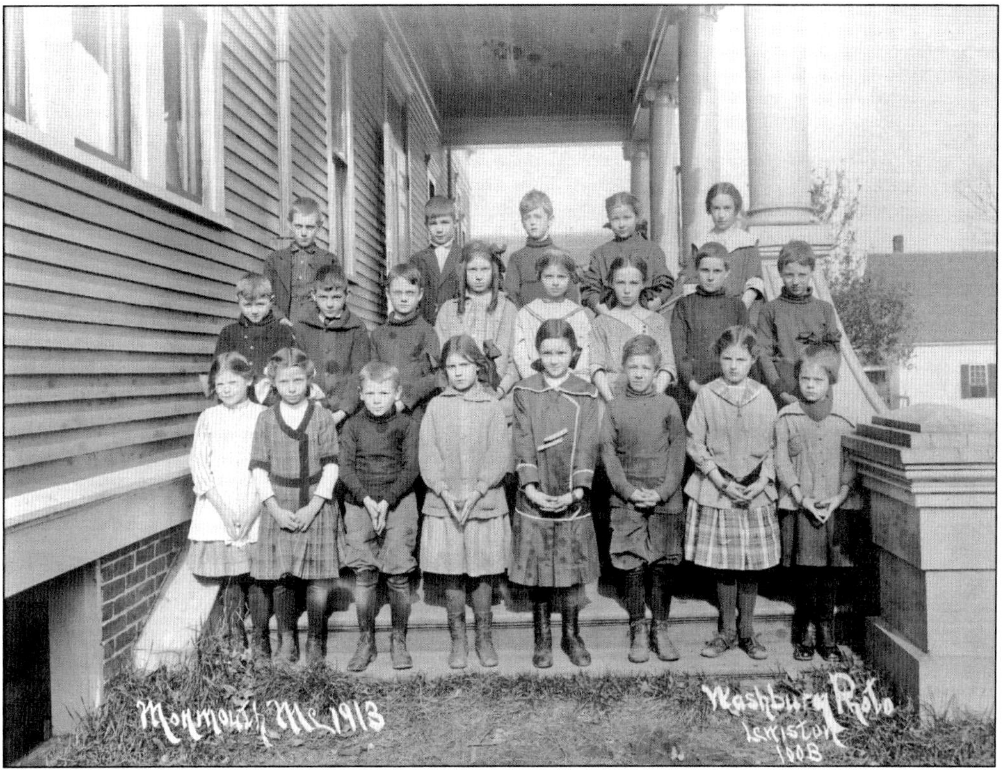

Washburn Photography, which was a father-and-daughter team from Lewiston, photographs a Monmouth Center School group in 1913. (Courtesy of the Monmouth Museum.)

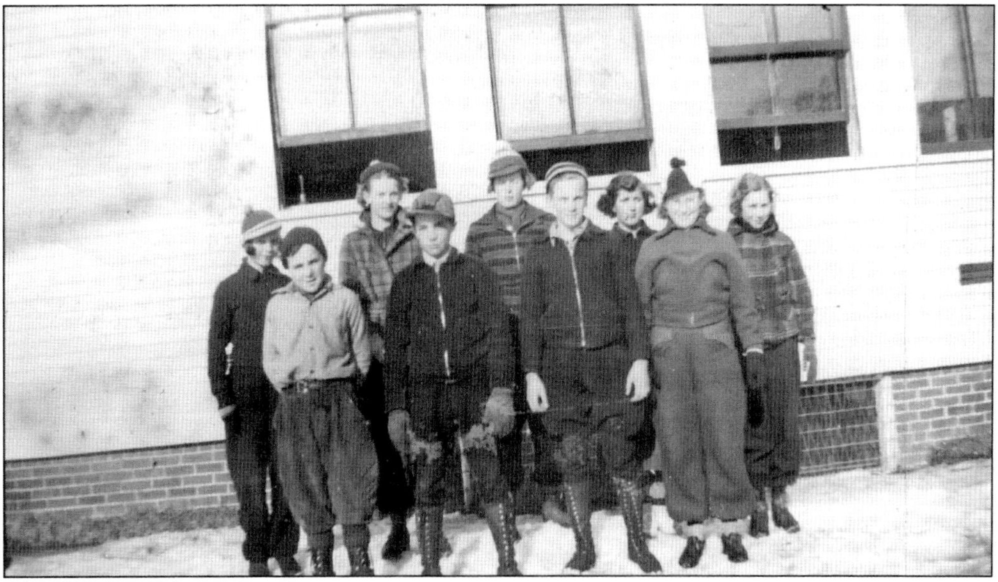

In 1938, this school group was photographed outside the Monmouth Center School. In the back row, second from the left, is Natalie Hall Jones. (Courtesy of Natalie Hall Jones.)

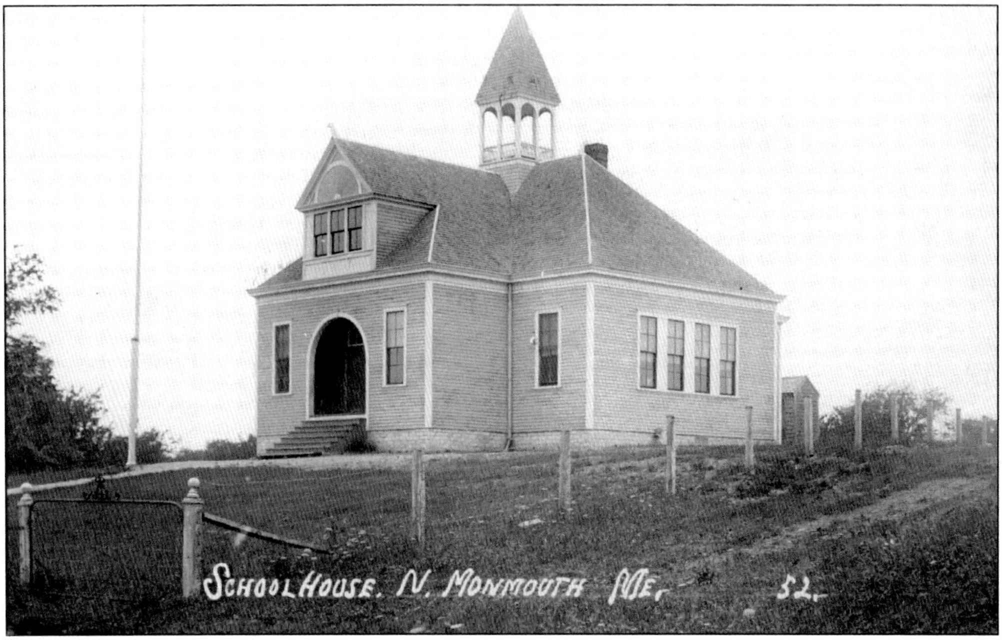

The new North Monmouth School opened in 1903. It replaced the little brick schoolhouse that was on Wilson Pond Road. (Courtesy of the author.)

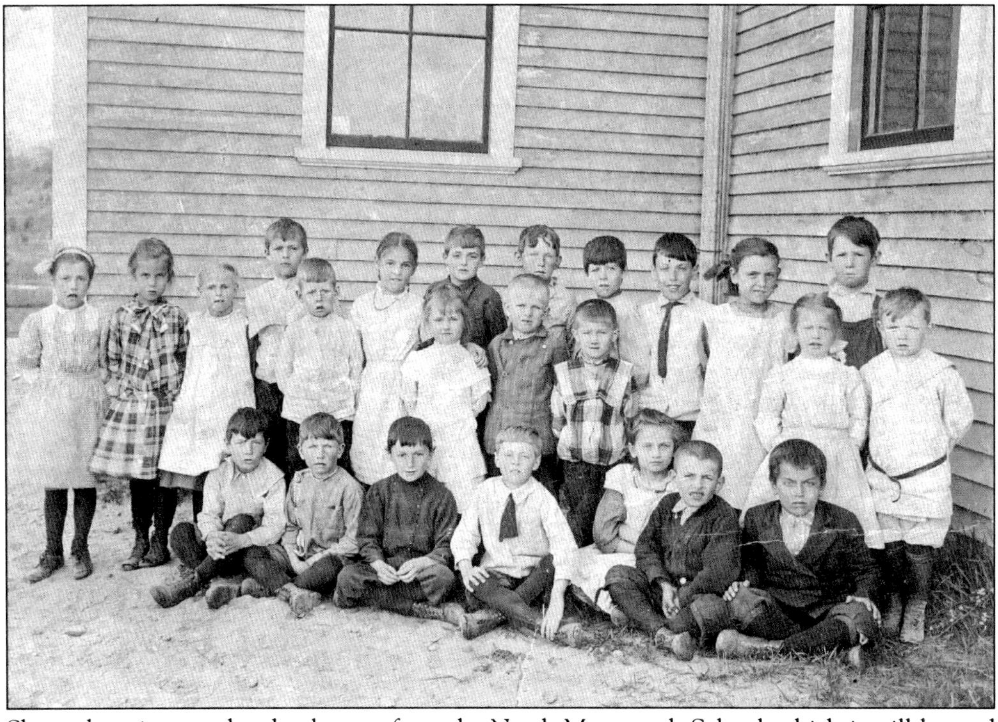

Shown here is an early school group from the North Monmouth School, which is still located on North Main Street. (Courtesy of the author.)

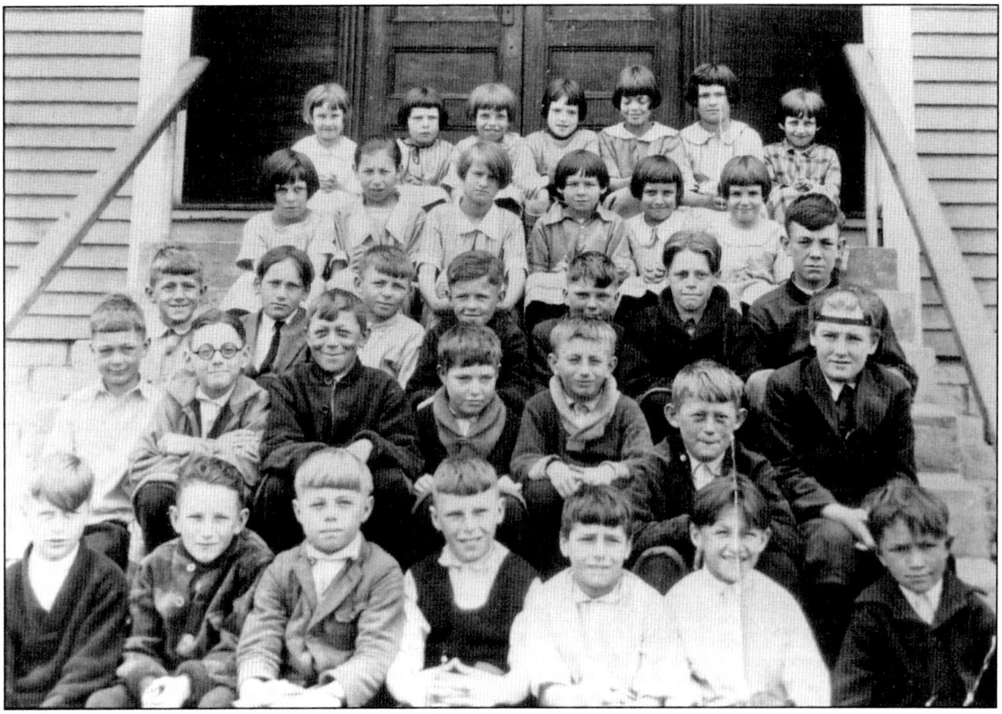

A class of North Monmouth students is on the front steps around 1925. (Courtesy of the late Alberta Keene.)

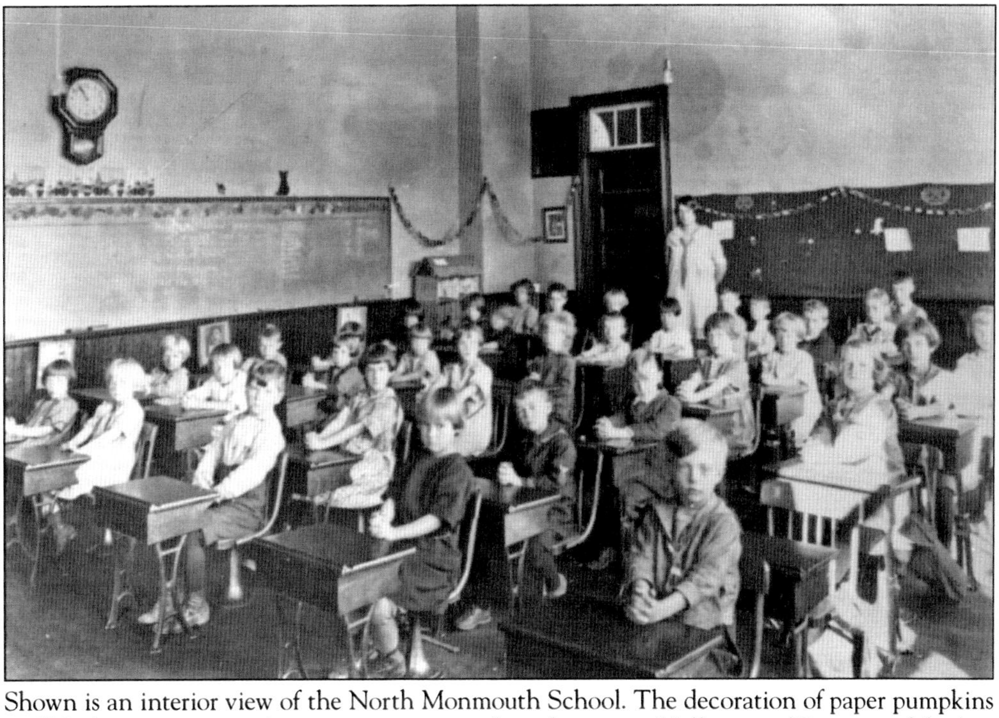

Shown is an interior view of the North Monmouth School. The decoration of paper pumpkins and black cats gives one the impression it must have been near Halloween. (Courtesy of the late Lewis Horzempa.)

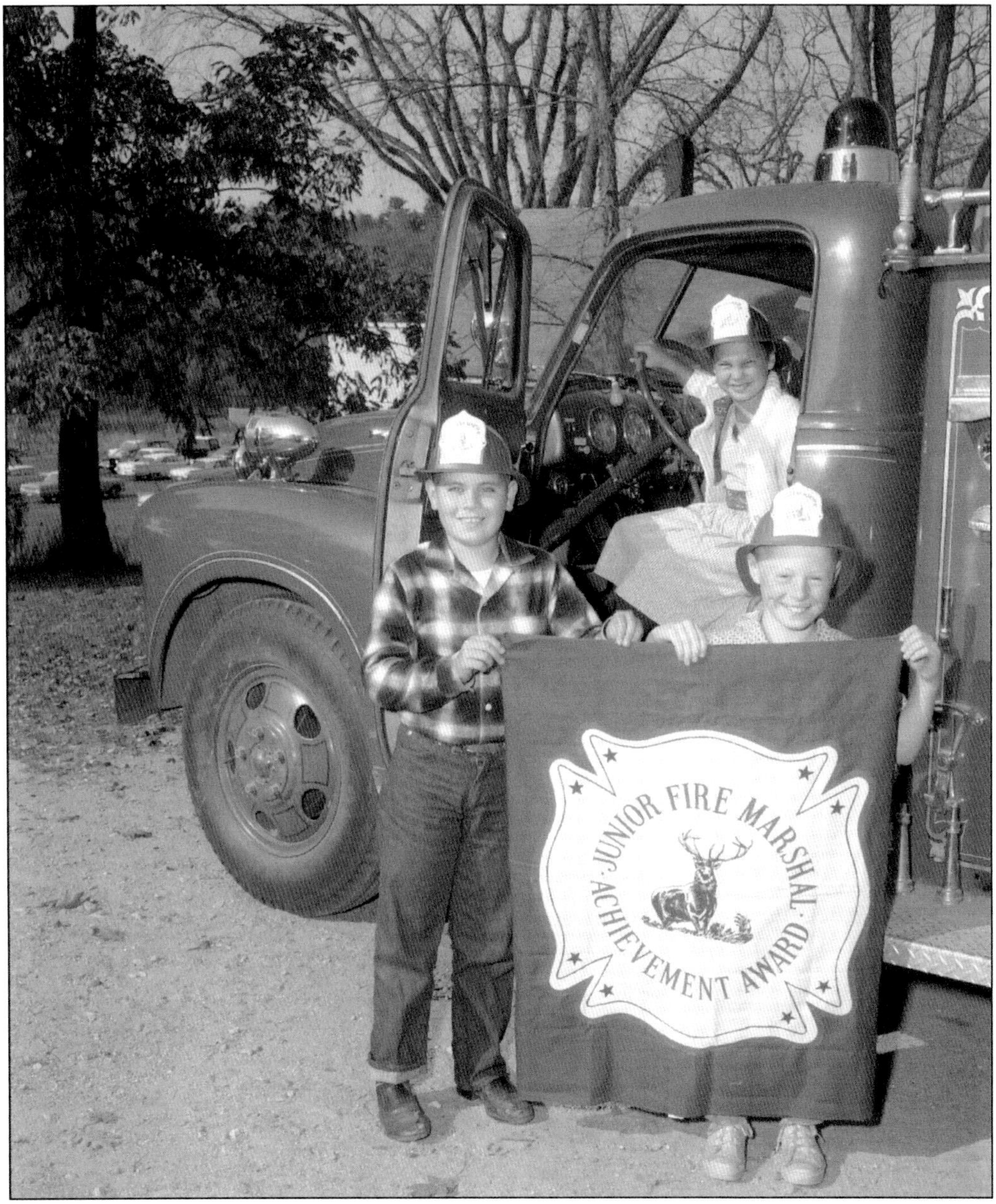

Monmouth insurance agent Leland Davis Jr. gave his third annual fire prevention program in October 1963. Fire helmets were presented to members of the North Monmouth Grade School. A special banner was given to Joan Stetson's third-grade class for having completed and promptly returned fire checklists, which were filled out by each student. The boys are eight-year-old Thomas Riggs (left) and nine-year-old Andrew Marsh. Seated at the wheel is nine-year-old Penny Smith. An article regarding this event ran in the *Lewiston Saturday* on October 12, 1963, and in the *Lewiston Daily Sun* on page 5. (Photograph by Roland LaVallee, courtesy of the Monmouth Museum.)

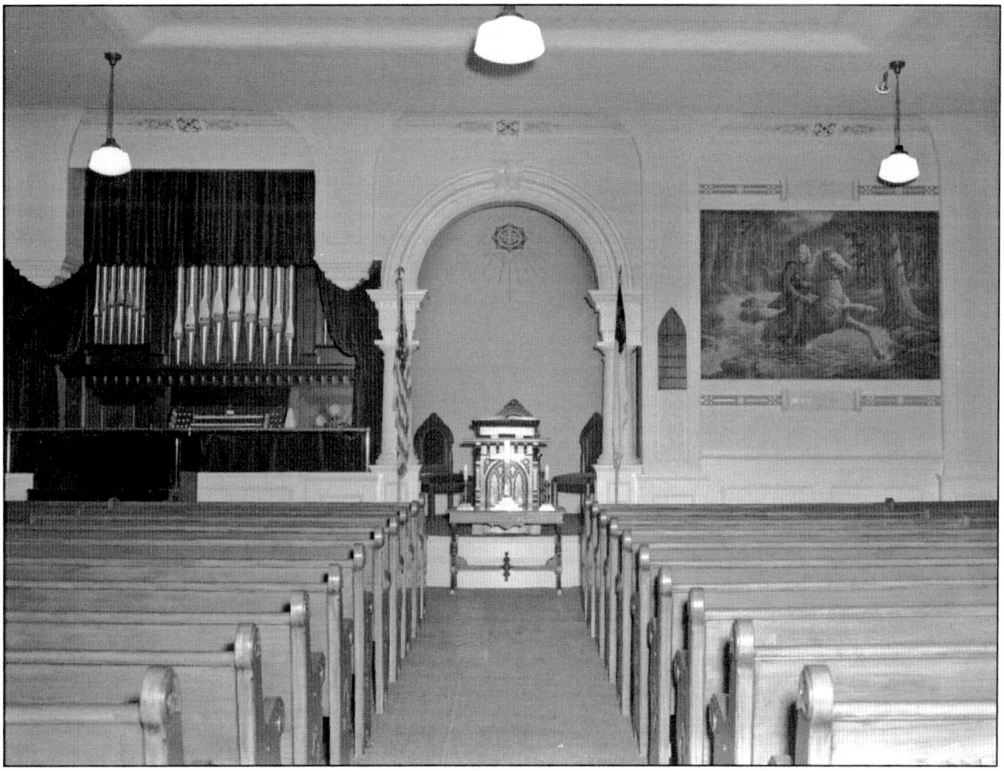

On September 25, 1952, this photograph was taken following the redecoration of the United Church on Main Street. The painting to the right is of Bishop Francis Asbury, painted by Harry Cochrane. It hangs in the United Church in Monmouth Center. Bishop Asbury came to Monmouth in 1802 for the New England Methodist Conference, which was held at the Old Fort. (Courtesy of the Monmouth Museum.)

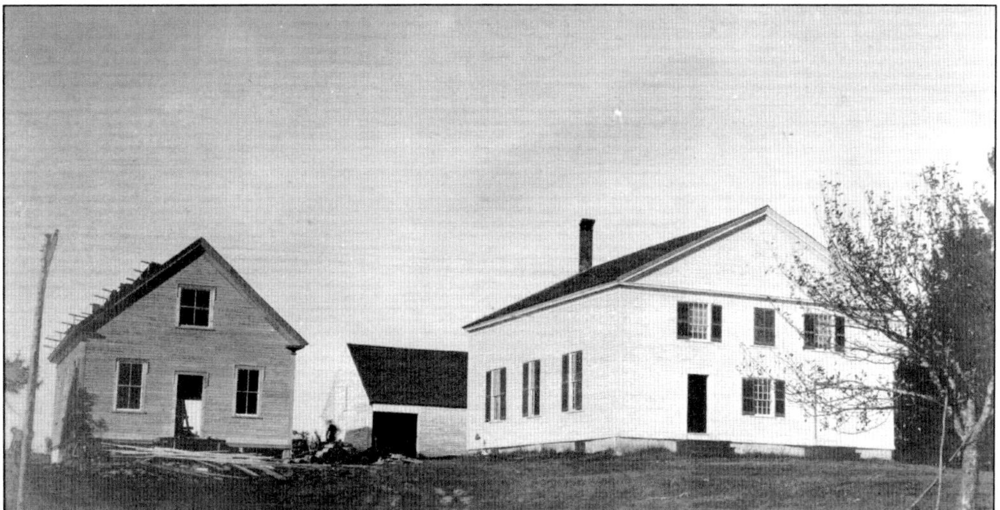

This photograph shows the building of the East Monmouth vestry next to the United Methodist church. The East Monmouth United Methodist Church is the oldest surviving church in Monmouth. (Courtesy of the Monmouth Museum.)

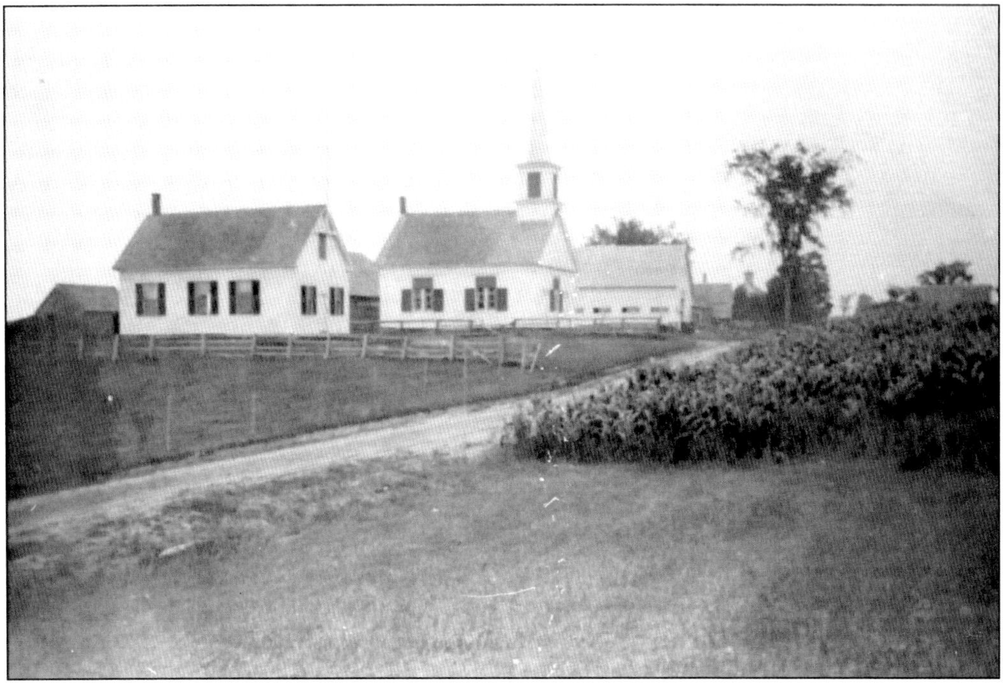

This view is of the South Monmouth School and the Baptist church. (Courtesy of Natalie Hall Jones.)

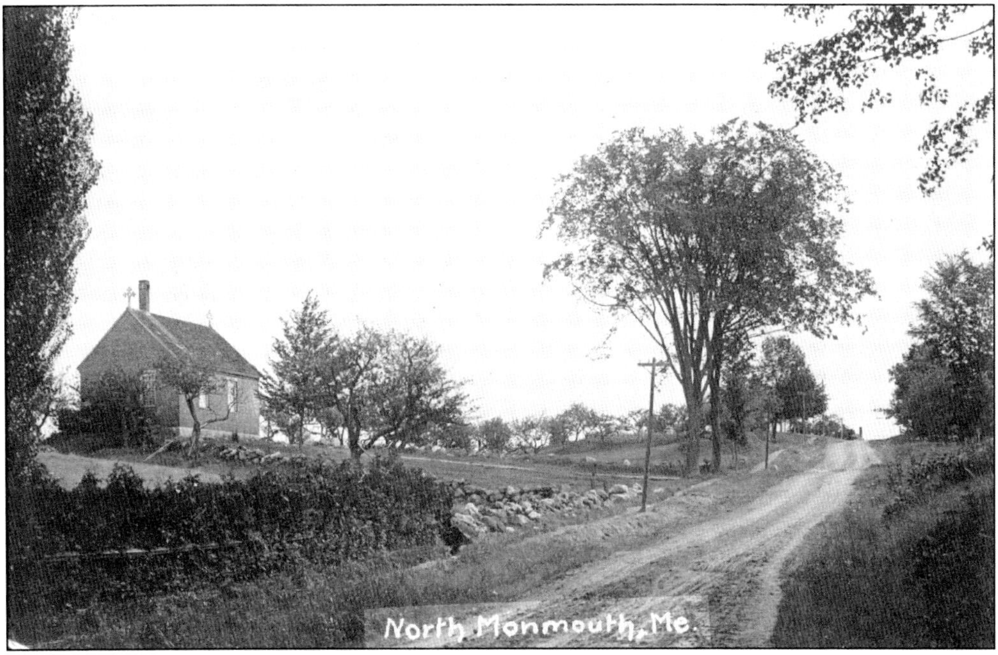

The first Catholic church in Monmouth was located on Wilson Pond Road just east of Joseph R. King's house. It was purchased by the Polish community around 1914. (Courtesy of the author.)

Six

Cumston Hall

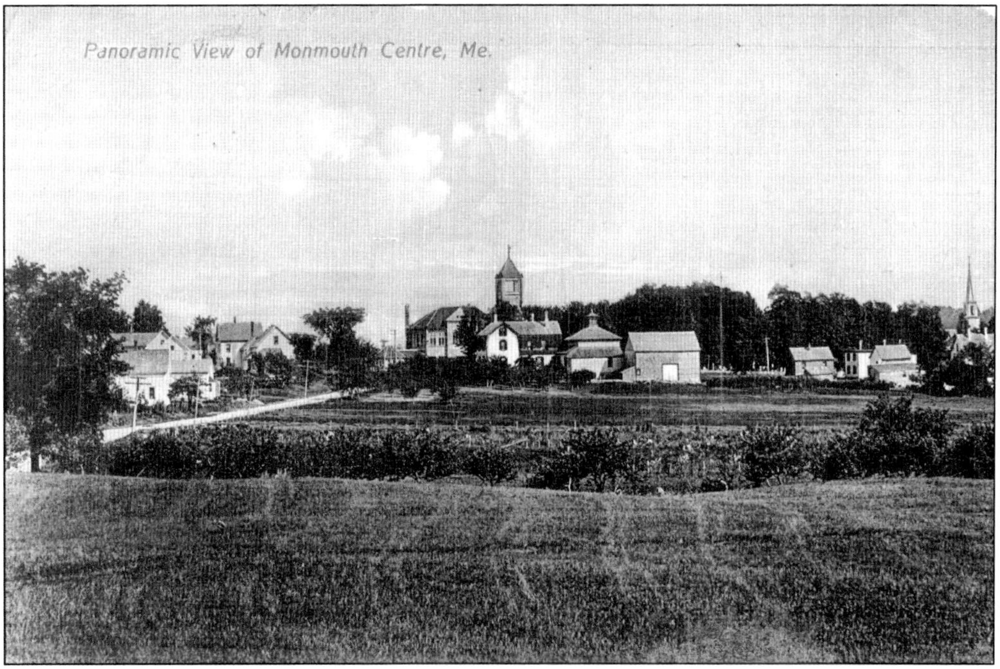

Back in the early 1900s, the view of Cumston Hall heading into Monmouth from Blue Road was a breathtaking. (Courtesy of the author.)

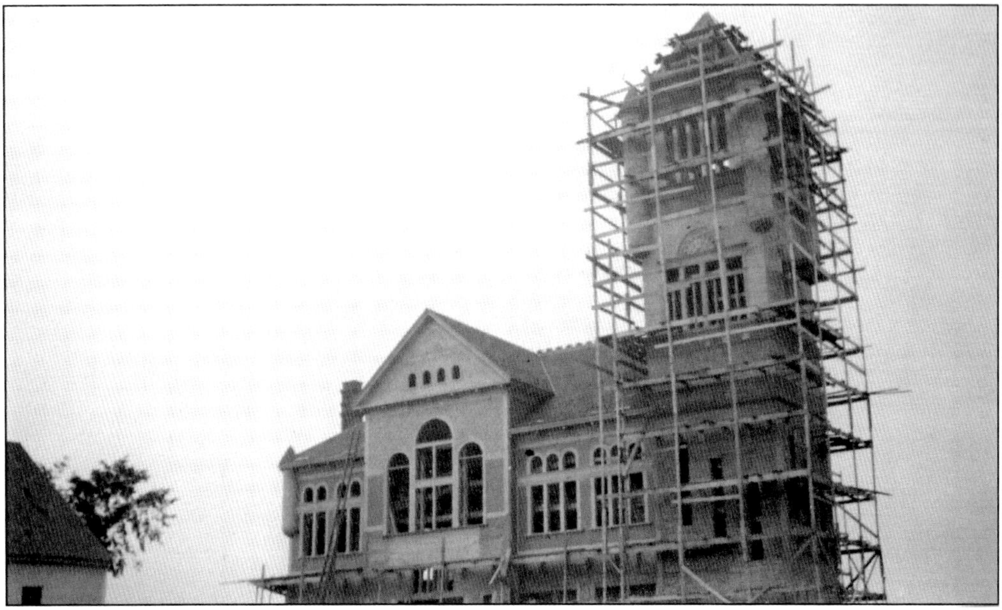

This is perhaps the only photograph of Cumston Hall under construction. It was completed in 1900. The building's designer, Harry H. Cochrane, was not an architect, but his plans were so thorough that barely any changes were necessary. The head carpenter on the project was Mellen J. Hanscom of Leeds, and the head plasterer was Daniel Kavanaugh of Lewiston. (Courtesy of Audrey and David Walker.)

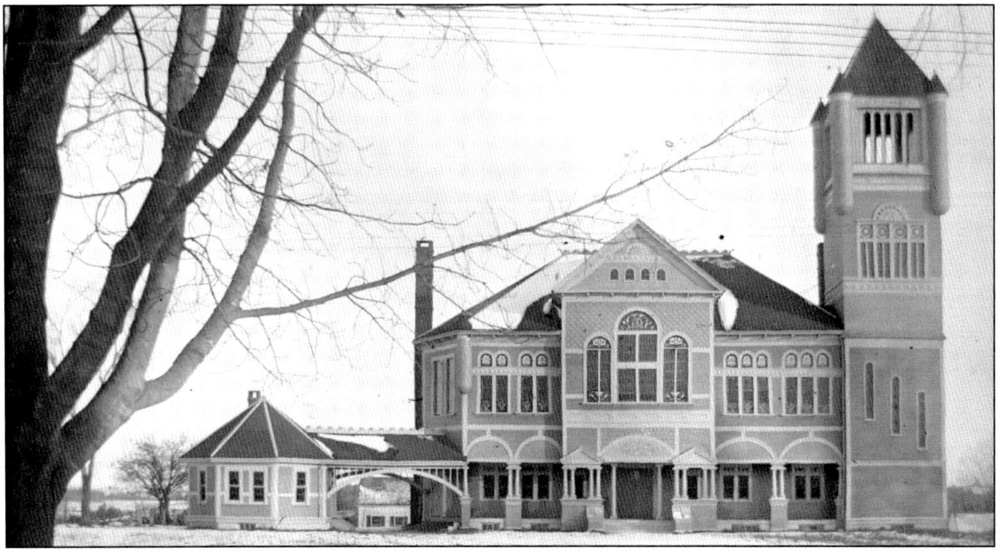

Cumston Hall was built as the town hall and the library of Monmouth. Harry H. Cochrane completed the plans in March 1899. The formal dedication took place on June 27, 1900. It now serves as the Theater of Monmouth and the town library. It was the first building in Monmouth to be lighted by electricity and was designed with its own private plant, supplied with power by a shingle mill. The small building on the left was designed as the selectmen's office, followed by a carriage porch. The architecture is a blend of Romanesque and Renaissance. The windows are leaded stained glass. The tower encloses the staircase leading to the second-floor opera house. (Courtesy of the Monmouth Museum.)

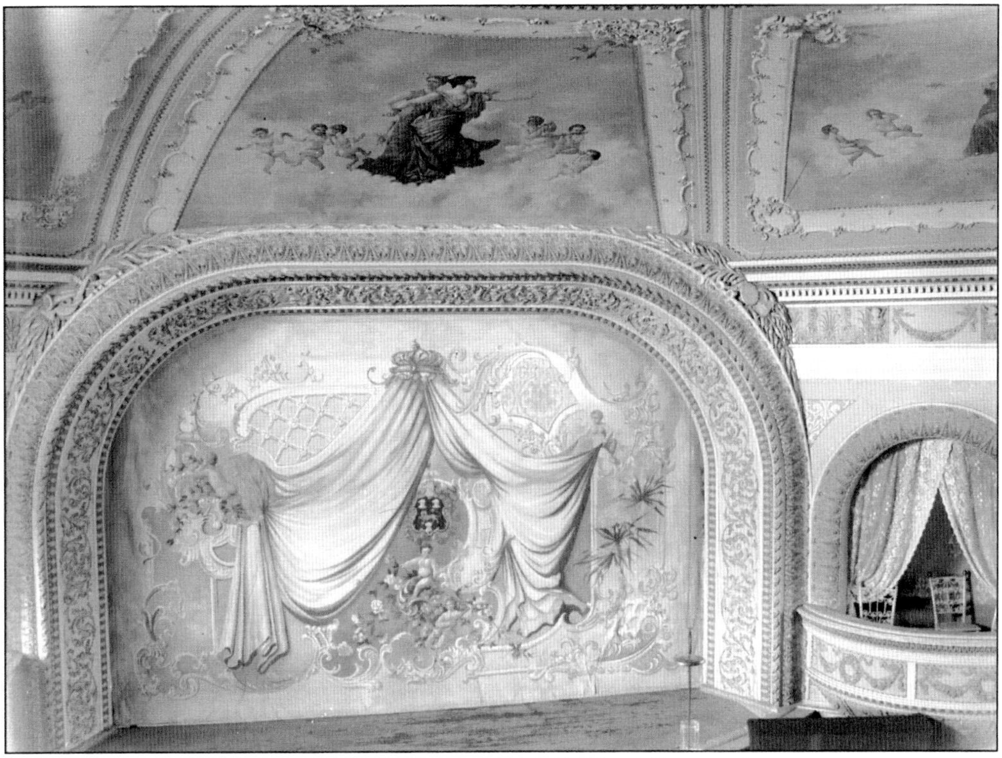

This is the interior of the second floor of Cumston Hall. The following descriptions are excerpted from the *Lewiston Journal* of May 1900. "This is opera house style, with sloping floor, balcony, stage, and boxes. Of course, the eye is first caught by the stage and the proscenium arch. Above the arch are three huge panels containing heroic figures. The panels, in order, represent Music, Drama [in the center], and Oratory." (Courtesy of the Monmouth Museum.)

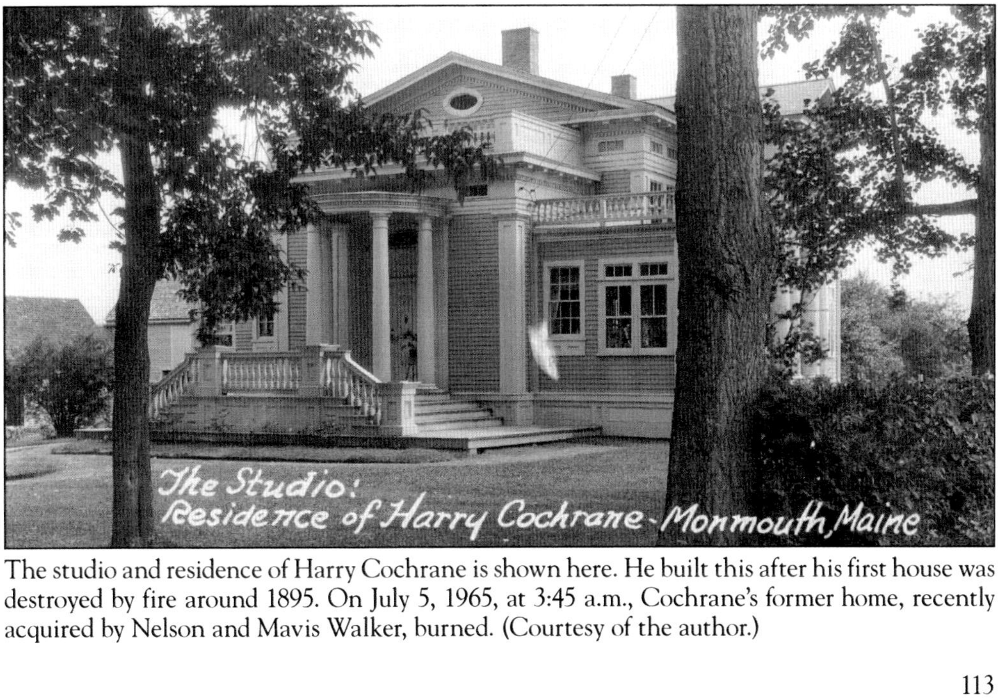

The studio and residence of Harry Cochrane is shown here. He built this after his first house was destroyed by fire around 1895. On July 5, 1965, at 3:45 a.m., Cochrane's former home, recently acquired by Nelson and Mavis Walker, burned. (Courtesy of the author.)

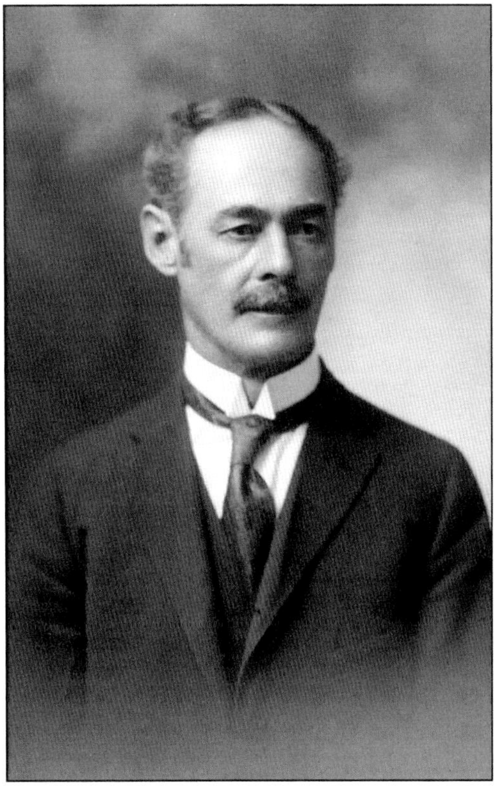

The son of Maj. James Henry Cochrane of Limington and Ellen M. Berry of Belfast, Harry H. Cochrane was born April 6, 1860, in Augusta. Harry was reared in the home of his grandparents, Dr. James Cochrane and Eliza McClure, in Monmouth and attended Monmouth Academy. He was an artist, architect, composer, conductor, musician, singer, writer, and poet. In 1927, he was the painter of the murals in the Kora Temple building in Lewiston. He was the designer, architect, and interior artist of the celebrated Cumston Hall in Monmouth and the writer of the two-volume book *History of Monmouth and Wales*, published in 1894. Harry L. Plummer was the photographer for this c. 1905 portrait of Harry. (Courtesy of the Monmouth Museum.)

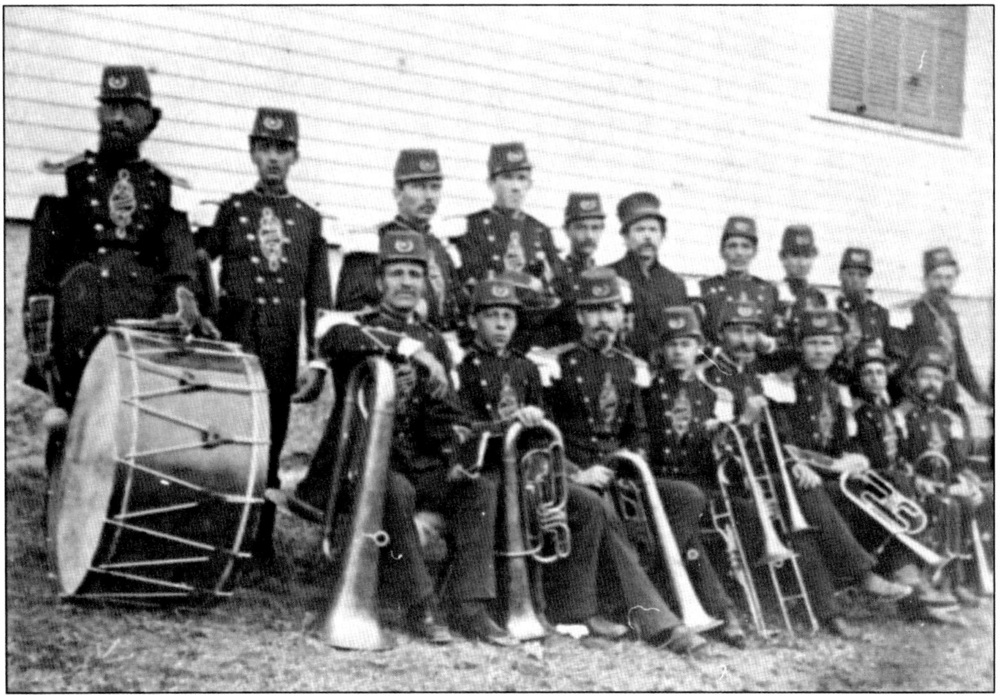

This photograph of the Monmouth Brass Band was taken in the mid- to late 1870s. In the front row, young Harry Cochrane is fourth from the left. (Courtesy of the Monmouth Museum.)

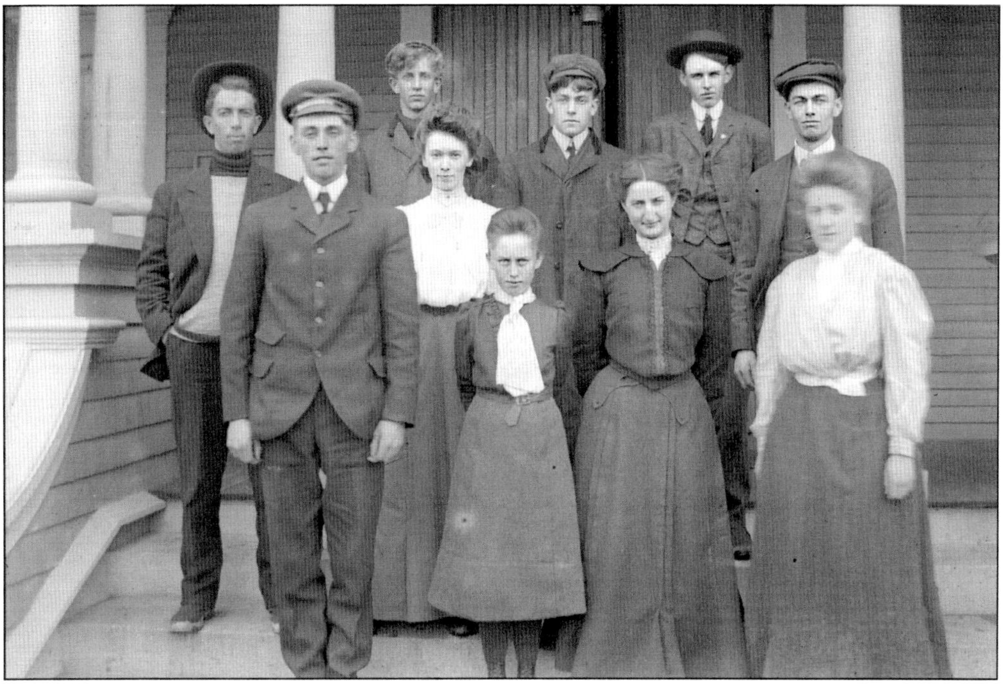

Here is a group of students on the steps of Cumston Hall. Boys are wearing coats, ties, and caps. The young girl in front is Ruby Day, and to her right is Eva McKechnie. In the back row, Frank Gilman at left. Frank would later marry Eva. Frank died in 1919 at the age of 30. (Courtesy of the Monmouth Museum.)

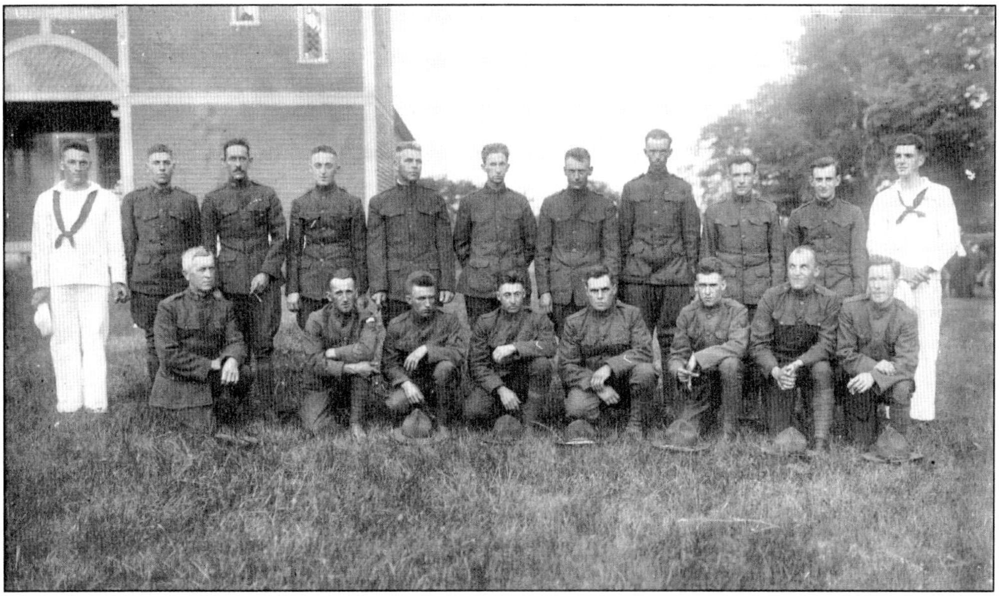

Monmouth's World War I veterans were photographed at the Fourth of July celebration that honored them at Cumston Hall in 1919. The known veterans in this photograph are the following: (first row) James Cochrane, left; Myron Prescott, second from right; and Millard Jackson, right; (second row) Ross Day, fifth from left; Clifton Loon, seventh from left; Guy Whittier, eighth from left; and Fred Hooker, ninth from left. (Courtesy of Audrey and David Walker.)

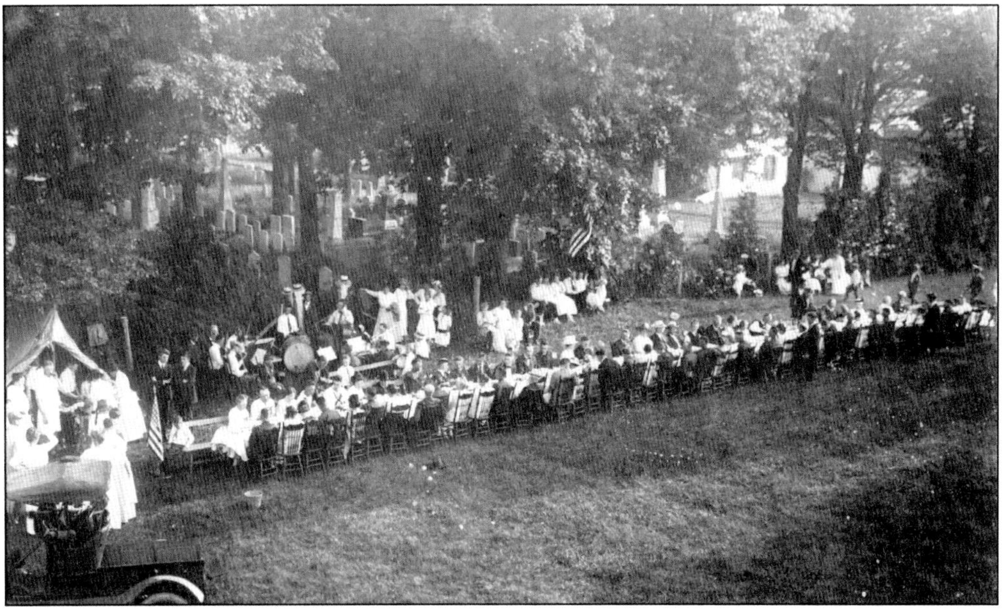

This photograph was taken from the top of Cumston Hall's tower before the windows were installed. The Fourth of July picnic was held in honor of the Monmouth men who had come home from World War I. The Center Cemetery is visible in the background. (Courtesy of Audrey and David Walker.)

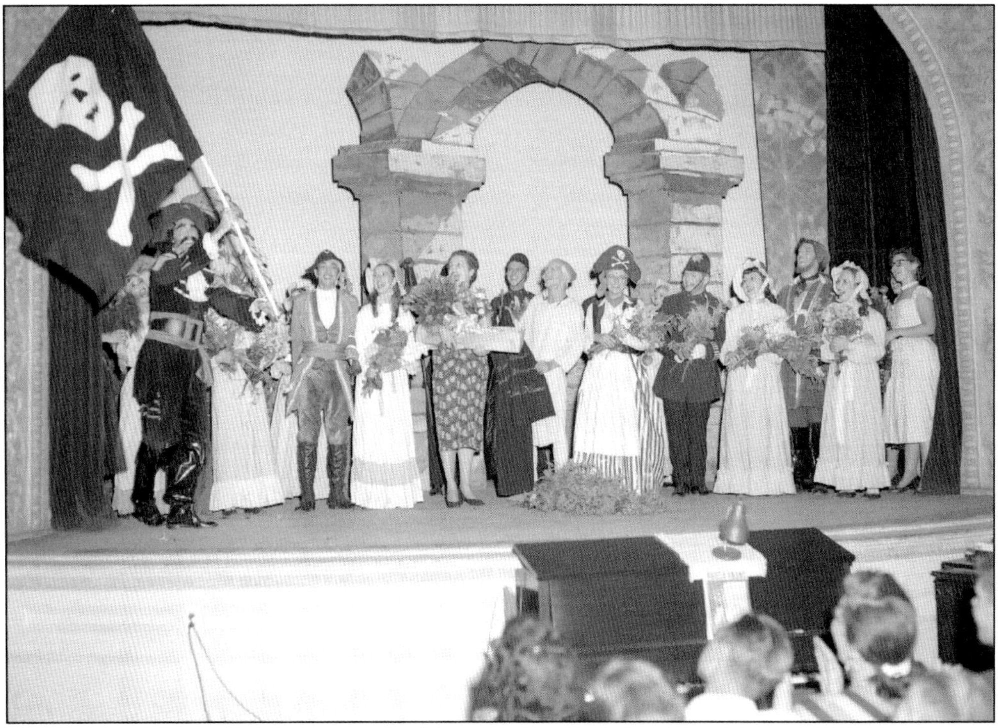

This is the final call in 1953 of the American Savoyards at Cumston Hall in their performance of Gilbert and Sullivan's *Pirates of Penzance.* (Photograph by Roland LaVallee, courtesy of the Monmouth Museum.)

Seven

Agriculture, Fairs, and Farms

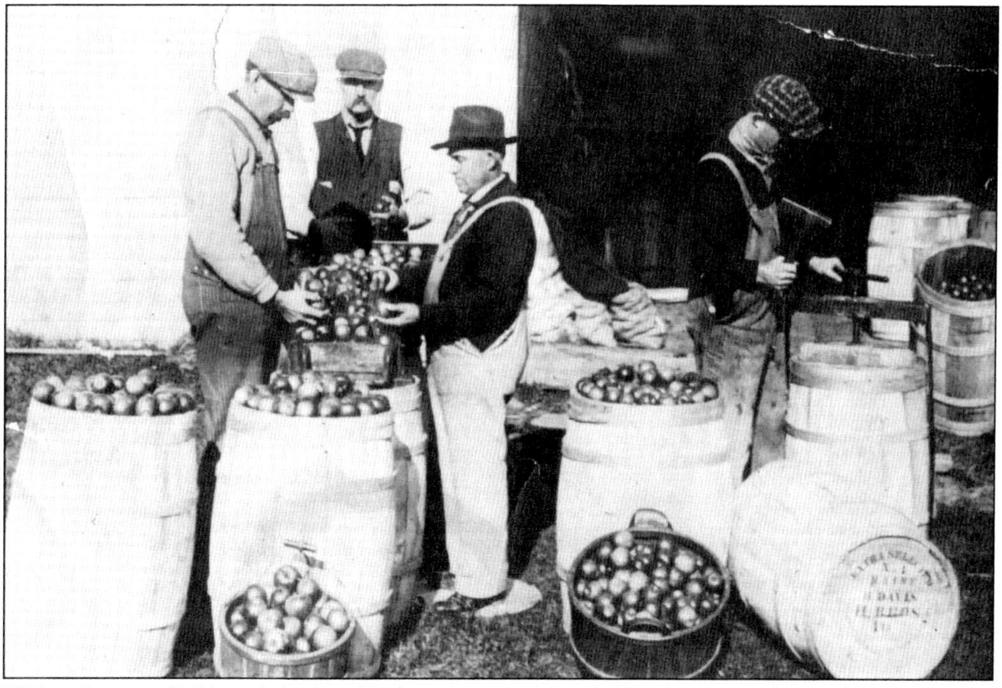

Walter Leavitt (left) and Arthur Hathaway sort through Ben Davis apples as they are placed in barrels and prepared for shipping. Built in 1904 and located just south of Monmouth Center on Main Street, Hathaway's Cider Mill was owned and operated by three generations. The Ben Davis apple was a hard apple that was softened by the salt air on its way to Europe, which made it more palatable. (Courtesy of Bertha Johnson.)

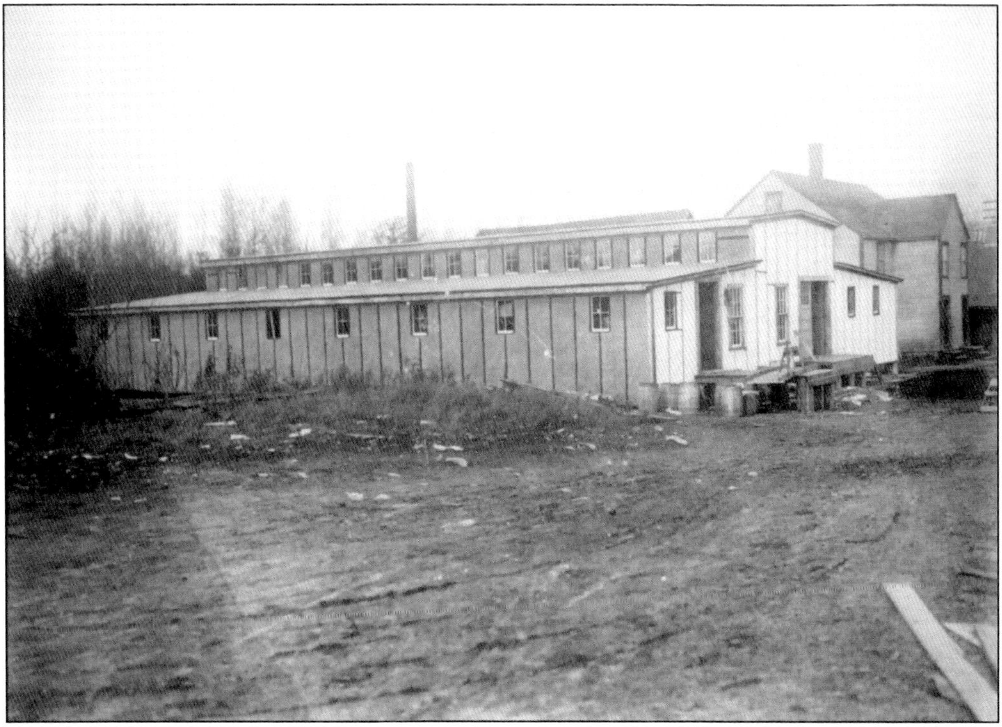

The Ham-Blake Apple Factory, located on what today is called Beach Road, operated out of this building during the 1920s. It canned apples and employed a large number of women from the town and the surrounding area. (Courtesy of Ted and Carol Johnson.)

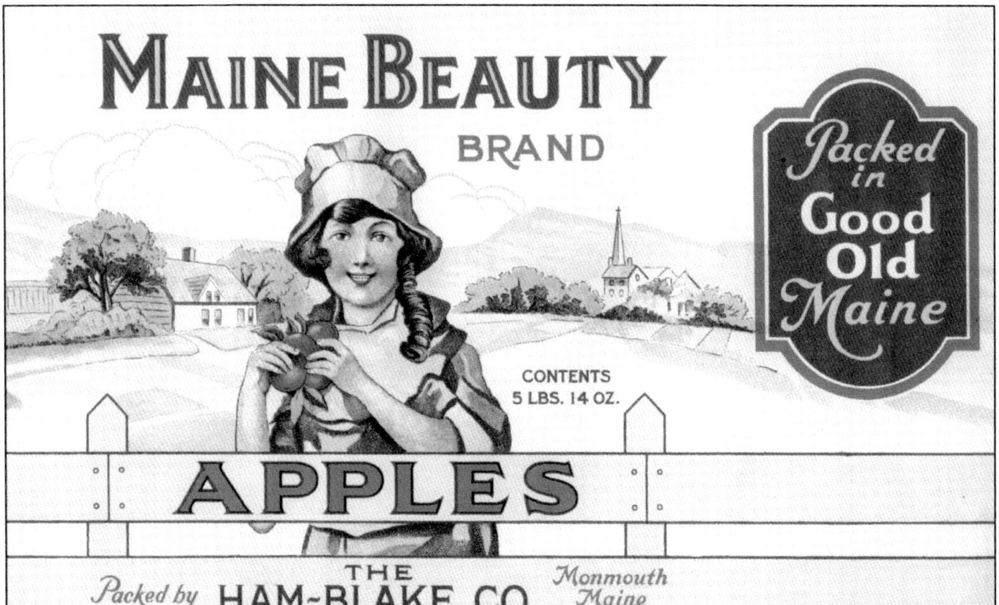

The Ham-Blake Apple Factory canned, as the label states, "Maine Beauty apples." The cans weighed 5 pounds, 14 ounces. (Courtesy of the author.)

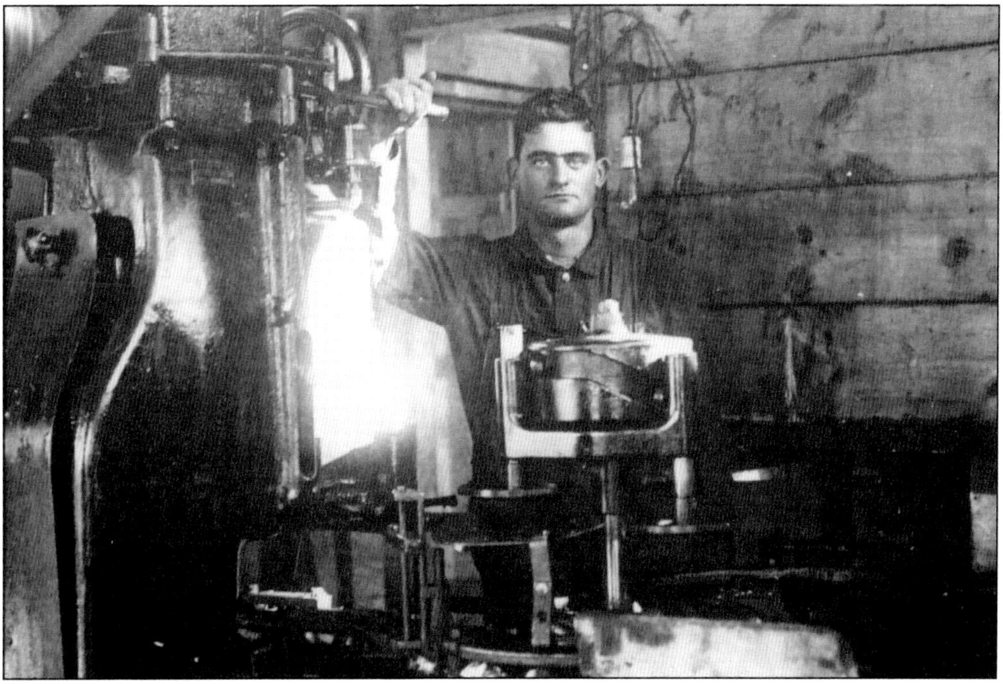

This interior view of the Ham-Blake Apple Factory shows Freemont Greenwood of Wales at work in the 1920s. (Courtesy of the George Greenwood.)

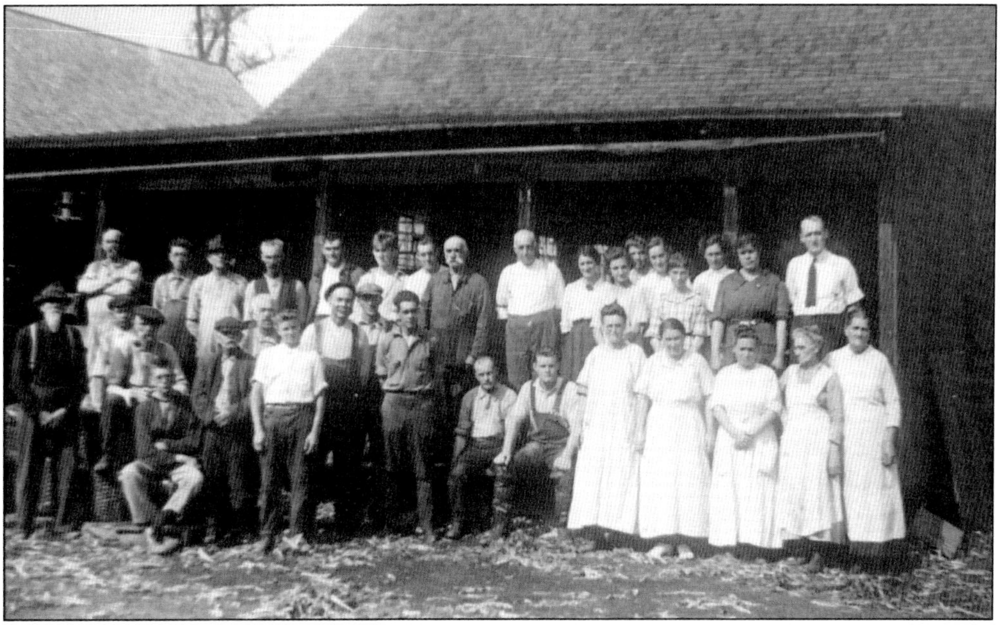

The Monmouth Canning Company was one of two corn shops in town. This photograph is of a group of workers outside the factory, which was located on the present-day Beach Road. Eugene Andrews, the father of the late Doris Andrews Johnson, was also the superintendent of the Monmouth Canning Company, which is also known as the Corn Shop. He is the man with the tie on the right side of the photograph. Andrews worked there from 1912 to 1936. The photograph was taken around 1912. (Courtesy of the late Doris Andrews Johnson.)

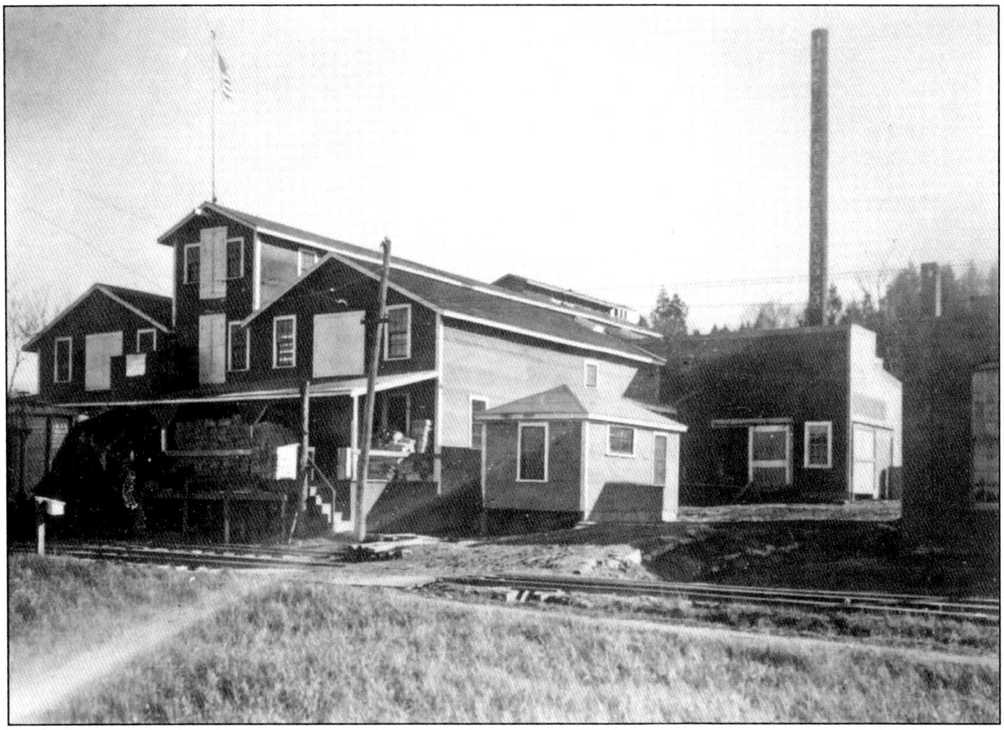

The first building erected by the Heart of Maine Canning Company at Days Corner was destroyed by fire in 1917. A second structure, pictured here, was constructed at the same location and was still in use at the time it was destroyed by fire in 1932. John T. McCarthy owned the Heart of Maine Canning Company, which concentrated in the canning of string beans, squash, corn, apples, and Irish stew. The name of the canning factory can be seen on the smoke stack. (Courtesy of Marcia Borphy.)

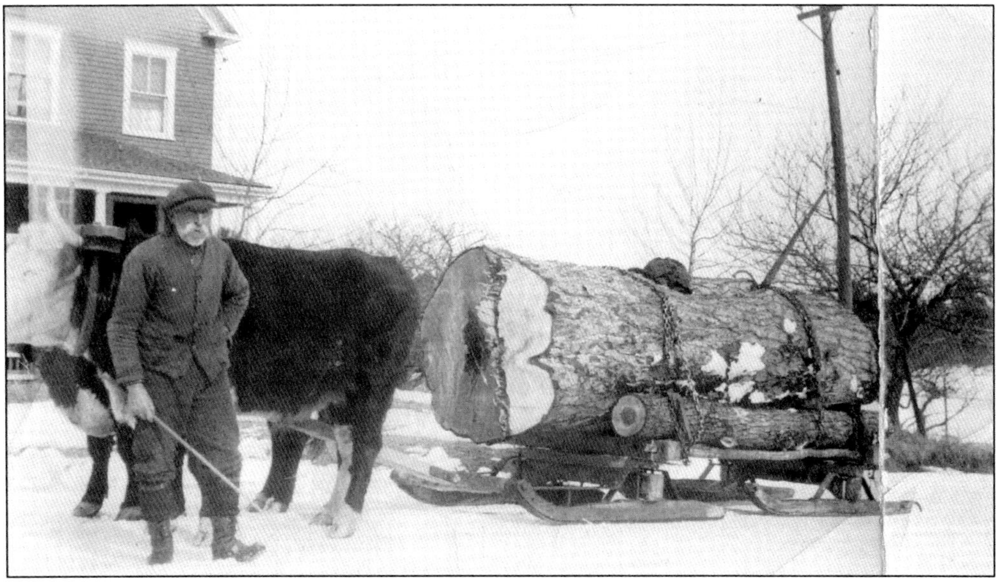

Oxen played an important role on the farms of Monmouth. This photograph shows Bill Curtis and his ox team moving a heavy load. (Courtesy of the Monmouth Museum.)

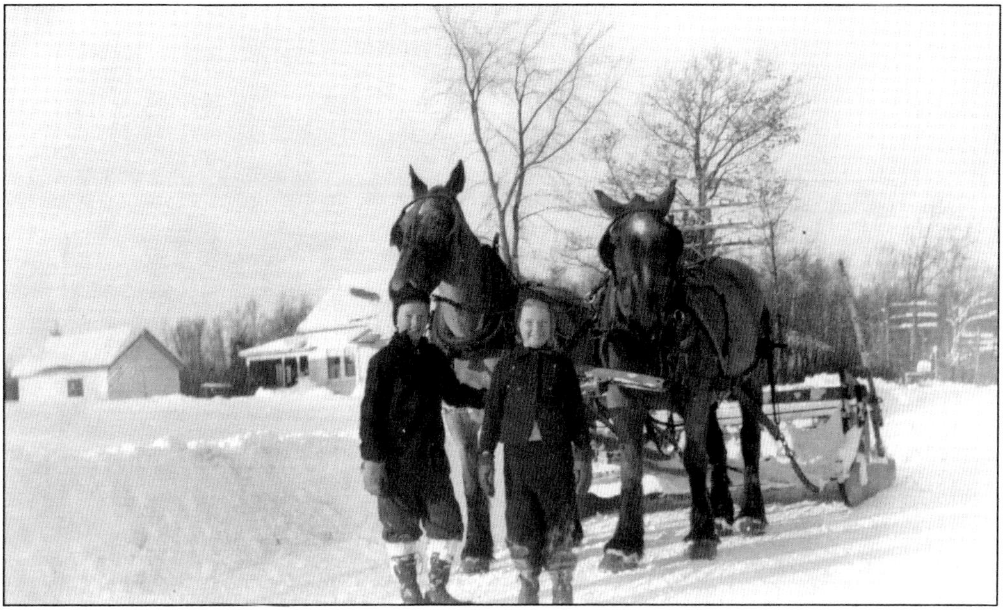

Gordon and Jayne Robinson, with their father's team, Tom and Jerry, are plowing snow with a Kennebec snow scoop just north of Monmouth Center. The snow scoops played a vital part in the ice-harvesting industry. (Courtesy of Jayne Robinson).

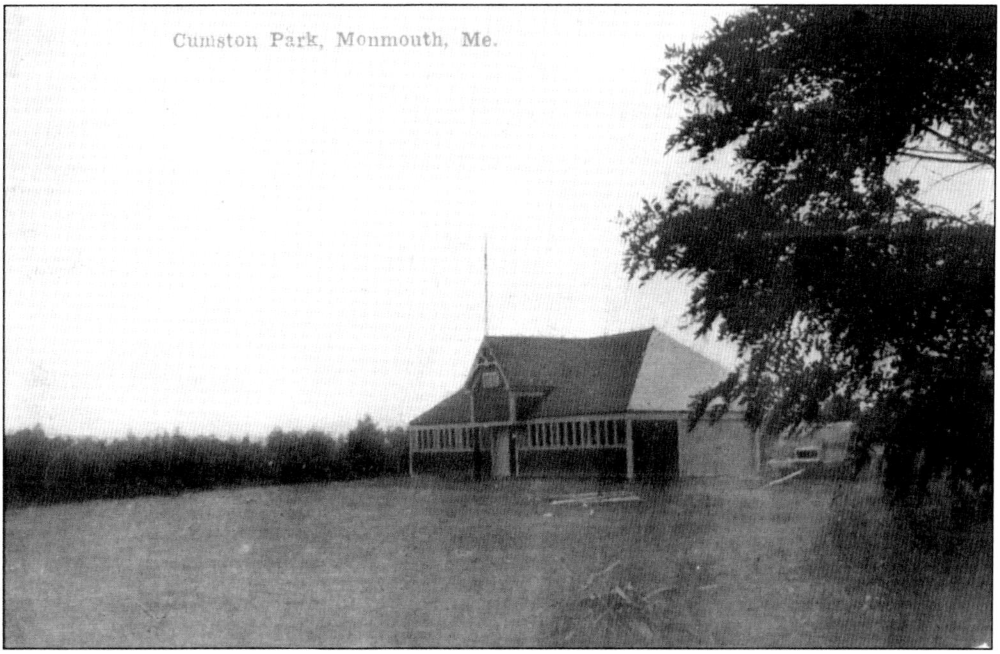

Dr. Charles Cumston, the benefactor who donated the money for the building of Cumston Hall in 1900, gave Cumston Park to the Town of Monmouth. The exhibition hall was first used at the Monmouth Fair in September 1909. According to the *Lewiston Evening Journal*, the town appropriated $500, and the remaining costs were covered by private subscriptions and free labor. To the right of the building is a snow roller. (Courtesy of the author.)

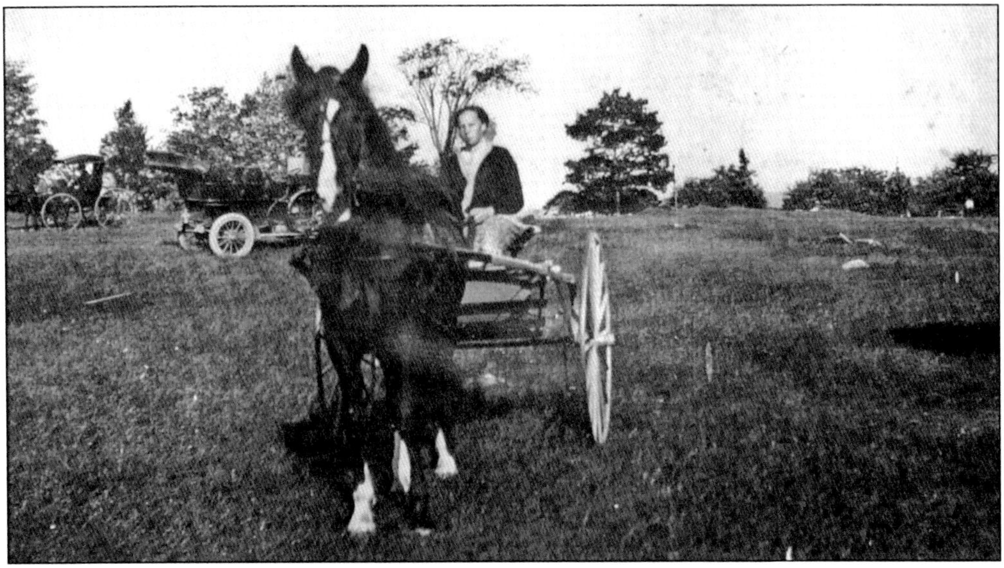

Tena Jacobs and her horse Pearl are at the Monmouth Fair Grounds in 1911. Tena, at the age of 16, was featured in an article that ran in the *Lewiston Magazine Section* on June 27, 1911, where her name was spelled "Tina" instead of "Tena." According to the article, Tena Jacobs had one of the finest henneries in town, with 1,000 hens and chicks. Tena M. Jacobs married Leon W. Prince on June 27, 1916. Together they had two children. Ivy was born on February 25, 1919, and Norman was born on November 7, 1920. Tena passed away at the age of 25 in 1920. In 1916, she was the first woman in Monmouth to have an automobile. (Courtesy of the late Ivy Prince Hillier.)

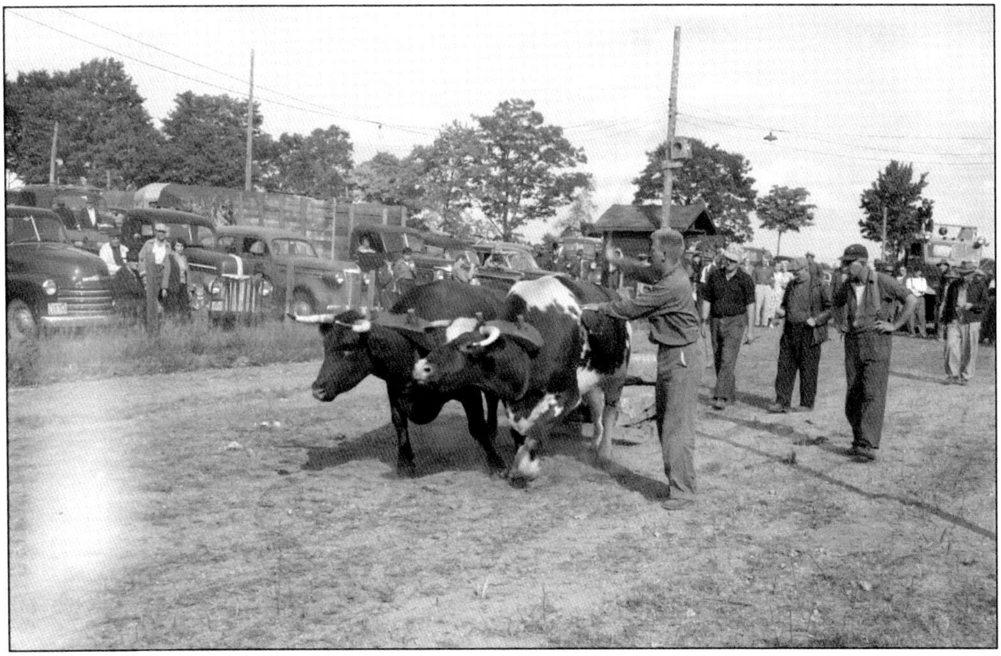

Oxen pulling is a longtime favorite attraction, pictured at the 1952 Monmouth Fair. In the background is Charles Henry Robinson, first from the right, and John Wesley Robinson, third from the right. Wesley dedicated many years working in the pulling ring at the fair. (Photograph by Roland LaVallee, courtesy of the Monmouth Museum.)

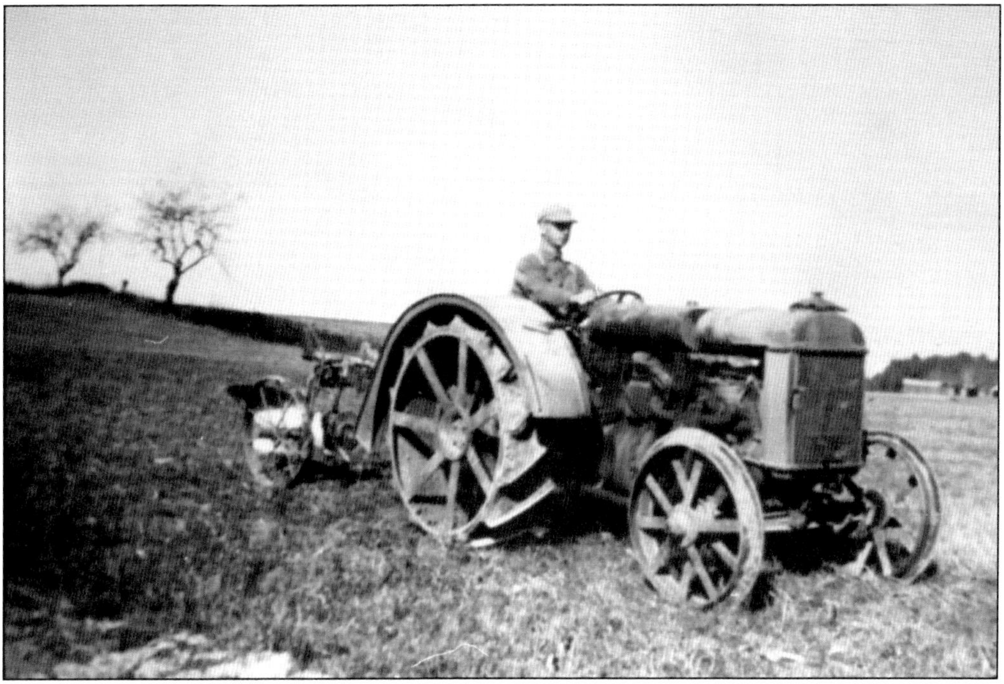

The first tractor in Monmouth was on the farm of Emil Peterson in South Monmouth. (Courtesy of the Monmouth Museum.)

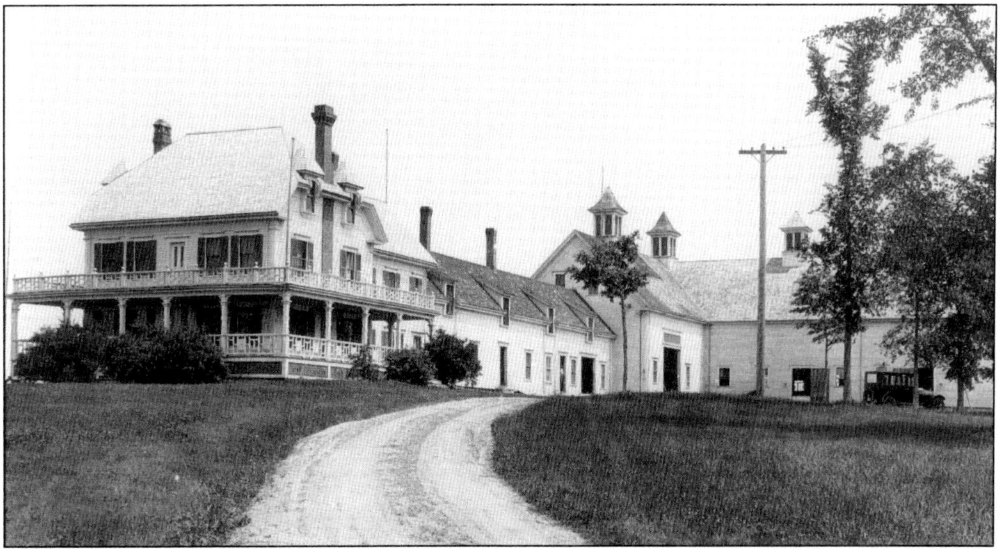

The Highmoor Farm is an experimental farm that is part of the University of Maine extension program. It was purchased by the State of Maine in 1909. (Courtesy of the author.)

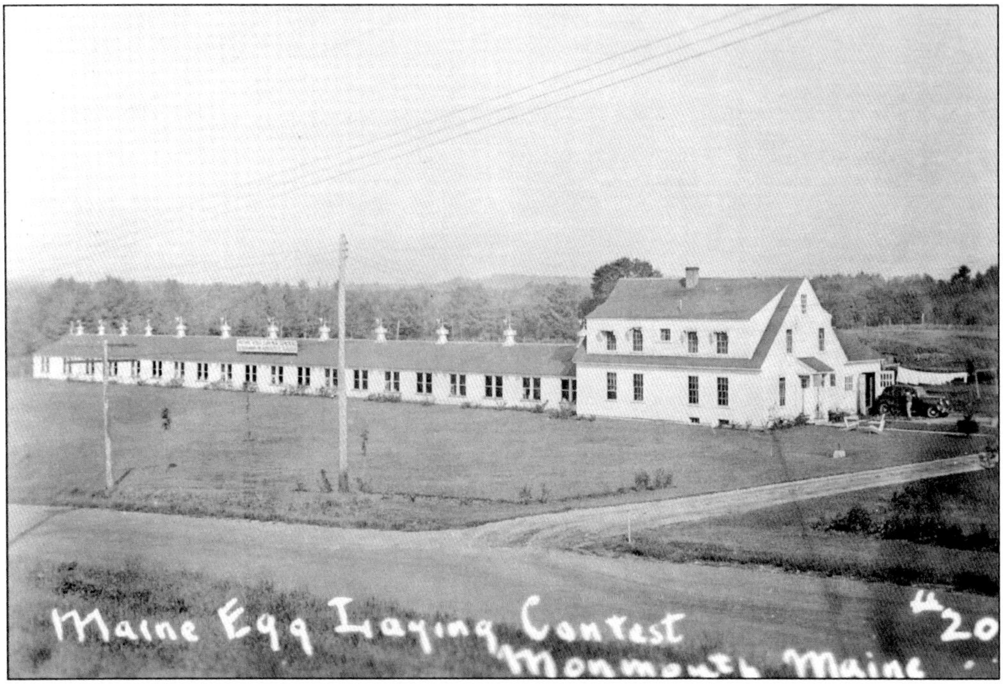

The Maine Department of Agriculture Maine Egg Laying Contest was on Route 202. It was southwest of the Highmoor Farm. The height of its operation was during the 1930s. (Courtesy of Stan DeOrsey.)

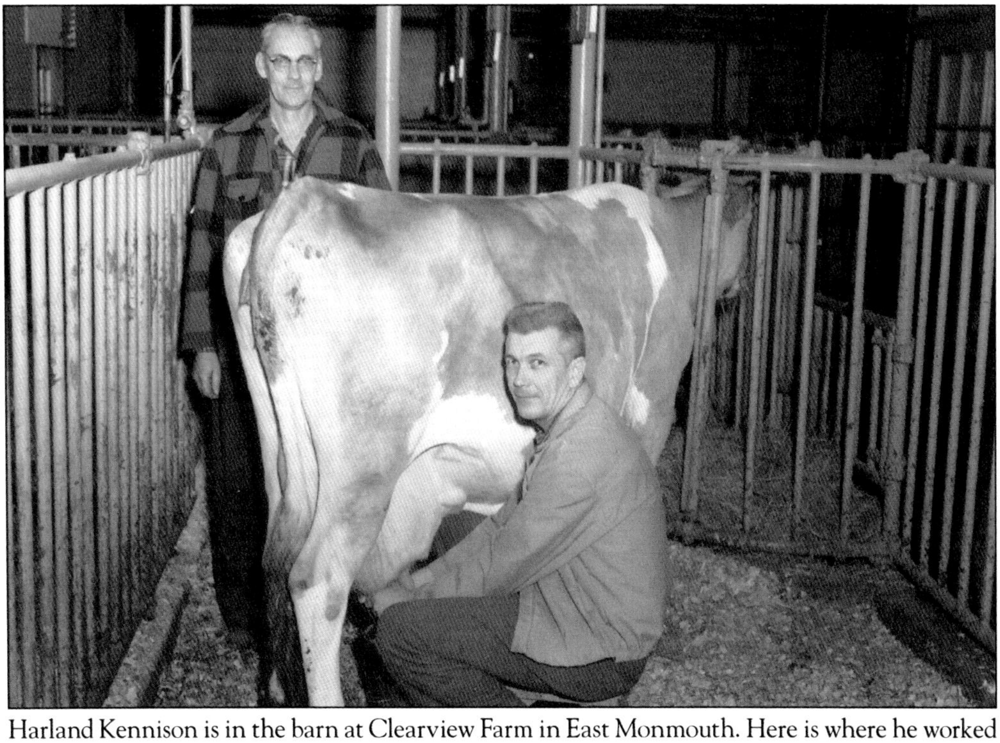

Harland Kennison is in the barn at Clearview Farm in East Monmouth. Here is where he worked with champion dairy animals. (Courtesy of Harland Kennison.)

Chick Orchards was producing 350,000 bushels of apples in the 1980s and held the title of having the largest orchards in the state at one time. This photograph of an unidentified man picking apples was taken in the early 1950s. (Photograph by Roland LaVallee, courtesy of the Monmouth Museum.)

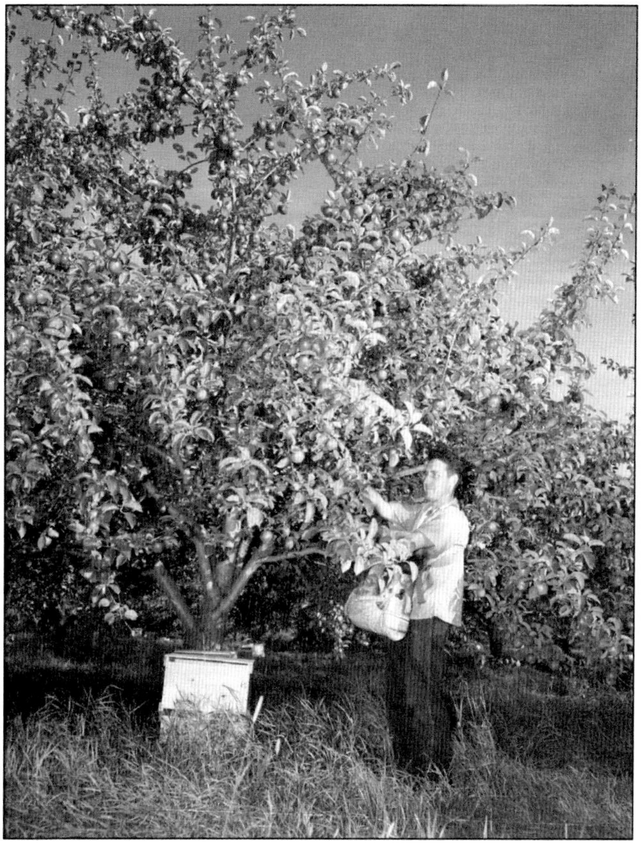

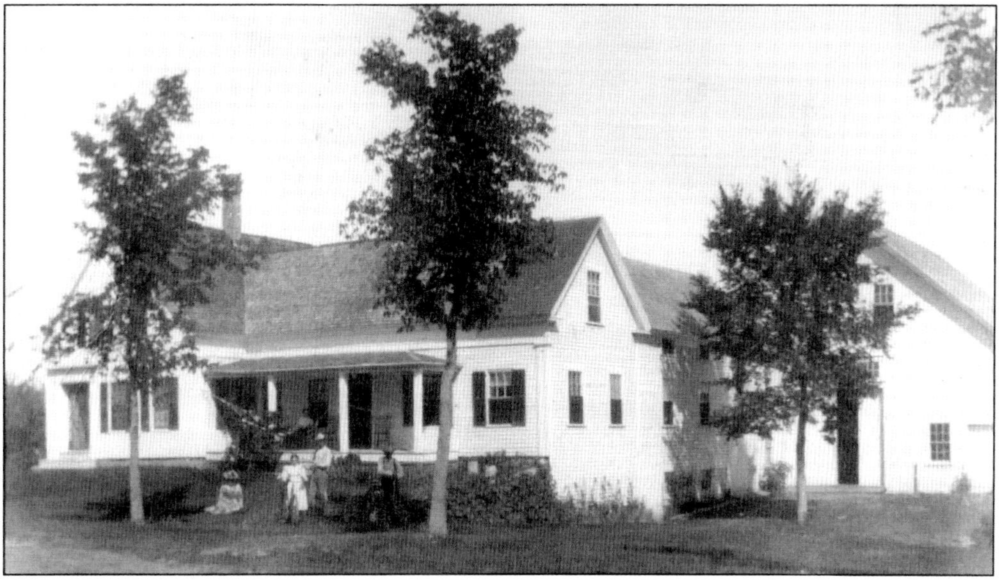

The Longfellow family owned this farm at the time the photograph was taken around 1900. Charles Henry Robinson ran a dairy business here for many years. The house, located north of Monmouth Center, still stands, but the barn is now gone. Note the gravestones leaning up against the house. (Courtesy of Mildred Robinson.)

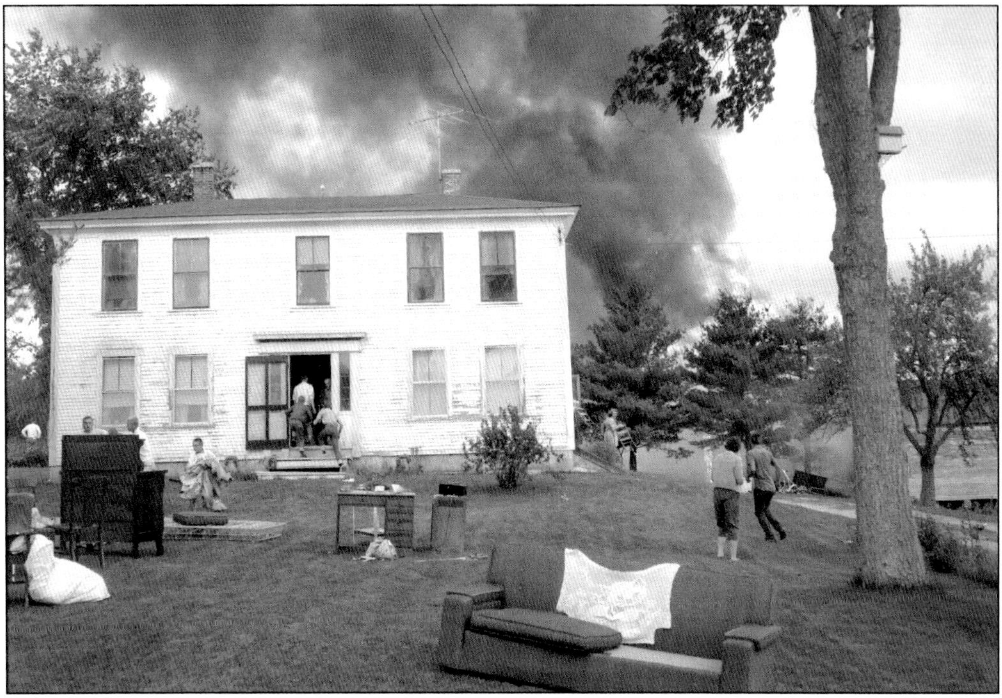

On July 6, 1962, flames came too close to the home of Clayton and Veneita Leonard on Norris Hill. The devastating fire burned the 80-foot-by-100-foot storage plant owned by Chick Orchards, Inc., to the ground. Roland LaVallee captured this dramatic photograph. Thankfully the Leonard Home was spared due to the fast firefighting of the Monmouth, Winthrop, Wayne, Leeds, and Greene volunteer fire departments. (Photograph by Roland LaVallee, courtesy of the Monmouth Museum.)

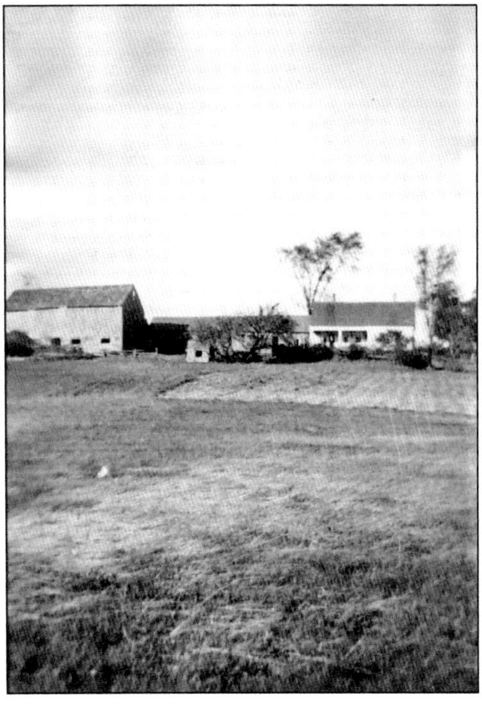

The James Cressey Farm was located on Cressey Road just before the railroad tracks. A fire destroyed it some time in the 1950s. An article that ran in the *Lewiston Saturday Journal* on May 18, 1907, reported that James Cressey, who moved to Monmouth around 1900, had 225 acres for his farm. In 1907, Cressey had only 20 acres of crops, and 10 of those acres were for potatoes. He had a herd of 35 cattle and 25 Chester white hogs. (Courtesy of Alberta Burnham.)

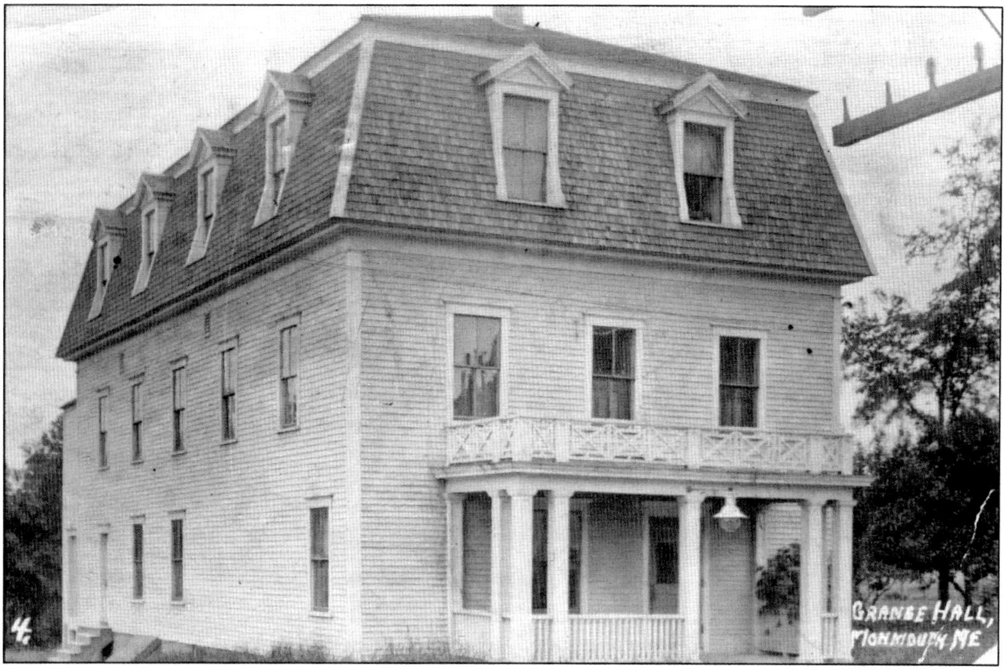

The Monmouth Grange was organized in 1874. A once-powerful organization for the agricultural community, the membership began to dwindle in the late 20th century. The Grange hall building was sold to the Theater of Monmouth in 1991. (Courtesy of the author.)

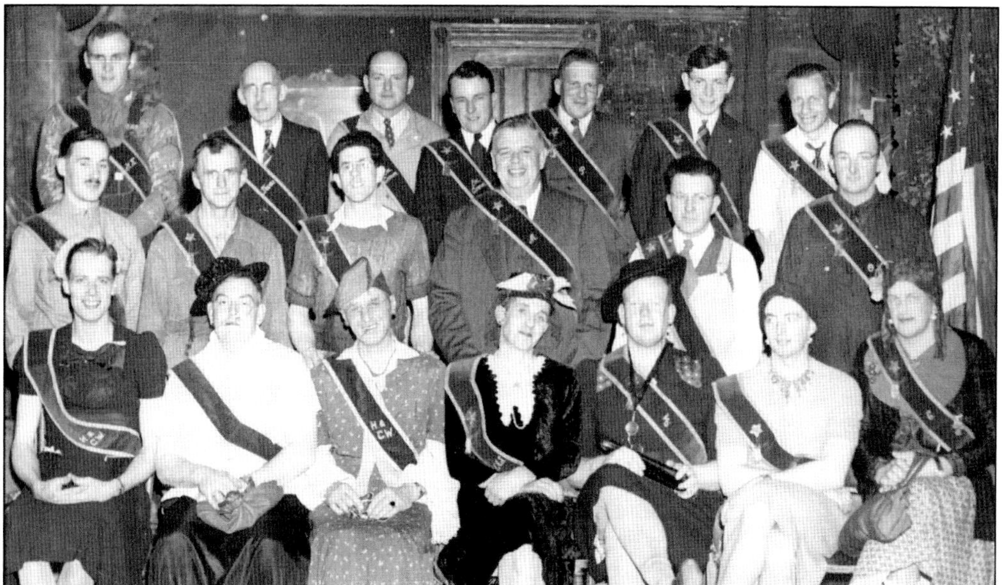

The photograph shows the officers of the Monmouth Grange No. 39 having a little fun. It is from the late 1940s or early 1950s. Those pictured are, from left to right, (first row) Robert Walker, Erlon Grover, Maynard Cole, Clarence Maxim, Earle Flanders, Clement Smith, and Robert Pettingill; (second row) Wesley Johnson, Merle Cooper, Thomas Peasley, Romie Marsans, Walter True, and Charles Henry Robinson; (third row) Gordon McKenney, Leon Dakin, Charles Walker, Edson Donnell, Ralph Glasnogg, Ernest Niles, and Eugene Tibbetts. (Courtesy of Marion Donnell.)

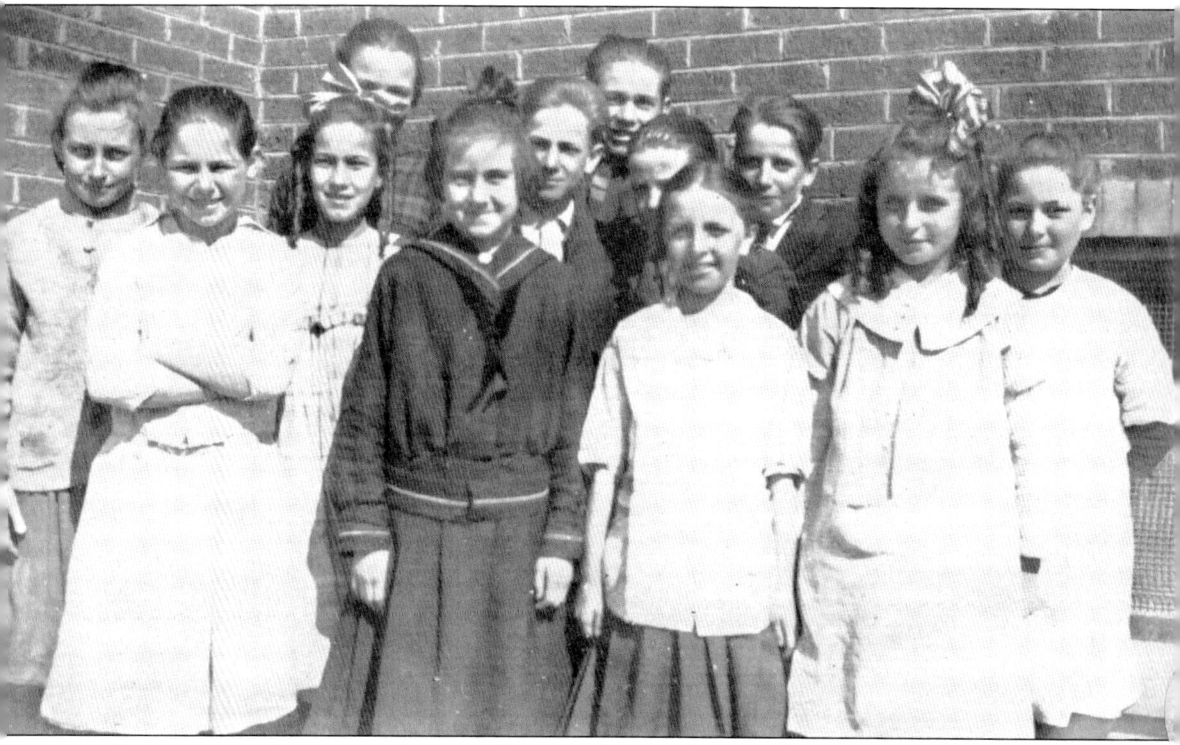

For the state-wide centennial project, Everett School sixth, seventh, and eighth graders produced an Everett community history in 1918 that included many descendants of pioneers of the 1830s and 1840s, family names that would reverberate through Lake Forest history: Margaret Sneddon, Anna Goergen, Mathilda Zieman, Rose Conway, Mary Carroll, Irvin Zieman, Joseph Carroll, Gene Seyl, Celia Klein, and Lloyd and Mary Yore. (Courtesy Lake County Discovery Museum & Archives.)

On the Cover: This 1927 Everett School picture shows the entire school. It was located on the south side of Everett Road west of Telegraph Road. (Courtesy Lake Forest-Lake Bluff Historical Society.)

IMAGES
of America

WEST LAKE FOREST

Susan L. Kelsey, Arthur H. Miller,
and Shirley M. Paddock

ARCADIA
PUBLISHING

ISBN 978-0-7385-9081-3

Published by Arcadia Publishing
Charleston, South Carolina

Printed in the United States of America

Library of Congress Control Number: 2012943306

For all general information, please contact Arcadia Publishing:
Telephone 843-853-2070
Fax 843-853-0044
E-mail sales@arcadiapublishing.com
For customer service and orders:
Toll-Free 1-888-313-2665

Visit us on the Internet at www.arcadiapublishing.com

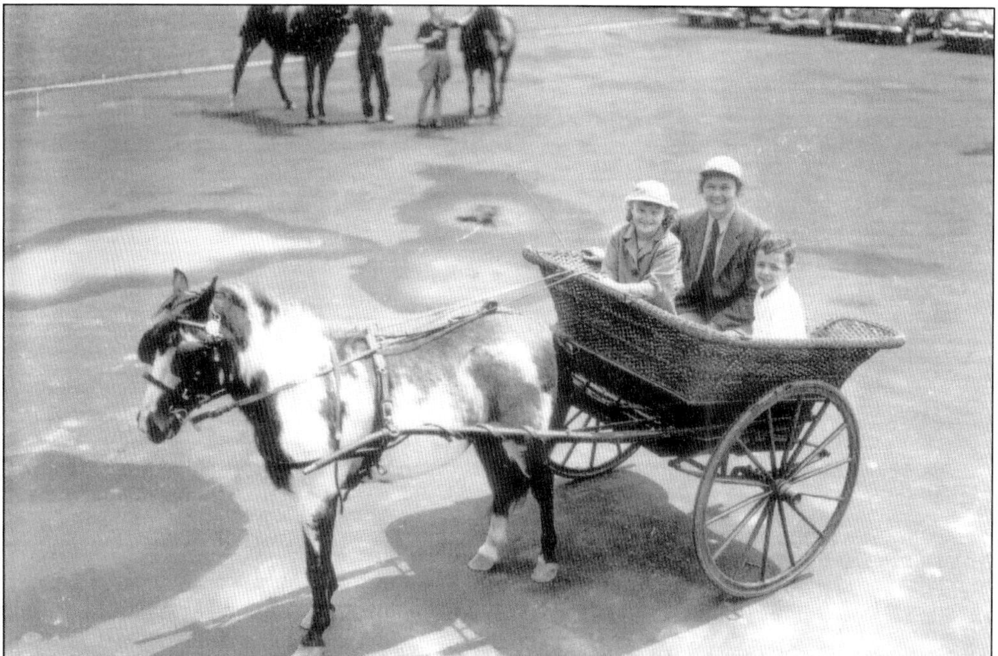

"I remember as a child attending the Everett School Country Fair in the 1940s. One year those of us from Lake Forest would perform acrobatics and the children from Everett would bring their pets," recounts Shirley McDonald Paddock. (Courtesy Shirley Paddock.)

Contents

Acknowledgments

Documenting Everett's history would not be possible without the contribution of so many families' personal collections. Lost history was pieced together with interviews, personal photographs, family connections, and the support of many individuals and organizations. Thank you to Janice Hack and Laurie Stein at the Lake Forest-Lake Bluff Historical Society for their continued support throughout the project. Readers should consider donating family collections to the historical society, stewards of Lake Forest history, and giving scans or allowing scans to be made. Also, thank you to Diana Dretske at the Lake County Discovery Museum and Archives for sharing photographs and the State of Illinois 1918 Centennial school histories. The Lake Forest College Special Collection and Archives provided images, research information, and authentication. Special thanks go to Rita MacAyeal at Lake Forest Academy for access to private collections.

Thanks are extended to Ronald Levitsky and Julie Morrison at West Deerfield Township for map research and support, Ambassador Robert D. Stuart and Mrs. Stuart for sharing their personal collection of Conway Farm and Topsfield Farm images, and to Jean McMasters Grost for contributing from a unique private collection of professional photographs taken by her parents, Ward and Mary McMasters, and for her ongoing stewardship of this resource. Of course, personal accounts from heritage family members were invaluable, including those of Chris Yore, Don Fiore, and Linda Biondi Conway. Special thanks are due to Bobbi Roe for scanning, Bob Musacchio for photographs, Dave Roe for research and support, and the authors' families generally.

Additional thanks go to David Mattoon, John Fincutter for all of his outreach to family members for historical facts, Paul Bergmann, the Stanley D. Anderson firm, James S. Anderson Surveyors, Robert Shaw, Joanne Miller, Karl and Barbara Nagel, Leanne and Rich Walther, Mayor James Cowhey, the City of Lake Forest, city manager Robert Kiely, Susan Banks, Leonard Gustafson, John Wawak, Phyllis Metcalf, Michael Caringello, Mike Rafferty, Mary Redmond Bertucci, Robert Shaw, Mike Ley, Charymane Kreuz, and Mary and Frank Robinson for their personal photographs.

A heartfelt thank-you to Lake Forest business owners and family businesses: Ed and Mike Pasquesi from Pasquesi Home and Gardens in Lake Forest and to John E. Cortesi from Sunset Foods in west Lake Forest. Thanks to local media for their support and promotion of our search for historical photographs, and special thanks to Linda Blaser with the *Lake Forester*, John Conatser with *Forest & Bluff* magazine, and Adrienne Fawcett with Gazebonews.com and Jim Powers with Patch.com.

As the authors were researching this book, as with many projects, a number of additional stories came up that were beyond the scope and dimensions of this initial project. Many of the founding families still have roots in Lake Forest, and learning about their heritage and family trees would be interesting and serve as additional resource points to document the history of the Everett area and Lake Forest. As the authors walked the trails, former roads, Corduroy Bridge, and Middlefork Branch of the Chicago River, they could not help but feel connected to the historic former Everett and northwestern areas of the city. Remnants of pioneers and where they lived and worked, their hardships, history, and stories are all around; readers have only to look for them here and also virtually, including on social media. Copies of the research material for this project will be deposited locally so that others in the future can enjoy and benefit from the fascinating stories.

Introduction

The west prairie side of modern Lake Forest, Illinois, was more thoroughly settled earlier by European immigrants and their descendants than was the east, forested and ravine-crossed bluff-top terrain facing the lake. The broad prairie was perfect farming country, and it attracted a community of recent immigrants from Ireland in 1836. As soon as the Chicago treaty of 1833 with the Native Americans (here Potawatomis) removed the tribesmen, pioneer settlement began. This book is the first to focus exclusively on the history of this community and the adjacent lands west of the wooded and ravine-punctuated lakefront town. (This west side now also is part of Lake Forest.)

Irish workers, attracted to Chicago by the ambitious public-works project to dig a canal from the Chicago River to the Illinois River system, the Illinois and Michigan Canal, streamed into the mid-1830s job-rich construction environment at Chicago and then went looking for land nearby. A significant, mostly Roman Catholic, Irish settlement grew up around the present-day intersection of Waukegan and Everett Roads as early as 1836. The small settlement was known as Meehan's Settlement, Corduroy, Irish Settlement, Lancasterville, and then Everett before being annexed by the City of Lake Forest in 1926. This signaled the transition from farm and later estate/foxhunt territory to early suburban development, soon to follow the North Shore Line's west line, completed in 1927, parallel to what now is Route 41, and spreading west.

The most distinctive feature dividing east and west is geographic character, marked by the continental divide today at Green Bay Road separating the prairie to the west from the east side bluffs above the lake. Water on the east side flows to Lake Michigan, into the St. Lawrence River system, and the Atlantic. Since 1900, water on the west side has flowed south into the Illinois River, the Mississippi, and the Gulf of Mexico. Lake Forest's terrain is made up of sandbars formed about 13,000 years ago by an ancient glacial lake and its various ridges as it receded to today's lakefront line, guarded by the 1980s beach and many private landowners' efforts.

The big ridge is at Green Bay Road, but other sandbars are at Ahwahnee Road/Ridge Road, west of Waukegan Road, and at Lake Forest Academy and Estate Lane farther south and west. East, the rainwater runs east to the lake, descending rapidly to the shore in ever-deeper ravines, with 10 cuts of over 80 feet through the bluff in town. These tablelands originally were heavily wooded. West, the water runs south in the sloughs between the ridges: the Skokie River (east branch of the Chicago River), the former creek bed at Route 41, and the Middlefork Branch of the Chicago River. This west land was prairie grasses sloping into marshland in the sloughs, shelter for birds and animals. So, the natural geographic dividing point is between these distinctive character traits.

Of course, other factors also enter into defining this difference between east and west. Most of the land east of Waukegan Road, north of Route 60, east of the Skokie on the south to Old Elm, and south of Middlefork Road on the north, plus the Knollwood and Lasker Estate areas, was developed with housing from the 1920s to the 1980s. This "middle kingdom" was supplemented by a few scattered neighborhoods, more former estates. In general, the mid-century "plan" was the development of early-20th-century estates as parcels—with roads and even private drives into but not across these communities: Winwood off Waukegan and King Muir off Deerpath, for example. Lots west, too, were larger from the 1920s and influenced by the Lake Forest Plan Commission, established in 1929, and its first chair, the eminent planner of cities, resident Edward H. Bennett, who also laid out the Knollwood Club in the natural park manner of east Lake Forest.

The estate era's foxhunting attraction, west of established Lake Forest and Onwentsia for the first quarter of the last century, contributed to the sense of unity of Lake Forest with the countryside to the west. Thus, only at Lake Forest does the lakefront suburb reach west of the 1930s Route 41 and, in recent years, to the Illinois tri-state tollway Interstate 94. South and north there are separate communities along Waukegan Road. But Lake Forest is unique in uniting these two distinct terrains into one community now for almost a century.

Most of the historical interest in Lake Forest to date has been with the east and the estate areas as they spread west and has included, but not focused on, the earlier population of what is now west Lake Forest, centered on the former Everett area to the southwest. Now, as then, this area has its own commercial center, named Settler's Square after its redevelopment with a Tax Increment Financing District in the 1990s. This book attempts to correct this imbalance, and to turn attention to the distinctive, even fascinating, past of this sunset side of Lake Forest and the epic of 175 years of unusual development there.

One

Early Pioneers and Everett-area Homesteaders

The 1833 treaty with Potawatomi and other Native American tribes gave title to land in Lake County to the United States, opening this territory to European immigrant and European-American settlement in 1836. One of the first settlers on record in Deerfield Township, today including the southern section of west Lake Forest, was Michael Meehan. Born in County Meath, Ireland, in 1808, he married Bridget Monahan in 1830 and settled in Lake County in 1835, presumably ahead of treaty permissions. Another early settler was Michael Yore, arriving in Lake Forest in 1836. He traveled from Ireland by way of the Erie Canal and then the Great Lakes. Michael Yore would travel to Chicago four times a week to sell wood, butter, and eggs. The Yore house became a stagecoach stop, located at present-day Old Mill and Telegraph Roads.

The I&M Canal was being built in 1836 and, according to the Canal Corridor Association, faced a shortage of workers. By 1837, a national financial panic stalled progress for a century. Irish, German, Swedish, and other immigrants dug the canal by hand, and finally, it was finished in 1848. The canal and Irish immigrants impacted the growth of Chicago and suburban communities like Lake Forest, providing rich farmland on which immigrants could settle their families and pursue the American Dream.

By 1846, the first mail stop was called Emmet Post Office and was located at present-day Everett and Waukegan Roads. From 1848 to 1855, the California Gold Rush was a national focus, and many of the Everett area men went out to California seeking riches. Three Steele boys—with a Steele farmhouse still on Waukegan Road north of Middlefork Drive—returned in 1849 with $100,000 and then went again. Anthony Melody went in 1850 and sent back $7,000. Other men who went included John Burns, Jimmie Connell, Lawrence Dorsey, M. Meehan, James O'Connor, Jim Redmond, Martin Sullivan, and John and Pete Yore.

In 1860, the *Lady Elgin* sank in Lake Michigan several miles out from Winnetka, its wreck discovered in 1989. Many of the Everett-area residents went east to rescue people from the ship near Highwood (then Port Clinton) but found only bodies, some of which were then buried in St. Patrick cemetery. The gravestones are located on the northwest corner of this venerable burial ground.

In 1872, a railroad track was put through from Chicago to Milwaukee, the Gilded Age Chicago, Milwaukee & St. Paul line of William Rockefeller and others. Its first station was in the area of the James Lancaster house at Everett Road until 1886, when the depot was built. The station location was called Lancaster, or Lancaster Station, for several years until a post office was located in Everett. Sources state that Tom Doyle named the town Everett after the son of the Chicago, Milwaukee & St. Paul general ticket agent, Marsh Everett.

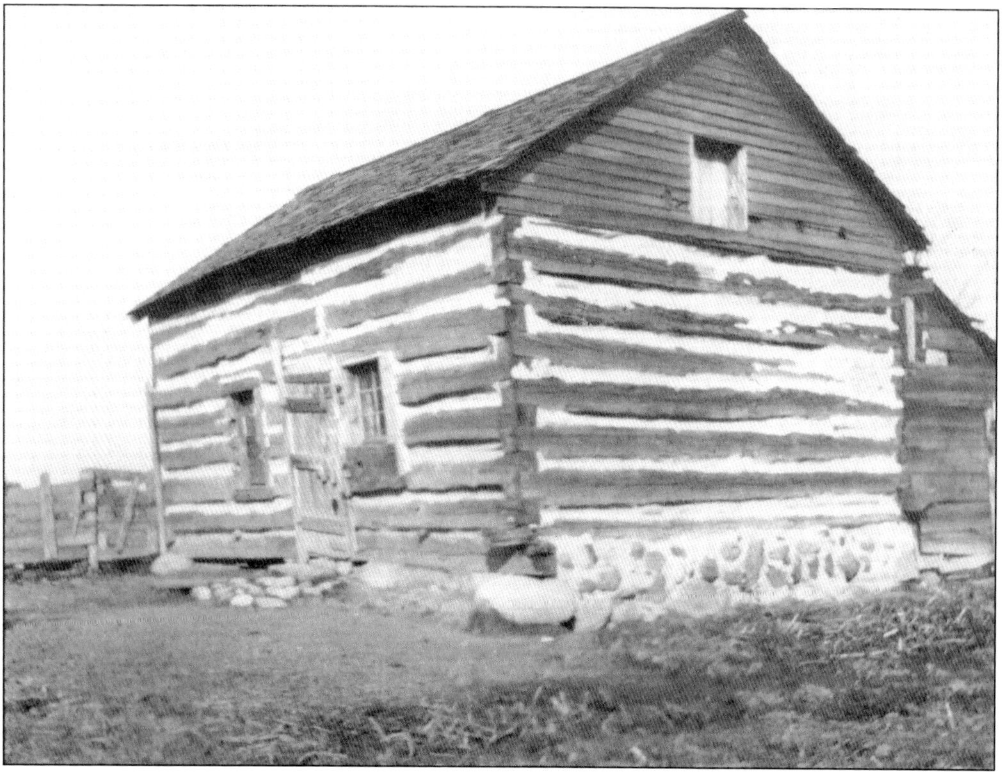

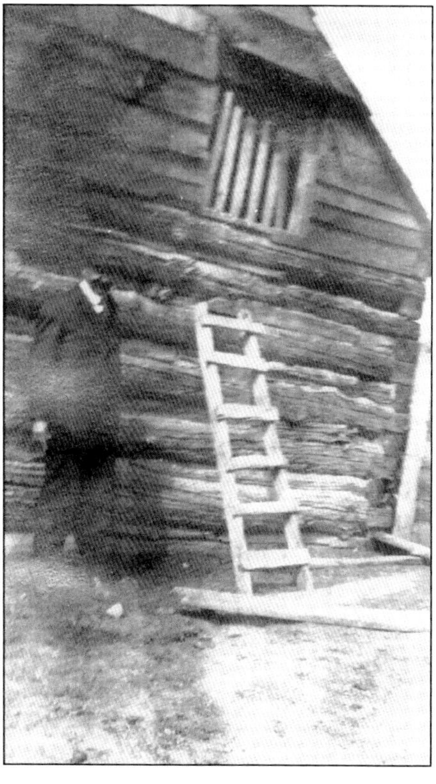

As early as 1835, Michael Meehan (1808–1892) built one of the first homesteads—similar to the McIntyre log house pictured here—on the west side of current Lake Forest, near Telegraph Road. Meehan gave one of the earliest Irish place names to the area: Meehan's Settlement, named for himself and his wife Bridget (née Monahan), from County Meath, Ireland. (Courtesy Lake County Discovery Museum and Archives.)

Shown in this 1918 image is Mike O'Boyle, an Everett resident, next to his log house, also known as the McIntyre Place. (Courtesy Lake County Discovery Museum and Archives.)

John Burns, one of the early residents of Everett in 1873, had a farm located at the present-day northeast corner of Everett and Waukegan Roads. Fortunately, first-hand accounts of life in this community were preserved by Everett School children, recording and documenting them for the 1918 Illinois centennial. (Courtesy Lake County Discovery Museum and Archives.)

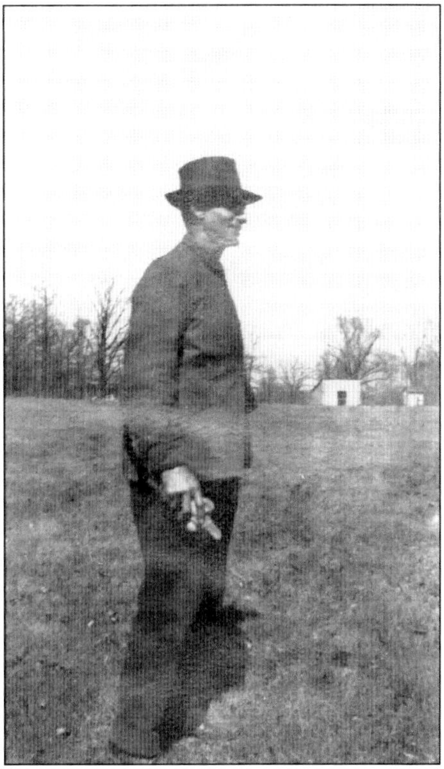

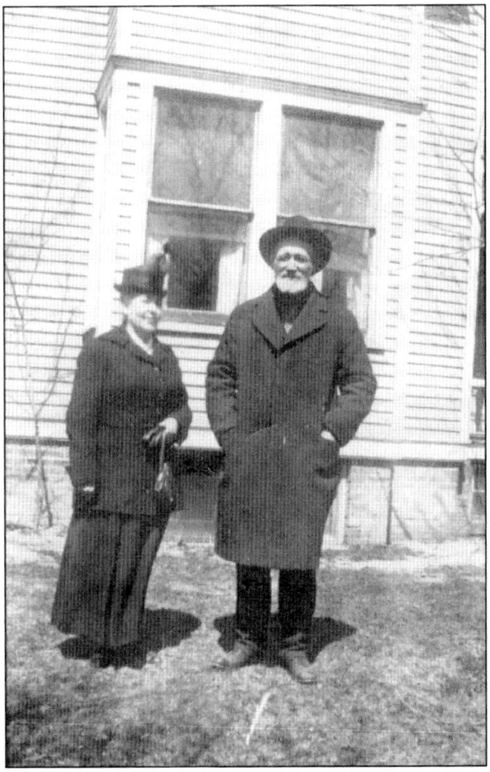

Pictured are Mr. and Mrs. Dennis E. Gibbons in 1918. According to the Illinois centennial school history, in the *1904–1905 Illinois Blue Book*, Gibbons represented the district in the general assembly as a Democrat. His service spanned the 44th and 45th general assemblies. He also served as a local fire marshal. Mrs. Gibbons was the daughter of Mrs. John Conway and the granddaughter of Patrick Melody. (Courtesy Lake County Discovery Museum and Archives.)

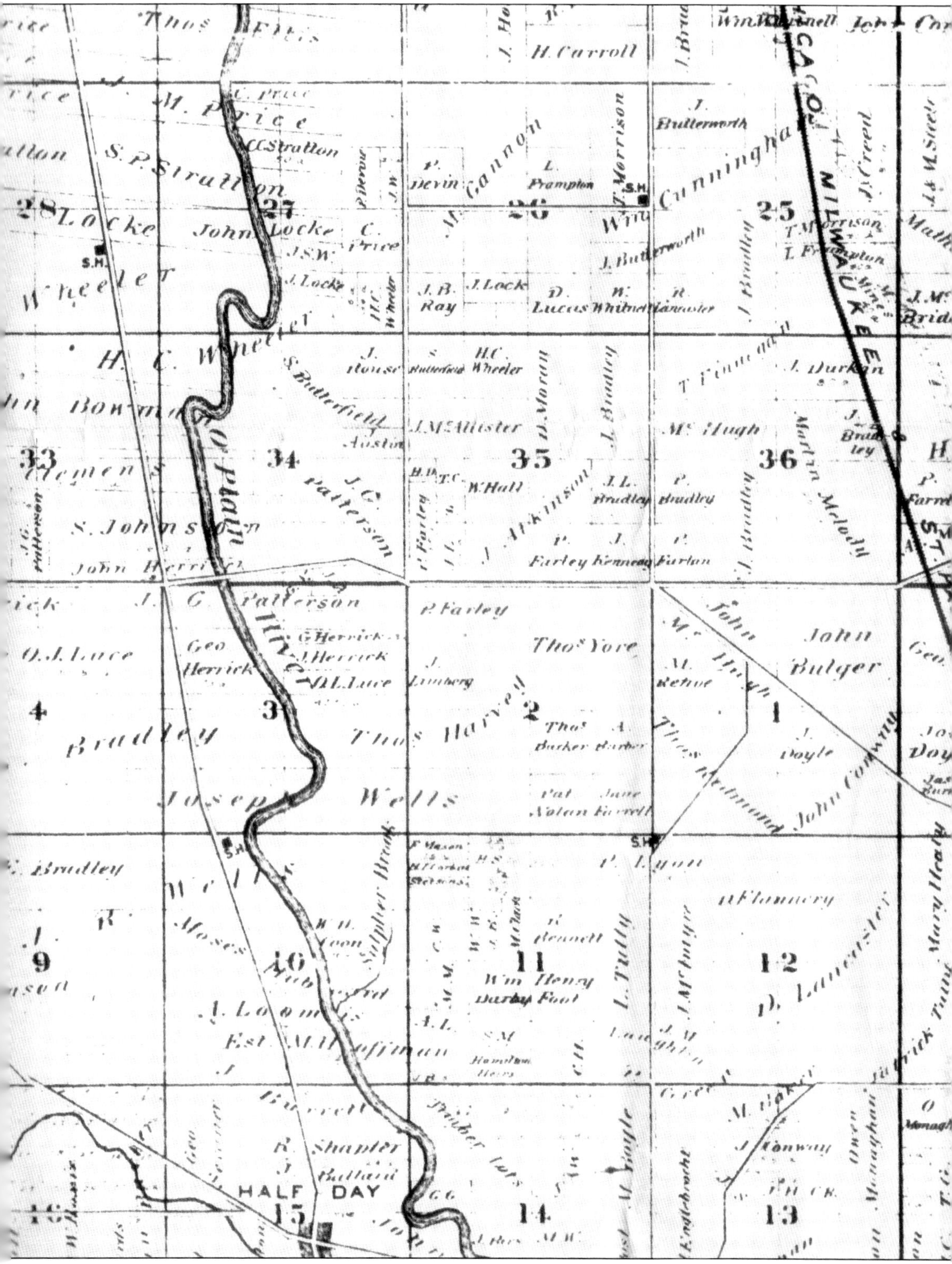

H. Carroll
M. Price
S. P. Stratton
C. Stratton
John Locke
Locke
Wheeler
H. C. Wheeler
Bowman
Clemens
S. Johnson
John Herrick
J. G. Patterson
O. J. Luce
Geo Herrick
G. Herrick
J. Herrick
M. L. Luce
Bradley
Joseph Wells
Thos Harvey
Wells
Moses Hubbard
A. Loomis
Est. M. Hoffman
R. Shapter
J. Ballard
HALF DAY
Des Plaines River
Sulpher Brook
Farley
P. Farley
Thos Yore
J. Limberg
Thos Barker
A. Barker
Pat Nolan
Jane Farrell
J. M. Allister
Austin
W. Hall
J. Atkinson
Patterson
J. Rouse
Butterfield
H. C. Wheeler
J. B. Ray
J. Lock
D. Lucas
W. Whitney
R. Lancaster
P. Devin
L. Frampton
McGannon
T. Morrison
J. Butterworth
Wm Cunningham
J. Bradley
T. Finnegan
McHugh
J. L. Bradley
P. Bradley
P. Farley
J. Kennedy
P. Farlan
D. Moran
J. Durkin
Martin Melody
J. Creed
T. Morrison
I. Frampton
John McHugh
John Bulger
M. Kehoe
Thos Redmond
John Conway
J. Doyle
P. Lyon
M. Flannery
D. Lancaster
J. McIntyre
L. Tully
Wm Henry
Darby Foot
J. Kennell
Patrick Tully
M. Baker
J. Conway
Owen Monaghan
Martin Healy
Englebrecht
CHICAGO MILWAUKEE ST. P.
S.H.
28
27
26
25
33
34
35
36
4
3
2
1
9
10
11
12
16
15
14
13

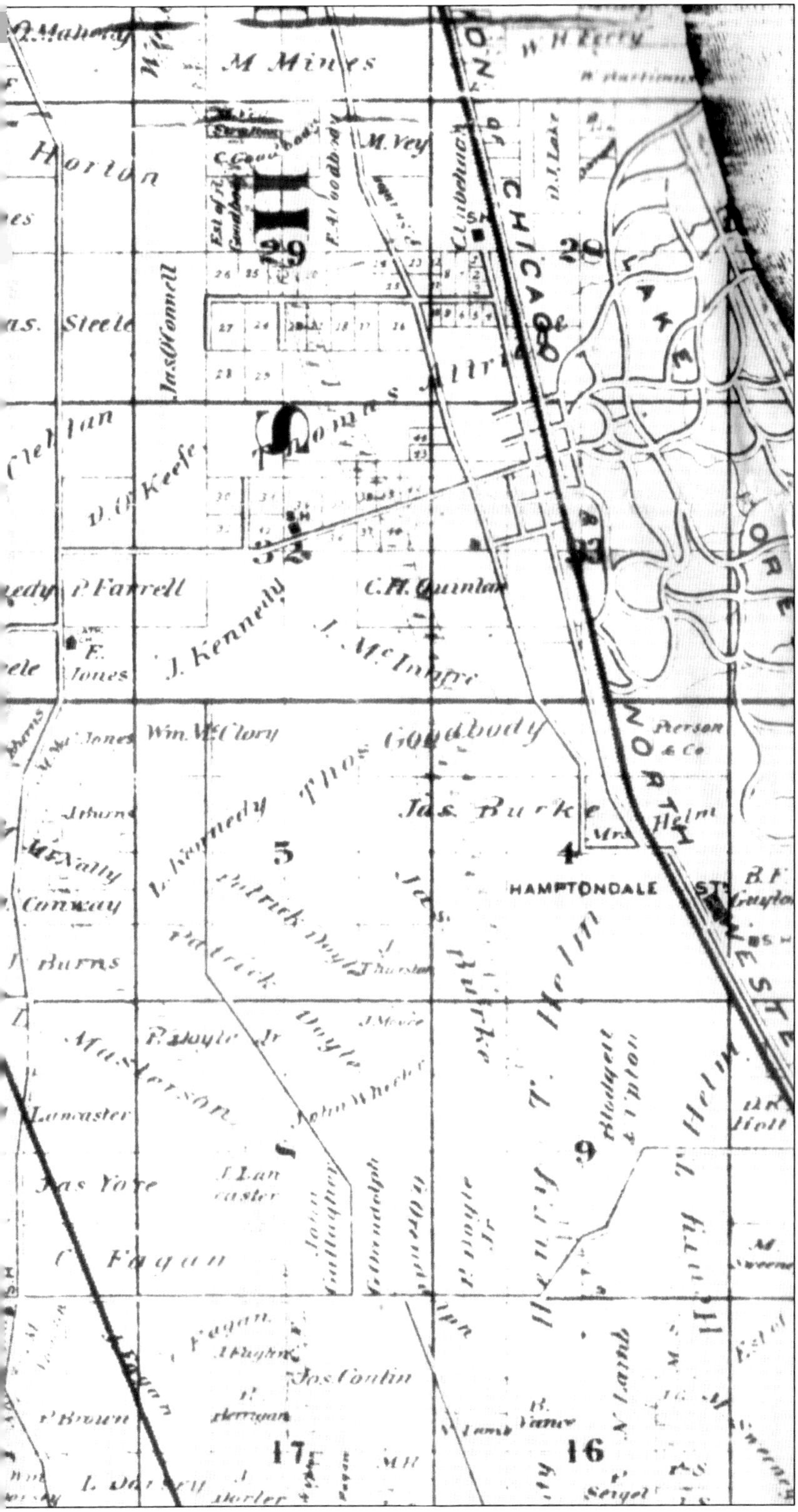

This 1873 map shows Lancaster Station/Everett-area property. The main north-south road through Everett was "Corduroy Road," now Waukegan Road. Also seen are Conway and Telegraph Roads, still in existence today. According to West Deerfield Township office records, property owners were required to perform road duty on a regular basis. Area farmers would often walk to Chicago or Waukegan to sell their farm goods. Records indicate a walk to Waukegan and back could be done in one day. (Courtesy Shirley M. Paddock.)

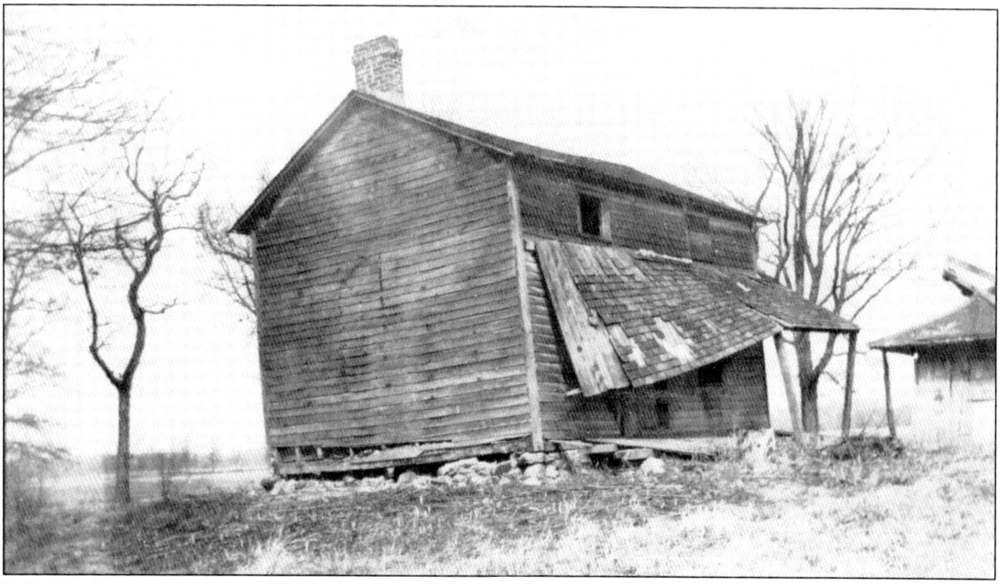

Life on the prairie was difficult. Pictured is Patrick Greene's house in Everett, which, by 1918, had already been standing for 50 years. The children's school history stories tell of Mrs. Yore watching for blackbirds from daylight to dark after the corn began to sprout, for three weeks until the corn was so big the birds couldn't pick it off. (Courtesy Lake County Discovery Museum and Archives.)

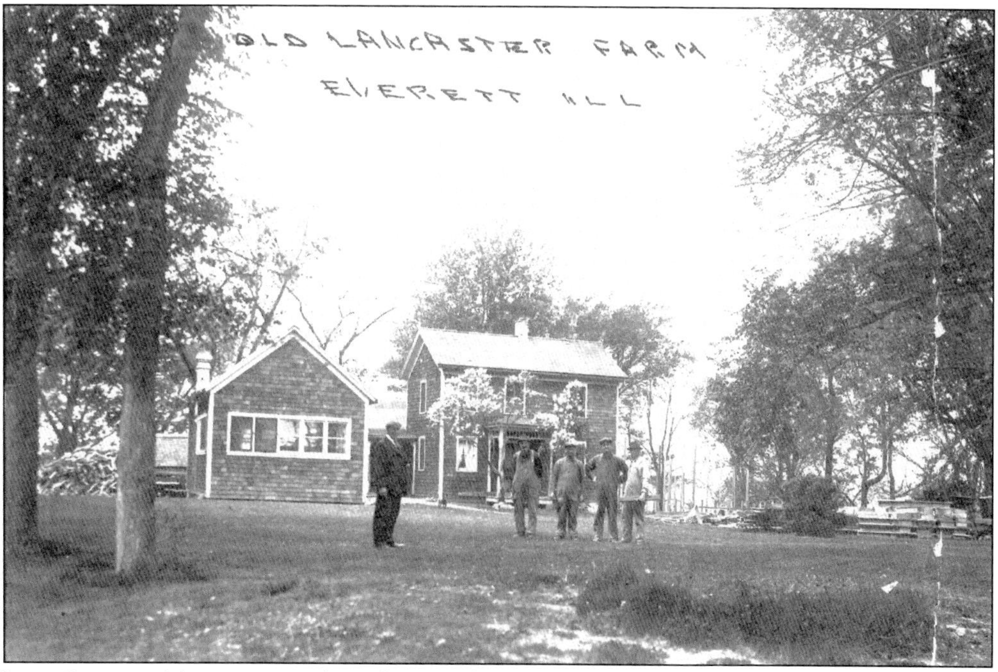

James Lancaster's house was used as a depot and stopping place until 1886, according to the *Chicago Daily News*. In 1905, Louis F. Swift purchased the Lancaster Farm on Everett Road (section 12 in the 1873 map on pages 12–13) as part of his Westleigh Farm, also known as the Everett Stock Farm. This enterprise had cattle, pigs, chickens and—according to the 1918 school account—deer. (Courtesy Lake Forest-Lake Bluff Historical Society.)

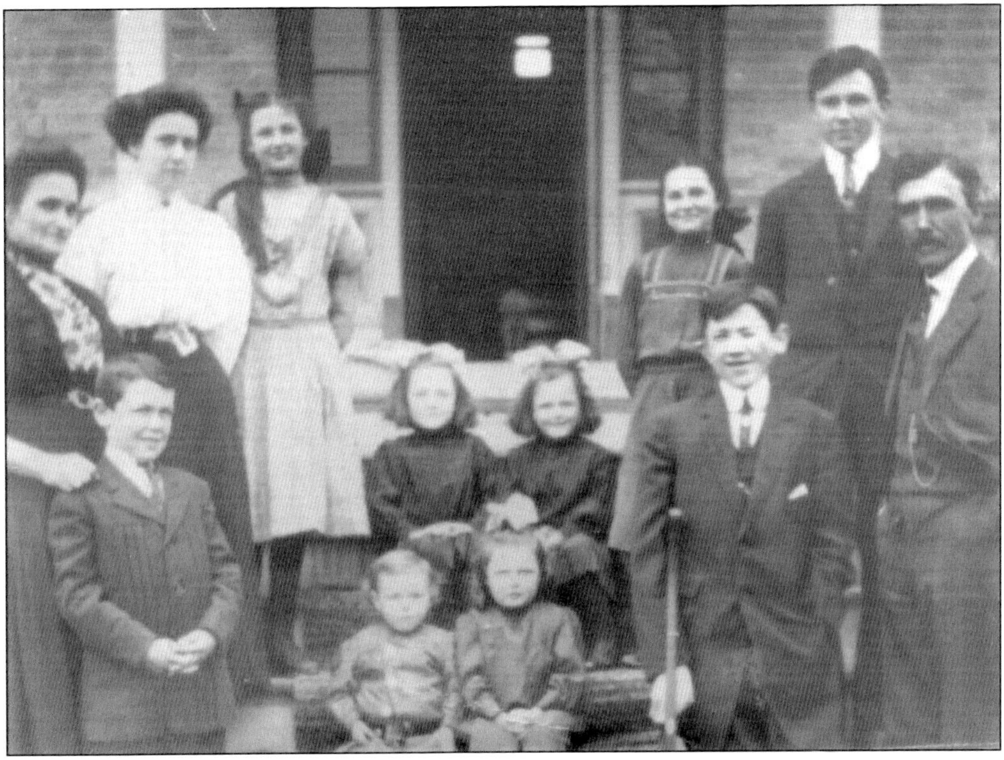

Mary (far left) and Myle Conway Jr. (far right), are pictured here with 10 of their 13 children. Linda Biondi, whose mother was a Conway, fondly remembers the old Conway house. (Courtesy Linda Biondi Conway.)

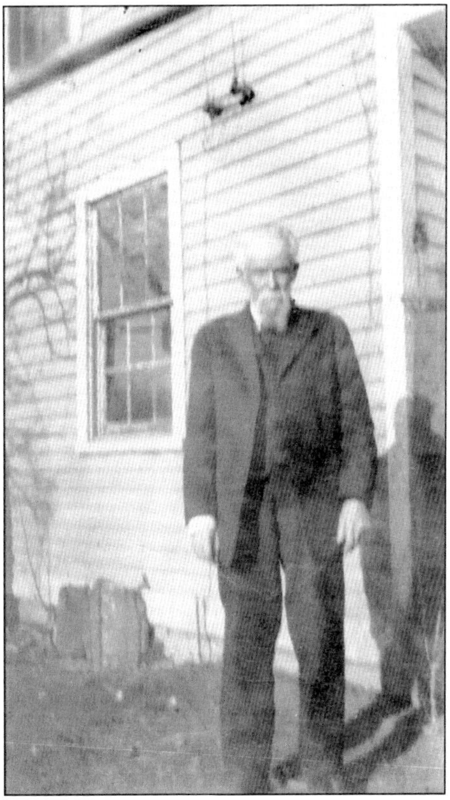

According to Chris Yore, his ancestor Michael Yore, pictured here in 1918 in his 90s, built a log cabin in 1841 near the current location of Telegraph and Old Mill Roads. Michael Yore donated the land for a church and cemetery, presently located on Telegraph Road. According to Halsey's 1912 *History of Lake County*, in 1854, Yore and Melody were the only farmers who had horses and would often help neighbors clear their fields. (Courtesy Lake County Discovery Museum and Archives.)

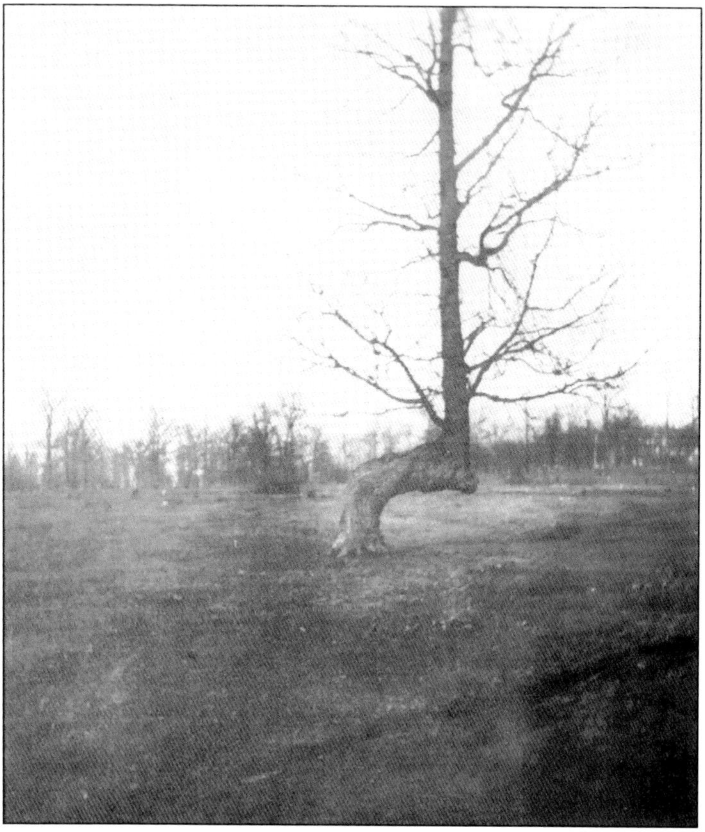

Native Americans populated this region into the 1830s. Potawatomi, Chippewa, and Ottawa peoples navigated through a network of trails by marking them with road signs known as "trail trees," typically oak or elms. Waterways such as Lake Michigan and the Des Plaines River were also used as thoroughfares. This trail tree is pictured in the early 1900s along Waukegan Road, west of North Chicago. (Photograph by Lake County historian Bess Bower Dunn; courtesy Lake County Discovery Museum and Archives.)

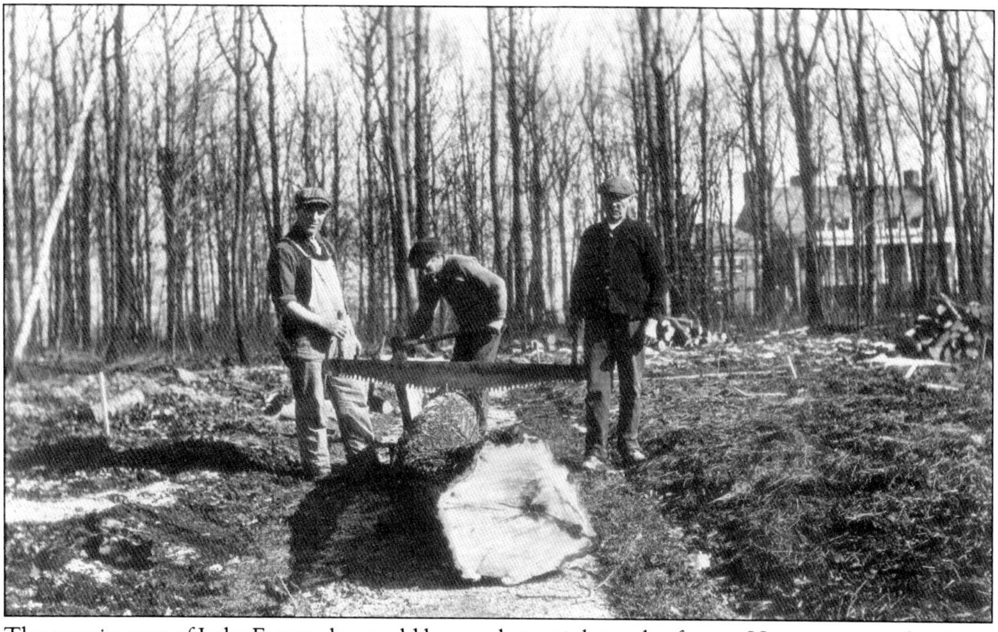

The terrain west of Lake Forest also could have substantial stands of trees. Here, men are clearing a field near Ridge Road. The Charles G. King estate house, built in 1905, is visible in the background. (Courtesy Leonard Gustafson.)

Mrs. Atkinson, age 71, is pictured here with her granddaughters. According to the 1918 school history, Mrs. Atkinson was a daughter of the Conway family. Stories from Mrs. Atkinson's youth include one about traveling by sleigh to attend a dance as far away as Buffalo Grove, eight miles from Everett. (Courtesy Lake County Discovery Museum and Archives.)

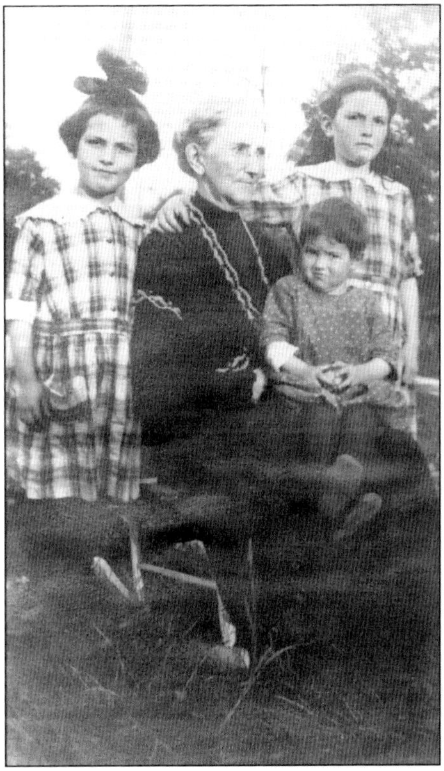

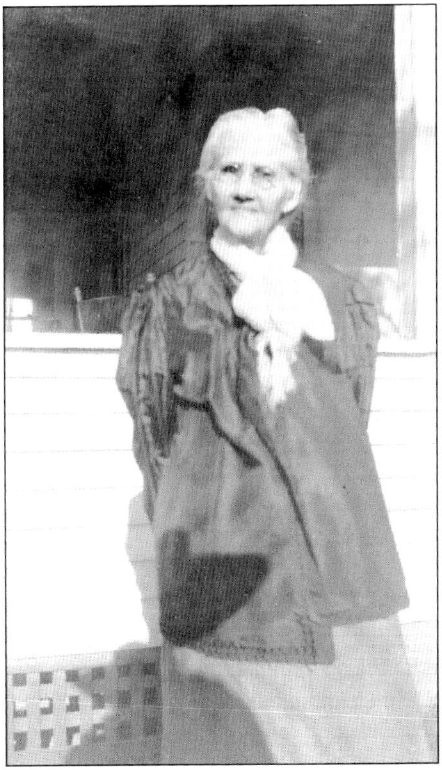

Theresa Devin Redmond was born in the Meehan Settlement on July 15, 1838. For this photograph, taken in 1918 by Everett School students, she may have put the blouse and scarf on over her day dress to look more presentable. The students wrote: "It is a pleasure to visit Mrs. Redmond. She is so lovable, active, and quick witted, a laugh as ringing as a girl's, and a keen sympathetic interest in her friends and neighbors." (Courtesy Lake County Discovery Museum and Archives.)

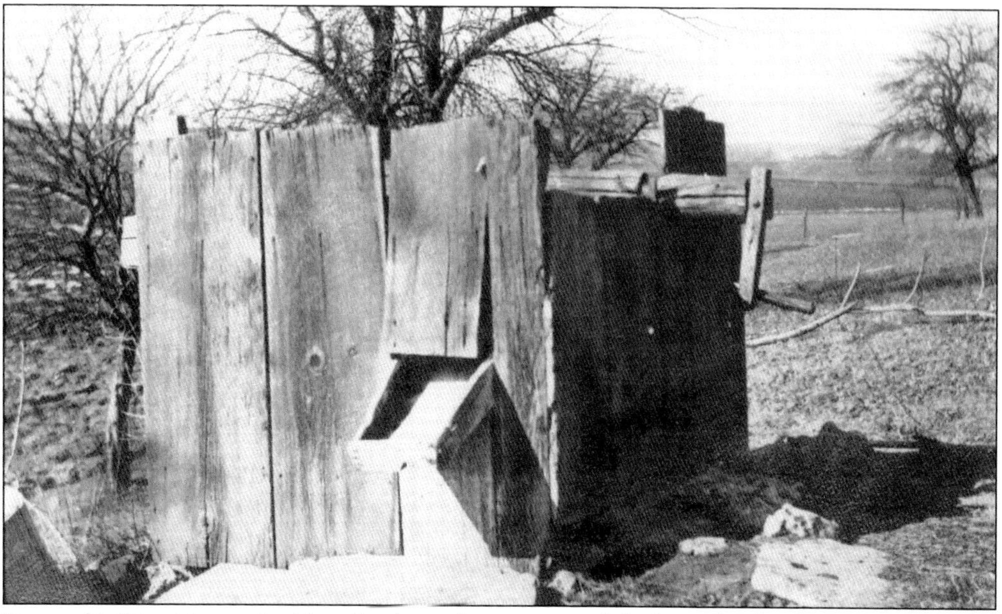

Pictured is Rita Conway's old well, where the water was lifted in a bucket by a windlass. The photograph shows the landscape as well: relatively flat, sparsely wooded, and with rich prairie soil for farming. The terrain east of the Skokie River, east of Route 41 today, to Lake Michigan was thick with woods and less desirable, requiring clearing in order to grow crops. (Courtesy Lake County Discovery Museum and Archives.)

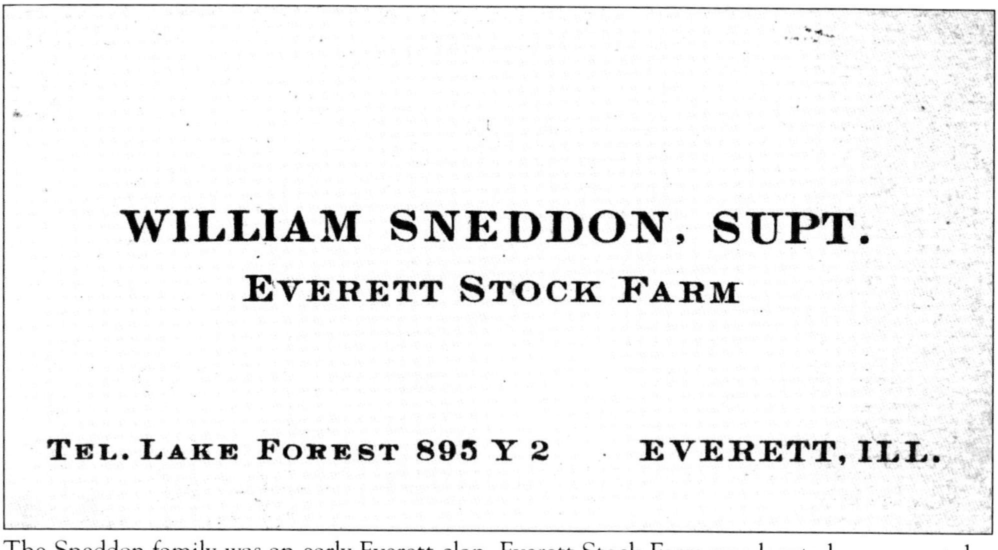

The Sneddon family was an early Everett clan. Everett Stock Farm was located on present-day Everett Road, west of Waukegan. In the 1918 school history, Bessie Sneddon recalls the 1849 Gold Rush and Everett boys who had traveled to California. Some fought Native Americans, some lost their lives traveling around South America, and some returned to Everett. (Courtesy Lake Forest-Lake Buff Historical Society.)

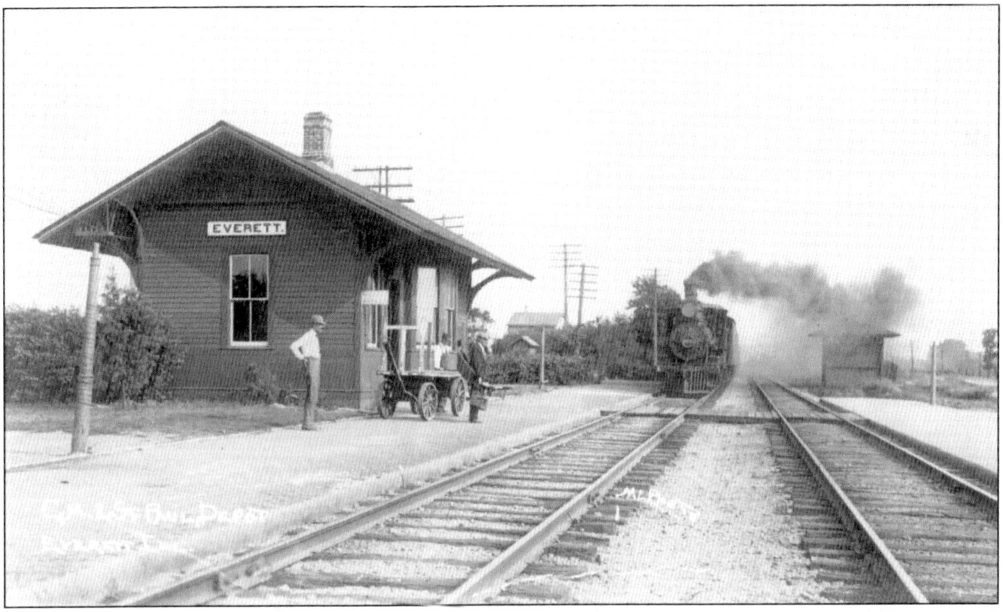

The original 1886 depot was located on the corner of the current intersection of Everett and Waukegan Roads on what is now the Lake Forest Fire Station parking lot. Driving south today on Telegraph Road, some early 20th century homes on the east side can be seen, backing up to the train tracks. These families served the growing estate community west of Lake Forest. The telegraph lines in the postcard ran along the west side of Waukegan Road. (Courtesy Lake Forest-Lake Bluff Historical Society.)

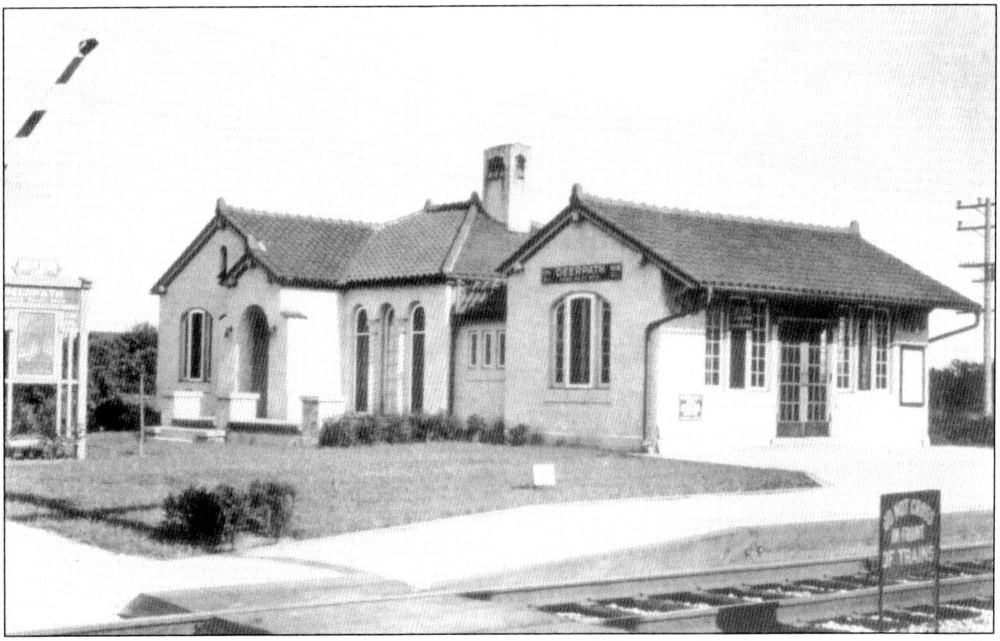

Pictured is the station and track for the west line of the North Shore Line (1926–1963), originally located at the underpass of Deerpath and present-day Route 41. The remains of the old concrete steps heading up to the site of the old station house can also be seen. (Courtesy Jean Grost McMasters.)

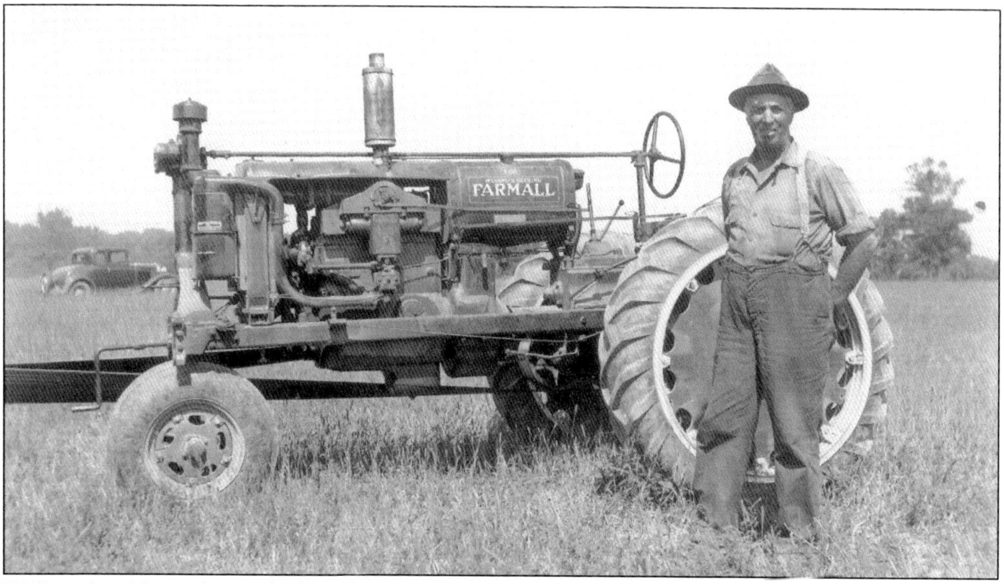

Willam Sneddon, who worked on the Everett Stock Farm, is seen standing in front of a McCormick Deering Farmall tractor sometime in the second quarter of the 20th century. (Courtesy Lake Forest-Lake Bluff Historical Society.)

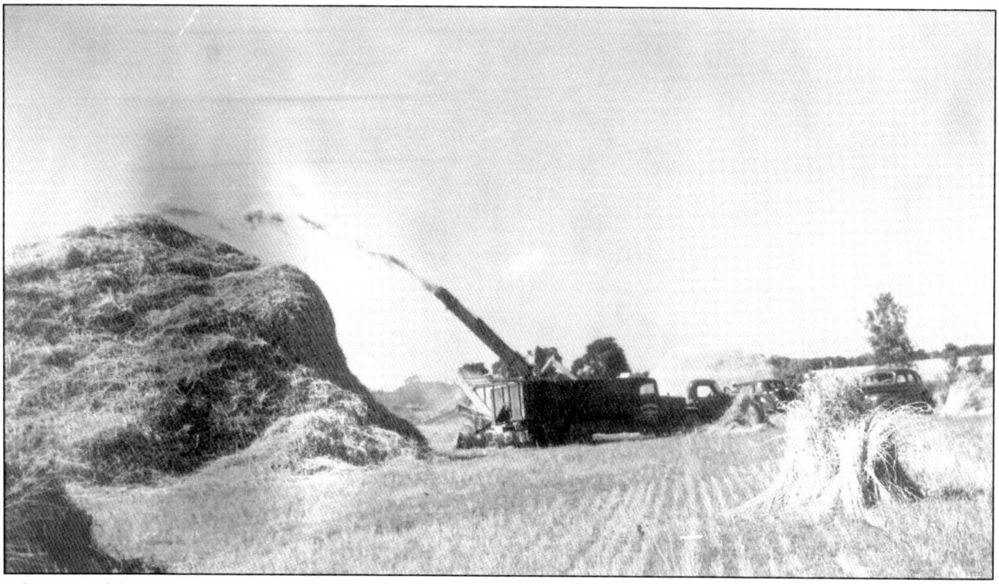

This Sneddon family picture shows the hay-harvesting season in Everett. (Courtesy Lake Forest-Lake Bluff Historical Society.)

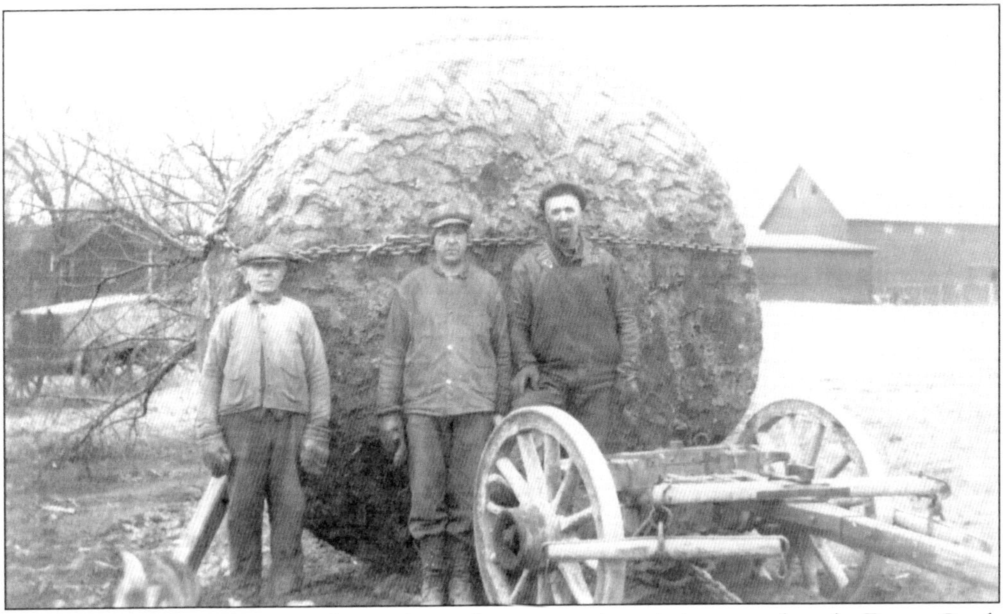

Three men are shown here standing in front of an uprooted tree being moved on the Everett Stock Farm. Trees on this scale were transferred to the 400-acre Lasker estate in the mid-1920s. Estate development in the area opened up new sources of income for the old farm families a century after the first settlement. (Courtesy Lake Forest-Lake Bluff Historical Society.)

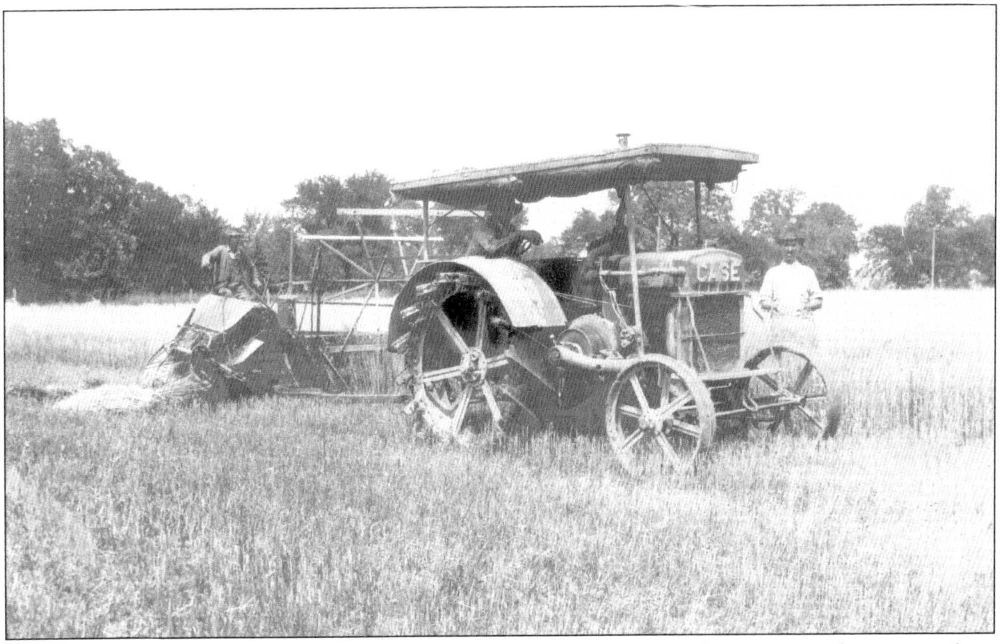

William Sneddon is pictured here with a Case tractor connected to a reaper for cutting hay. Steam and later gasoline tractors replaced horses for pulling the reapers introduced in the West by Cyrus McCormick's Chicago-based firm by the 1840s, dominating this business west of that city. Case tractors were made in nearby Racine by the late 19th century. Waves of such innovations improved farm life in the century following the original settlement. (Courtesy Lake Forest-Lake Bluff Historical Society.)

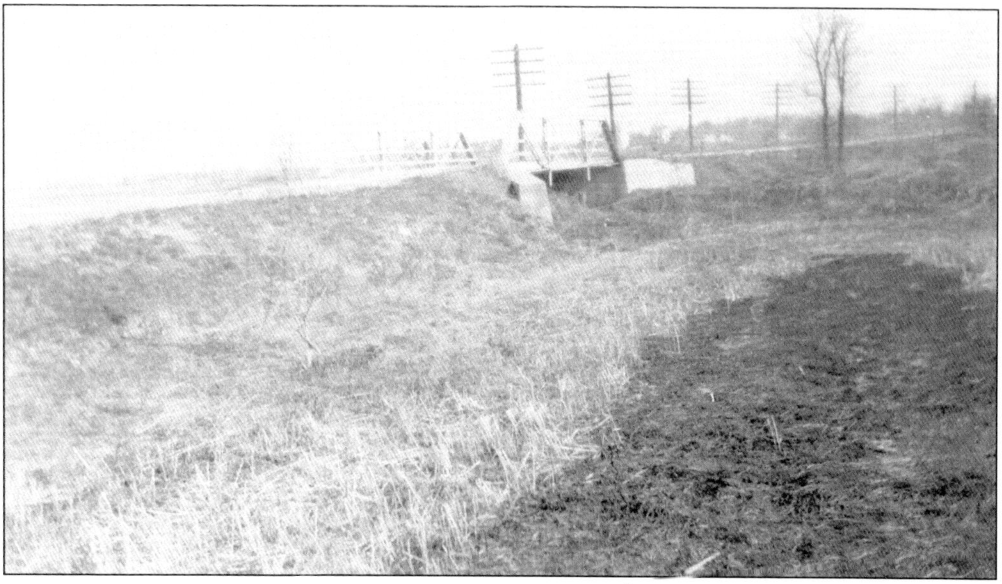

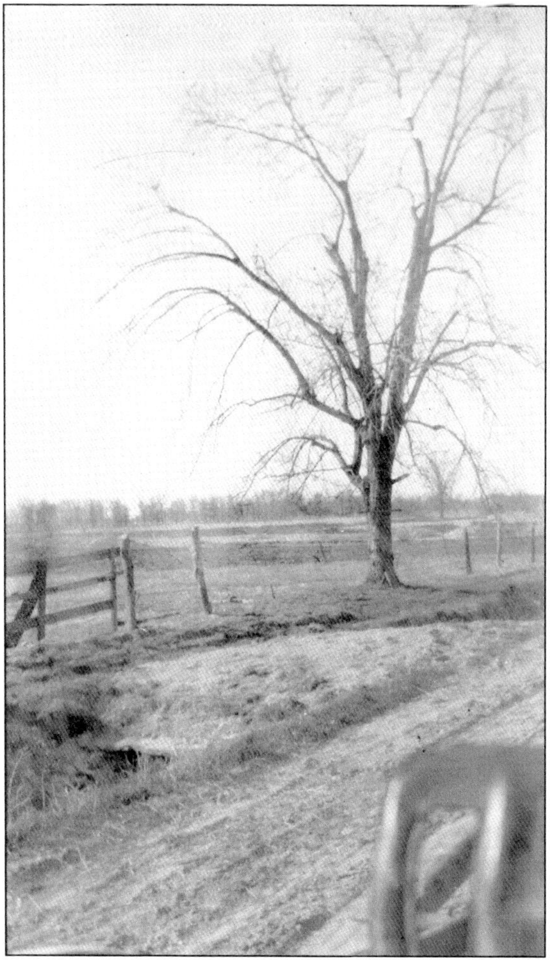

Corduroy Bridge, built of logs over the north branch of the Chicago River, was located on Waukegan Road, just south of Route 60, near today's Lake Forest High School West Campus. Two north-south roads, Corduroy (Waukegan) Road and the Green Bay Trail, served the forested terrain from the Middlefork branch of the Chicago River to the edge of Lake Michigan. (Courtesy Lake Forest-Lake Bluff Historical Society.)

Just south of Corduroy Bridge was Emmet's Hall—marked by the tree here—a post office, blacksmith shop, and tavern. The location of the Corduroy Bridge was determined by reading the 1918 accounts and comparing these stories with West Deerfield Township records. (Courtesy Lake County Discovery Museum and Archives.)

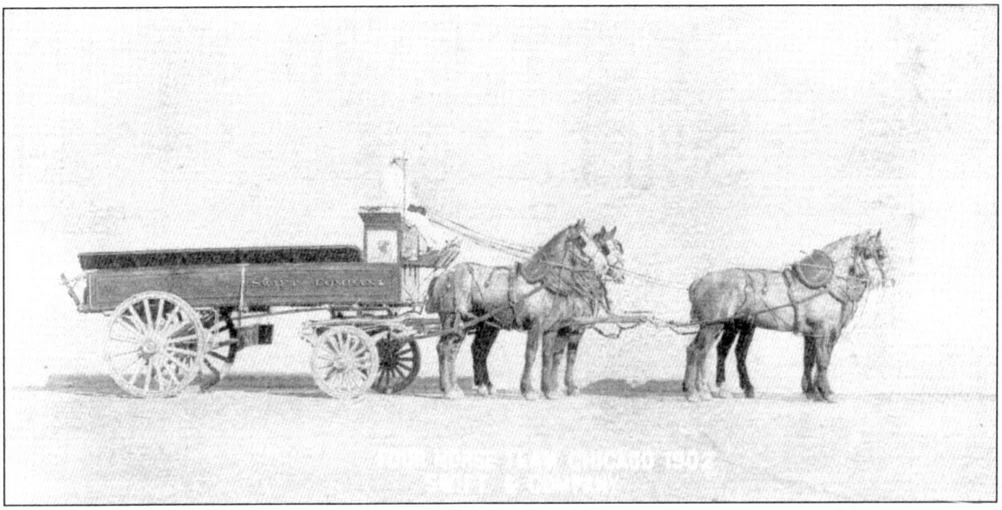

This is a 1902 postcard view showing a Louis F. Swift farm four-horse team. Swift was acquiring land west of Lake Forest in the early years of the 20th century, farming the land until development spread and he could sell his land for estates, such as Albert Lasker's in the mid-1920s. (Courtesy Shirley Paddock.)

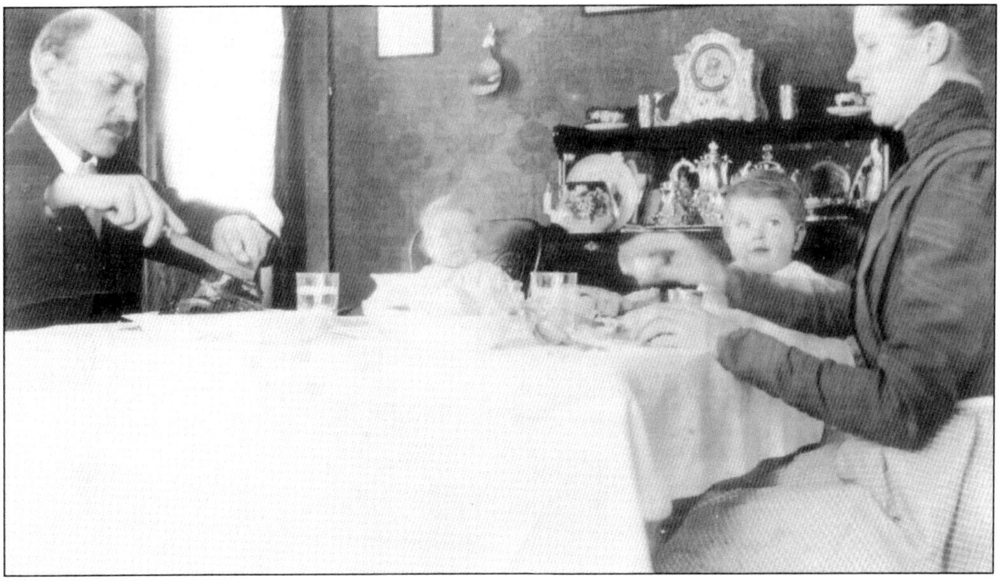

Shown here is the Gustafson family, with Henry on the left, his wife Charlotte on the right, and two of their children, at dinner apparently in the 1910s. Henry Gustafson was the gardener for the King estate on Ridge Road. He was born in Sweden in 1878, married in 1905, and lived in Everett from 1905 to 1924. His great-grandson, Leonard Gustafson, is a Lake Bluff resident in 2012. (Courtesy Leonard Gustafson.)

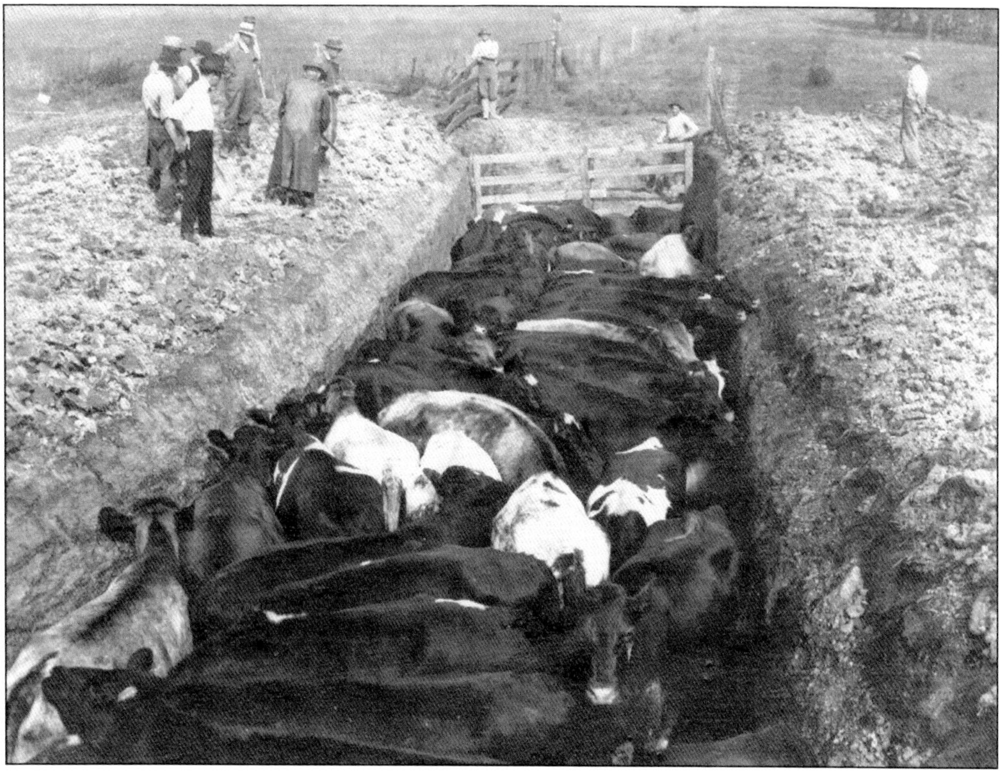

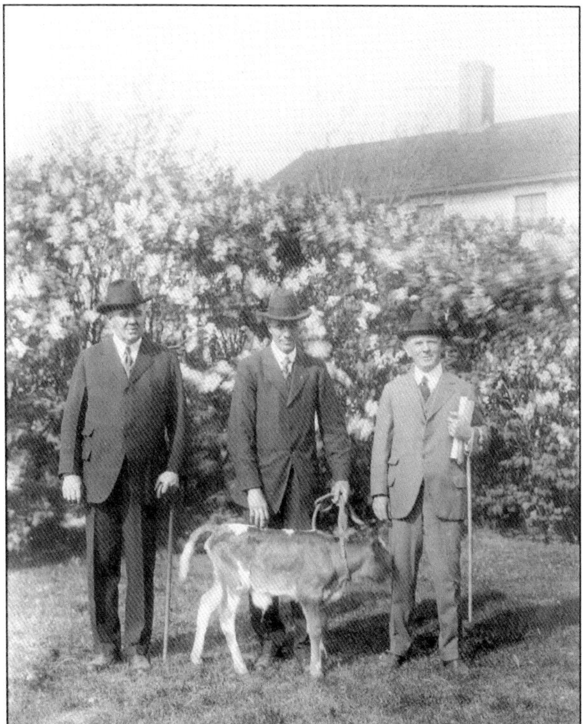

Hoof and mouth disease broke out in August 1915. Many farmers lost significant numbers of cows and hogs. Louis Swift's infested cattle, shot with a sporting rifle, were buried in trenches, as shown here, and then covered with lime followed by soil. The farmers had to wait six months before acquiring any replacement stock. (Courtesy Lake County Discovery Museum and Archives.)

Arthur Meeker is on the left with a heifer calf sold at auction in May 1918. Chicago executive and owner of Arcady Farm, Meeker was the packing associate of J. Ogden Armour and was Armour's neighbor on Waukegan Road. The Armour packing operation was at its all-time height of production and profitability at the time, supplying meat to Europe and to American forces in France during World War I. (Courtesy Lake Forest-Lake Bluff Historical Society.)

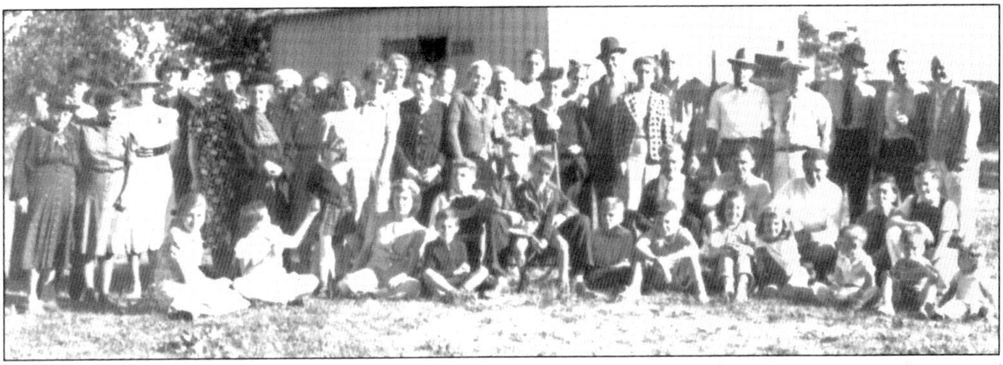

This 1948 photograph shows three generations of the Conway family on a picnic at the site of the farm. According to Linda Biondi Conway, both of the Conway homes—the first at the end of Conway Road, west of Waukegan Road, and the second located in Everett—had burned down. (Courtesy Lake Forest-Lake Bluff Historical Society.)

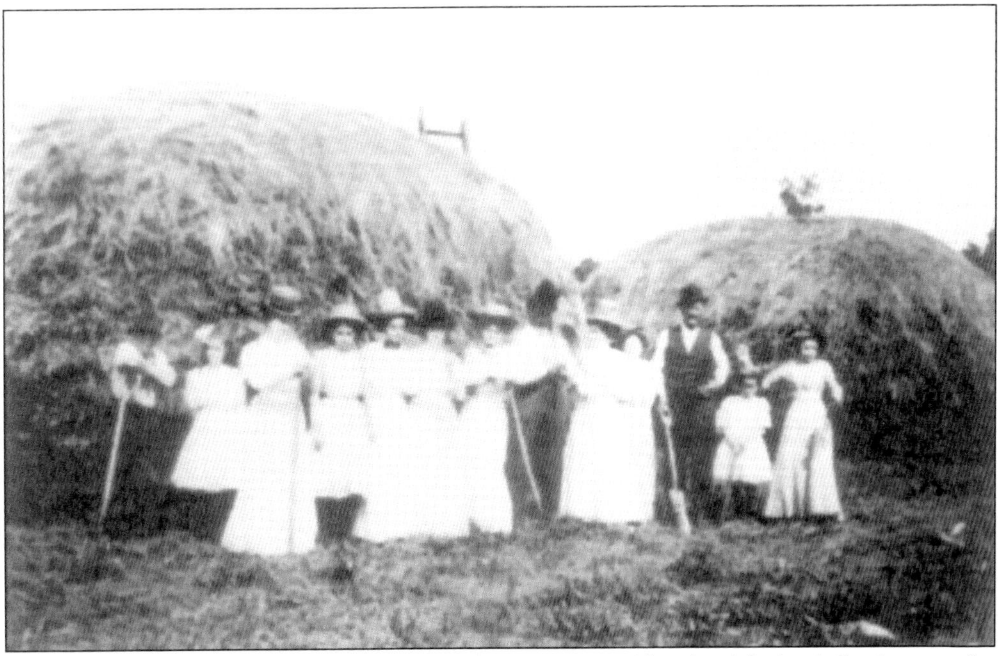

The Dawson family came to Deerfield Township in 1846 and lived in Meehan's Settlement, the Irish settlement north of Deerfield. In addition to highly productive wheat fields, shown here at harvest time with a family gathering, the prairie had red oak, white oak, and elm hickory trees, along with fruit orchards. (Courtesy Shirley Paddock.)

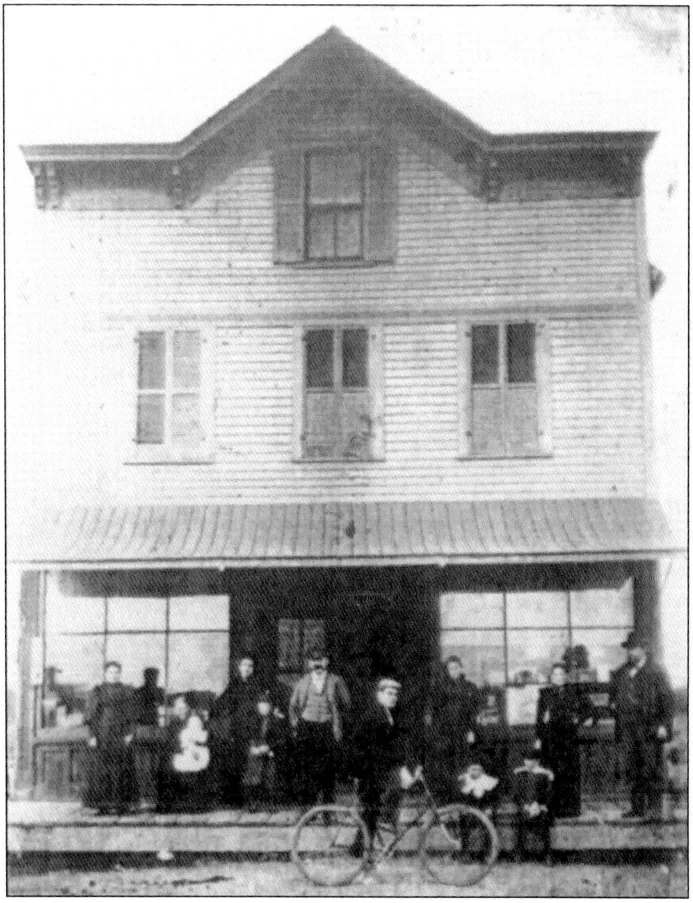

Lancaster's General Store was located east of the railroad tracks, north of Everett Road. Original pioneers to the region, over 50 Lancaster family members lived in the area. Until 1892, the community was called Lancasterville for homesteader James Lancaster, who ran a general store. (Courtesy Lake County Discovery Museum and Archives.)

This early photographic-process postcard shows the store around 1908–1910, several years after the town changed its name to Everett. This larger structure may be a second or a renovated Lancaster store, with the three left windows on the second floor the original section as shown left. (Courtesy Thomas Kinney.)

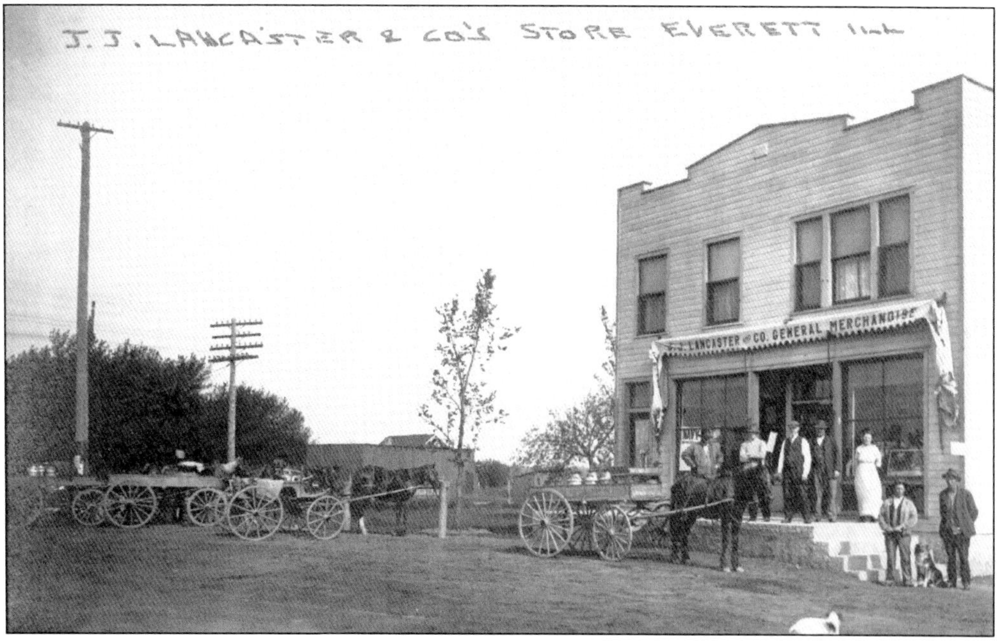

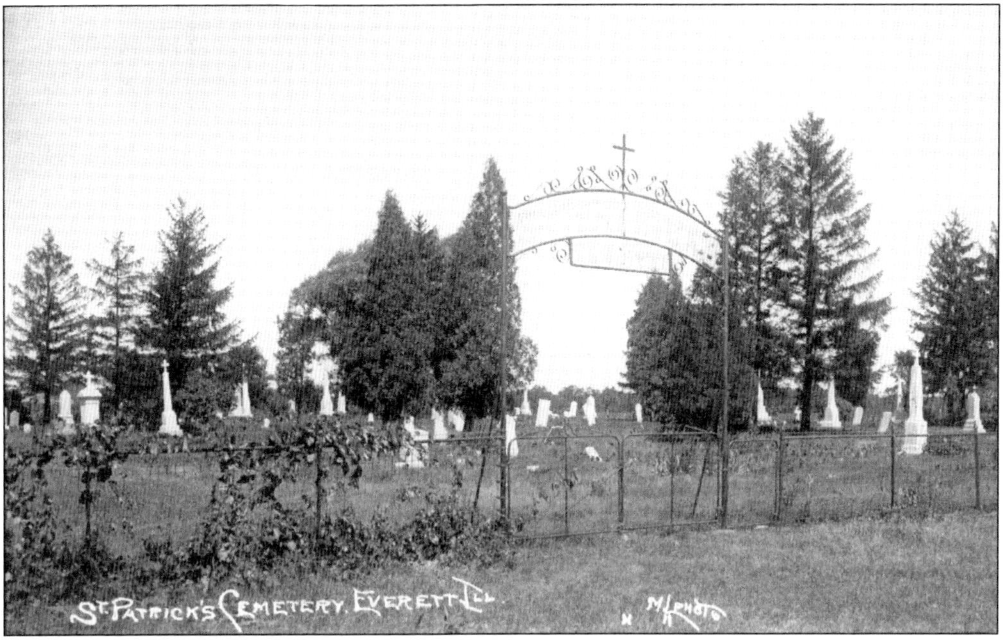

St. Patrick's cemetery was started in 1840 on land from Michael Yore with the rescued remains of several Irish Catholic sailors from nearby Lake Michigan. The cemetery, the oldest in Lake Forest, contains some of the earliest families in Everett: Atkinson, Bolan, Bradley, Burke, Burns, Carolan, Conway, Cooney, Dawson, Dickenson, Doyle, Fagan, Flannery, Kelley, Kennedy, Kerrigan, King, Lancaster, Ludlow, McLaughlin, Melody, Moran, Nolan, O'Connor, Sheridan, Sweeney, Tully, and Yore. (Courtesy Lake County Discovery Museum and Archives.)

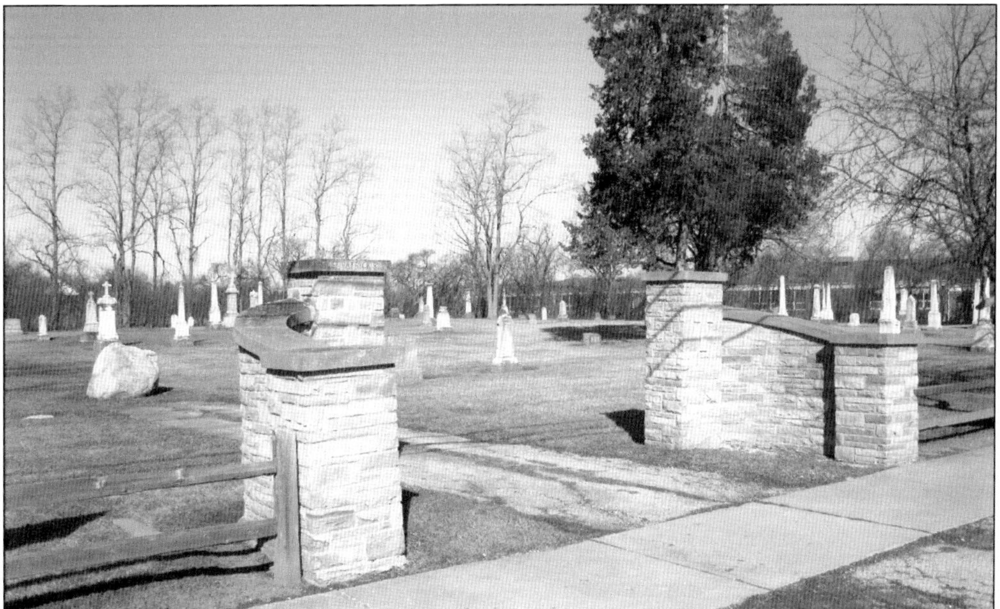

This photograph, taken in 2012, shows St. Patrick's cemetery, located still on Telegraph Road south of Everett Road, and little changed from the 1918 view above. The Yore family plot is found directly west-southwest, or back from the entrance and to the left. (Courtesy Susan Kelsey.)

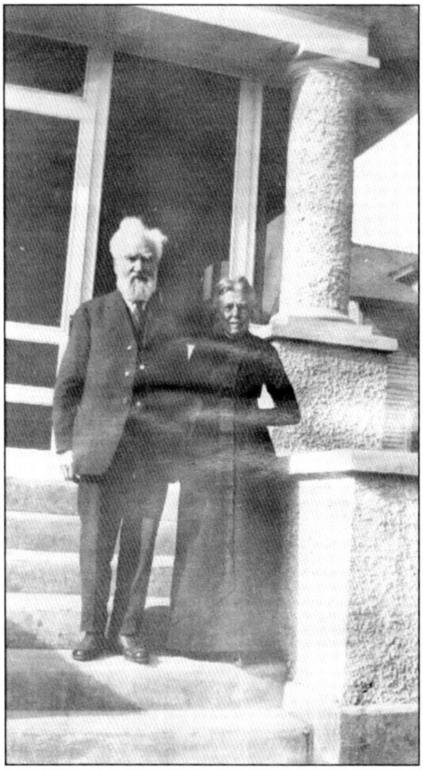

This photograph shows Martin Melody, 81 years old, and his sister Ellen Melody Doyle in 1918 at their home on Vine Avenue, east Lake Forest. Melody was one of the early settlers west of Lake Forest by the late 1850s, coming here as a child of four years. The Melody and Doyle properties were sold to J. Ogden Armour in 1904 and incorporated into his new Mellody Farm estate. (Courtesy Lake County Discovery Museum and Archives.)

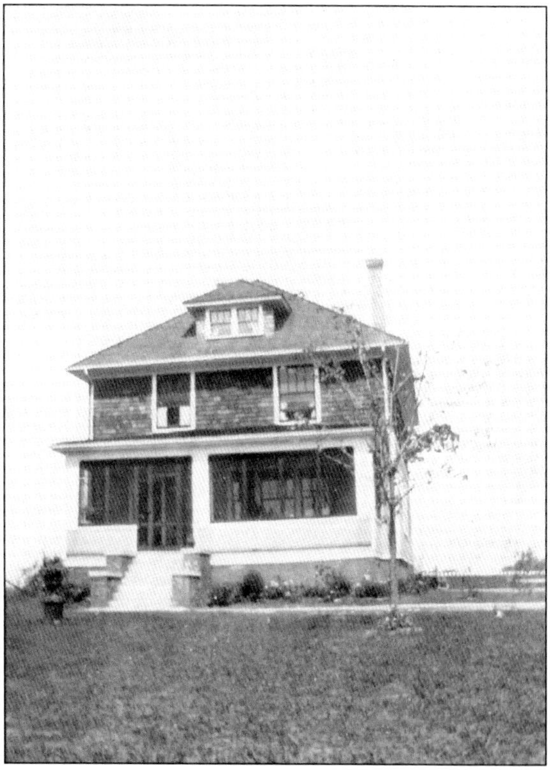

This second Conway family home in Everett was destroyed by fire in 1938. The American Four Square, two-story house, 36 by 30 feet, was wood-frame, finished in concrete and brick. It was comprised of a (lower level) boiler room, coal bin, vegetable room, storeroom, and laundry; (first floor) kitchen, dining room, living room and bedroom; (second floor) four bedrooms and a sanitary closet. Linda Biondi Conway remembers picnics on the front lawn. (Courtesy Lake County Discovery Museum and Archives.)

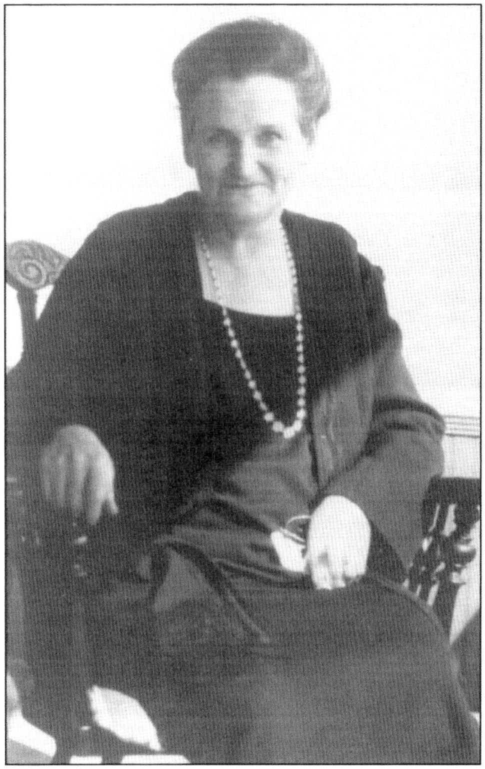

Dates are unknown for these photographs of Mary Melody Nolan Conway and Ambrose Conway, the latter shown in a late-19th-century cabinet photograph posed in an elegant studio, with the photographer's name prominently displayed below. The Conway family was one of the oldest in the Everett area. Their original home was located on Conway Road west of Waukegan Road. This road turns to the northwest, and the farm residence stands today at the end of the road, the original Conway homestead. (Courtesy Lake Forest Lake-Bluff Historical Society.)

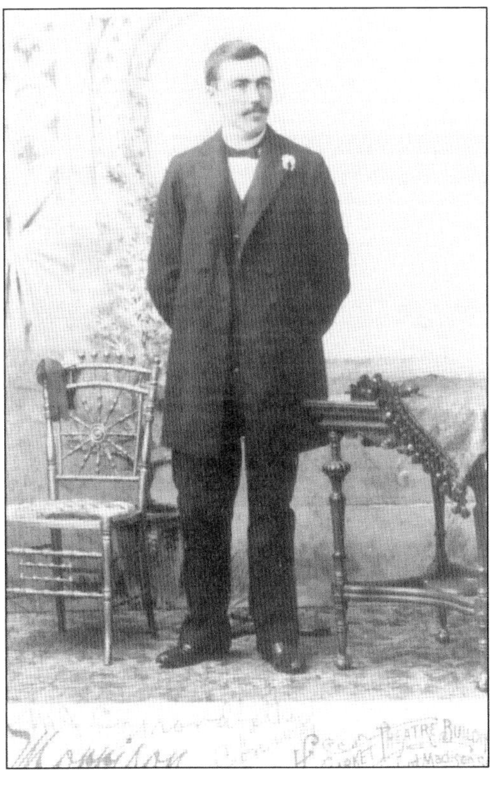

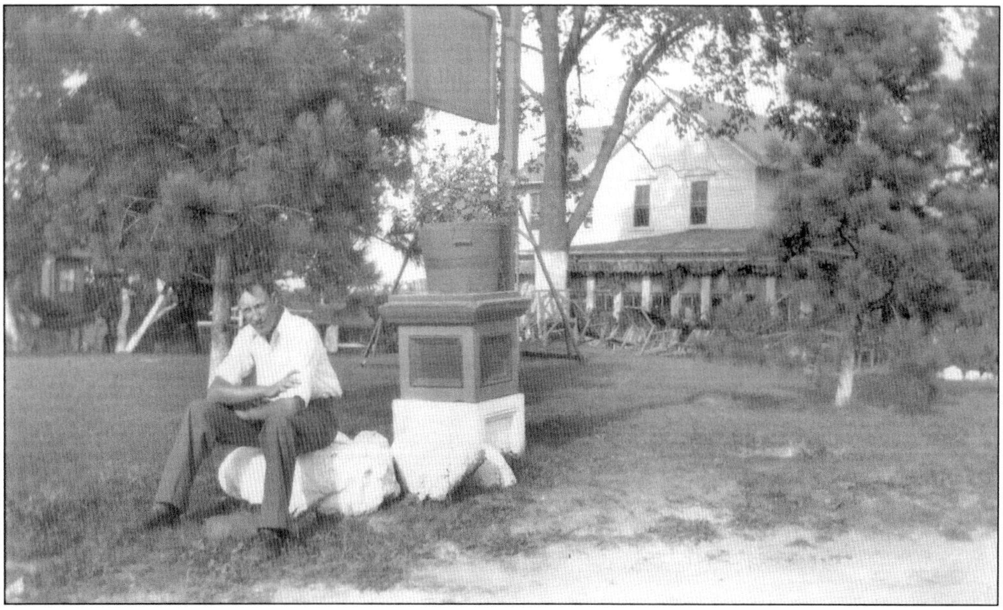

With the advent of an improved road, the Lancaster house was moved farther east, remodeled, and converted into the Green Tree Inn in 1922. Swift's house—moved from the Fritsch place and remodeled to modern requirements for the Kostail family—stood between the garage and the Green Tree Inn. Located at 1101 South Waukegan Road, a Lake Forest landmark, the structure burned to the ground January 23, 1935. (Courtesy Lake Forest-Lake Bluff Historical Society.)

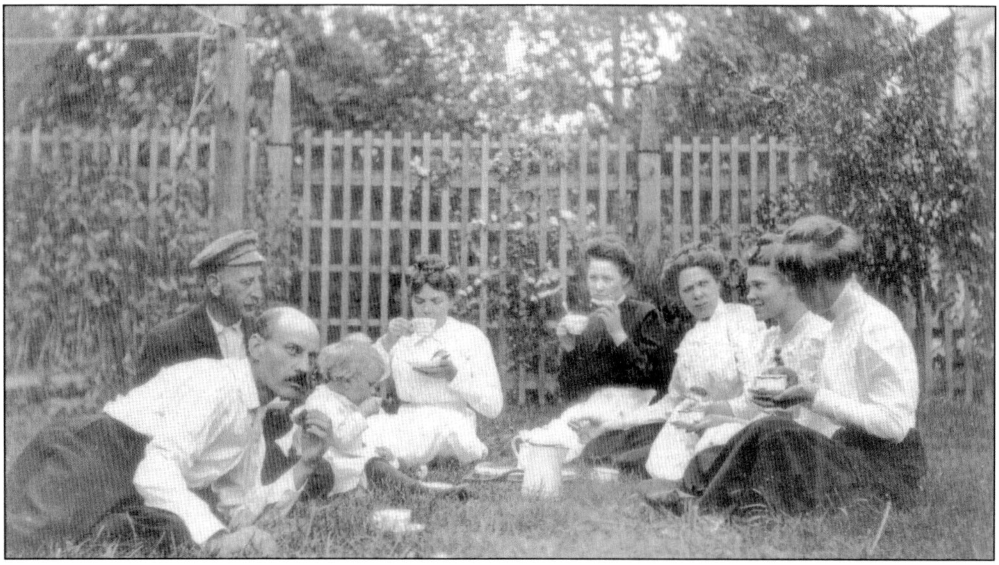

Henry Gustafson, left, enjoys a picnic with family members. Gustafson was the gardener for the Charles G. King estate and lived in the caretaker's cottage, designed by a young David Adler, and still located on Ridge Road adjacent to the polo stable, designed by Howard Van Doren Shaw for the King family. King's daughter Ginevra captivated the adolescent F. Scott Fitzgerald and his imagination in 1915, becoming a muse of his great writings of the 1920s and 1930s. (Courtesy Leonard Gustafson.)

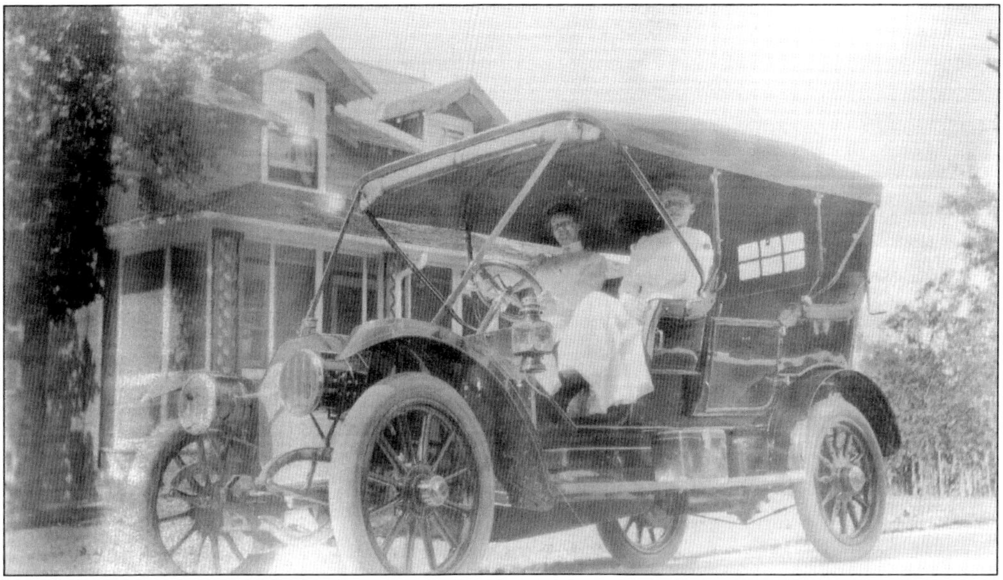

Shown here are the Gustafsons in an early car in front of the Kings' staff lodge, the Gustafsons' home. Automobiles were adopted by the estate group in 1904, and this led to the Kings' 1905 purchase of their estate southwest of Onwentsia on Ridge Road, the faster motorcar allowing for a greater distance from the east side train station for King when he commuted to the city. (Courtesy Leonard Gustafson.)

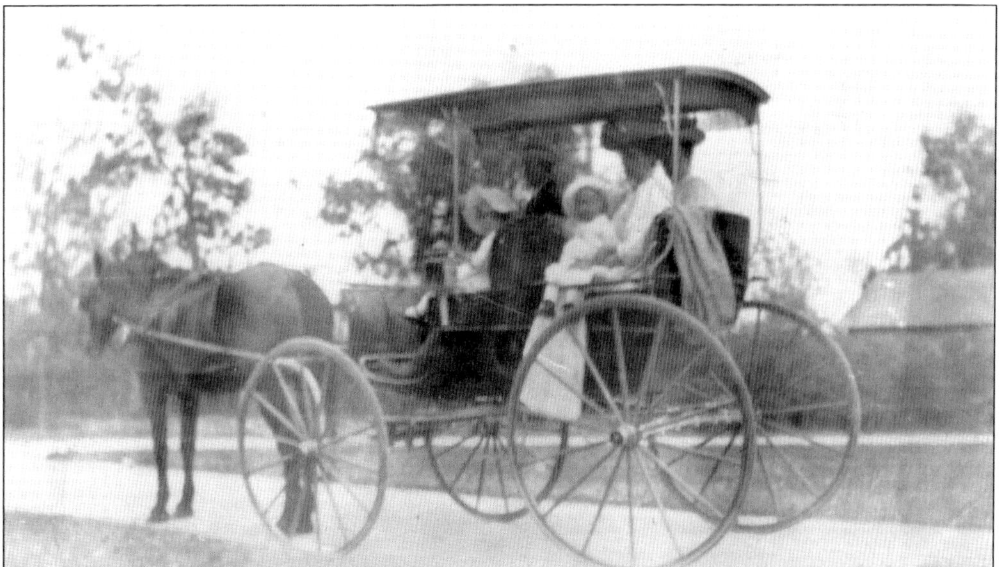

Henry Gustafson was the Kings' head gardener, and perhaps the stylish horse and carriage were readily available for this staff family for an outing while the Kings themselves traveled by the motorcar to Onwentsia or to visit friends. (Courtesy Leonard Gustafson.)

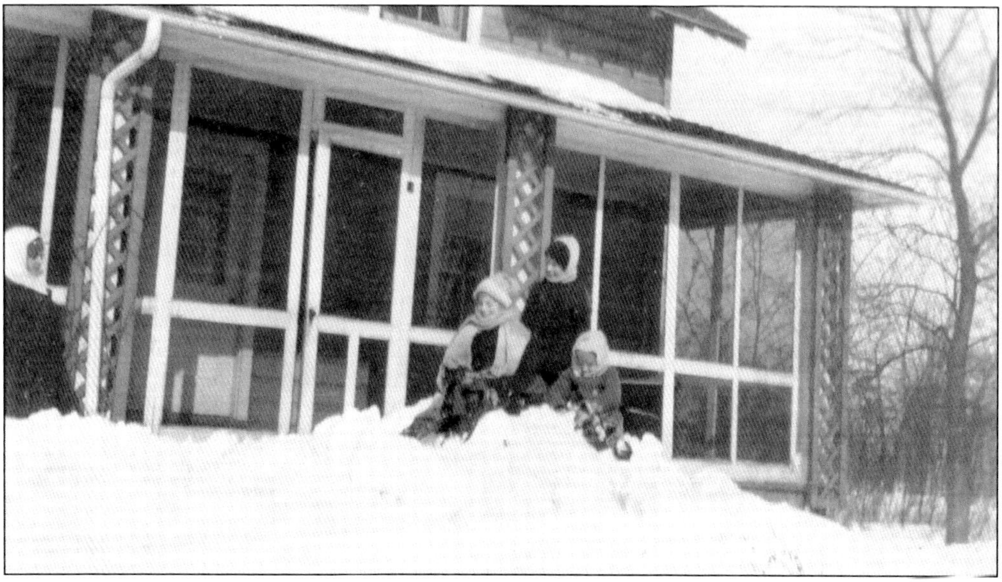

The Henry Gustafson children appear here playing in the snow in front of the caretaker's cottage on Ridge Road. In such winter weather, the King family would have been ensconced in their warm, commodious Astor Street mansion (since demolished) in the highest classic style of the day, the house having been designed by David Adler in 1914. Their activities would have included balls, theater parties, and rounds of visits. The Kings would have returned to the country in the spring when windows had to go up on Astor Street, letting in the inescapable odors of the stockyards to the southwest. (Courtesy Leonard Gustafson.)

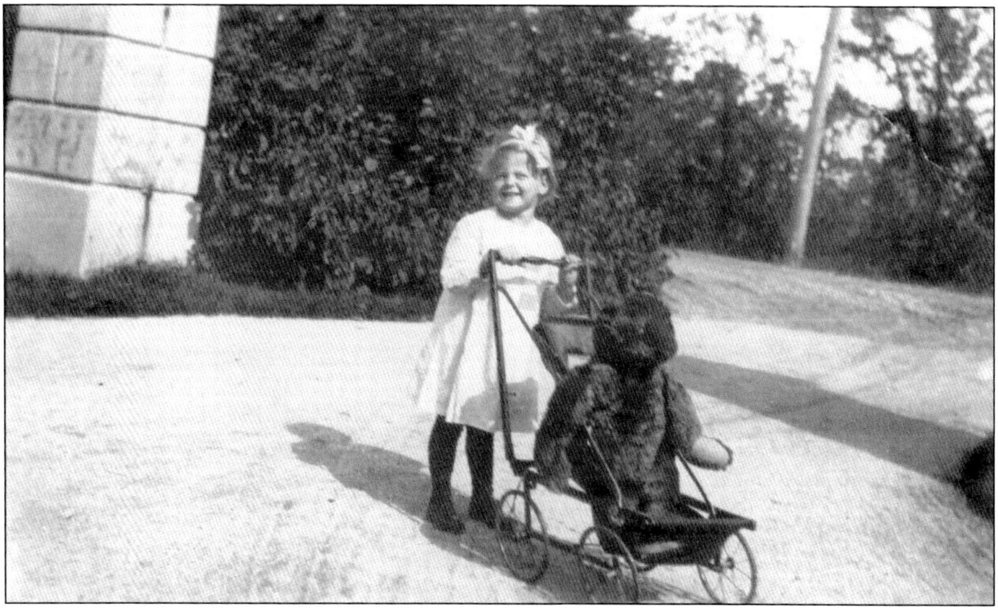

Pictured is a Gustafson youngster, aunt of Lake Bluff resident Leonard Gustafson, playing with her bear by the Ridge Road gateposts at the King country place on Ridge Road. Ridge Road, running north to south, followed one of the sandbars of the ancient glacial lake west of the divide (Green Bay Road). Estates on such high points caught cooling evening breezes during the hottest part of the summer. (Courtesy Leonard Gustafson.)

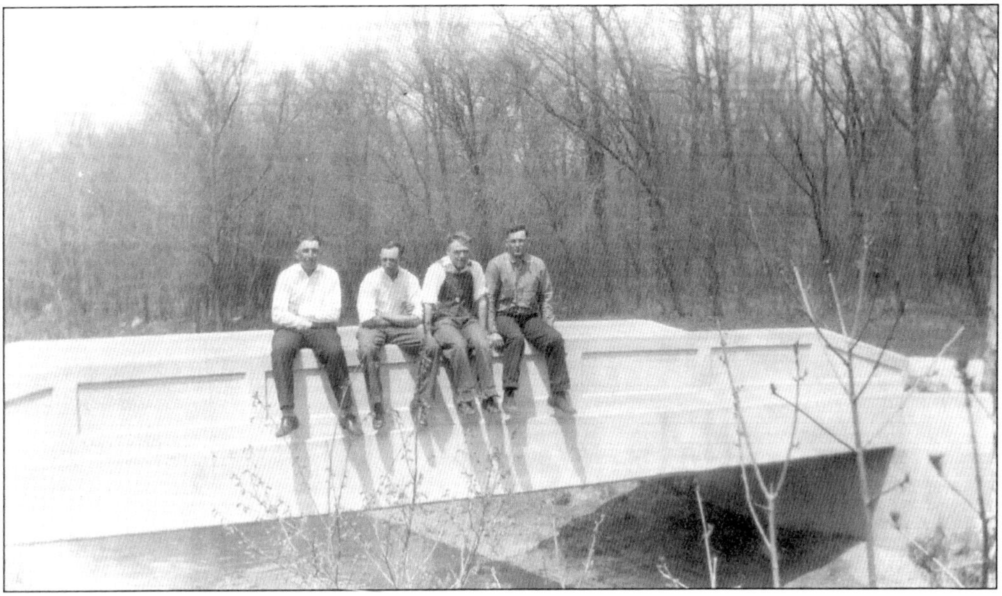

Four men are seen sitting on a bridge overlooking a river. The historical society believes this may be Elmwood Farm at 499 West Old Mill Road. (Courtesy Lake Forest-Lake Bluff Historical Society.)

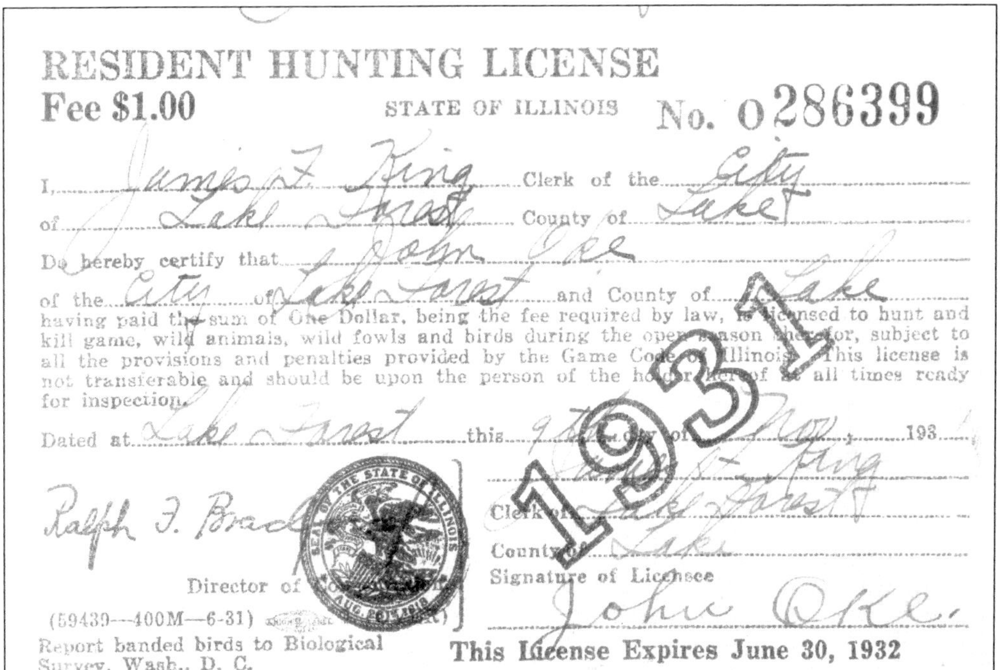

RESIDENT HUNTING LICENSE

Fee $1.00 STATE OF ILLINOIS No. 0286399

I, James F. King Clerk of the City
of Lake Forest County of Lake
Do hereby certify that John Oke
of the City of Lake Forest and County of Lake
having paid the sum of One Dollar, being the fee required by law, is licensed to hunt and kill game, wild animals, wild fowls and birds during the open season therefor, subject to all the provisions and penalties provided by the Game Code of Illinois. This license is not transferable and should be upon the person of the holder thereof at all times ready for inspection.

Dated at Lake Forest this 9th day of Nov., 1931

1931

Ralph F. Brad
Director of
(59439—400M—6-31)
Report banded birds to Biological Survey, Wash., D. C.

James F. King
Clerk of Lake Forest
County of Lake
Signature of Licensee
John Oke.

This License Expires June 30, 1932

The area was popular for hunting smaller game, such as birds and rabbits; a resident hunting license from 1931 is shown here. James F. King, city clerk from the 1890s to the 1930s, played a key role in shaping modern Lake Forest and annexing Everett in 1926. (Courtesy Shirley Paddock.)

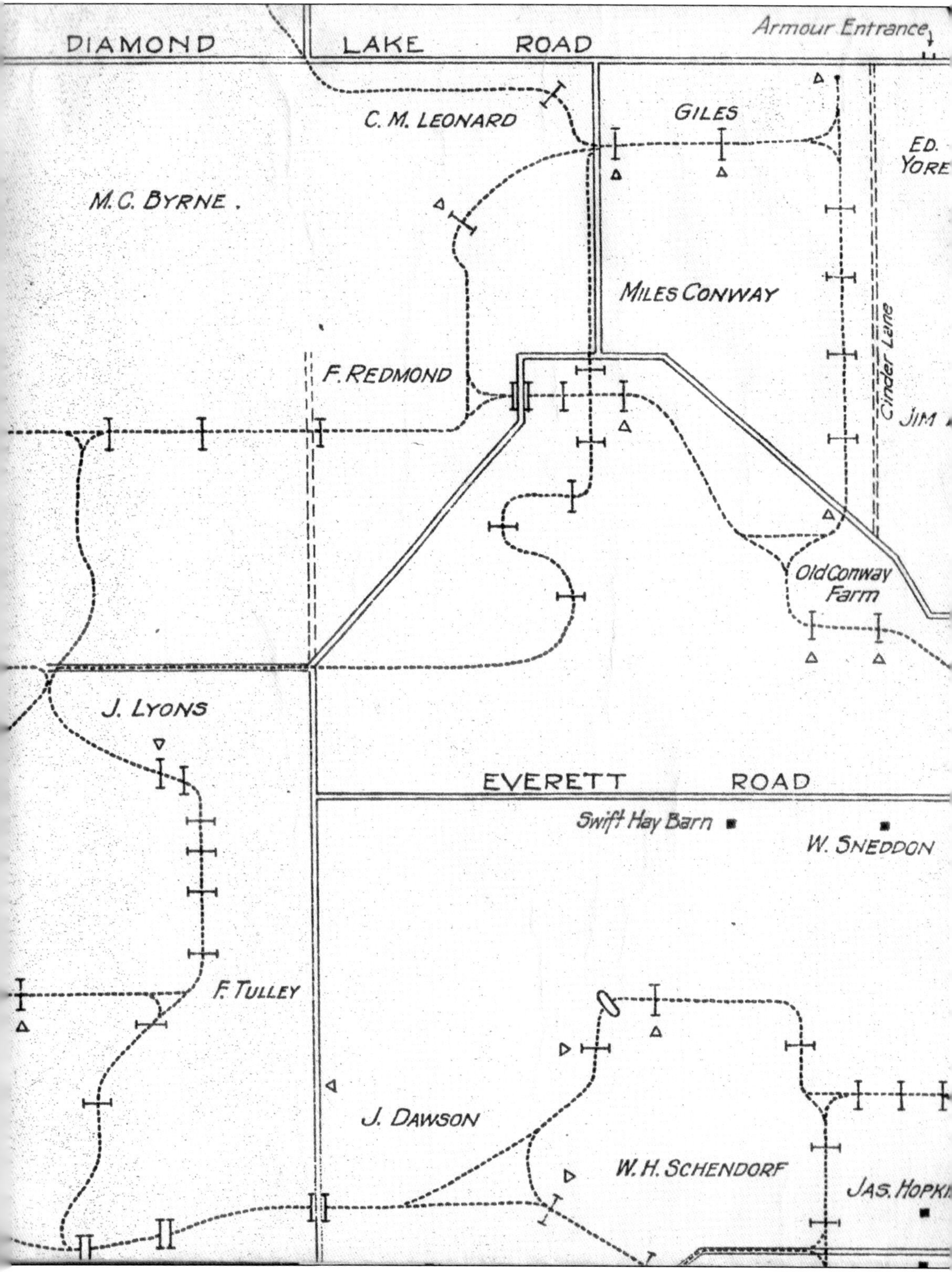
DIAMOND LAKE ROAD
Armour Entrance
C. M. LEONARD
GILES
ED. YORE
M.C. BYRNE.
MILES CONWAY
Cinder Lane
F. REDMOND
JIM
Old Conway Farm
J. LYONS
EVERETT ROAD
Swift Hay Barn
W. SNEDDON
F. TULLEY
J. DAWSON
W. H. SCHENDORF

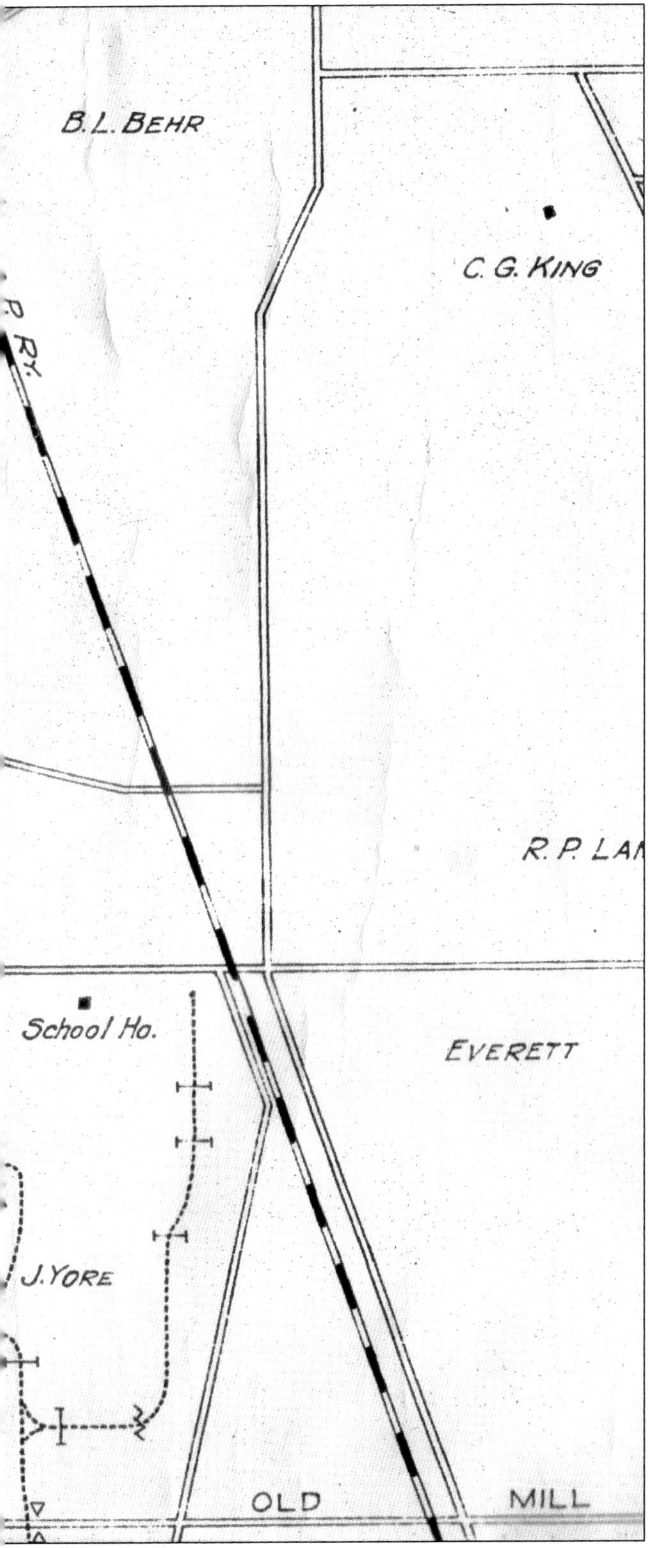

Foxhunts and paper chases (riders on horseback following clues from one prize to the next) were popular west of Lake Forest. An Onwentsia Hunt Club steeplechase course covered 1.75 miles, including five four-foot fence jumps, two 10-foot water jumps across the Chicago River's Middlefork branch, and one five-foot brush jump at the finish. A newspaper clipping from November 2, 1902, states: "Fox hunting made a record at Lake Forest when forty-seven riders started in the chase which covered seven miles across fields. Several local farmers took part in the hunt too. All along the route of the chase, residents of the country flocked to the path of the hunt and cheered the riders as they dashed by." John Doyle's farm, near Everett, was the scene of the meet. The chase took a southeasterly course through the farm of Miles Conway and ended in a big slough west of the Milwaukee and St. Paul tracks. (Courtesy Shirley Paddock.)

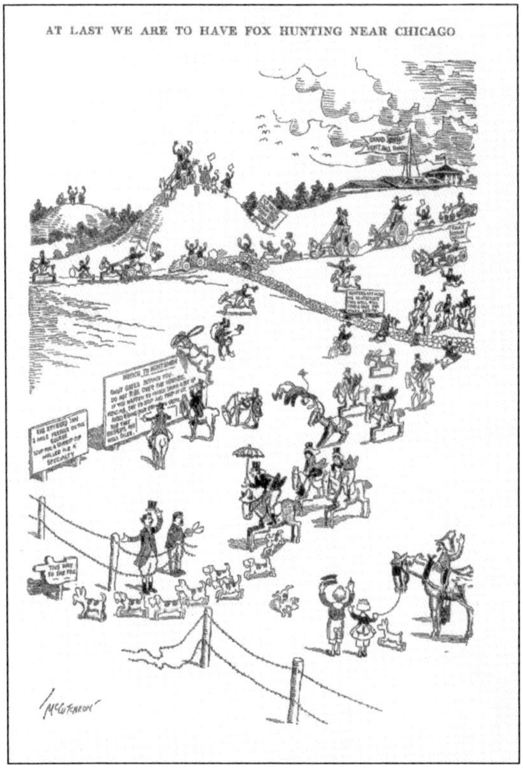

Foxhunting in the early years of the 20th century was wildly popular with the new suburban set, as featured in this cartoon by *Chicago Tribune* artist and writer John T. McCutcheon (1870–1949). Hoosier farm lad McCutcheon tended to identify as much with the area farmers who were bemused by the new sport as he did with his Onwentsia society friends who had jumped on this Anglophilic blood sport bandwagon with all its trappings. (Courtesy Shirley Paddock.)

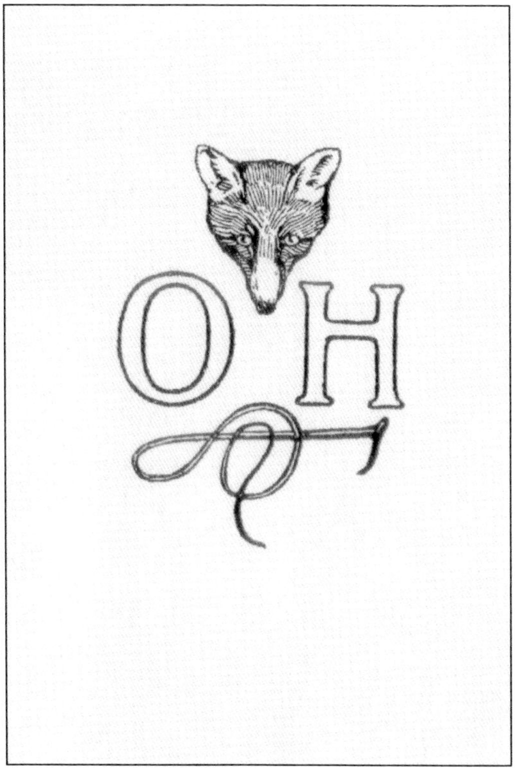

Lake Forest's Onwentsia Hunt began in 1900 and ranged west of the club across the farmland there, countryside that soon became estates and gentlemen's farms. It followed the classic English and east coast modes of dress and activities—on horseback in specific riding attire, with hounds trained to find foxes. In 1928, the hunt moved 12 miles north and west to Milburn. (Courtesy Shirley Paddock.)

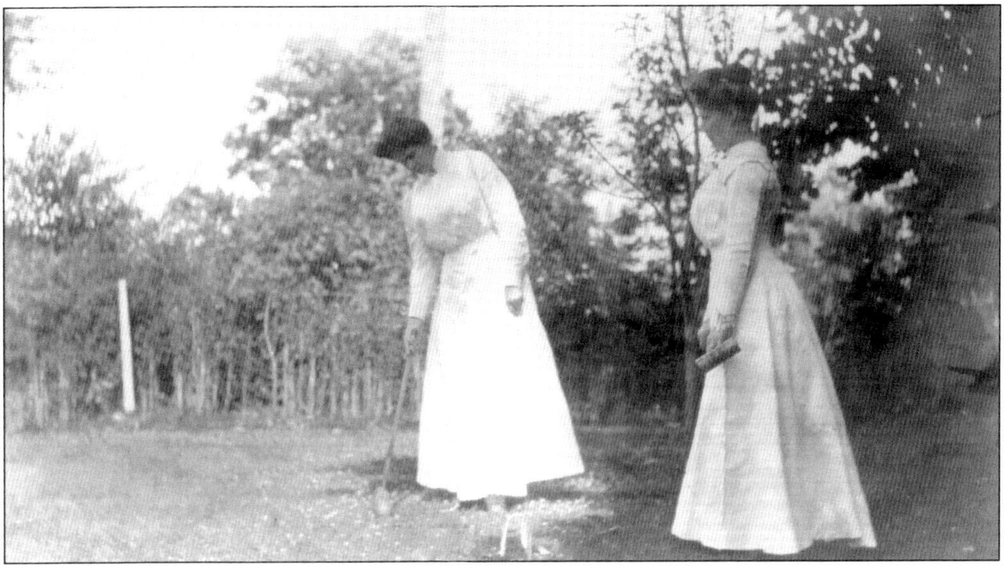

Croquet was a popular pastime all across Lake Forest a century ago. The players appear to be the Gustafsons and their friends. The activity, related to European lawn bowling games, was accessible to many, unlike expensive foxhunting with its horses, hounds, land, and proscribed dress. (Courtesy Leonard Gustafson.)

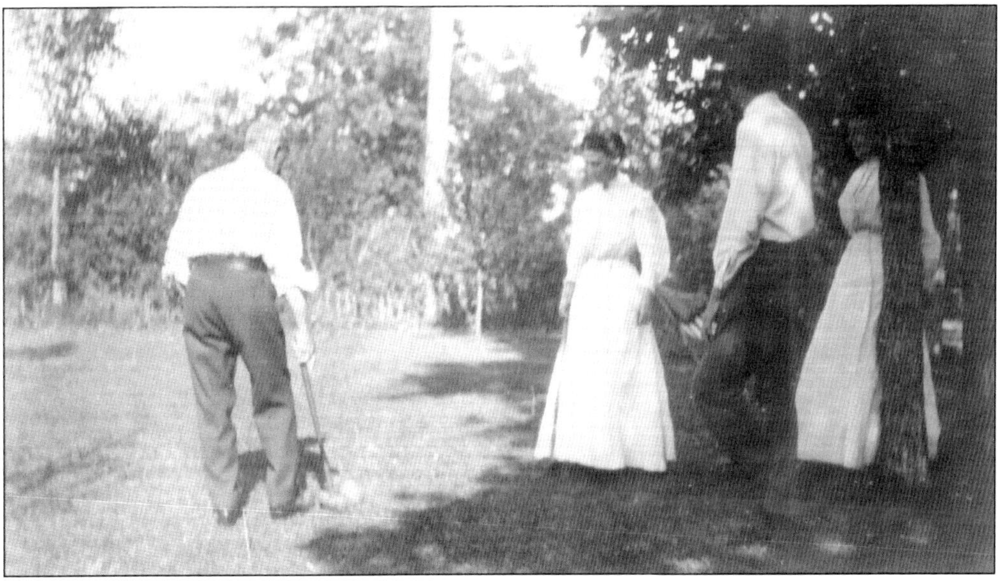

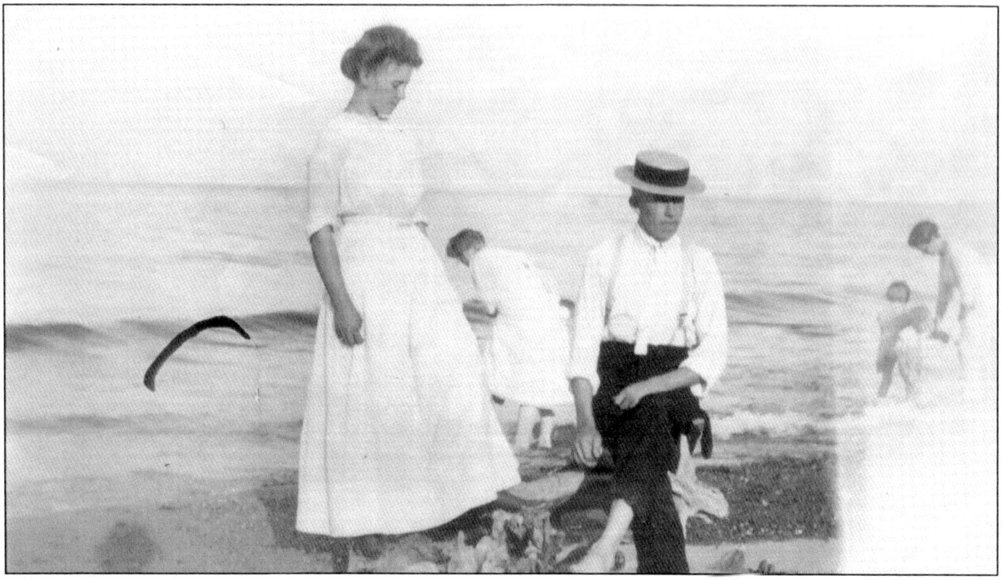

The Gustafson family enjoys a pleasant afternoon at the nearby Lake Michigan beach. West Lake Forest was only a few miles from the Lake Forest beaches on Lake Michigan. There were five lakefront access points then—including at the east end of Illinois Road and just south of the cemetery. (Courtesy Leonard Gustafson.)

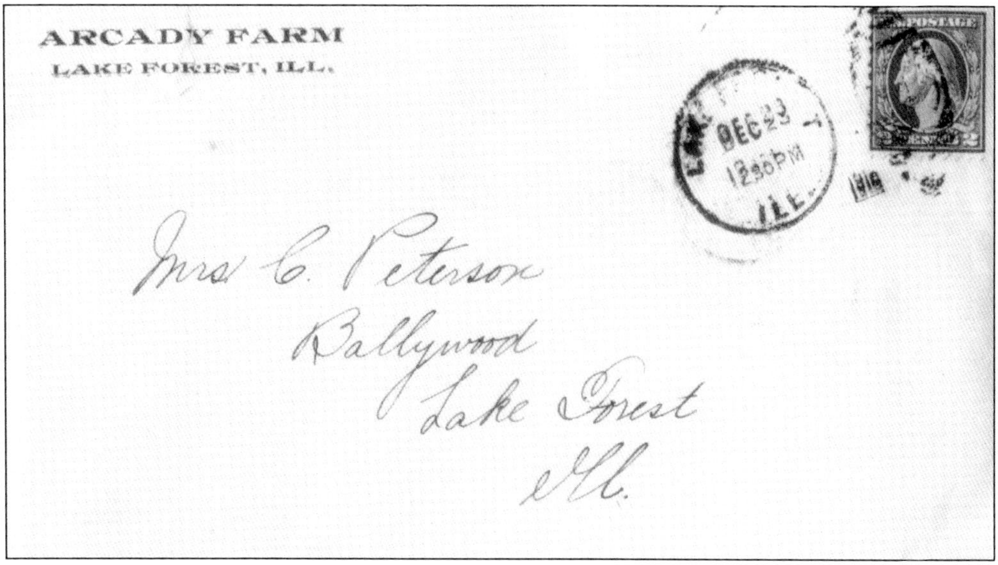

ARCADY FARM
LAKE FOREST, ILL.

Mrs C. Peterson
Ballywood
Lake Forest
Ill.

A 1918 letter on Arcady Farm stationery is shown here, addressed to a member of the staff on the Ernest Hamills' estate on Mayflower Road. Notable is the lack of any street address, much less a late-20th-century zip code for machine processing of the envelope. Local postal authorities knew who was who among the local residents and estates, including staff members and their families. In this case, the estate name was written incorrectly. It should be Ballyatwood. (Courtesy Shirley M. Paddock.)

Two

Churches, Schools, Children, and Townspeople

Starting in 1842, the settlers built their first church in what was called Meehan's Settlement. It was built of logs and located in the northeast corner of the present-day cemetery on Telegraph Road. Mass was said once a month, when French missionaries would come from Waukegan. On weekdays, the church was used as a school.

The Everett church had a total of four locations and two names. The first church in 1844 was located in the northeast corner of the present-day cemetery and was a log cabin. This church was called St. Michael's and sources say it was probably named after Michael Meehan. The parish was founded in 1849. The church burned down and a second church was built on Mahoney property, which would be located near the intersection of present-day northeast corner of Waukegan Road and Route 60. While the new church was being built, mass was said in the Gibbons home. In 1895, lighting struck and destroyed the church. The third church, now called St. Patrick's, was built in 1910 at the present-day location of St. Patrick's Church. This church burned down in 1910 and a fourth church was built, which stands today at Waukegan and Everett Roads. The town was known as Corduroy, based on the bridge on present-day Waukegan Road over the Skokie River.

There have been four Everett schools. The first was located in the St. Michael's church and log cabin in the northeast corner of the present-day St. Patrick's cemetery. The second Everett school was located on the Lancaster property (see page 14 to compare pictures), around the intersection of present day Waukegan and Everett Roads. In 1914, the Everett school district and Lyons district were consolidated and a two-room brick school building was erected about 330 feet west of the old railroad depot. This third school was located south of Everett, west of Telegraph Road. The fourth Everett School was built at its present-day location on Telegraph Road.

Children have been an organizing element of west Lake Forest, as they were in the mid-19th century on the east side. By the mid-20th century, there were two boarding schools west: Lake Forest Academy at the former J.O. Armour estate and the Grove School, a special education facility in the former Ridge Farm Preventorium—following the elimination of tuberculosis with antibiotics by the 1950s. Children lived on farms, around local businesses, at school, and on the estates that were their parents' employers. Their open-air, relatively free countryside lifestyles allowed them to thrive. Common to them all was access to open space with woods, fields, and streams year-round. At the turn of the century, children had become a focus of middle-class life, from English garden designer Gertrude Jekyll's 1908 book, *Children and Gardens*, to Swedish artist Carl Larsson's book, *Our Home* (1902), about the charms of simple life on a rural farm. This idealized life drew children of all social backgrounds to west Lake Forest's rural, garden, and educational opportunities.

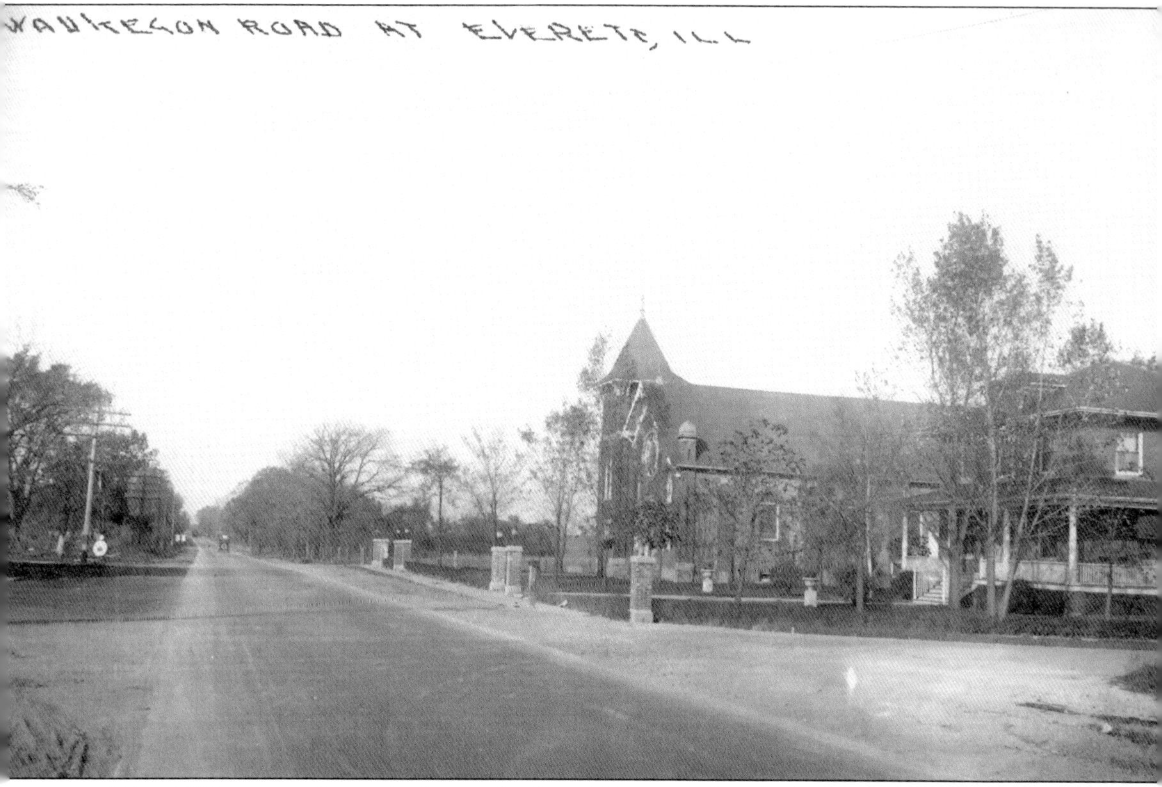

This 1910s postcard view looks north along Waukegan Road, showing the parish house and church soon after they were completed. The names of 1840s pioneers such as Conway, Dwyer, Kennedy, Keough, Melody, and Yore still are to be found on the parish rolls, among the 1,780 families enrolled there and using the campus and church completed in 1998. (Courtesy Lake Forest-Lake Bluff Historical Society.)

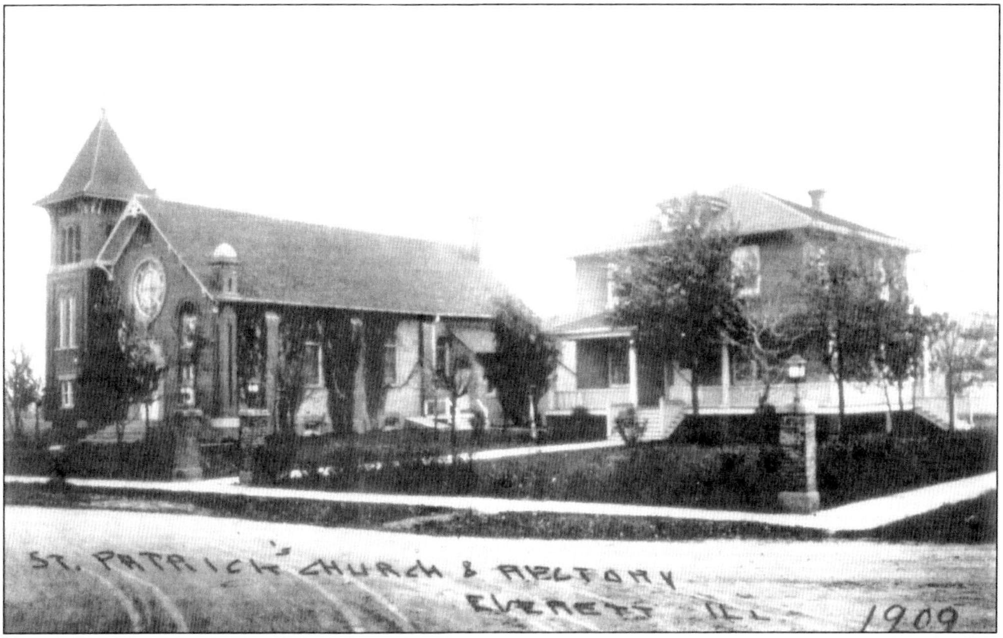

This close-up postcard view of the newly completed St. Patrick's Church shows the church and rectory, the only buildings left of Everett, Illinois. (Courtesy Lake Forest-Lake Bluff Historical Society.)

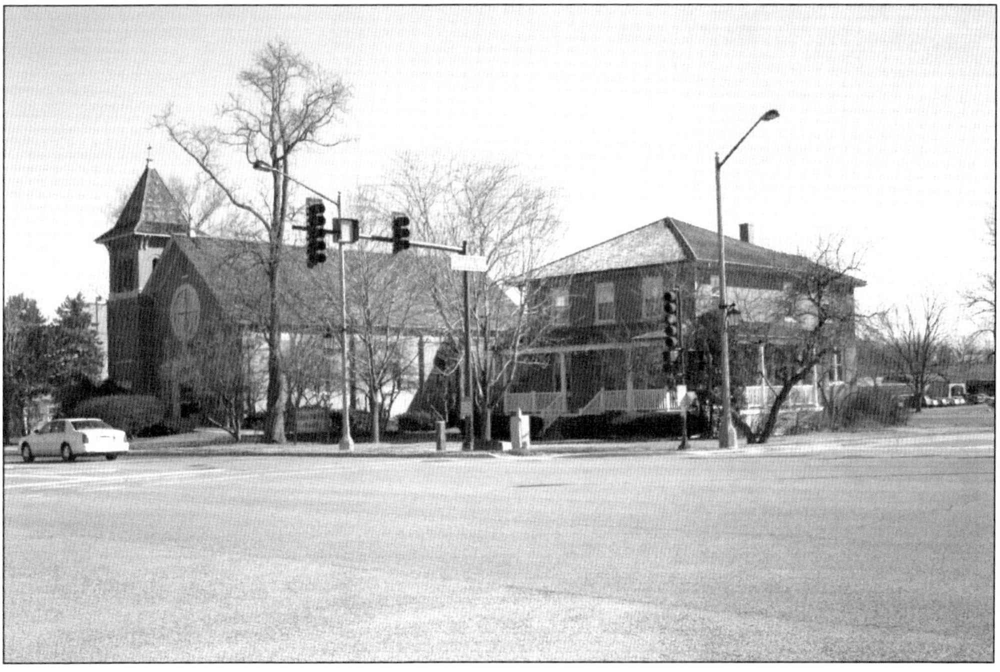

This 2012 image from a similar angle and distance as the view above shows how well preserved these two iconic west Lake Forest religious buildings are today, even though the greatly expanded parish is served by a campus of buildings to the immediate east of these. They apparently are the only buildings left from a century ago of this central section of Everett. (Courtesy Susan Kelsey.)

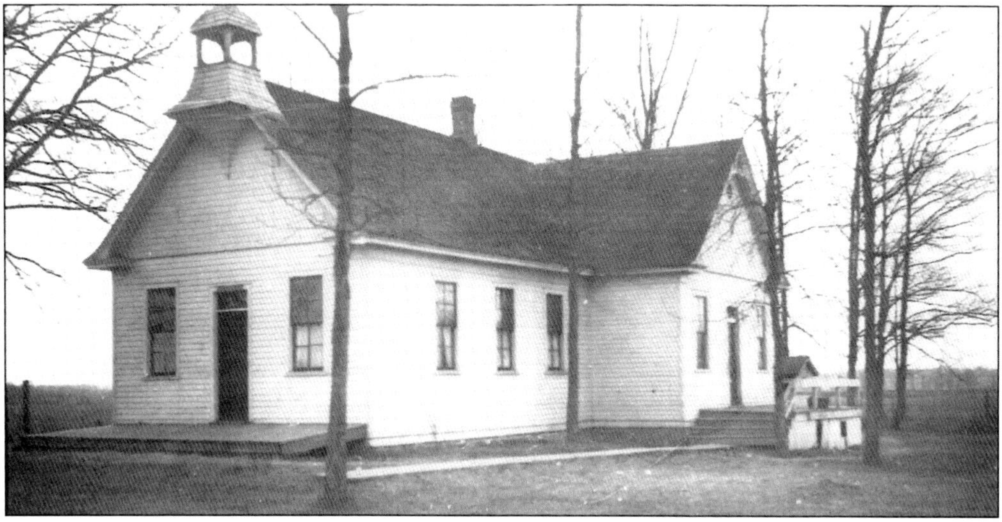

An early school, a frame building, stood on the Matthew Steele Farm on Telegraph Road (now Waukegan Road) north of Deerpath on the east side. The furniture consisted of a teacher's table, a wood stove, and the board benches for the pupils, each long enough to seat four children. Jeanette Simpson was the first teacher in District 66. The school was moved to land given by Henry Vickerman and renamed The Vickerman School. It housed one teacher and 10 students. (Courtesy Lake County Discovery Museum and Archives.)

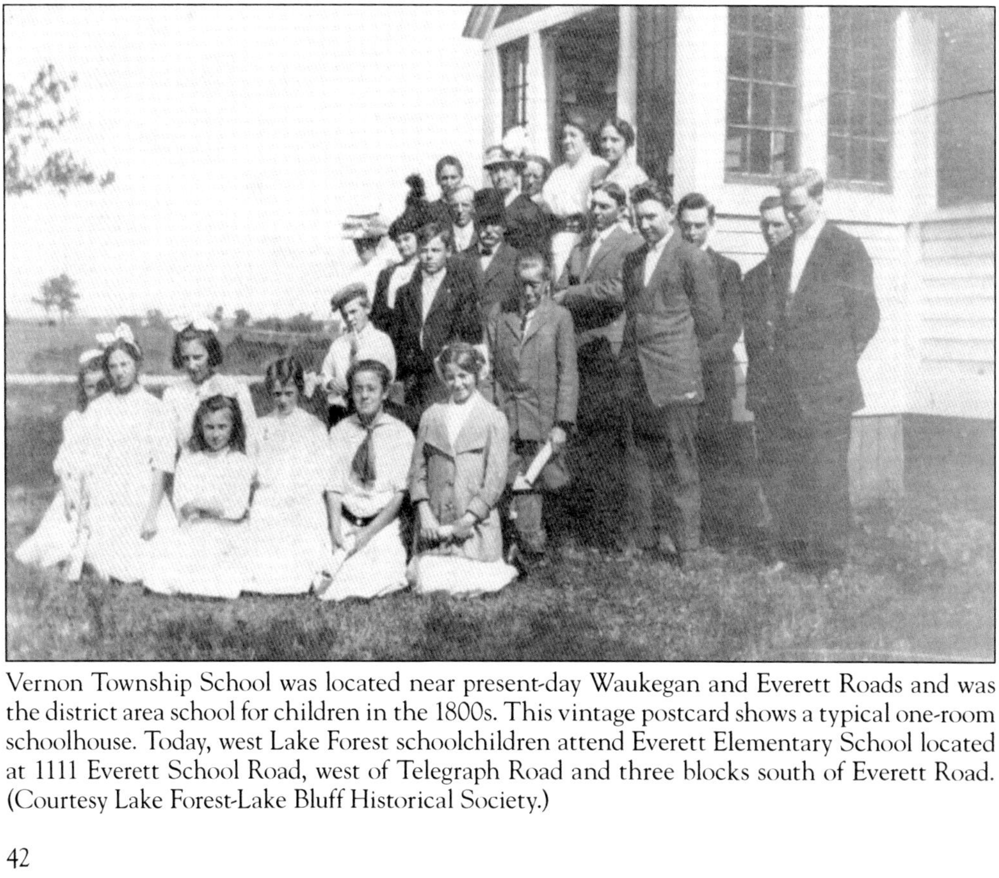

Vernon Township School was located near present-day Waukegan and Everett Roads and was the district area school for children in the 1800s. This vintage postcard shows a typical one-room schoolhouse. Today, west Lake Forest schoolchildren attend Everett Elementary School located at 1111 Everett School Road, west of Telegraph Road and three blocks south of Everett Road. (Courtesy Lake Forest-Lake Bluff Historical Society.)

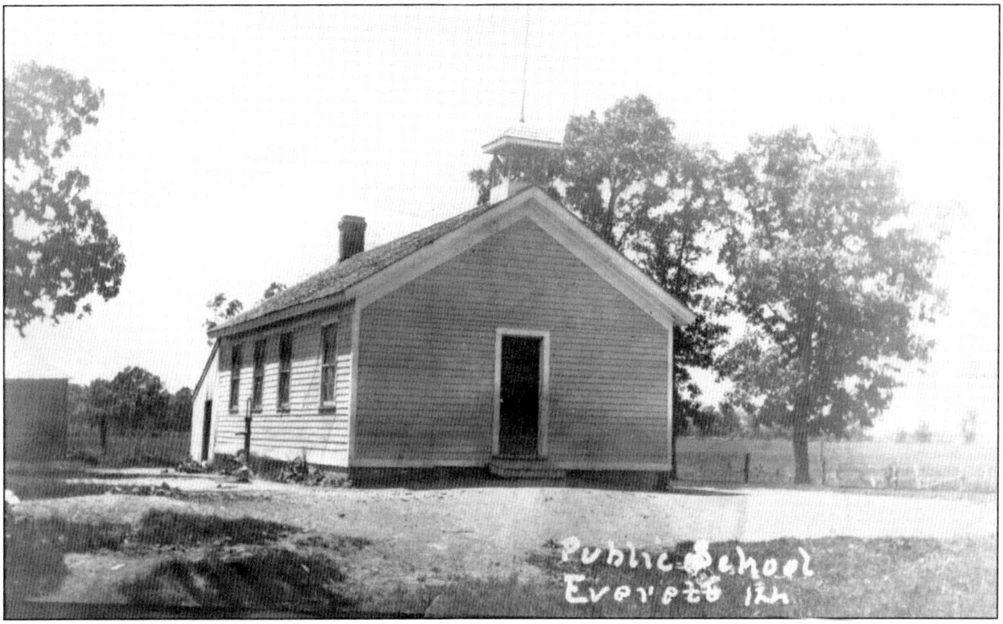

The old Lyons school was built in 1866, using planks for benches. Native Americans and settlers, it is reported, attended school together in Everett. The image above is from a c. 1910 photo-process postcard. The image below is from the 1918 Everett School history. By this time, classes had moved to the new brick school building on Everett Road. It is pictured here without its cupola and apparently not in use. (Both courtesy Lake County Discovery Museum and Archives.)

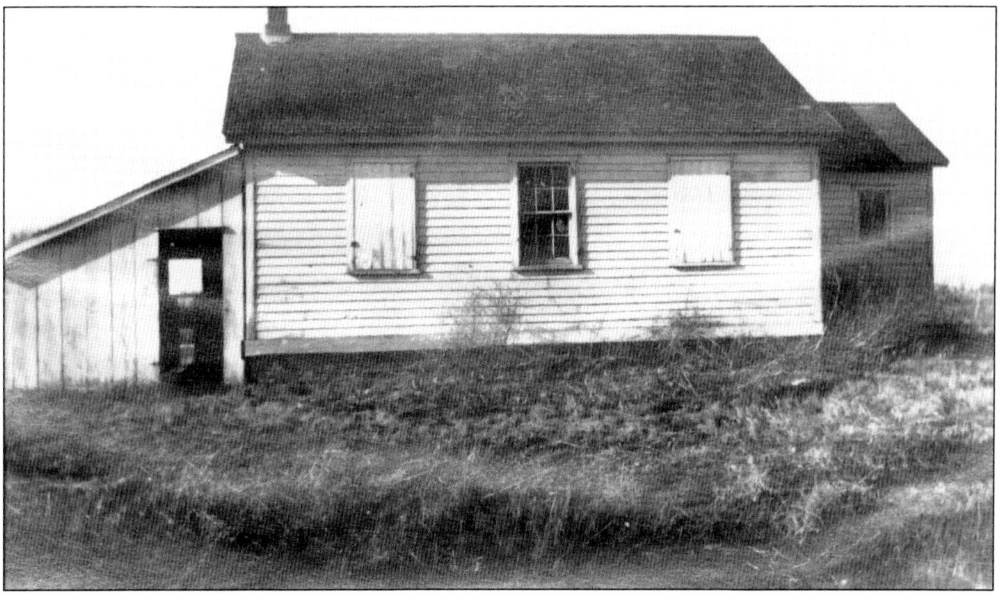

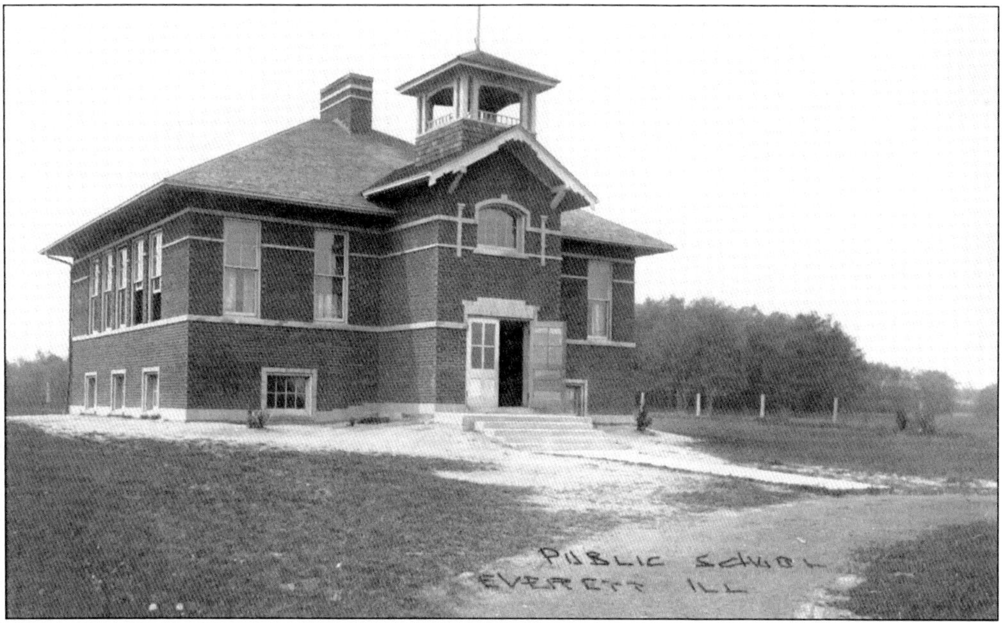

The brick replacement Everett School was built on the southwest corner of Everett and Telegraph Roads. The school was built in 1914 and later became a fire station until 1993, when the building was razed. Today, over 1,000 children attend the fourth and newest Everett School, located on Everett School Road, just south of Everett Road. The old school bell that used to call the children was restored by the Lake Forest Preservation Foundation and is now housed at Deerpath Middle School. (Courtesy Lake County Discovery Museum and Archives.)

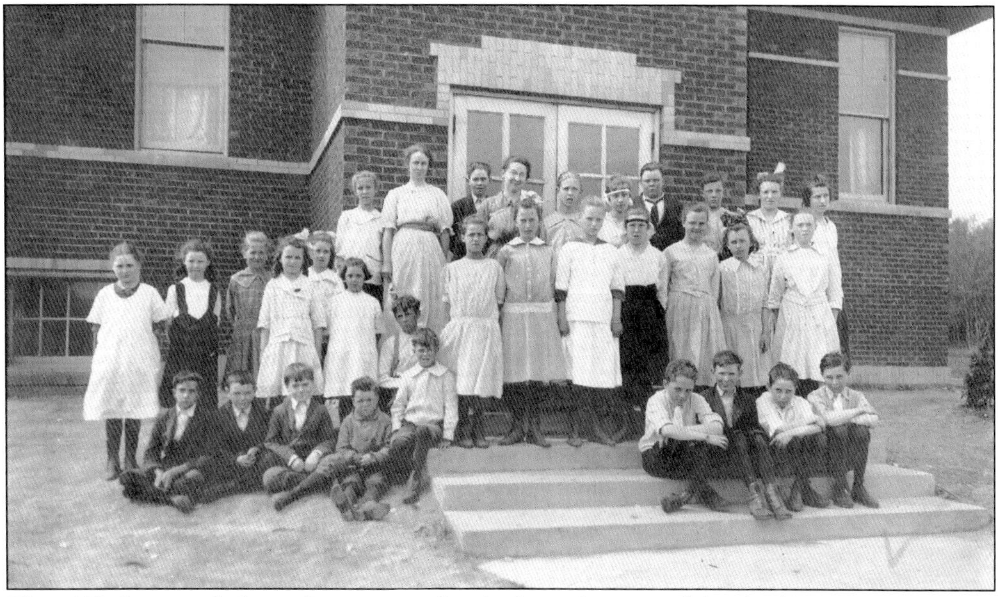

This 1927 photograph shows the entire student body on the stairs of the third Everett School. The school was located on former Louis F. Swift farmland west of the southwest corner of present-day Everett and Telegraph Roads. There were two rooms on the first floor, a basement below for the children's physical education and recess, when weather dictated, and a large furnace to heat the rooms. (Courtesy Lake Forest-Lake Bluff Historical Society.)

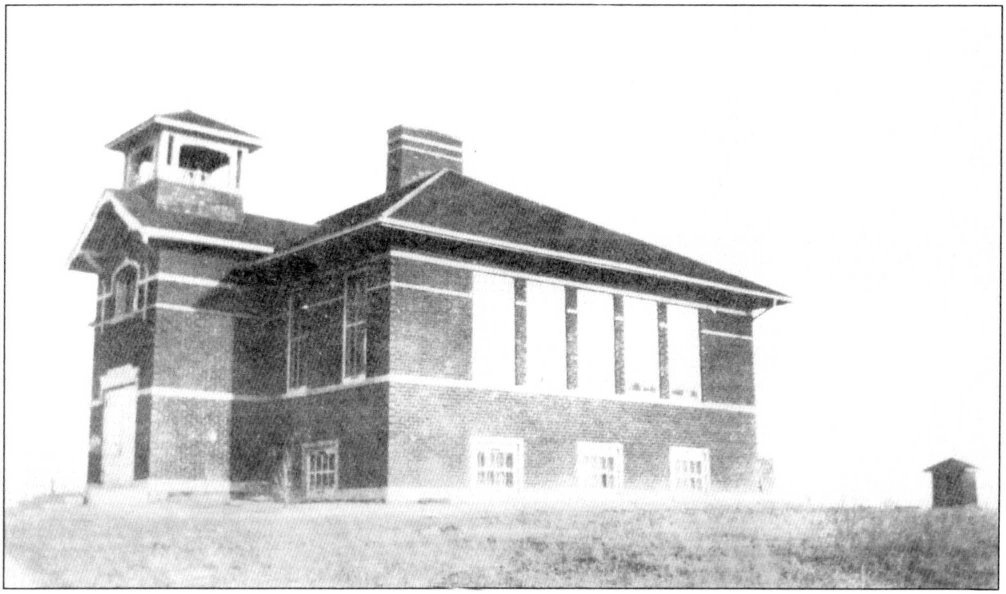

The horizontal banding around the 1914 building's exterior suggests a Prairie School style palette, located as it was on the broad and rich prairie lands west of the wooded lake shore area. Early teachers at the Everett school were Nellie Keough, from a local farm family, who taught the four upper grades, and Marie Kelly, who taught the four lower grades. (Courtesy Lake County Discovery Museum and Archives.)

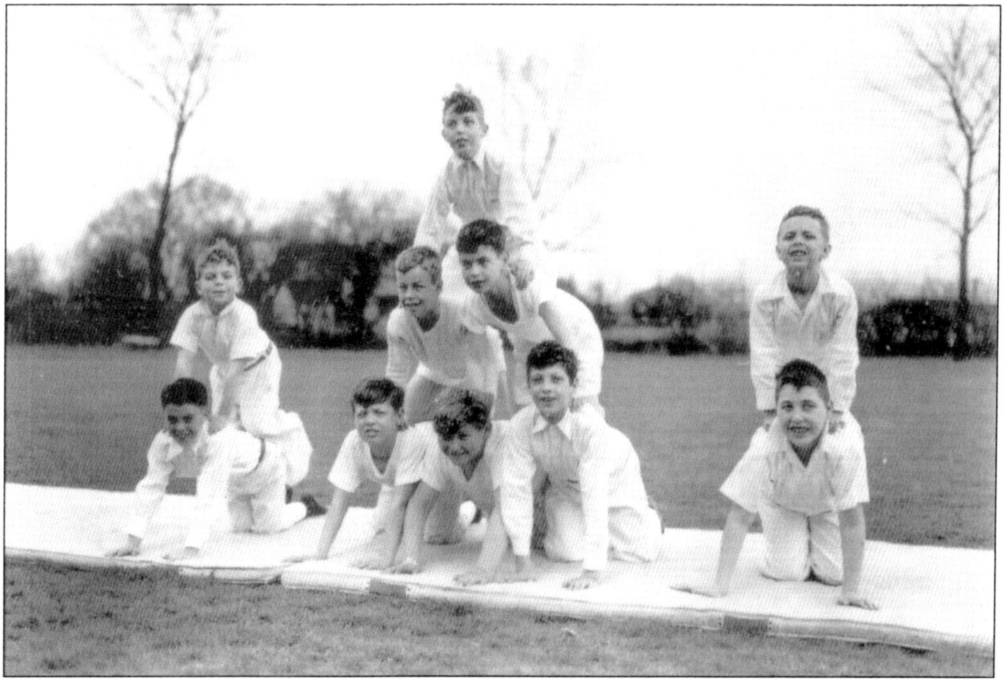

This 1940s image shows youngsters performing tumbling tricks at the Everett School Country Fair, the fruits of physical education classes. Now likely in their 70s or even 80s, these cheerful children are forever young and forever free from wartime and postwar cares in this moment frozen in time. (Courtesy Shirley Paddock.)

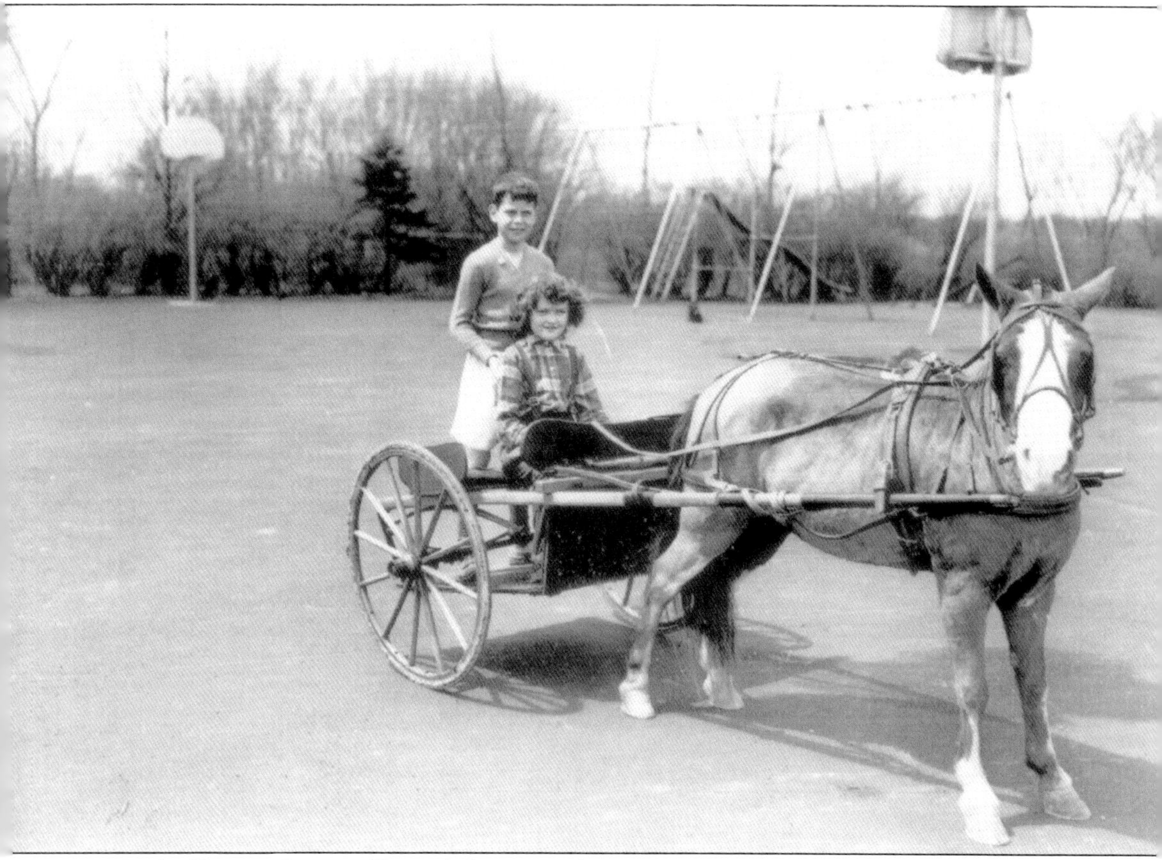

At the Everett Country Fair exhibition in the 1940s is a pony cart with its young driver and passenger. These fairs corresponded to 1920s Onwentsia children's fundraisers and summer dog and pony shows, as at the first Cudahy estate pictured in *Classic Country Estates of Lake Forest*. (Courtesy Shirley Paddock.)

This road leads to an old foundation from pioneer days, just off Old Mill Road. (Courtesy Susan Kelsey.)

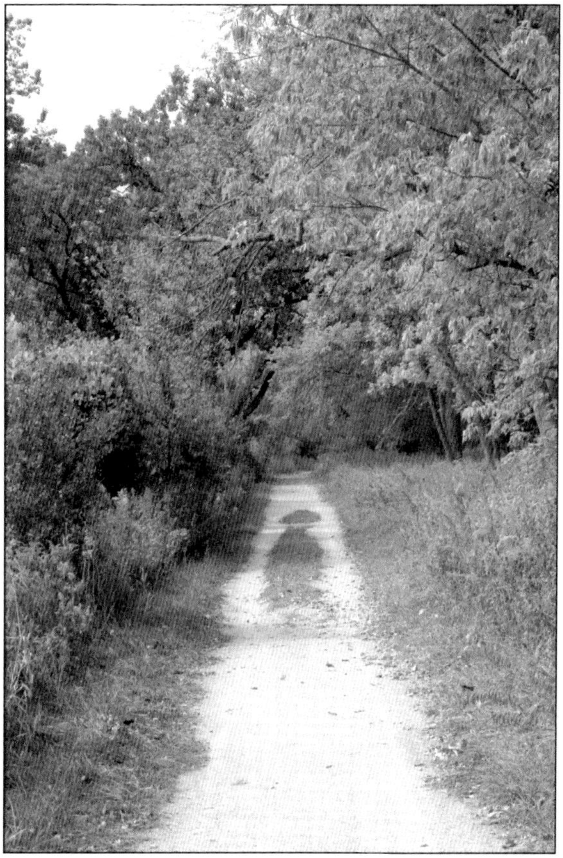

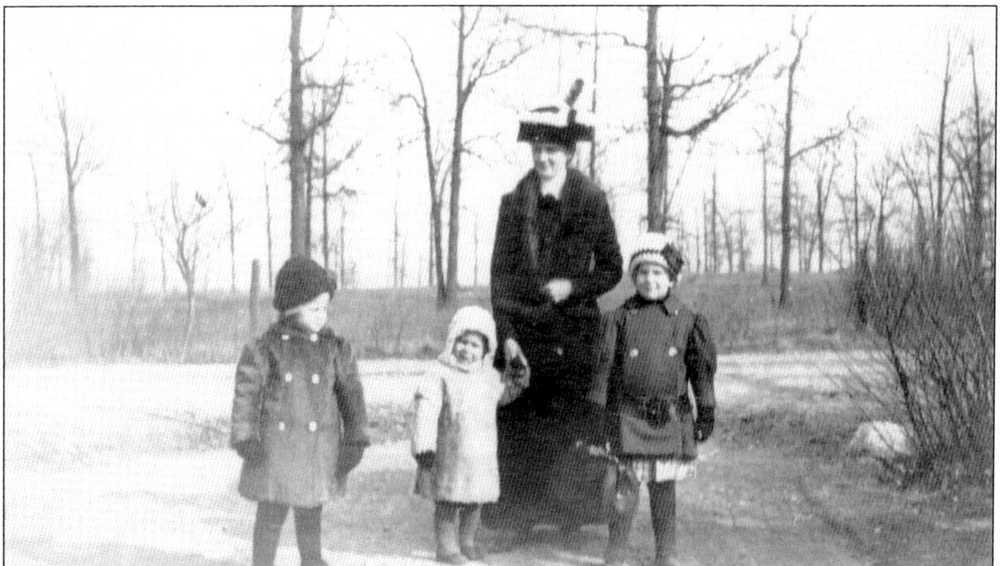

This photograph provides good insight into what the area looked like during the early 1900s. The Gustafson family is facing west on Ridge Road with the east to their backs. There are fewer trees than today. (Courtesy Leonard Gustafson.)

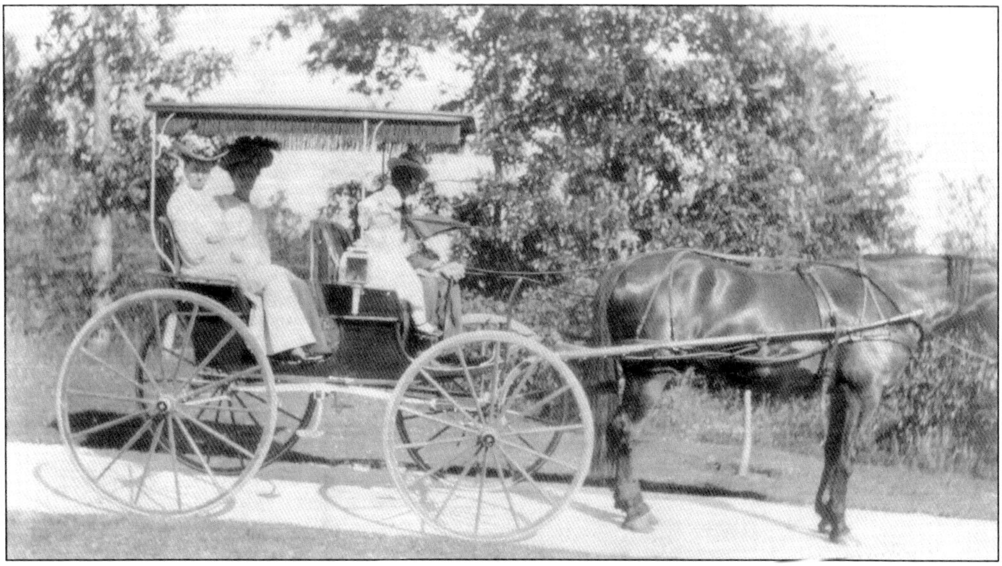

Shown here are the Gustafsons, dressed for a social occasion and riding in the same carriage pictured on page 31. Since the 1850s, trained estate workers like these had enjoyed an elevated status locally, and the arrival of Onwentsia in the mid-1890s brought this phenomenon with the estates into the west Lake Forest area. (Courtesy Leonard Gustafson.)

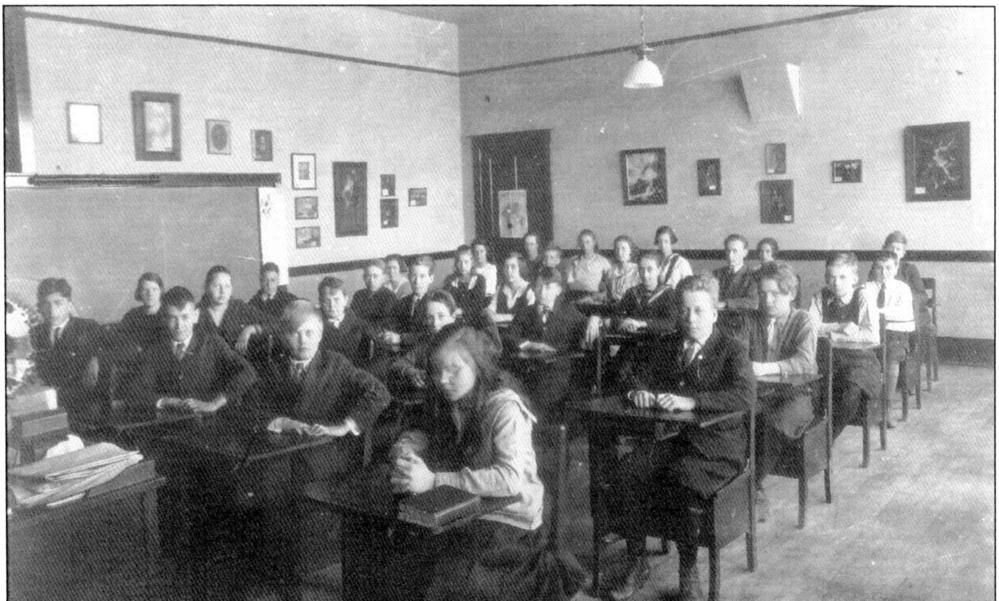

While this photograph shows Halsey school, located on the east side of Lake Forest, it also represents the inside of a typical classroom during the early 1900s, similar to what Everett School looked like. (Courtesy Leonard Gustafson.)

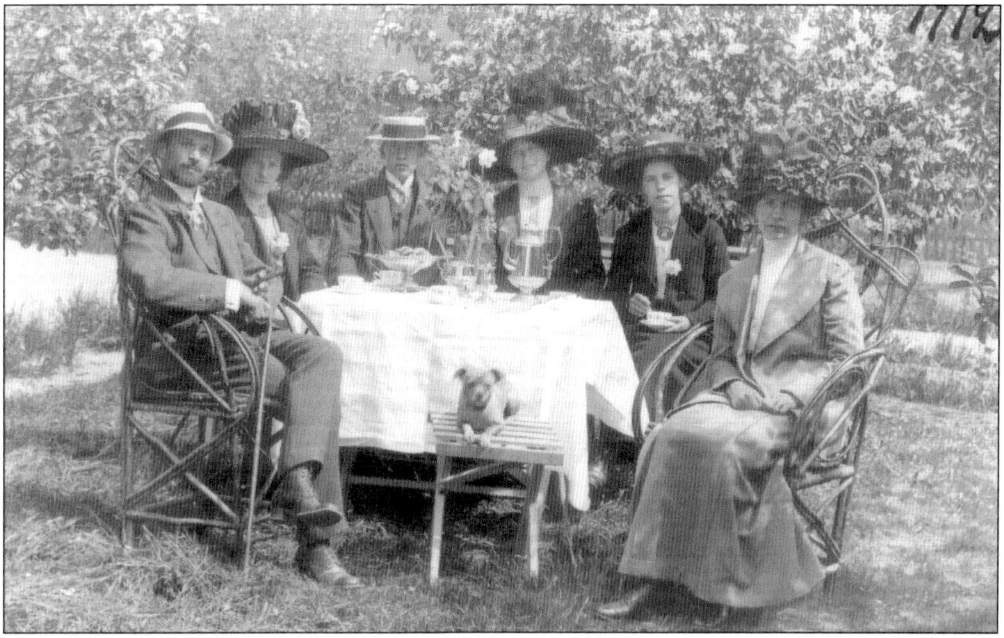

This refined party reflects the sophistication of the new wave of middle class estate workers and their families staffing the new west of Lake Forest estates. Charles King himself was a successful banker and broker and his daughter Ginevra, through her impact on author F. Scott Fitzgerald in the mid-1910s, was an iconic American figure of wealth and privilege. The specialist chosen to maintain the Kings' gardens and grounds, too, would have been at the top of his field. (Courtesy Leonard Gustafson.)

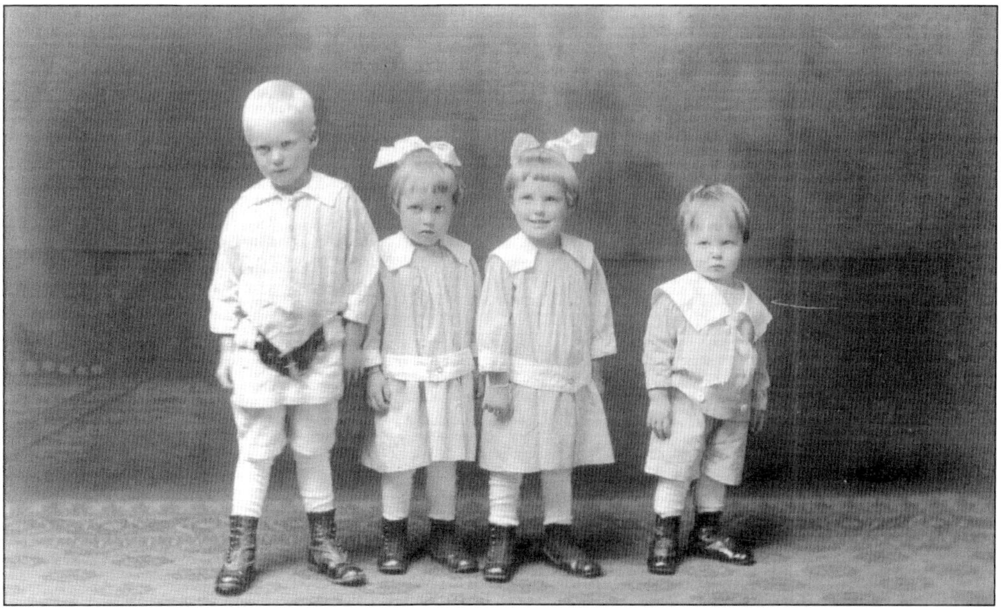

Further establishing this distinction for staff families of west of Lake Forest estates in the early 20th century, this view shows four Gustafson children well-dressed and posed for this formal portrait, perhaps to send to relatives, such as grandparents, elsewhere in this country and in Europe. (Courtesy Leonard Gustafson.)

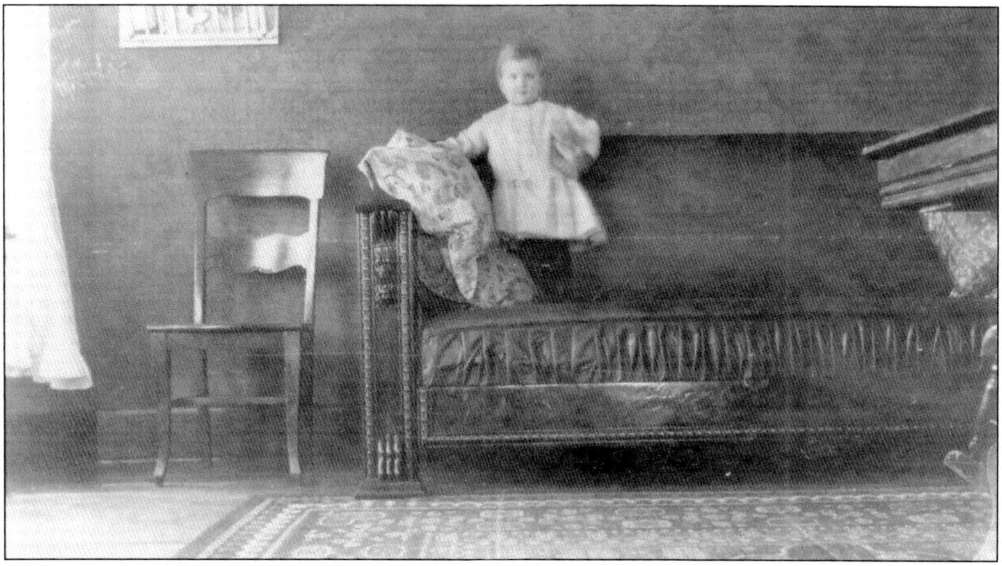

This photograph shows a Gustafson child posed on a couch in the parlor or living room of the Adler cottage of the Kings. The room appears to be well furnished indeed, in appropriate middle-class taste, and the couch very likely more comfortable than the one that served in the period at Howard Shaw's Ragdale living room, it not surviving the recent restoration there. (Courtesy Leonard Gustafson.)

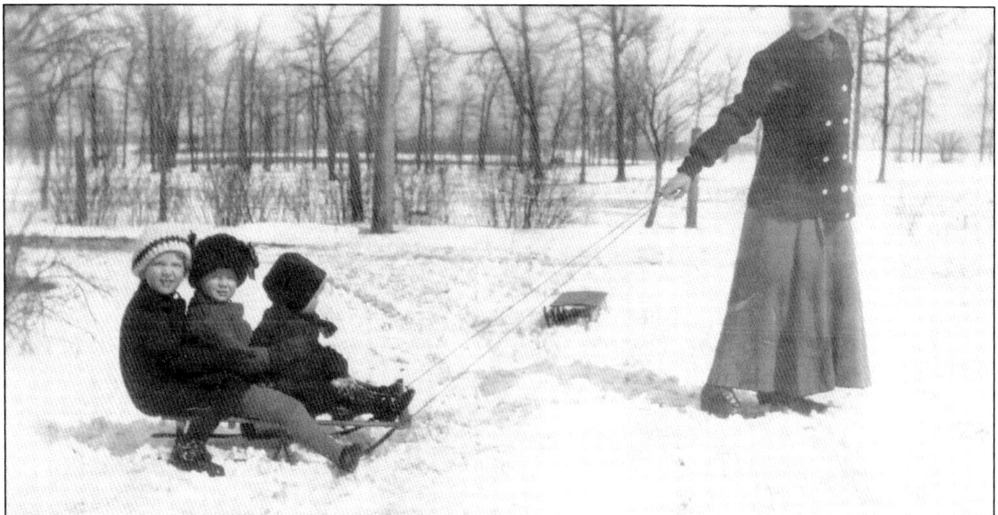

Abundant open space in west Lake Forest gave staff families like the Gustafsons lots of room to play, recalling here a scene from Swedish artist Carl Larsson's 1890s painting, "The Yard and the Washhouse (Brita with the Sleigh)." Larsson's evocative images of country life in Sweden may have inspired in that period Howard Shaw at Ragdale and also Alfred Lunt, at his Ten Chimneys nearby at Genesee Depot, Wisconsin. (Courtesy Leonard Gustafson.)

Shown here are young men dining in Lake Forest Academy's Reid Hall Garden Room in the 1950s. The academy moved to the former J. Ogden Armour estate in 1948, leaving East Lake Forest, the school's base for 90 years. The room pictured is the Armour Winter Garden, designed by Elsie DeWolf. (Courtesy Lake Forest Academy.)

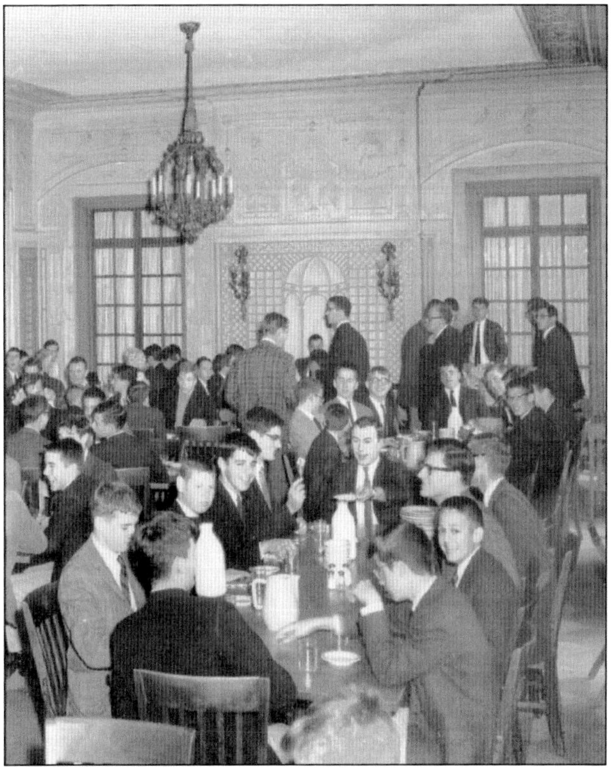

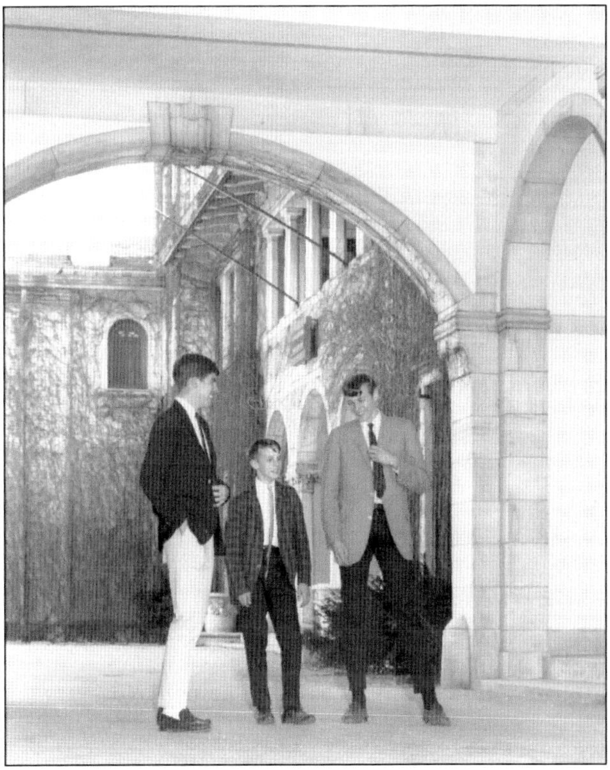

Students are seen here around the 1950s standing outside of Reid Hall, the former Armour mansion. Not long before this, noted novelist and then Knollwood Club resident Ward Just had daydreamed during academy classes of Gatsby-like characters walking the same halls and paths that he was traversing. Ward Just spoke about this at Lake Forest Library for the Friends of the Library in 1985. (Courtesy Lake Forest Academy.)

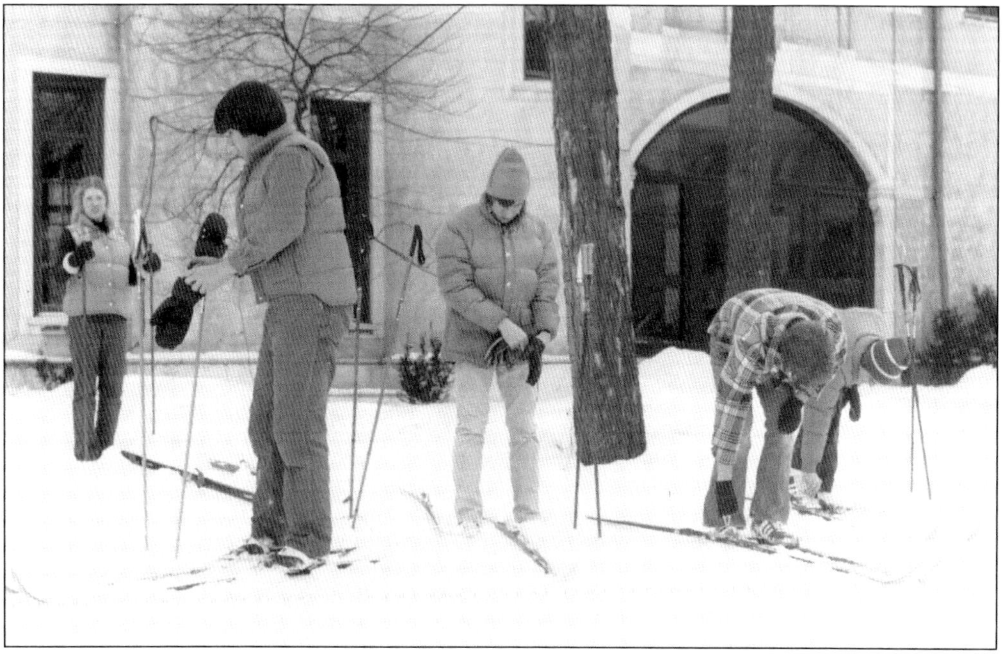

Lake Forest Academy boys' preparatory school was founded in 1857 east of the tracks in town, located in four places there in 90 years, and then relocated west of town on the former Armour property after a disastrous 1946 school fire. Here, boarding and day students both try cross-country skiing on the spacious grounds of the school around the 1980s. (Courtesy Lake Forest Academy.)

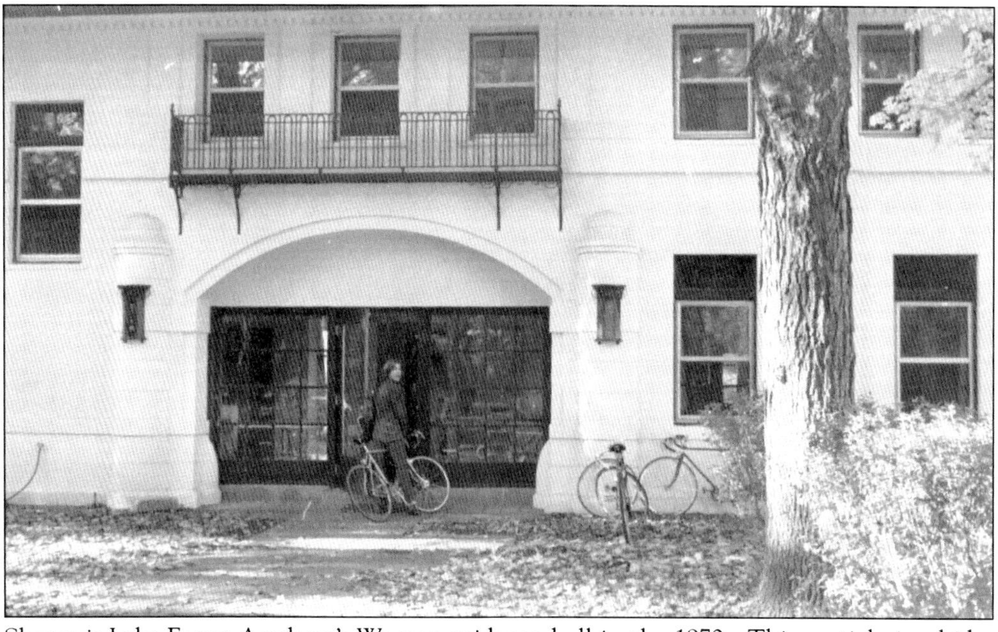

Shown is Lake Forest Academy's Warner residence hall in the 1970s. This partial view hides the scale of the structure, the Armours' stables and staff lodge north of the house, illustrated in *Classic Country Estates of Lake Forest*. In the 1940s and early 1950s, the academy reconfigured the massive estate buildings for school use. Author Ward Just describes the house in his 2011 novel *Rodin's Debutante* as adapted to a boys' school. (Courtesy Lake Forest Academy.)

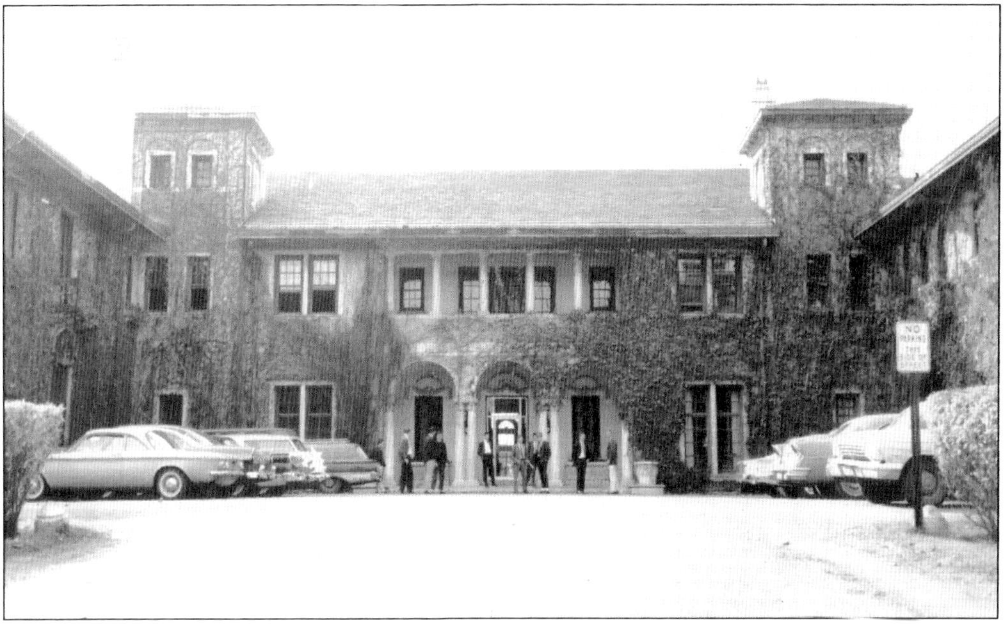

This view of the east entry facade of the Armour estate, a half-century after its heyday, shows what by the 1950s was Reid Hall. Unchanged, it fueled the dreams of Ward Just. (Courtesy Lake Forest Academy.)

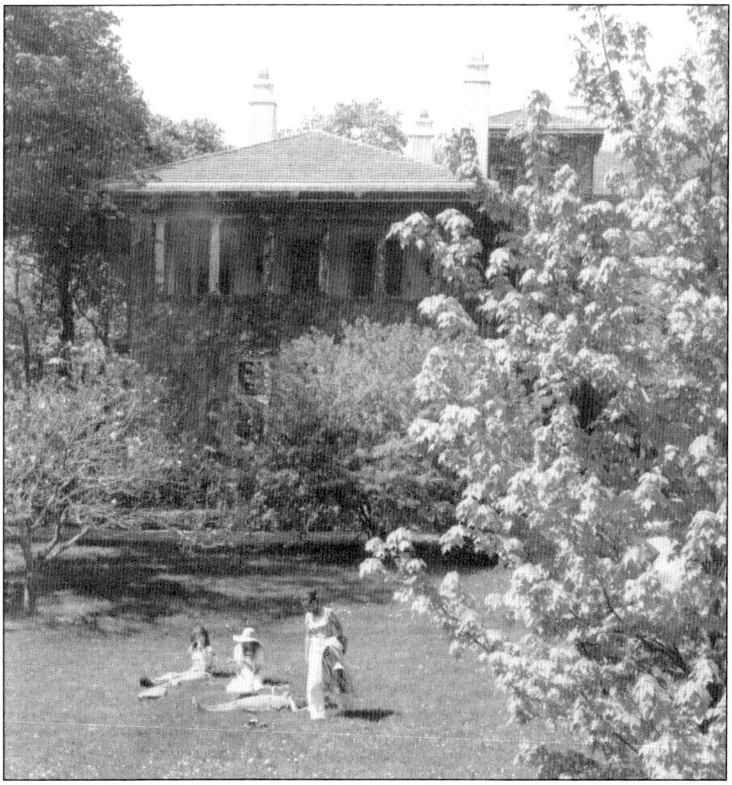

By the 1970s, young women also had joined the academy men, as the school briefly was known as Lake Forest Academy-Ferry Hall, reflecting the 1974 merger of the two venerable east Lake Forest institutions. The 1960s had brought dramatic changes in youth culture, and the schools pooled their resources and heritages, soon comfortably dropping Ferry Hall from the academy name, as coeducation became the norm in private independent schools. (Courtesy Lake Forest Academy.)

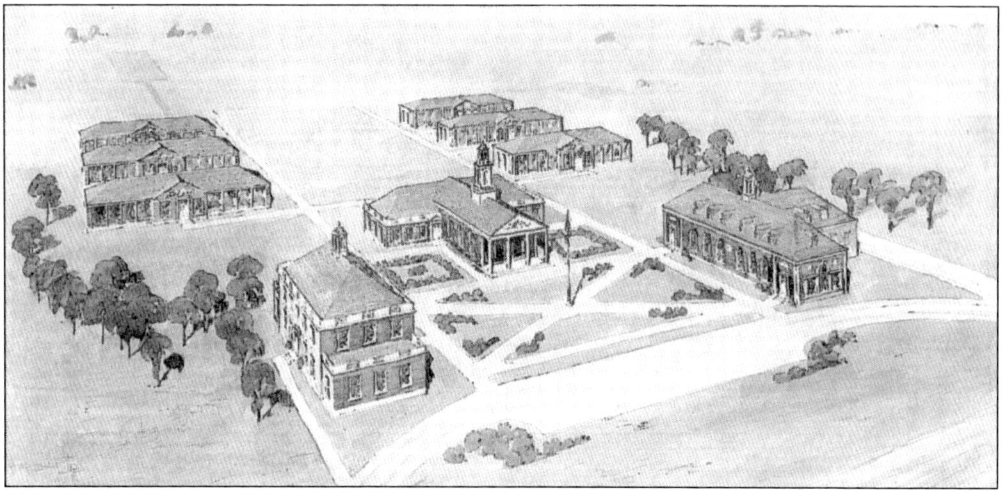

Historic buildings on the city's Grove School cultural campus now house the senior center in Dickenson Hall, the music institute, the pottery studio in Stirling Hall, and the career resource center, along with other activities and structures. The Ridge Farm Preventorium, established in 1914, treated children at risk for tuberculosis for almost half a century. Architecturally significant, the buildings after 1930 were designed by Edwin H. Clark and the Stanley D. Anderson firm. The buildings are located on 27 acres at 40 East Old Mill Road, east of Ridge Road. (Courtesy Lake Forest Senior Center.)

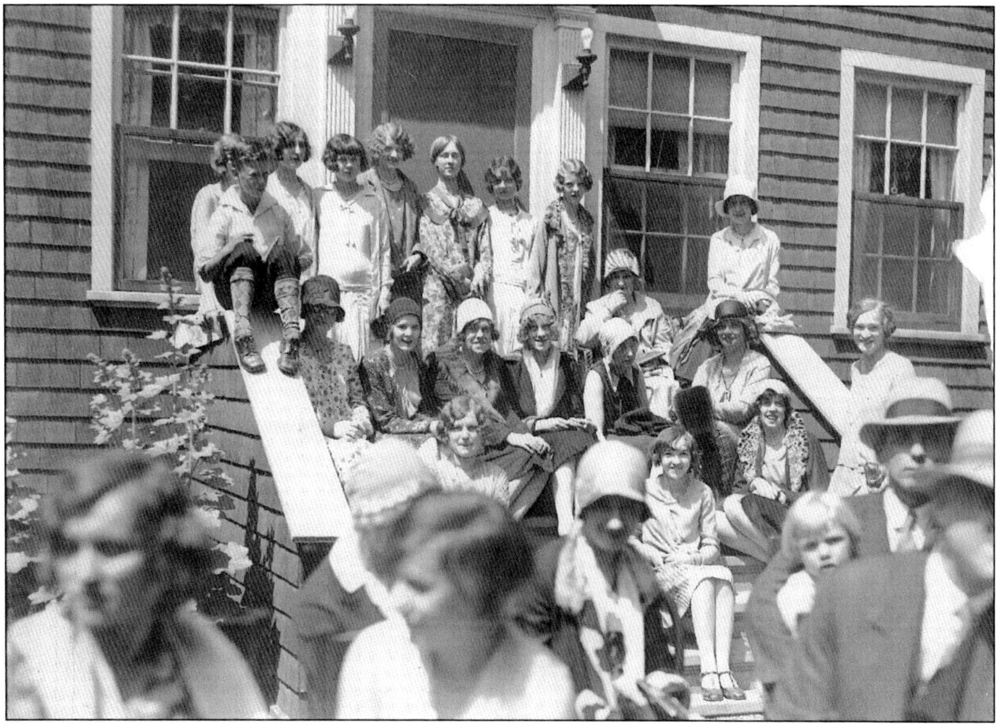

In the era before antibiotics, tuberculosis was a scourge that plagued Chicago, spreading in crowded neighborhoods. This building shows some of the early at-risk young people who were enjoying the fresh air of the country at the Preventorium. (Photograph by Mary McMasters, courtesy Jean McMasters Grost collection.)

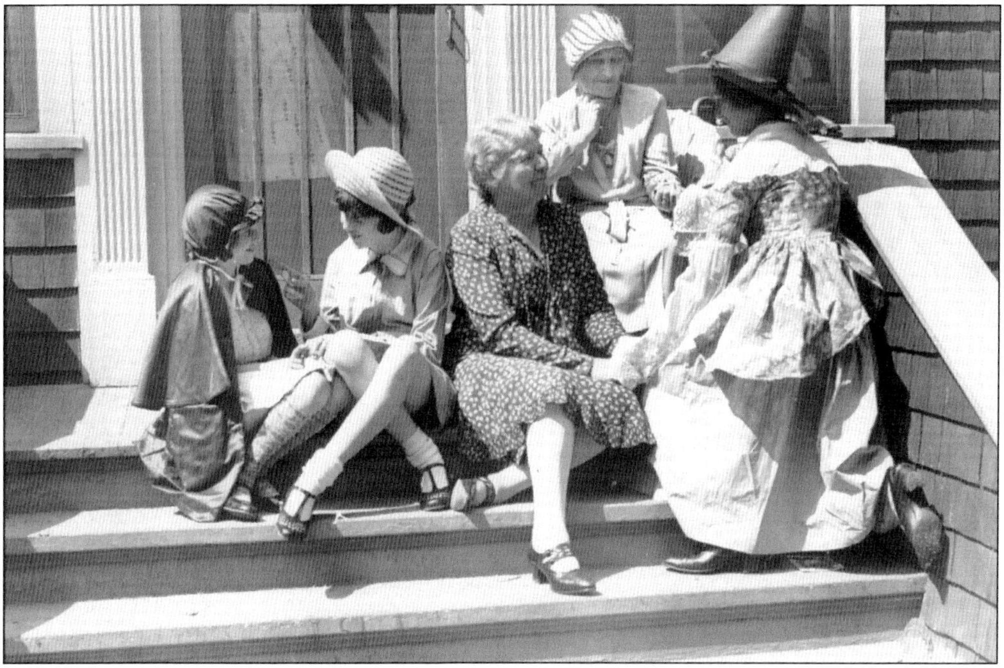

Here, a Halloween party is shown at this no longer extant structure in the early 1940s. Other such escapes for city children to the country nearby included Waukegan's Bowen Country Club (for Hull House), an Association House camp at Diamond Lake, and the Gads Hill settlement camp for mothers and children (formerly also Arden Shore), Lake Bluff lakefront. (Photograph by Mary McMasters, courtesy Jean McMasters Grost collection.)

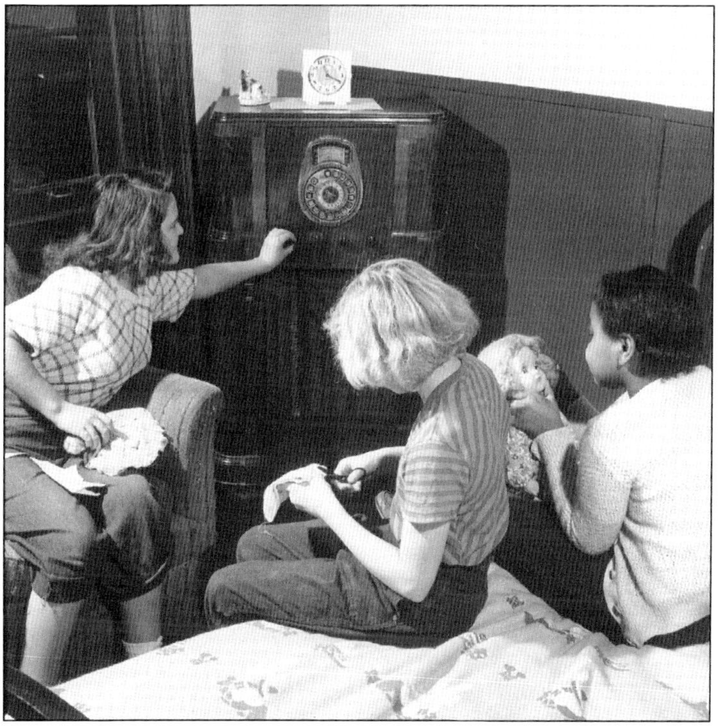

These Ridge Farm young women, gathered around a radio, show the middle class lifestyle that the retreat offered for these city children. A health initiative, it also offered to the young people a glimpse of a more orderly, less hand-to-mouth existence than might have been the norm in their neighborhood in 1930s and 1940s Chicago, like those characterized in novels by Chicagoans James T. Farrell and Saul Bellow. (Photograph by Mary McMasters, courtesy Jean McMasters Grost collection.)

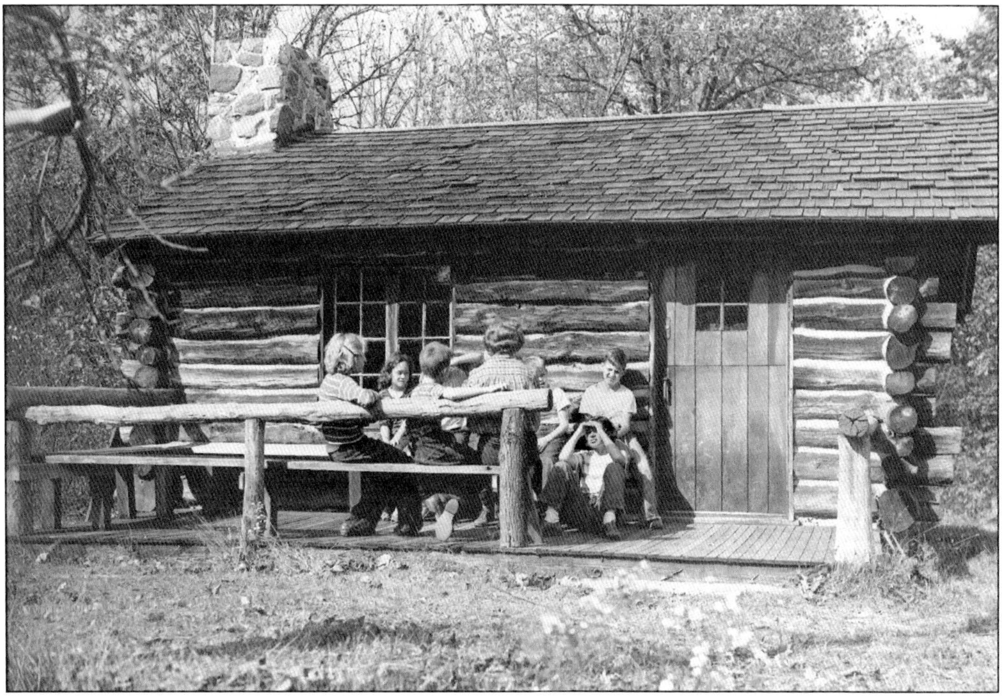

This 1930s log cabin at Ridge Farm reflected the estate ambiance of this campus on Old Mill Road just east of Ridge. The 1920s and 1930s saw an Americana architectural revival, including cabins on many of the estates east and west, with a whole cluster of them at what now is the Ryerson Woods Nature Preserve, Riverwoods, formerly the E.L. Ryerson Jr. Brushwood Farm, also involving architect Ambrose Cramer in 1941. (Photograph by Mary McMasters, courtesy Jean McMasters Grost collection.)

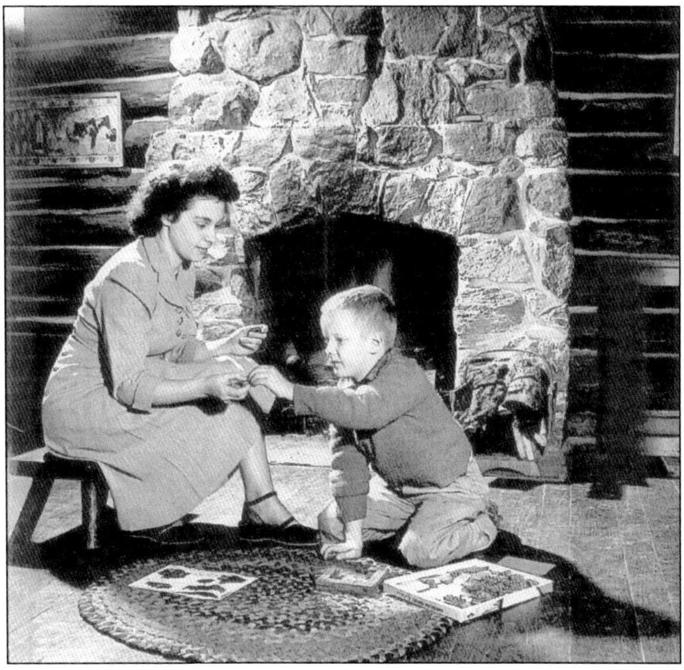

This teacher and a patient/student at the Preventorium's 1930 rustic, camp-like log cabin, again reflects the rich cultural experience of a stay at the health retreat. Not just for the middle class, cabins were in vogue in the 1930s and 1940s among the estate families of the nearby countryside. (Photograph by Mary McMasters, courtesy Jean McMasters Grost collection.)

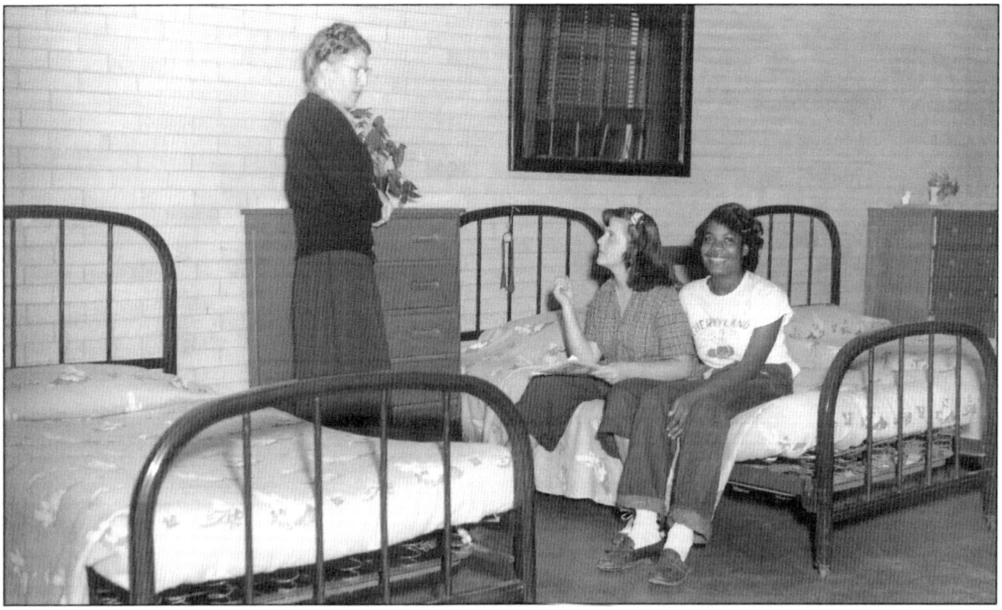

This is one of a group of photographs taken by the artistic Mary McMasters, who herself had been a volunteer (1926–1929) at Jane Addams's Hull House and understood the settlement house mission in Chicago. Probably part of a series of publicity shots for potential donors, this image shows a Spartan (apparently shared-bed) dormitory, though kept with rigorous cleanliness and order. (Photograph by Mary McMasters, courtesy Jean McMasters Grost collection.)

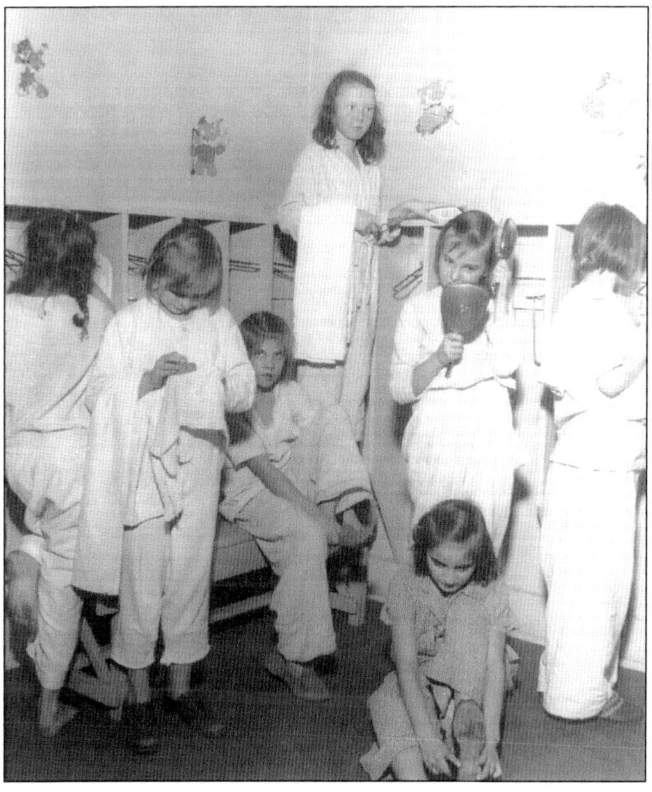

This 1940s photograph by Mary McMasters shows that the group lifestyle of the children while at the Preventorium was not unlike rustic summer camp for middle-class youngsters then and now. (Photograph by Mary McMasters, courtesy Jean McMasters Grost collection.)

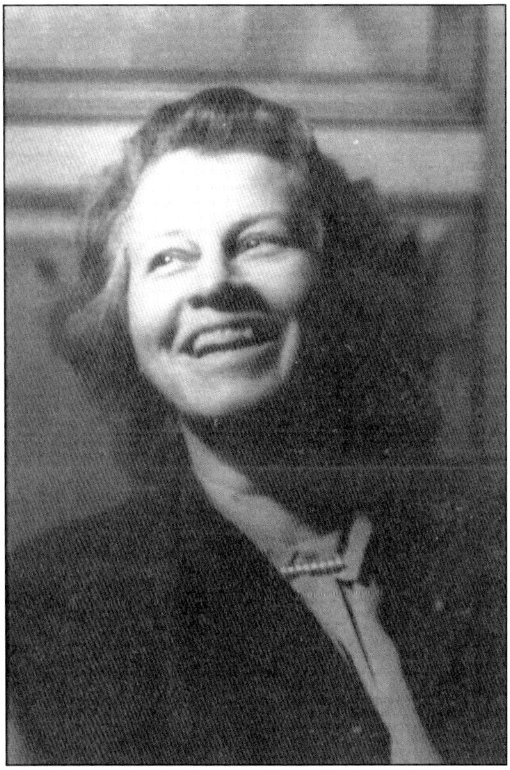

This is a striking portrait of director Charlena Elliott of the Ridge Farm Preventorium at its zenith in the 1930s and 1940s, after the new facilities were built and before antibiotics ended the mortal danger for children with tuberculosis. She represented the fine teachers and administrators who lived and worked in Lake Forest but may not have owned property or continued to live in town after retirement. (Photograph by Mary McMasters, courtesy Jean McMasters Grost.)

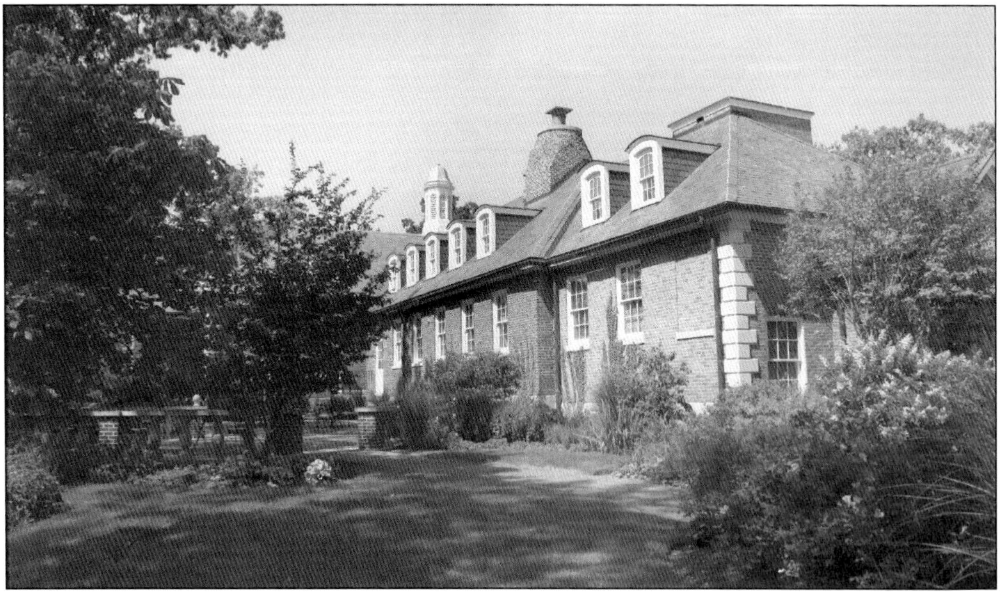

This is a view of Dickinson Hall (1930), built in the William and Mary Christopher Wren style then being recreated at Williamsburg; it now houses program activities of the Lake Forest-Lake Bluff Senior Center and also serves the unincorporated Knollwood community, north of the city of Lake Forest. With its superb architectural detailing, it joins the Armour estate in being a significant west Lake Forest structure devoted to not-for-profit and, later, public use. (Courtesy Susan Kelsey.)

Three

Gentlemen's Farms and Dairy Farms

John Conway, one of the earliest settlers in Lake County, had his dairy farm straddling present-day Conway Road, just west of Waukegan Road. According to Diana Dretske, historian with the Lake County Discovery Museum and Archives, dairy farms grew in popularity after the Civil War ended in 1865. There were several dairy farms in the area, Mellody Dairy Farm notably. Dretske states that "the most famous dairy in the United States" was Crab Tree Farm on Sheridan Road north of central Lake Bluff, begun in 1905 and led by the high profile and formidable entrepreneur Grace Durand (Scott).

The gentlemen's farms locally grew out of, in part, the wish to free up farmland west of Lake Forest for foxhunting and paper chases. The land was bought from the pioneer families who otherwise could not work it while putting up with the intrusions of the riders. In general, this was part of a larger reform-era trend in providing local, fresh, unadulterated food for families. These farms did not depend on selling crops for their existence, but rather often on subsidies from resources gained elsewhere to make ends meet. If money was generated, that was fine, but it was expected in most or many cases that the land could not be entirely profitable. A central purpose of gentlemen's farms was the study and promotion of "scientific farming," to increase productivity and ensure cleanliness and sanitary production of food, especially dairy products.

Over the years, many gentlemen farmers were executives or owners of Chicago businesses or the children of prominent Chicago industrial and trade families. Their farms transformed the landscape of Lake County from homesteads with traditional white clapboard farmhouses to estate houses and elaborate gardens designed by famous architects and landscape gardeners. Among these farms were Cyrus McCormick's Walden with farmland to the west as well as on the lakefront, Arthur Meeker's Arcady Farm, Grace Durand's Crab Tree Farm (more self-supporting than most), Robert Leatherbee's Brae Burn Farm (Green Bay Road, north of Lake Bluff), and Malcolm Boyle's Lakewood Farm. Samuel Insull's place, now the Cuneo Museum and Gardens, Vernon Hills, was outstanding for its efforts to demonstrate the advantages to farmers of electric power, and it caused Lake County to be the first such area to gain rural electrification by 1910, a quarter century before the rest of the country with the 1930s New Deal.

In this period, the first two thirds of the 20th century, west Lake Forest was a distinctly post–family farm, specialized retreat region for Chicago's business and social elite. Landmarks of this phenomenon continue to define the character of west Lake Forest, from the Lasker estate in the southwest to the Knollwood Club in the north, with the Armour estate and Elawa farm in between.

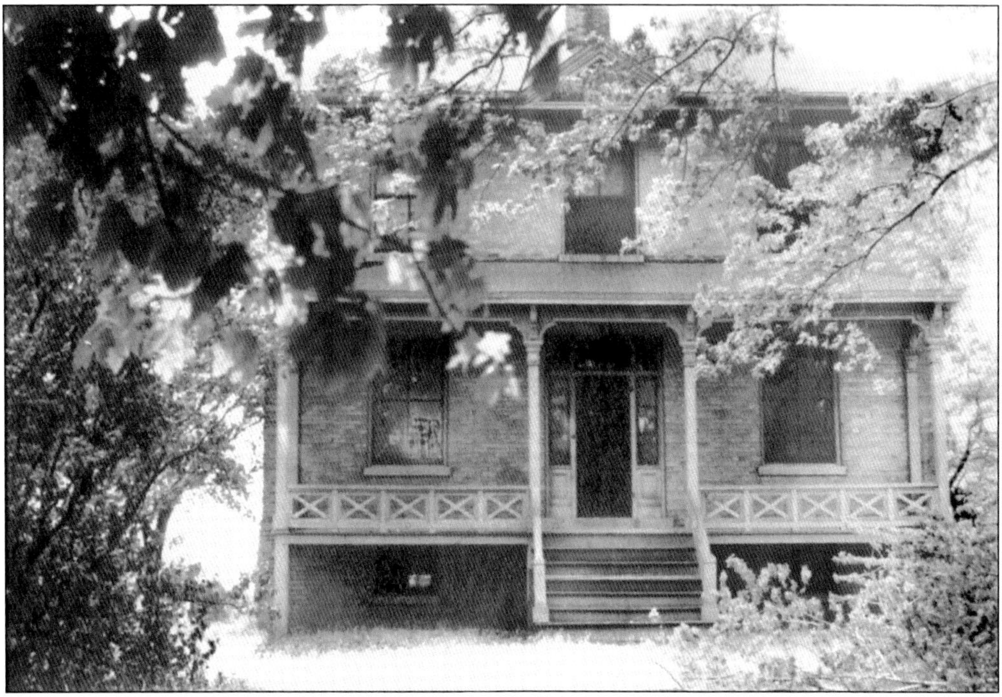

An original Conway family farmhouse was this one-and-a-half-story bungalow-style dwelling, perhaps incorporating earlier versions. (Courtesy Ambassador and Mrs. Robert Stuart private collection.)

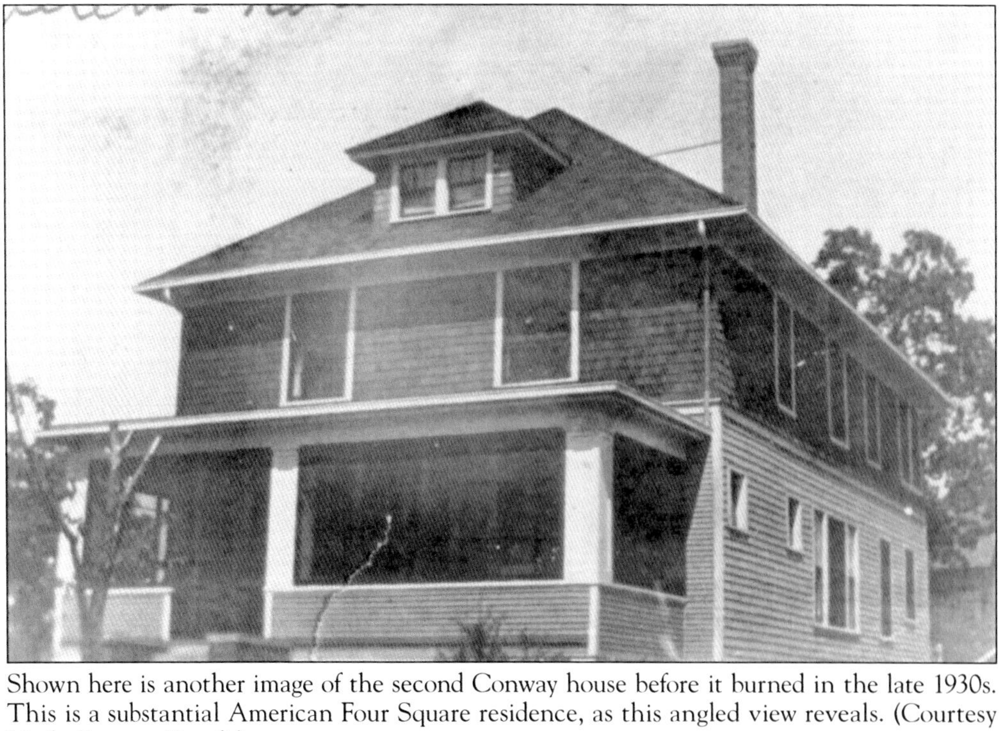

Shown here is another image of the second Conway house before it burned in the late 1930s. This is a substantial American Four Square residence, as this angled view reveals. (Courtesy Linda Conway Biondi.)

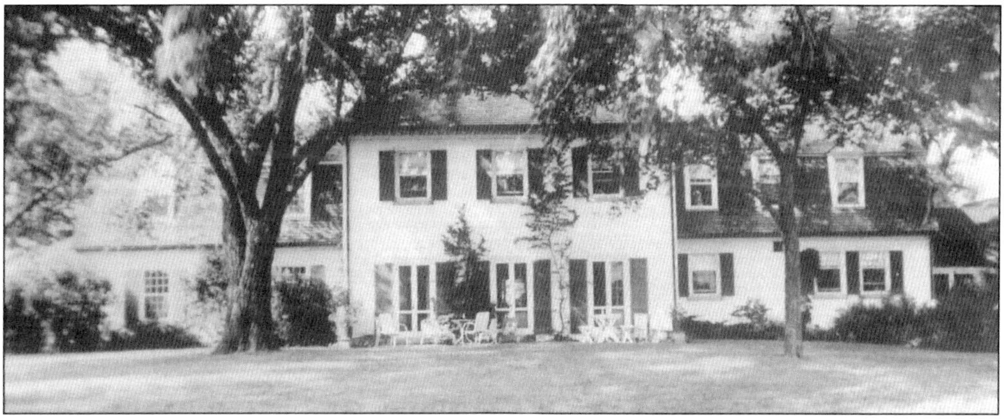

This image shows Topsfield Farm, as it was renovated on the Conway homestead beginning in 1955 by architect Stanley D. Anderson's firm for Ambassador Robert Douglas Stuart, his first (late) spouse, and their young family. Stuart, now in his mid-90s, is the son of R. Douglas Stuart and Harriet McClure Stuart, of Mayflower Road. R. Douglas with his brother John ran Quaker Oats in the mid-20th century, a firm assembled in the trust era, over a century ago, combining many oats processers. Originally based in Cedar Rapids, Iowa, the Stuarts moved their operations headquarters to Chicago around 1900 and lived in Winnetka. Young Robert D., a Yale law graduate, launched America First in 1940, prior to Pearl Harbor, to keep the United States from getting directly entangled in the war in Europe. The December 7, 1941, attack on Hawaii ended that aspiration, and the Cold War Soviet occupation of much of Europe until the end of the 1980s fulfilled some of the worst fears of the idealistic America First. This group had included many well-meaning and intelligent locals, backed up by the *Chicago Tribune* editorial policy of balancing Hitler against the anti–business class, take-no-prisoners Soviets. Robert D. followed his father in leadership of the Quaker concern and later, was ambassador to Norway, where he met his second spouse, Lillian Løvenskiold. (Courtesy Ambassador and Mrs. Robert Stuart collection.)

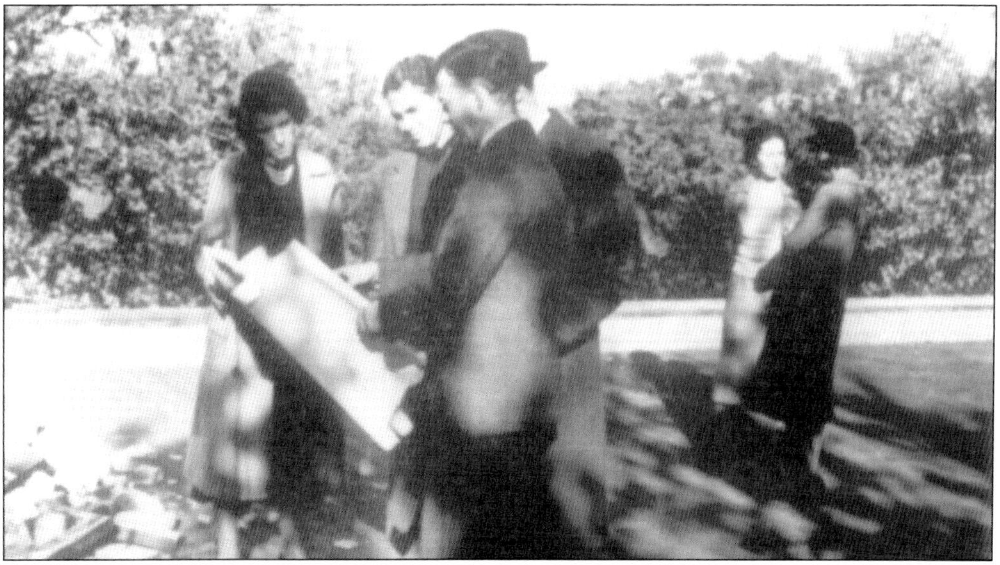

This photograph appears to show the Stuart family and perhaps Anderson or his associate William Bergmann going over the plans for Topsfield Farm. In 1936, Stanley D. Anderson converted the Conway farmhouse into an elegant estate house for John G. Beadle, CFO for the A.B. Dick Company. (Courtesy Ambassador and Mrs. Robert Stuart private collection.)

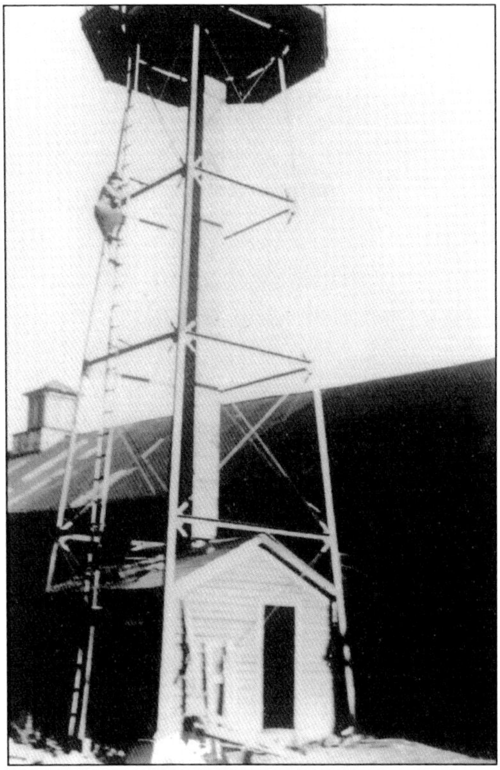

This old water tower, typical of the era, was located on the Conway farm property. Water would be pumped to the tank using the power of a windmill, stored for future use, and then, using gravity, would water the gardens or animals. (Courtesy Ambassador and Mrs. Robert Stuart private collection.)

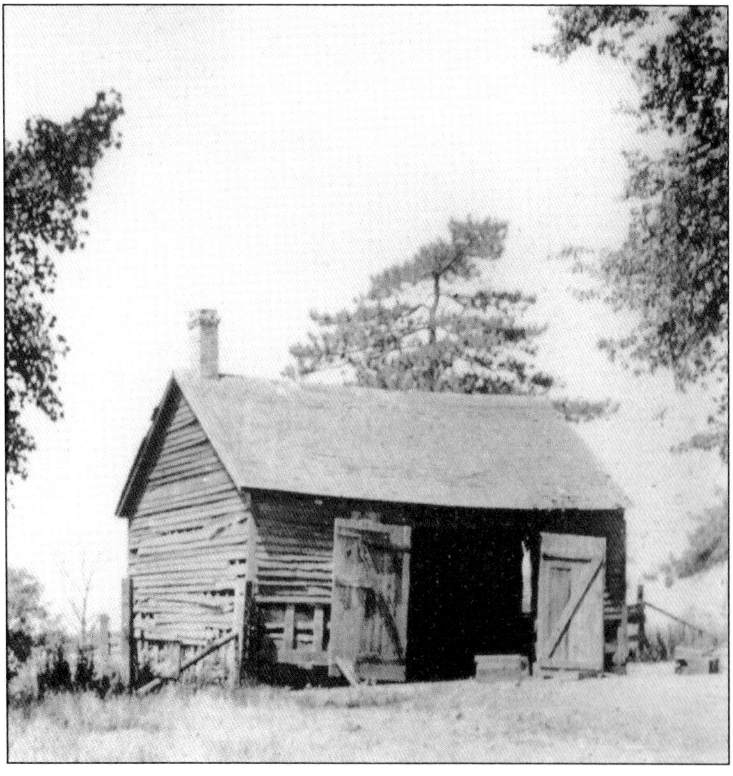

This early Conway family farm log outbuilding was a survivor into the mid-20th century. (Courtesy Ambassador and Mrs. Robert Stuart private collection.)

This 1950s photograph of the Topsfield Farm lawn looks west across the undeveloped fields of what are today the Conway Farms residential development and its stellar golf course of the 1990s, site of national golf tournaments. This also precedes the late 1950s construction of the tollway that divided the countryside west of Lake Forest, former foxhunting terrain, into what has become Lake Forest proper on the east side and Mettawa on the west side, still with Lake Forest postal addresses. Estate-era Lake Forest anglophiles from the early 1900s through the 1970s may have fancied this landscape similar to that of the English countryside. The Stuart family, rooted locally back to the arrival of Dr. James G.K. McClure and Phoebe Dixon McClure in 1881, claimed the status of landed gentry. Phoebe especially claimed a heritage older than the republic of elite economic, political, and social position in Connecticut and western Rhode Island (where the McClure family summered over a century ago). (Courtesy Ambassador and Mrs. Robert Stuart private to collection.)

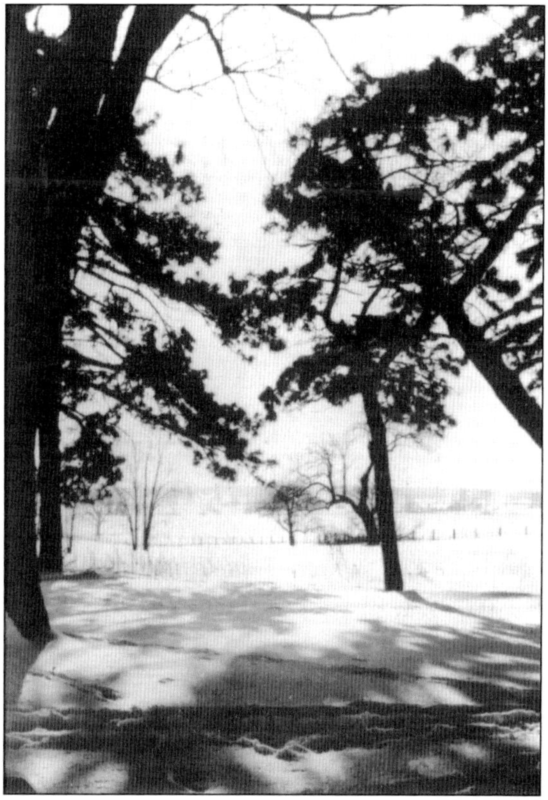

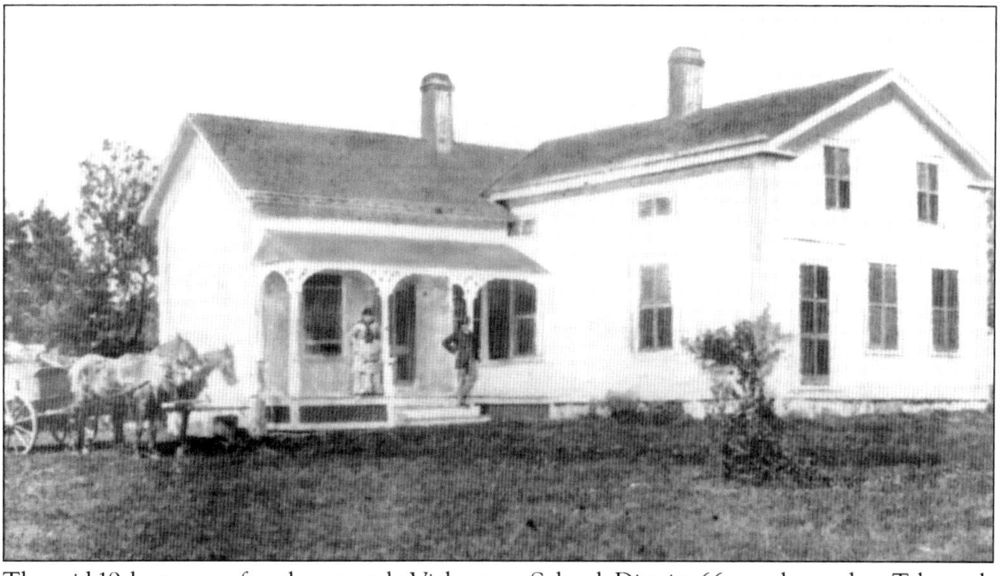

The mid-19th century, farmhouse-style Vickerman School, District 66, was located on Telegraph Road, now North Waukegan Road. It reflects the prosperous farm economy of west of Lake Forest by the time Chicago Presbyterians were establishing their chic lakefront, natural-landscape town for millionaires with its distinctive, curvilinear streets. Either part of the farmhouse/school could have been a log house that was covered by mill-cut clapboards after the 1855 train line at Lake Forest made this practical and affordable. (Courtesy Elawa Farm Foundation.)

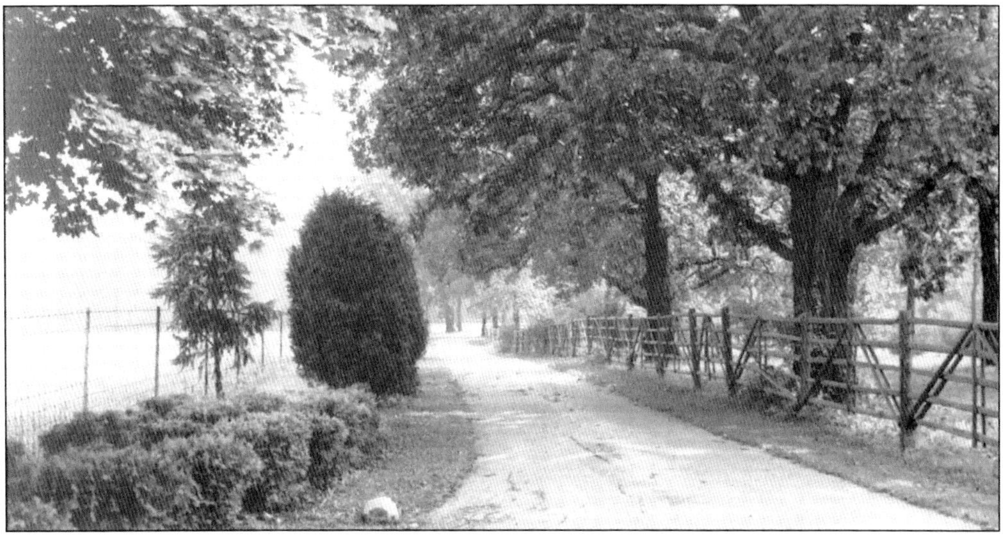

This handsome country lane led from North Waukegan Road west and down the gentle slope toward the Middlefork slough to the 1915 farm group designed by New York stable block specialist, architect Alfred Hopkins, for the A. Watson Armours. This lane, a direct result of this exchange of wealth, recalls calmer times on English or French estates and farms. The Amour clan—new money compared to the McClure/Stuarts, Farwells, and Durands of east Lake Forest, though with a fortune eclipsed only by that of the Rockefellers at the time—was able to build on a grand scale, as cousin J. Ogden Armour had demonstrated with his 1904–1910 Mellody Farms, not too far south. (Courtesy Elawa Farm Foundation.)

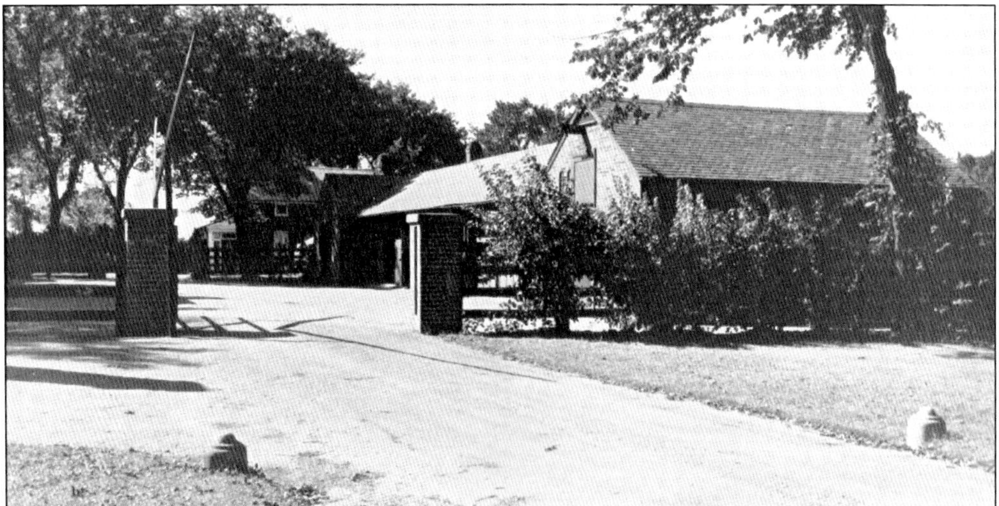

Shown here is the destination at the end of the long drive west to Elawa Farm, the central block of Hopkins's brick farm group, recalling Georgian predecessors in England. The landscape design was accomplished by Ralph Rodney Root of Root & Hollister, first in the summer of 1916 in Lake Forest to teach in the first "beta test" summer-session school for landscape architectural students, meeting at Gorton and housed at the college while funded and organized by the Garden Club of Illinois, the Lake Forest Garden Club by 1922. Later significant figures who were students that summer were Annette Hoyt Flanders, Charles W. Wagstaff, and Helen Brown (Milman). (Courtesy Elawa Farm Foundation.)

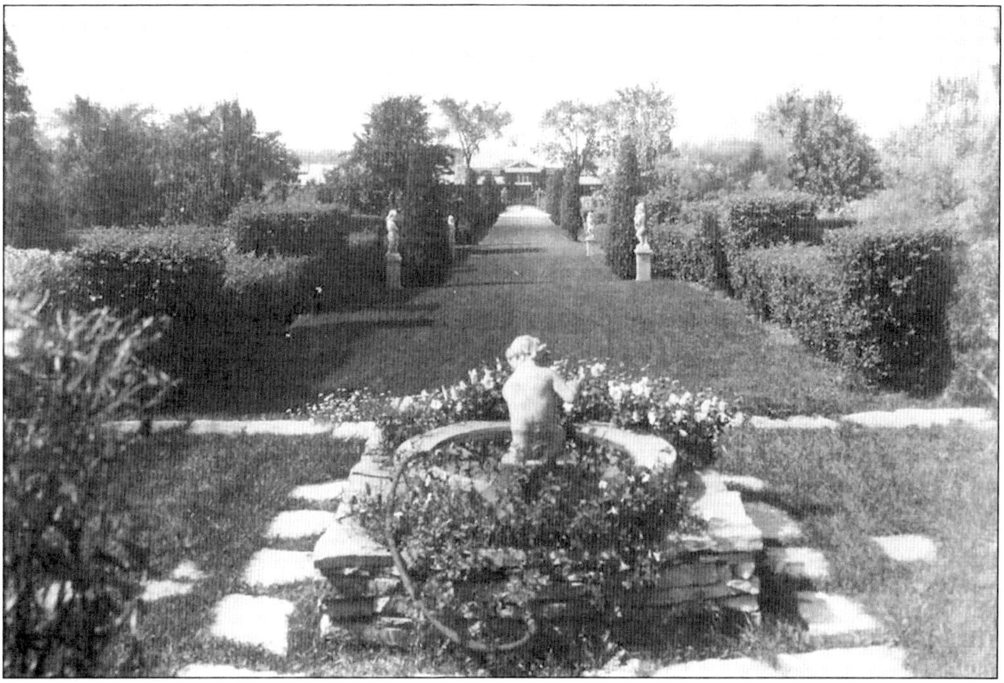

This garden, east and uphill from the Hopkins farm group's Georgian central stable block, shows Root's formal garden for the Armours, today the site of a restored vegetable garden, among other things, and an attraction on Garden Conservancy Open Days, held here annually. The architectural, squared hedges, with two levels, were quite similar to the presumably-extant privet hedges of the Eugene Pike second house and garden at 955 North Lake Road, accomplished with David Adler and Robert E. Work in 1917. (Courtesy Elawa Farm Foundation.)

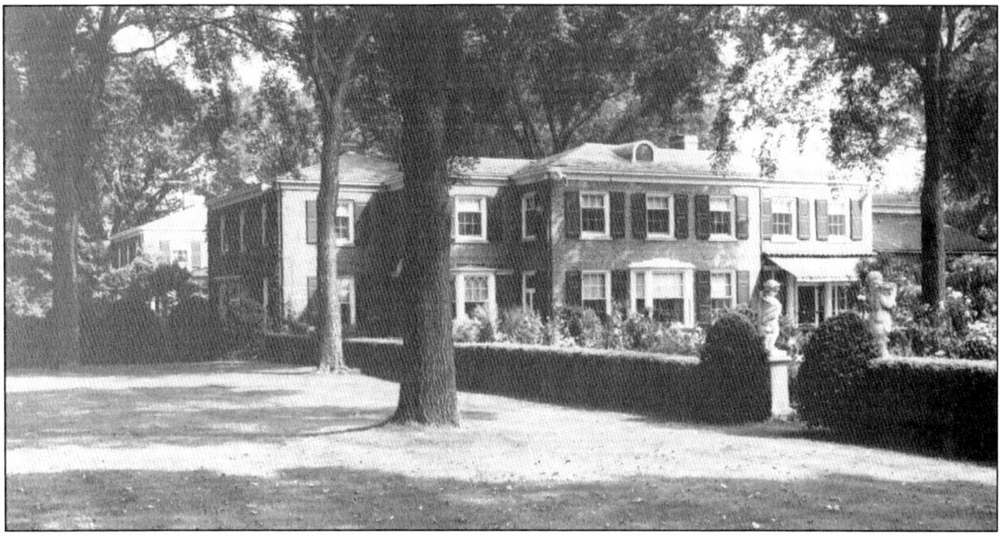

This is a view dating from the Armour period from the northwest showing the westernmost of two staff cottages of the pre-1917 period by architect David Adler, with a garden hedge again by Root & Hollister. The story of the rise and fall of the Armour fortune is told elsewhere, but the main house by Adler was never built, and instead the A. Watson Armours at first "camped out" weekends in the cottages (as did Mrs. Morse Ely and Philip Armour in Lake Bluff) and then settled in after the Armour fortune evaporated in the early 1920s. When the fortune was restored in the early 1930s, these Armours had accommodated themselves quite well to this little cluster of cottages, and only in the later 1930s had Adler build a tunnel between the two for rainy and wintry days. Perhaps until then, they were still thinking of building the great house. Today, the cottages and gardens are being restored by old-garden whisperer, Craig Bergmann, for his own home and professional studio. These, with the farm group, were preserved in the second half of the 20th century as Lewa Farm by the Carroll family. The Lewa name was taken from the names Leila and Wallace Carroll. (Courtesy Elawa Farm Foundation.)

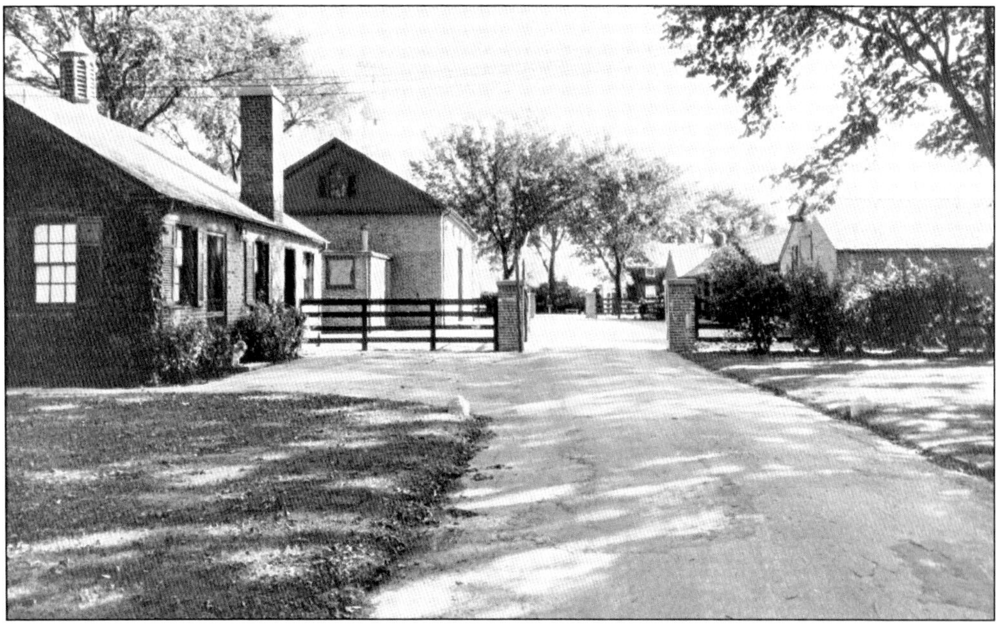

Lewa Farm, owned by the Carrolls from 1954 through the rest of the century, was a working gentleman's farm through the 1980s, according to a story in the June 20, 1999, business section of the *Chicago Tribune*. Barry Carroll's father bought 125 acres initially, which ultimately grew to 600. By 1992, though, the forest preserve was setting out to condemn the Carroll acreage as preserved open land. Carroll, to manage this process, began developing the land with homes and contributing acreage to the forest preserves, Lake Forest Open Lands, and the city. These mid-century views show Lewa Farm Connemara horses imported from Ireland with Kim Robinson, daughter of Mary. Mary Robinson published *The Modern Horseman* magazine and featured the Connemaras in June 1960. (Courtesy Mary Robinson.)

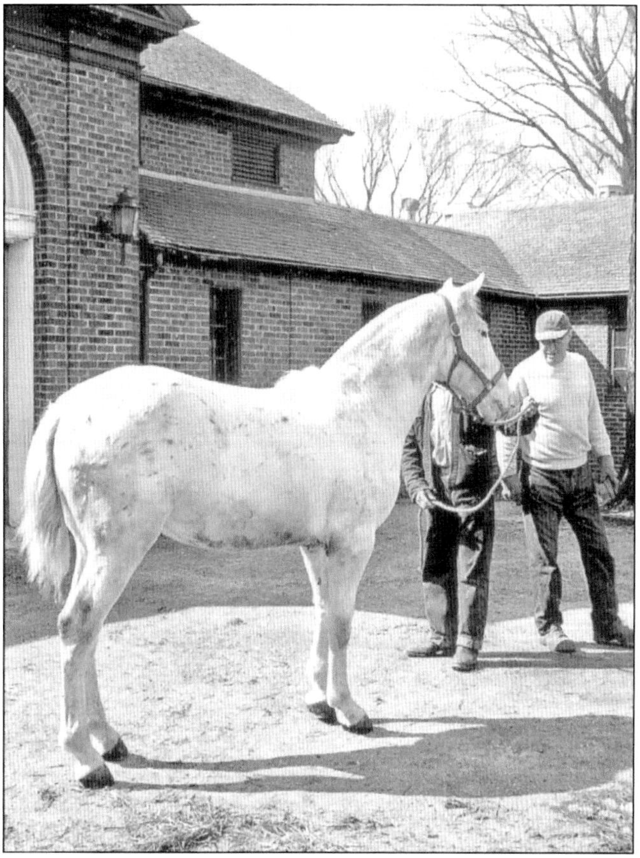

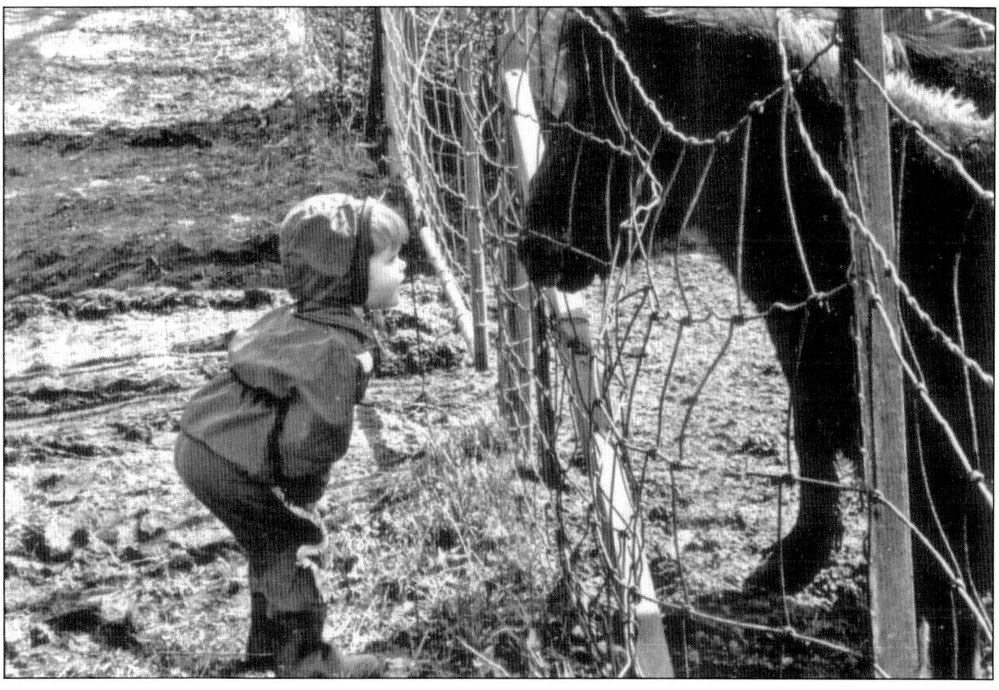

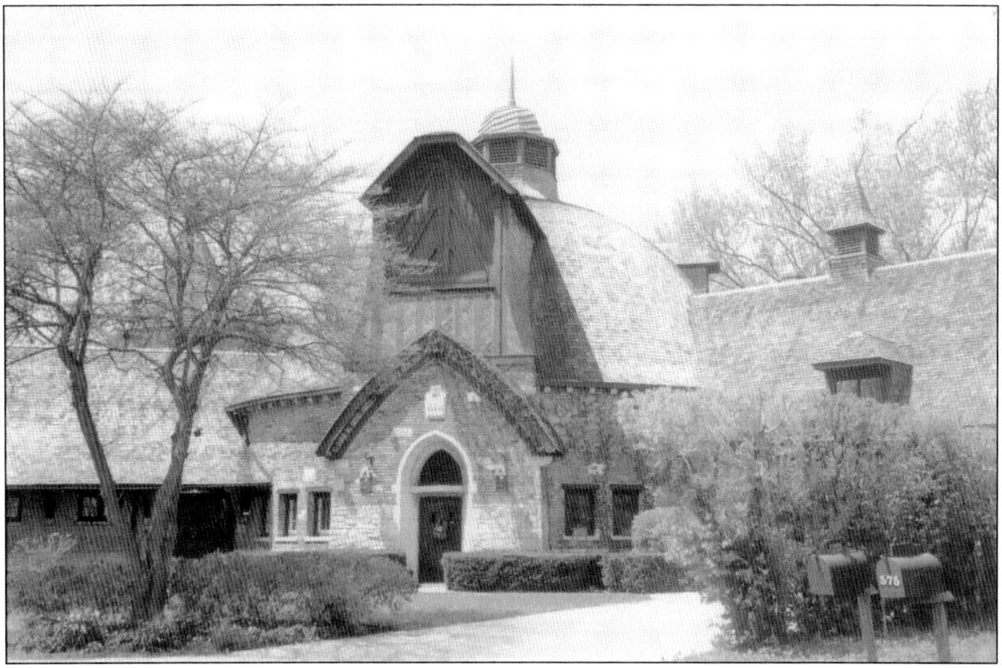

Dairy barns, or this part of them, were located on the west side of Waukegan Road. This had been the Leonard/Ewing place earlier, the latter when combined with Helen Culver's 1900 Pond & Pond brick country house, on Ashlawn today, in the 1920s by Culver's nephew and real estate business partner, Charles Ewing. The five-building dairy farm is now five private homes, as shown above. These dairy barns were designed by architect Ralph Varney. (Courtesy Jean Grost McMasters.)

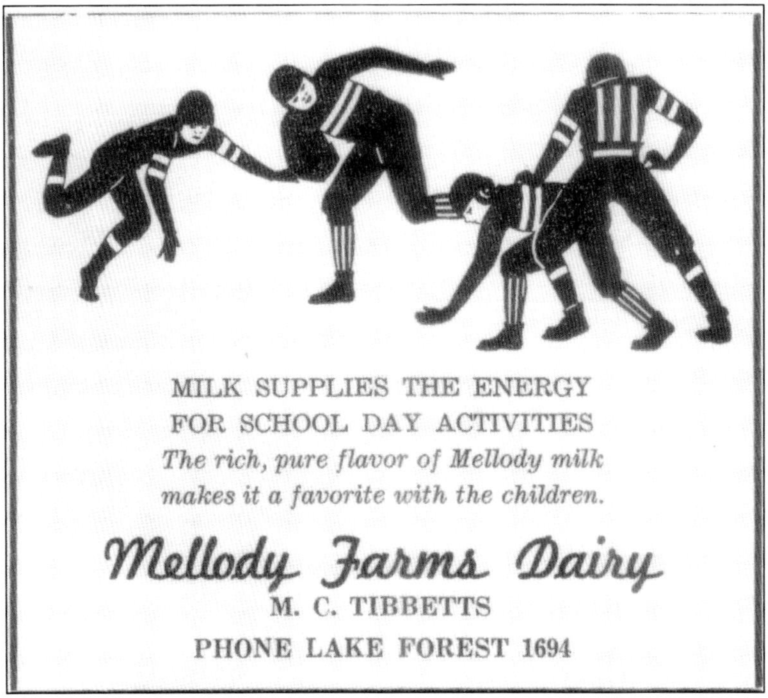

This 1930s advertisement (note the simple phone number) is for Mellody farms milk, and promotes milk as a healthy energy booster. The Hawthorn Mellody Farms organization still produces milk and dairy products in the Midwest. (Courtesy Shirley Paddock.)

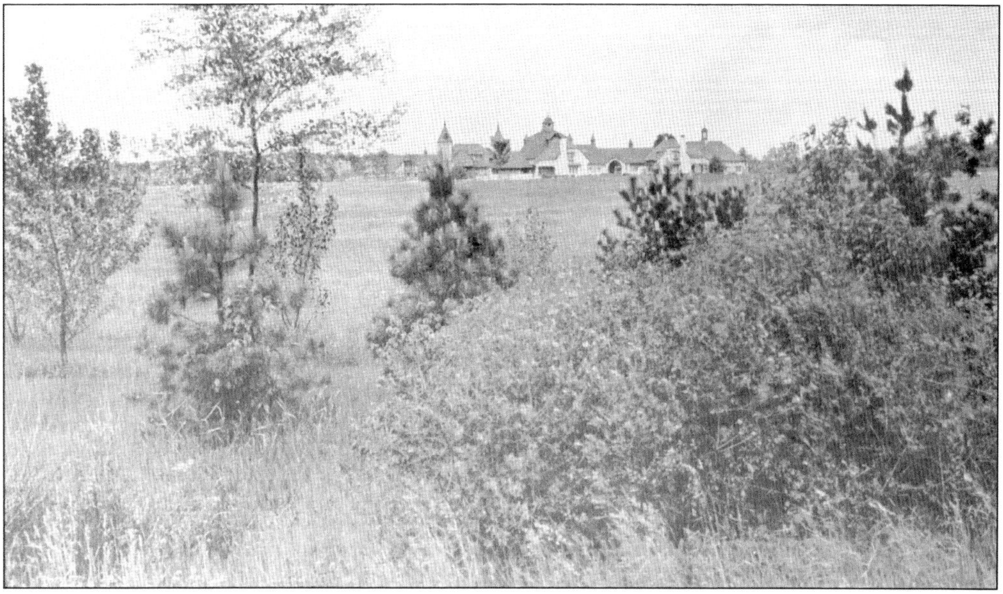

Meadowood was the name of Clifford Leonard's estate farm group just north and west of the intersection of Waukegan and Deerpath Roads. It was a 1923 Normandy farm designed by architect Ralph Varney, with seven buildings: three barns, three cottages for employees, and a poultry house. The landscaping was by Prairie Style master Jens Jensen. The main house was never built, and now all the buildings are personal residences listed in the National Register of Historic Places. Following World War I, many service men and their architects, such as the École des Beaux Arts–trained Varney, returned wanting to recreate some of the charming French country farm architecture they discovered in their travels around the northeastern French countryside. Both photographs on this page are from the 1930s. (Courtesy Lake Forest-Lake Bluff Historical Society.)

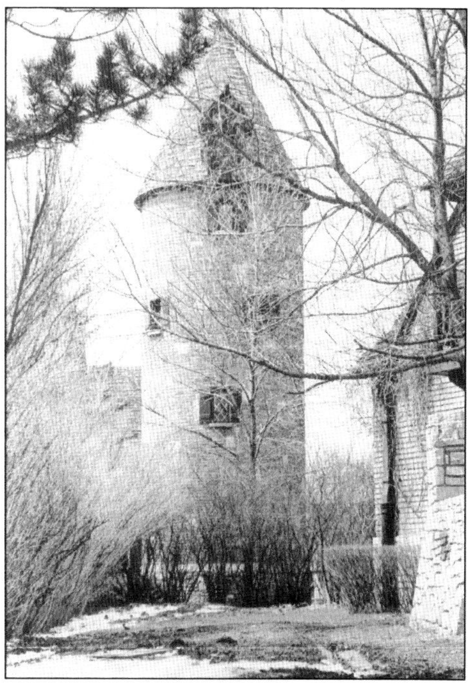

This tower/silo was part of the Varney-designed Meadowood cluster of farm structures of the early 1920s. (Courtesy Lake Forest-Lake Bluff Historical Society.)

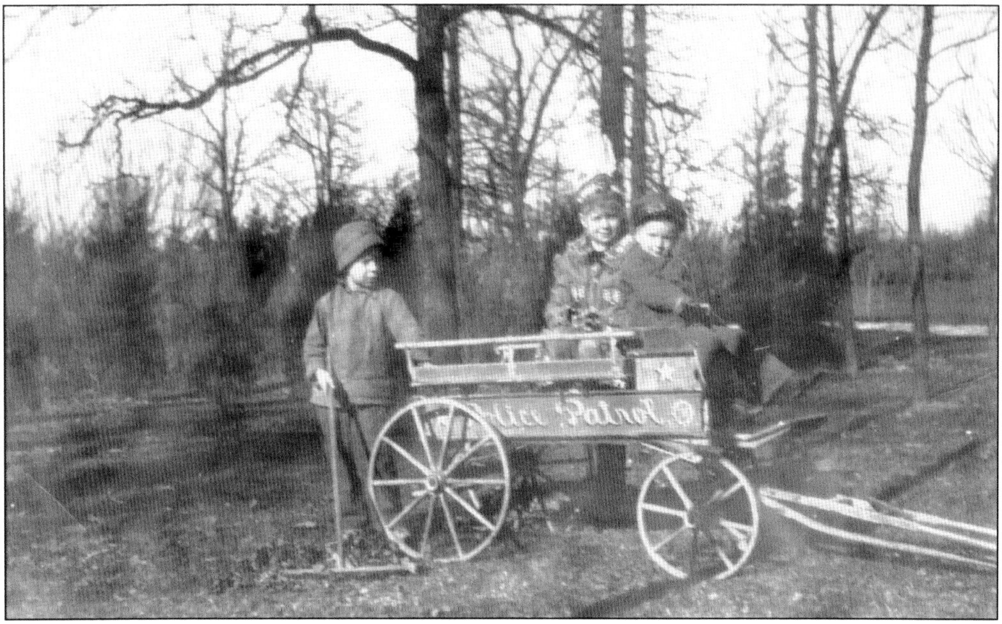

Life for staff children on these great west of Lake Forest estates, like for these Gustafson youngsters on the King estate on Ridge Road, was not unlike that for the Everett area pioneer children a half century previous and earlier. They were able to play on the open spaces these estates offered, previously farms. (Courtesy Leonard Gustafson.)

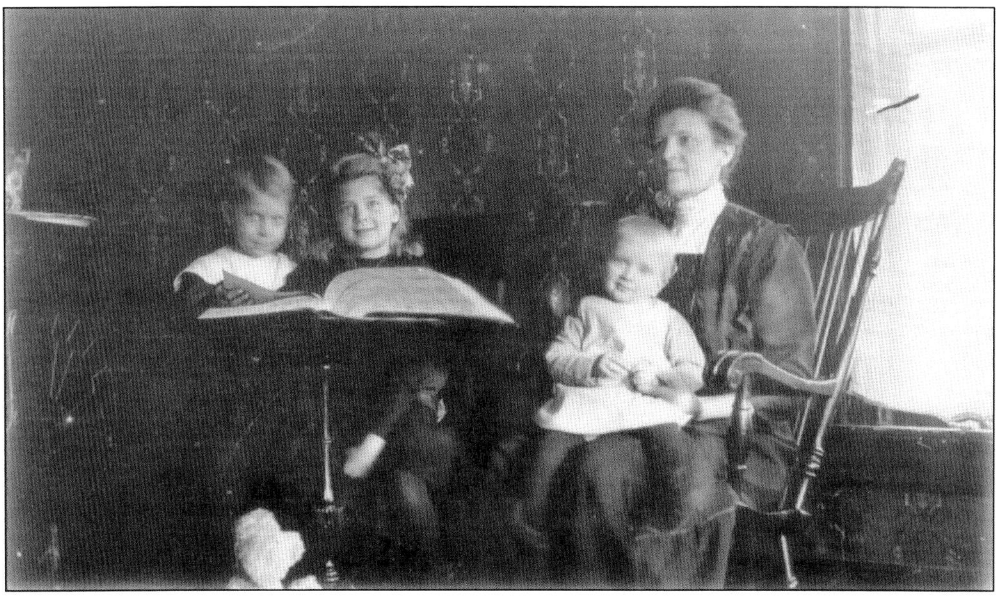

This image shows Charlotte Gustafson and her children, posed reading in the parlor/living room of the 1912, Adler-designed staff cottage on Ridge Road, south of the Kings' 1905 main house. Staff families led middle class lives on these properties, when the employee brought sought-after specialized knowledge to his or her position, in this case perhaps caring for elite polo and equestrian ponies and horses nearby. (Courtesy Leonard Gustafson.)

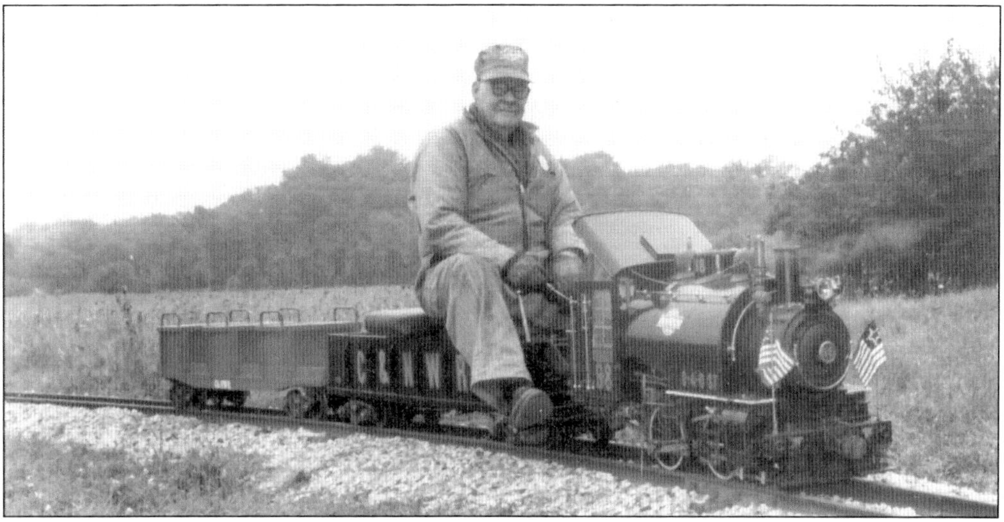

Printing-family scion and serious rail fan Elliott Donnelley and his spouse Ann Steinwedel Donnelley, who had raised their family in a 1934 colonial house on Ridge Lane just west of the east-side commercial district, moved to a larger parcel of former Mellody Farm entry landscape in the mid-1950s. Here, they built a modern, one-story, but quite commodious house by Walter Frazier of Frazier and Raftery, according to *Walter Frazier* by Kim Coventry and Arthur Hawks Miller. Presumably, the move was occasioned in part by Donnelley's wish to set up a live garden-scale steam railroad for himself and his hobbyist buddies. This image shows one of these friends, Stanley Wells, running one of the trains on Elliott's tracks. After 1975, this was moved west along Route 60 to its present location. (Photograph from Stanley Wells; courtesy Lake Forest-Lake Bluff Historical Society.)

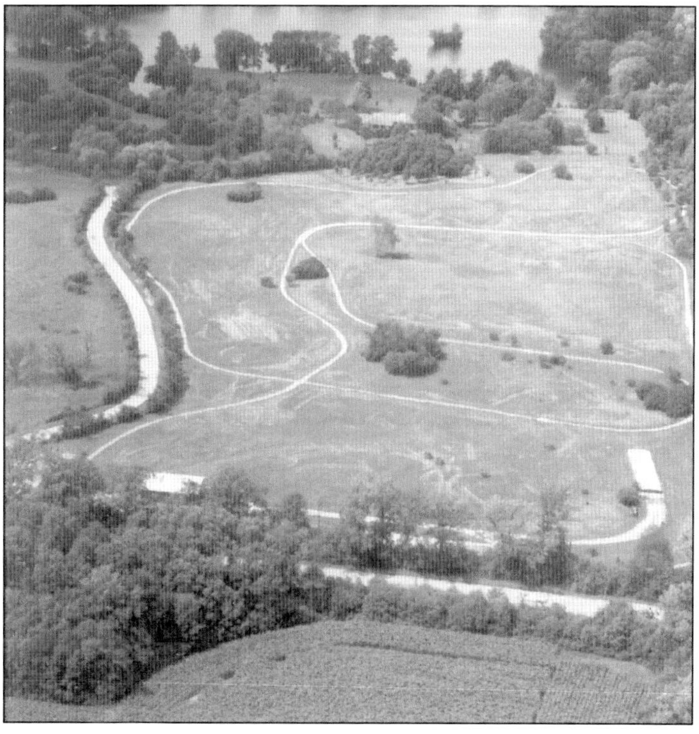

This Stanley Wells aerial photograph shows the Donnelley property garden train layout north of Melody Lane and west of Waukegan Road. (Courtesy Lake Forest-Lake Bluff Historical Society.)

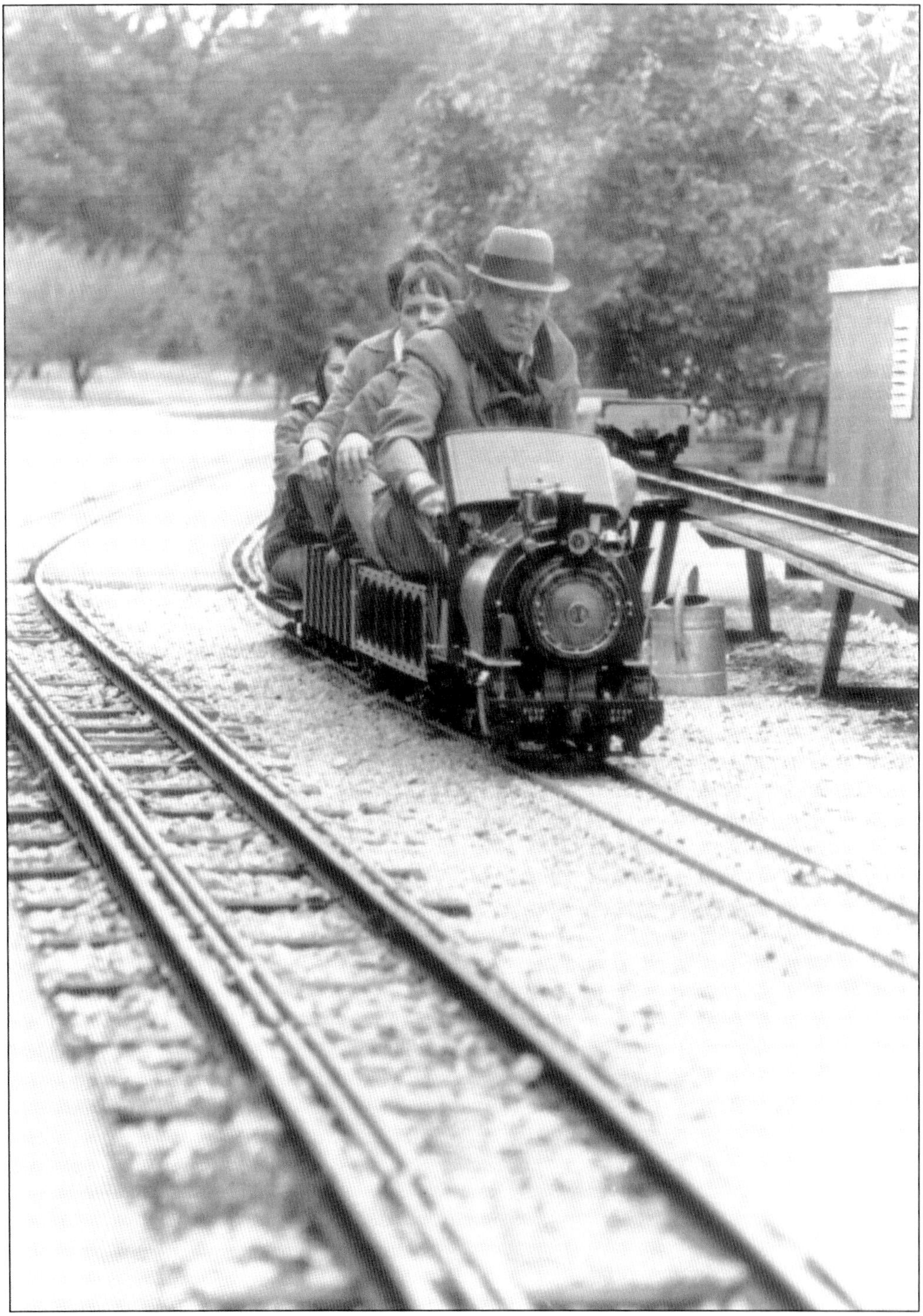

Here, under full steam on the Donnelley layout are (from front to back) Benjamin B. Bryan at the controls, Romaine Scoppos, photographer Mary McMasters, and her daughter Jean McMasters (Grost). (Both courtesy Jean McMasters Grost.)

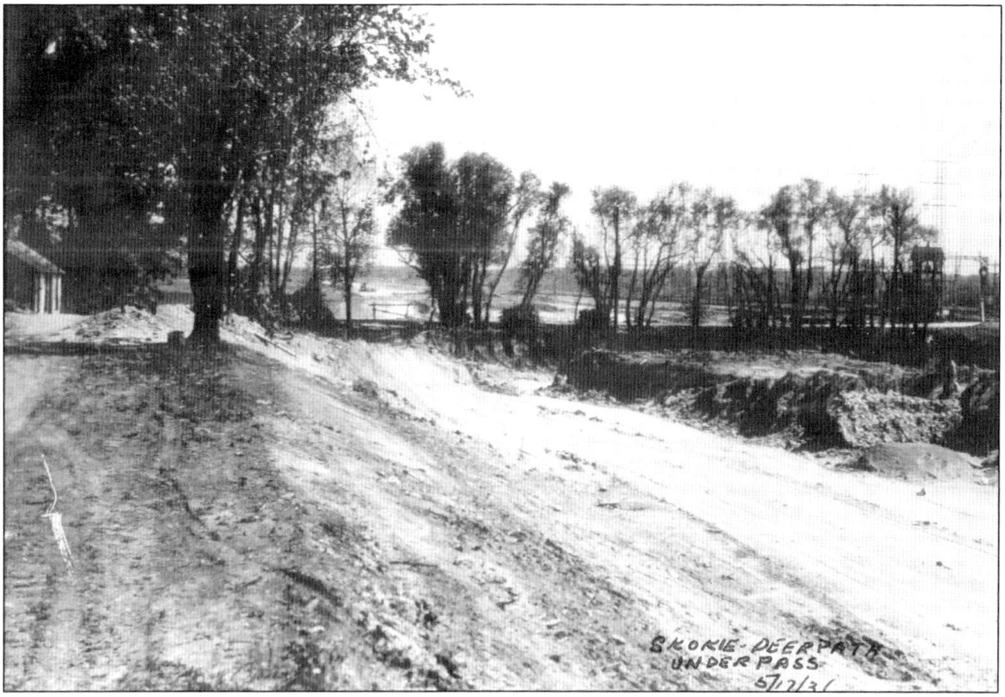

By the 1930s, work was underway to create a new truck route around east Lake Forest, today's Route 41. Lake Forest tripled in size with the 1920s annexation of country club and country estate land west of the town. Louis F. Swift, owner of Westleigh Farms, owned more than 1,000 acres in the annexation. He was the largest single property owner. At the time, Everett, with a population of 50, was added, with Old Elm to the east (Highland Park) along with Onwentsia country clubs and the estates of A. Watson Armour, J. Ogden Armour, Arthur Meeker, L.H. McCormick, and Cyrus H. McCormick. (Courtesy Shirley Paddock.)

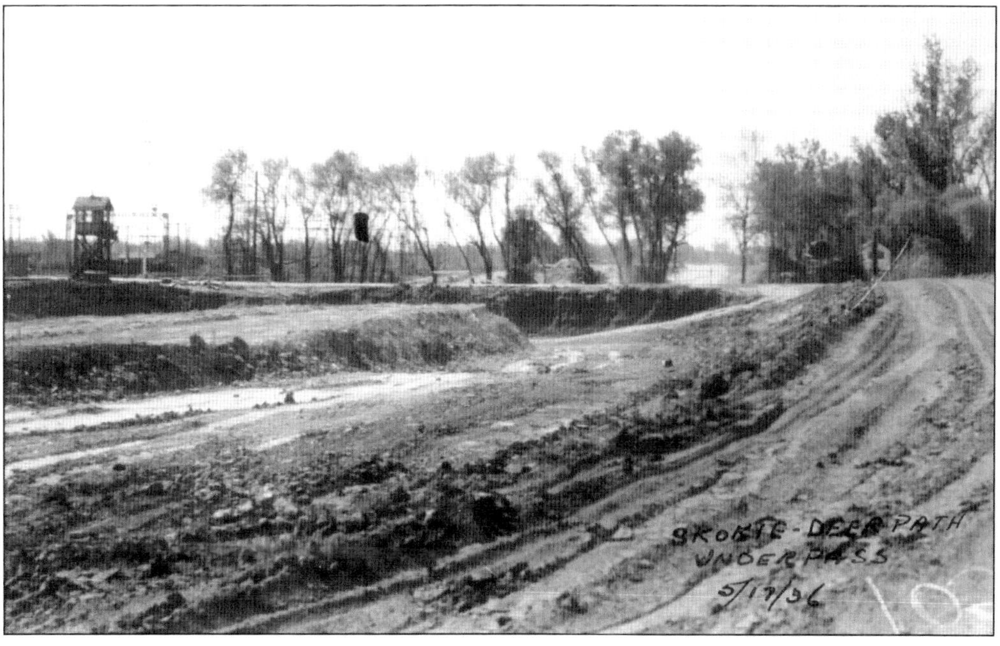

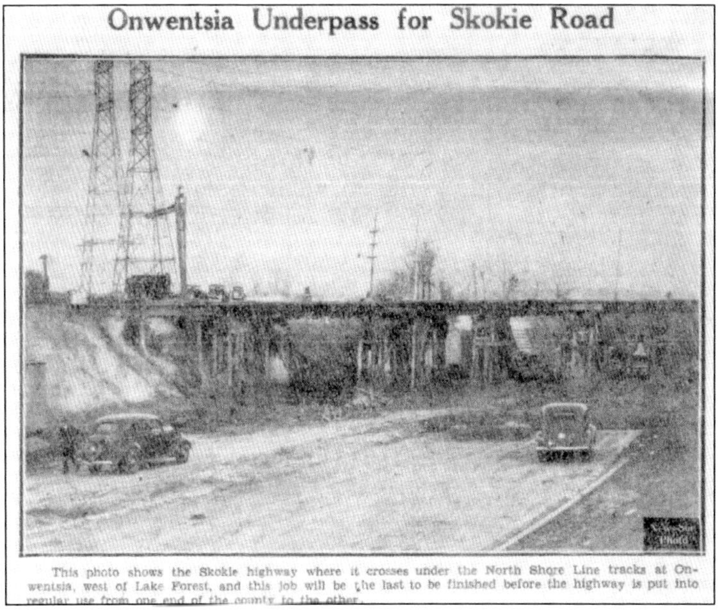
Onwentsia Underpass for Skokie Road

This photo shows the Skokie highway where it crosses under the North Shore Line tracks at Onwentsia, west of Lake Forest, and this job will be the last to be finished before the highway is put into regular use from one end of the county to the other.

Everett and much of west Lake Forest were annexed to Lake Forest in 1926. The major road project bisecting Lake Forest in the 1930s was the creation of the Route 41 highway from a former creek bed/slough between ancient sandbars. Pictured is the Skokie and Deerpath Roads underpass construction, ongoing in May 1936, presumably with federal stimulus funds. (Courtesy Shirley Paddock.)

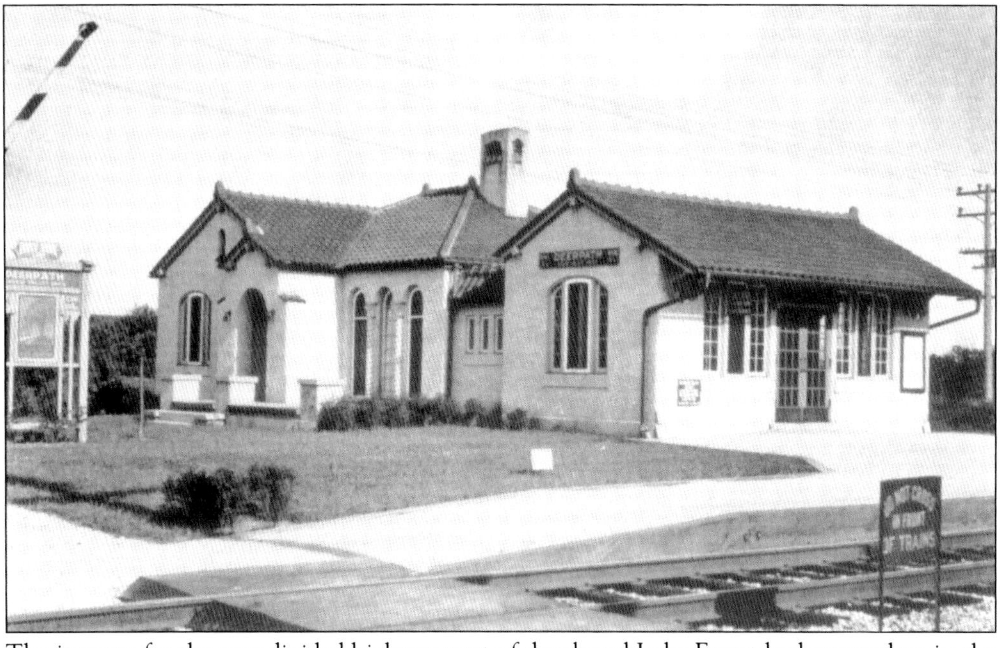

The impetus for the new divided highway west of developed Lake Forest had cropped up in the 1920s, when the Pennsylvania Railroad, constrained from running trains up to Milwaukee, started a trucking line to connect that city with the freight terminus in Chicago. The line quietly gained permission to run trucks on Sheridan and Green Bay Roads and for them to be expanded to four lanes each. This led the estate owners all along the shoreline north of the city to organize the North Shore Property Owners Association to fight this "invasion." Each town had its own committee, and Lake Forest's Edward H. Bennett, the highest-profile planner in the United States in the period, was a consulting member of the committee. To this day in Lake Forest, no trucks are allowed on Green Bay Road (signs still make this clear), and the new truck route was built west of Onwentsia and its surrounding member places. (Courtesy Shirley Paddock.)

Four

Magnificent Estates

Gentlemen's farms typically were weekend escapes from the city for the families of wealthy industrial and commercial companies. Some raised stock, advanced safe food culture, and created wonderful gardens, such as those that graced the A. Watson Armours' Elawa Farm from the 1910s to the early 1950s. One that was considered to be of both types was that of Joseph Medill Patterson and his spouse, Alice Higinbotham Patterson—located on the northwest corner of Milwaukee Avenue and Route 60, now Vernon Hills but a century ago considered Lake Forest countryside (a code name for Onwentsia members' country places). This was one of Lake Forest's memorable couples, but their disagreement about their place illustrates the blurred boundary between farms and estates, to some extent even today (Crab Tree Farm, Lake Bluff). *Chicago Tribune* family scion and reformer Joseph wanted an experimental farm and raised great Percheron horses with barns on the northeast corner of that intersection. (The estate also extended east across the river, with bridal paths there still visible from the road.) He also planted experimental wheat crops in carefully labeled sections, for controlled experiments. Alice, though, wanted an English estate, and she called their place Westwood, with its Howard Shaw house of 1905. She hired Ralph R. Root (Root & Hollister) to design a grand and straight divided allee from Milwaukee Road up to her house, about where J.C. Penney's is today, with young elms to shade the way in the European manner. Joseph, upset with the shade impact on his trials in the fields, had the trees cut down.

Everything was not this contentious west of the town of Lake Forest, certainly. But some places were more grand centers for entertaining and perhaps catching press coverage, while others were closer to working farms. The examples in this chapter will show some of the often nationally significant country properties of Chicago's great leaders.

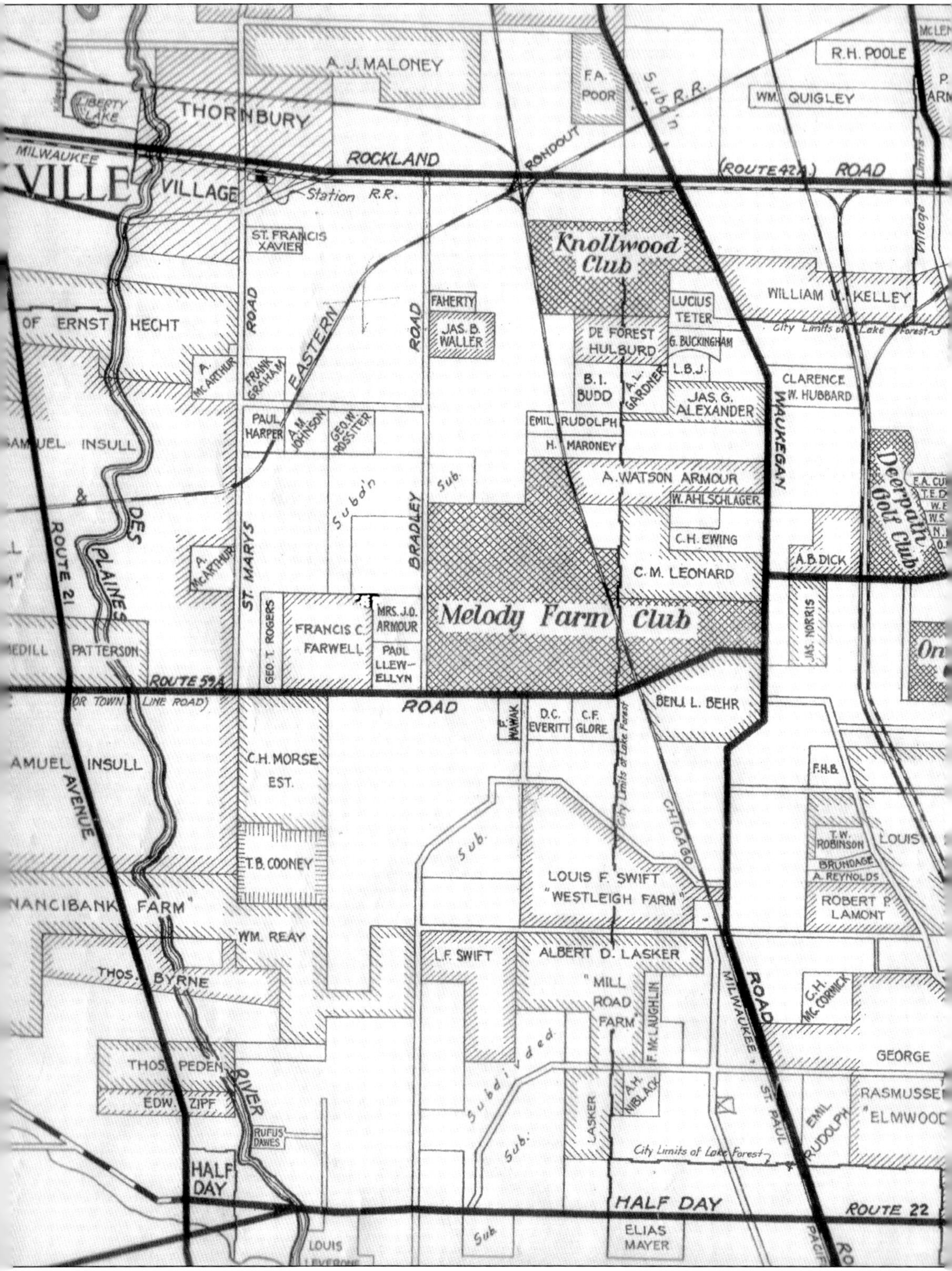
A. J. MALONEY
THORNBURY
LIBERTY LAKE
MILWAUKEE
VILLE
VILLAGE
ROCKLAND
Station R.R.
RONDOUT
F.A. POOR
R.R.
Subd'n
(ROUTE 42A) ROAD
R.H. POOLE
WM. QUIGLEY
Village Limits
ST. FRANCIS XAVIER
Knollwood Club
WILLIAM V. KELLEY
City Limits of Lake Forest
OF ERNST HECHT
ROAD
EASTERN
FAHERTY
JAS. B. WALLER
LUCIUS TETER
DE FOREST HULBURD
G. BUCKINGHAM
A. McARTHUR
FRANK GRAHAM
B. I. BUDD
A. L. GARDNER
L.B.J.
JAS. G. ALEXANDER
CLARENCE W. HUBBARD
WAUKEGAN
PAUL HARPER
A. M. JOHNSON
GEO. W. ROSSITER
EMIL RUDOLPH
H. MARONEY
SAMUEL INSULL
Deerpath Golf Club
A. WATSON ARMOUR
W. AHLSCHLAGER
Sub.
Subd'n
BRADLEY
DES PLAINES
ROUTE 21
A. McARTHUR
ST. MARYS
C. H. EWING
A. B. DICK
C. M. LEONARD
GEO. T. ROGERS
FRANCIS C. FARWELL
MRS. J. O. ARMOUR
PAUL LLEW-ELLYN
Melody Farm Club
JAS. NORRIS
MEDILL PATTERSON
ROUTE 59A
(OR TOWN LINE ROAD)
ROAD
D.C. EVERITT
C.F. GLORE
BENJ. L. BEHR
SAMUEL INSULL
AVENUE
C. H. MORSE EST.
City Limits of Lake Forest
F.H.B.
CHICAGO
Sub.
T. B. COONEY
LOUIS F. SWIFT "WESTLEIGH FARM"
T. W. ROBINSON
LOUIS
BRUNDAGE
A. REYNOLDS
ROBERT P. LAMONT
NANCIBANK FARM"
WM. REAY
L.F. SWIFT
ALBERT D. LASKER "MILL ROAD FARM"
F. McLAUGHLIN
THOS. BYRNE
MILWAUKEE
ROAD
C. H. McCORMICK
Subdivided
THOS. PEDEN
RIVER
EDW. ZIPF
LASKER
A. H. NIBLACK
ST. PAUL
EMIL RUDOLPH
GEORGE
RASMUSSE
"ELMWOOD
RUFUS DAWES
Sub.
City Limits of Lake Forest
HALF DAY
HALF DAY
ROUTE 22
Sub.
ELIAS MAYER
LOUIS LEVERONE
PACIF

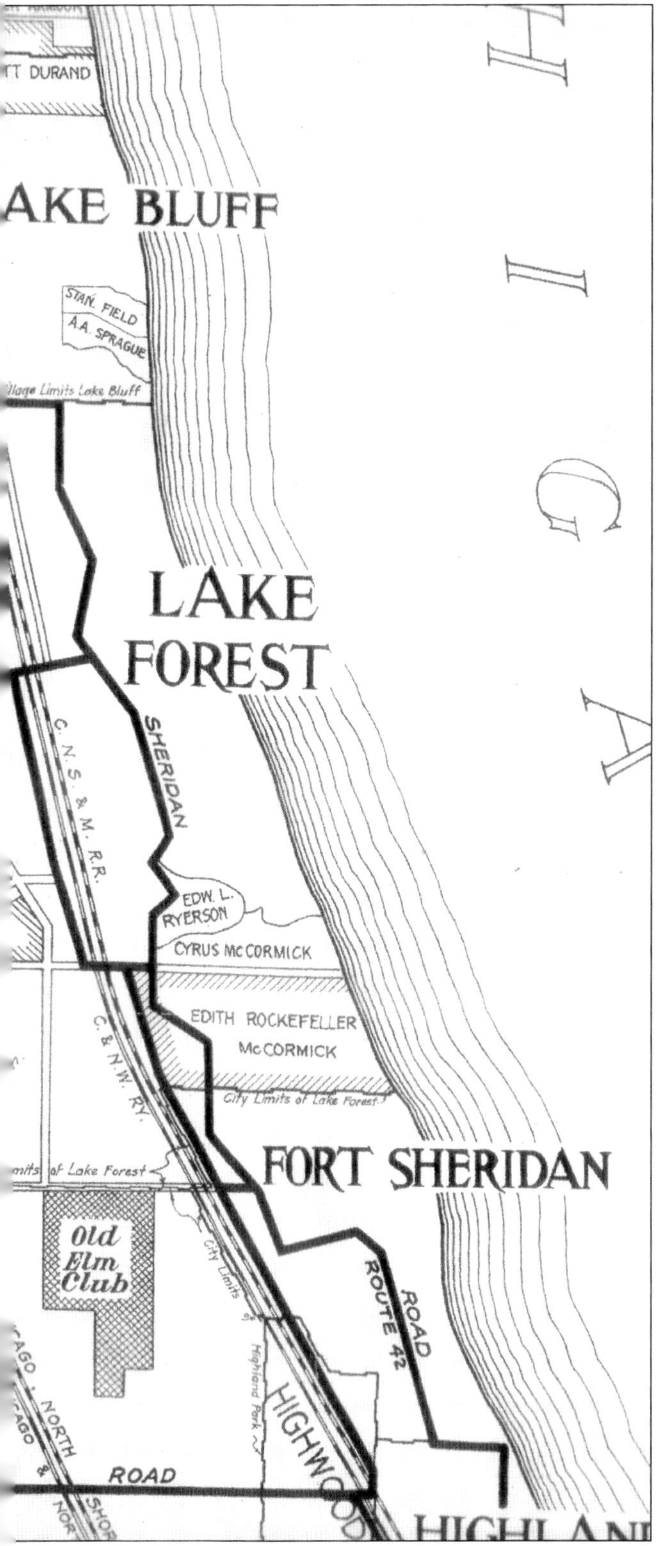

A 1930s estate map shows the changes in west Lake Forest. Everett, annexed in 1926, and large, beautiful estates were developing on the west side. (Courtesy James Anderson Surveying Company.)

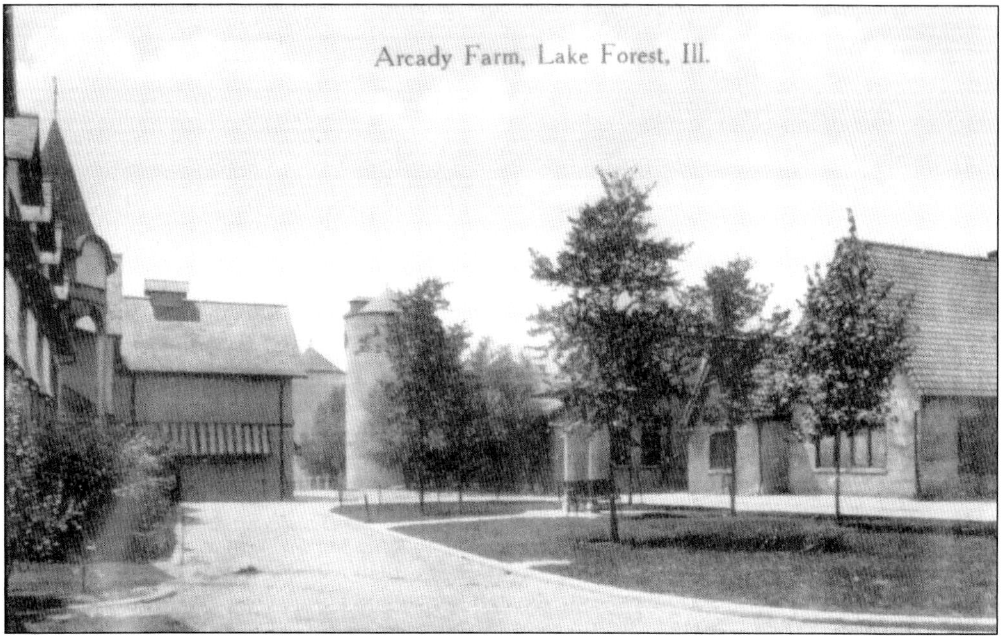

When Arthur Meeker Sr., a senior associate to J. Ogden Armour at his meatpacking concern, built his Arcady Farm in 1907, three years after his employer began his Mellody Farm immediately north and west, he perhaps had in mind the fate of Nicolas Fouquet. Fouquet, treasurer to Louis XIV, built such an elegant palace that the King seized it for his own. Arcady Farm is less Italianate than Mellody Farm and its farm buildings are simple French or English countryside half-timbered structures. Meeker played his cards well by emphasizing the farm character of his smaller place in the shadow of the greater Mellody Farm next door. (Courtesy Lake County Discovery Museum and Archives.)

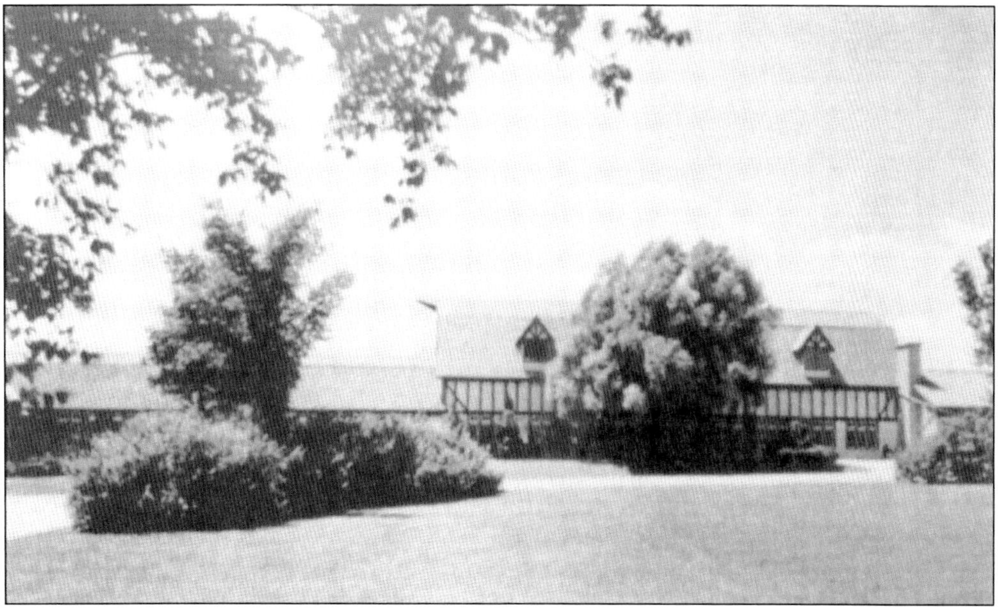

The whole farm complex, nevertheless, was set in an elegant country landscape—the work of Jens Jensen. (Courtesy Lake County Discovery Museum and Archives.)

In 1936, Arcady Farm was 125 acres on the northwest corner of Waukegan and Diamond Lake (now Route 60) Roads. A long shady drive led the visitor past an abundance of Jensen's plantings of oaks (some very likely survivors from the farm era), elms, poplars, maples, pines, and spruce trees. By this date, Arcady Farm was a horse hobby farm for Mr. and Mrs. Benjamin Leslie Behr. The stable housed stalls for 30 horses with fine saddles and bridles hung from wood-paneled walls. The Behrs' granddaughter Barbara married Tom Donnelley, whose family owned the estate just to the north. (Courtesy Shirley Paddock.)

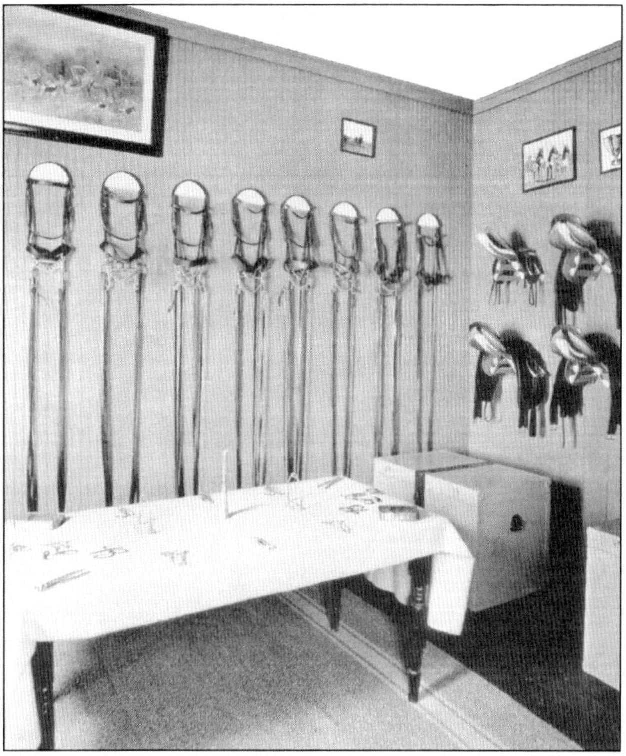

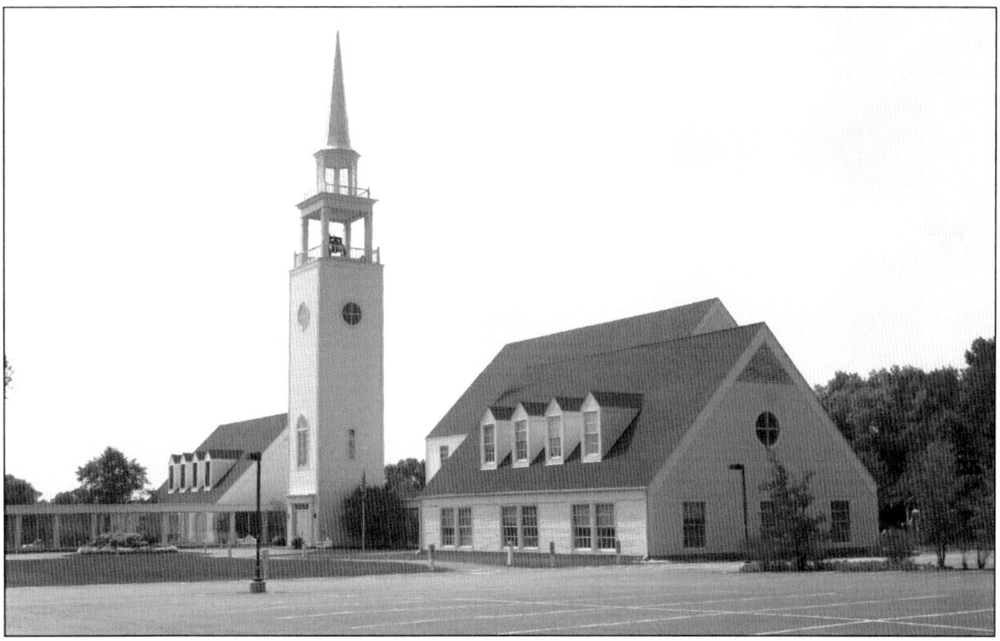

Today, the Arcady site is known for the unaffiliated Protestant Christ Church, built in the 1980s, and the adjacent Foret de Dieu subdivision. The architecture is postmodern, with simple modernist lines recalling historic New England churches in its whiteness, tall tower, and essential simplicity. It is supported by a growing congregation. An early 19th century version of St. Patrick's Catholic Church previously stood in this vicinity. (Courtesy Susan Kelsey.)

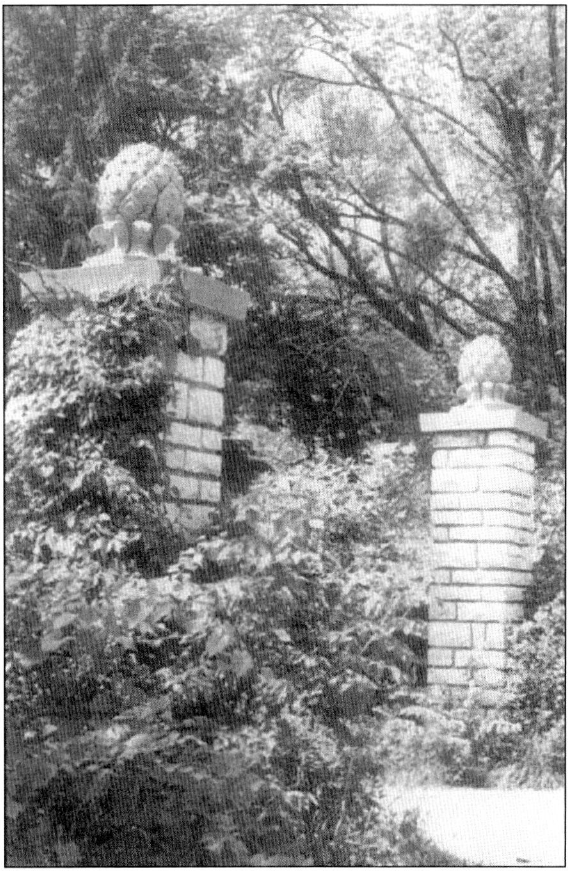

This is a historic view of the entry gate to Arcady, the former Meeker and Behr estate. (Courtesy Shirley Paddock.)

The gateposts and gates have been preserved, though not the angled approach to the 1907 Arcady house, designed by architect Arthur Heun. Jensen laid out the grounds. Through the gate can be seen one of the 1980s houses in the development that helped fund the construction of the nearby church. (Courtesy Susan Kelsey.)

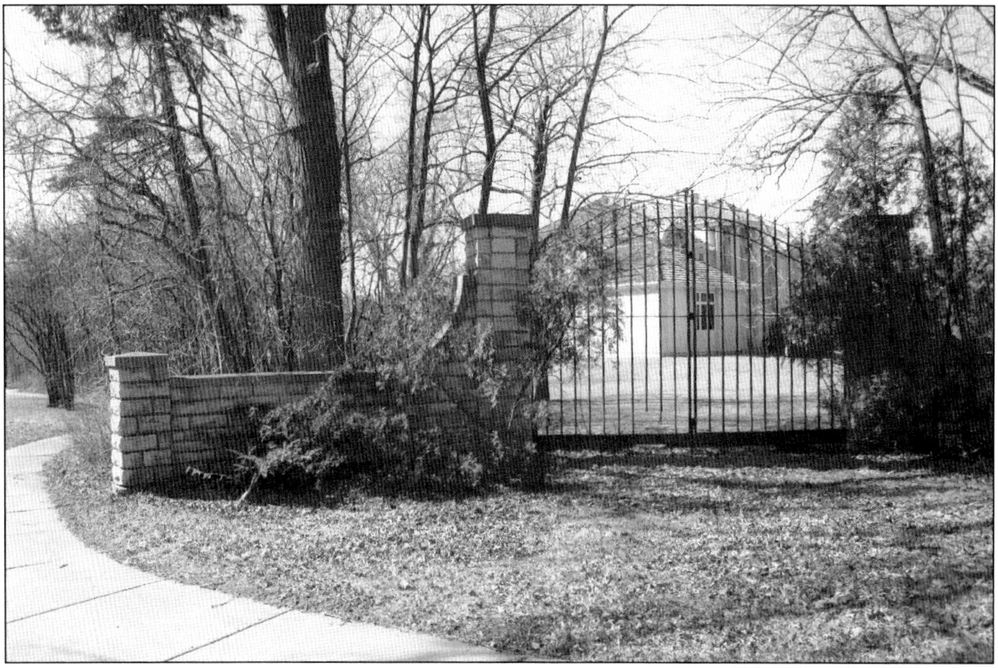

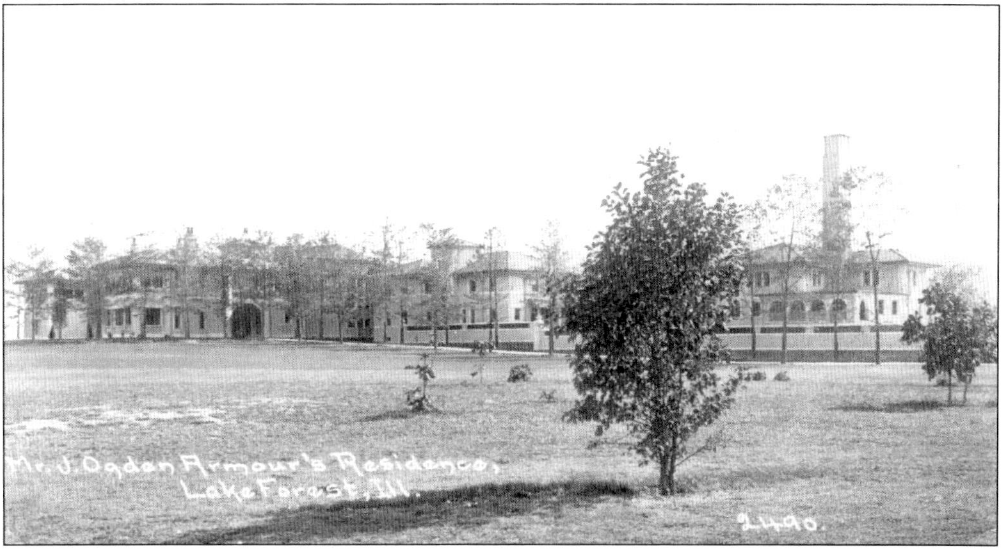

Mellody Farm, the J. Ogden Armour estate, was built from 1904 to 1910 on the north side of Route 60, or at the time, Diamond Lake Road, and the west side of Waukegan Road south of Deerpath Road. The main architect was Arthur Heun, who had been an associate of Francis M. Whitehouse, who in turn was a partner of Bauer and designed Chicago's Nickerson mansion in 1880, now the Driehaus Museum. The estate's great house was built at a cost of $6 million and features Italian marble entrances and window trim throughout. The long gallery running north from the flying divided stairway to the south recalls the hallway and stairs of the Nickerson mansion.

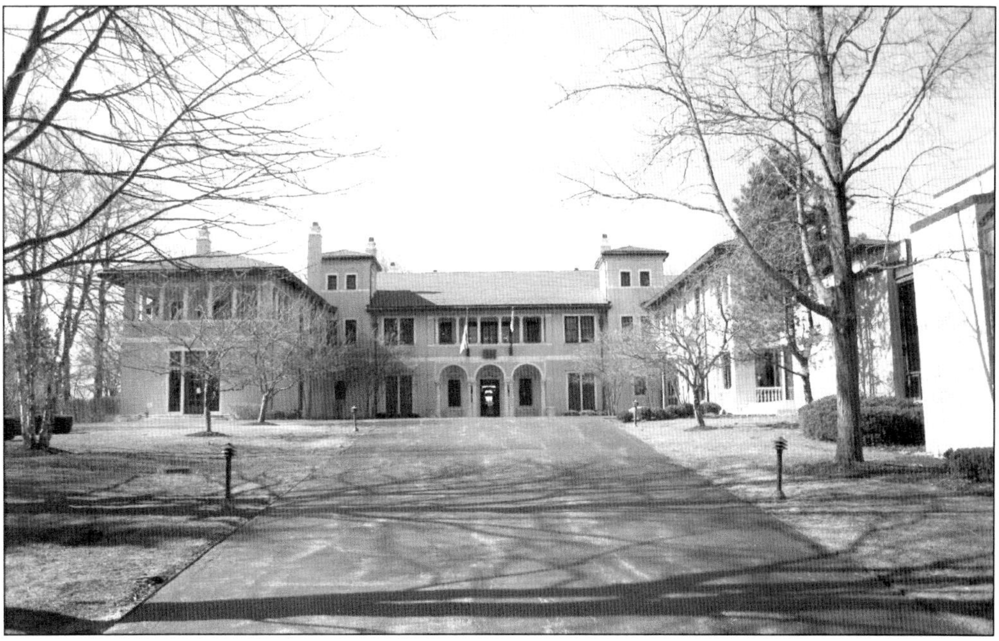

In 1948, the estate house and much of the surrounding Mellody Farm gardens and landscape became Lake Forest Academy, and this entry facade appears unchanged after a century. Actor Vince Vaughn was married at the Mellody Farm house in 2010, demonstrating that the larger-than-life, fairy-tale quality of the estate has survived. (Courtesy Lake Forest-Lake Bluff Historical Society (Courtesy Susan Kelsey.)

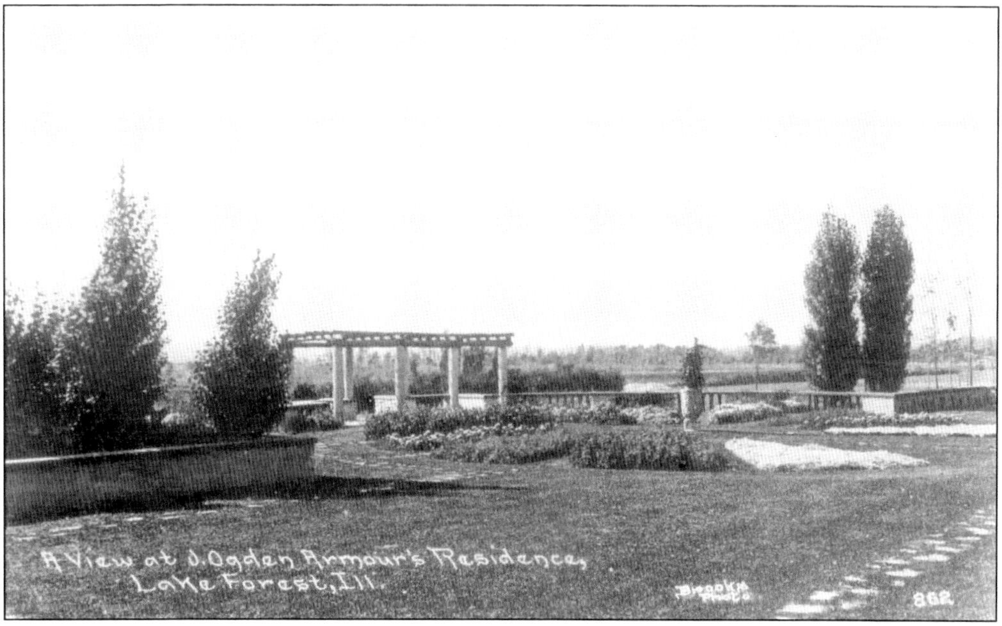

The casino on a high point to the west, a terminus to the view from the house across exquisite Heun-designed garden spaces, was built in 1908 and recalls today the golden era of Lake Forest, with its unique gardens planted by O.C. Simonds and apparently later by Jens Jensen. The two artificial lakes drain into the Middlefork of the Chicago River. (Courtesy Lake Forest-Lake Bluff Historical Society.)

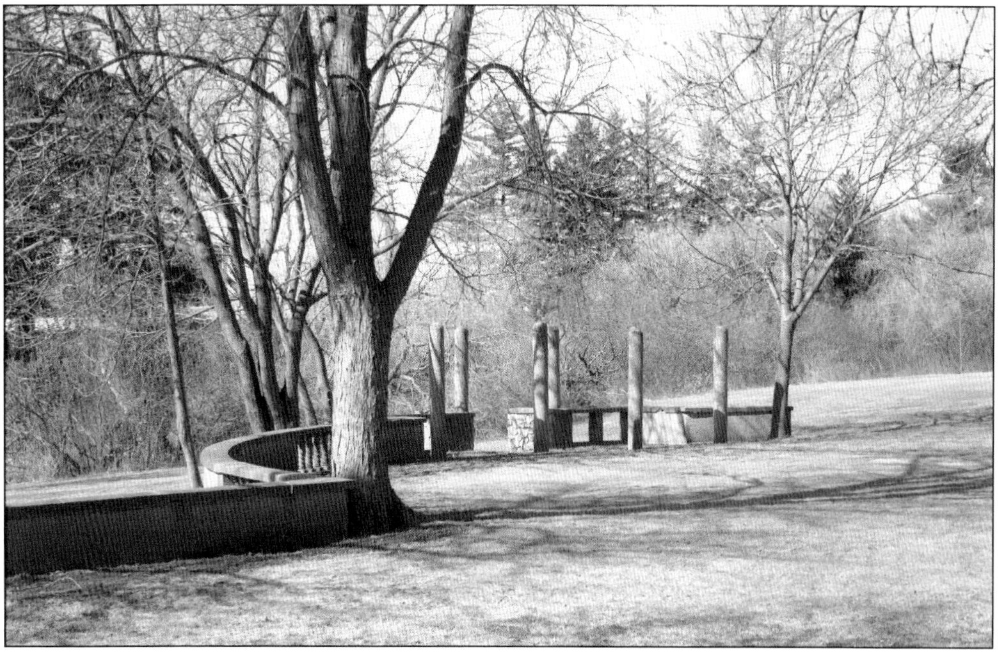

The classic, formal gardens at the Armour estate, now the Lake Forest Academy, are still visible today and the reflecting pools are partially restored. Even after most of a century of benign neglect, the pond edge here recalls naturalistic work by Simonds at Graceland Cemetery, Chicago, and by Jensen in that city's west side parks. (Courtesy Susan Kelsey.)

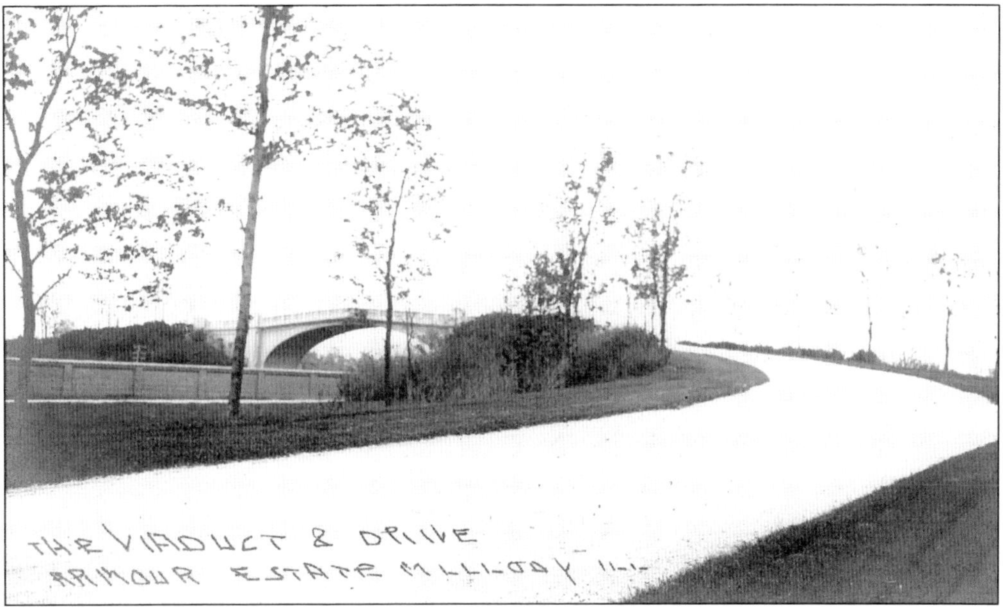

Very likely, University of Michigan-trained engineer O.C. Simonds designed the elegant stone bridge over the train tracks bisecting Mellody Farm and its mile-long drive from Waukegan Road to the house. Armour also had built a masonry barrier between his residence and the train tracks to both reduce the noise and improve the view. He had wanted to build his new house west of all five railroad lines then passing through Lake Forest. (Courtesy Lake Forest College Library Special Collections.)

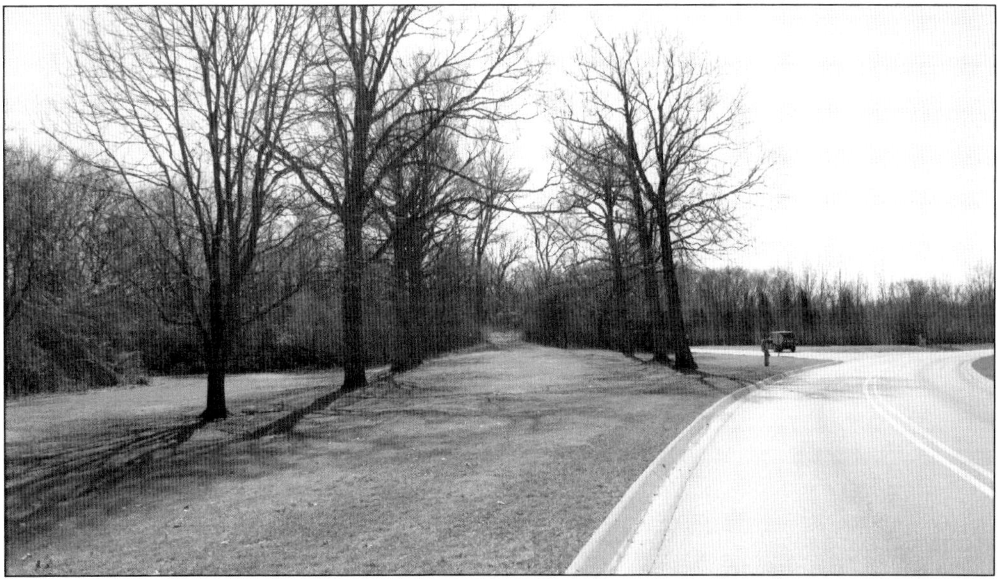

The approach to the academy today is from a new entry on Route 60, all west of the Chicago, Milwaukee & St. Paul Railroad tracks. This view shows the old drive through the tree-lined landscape that Simonds and Jensen created leading to the academy centered on the 1910 completed main house for Mellody Farm, now Reid Hall, and also to the Academy Woods development of the early 1990s that generated funds for new buildings for the academy. (Courtesy Lake Forest-Lake Bluff Historical Society.)

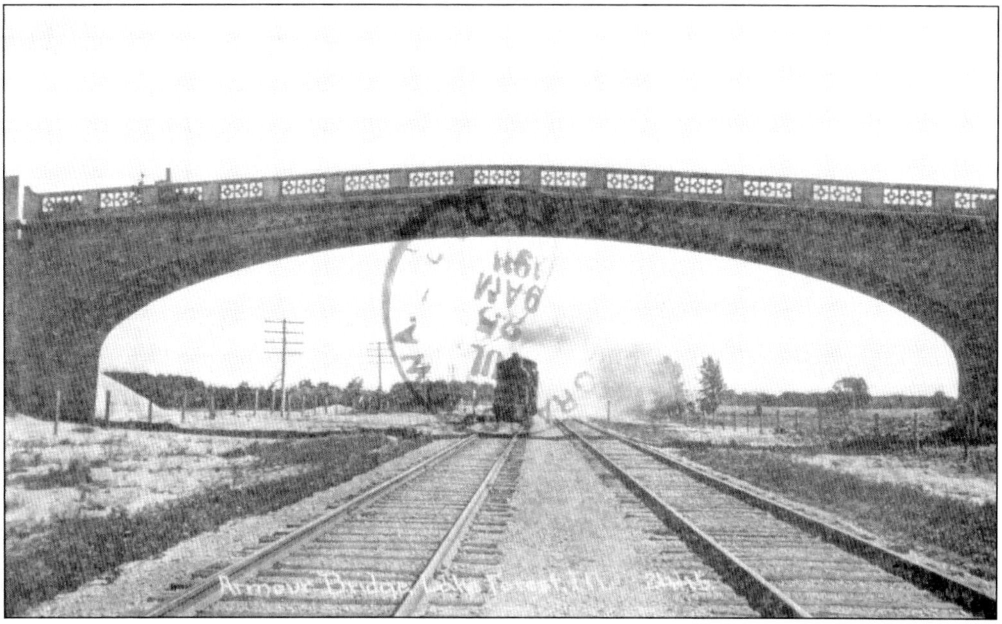

This is an early postcard view of the Armour Mellody Farm Bridge that brought guests to the estate through a one-mile drive starting from Waukegan Road. Armour used over 400 men to bring in soil, horses, and equipment to build the bridge, some on tracks laid for the purpose and later taken up. (Courtesy Shirley Paddock.)

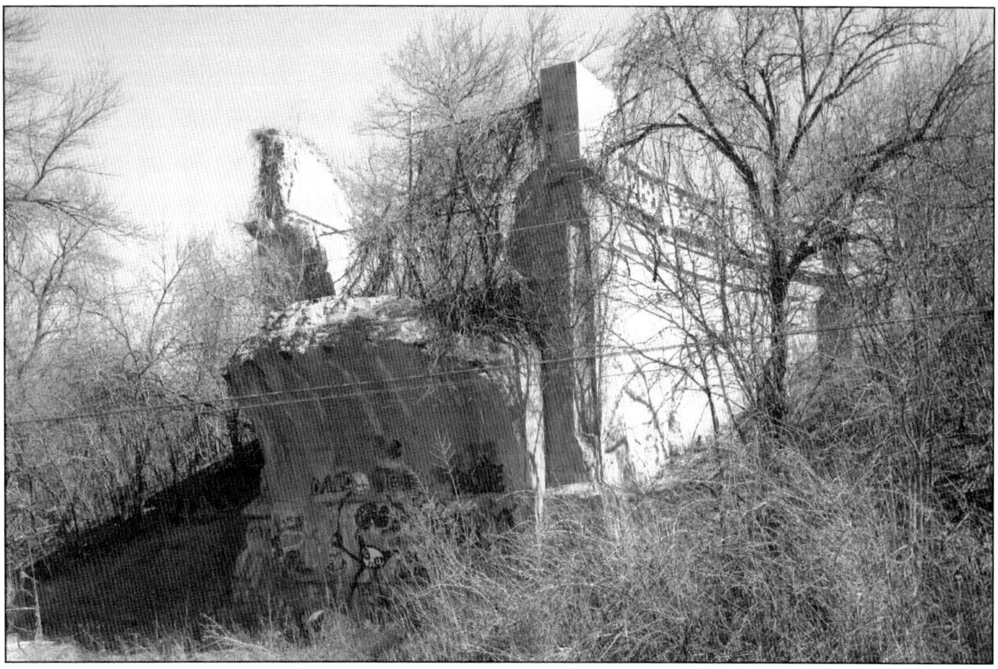

Between the early 1950s and 1960, according to David Mattoon, the Armour Bridge of a half-century earlier was demolished. Shown here is a surviving heavy masonry abutment of the once proud engineering feat with its broad span. (Courtesy Susan Kelsey.)

Jonathan Ogden Armour, son of the brilliant trader and packer Philip Danforth Armour, is shown here in Chicago. The younger man grew his father's firm enormously in the early years of the 20th century, so that by 1917, his family's wealth was second only to Rockefeller's in this country. But a series of reverses and bad commodities trades in the early 1920s wiped it all away, though he was never bankrupted, only sold out by his creditors. This was a cycle—boom and bust—repeated by others in Lake Forest in the 1930s and again in the 2000s, but none other on such Herculean scale. (Courtesy Chicago Historical Society.)

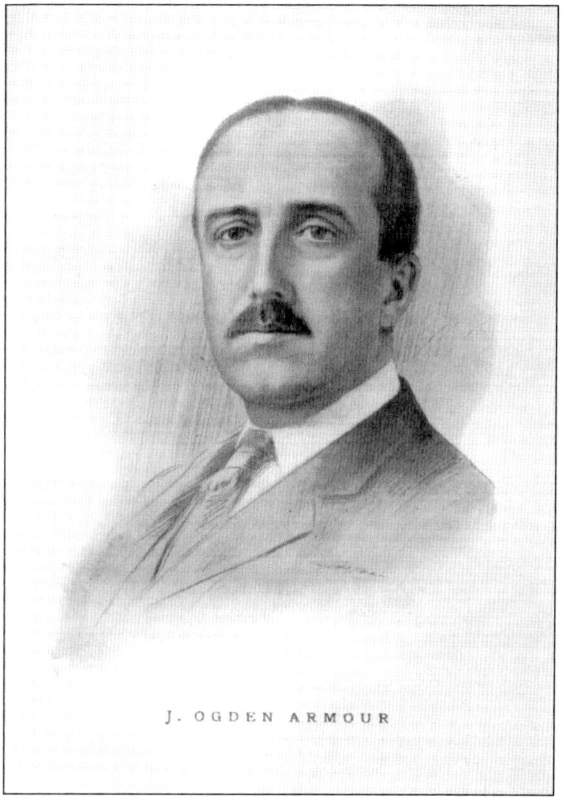

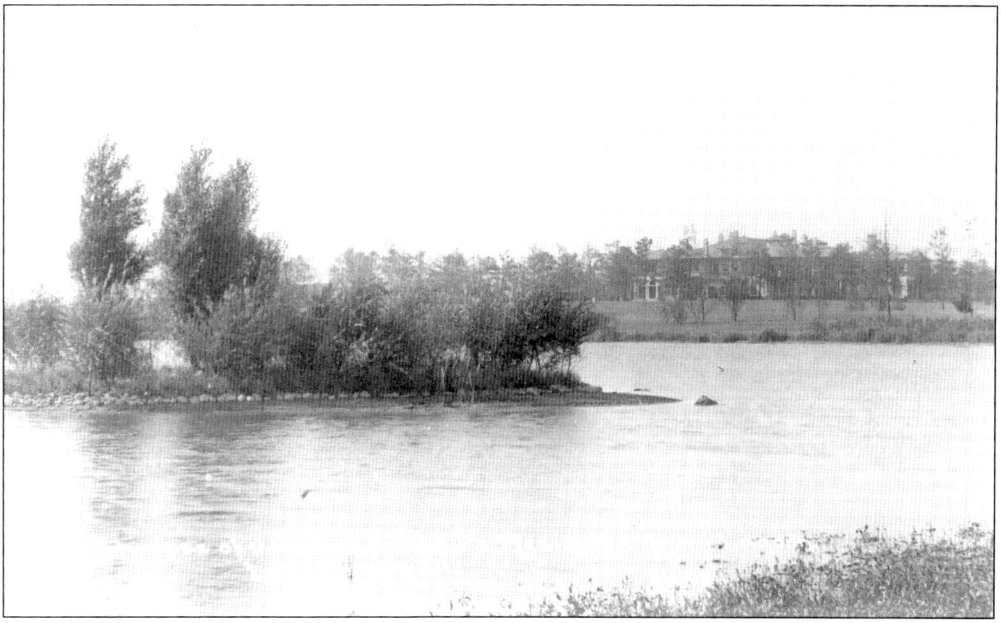

Armour lost his famous country place by 1923, including its beautiful lagoons along the later approach road shown here, and died in 1927. Mrs. J. Ogden Armour was living in a home she built on Vine Avenue, provided by the Laurance Armours of Two Gables on Green Bay Road. (Courtesy Lake Forest-Lake Bluff Historical Society.)

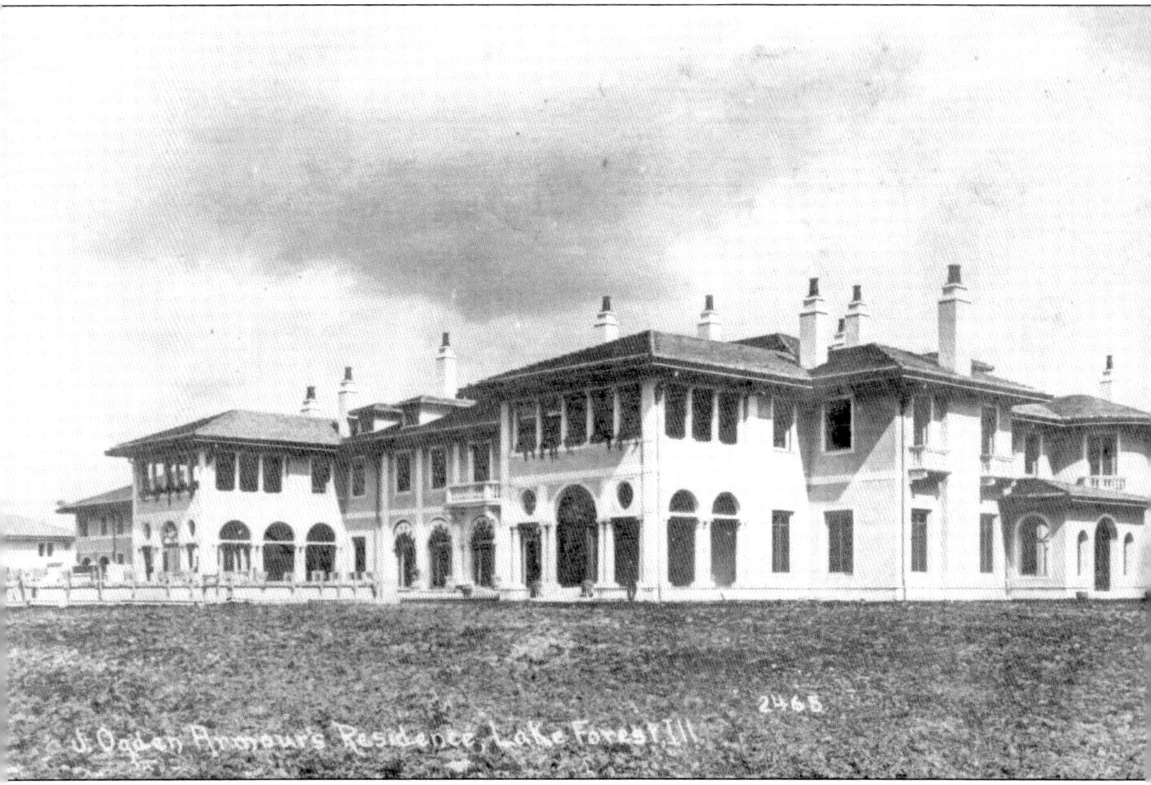

J. Ogden Armour's Mellody Farm, now Lake Forest Academy, is pictured here from the west. The estate was located on 1,000 acres of reclaimed marsh and prairie land and was part of the Gibbons farm. Mrs. Gibbon was a pioneer settler and Patrick Melody's granddaughter. The estate induded a main house, formal gardens, stables, working farm, power plant, and railroad stop. The American Renaissance country house is in the form of a letter "H" and contained 29,000 square feet of living space. Construction took place between 1905 and when the family tentatively moved in on May 5, 1908, though work undoubtedly continued atter that. The general contractor was Chicago-based W.J. Newman, according to a contemporary newspaper article found among the Griffith, Grant, and Lackie archives by Shirley M. Paddock. Newman invented and built a "powerful steam shovel" to excavate the extensive basement and foundation from the top, rather than from below, as was typical. Fifty men and twenty-five teams of horses were engaged in the earth excavations, with a temporary village of boarding houses, shops, and stables. An embankment 22 feet tall and a half mile long shielded the house from the CM&SP rail line traversing the property north to south, east of the house and gardens. The house and grounds were thought to have cost $10 million. (Courtesy Shirley Paddock.)

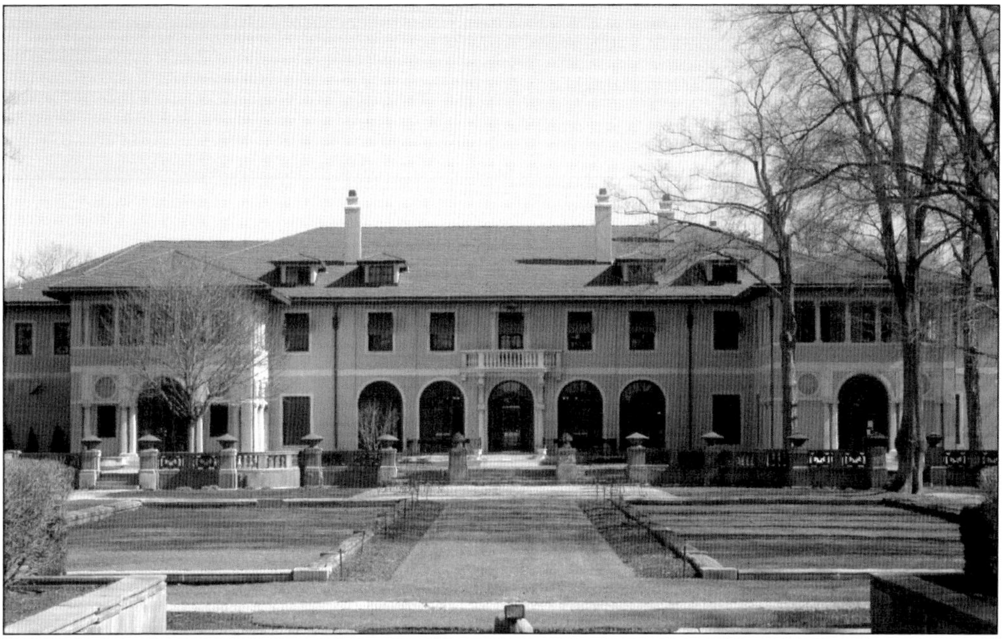

The Armour country place west of Lake Forest began in 1904, coinciding with the arrival of cars in lake Forest. The view from the west above featured a grand loggia or winter garden embellished by a central balcony and located on axis with the gardens and reflecting pool. Pictured below are the remains of a garden path. (Both, courtesy Susan Kelsey.)

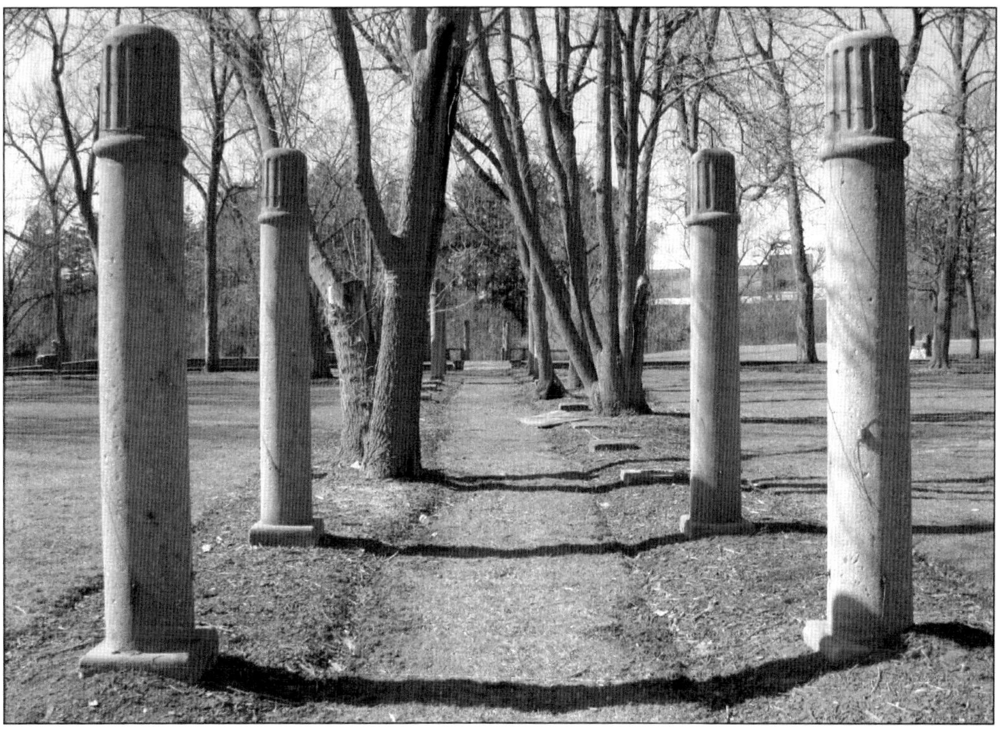

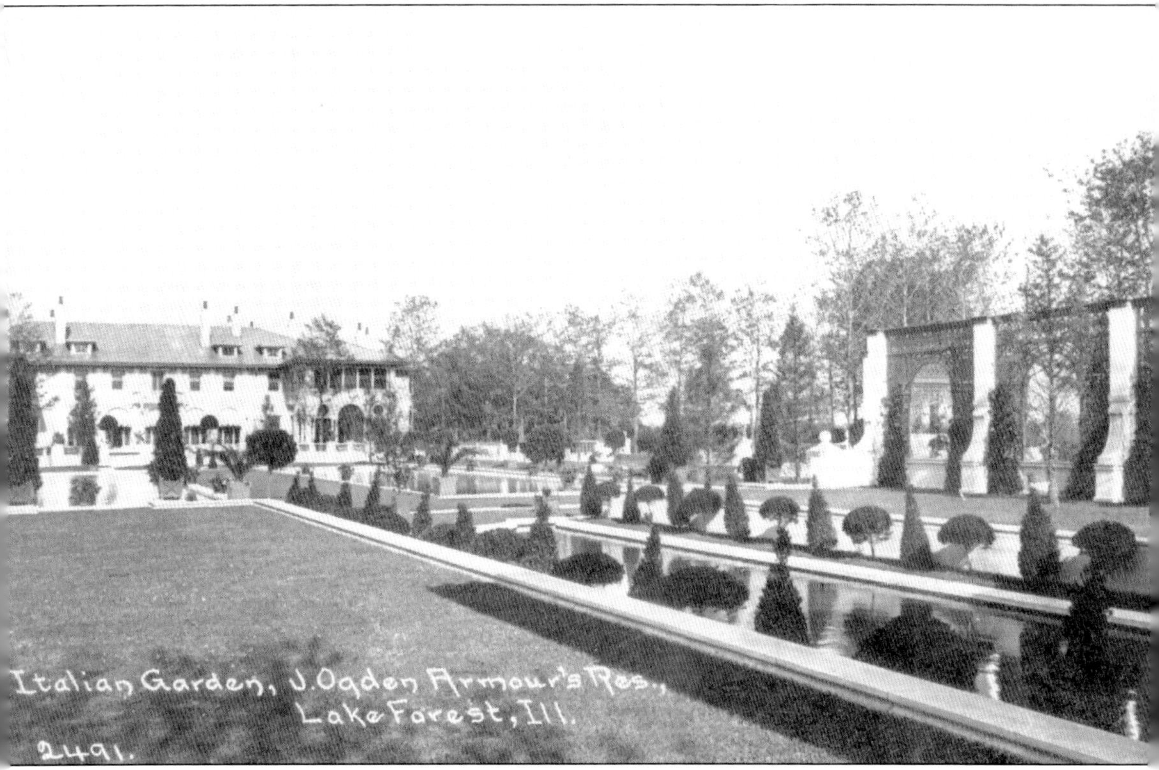

This view from the northwest, perhaps in the early 1910s, shows the mannerist formal Italian garden architecture of Arthur Heun, with plantings at this stage perhaps by Simonds. (Courtesy Shirley Paddock.)

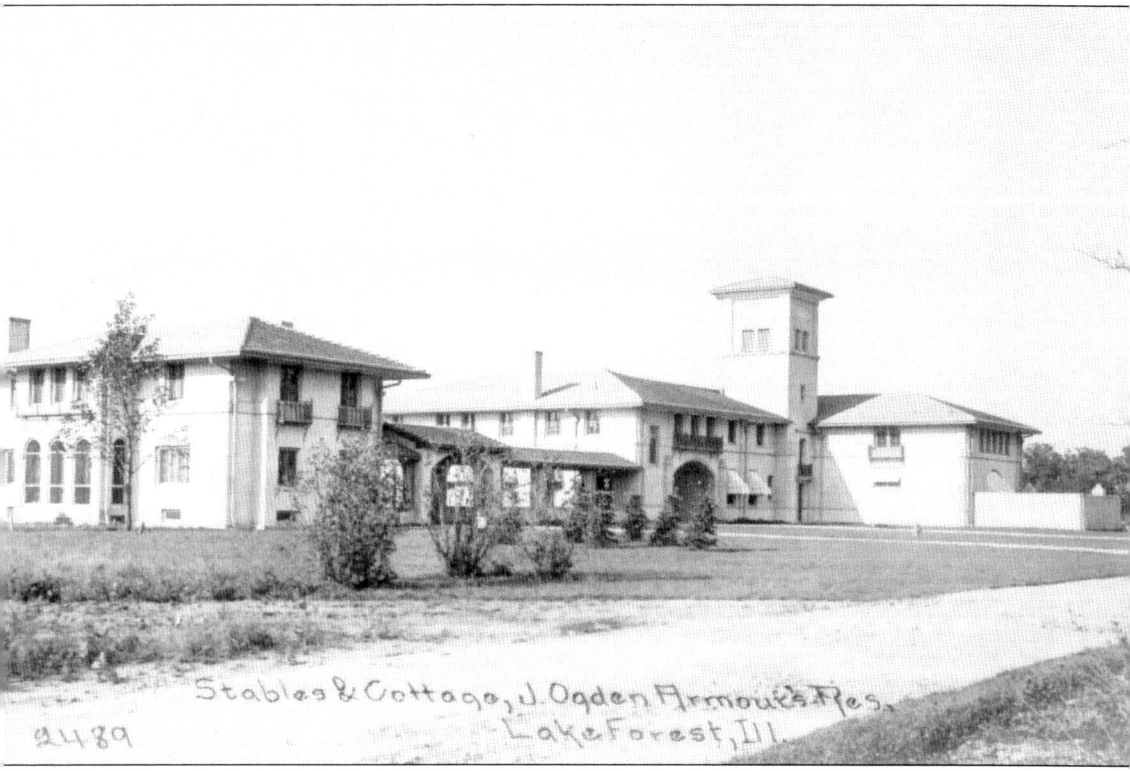

This early postcard view of the stables and "cottages" for staff north of the new villa for J. Ogden Armour illustrates the scale of the whole enterprise. These support buildings were required for the 400-foot-long main house nearby. (Courtesy Shirley Paddock.)

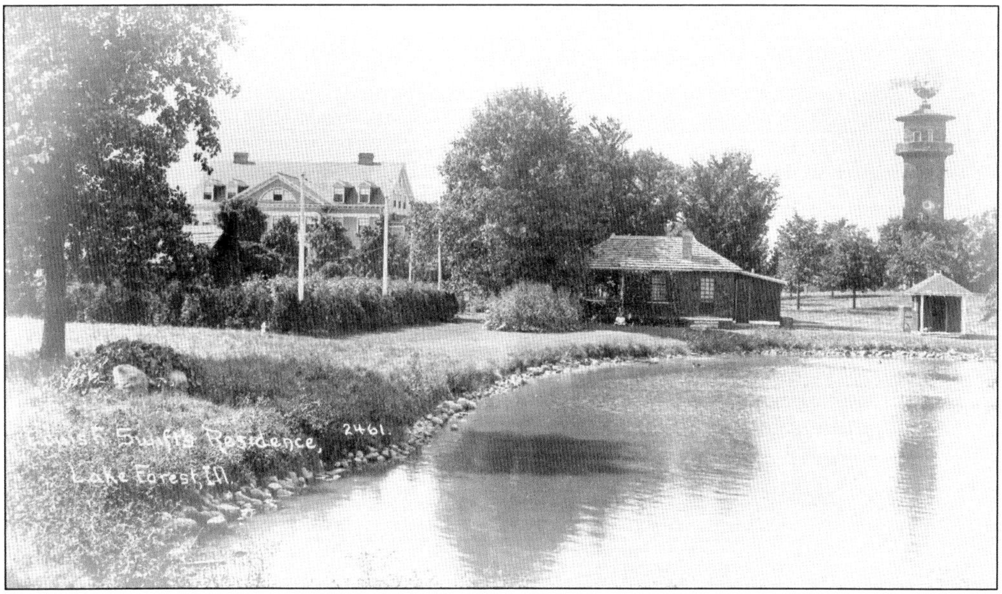

Louis F. Swift, like Armour a second-generation Chicago meatpacker following his father Gustavus Swift, built his own country home and estate, Westleigh, on Green Bay Road south of the Onwentsia Club in Lake Forest. The classic frame house, completed in 1899, was designed by architect William Carbys Zimmerman. Early in the new century, the state architect Zimmerman added a Shaw-designed stone masonry wing in 1916, not shown here, which survives on Foster Place. The Stanley D. Anderson firm demolished the Zimmerman main house and converted the Shaw-designed addition into a standalone residence in 1956. (Courtesy Lake Forest-Lake Bluff Historical Society.)

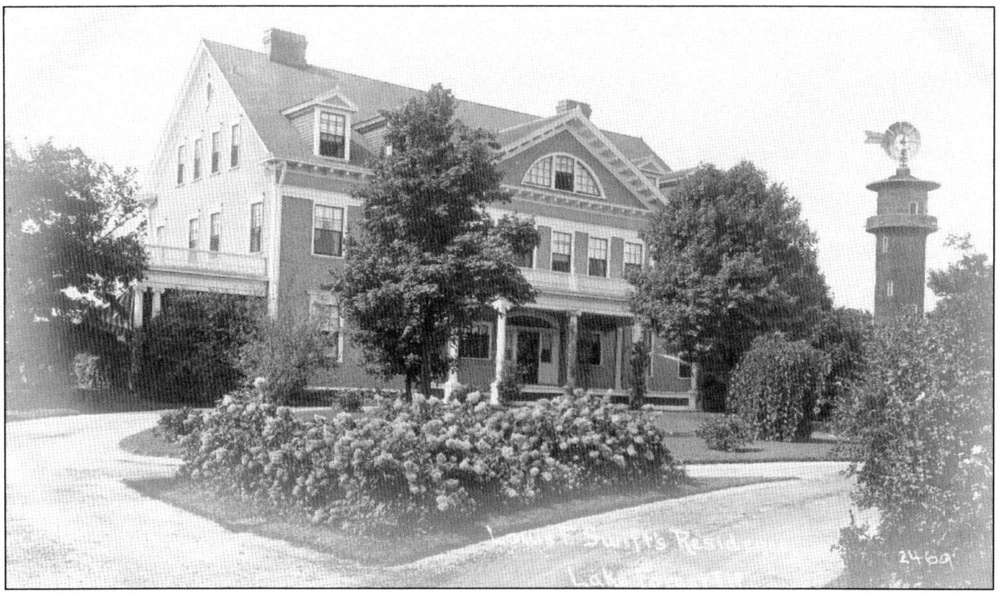

Swift's house was perched high on the ridge or ancient sandbar near Green Bay Road and looked west toward the slough or marshes of the Skokie River. As Armour would do later at his place, Swift had this lowland area reconfigured with ponds. A great water tower is seen on the right. (Courtesy Lake Forest-Lake Bluff Historical Society.)

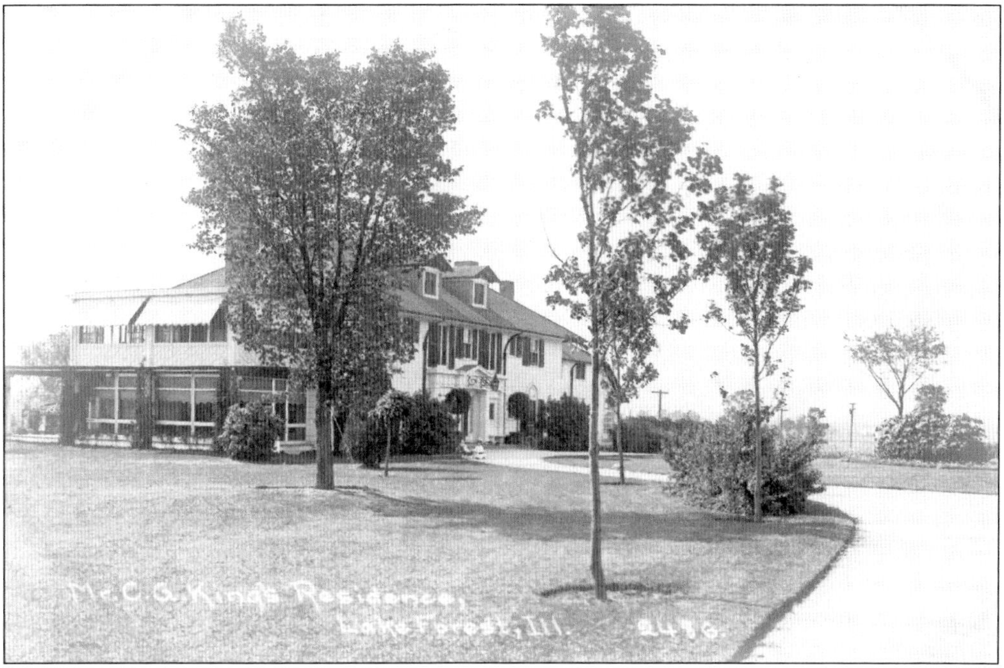

Cars came into vogue in Lake Forest by 1904 and widened the range of easy access to the train station locally. Swift sold a western part of his Westleigh Farm, on Ridge Road west of what today is Route 41, to the successful Chicago broker and banker Charles Garfield King, the father of Ginevra King, muse of future author F. Scott Fitzgerald. King's two-story residence, designed in 1905 by Howard Van Doren Shaw with awnings and circular drive, was a large, rambling country place that is still standing. (Courtesy Lake Forest-Lake Bluff Historical Society.)

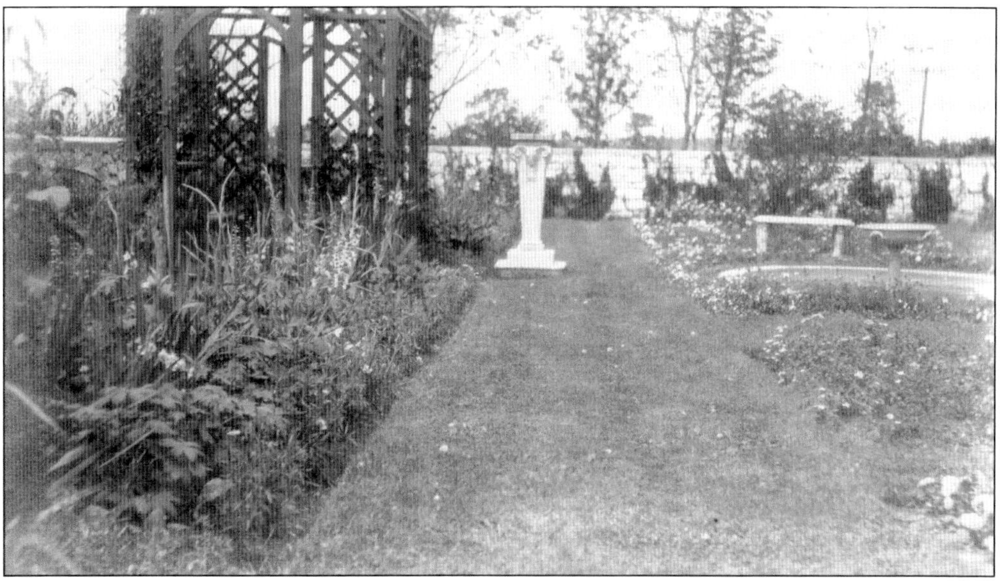

The Charles Garfield King family also had a classically formal garden with a fountain in the middle and latticework gazebo, all surrounded by a stone wall. This outdoor room for entertaining stood between the house and the prairie land to the west. (Courtesy Lake Forest-Lake Bluff Historical Society.)

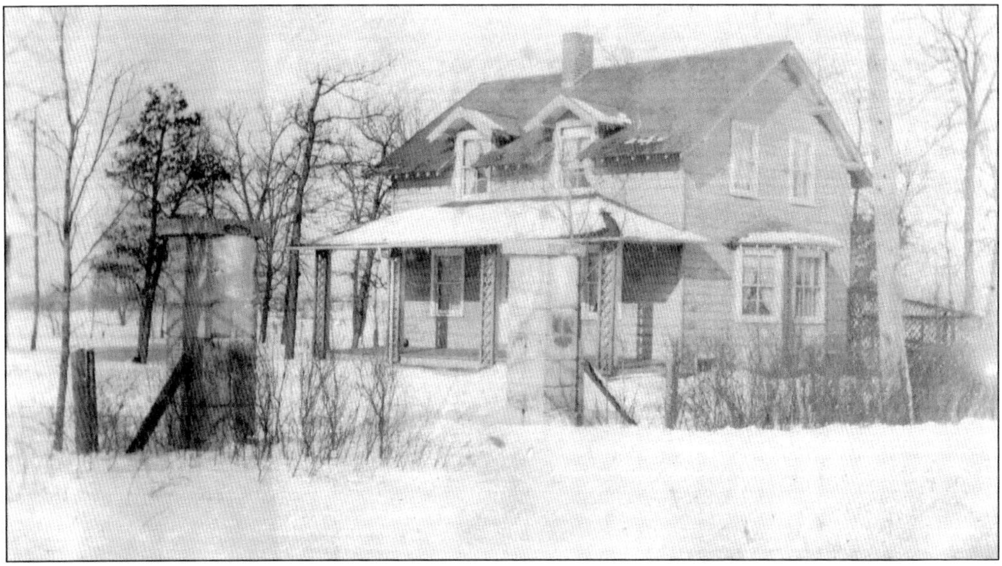

This is an early 20th century exterior view of the small staff lodge (compare to Armour's), designed by the young architects David Adler and Henry Dangler in 1912 while still working for Howard Van Doren Shaw's firm. It remains essentially unchanged today, south of the main King house on Ridge Road. (Courtesy Leonard Gustafson.)

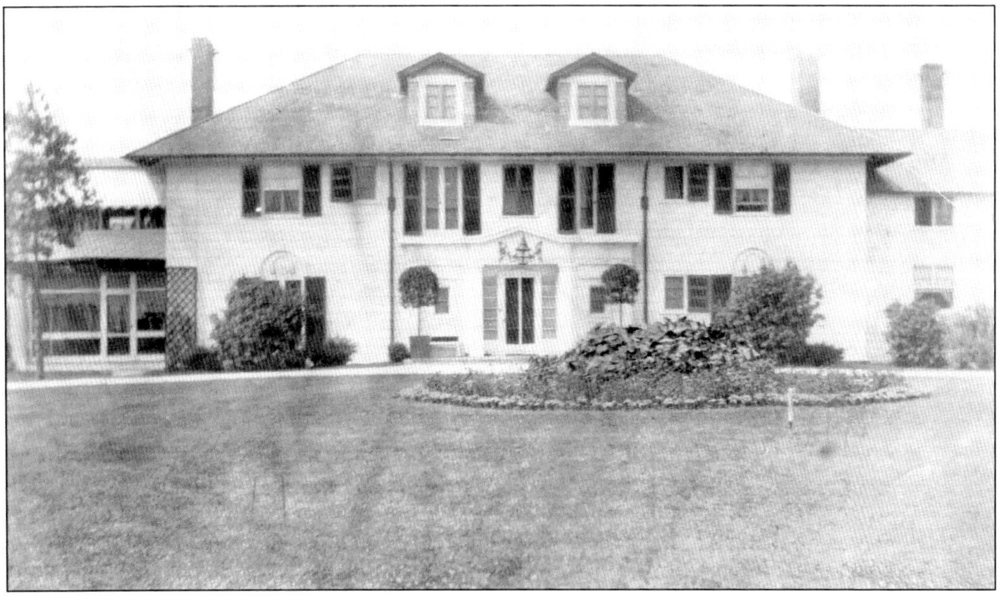

This is a view of the front or east facade of the two-and-a-half-story 1905 King home (extant), typical of Shaw's designs in those years. The architect had similar small trees in pots at the entry to his own Ragdale house, North Green Bay Road. He also designed a similarly massed frame home for Swift's daughter Bessie in 1909 on Ahwahnee Road immediately west of the Onwentsia golf course and polo grounds, on a ridge—a continuation of the same ancient sandbar system to the northeast (now across Route 41) to the King place a few years earlier. (Courtesy Leonard Gustafson.)

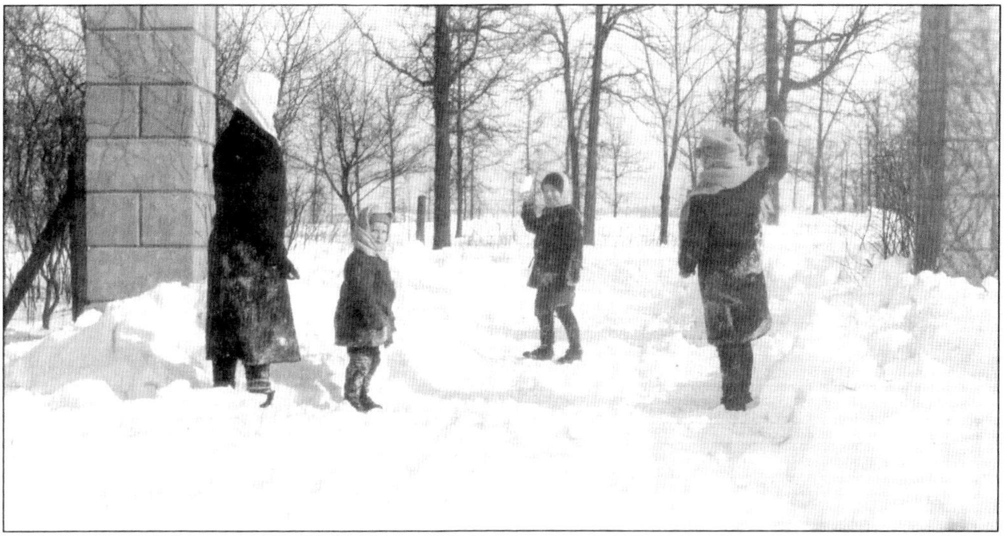

The Gustafsons lived in the staff lodge and are seen here playing near the gate to the polo barn and cottage complex south of the main house on Ridge Road early in the 20th century. (Courtesy Leonard Gustafson.)

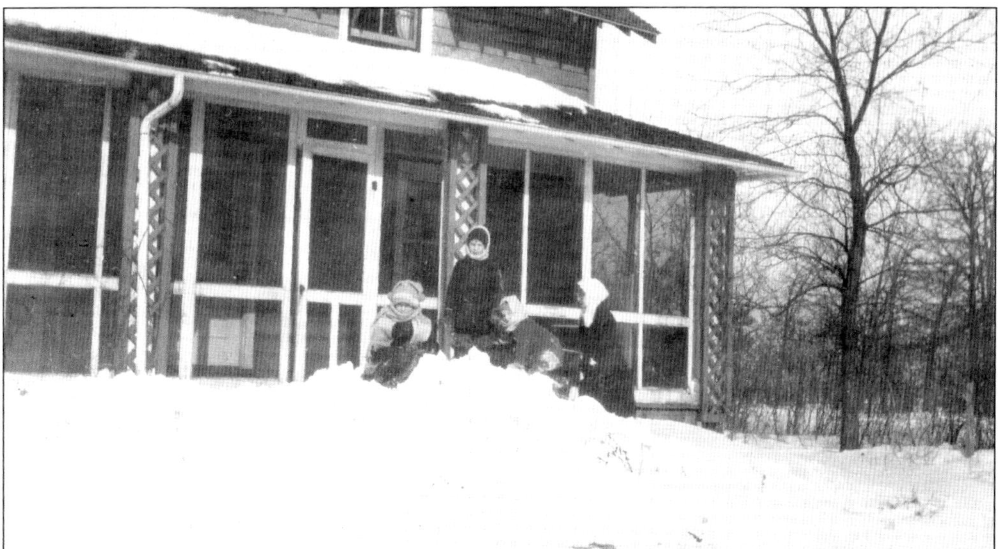

This is a winter view of the Adler-designed early staff cottage for the King place. (Courtesy Leonard Gustafson.)

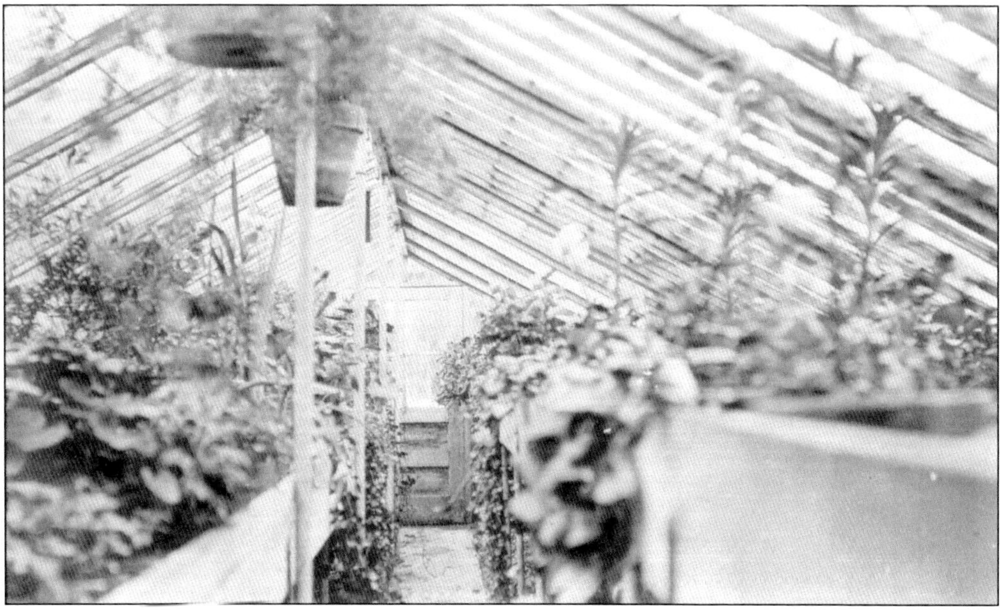

Shown here is the interior of the Ginevra and Charles Garfield King estate greenhouse. Such warm places for delicate plants had been part of Lake Forest form the start, around 1860, and allowed for early-starting annuals, wintering-over plants for the formal gardens, and also fresh vegetables and fruit. (Courtesy Leonard Gustafson.)

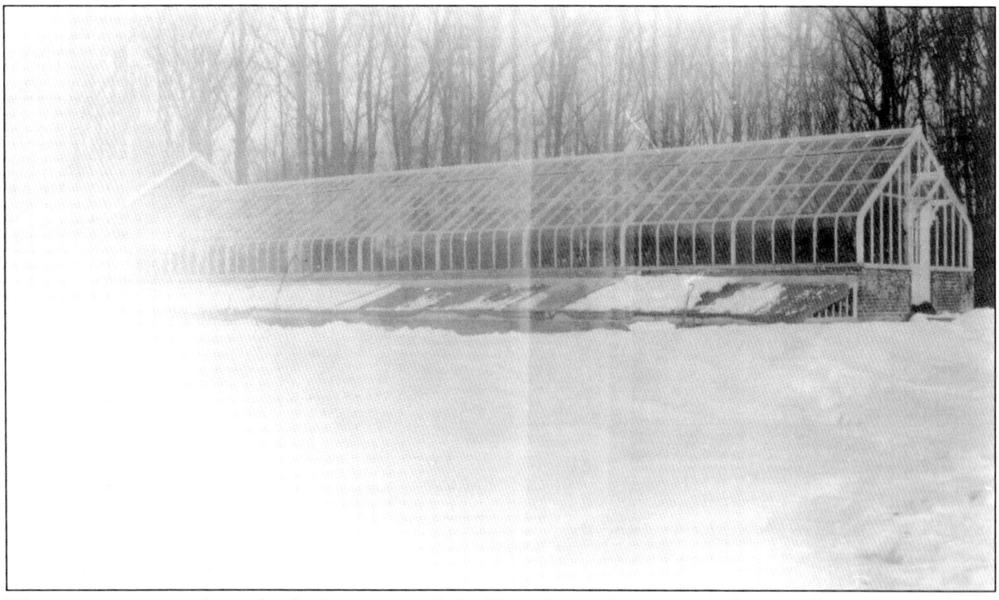

This winter image shows both the extent of the Kings' greenhouse and also its relation to the head house, on the left, where a furnace kept the plants warm through the cold months. (Courtesy Leonard Gustafson.)

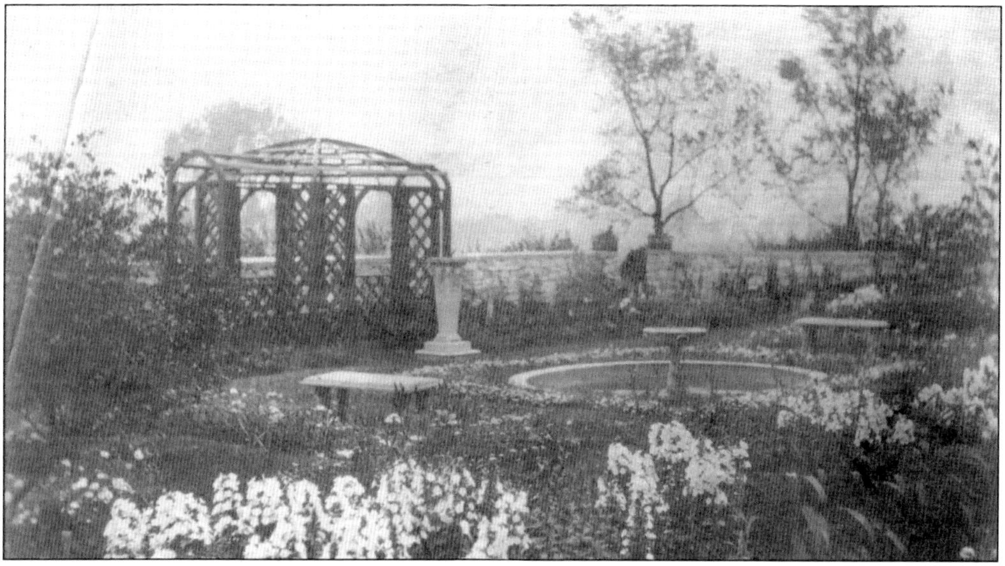

The King garden is shown here in a close-up view of its central features, with a view to the west in the rear. The trellised arbor or summerhouse looks both into the garden and beyond it to the landscape. The central fountain in a reflecting pool recalls Howard Shaw's Ragdale fountain and pool of 1905 south of the house, which is presumed to be Lake Forest's oldest continuously operating such feature. (Courtesy Leonard Gustafson.)

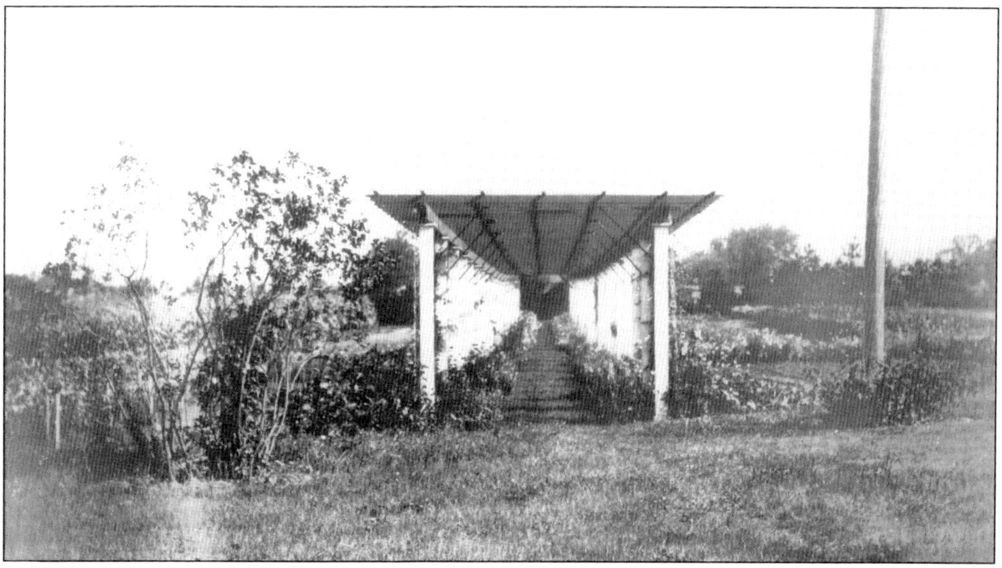

The Kings' arbor is another early example of its type. Shaw also had such a feature in his 1910s Ragdale garden (demolished), and Jensen employed these at his 1906 Norton House garden (demolished), 555 East Deerpath, and at the 1910 Hasler place garden (restored) on the southeast corner of Green Bay Road and Vine Avenue. Formal gardens relating to houses were advocated in 1892 in *The Formal Garden in England* by Reginald Blomfield, a book owned by Shaw. (Courtesy Leonard Gustafson.)

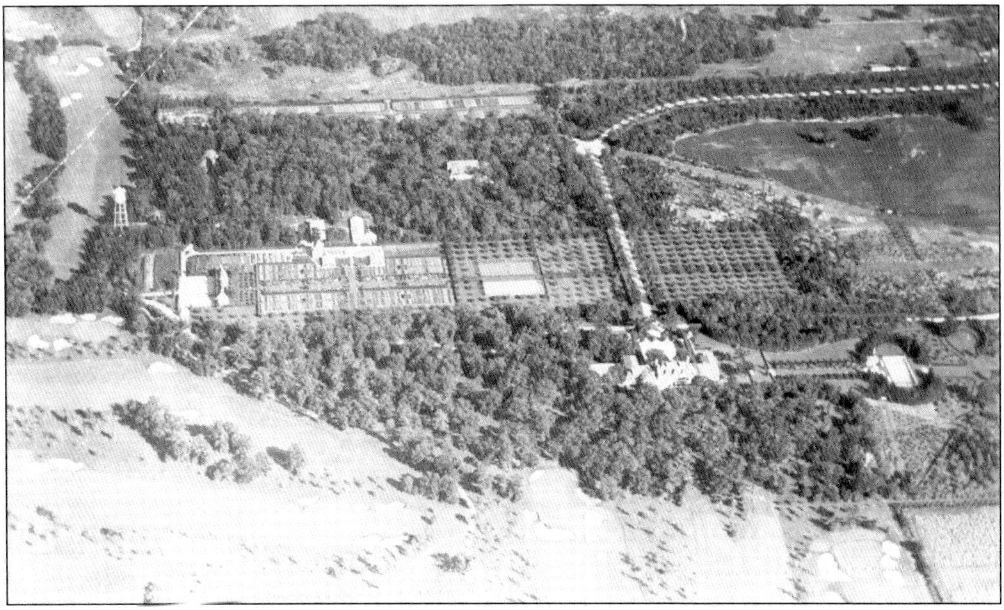

The Albert Lasker estate, started in 1926, was a 480-acre rambling country place located north of Half Day Road to Everett Road, and from Telegraph Road to what would be the tri-state tollway by the later 1950s. Called Mill Road Farm, the estate had more than 27 outbuildings, designed by David Adler. The estate was also a working farm, and housed polo ponies, 2,000 chickens, and dairy cows. A major feature was the legendary 18-hole golf course, with long holes that challenged the best players of the day. The course, visible toward the bottom of the photograph, was built after trying 50 different types of experimental grasses. No longer extant, the course is documented in golf history for its remarkable layout. (Courtesy Lake Forest-Lake Bluff Historical Society.)

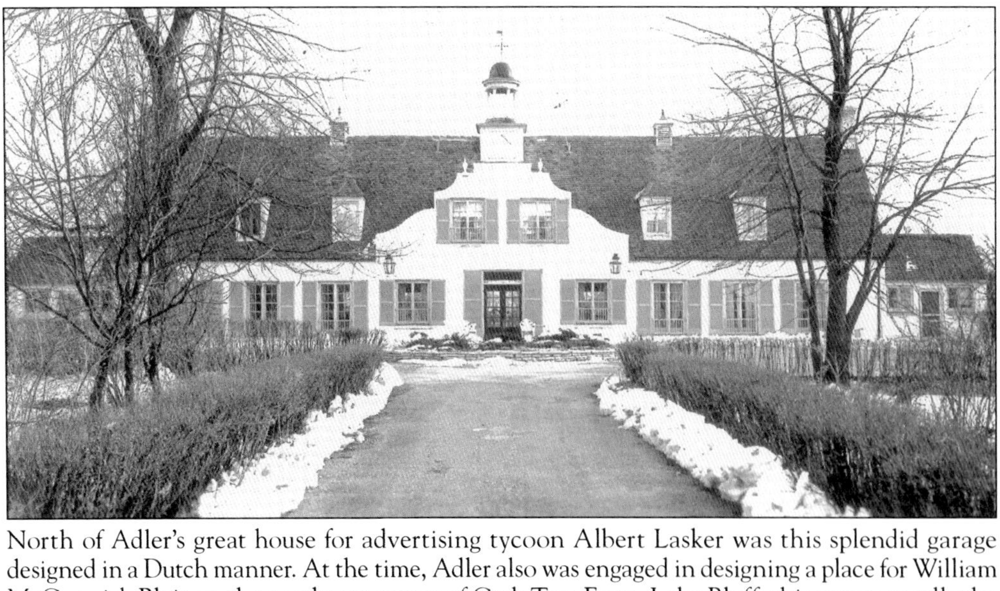

North of Adler's great house for advertising tycoon Albert Lasker was this splendid garage designed in a Dutch manner. At the time, Adler also was engaged in designing a place for William McCormick Blair on the northeast corner of Crab Tree Farm, Lake Bluff; this garage recalls the style and proportions of Solon S. Beman's 1911 Dutch-style barns for Grace Durand. (Courtesy Lake Forest-Lake Bluff Historical Society.)

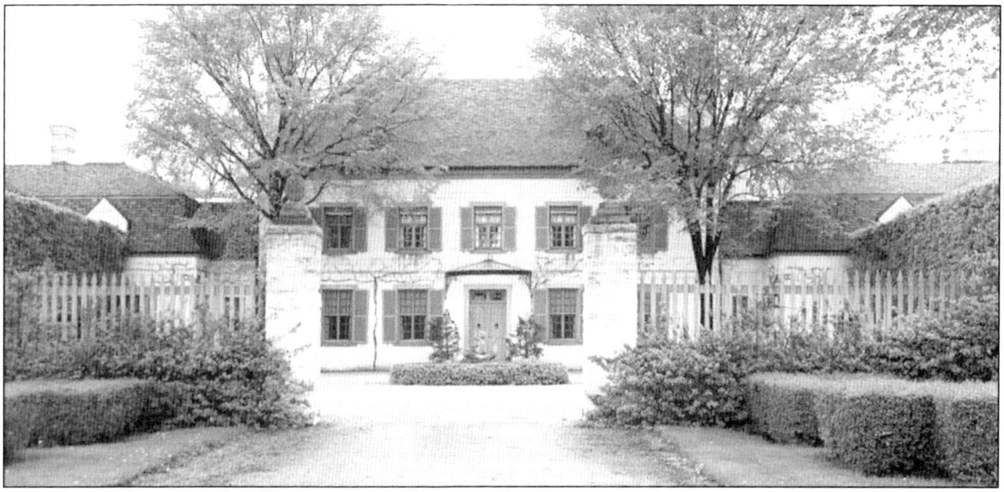

Lasker was a brilliant innovator in the field of advertising, and pioneered ads for radio, new in the mid-1920s. Shown here is an image of the front or east facade of the Albert Lasker French-style manor house, Mill Road Farm. To maintain the farm, Lasker had a staff of over 50, including the gardeners and golf staff. He was the largest employer in the area at the time, with some staff living on the farm and others shuttled on a bus from Highwood. (Courtesy Lake Forest-Lake Bluff Historical Society.)

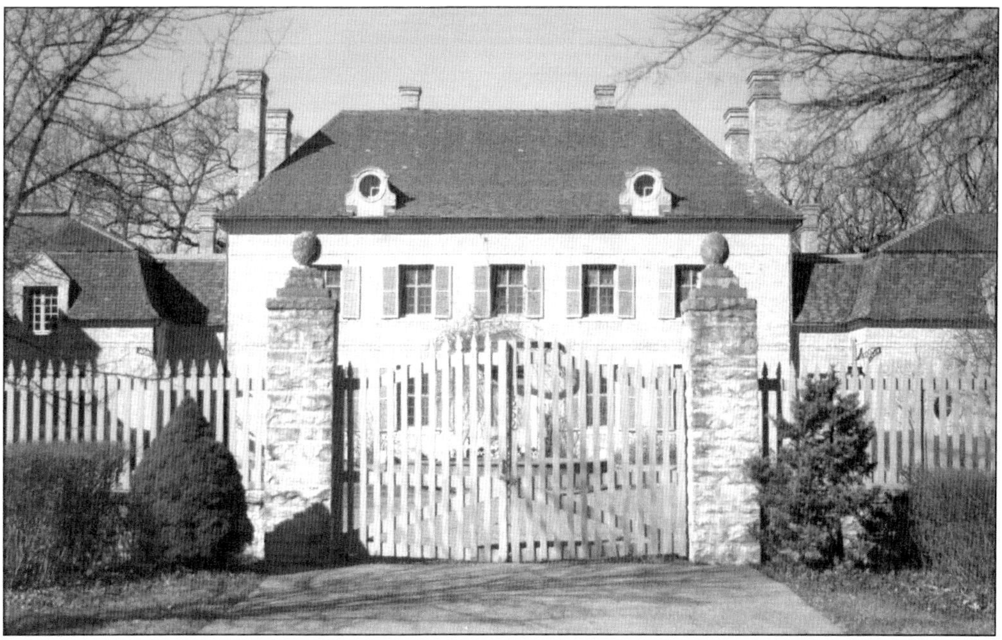

Today, the French manor house, now at 1352 Estate Lane, looks much as it did in the 1920s, except that the whitewashed stucco has been removed from the common brick exterior surface. The topiary-trained band of vines between the two stories of the house, seen in the earlier view, also was employed at Crab Tree Farm's Adler house of the late 1920s, and can be seen there still. By the end of the 1930s, Mrs. Lasker had passed away, Albert had remarried and moved to New York, and the whole estate was donated to the University of Chicago, to gradually be broken up into parcels in the next decade. High federal income taxes after 1933 also would have been a factor in Lasker's abandonment of his great country place. (Courtesy Susan Kelsey.)

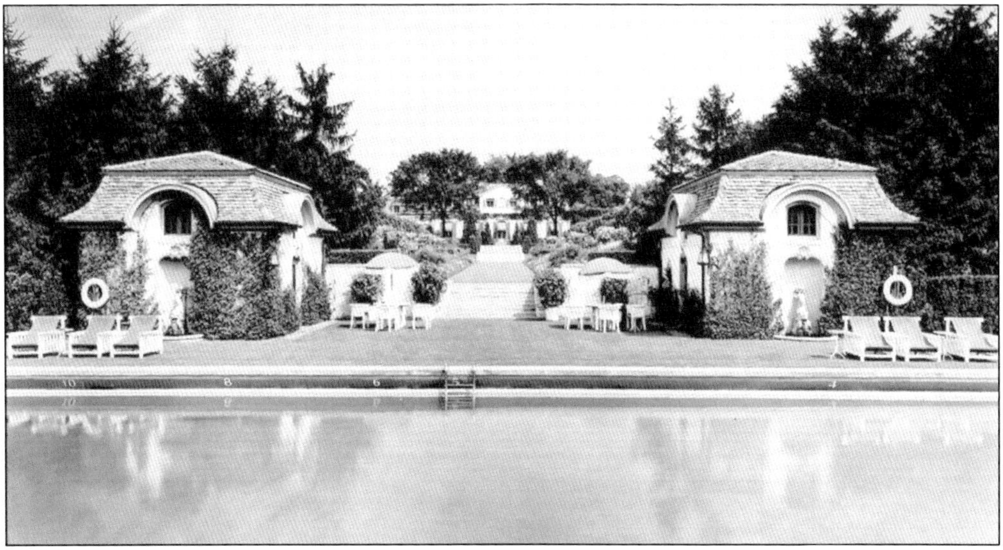

From the Lasker manor house Adler planned a great vista south across a swimming pool and terminating near Old Mill Road. This view from June 14, 1941, shows the two extant pool pavilions or changing rooms on the north side and a view north to the living room facade of the 18th-century French country manor. The swimming pool measured 100 feet by 40 feet, and there was a cocktail lounge above and to the west, still extant. The pool today has a one-story, mid-century modern house built in its footprint and blocking the vista south, otherwise not built over and with potential for restoration. (Courtesy Special Collections Research Center, University of Chicago Library.)

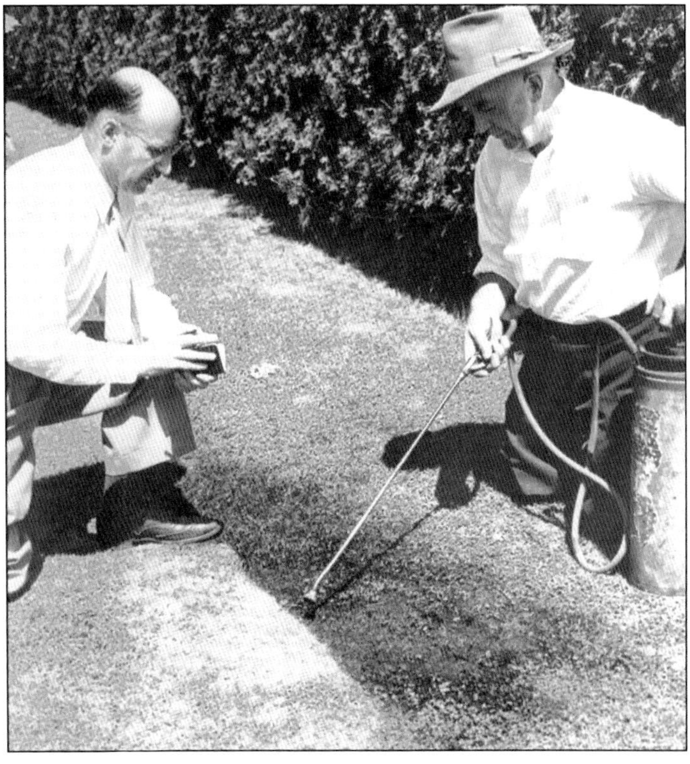

Cyril A. Tregillus (left), manager of the University of Chicago's Mill Road Gardens, assists gardener Robert Brydon in "painting out" brown spots on the estate's lawn. An aqua-green spray is used in the treatment, the chemical serving to revive grass that is not already dead. (Courtesy Special Collections Research Center, University of Chicago Library.)

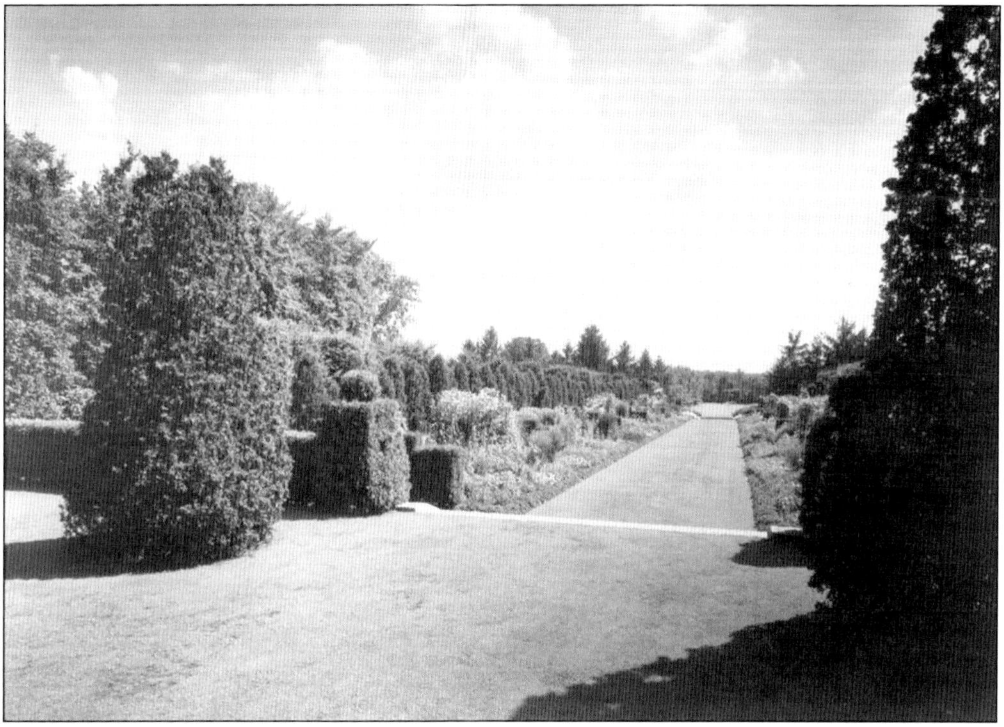

This is the vista south from near the Lasker living room. About 250 acres, more than half the total acreage, were landscaped. There were six miles of clipped hedges, trees planted symmetrically in careful relation to the landscape, and acres of grass manicured to the roots, according to John Guenther in *Taken at the Flood.* (Courtesy Special Collections Research Center, University of Chicago Library.)

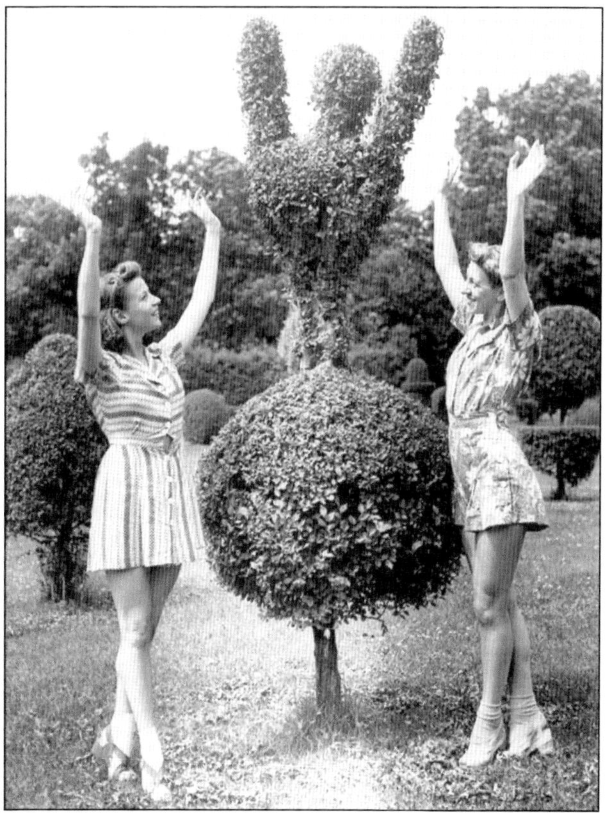

Topiary, formal flower gardens, and greenhouses on the property were some of the finest in the Midwest. The farm was considered one of the most beautiful estates in the country, both elegant and comfortable. This publicity photograph with female students is from the University of Chicago ownership period, when the gardens were opened to the public in the summer. (Courtesy Special Collections Research Center, University of Chicago Library.)

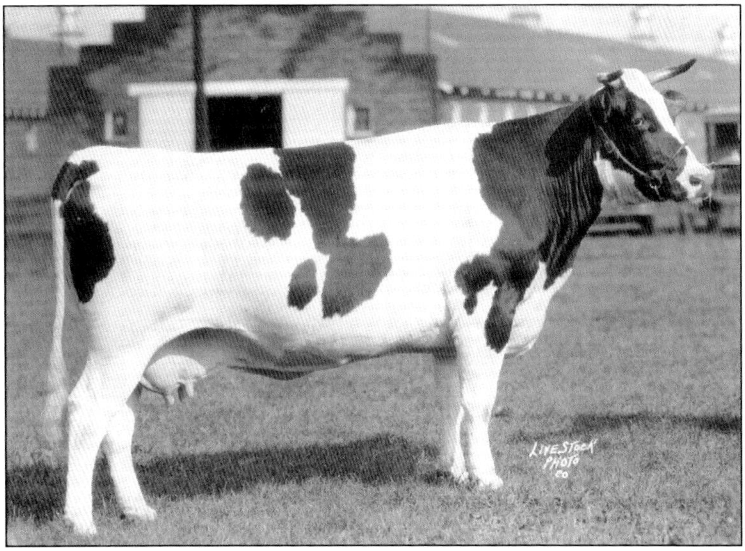

Today, there is a 1920s farm on the east end of Old Mill Road, built by the Rosencrans Baldwins. This Mill Road Farm was preceded by a farm owned by the Rudolph family. The farm raised prize cattle such as the one shown here. (Courtesy Lake Forest College Library Special Collections.)

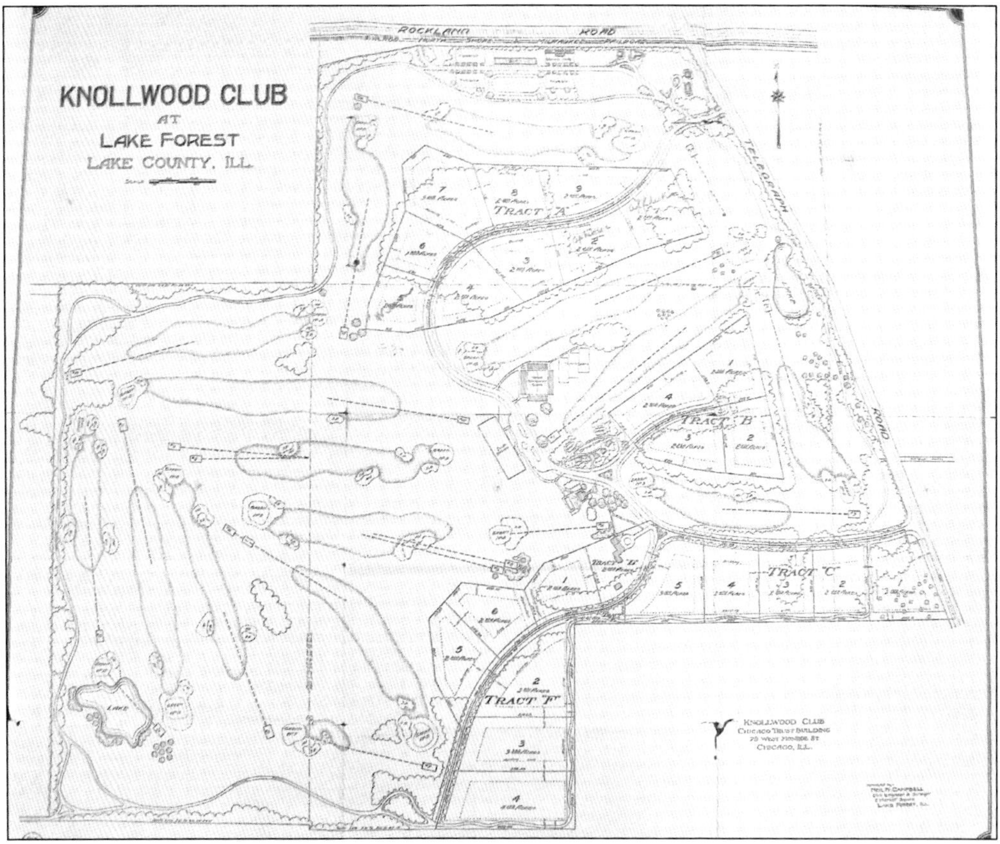

Knollwood Country Club was founded in 1924 on the Knollwood Farm, on over 200 acres at the corner of present-day Waukegan Road and Route 176. Some of the original club buildings still exist on the north end of the property. This 1925 plan by local resident and Grant Park's creator Edward H. Bennett is distinguished for its curving street layout, a continuation of the east side of Lake Forest. (Courtesy Lake Forest College Library Special Collections.)

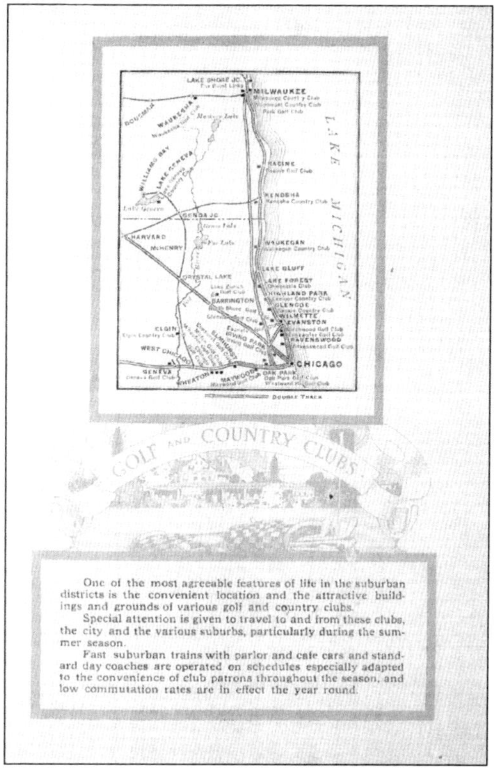

The Knollwood Club lots as configured by Bennett were 2 or 2.5 acres and overlooked the golf course. Lot 5, with the golf course on the southwest and northwest, was a prime site, and here was built this 1929 house, designed by architects Russell Walcott and Robert Work (the latter Shaw's first draftsman and Adler's former partner), with a landscape by R.R. Root of Root & Hollister, with a long-framed vista west of this French Provencal farmhouse across the golf course. (Courtesy Lake Forest College Library Special Collections.)

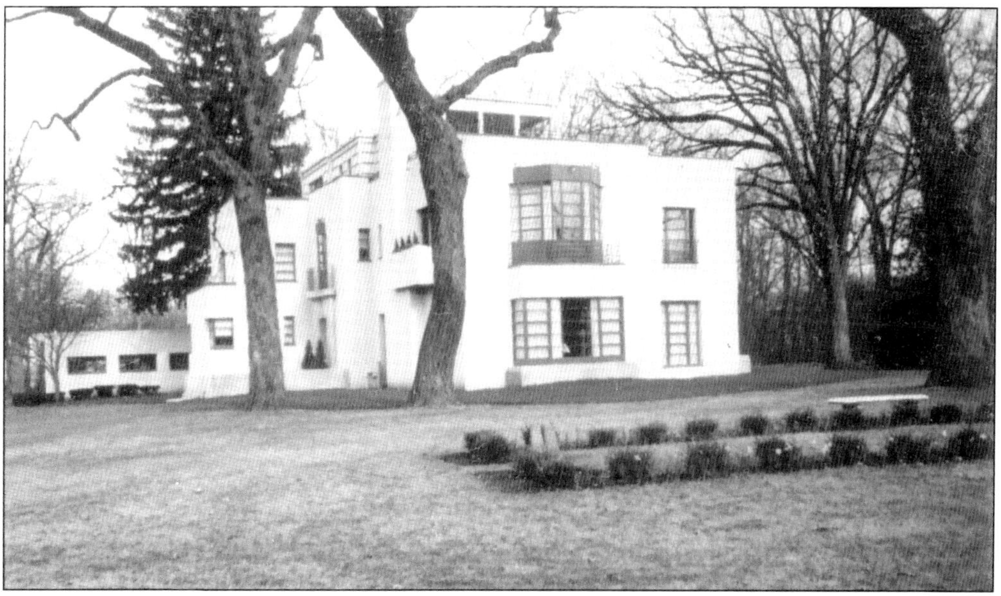

This is the Art Deco 1931 Col. Robert Hosmer Morse house and landscape on Knollwood Circle in the heart of the Knollwood Club golf course and neighborhood. Designed by Zimmerman, Sachs & Zimmerman for the head of the mighty Fairbanks Morse industrial empire, the house was ideal for business entertaining with a golf locker room in the basement and a guest dormitory on the third floor. Also, the Art Deco landscape and garden, right, are by North Shore landscape architect C.G. Wagstaff. (Courtesy Lake Forest College Library Special Collections.)

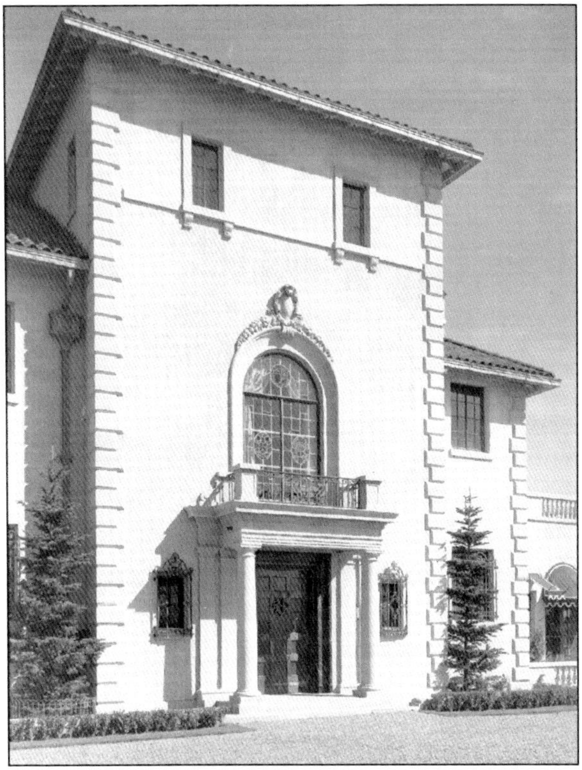

The plans for this grand late 1920s Italian villa for the Arthur Jacksons indicate that the house was the creation of New York's H.F. Huber & Co., decorators, also responsible for the interior of Stan Hywet, the Seiberling mansion at Akron, Ohio, now a museum. This view shows the west-facing facade greeting visitors. The Huber firm's associated local architect was Highland Park architect John S. Van Bergen (1885–1969), noted for his Prairie School work. (Courtesy Lake Forest College Library Special Collections.)

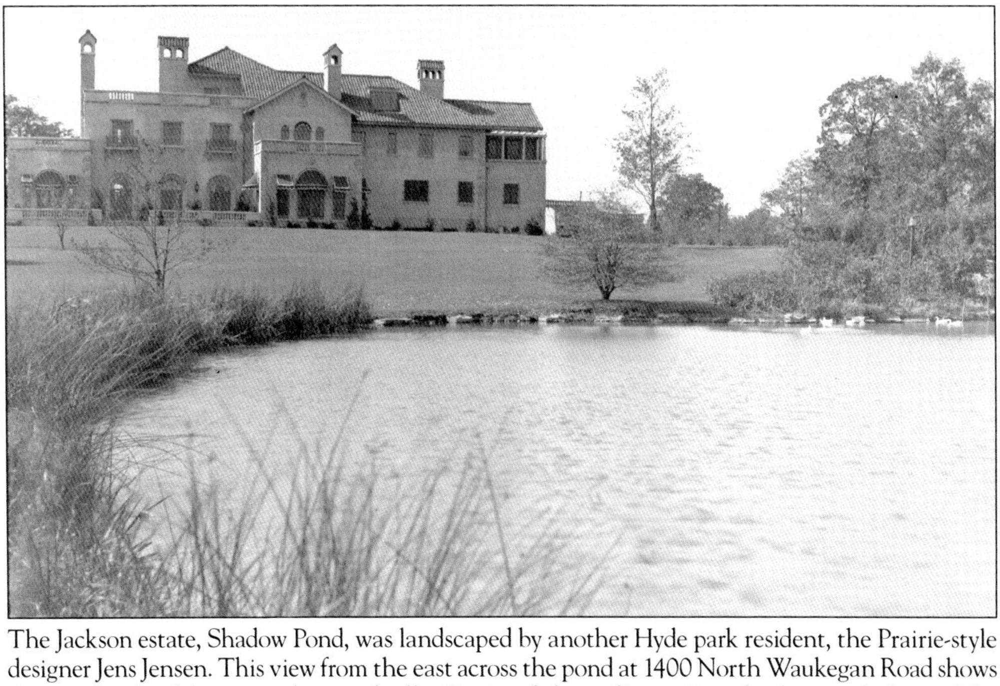

The Jackson estate, Shadow Pond, was landscaped by another Hyde park resident, the Prairie-style designer Jens Jensen. This view from the east across the pond at 1400 North Waukegan Road shows the east facade of this very substantial villa. Copies of plans of Jensen's work, along with those of the house, are now located in Lake Forest College's special collections. Another Jensen landscape was the Rasmussen place on Old Mill Road. (Courtesy Lake Forest College Library Special Collections.)

Five

Businesses and the Green Bay Trail

The intersection of Everett and Waukegan Roads has been a commercial center since the 1830s and perhaps even earlier than that, since the roads follow old Indian trails, which in turn followed old animal trails.

Beginning as a stagecoach stop, later adding a railroad track through the area, the community centered on the intersections of Everett. What now is Waukegan Road is the earliest commercial district included in today's city of Lake Forest. Eclipsed by the more robust east Lake Forest central business district by early in the last century, once again it is a bustling commercial cluster located on what is now the west side of Lake Forest: the Settler's Square group of shopping centers and free-standing operations. Capt. James Lovell, Apollo 13 astronaut, along with his chef son launched the fine-dining restaurant Lovell's near the northeast corner of the historic intersection of Everett and Waukegan Roads. Sunset Foods developed the shopping area north of Lovell's, with Sunset Foods grocery as the anchor store along with several other retail establishments. A new retail shopping center west of this across Waukegan Road was built in the 2000s, Forest Square. A new pedestrian path serving the 1990s train station will be created for safe commuting on the train line and possibly on Amtrak in the future. The 1990s fire station was built south of Everett Road and west of the tracks, just east of Telegraph Road, and is in the same location as several former Everett businesses. There is one remaining corner to be redeveloped on the southeast, with many proposals being explored. This all serves the recently developed residential area, formerly farms and then estates.

A drive north on Waukegan Road from this commercial center toward Route 60 illustrates the changes. An observer can try to imagine a one-lane road: as a carriage approaches, one must pull off to the side to let the southbound equipage pass. Continuing on, there is a crossover on the Corduroy Bridge, now next to the soccer fields and hardly noticeable by today's standards. One can imagine crossing over this branch of the Chicago River on logs or planks, the crudely cut wooden surface shaking as one moves over them. For over 175 years, west Lake Forest has been a significant community, with a commercial district serving the succeeding farm, estate, and suburban communities of Corduroy, Lancaster Station, Everett, and since 1926, Lake Forest.

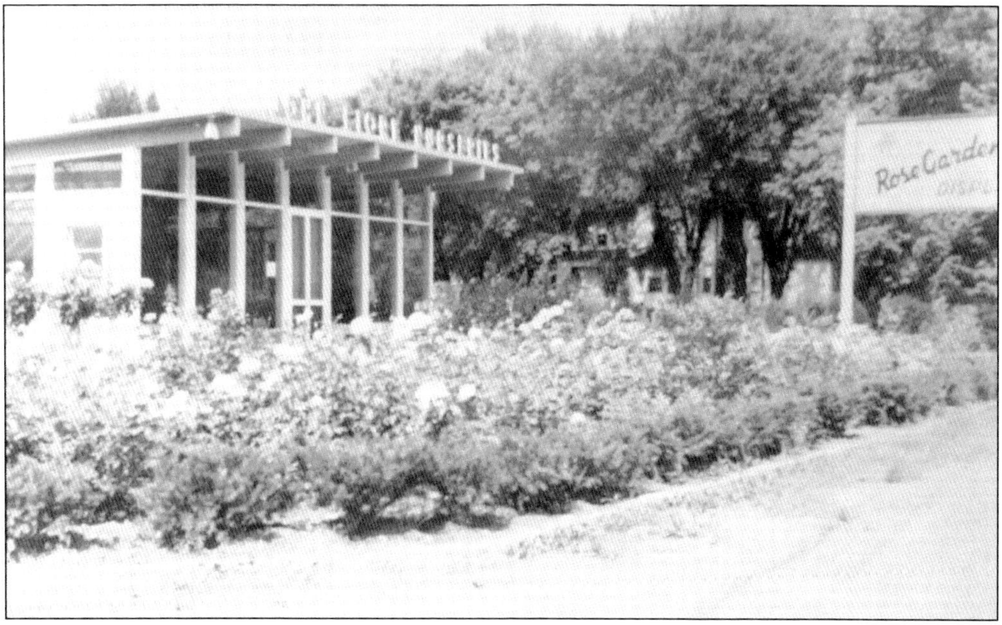

The Fiore family has been in Lake Forest for over 70 years. Don Fiore and brother John Fiore fondly remember growing up on the west side. Pictured here is the Fiore business designed by William Bergmann of Stanley D. Anderson in 1958, previously located on the west side of Waukegan, just north of Everett in the present-day Forest Square shopping plaza. (Courtesy John Fiore)

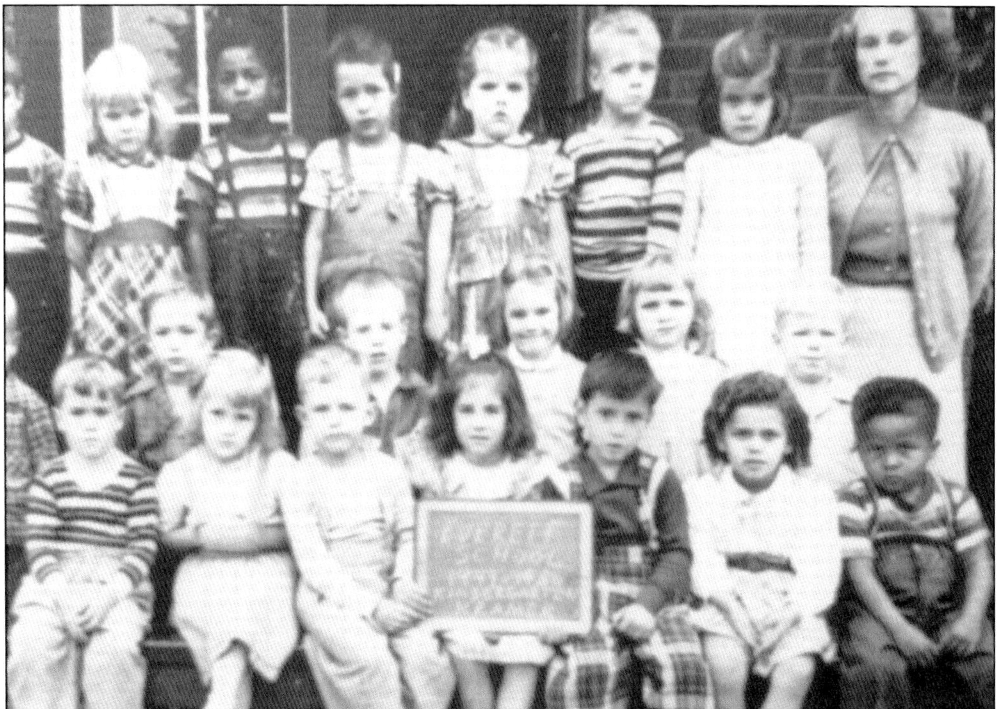

John Fiore attended Everett Elementary School and is featured in this class photograph in the front row with plaid pants. (Courtesy John Fiore)

The intersection of Waukegan and Everett Roads has always been a hub for commerce. Sunset Foods, owner of Settlers Square, features the finest customer service. Sunset Foods is a family-owned grocery store founded in 1937. Sunset offers a wide selection of organic, gourmet, specialty, and fresh food items and is committed to outstanding customer service and community involvement. Today, Sunset has five locations, with stores in Northbrook, Lake Forest, Libertyville, and Long Grove that employ approximately 900. (Right, courtesy Lake Forest-Lake Bluff Historical Society; below, courtesy Sunset Foods.)

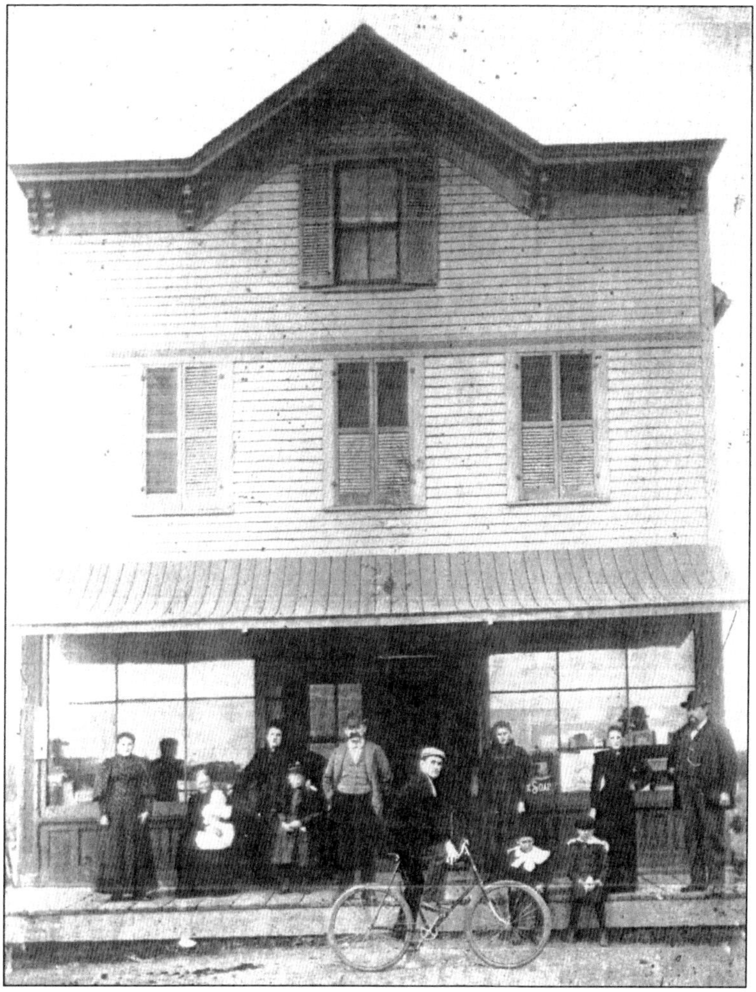

SUNSET
FOODS

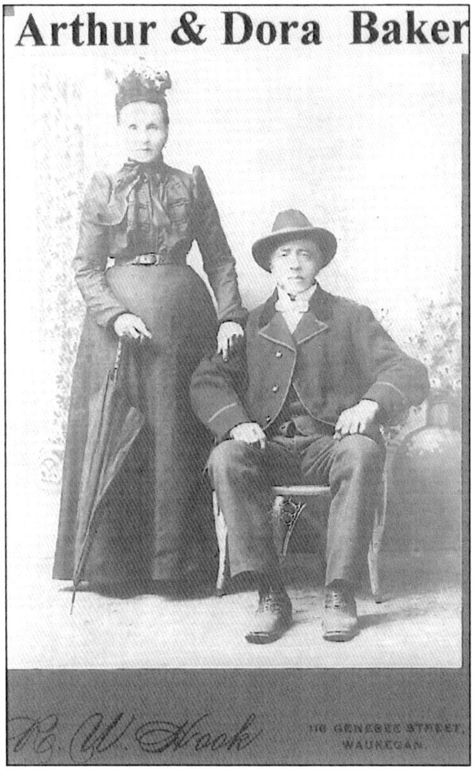

Mike Rafferty, son of Elizabeth Baker from the Peter and Sarah Fagan Baker family, recalls his family business that had been located on the present-day west Lake Forest Metra station, on both sides of Conway Road. Also pictured are Peter Baker's parents, Arthur and Dora Baker. (Both courtesy Mike Rafferty.)

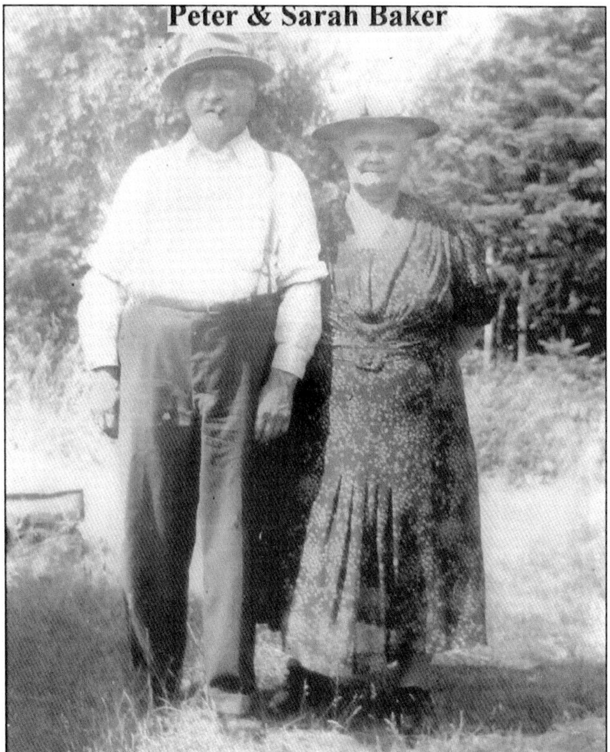

Pictured is James Fagan in front of his daughter Sarah Fagen Baker's Washington Circle home around the 1920s. The Peter Baker & Son asphalt plant was located at the present-day Metra parking lot, west of the tracks. The tracks to deliver the asphalt materials can still be seen by Everett road in 2012. (Courtesy Mike Rafferty.)

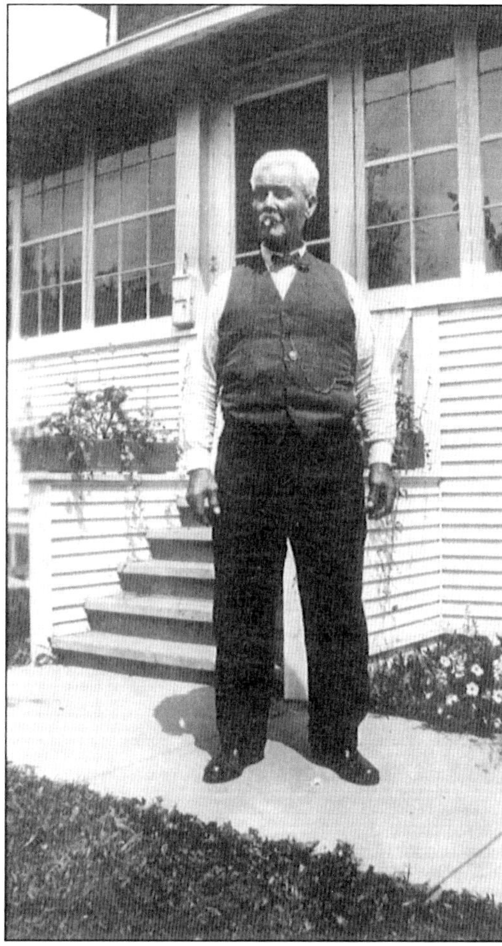

Asphalt work in 1918 was labor intensive. West Deerfield Township records show that each Everett resident had road duty as part of their community responsibility to create and improve roads in Lake County. First gravel would be laid on the road, followed by hot asphalt from the drum. Spigots would fill asphalt buckets, as shown on the lower left, and all was applied manually. (Courtesy Mike Rafferty.)

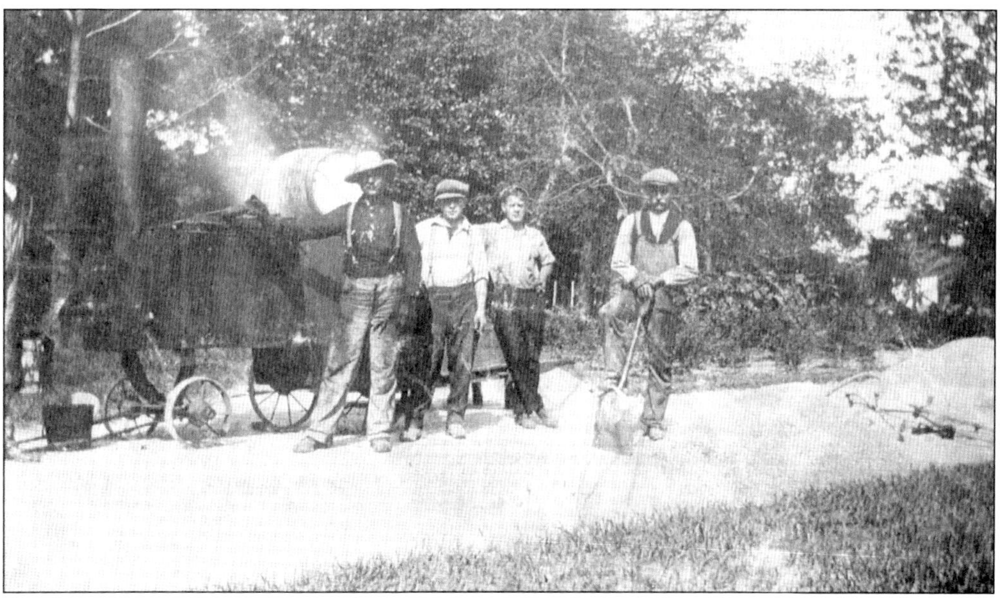

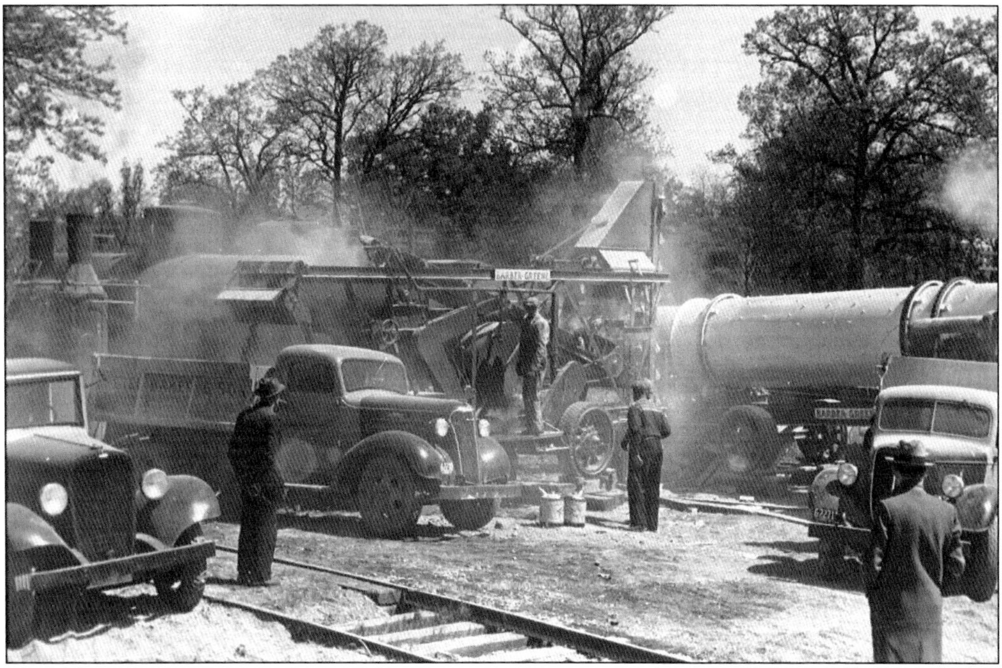

Baker Asphalt, previously located in the present-day Metra train parking lot, paved many of Lake Forest roads. Pictured here in 1940 is a long dryer to heat the stone aggregate. The truck is being loaded with blacktop from the asphalt plant pug mill. Many of the streets in Lake Forest were paved by Peter Baker & Son. (Both courtesy Mike Rafferty.)

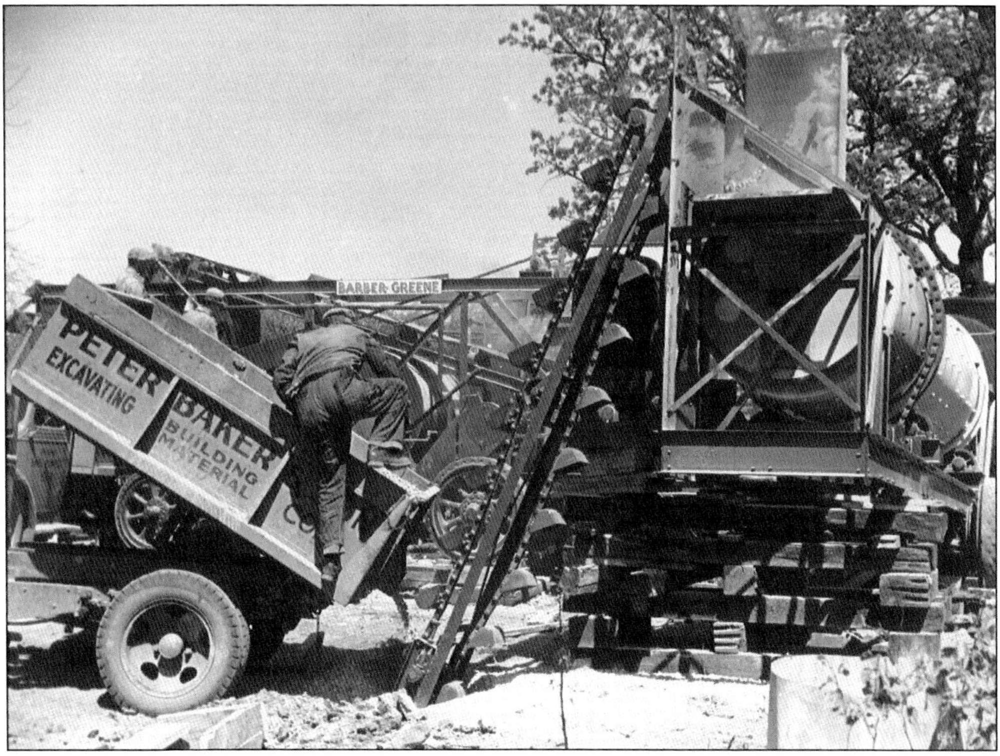

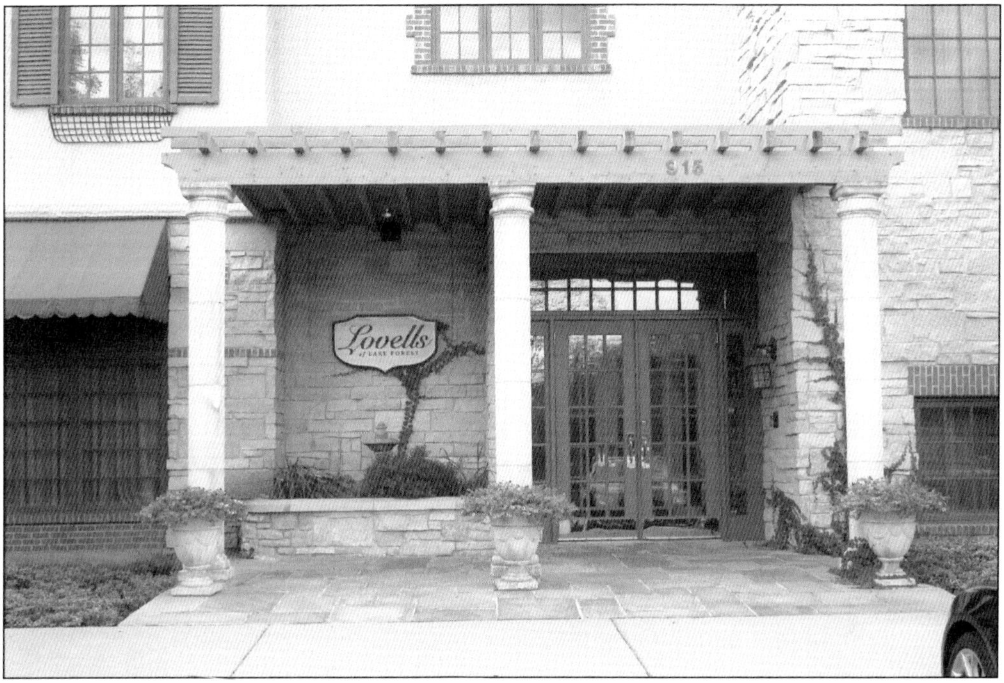

Capt. James A. Lovell of Apollo 13 opened Lovell's of Lake Forest on the west side of Lake Forest in 1999. The restaurant houses famous artwork and space program memorabilia, such as the "Steeds of Apollo" mural, Captain Lovell's awards, a moon rock, Apollo 13 movie items, and collectibles. (Both courtesy Susan Kelsey.)

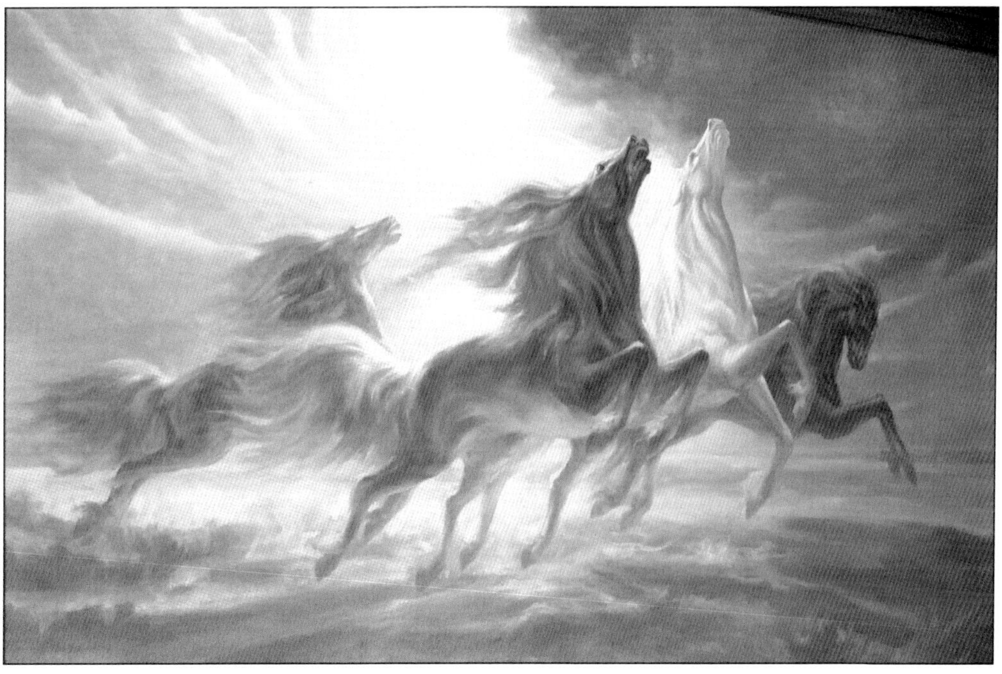

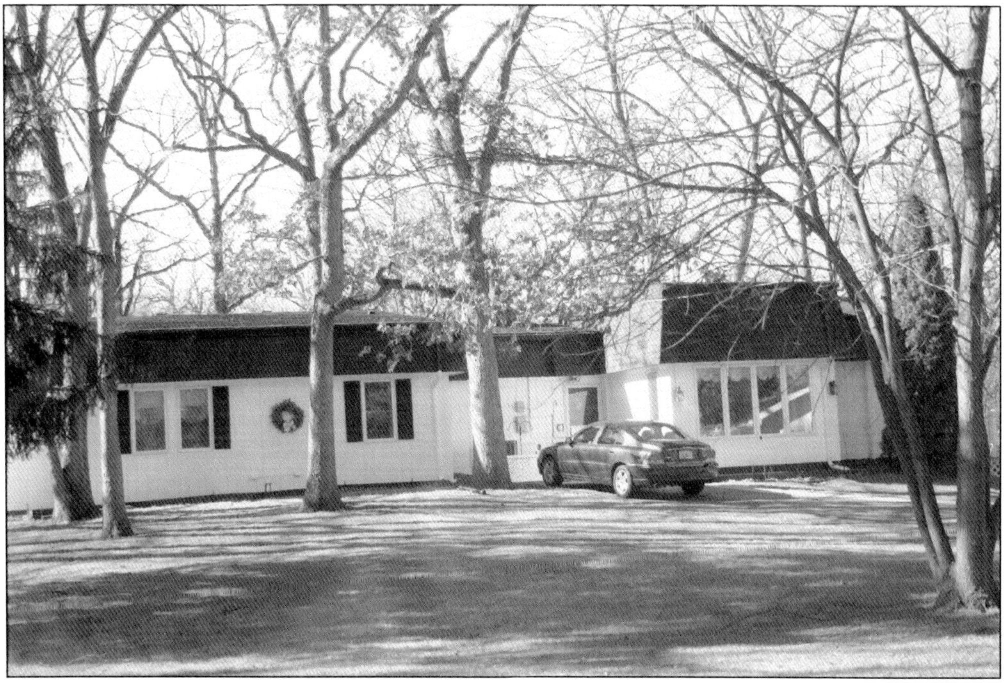

Five prefabricated, steel-frame homes originally furnished and decorated by Marshall Field & Co. and built by Fred D. Sadler of Lake Forest constitute the first community development of modern prefabricated homes in the area; it was called the Acorn Knoll estates. (Courtesy Susan Kelsey.)

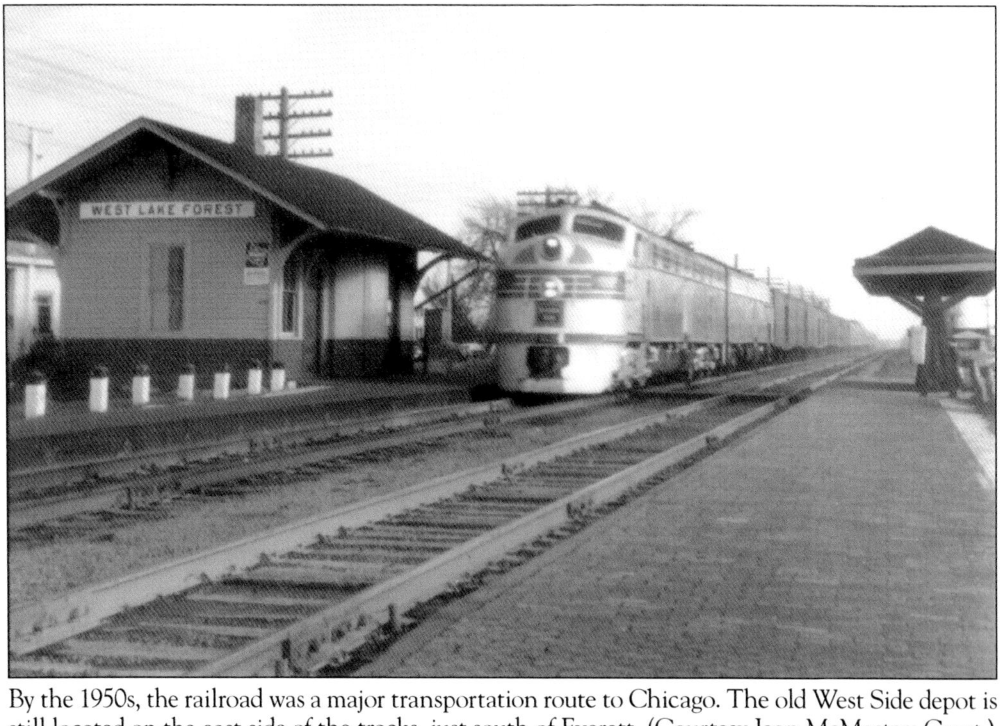

By the 1950s, the railroad was a major transportation route to Chicago. The old West Side depot is still located on the east side of the tracks, just south of Everett. (Courtesy Jean McMasters Grost.)

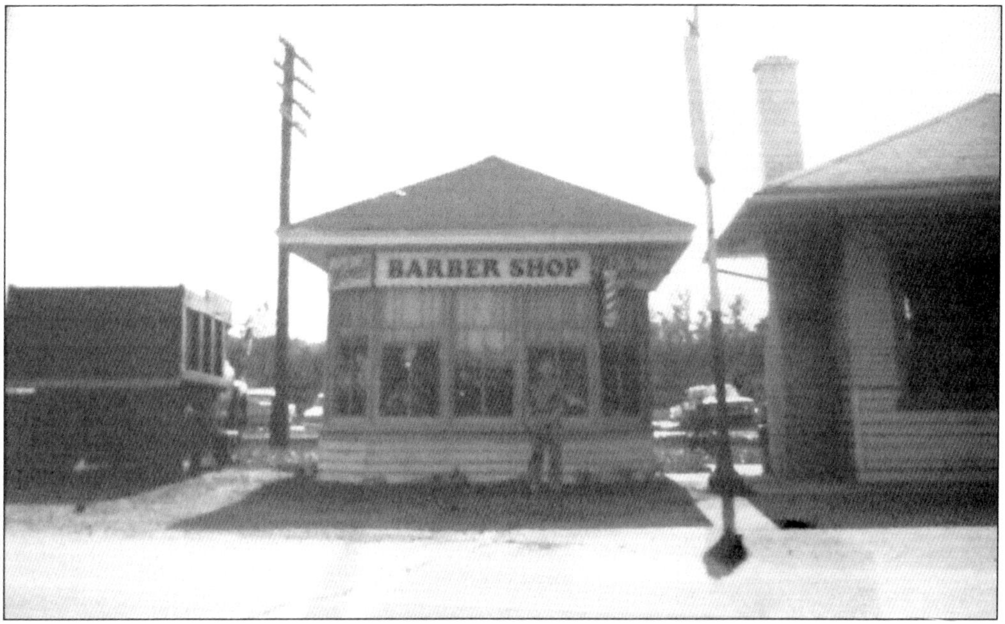

Pictured above is Michael Caringello's former barbershop. It was located on Waukegan's west side, just south of Everett Road. Michael's barbershop is now located at 950 North Western Avenue; he has been in business over 50 years. Steve Kostele's Garage was previously located on Waukegan Road where McDonald's is currently. Mark McMahon, a local artist and Ridge Road resident, designed the wall mural in McDonald's. (Above, courtesy Michael Caringello; below, courtesy Mark McMahon.)

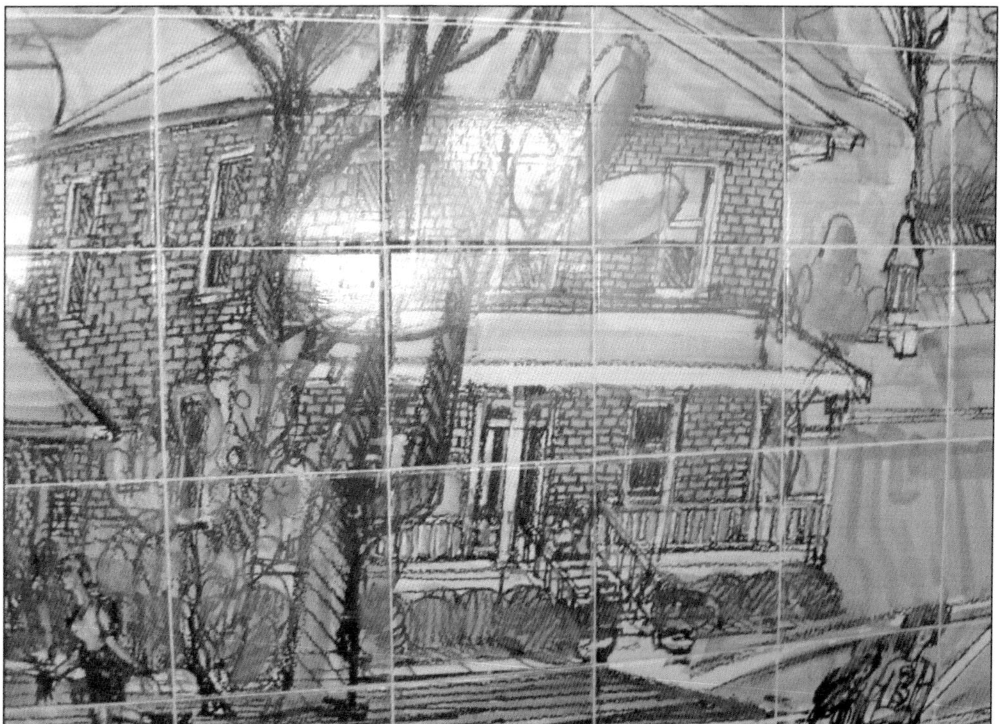

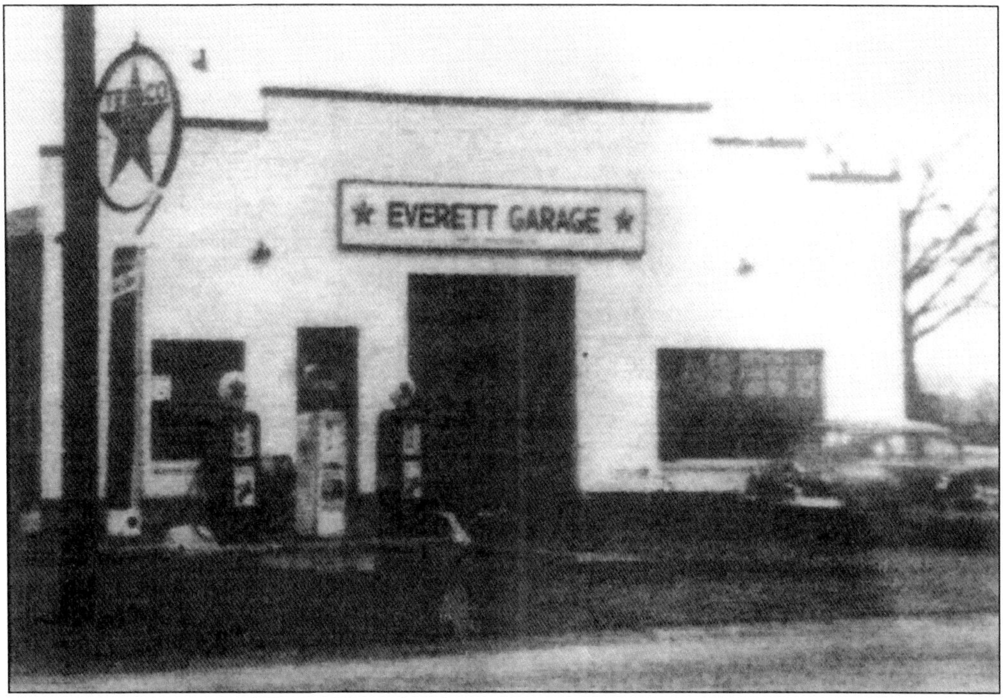

Everett Garage occupied the building that housed Pasquesi Home and Farm Supply on Waukegan Road south of Everett. It had also housed a blacksmith shop in the back. (Courtesy Lake Forest-Lake Bluff Historical Society.)

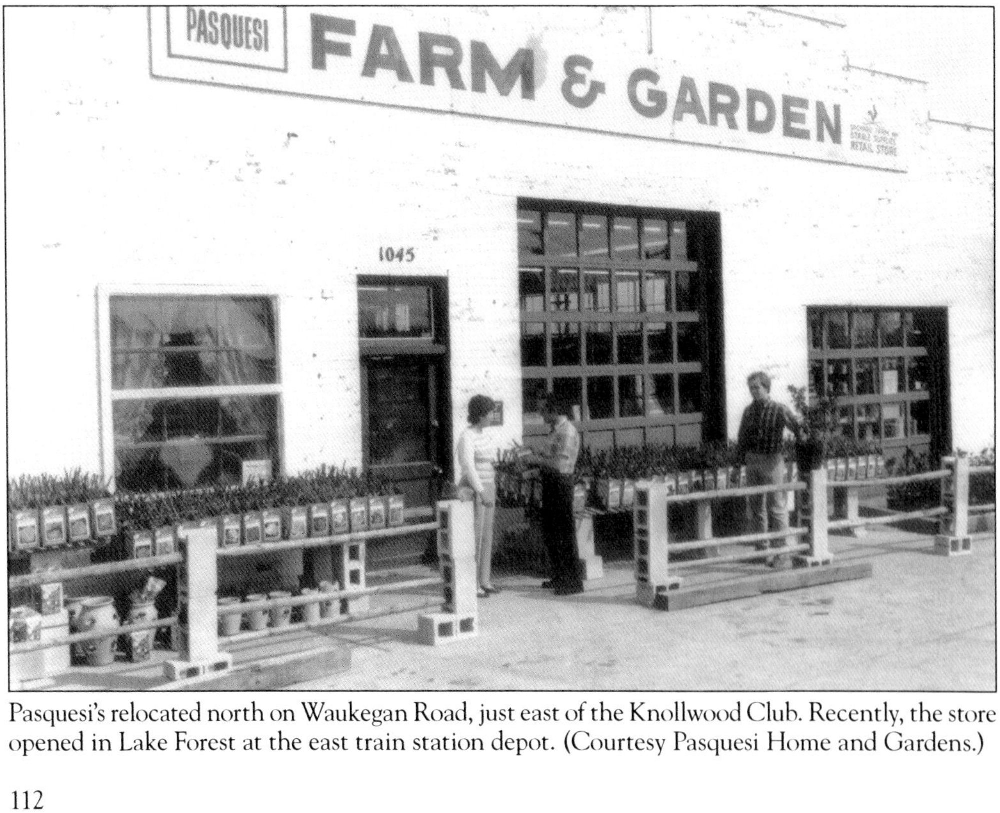

Pasquesi's relocated north on Waukegan Road, just east of the Knollwood Club. Recently, the store opened in Lake Forest at the east train station depot. (Courtesy Pasquesi Home and Gardens.)

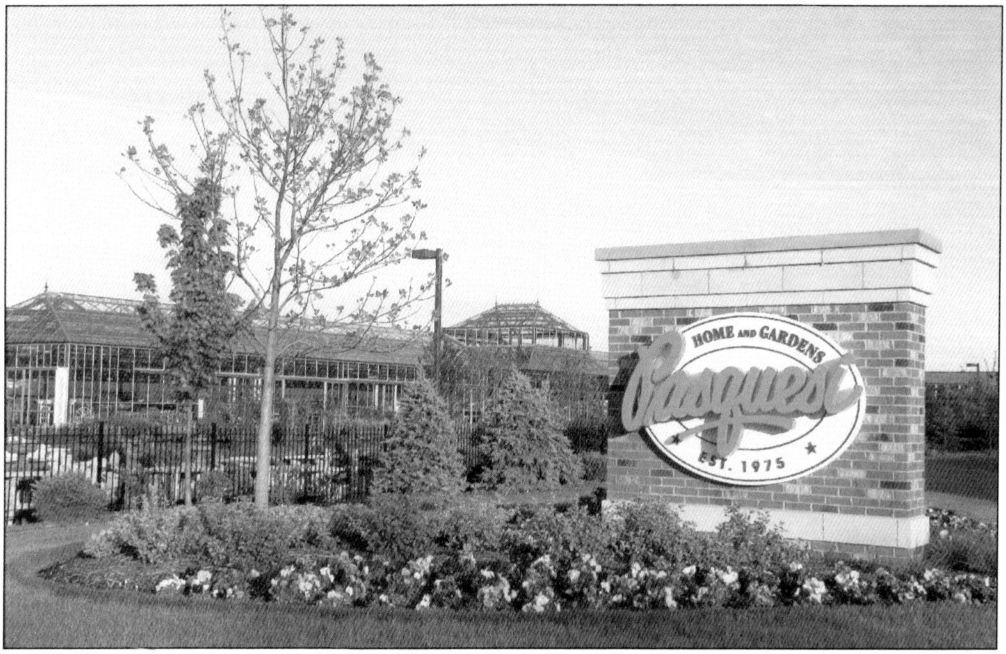

In 2006, the Lake Forest Pasquesi Home and Gardens store relocated to Lake Bluff and in 2012, a third location was opened downtown at the historic east Lake Forest train station.

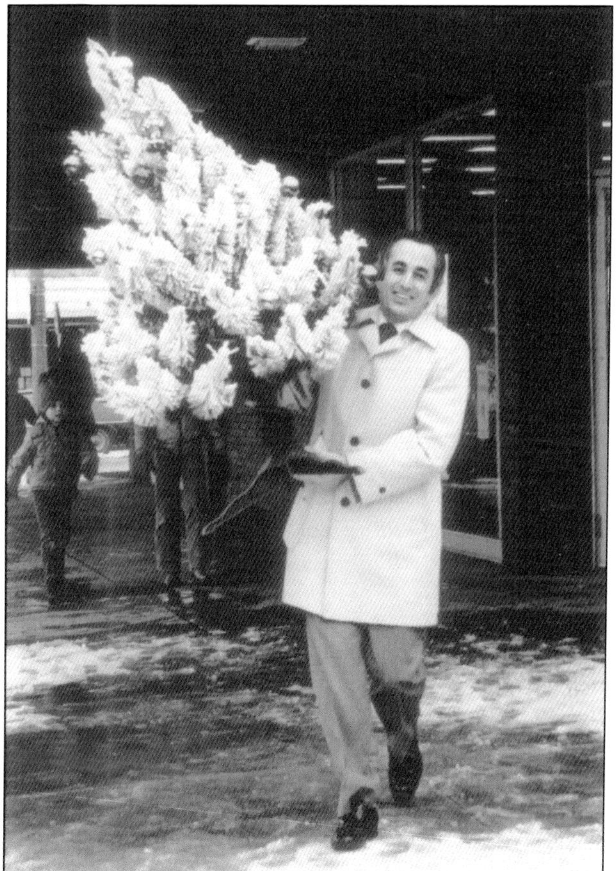

Ed Pasquesi is pictured here carrying a holiday tree to a customer in the 1970s. (Courtesy Pasquesi Home and Gardens.)

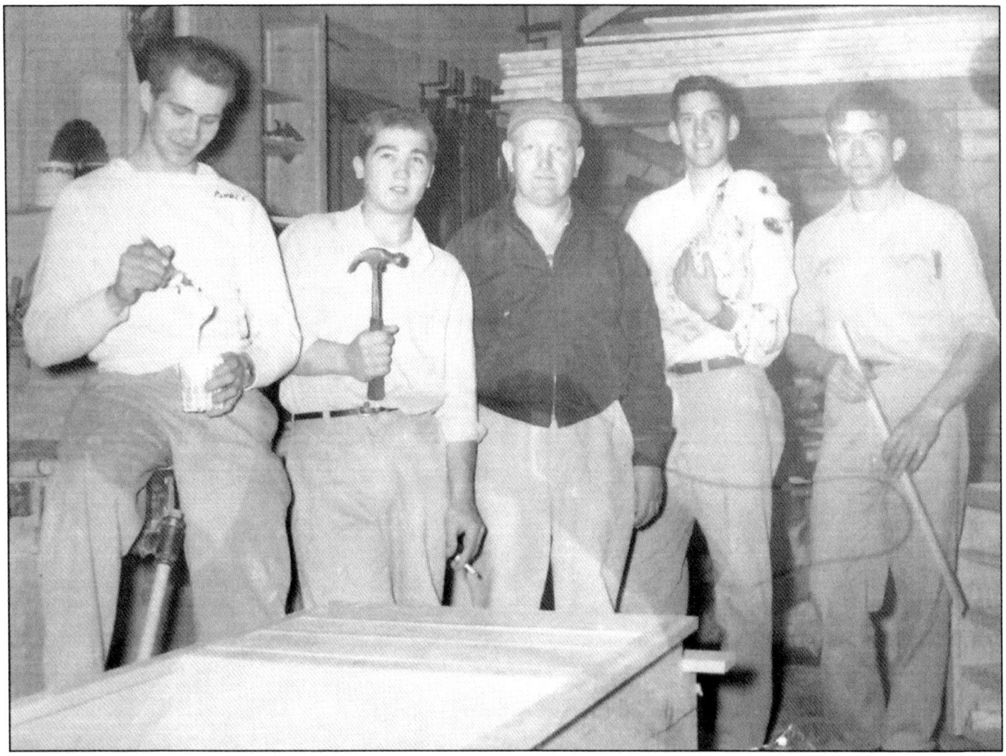

Karl Nagel Sr., now 100 years old and living in Lake Forest, is pictured here (center, dark jacket) in his business called Lake Forest Millwork. Also pictured is his son Karl Nagel, second from the right, holding his dog. (Courtesy Karl Nagel family.)

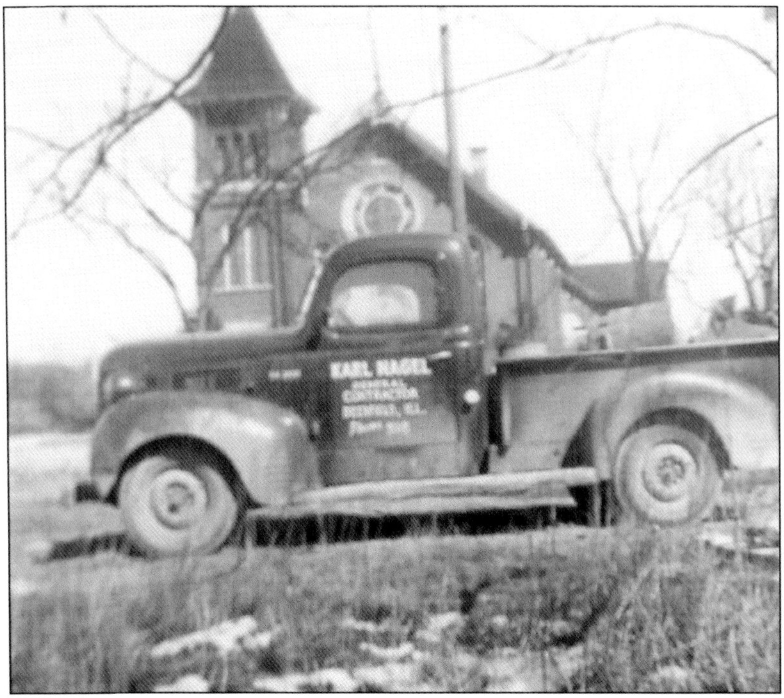

Karl Nagel Sr. arrived in Lake Forest in 1928 after seeing an advertisement to live on the west side. He started Lake Forest Millwork and soon built the St. Patrick's Church altar and the front doors of the church. Pictured here is his truck in front of St. Patrick's. (Courtesy Karl Nagle family.)

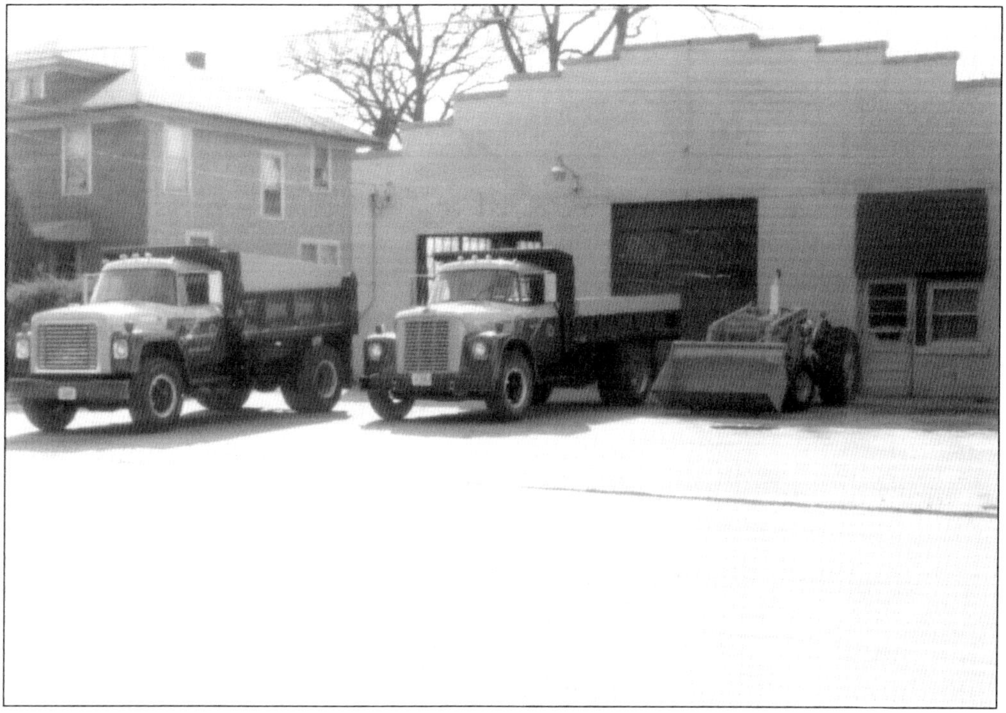

At right, John Fiore Jr. is standing next to a log cabin on the west side of Lake Forest. John is holding his sailor's cap, which he remembers he used to wear all the time. John and Don Fiore remember riding their bikes down Everett Road to Estate Lane, down to Old Mill Road and up Telegraph, the only roads that existed in 1940s. With his brother Don, they used to roam around the area and play in the relics of those lost pioneer days. The Fiores owned, until recent years, a nursery outlet on Waukegan Road (above), now a shopping center north of the McDonald's. (Above, courtesy John Fiore; right, courtesy Shirley Paddock.)

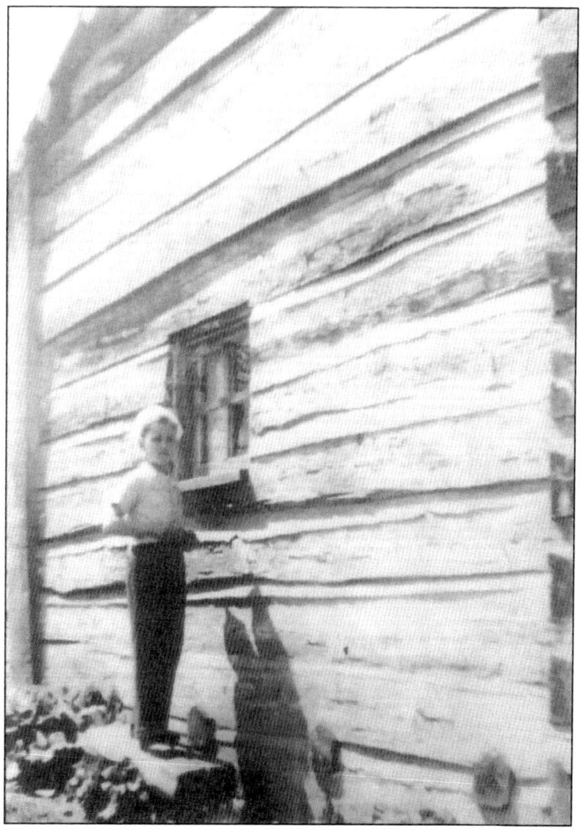

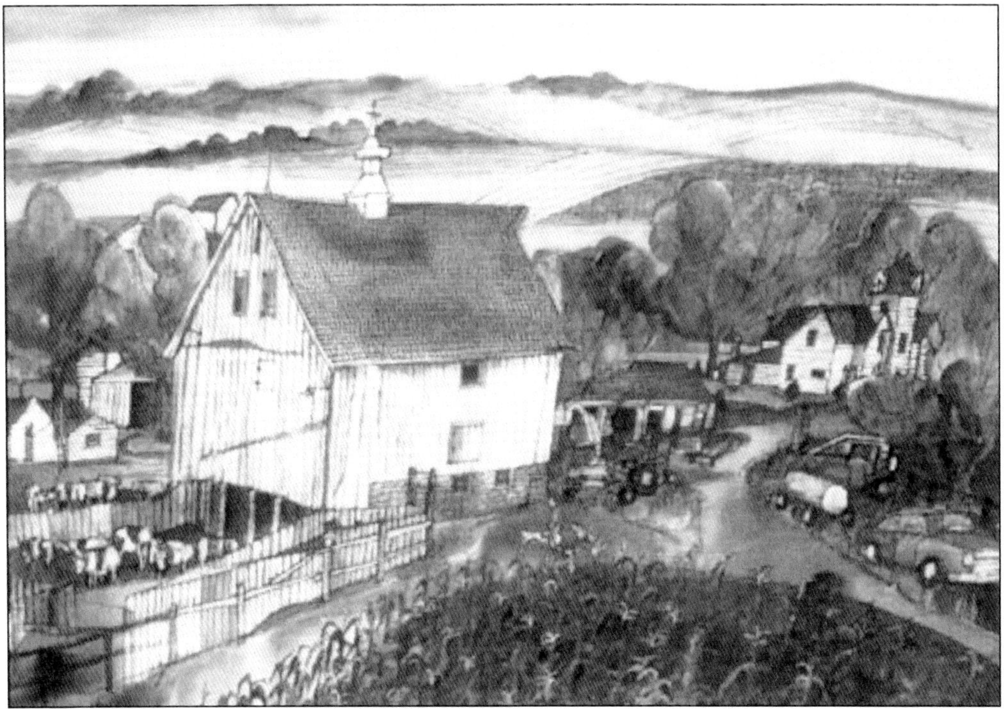

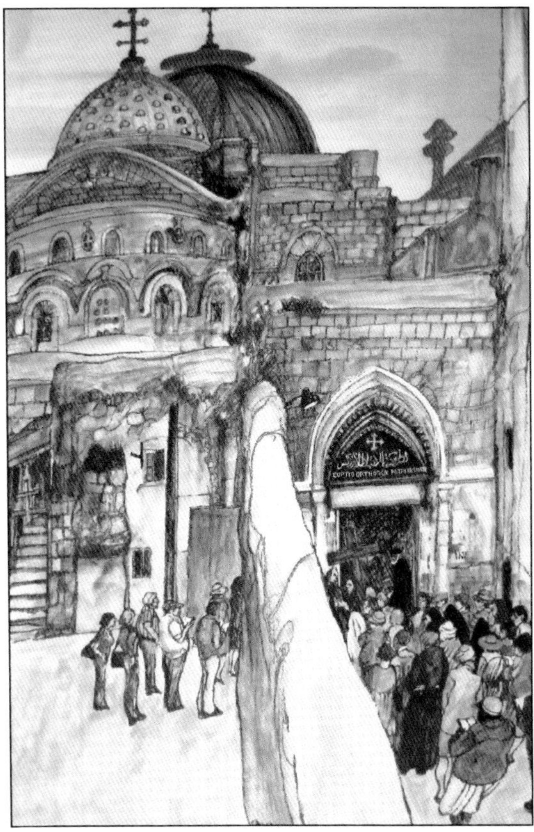

Mark McMahon and his father, Franklin McMahon (1921–2012), are Lake Forest artists who contribute greatly to the community. The west-side McDonald's on Waukegan has a beautiful wall of hand-painted tiles displaying Mark and Irene Leahy McMahon's artistry. Visitors can see Franklin McMahon's Stations of the Cross tiles at St. Patrick's Church, located at Waukegan and Everett Roads. Moving to Lake Forest in 1951, Franklin McMahon had nine children: William Franklin, Mark, Mary, Debbie, Patrick, Hugh, Margo, Michelle, and Michael. The family of artists continues with Carolyn McGregor McMahon and Mark McMahon and their three children, Meryl, Andrew, and Elise. (Above, courtesy Mark McMahon; left, courtesy Franklin McMahon.)

Six

Estate-Era Legacy to 21st Century West Lake Forest

This first survey of west Lake Forest has defined the area characterized by this designation. West Lake Forest largely is found beyond Onwentsia and the Green Bay Road estates of the 1890s. This boundary is west of the estate area easily accessible by the elite Chicagoans prior to the general adoption of automobiles by 1904. Motor cars allowed a wider reach from the east side train station. This west side region in the 19th century and also later was an agricultural community, the province of pioneer settler families and their working farms. This was centered on the small rural trading and transportation center at Corduroy, Lancaster Center, and by the 1880s, Everett.

The estates spread rapidly west after the beginning of the 20th century, with a few landowners buying large parcels—Swift, Armour, and later, Lasker—including Albert Blake Dick, one of the subjects of this final chapter. By the 1920s, too, midsize estate-like places were introduced at the Deerpath Hills Estates developments north and south of Deerpath and east of Waukegan Road, north on the former McKinlock estate of 1900. Both of these examples provide guidance for the future—the former as the estate compatibly transitioned to a hospital and a neighborhood and the latter as an example of a classically planned and carried out project of coordinated development to preserve harmonious visual character.

The Alice Home cottage hospital, built in 1899 on the North Campus of Lake Forest College, needed to grow by the later 1930s. It moved to the A.B. Dick Westmoreland estate of 1903, and opened October 31, 1942. The A.B. Dick family donated 25 acres, which has grown to 160 acres. Opened with 41 beds and 28 physicians in 1942, the new Lake Forest Hospital designed by the Stanley D. Anderson firm cost $566,000, with the funds raised by local citizens. This local health care center has grown into a 205-bed facility. In 2011, the venerable local institution, organized in 1899, merged with Northwestern Hospital, becoming Northwestern Lake Forest Hospital, beginning a new chapter of service in the expanding area.

Deerpath Hills Estates was conceived in the late 1920s as a cluster of small estate-like properties of two acres or so, not unlike the original 300 east Lake Forest lots' scale in 1857. This time it was to be across from a new country club on the former Mellody Farm property, across Waukegan Road to the west. The main artery is King Muir Road, on the north side passing a large home replacing the 1900 McKinlock Shingle-style place. (The gateposts still can be seen on the north side of Deerpath, west of King Muir.) Architect Stanley D. Anderson (1896–1960), a former Howard Shaw associate and alumnus of Lake Forest College (1916), the University of Illinois architecture program, and the Atelier Laloux of the École des Beaux-Arts (Paris), oversaw the architecture and managed the new houses' roof pitches, angles, gardens, and more to be compatible, private, and varied enough for interest among French, Scottish, and English Half-Timbered Revival styles. The plan and the central authority were essentially classic French in conception, and careful study by planners today would be well worth the effort.

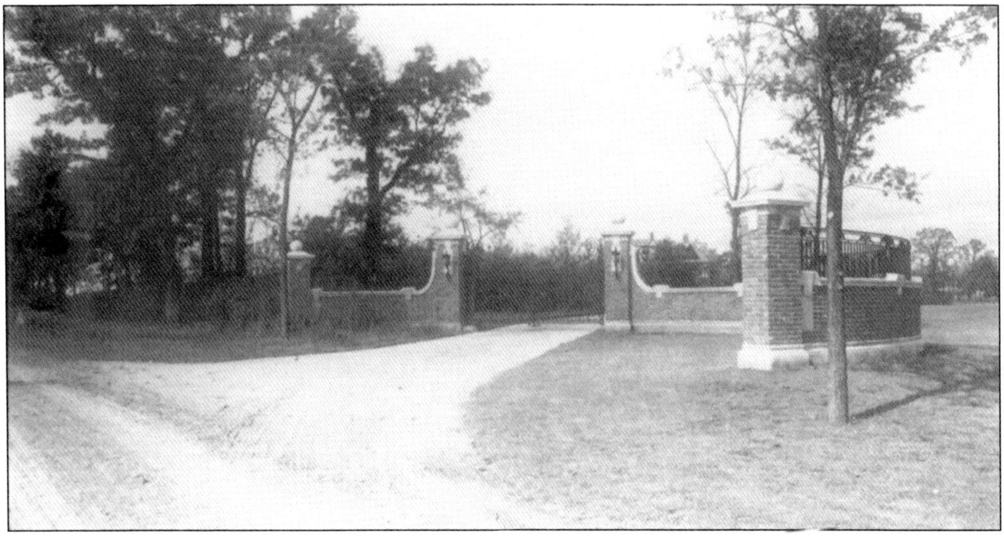

This early 20th century postcard view shows the entrance to Westmoreland, the 1903 American Renaissance estate, as it was dubbed by architectural reviewer Peter B. Wight, estate of mimeograph entrepreneur Albert Blake Dick. The estate's architect was École des Beaux Arts diploma recipient James Gamble Rogers (1867–1947), who married into the local Day family with McCormick ties. The landscape conception was informal, English estate style, and this entry gateway by Rogers with plantings in the manner of the Olmsted firm or of O.C. Simonds, perhaps, shows the interplay of masonry and softening deciduous shrubbery. (Courtesy Lake Forest-Lake Bluff Historical Society.)

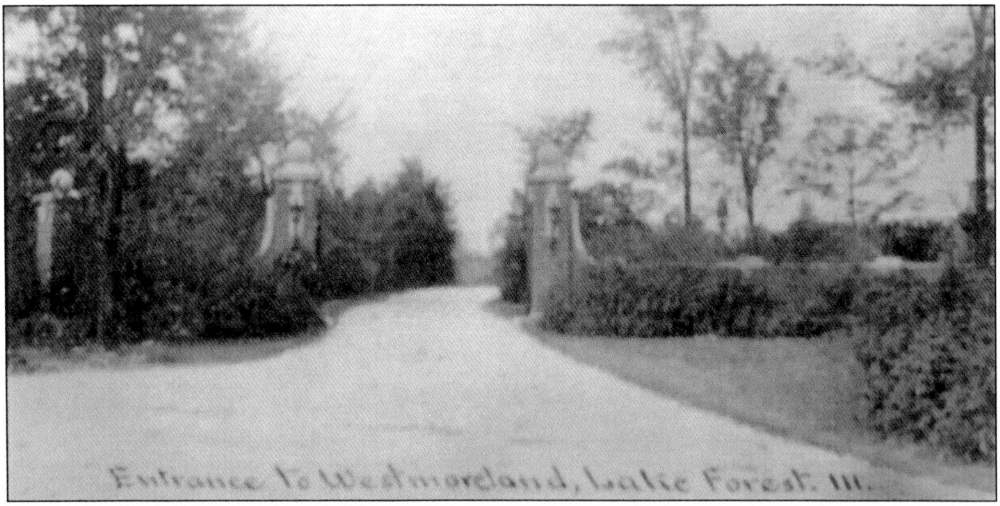

In contrast to the later image above, this is an earlier view of the entryway on the north side of Deerpath. Just west of the slough or creek bed that by the 1930s became Route 41, it shows the effect of the masonry alone before it was landscaped—much more austere. These two early views illustrate the importance of sensitive, in this case mitigating, landscape design in completing any lasting notable project. Too tightly clipped evergreen plantings would not have achieved the same complementary effect with the very firm brick and stone structure. By the 1920s, the local Foundation for Architecture and Landscape Architecture would be working summers with students in both fields to encourage collaboration for the best effects on estates. (Courtesy Lake Forest-Lake Bluff Historical Society.)

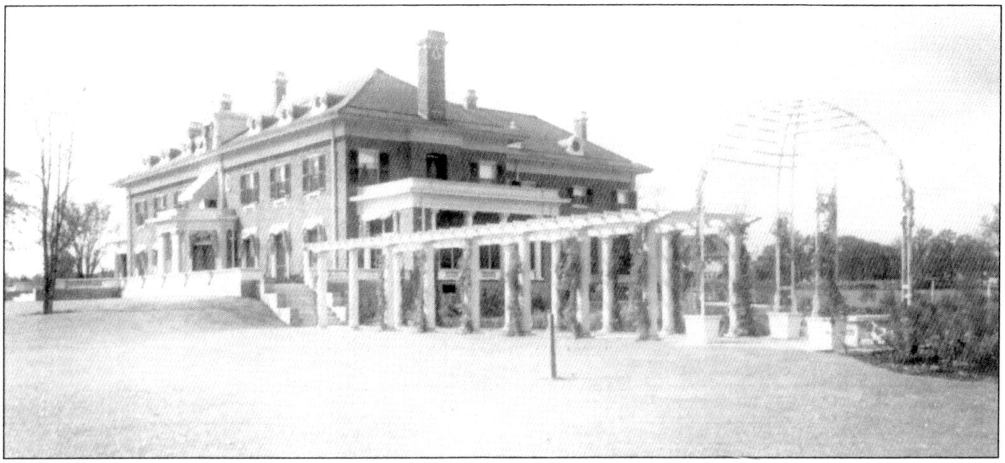

This view of the great brick house at Westmoreland (demolished), with its garden and landscape setting, shows the classic, Georgian Revival, two-and-a-half-story west facade with open meadow beyond to the left. Emphasized by the angle is the terrace overlook to the west. This photograph only suggests, on the right, the "L" shaped plan of Rogers's house for the Dicks with its entry at the point where the two wings meet, facing east and south. This view recalls the massing, style, and scale of The Mount, the Berkshires clapboard house of opinion leader on matters of design and author Edith Wharton. The Westmoreland terrace, too, echoes that at The Mount, though a first floor, centered peristyle of columns provides the interest here vs. the roof-level central pediment at the Berkshires house. (Courtesy Lake Forest-Lake Bluff Historical Society.)

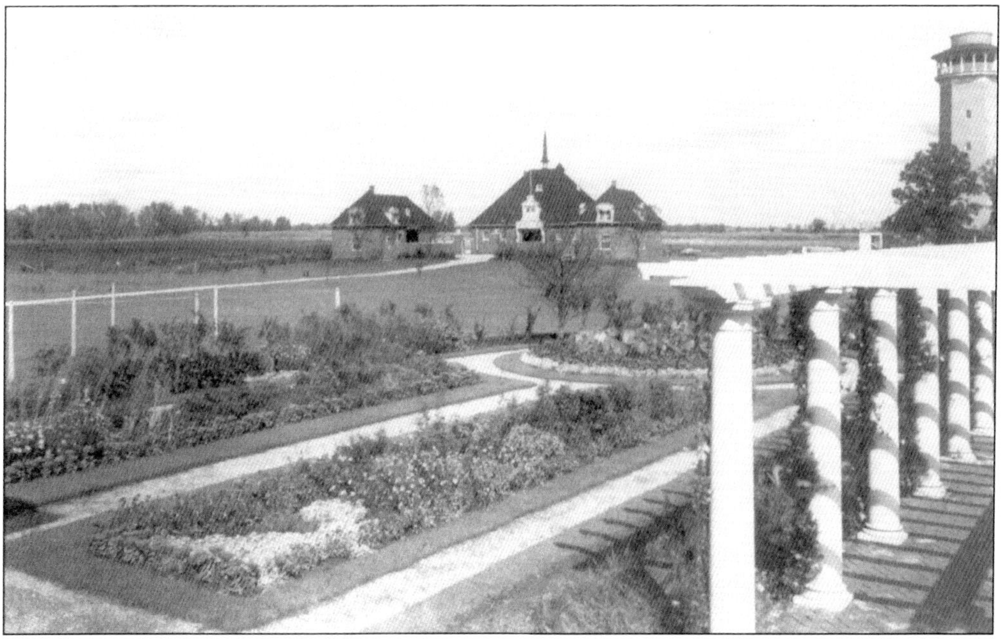

This angle shows the formal garden on the south and west side of the house, with a view of the stable and staff cottage group at center rear. On the right is the water tower. If this garden, with its arbors and trellis, was created at the time of completion of the estate house, it would be one of the earlier large formal gardens locally, with Rogers providing the design oversight for this Beaux Arts extension of the house, an outdoor room, or "Arts and Crafts" garden, as it is typically termed in this century. (Courtesy Lake Forest-Lake Bluff Historical Society.)

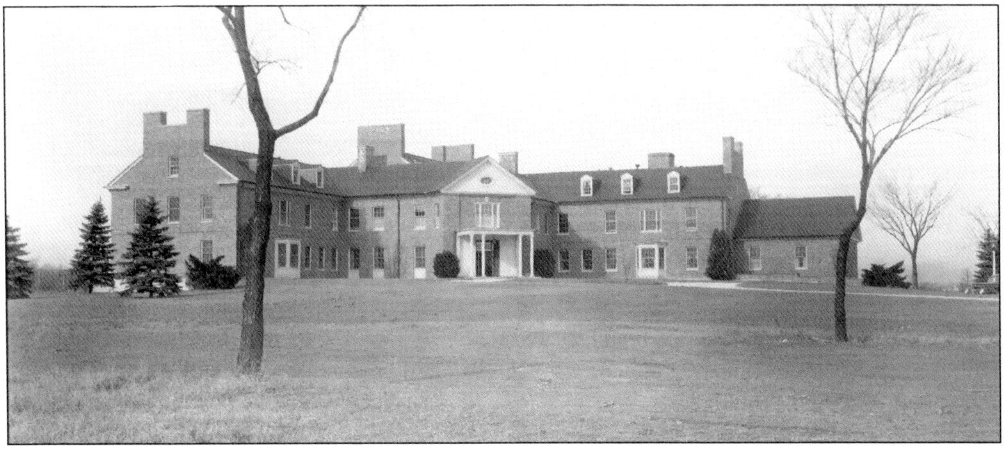

The 1942 brick, distinctively "L" planned Lake Forest Hospital, west of the new Route 41, was built northeast of the main Westmoreland house, by that time doomed to demolition by mid-20th-century high income, estate, and property taxes. So the similar style and plan of this new hospital building preserved the genius of Rogers's mansion, completed in 1903, through the mastery by Stanley D. Anderson of the Anderson & Ticknor architectural firm of the Georgian classic design vocabulary, as they had previously demonstrated at Lake Forest High School in 1935. This original main block survives, though perhaps not equaled in taste and sophistication in recent, post–Anderson and postmodern additions. (Courtesy Shirley Paddock.)

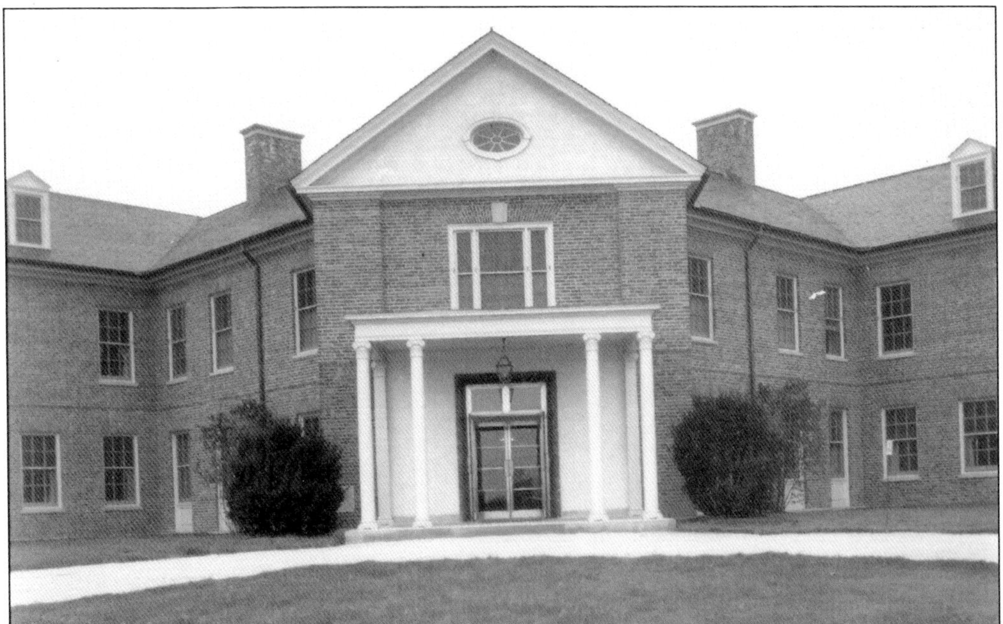

The curving English-landscape style roadway to the Westmoreland estate house contributed to the sense of a new landed gentry for Lake Forest, its design impulse springing from the same informal roots as the 1857 plan for Lake Forest, by landscape gardener Almerin Hotchkiss. Thus, east Lake Forest was carried west to beyond the slough at the future Route 41 by a new generation of architects and landscape designers. Though not surviving, its spirit is replicated in the curving, informal approach from Deerpath Road north to the hospital today, Westmoreland Road. (Courtesy Shirley Paddock.)

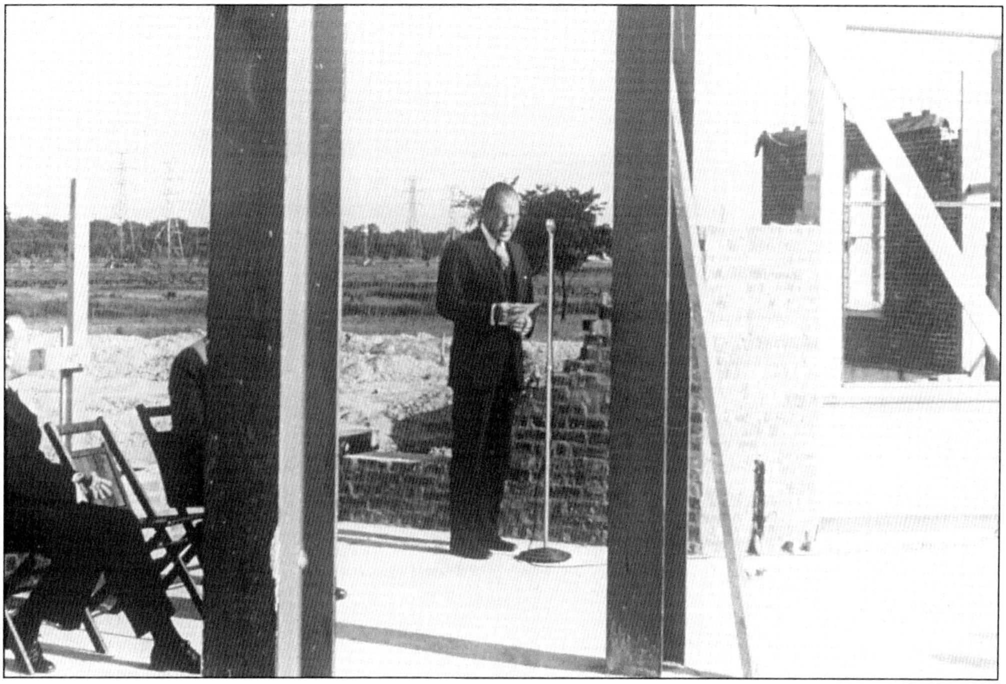

Albert Blake Dick Jr. is shown speaking at the 1941 cornerstone-laying ceremony for the new hospital. The A.B. Dick mimeograph continued to dominate small-scale printing and duplicating through most of the 1950s, until it was succeeded by the Xerox photocopier. The Dick family has continued to be major supporters of the hospital that sprouted on their soil, a baby chick to the Westmoreland estate house mother hen. (Courtesy Jean McMasters Grost.)

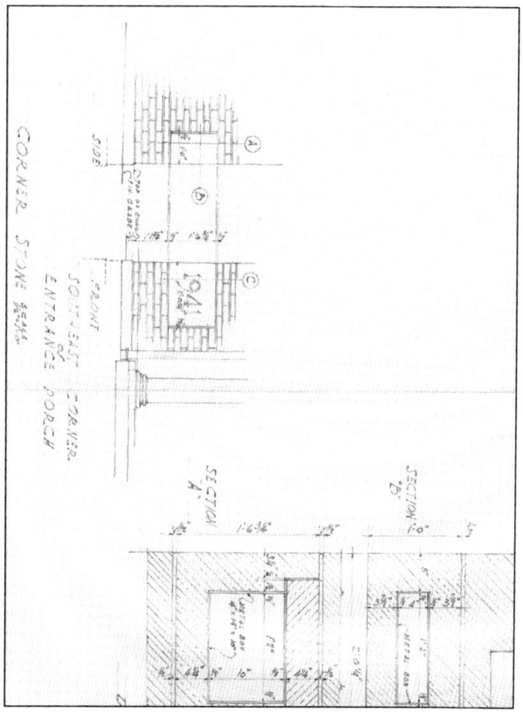

Peter B. Wight, who wrote about Westmoreland early in the last century; Rogers, who designed the estate and its great house; and Stanley D. Anderson, who designed the "new" hospital—now 70 years old—in the classic style of the 1903 house, all appreciated the legacy of timeless design precepts, rules, and constraints derived from the Renaissance. These included proportion, scale, composition, and harmony. This section of a plan by the Anderson firm illustrates this attention to detail that goes back to Greece and Rome. It provides a challenge to the creators of the projected Northwestern Lake Forest Hospital to respect and honor this heritage as they plan for the rest of this century. (Courtesy Paul Bergmann, Stanley D. Anderson archives.)

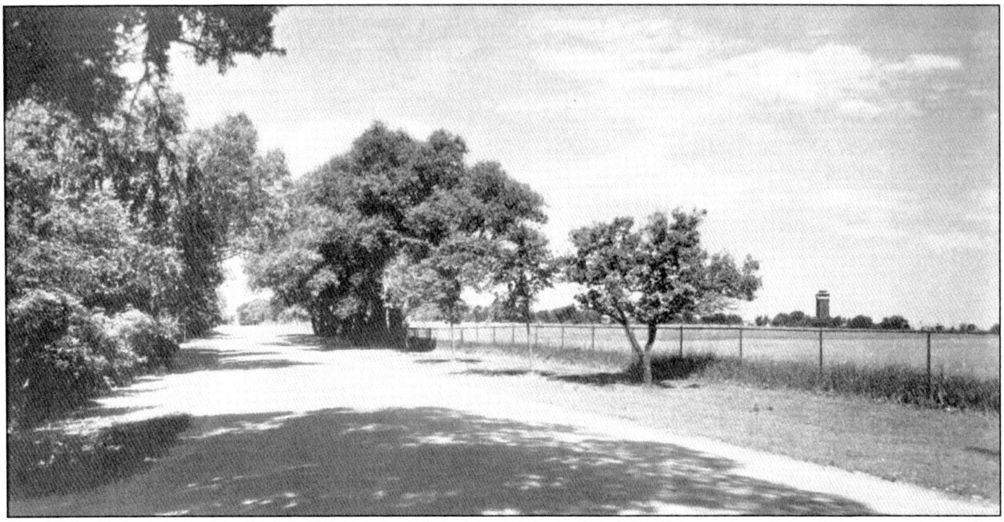

the Deerpath Hills Estates neighborhood was developed in the late 1920s on the east side of the intersection of the north-south Waukegan Road, earlier Telegraph Road, with Deerpath Road. These smaller estate properties typically were on parcels of about two acres. Planned here by the developer Henry K. Turnbull, designed and supervised by architect Stanley D. Anderson, was a community within walking distance of the mid-1920s west track of the North Shore Line Railroad light rail (1926–1963) for commuting to loop offices. Civil engineering was done by Stanley D. Anderson's cousin James S. Anderson Surveyors, still in business for over 100 years. This also would be just east of a new country club on the former Mellody Farm estate of J. Ogden Armour, who had lost the property in 1923 due to financial reverses of epic scale. (Courtesy Paul Bergmann, Stanley D. Anderson Archives.)

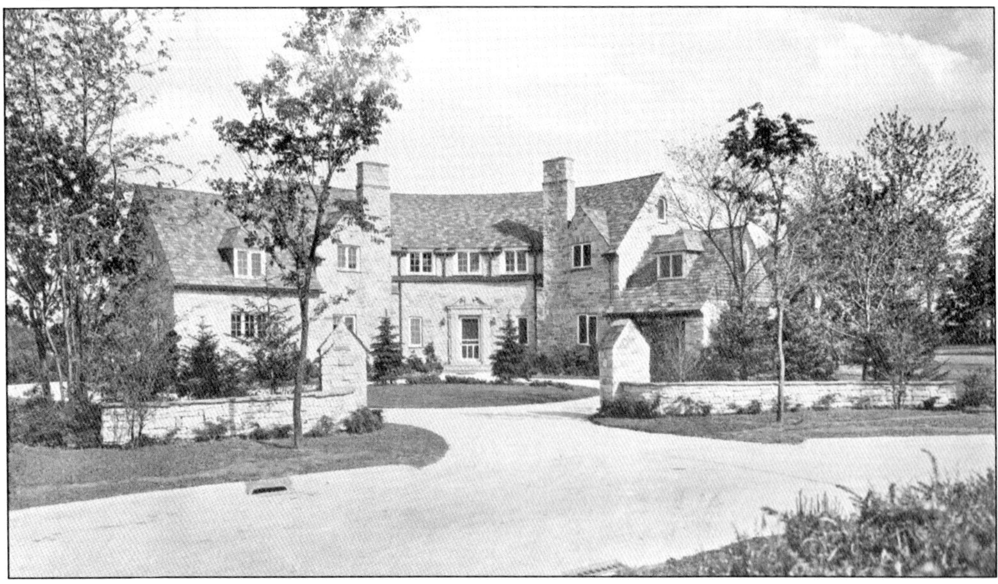

The scale, character, and quality of estate homes envisioned by Turnbull and Anderson is shown in this view of the Grary Walls Gullan, completed in 1929, on the circle south of Deerpath on King Muir Road. It was modeled on a Scottish estate house of the same name at Gullane, Lothian (architect Sir Edwin Lutyens, 1901). Today, it is part of the neighborhood's National Register Historic District. (Courtesy Paul Bergmann, Stanley D. Anderson Archives.)

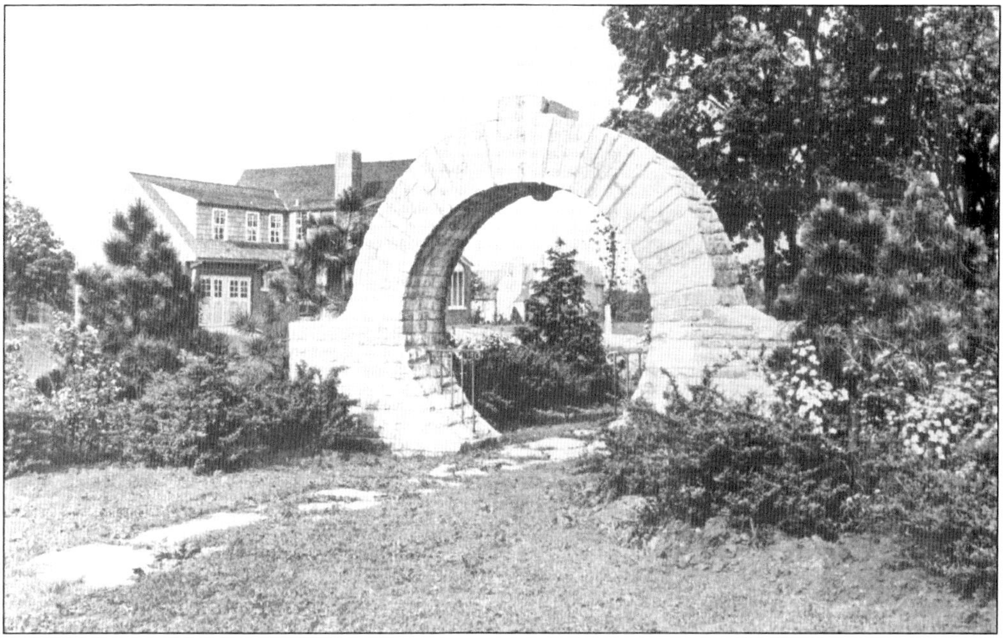

This Chinese Moon Gate by Anderson, a pedestrian gate leading from the Deerpath Hills development to Waukegan Road and the proposed country club on the thoroughfare's west side, still stands on one of the properties at the west end of Verda Lane. The French Provincial home to the left is 970 Verda Lane, designed by an unknown architect in 1928. Today, the mature landscaping and fence hide this from view on Waukegan Road. (Courtesy Paul Bergmann, Stanley D. Anderson Archives.)

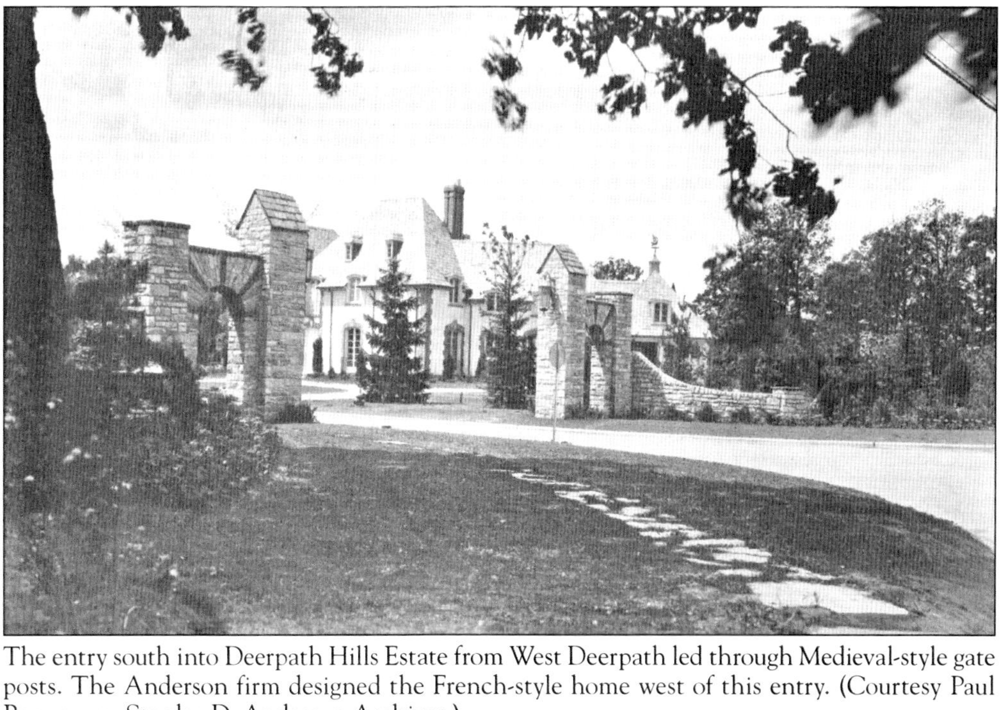

The entry south into Deerpath Hills Estate from West Deerpath led through Medieval-style gate posts. The Anderson firm designed the French-style home west of this entry. (Courtesy Paul Bergmann, Stanley D. Anderson Archives.)

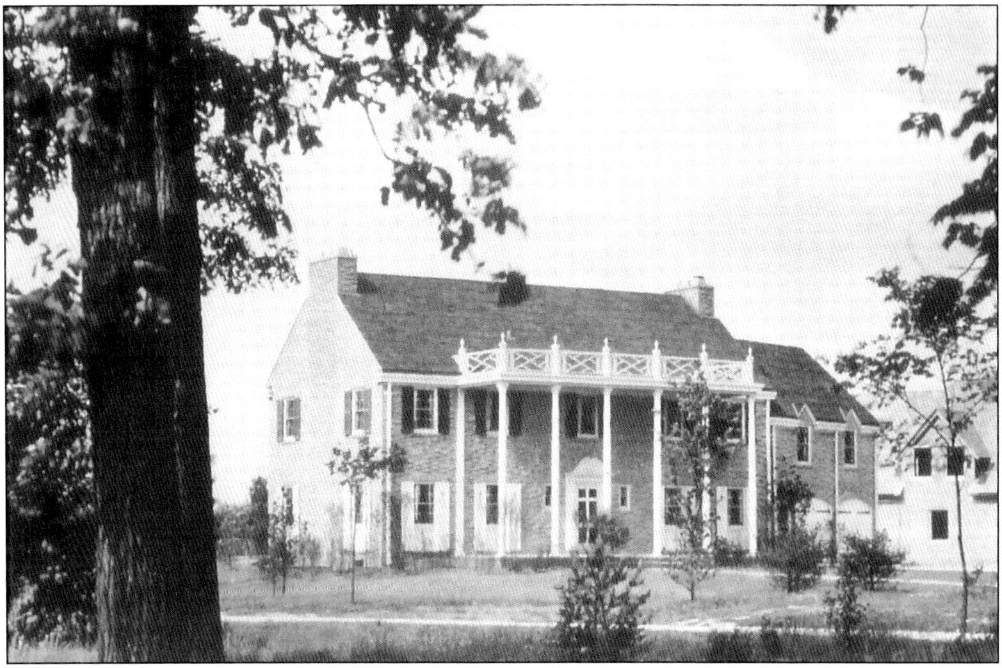

This 1929 classic colonial-revival house designed by an unknown architect is located at 190 King Muir Road. (Courtesy Paul Bergmann, Stanley D. Anderson archives.)

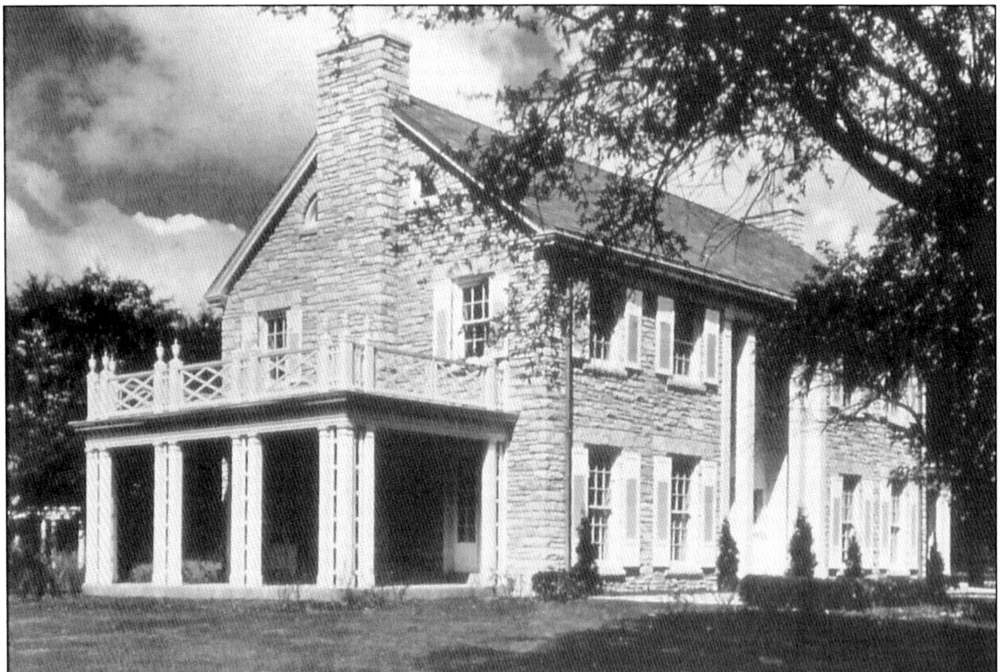

This 1929 house by William Braun at 340 King Muir Road is one of the structures listed in the Deerpath Hills Estates National Register Historic District. (Courtesy Paul Bergmann, Stanley D. Anderson archives.)

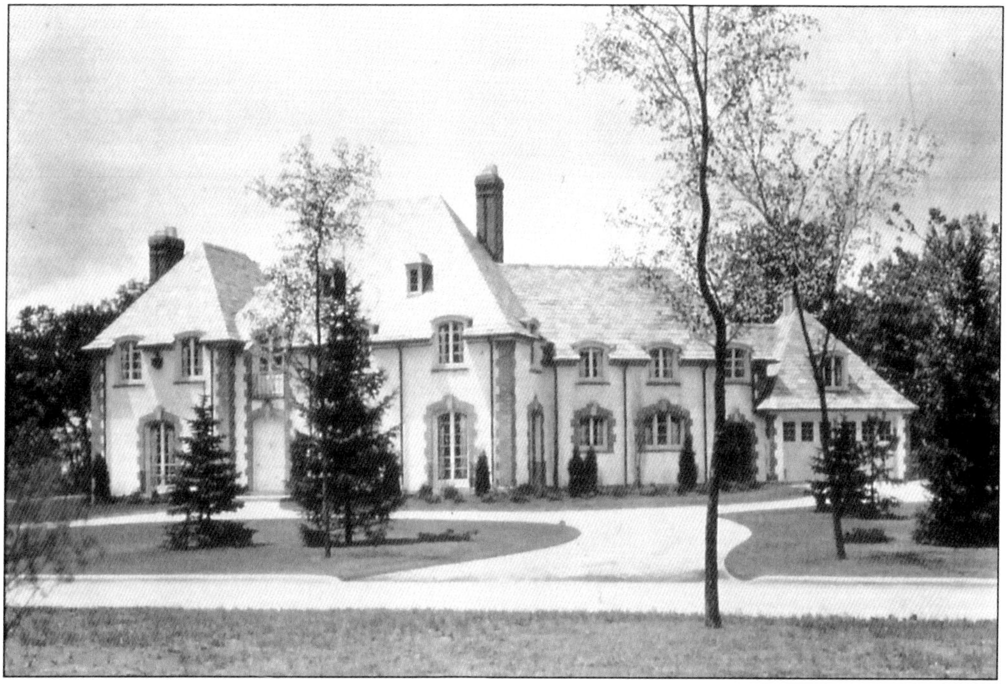

Most prominent among the south of Deerpath King Muir Road houses is 380 King Muir Road, a two-and-a-half-story French-style manor house designed by Anderson & Ticknor in 1929. (Courtesy Paul Bergmann, Stanley D. Anderson archives.)

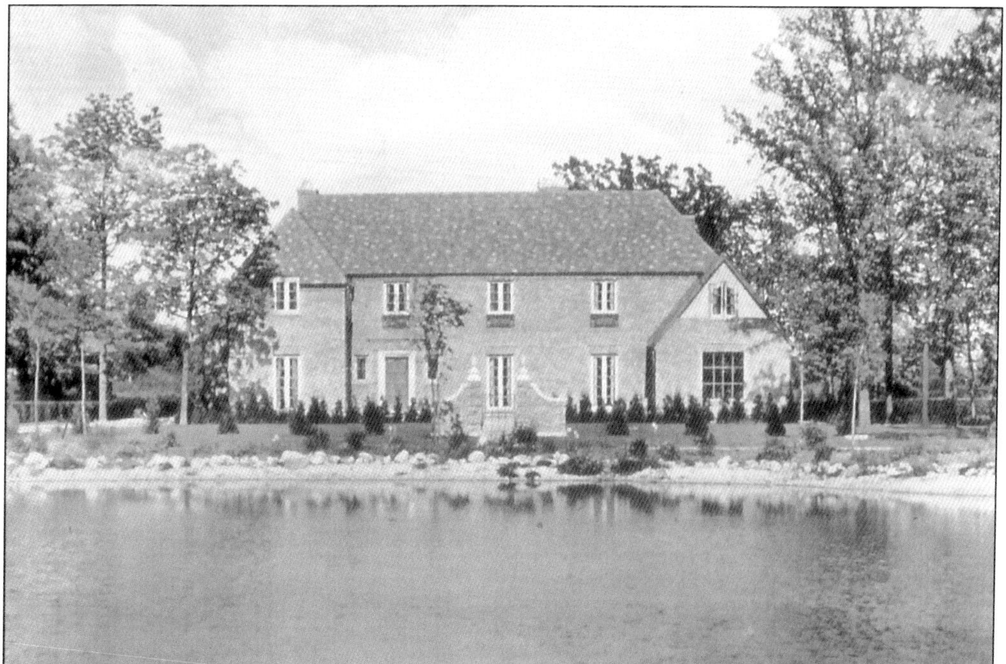

Across this no longer extant pond is 251 King Muir Road, designed by architect Howard Irwin in 1929. Well preserved, the Lake Forest Preservation Foundation gave it an award. (Courtesy Paul Bergmann, Stanley D. Anderson archives.)

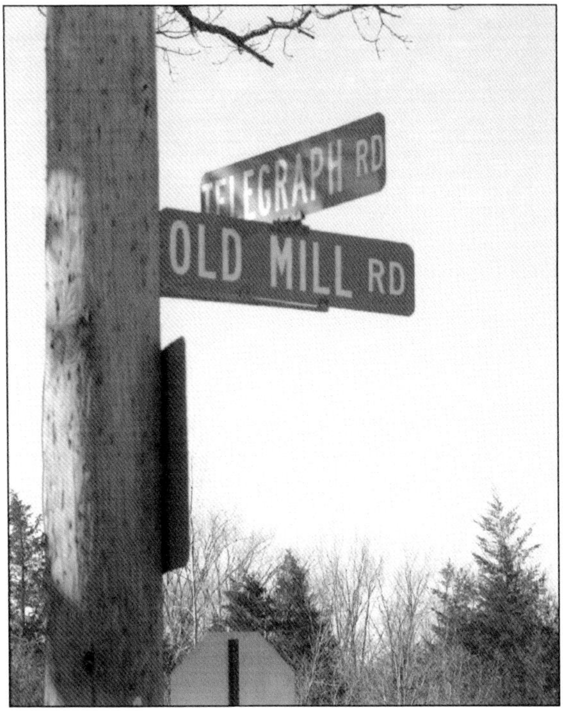

The Everett story begins at Telegraph and Old Mill Roads, the original location of Michael Yore's and Michael Meehan's log cabins. Using local resources, we pieced together the exact location of the cabins on historic Telegraph Road, but the story does not end here. Preservation of Lake Forest history is important to future generations so that we as a community can cherish the dreams and ambitions of those who chose to live in this area. Early pioneers of Everett endured many hardships in order to live the American dream. Historic landmarks are important to the community and our history. We encourage children to get excited about history, explore historic landmarks, and learn how we are all connected by this beautiful community over the span of over 175 years. (Both, courtesy Susan Kelsey.)

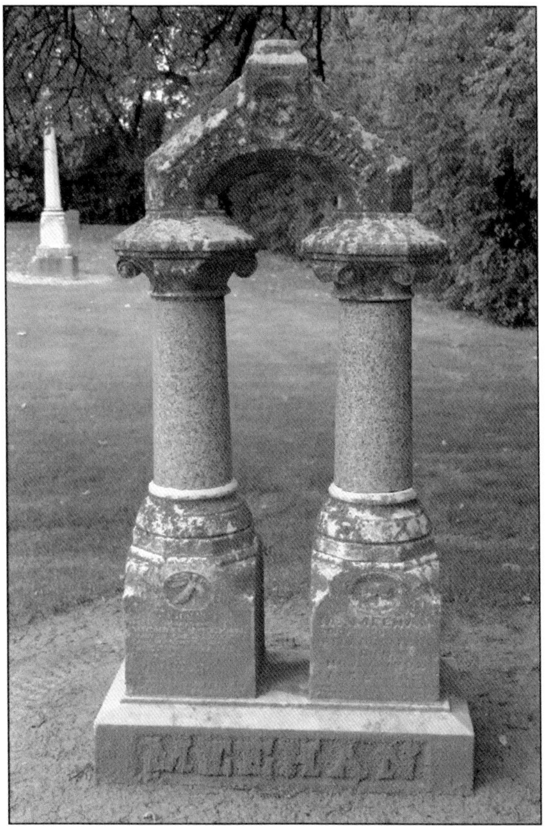

Selected Bibliography

Arpee, Edward. *Lake Forest, Illinois: History and Reminiscences, 1861-1961*. Lake Forest: Lake Forest-Lake Bluff Historical Society, 1991. With Supplement, Susan Dart, ed.

Banks, Susan, Susan Kelsey, and Arthur H. Miller, eds. *Celebrating Lake Forest's 150 Years, 1861-2011*. Northbrook: 2011.

Cohen, Stuart and Susan Benjamin. *Houses of the Lakefront Suburbs: 1890-1940*. New York: Acanthus Press, 2004.

Coventry, Kim, Daniel Meyer, and Arthur H. Miller. *Classic Country Estates of Lake Forest, Architecture and Design: 1856-1940*. New York: W.W. Norton, 2003.

Dretzke, Diana. *Lake County: An Illustrated History*. Wauconda: Lake County Discovery Museum, 2007.

Gunther, John. *Taken at the Flood: the Story of Albert D. Lasker*. New York: Harper, 1960.

Halsey, John J. *History of Lake County, Illinois*. Waukegan: Bates, 1912.

www.lakeforest.edu/library/archives/lf-country-places/index.php

www.lflbhistory.org/research-timeline

Miller, Arthur H. and Shirley M. Paddock. *Lake Forest: Estates, People and Culture*. Charleston, SC: Arcadia Publishing, 2000.

Miller, Arthur H. "Overviews: the Campus Planned," *Lake Forest College: A Guide to the Campus*. Christopher Reed and Arthur H. Miller, eds. Lake Forest: 2007.

Salny, Stephen M. *The Country Houses of David Adler*. New York: W.W. Norton, 2001.

Shafer, Mary A. *Rural America*. Minocqua, WI: Willow Creek Press, 1995.

Wittelle, Marvyn. *Pioneer to Commuter*. Highland Park: Rotary Club, 1958.

Index

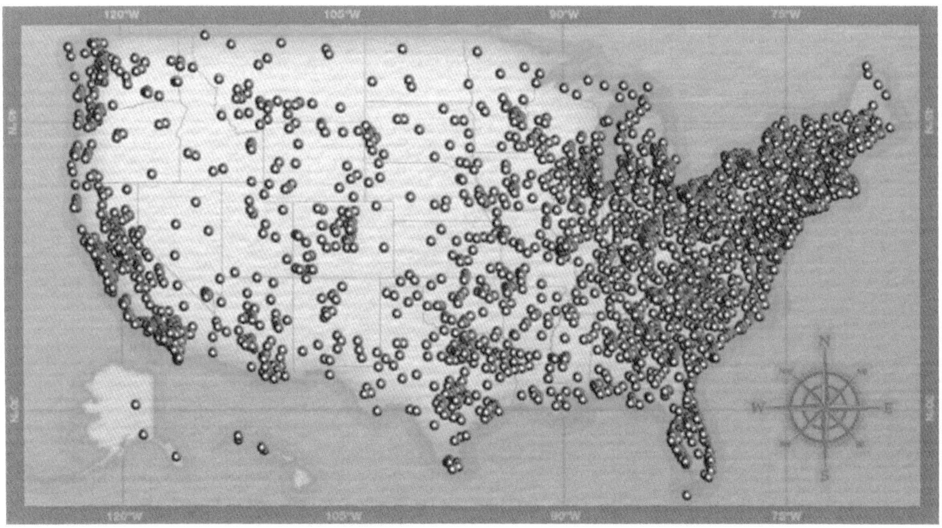